# Life-Span Development
# and Behavior

## VOLUME 6

# Life-Span Development and Behavior

## VOLUME 6

Edited by

### *Paul B. Baltes*

Max Planck Institute for
Human Development and Education
Berlin, Federal Republic of Germany

and

### *Orville G. Brim, Jr.*

Foundation for Child Development
New York, New York

1984

## ACADEMIC PRESS, INC.

(Harcourt Brace Jovanovich, Publishers)
Orlando   San Diego   New York   London
Toronto   Montreal   Sydney   Tokyo

BF
712
.L725
1984
v.6 / 58,846

ACADEMIC PRESS, INC.
Orlando, Florida 32887

United Kingdom Edition published by
ACADEMIC PRESS, INC. (LONDON) LTD.
24/28 Oval Road, London NW1 7DX

LIBRARY OF CONGRESS CATALOG CARD NUMBER: 77-0531

ISBN 0-12-431806-1

PRINTED IN THE UNITED STATES OF AMERICA

84 85 86 87    9 8 7 6 5 4 3 2 1

# Contents

**Personal and Social Control over Development: Some Implications of an Action Perspective in Life-Span Developmental Psychology**

*Jochen Brandtstädter*

**New Perspectives on the Development of Intelligence in Adulthood: Toward a Dual-Process Conception and a Model of Selective Optimization with Compensation**

*Paul B. Baltes, Freya Dittmann-Kohli, and Roger A. Dixon*

v

**Memory for Text Materials in Adulthood**

*David F. Hultsch and Roger A. Dixon*

**Parent–Child Behavior in the Great Depression: Life Course and Intergenerational Influences**

*Glen H. Elder, Jr., Jeffrey K. Liker, and Catherine E. Cross*

**Entry into Adulthood: Profiles of Young Men in the 1950s**

*David L. Featherman, Dennis P. Hogan, and Aage B. Sørensen*

## Mental Illness and the Life Course

### John A. Clausen

## Personality Development from the Inside: The Subjective Experience of Change in Adulthood and Aging

### Carol D. Ryff

## Change in Self in Adulthood: The Example of Sense of Control

### Patricia Gurin and Orville G. Brim, Jr.

**Sibling Studies and the Developmental Impact of Critical Incidents**

*Judy Dunn*

**Peer Interaction and Communication: A Life-Span Perspective**

*Joan E. Norris and Kenneth H. Rubin*

# Contributors

Numbers in parentheses indicate the pages on which the authors' contributions begin.

*Paul B. Baltes* (33), Max Planck Institute for Human Development and Education, 1000 Berlin 33, Federal Republic of Germany

*Jochen Brandtstädter* (1), Department of Psychology, University of Trier, 5500 Trier, Federal Republic of Germany, and Institute for Advanced Study, D-1000 Berlin 33, Federal Republic of Germany

*Orville G. Brim, Jr.* (281), Foundation for Child Development, New York, New York 10017

*John A. Clausen* (203), Institute of Human Development, University of California, Berkeley, California 94720

*Catherine E. Cross* (109), Department of Human Development and Family Studies, Cornell University, Ithaca, New York 14853

*Freya Dittmann-Kohli* (33), Max Planck Institute for Human Development and Education, 1000 Berlin 33, Federal Republic of Germany

*Roger A. Dixon* (33, 77), Max Planck Institute for Human Development and Education, 1000 Berlin 33, Federal Republic of Germany

*Judy Dunn* (335), MRC Unit on the Development and Integration of Behaviour, University of Cambridge, Madingley, Cambridge CB3 8AA, England

*Glen H. Elder, Jr.* (109), Department of Sociology, University of North Carolina, Chapel Hill, North Carolina 27514

*David L. Featherman* (159), Department of Sociology, University of Wisconsin, Madison, Wisconsin 53706

*Patricia Gurin* (281), Department of Psychology, The University of Michigan, Ann Arbor, Michigan 48109, and Russell Sage Foundation, New York, New York 10021

*Dennis P. Hogan* (159), Department of Sociology, University of Chicago, Chicago, Illinois 60637

*David F. Hultsch* (77), Department of Psychology, University of Victoria, Victoria, British Columbia V8W 2Y2, Canada

*Jeffrey K. Liker* (109), Department of Sociology, University of Michigan, Ann Arbor, Michigan 48109

*Joan E. Norris* (355), Department of Family Studies, University of Guelph, Guelph, Ontario N1G 2W1, Canada

*Kenneth H. Rubin* (355), Department of Psychology, University of Waterloo, Waterloo, Ontario N2L 3G1, Canada

*Carol D. Ryff* (243), Department of Psychology, Graduate School of Arts and Sciences, Fordham University, Bronx, New York 10458

*Aage B. Sørensen* (159), Department of Sociology, Harvard University, Cambridge, Massachusetts 02138

# Preface

The serial publication *Life-Span Development and Behavior* is aimed at reviewing life-span research and theory in the behavioral and social sciences, with a particular focus on contributions by psychologists and sociologists. As editors we do not attempt to organize each volume around a particular topic or theme. Rather, we solicit manuscripts from investigators who are conducting programmatic research on current problems or are interested in refining particular theoretical positions. Occasionally authors are invited to identify new areas of concern worthy of theoretical articulation or exploration. The lack of substantive focus of any given volume resulting from our editorial policy is somewhat compensated by listing the contents of previous volumes of the series in each new volume. Thus, it is possible to link articles from the entire series along substantive or theoretical dimensions of particular interest.

The prefaces to the five preceding volumes stated the purposes of introducing more empirical research into the field of life-span development and of increasing its interdisciplinary character. These two purposes are reaffirmed in the current volume. Life-span research on human development contributes to a variety of intellectual positions, some of which deserve particular elaboration at this time.

First, in the past few years research and theory in life-span development have given increased attention to the issue of constancy and change in human development. For example, the assumption that the experiences of infancy and early childhood have a lasting and generalized effect on adulthood and personality is under increasing challenge by careful studies of the effects of early experiences, the results of which have not been entirely supportive of the simple view of continuity. While a life-span approach, then, acknowledges the need for and existence of interconnection between age or developmental periods, it focuses also on conditions for possibly discontinuous development that emerge at later periods and exhibit less generality in terms of sequencing and occurrence than is true for many facets of child development such as physical and cognitive growth. A concern with nonnormative and atypical life events as major contributing factors to life-span change is a case in point.

Second, life-span development scholars are sensitive to the restrictive consequences of studying only specific age periods such as old age, infancy, or adolescence. A life-span development view encourages each scholar to relate the facts about one age group to similar facts about other age groups, and to move toward the study of transformation of characteristics and processes over the life span. A third issue of high salience in current life-span research is the relationship between individual development and historical change. The course of history influences the life patterns of different birth cohorts, and we see that each birth cohort has features of uniqueness because it shares the experience of certain events and conditions at the same age as it moves through its lifetime. These perspectives and others are evident in the articles in this volume.

The editors wish to acknowledge with gratitude and respect the contributions of many colleagues who assisted in making the volume what it is. In addition to our advisory editors, a number of ad hoc reviewers provided valuable comments and suggestions to the contributors before final chapters were prepared:

| | |
|---|---|
| Gerald R. Adams | Kurt Kreppner |
| Toni Antonucci | Michael E. Lamb |
| Margret M. Baltes | Richard M. Lerner |
| Jay Belsky | John A. Meacham |
| Hans Bertram | Bonnie J. F. Meyer |
| Bertram Cohler | Hayne W. Reese |
| Steven W. Cornelius | Lee Robins |
| Fergus I. M. Craik | David L. Rosenhan |
| Roger A. Dixon | Carol D. Ryff |
| Gregg Duncan | Irving E. Sigel |
| Kenneth J. Gergen | Ellen Skinner |
| James Greenley | M. Brewster Smith |
| Willard W. Hartup | Graham Spanier |
| Walter Kintsch | Lillian E. Troll |

Our special thanks go to Amy Michéle for her editorial assistance, and to Jacqueline English, Helga Kaiser, and Joan Pifer for their splendid secretarial work. The next two volumes of the series will be coedited by sociologist David L. Featherman, University of Wisconsin at Madison, and psychologist Richard M. Lerner, The Pennsylvania State University. We thank them for their willingness to give us a respite from our editorial duties and wish them well.

# Contents of Previous Volumes

## VOLUME 3

# Life-Span Development and Behavior

## VOLUME 6

# Personal and Social Control over Development: Some Implications of an Action Perspective in Life-Span Developmental Psychology

## Jochen Brandtstädter

UNIVERSITY OF TRIER
TRIER, FEDERAL REPUBLIC OF GERMANY
AND
INSTITUTE FOR ADVANCED STUDY
BERLIN, FEDERAL REPUBLIC OF GERMANY

## Abstract

Development across the life span is a culture-bound process constituted and regulated through individual and social action. This article discusses some theoretical, methodological, and practical implications of an action-based conception of life-span developmental psychology. Developmental sequences involving an actional nexus are not nomologically universalizable, but possess only local validity. Nevertheless the aspects of contextual variability and invariance can be conceptually integrated in an action–theoretical framework that distinguishes between generated and generating developmental functions. The idea of an unlimited developmental relativism and voluntarism is rejected. Action is conceived of as an interpretative construct which is constituted (rather than determined) through certain attributes such as expectations, values, and control beliefs. This conception involves certain problems for the causal explanation of action and of action-dependent developmental patterns.

Although an action-oriented developmental perspective cannot be based upon a unitary action theory, it offers a conceptual framework of great heuristic and integrative worth. As examples, some topics of life-span developmental research are considered. Finally, an action perspective provides some novel outlooks for an applied developmental psychology. Developmental crises and conflicts on individual, social, and institutional levels may be explicated as problems of readjusting developmental action orientations; this highlights the importance of a life-span-oriented developmental counseling as a supplement to traditional modes of intervention.

## I. Introduction

Individual development across the entire life span is embedded in and dependent upon a highly complex, dynamic, and conflicting structure of personal goals and potentials and of social demands and opportunities. These personal and social controls and constraints of development become effective primarily through the medium of development-related actions. The spectrum of development-related action includes not only the familiar contexts of education and socialization, but it also reaches from the individuals' everyday efforts to influence their own development up to professional interventions in therapy or prevention. Development-related actions, and therefore developmental processes themselves, are culturally formed and at the same time constitutive of culture. They are relative to historical, cultural, and social action orientations and potentials: to the skills, value structures, technical resources, and normative restrictions inherent in given social or societal contexts. The developmental sciences themselves are necessarily involved in the formation of these contextual conditions, insofar as their empirical and theoretical contributions shape and influence development-related decisions on the personal, institutional, and social level.

These insights are neither novel nor revolutionary. Nevertheless, they have important implications for the understanding of developmental processes across the life span. The individual's contribution to the formation of his or her own development has recently gained increasing attention (e.g., Lerner & Busch-Rossnagel, 1981). This article attempts to work out in greater detail some implications and problems of an action-oriented perspective for research, theory, and application within life-span developmental psychology.

## II. Development as a Cultural Product

The concepts of action and culture are closely related to each other. The culture concept comprises foremost those conditions of life and development which, on the basis of natural preconditions, are transformed through purposeful action according to the needs, requirements, and ideals of human life and social existence (cf. Klaus & Buhr, 1971). On the other hand, action as a process both controlled and constituted through social rules is itself bound to certain institutions and forms of life, hence to culture. Thus, we may expect that under an action perspective, the cultural as contrasted to the "natural" aspects of developmental processes will be more prominently displayed. As cultural aspects of development we have to consider all those aspects of development that can be reconstructed as direct or indirect effects or side effects of personal or social actions and decisions and, therefore, may be interpreted as "objectifications" of individual and institutional action orientations (Leontjew, 1977).

To be sure, a clear division of developmental conditions and phenomena into natural and cultural aspects proves to be problematic. On the one hand, cultural products do not stand outside nature; they remain subject to natural laws (Lenk, 1982). On the other hand, many seemingly "natural" givens are already involved in cultural action contexts and, thus, are accessible to corresponding interpretations (cf. Boesch, 1980; Warren, 1980): The tree outside my window, even if it has not been planted, but only thus far left to stand, is already a part of a civilized landscape; the weeds on the lawn may call to mind a cut in the university's gardening budget; the blue sky today would perhaps be gray, if it were not for pollution control regulations. Even the butterflies and birds in a certain sense appear already as cultural artifacts, since they are presumably a product of a culturally molded evolution. The idea of a precultural, "untouched" nature is definitively rendered questionable by the fact that the natural is accessible to us only through conceptual and epistemic devices which are themselves culturally constituted. As Gehlen (1971) stated, the human individual as a "Mängelwesen" (deficient creature), being largely unspecialized and devoid of instinctual resources, is by his very nature dependent on culture to secure his life. The cultural environment for him thus becomes a "second nature" as it were: "Man lives essentially in a 'second nature,' in a world transformed by himself and changed to serve *his* needs. . . . We live moreover not merely in an artificial, but in a 'cultivated' nature, in that we extract possibilities from nature which she would not have come upon if . . . left to herself'' (Gehlen, 1971, p. 103, my translation).

These insights also apply without reservation to the realm of human development. Development is made possible through the cultural stabilization and regulation of critical developmental conditions and is impossible without the active contribution of the individual and his sociocultural environment. This is valid not only for the elementary aspects of biological sustenance of life, but all the more for development in the demanding sense of successful or optimal development. An action perspective on development indicated that what we often prematurely label a ''normal'' developmental phenomenon occurs in the observed manner only in a highly artificial, thoroughly controlled ecology (even if this ecology—in contrast to artificial laboratory environments—is often and misleadingly characterized as ''natural environment''). Even maturational processes—from prenatal development through sensory and somatic development in childhood and youth to physiological involution processes in old age—are by no means to be viewed as invariant sequences following laws of nature, but have to be structurally and functionally related to the prevailing interests, possibilities, and limitations of given historical, cultural, and social action contexts (see also Baltes & Baltes, 1980; Garn, 1980). If development is explicated as a joint product of hereditary and environmental conditions, the fact that environment can be conceptualized only as a cultural ecology, which is constituted and permanently transformed through individual and social action, must be emphasized and theoretically taken into account. This may be considered as the central tenet of an action perspective on human development. Some of the methodological and theoretical consequences of this perspective—which is not a theory, but rather a prototheoretical posture—can be elaborated already on the basis of a common-sense understanding of the action concept, so that issues of definition and terminology can be deferred for a while.

### III. Action Contexts as Systems Generating Development

As a general heuristic and explanatory posture, an action perspective suggests the reconstruction of observed developmental patterns as action-dependent, modifiable, thus also merely ''locally generalizable'' phenomena. It will be demonstrated that such a heuristic stance does not amount to an unlimited contextual relativism.

#### A. PLASTICITY AND VARIABILITY AS CONTEXT-RELATED
#### ATTRIBUTES OF DEVELOPMENT

A controversial issue which can profitably be approached from an action perspective concerns the questions of stability and variability and of plasticity or universality of developmental processes. Evidence from developmental studies comparing cultures, cohorts, or social classes shows that the transcontextual "generalizability" of numerous developmental patterns and functions is rather limited (see Baltes, Reese, & Lipsitt, 1980; Brim & Kagan, 1980). Since the search for developmental invariances has led to recurring frustrations, it is understandable that one has begun to see the results positively and to take them as indicative of a fundamental plasticity and contextual variability of human development. In the light of empirical evidence, it seems reasonable that conceptions of development emphasizing plasticity and malleability of human development ("aleatory" conceptions, "contextualistic" approaches, see Gergen, 1980; Lerner, 1984) gain ground over stability and ordered-change orientations. "Contextualistic" or "aleatory" paradigms are certainly close to an action-oriented developmental perspective; the latter, however, focuses more explicitly on the constructive and mediating function of human action in relating contextual and developmental factors.

The transcontextual variability of many developmental functions or patterns provides a strong argument for an action perspective, since the main sources of variation are cultural-historical factors that depend on and in turn influence action: nutritional resources, learning opportunities, developmental value orientations, and so on. From this point of view, the greater or lesser variability and malleability of developmental characteristics or functions is not an absolute property, but a relational one, that must be related to cultural, social, and individual action systems with their inherent control interests and potentials. The boundaries between "stable" or unmodifiable and "plastic" or malleable aspects of development can shift dramatically in the wake of cultural and scientific change. An impressive example is the hereditary metabolic disease phenylketonuria. While mental retardation long seemed to be an invariant sequel of this disease, our knowledge of the metabolic mechanisms involved now enables us to suppress the negative side effects of this disease on cognitive development. It is clear from this and many other examples that one should suspend the nomological generalization of developmental regularities as long as the possibility cannot be ruled out that the observed developmental sequences are dependent upon the execution or nonexecution of certain actions.

These reservations generally hold for all attempts to infer a greater or lesser stability, modifiability, or plasticity of developmental functions from observed inter- and intraindividual variability. A well-known example is the attempt to infer "sensitive phases" of cognitive development from longitudinal $t$ correlations (see Bloom, 1964). This argument seems defective since it confuses realized with possible variability. For the same reason, arguments which try to derive generalizing assumptions about the modifiability or environmental plasticity of developmental variables from statistical estimates of heritability are questionable: the ratio of genetically determined variation to phenotypic variation is known to be relative to the factual variation of developmental conditions realized in the sample. Equally dubious are attempts to evaluate the developmental adequacy of educational demands or developmental tasks with reference to descriptive–statistical developmental norms, as frequently occurs in diagnostic or instructional contexts. Arguments of this kind do not account for the fact that observed distributions and variability ranges originate in action, and that they are, in other words, relative to specific cultural settings with their specific demands, learning opportunities, development stereotypes, and so on. If this is overlooked, stereotyped conceptions of "normal development" may readily become self-fulfilling prophecies.

## B. CAUSAL VERSUS "ACTIONAL" NEXUS OF DEVELOPMENTAL PHENOMENA

Wherever an empirical connection between developmental phenomena can be established or (as in the case of prevention) interrupted through "intervening" actions, it does not seem possible to interpret this relation nomologically. Such a relation is not based on a "causal nexus" (Kagan, 1980), but on an *actional* nexus (as we might call it) which, as such, can in principle be altered.

Such an actional nexus may well be assumed for most developmental trajectories. Consider, for example, the controversial issue of intellectual development in adulthood and old age. Schaie (1974) and Baltes and Schaie (1974) have argued against the stereotype of a general and universal decline in intellectual functions in middle and old age. On the basis of cross-sequential research findings, they postulate that observed functional losses in large part result from contingent contextual conditions such as health problems or insufficient opportunities for training and education in old age, and consequently could be counteracted through a compensatory or preventative elimination of these "unnecessary causes of decline" (Baltes & Schaie, 1974, p. 40). In contrast, Horn and Donaldson (1976) have maintained that valid generalizations about intellectual development in old age should also account for age-related differences in such extrinsic contextual conditions. This objection seems justified as long as the main concern is a representative statistical description of developmental functions for a given cultural situation. According to the considerations above, such statistical descriptions must be interpreted with a contextual reservation and cannot be nomologically generalized. To pass from purely local descriptions to nomological universalizations, the invariance of the relevant contextual conditions would have to be supposed—invariance not only in a factual, but in the strict sense. In the argument considered above, which refers to conditions of health care, cultural learning opportunities, and so on, such an assumption is quite untenable. It becomes evident at this juncture that statistically based conceptions about the "normal" or "common" course of development often already involve tacit assumptions about action possibilities and potentials for developmental modification and change in a given cultural situation.

It follows that observed transcontextual stability of a developmental pattern does not in itself justify a nomological universalization. One reason is that transcontextual generalizability studies can always span only a limited range of variation; thus, they cannot yield a conclusive answer to the generalizability question, but are themselves subject to problems of generalizability. Second and perhaps more important, the nomological law concept seems to presuppose not only universality, but also necessity of a relationship (e.g., Bunge, 1979): nomological universality claims seem unwarranted unless supported by cogent arguments that exclude any exceptions from the observed regularity.

### C. BOUNDS OF PLASTICITY: LIMITATIONS OF A VOLUNTARISTIC CONCEPTION OF DEVELOPMENT

The foregoing considerations seem to justify a "voluntaristic" reservation[1] in propositions about developmental antecedent–consequent relations: If A, then B—as long as the relevant social context has neither the interest nor the possibility to change this relation (cf. Watkins, 1957). A voluntaristic position, if formulated in this way, can always be defended, since it has tautological character. Nevertheless, it makes sense to ask whether there are strictly immutable relationships to which such a voluntaristic reservation does not apply.

To deal with this question, one has to distinguish factual limits of intervention and change from strict or necessary ones (Brandtstädter, 1980). Social–normative restrictions, technical or theoretical deficits, and so on do not pose invariant constraints on action and change, but must count as limitations which are modifiable in principle. As was intimated above, developmental processes cannot be nomologically universalized insofar as they depend on such factual limitations.

In contrast to cultural restrictions, laws of nature, according to common understanding, are not open to voluntary change. This is not an empirical fact, but seems to be implied in the nomological interpretation of the concept of natural law. To be sure, we can "apply" natural laws technologically to generate certain intended effects, and we can stop their application; we cannot, however, modify them.[2] Next to such "nomological" boundaries, logical limitations seem to constitute a second type of strong or necessary limitation. Developmental states which are logically incompatible cannot be realized simultaneously. Thus, nomological and logical restrictions strictly curtail the range of developmental

---

[1]Here and in the following, the term of "voluntarism" is taken to denote a programmatic posture that emphasizes the openness of developmental relationships to voluntary modification.

[2]This argument remains valid of course if we accept the hypothesis of an "evolutionary change" of natural laws.

modifications. To these two types of restrictions, a third one has to be added that may be termed a "structural" limitation. Most interesting in the present context are structural limitations that are imposed by terminological rule systems. Such rule systems are of course culturally constituted, nevertheless they pose limitations that, within an established language game, seem strict and necessary. For example, the possibility that a certain developmental task $T_a$ can be achieved before a task $T_b$ can be excluded a priori (in the sense of a linguistic a priori; cf. Ashby, 1967) if $T_b$ is conceptually entailed by $T_a$ (according to established language rules that determine the use and intensional meaning of the task concept $T_a$).

Considering such nomological, logical, and structural restrictions, a voluntaristic posture can hardly be defended, if it goes so far as to assume that developmental patterns are open to voluntary change not only in some, but principally in all aspects. The consideration of structural restrictions also becomes relevant for evaluating claims of invariance and universality in life-span development. We will return to this point in Section IV,B.

## D. THE COMPATIBILITY OF VARIABILITY AND INVARIANCE

Contrary to widespread opinion, the notorious difficulties of a transcontextual "generalization" of developmental processes and patterns provide no sufficient reason for abandoning the epistemological ideal of lawful invariance and universal validity. It is a common complaint that textbooks in developmental psychology must be written anew from one generation to the next in view of the great contextual specificity of developmental patterns—if they are not already obsolete at the time of publication (e.g., Bell & Hertz, 1976). Of course all developmental psychological research that remains at the level of description and inductive generalization runs this risk of obsolescence—quite apart from the fact that developmental psychology is itself a developing field. However, transcontextual variability and instability of empirical patterns of development do not exclude invariances on more basic levels of functioning. The juxtaposition of stability-oriented and plasticity-oriented accounts of development as radical alternatives appears misplaced, since it fosters the confusion of different epistemological levels—the data level and the level of data-generating systems (mechanisms, principles). Developmental psychological research and theory should attempt to relate both levels, i.e., to reconstruct the contextual variability at the data level through the modeling of the underlying generative systems and mechanisms.

Formulated very generally, such a reconstruction is achieved by assigning a generative system G (of generative rules, principles, mechanisms) and a set C of contextual conditions to an empirical pattern D of developmental data so that G and C together reproduce D. This reconstruction may differ according to whether we assume a causal or an actional nexus for the observed pattern of development, or whether we want to provide "connective" or "essential" explanations (Pörn, 1977). Let us consider the following simple example: In some longitudinal studies (e.g., Macfarlane, Allen, & Honzik, 1954), early childhood aggression in girls seemed to be less persistent than in boys. Even if this is a rather stable and well-replicated finding, there is no reason to assume that it is invariant or immutable in a strict nomological sense. Thus, one might speculate that the relationship depends on specific conditions of the socialization context; for example, the social desirability and, accordingly, the social control of aggression in boys and girls may differ across historical and cultural contexts. If such differences could be empirically confirmed, it should be possible to formulate a generative model that reconstructs not only the singular context-specific findings, but even their contextual variation. It is clear that such reconstructive efforts may continue on higher levels in order to achieve a wider scope of explanation.

These methodological remarks by no means deny the practical importance of context-specific "quasi-laws." The knowledge of quasi-lawful regularities in development is certainly indispensable for prediction, (quasi-)explanation, and modification of development in a given context—one thinks of culture-specific patterns of educational behavior, of context-specific age–risk functions for critical life events, and so fourth. Our doubts do not refer to quasi-laws as such, but rather to the nomological misinterpretation of quasi-laws, as well as to a research which does not attempt to transcend the level of context-specific quasi-laws.

It could at this point be said that the arguments presented up to now add little that is new to the familiar admonition that research in developmental psychology should not stop at the level of descriptions, but seek explanations for observed data. In this methodological commonplace, the term "explanation" is usually taken to mean causal–nomological systematizations. Whether this type of explanation can be applied to actions and action-generated development is, however, controversial.

## IV. Problems of the Nomological Interpretation of an Action Perspective on Development

In the preceding sections, the action concept has been used in a largely unexplicated, commonsense way. To deal with questions of action explanation, however, a more explicit consideration of conceptual issues is necessary.

In spite of earlier attempts at integration (e.g., Parsons & Shils, 1951), there is up to now no general and comprehensive action theory to which an action-oriented developmental perspective could refer. Action theory and research on action at present form a ramified and conceptually heterogeneous, multidisciplinary research program.

Perhaps the most prominent group of action theories in the narrower field of psychology are the expectancy–value models and attribution research approaches in the tradition of Tolman, Lewin, and Heider (e.g., Feather, 1982). Alongside them are cognitive–structuralist action theories in the tradition of Piaget and Bruner (e.g., Aebli, 1980) as well as system–analytical approaches which are influenced by the pioneer work of Miller, Galanter, and Pribram (1960) and draw on concepts from systems theory and cybernetics (e.g., Volpert, 1981). Important contributions also come from sociology (symbolic interactionism, ethnomethodological approaches), as well as from biology and anthropology. Last but not least, one should mention the contributions of analytic action philosophy which has branched off from ordinary language philosophy and the late work of Wittgenstein (e.g., Von Wright, 1971; see also Gauld & Shotter, 1977). It is probably not unfair to say that understanding between the various intra- and interdisciplinary branches of action theory is quite limited. The different approaches share at best a small set of common assumptions. For the purpose of orientation and without regard to the facets of specific theories, an attempt will be made to work out some very general tenets of an action perspective.

## A. ON THE STRUCTURE OF THE CONCEPT OF ACTION

Most formulations of action theory presuppose that action is not simply behavior, but rather self-planned behavior that can be interpreted as a means to achieve certain goals, to express certain values, or to solve certain problems, and that is—within certain boundaries—freely (or at least subjectively freely) chosen on the basis of certain beliefs and values. As a constitutive characteristic of the action concept, the aspect of personal control is frequently stressed. Actions are distinguished from behavioral events that lie outside the agent's control and which, therefore, simply occur or happen to him (cf. Buss, 1978). As is well known, the difference between controlled action and noncontrolled or involuntary behavior is of central importance in the context of moral and legal evaluation; attributions of guilt and responsibility presuppose (not causally, but conceptually) the assumption of controllability. Attribution research has traced out these conceptual relations empirically (e.g., Weiner, 1980).

The concept of action is often brought into a close relationship with the concept of rules (e.g., Smith, 1982; Toulmin, 1974). In this connection, the distinction (already formulated by Kant) between regulative and constitutive rules seems important.

1. *Regulative rules:* Individual action is regulated by formal and informal

cultural prescriptions and restrictions (laws, norms, social expectations, etc.). Such regulative cultural constraints, in contrast to natural laws, can be violated. Whereas the deviation from a theoretical law proposition is charged to the proposition, but not to the observed phenomenon, the violating of rules, if discovered, results in corrective countermeasures or sanctions. As Toulmin (1969) remarks, rules possess a "normative force" in contrast to natural laws. This fact is basic for the understanding of development and socialization in cultural contexts (cf. the concept of "developmental adaptational traits," Kohlberg, LaCrosse, & Ricks, 1972). It has also proved itself fruitful for the explanation of aging processes: age-related role expectancies and developmental tasks in age-graded societies have a clearly regulative normative force on processes of aging (cf. Neugarten & Hagestad, 1976).

2. *Constitutive rules:* If we consider, for example, types of action such as lying, excusing oneself, praying, promising something, or playing chess, it is evident that these actions are not only regulated, but in a stricter sense constituted by rules. One can play chess only within the rules of the game, and one can similarly lie, pray, excuse oneself, greet someone, and so forth only in the framework of certain social and semantic rules that constitute the respective types of action. To interpret a certain behavior, such as a hand movement, as an act of greeting, one has to relate the behavior to the constituting rules of the respective action type with regard to the way in which it is carried out, the context in which it is embedded, and so forth. The system of social and semantic rules constituting an action type is comparable to a "script" in the sense of Schank and Abelson (1977). In this connection, it becomes evident that an understanding of actions presupposes familiarity with the relevant social–cultural context of rules and institutions (see also Winch, 1958). Constitutive rules obviously cannot be violated through actions that are constituted by these very rules (cf. the above-mentioned concept of structural limitations). For example, one can certainly violate the rules of chess, but then one no longer plays chess.[3]

In sum, the central significance of the rule concept for an action-oriented developmental perspective must be underscored. The significance of regulative rules for the personal and social control of developmental processes has already been stressed. As we will show in the following, the concept of constitutive rules becomes methodologically relevant especially in connection with the analysis of ontogenetic sequences.

[3]These considerations may seem sophistic. Nevertheless, it may not be completely beside the point to reflect on analogies between the "force" that constitutive rules exert on an action constituted by them and the nomological force attributed to natural laws. Certain similarities might be seen at least from the view of a conventionalistic or constructivistic conception of science.

## B. CONSTITUTIVE RULES AND ONTOGENETIC SEQUENCES

The significance of constitutive rules for the analysis of ontogenetic sequences is particularly evident in connection with questions of competence development, which represent a central research topic for an action-oriented developmental perspective. Relevant research programs in life-span developmental psychology are concerned with questions of social-cognitive and communicative competencies (e.g., Flavell & Ross, 1981), of competencies in moral judgment (e.g., Kohlberg, 1976), and of competencies in coping with anxiety, stress, and critical life events (e.g., Lazarus, 1980), and with questions of the development and the development-regulating functions of subjective control beliefs (e.g., Bandura, 1981; Garber & Seligman, 1980), or with the development of wisdom across the life span (e.g., Clayton & Birren, 1980). The respective core concepts of these research programs—justice, responsibility, wisdom, coping, and so forth—have a certain meaning and therefore a certain conceptual and semantic structure. Before starting empirical research, it seems important to explicate this conceptual structure; one can meaningfully ask empirical questions and develop conceptually valid measuring devices only if one has structured the meaning of the concept to be investigated at least in its core aspects. Such preparatory conceptual work has to go beyond simple operational definitions or empirical descriptions of a factual language use. Rather, a conceptual reconstruction from the standpoint of a competent language use is needed. Kohlberg (1976) recognized this, for example, in starting from a philosophical analysis of the concept of justice rather than with operationalizations or descriptions of everyday concepts of justice. This conceptual analysis provided the standard to evaluate empirical moral judgments and to bring them into a qualitative structural sequence. As noted above, the semantic structure of a concept—that is, the rules constituting the competent use of a concept—implies also developmental priorities.

If, for example, the concept of "trading" semantically implies the concept of "giving" and "taking," then clearly the achievement of this concept presupposes the achievement of semantically implied concepts in the ontogenetic sequence as well (for empirical evidence on this point, see Gentner, 1975). Or if the competent use of the concept of responsibility presupposes the differentiation of intentional action and unintentional behavior, then the ontogenetic development of the responsibility concept—which terminates with a competent rather than an arbitrary concept use—likewise seems to presuppose the prior development of the concept of intention (see Shaw & Sulzer, 1964). Developmental sequences of this nature do not represent empirical laws, but rather structural implications (cf. Lenk, 1975); that is, they can be derived a priori from established logical or semantic rules which constitute the concepts under investigation (Brandtstädter, 1982; Smedslund, 1980).

There are reasons to assume that sequential invariances such as those postulated by Piaget for intellectual development or by Kohlberg for moral development can be reconstructed more appropriately as structural implications in the described sense rather than as causal–nomological regularities. The distinction between structural implications and empirical causal relations may contribute to the clarification of long-standing controversies about the empirical and epistemological status of such stage models. Evidently, such a distinction presupposes explicit structural analyses: Piaget has given excellent examples, although to be sure he focused primarily on logicomathematical rather than on semantic structures.

To prevent misunderstandings it should be added that the considerations above by no means imply that empirical developmental research can or should be replaced by conceptual analyses (which, to be sure, are not independent of experience). By the same token, however, it would be methodologically incorrect to believe that conceptual analyses can be reduced to a purely descriptive hypothesis testing.

## C. PROBLEMS IN ACTION EXPLANATION

It has been stipulated that action is not simply behavior, but behavior that is interpreted with regard to certain constitutive aspects such as controllability, intentionality, freedom of choice, and so forth. It is thus possible that outwardly identical behavioral events may represent different types of action. A certain movement of the hand, for example, could be interpreted as a greeting, as a fanning of the air, and so on, according to the situational context. Conversely, different patterns of behavior can represent the same type of action. Accordingly, actions are not to be conceived as isolated behavioral events, but as "interpretative constructs" (cf. Lenk, 1978; Thalberg, 1977). It seems questionable, then, whether action explanations can be given according to the traditional covering law scheme of event explanations (Hempel & Oppenheim, 1948).

In common linguistic practice, actions are usually explained by relating them to cognitive orientations (expectations, beliefs, etc.) and volitional orientations (goals, intentions, etc.) of the agent. This basic scheme of explanation is already found in Aristotle's writings (cf. Kenny, 1975); it also lies at the heart of recent action–theoretical formulations (especially of the expectancy–value type; see Feather, 1982). As an explication of such "intentional" action explanations, Von Wright (1971) proposed the scheme of practical syllogism: "$S$ intends to bring about $x$" (volitional premise); "$S$ believes that he can bring about $x$ only by doing $y$" (cognitive premise); "therefore, $S$ proceeds to do $y$" (practical conclusion). Numerous variants of this scheme exist. Undoubtedly, in the given simplified format it can count only as a rudimentary form of an action explanation that requires certain refinements (see Meggle, 1977). Obviously, additional conditions must be fulfilled, before it comes to an action: Above all, S must be objectively as well as subjectively in the position (be able, free, etc.) to perform the respective action. This very straightforward, perhaps even tautological or analytical proposition forms the the central notion of recent efficacy–theoretical formulations (e.g., Bandura, 1977).

Von Wright (1971) maintains that intentional action explanations of the given type can not be causally interpreted or conceptualized as deductive–nomological explanations. He argues that the components of such explanations (expectations, goals, action tendencies, etc.) cannot be determined methodologically independent from one another. For example, in order to validly assess the intentions of an individual, one must take his beliefs and action tendencies into consideration. Consequently, the relationships involved should be considered not as causal (in the traditional Humean sense), but rather as logical–conceptual relations.

This argument has numerous adherents as well as opponents. This is not the place to go into detail on this controversy. At any rate, attempts to modify the practical syllogism as an explanatory scheme so that it fits the traditional deductive–nomological model of explanation meet serious difficulties (see Brandtstädter, 1984a). It is noteworthy that some "causal" counterpositions presuppose a concept of causality in which the traditional requirement of logical independence between causes and effects is abandoned or at least relaxed (see Beckermann, 1979). It therefore does not seem impossible that a position between strict causalism and logical intentionalism can be established. Such an intermediate position is suggested by the fact that the interpretative analysis of action–theoretical terms such as intentions, goals, beliefs, etc. via measurement rules or reduction statements leads neither to purely empirical–hypothetical nor to purely logical or analytical statements, but rather to "quasi-analytic" propositional systems (Stegmüller, 1969). Within such a quasi-analytic system, certain interpretative propositions may be discarded in the light of empirical evidence while other, more central or constitutive meaning propositions cannot be disposed of. This comes close to a structuralist position, that conceives of theories not as systems of statements, but as ideal conceptual constructions or conceptual core structures that cannot be empirically refuted in the traditional sense, but can only be more or less successfully applied to selected domains through interpretative extensions (cf. Herrmann, 1976; Stegmüller, 1979, 1980).

In sum, it appears that the problems addressed above can be accounted for more appropriately on the basis of an action concept that explains actions through reconstruction of the actor's argumentative orientation base (cognitions, values, etc.) rather than as physical consequences of causal antecedents. Within such an approach, rationality is conceptualized not as an empirical disposition, but as an idealized methodological principle which is used in the construction of action explanations (see Schwemmer, 1976).

## V. Some Research Topics of an Action Perspective on Development

An action-oriented developmental perspective offers a conceptual framework of high integrative and heuristic value for life-span developmental research and theory. In this section some research topics are addressed in an exemplary fashion that may be approached and integrated within an action–theoretical rationale.

### A. PERSONAL REGULATION OF DEVELOPMENTAL AND AGING PROCESSES

We have already noticed that developmental changes in social contexts are related to specific constellations of age-graded behavioral expectations, developmental tasks, role patterns, and so on. This implies that such changes are produced to a considerable extent by developmental and age-related action constraints of the personal and social level. Such considerations lead us to assume that subjects do not only behave according to such constraints, but try to actively control their development in functional aspects—such as bodily conditions, sensory functioning, social and cognitive competencies—that, in turn, are important boundary conditions of personal action potentials at a respective age level or developmental stage. In an action theoretical framework that combines elements of expectancy–value theories, attribution research, social learning theory, and more recent theories of subjective efficacy, such personal interventions in development may be accounted for by the following molar categories of action orientations.

1. *Expectations about age-related changes and developmental outcomes:* Such expectations may, for example, be influenced by cultural aging stereotypes as well as by personal or vicarious developmental experiences. One has to distinguish between initial expectations, which do not yet take into account the subject's actions but may instigate such actions, and revised expectations, which already include the anticipated effects of personal interventions in development. Obviously, the difference between initial and revised expectancies is a function of the individual's subjective control potential (see also Weiner & Litman-Adizes, 1980).

2. *Subjective evaluations of expected developmental and age-related events:* Evaluations of anticipated developmental and age-related outcomes depend on the final and instrumental value orientations of the individual and on his "role themes" and "life themes," which continuously generate goals of development and action propensities across the life span (cf. Schank & Abelson, 1977; also

Bühler & Massarik, 1969) and which are, to be sure, themselves subject to change over the life span.

3. *Developmental and age-related control beliefs:* To this category belong subjective assumptions about the availability and efficiency of personal interventions in development in a given action context. Such assumptions may reflect generalized or specific self-efficacy beliefs or attributive orientations (e.g., internal vs external control beliefs) as well as more or less informed hypotheses about the stability and plasticity of certain developmental functions or variables.

Such a conceptual framework, which is of course only generally sketched here and needs further elaboration, generates numerous research questions. It may be deduced that efforts toward the maintenance of sensorial and intellectual functions, of physical health, sexual activity, and so forth essentially depend on the personal and social expectancies, beliefs, and values related to these areas of functioning. It may be further assumed that a subjective conception of development that emphasizes plasticity and modifiability fosters a high motivation for personal control of development, particularly if it is supported by cognitions of self-efficacy. These assumptions seem to offer at least a partial explanation for the frequently observed variability of developmental functions across cultures, cohorts, and social classes.

## B. SUBJECTIVE POTENTIALS OF DEVELOPMENTAL CONTROL

An action–theoretical rationale as sketched above highlights the central significance of subjective control potentials and effectance beliefs for the personal regulation of development. Such cognitions and beliefs are necessary (but not sufficient) conditions for subjective endeavors toward active developmental change. They determine, for example, the subject's effort in counteracting negative developmental outcomes; they motivate a person's reactance against expected functional losses and determine the individual's persistence in the face of apparent failure; and they account for differential risk preferences in exposing oneself to challenging and potentially enriching activities or situations. It becomes evident at this point how stereotyped beliefs about the loss of certain control competencies in old age can turn into self-fulfilling prophecies. Together with other variables of action control, subjective control potentials constitute a controlling overlayer of development, that of course itself is subject to developmental changes. It follows that development over the life span has to be considered not only as a multidimensional and multidirectional, but also as a multilevel process in which functionally interrelated levels of regulation must be differentiated. The development and change of subjective control beliefs thus appear as a theme of key importance in life-span developmental research (see Bandura, 1981).

The topic of personal control and subjective control beliefs constitutes a nodal point in the conceptual network of an action perspective on development, from which threads lead to various other research topics. In the following, we take up two of these conceptual threads and discuss them briefly: One leads to questions of the emotional–affective experience of developmental and aging processes (Section V,C) and another to the theme of developmental crises and conflicts (Section V,D).

## C. EMOTIONAL ASPECTS OF DEVELOPMENTAL AND AGING EXPERIENCES

Closely connected to the subject's control beliefs, values, and expectations about development and aging are the emotional–affective experiences of development and aging processes. Emotional reactions are not actions, but are closely related to processes of action regulation. In the actual genesis of emotions, the attributional analysis of action situations and outcomes, in particular the appraisal of one's own potentials for action, is of central significance. Positive and negative emotions such as joy, pride, confidence, annoyance, anxiety, worry, helplessness seem to be conceptually dependent on the subject's appraisal of his control potentials (high or low subjective control, gain or loss of control) in personally relevant fields of action. This is a point in which theories of coping, helplessness, and effectance converge with recent attributional work on cognition–affect relations (Lazarus, 1980; Weiner, 1982). Accordingly, along with subjective evaluations of perceived or anticipated developmental changes, personal assumptions regarding the modifiability (plasticity, reversibility) of the corresponding developmental outcomes and sequences as well as related perceptions of self-efficacy should also play an important role in one's emotional attitude toward such changes. These notions can be extended to the area of aging. From this perspective, the fostering and maintenance of subjective control beliefs relating to development appear as key problems of successful aging (Lehr, 1984; Schulz, 1980; Thomae, 1980).

Figure 1 summarizes and extends some of the arguments presented in the last sections. It offers a rough heuristic framework from which propositions concerning the interrelationships of cognitive, emotional, and actional orientations in the control of personal development and aging may be derived. To substantiate and further elaborate these propositions theoretically, we can refer to diverse action–theoretical approaches centering on the theme of personal control: theories of coping, effectance and helplessness, expectancy–value models, social learning, and attribution–theoretical formulations (see above; cf. also Garber & Seligman, 1980; Krampen, 1982).

Figure 1 may be read as a sequence of more or less complex implications: for example, if the aging individual perceives his developmental prospects as un-

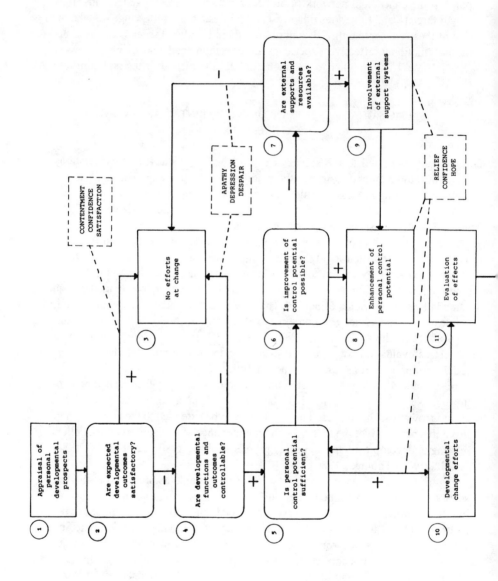

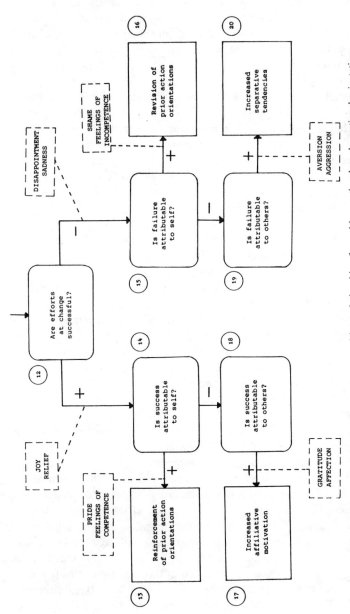

**Fig. 1.** Personal control of development: structure and interrelationship of cognitive, actional, and emotional orientations.

19

satisfactory with regard to his personal aspirations, values, or life plans (1, 2−), and believes that there is no chance to influence positively the initially anticipated course of development (4−) or, alternatively, considers the anticipated course of development as alterable but, at the same time, believes that his actual control potential or efficacy is insufficient (4+, 5−) and that there is no way to augment his control potential—for example, through information seeking, skill training, or external supports (6−, 7−)—then he will make no efforts to change his developmental fate (3) and, presumably, will experience feelings of apathy, depression, or despair. As an aside, it may again be questioned whether such research-guiding propositions have to be interpreted as causal hypotheses—in this case, "antecedents" and "consequents" should be logically and/or terminologically independent—or as conceptual or structural implications in the sense mentioned earlier. Elsewhere, I have advanced arguments in favor of the latter point of view (Brandtstädter 1982, 1984c).

## D. DEVELOPMENTAL CRISES AND CONFLICTS AS PROBLEMS OF ACTION ORIENTATION

Developmental crises and conflicts must be conceived in a relational or "transactional" sense as situations that are characterized by a discrepancy between (subjective) demands of the situation and (subjective) potentials for mastery. Such discrepancies may arise, for example, in the confrontation with new developmental tasks and life tasks, in phases of rapid cultural change involving problems of alienation and obsolescence, or in connection with normative and nonnormative life transitions. Recent formulations have stressed the potentially productive and competence-enhancing functions of developmental crises and critical life events (e.g., Filipp, 1981; Riegel, 1975).

An actional perspective offers a point of departure for the further elaboration of this viewpoint, since crises and critical life events may be readily explicated as problems of action orientation. Such orientation problems are likely to occur during radical changes in personally relevant areas, which alter the instrumental or expressive value of habitualized action patterns and thus lead to a destabilization of prior action orientations (expectancies, values, efficacy beliefs, etc.); in more serious cases, basic life themes may be threatened, so that the individual's whole organization of action loses its personal meaning and identity. Such adaptive crises may activate control processes at higher functional levels which aim at the reorientation of action. Adaptive regulations of this type were already postulated in older theories of personal competence (e.g., White, 1959) and cognitive consistency (e.g., Festinger, 1964); in the cybernetic theory of self-regulating systems, such processes are addressed in the concepts of ultra- and multistability (see W. R. Ashby, 1960). Subjective coping efforts can accordingly be interpreted as processes of the restructuring and restabilization of action orientations, which may include processes of affective reevaluation, problem solving, information seeking, and so forth (Lazarus & Launier, 1978). Subjective effectance beliefs again play an important role in this connection. Crises and conflicts may have an enhancing impact inasmuch as the individual's reorientation efforts on development involve attempts to develop new skills and to improve his knowledge. Parenthetically it should be noted that situations of crisis and conflict often are characterized by an intensified need for information and counseling; we will come back to this point in Section VI,B.

## E. ANALYZING HISTORICAL AND CULTURAL CHANGE IN DEVELOPMENT-RELATED ACTION ORIENTATIONS

As postulated at the beginning, cultural products can be considered results or "objectifications" of action and decision processes. According to this supposition, an action–theoretical approach also becomes relevant for the analysis and explanation of historical and cultural change in development-related action orientations. The action perspective thus seems to offer a common methodological format for the analysis of ontogenetic and historical developmental change and an opportunity to relate both levels to each other in the sense of cross-level theorizing.

It has been argued that action explanations essentially require an assessment of the agents' normative and cognitive orientations. This implies that the preparatory phase of an action, in which stable action orientations are not yet established, involves explicit or implicit deliberations in which alternative courses of action are considered and evaluated with regard to their possible effects and side effects, to their feasibility and compatibility, to their instrumental effectiveness, and so on. Accordingly, the explanation of historical and cultural changes requires a methodically controlled reconstruction and reactualization of the argumentative suppositions upon which these changes or the associated actions and decisions are based.

In contrast to preparatory phases of action, habitualized or routine action, in which the actor has already achieved stable action orientations, is rather unburdened of reflexive deliberations of the kind mentioned above. But it would be a mistake to consider routine action as a less rational or even irrational type of action, as some authors seem to do (see Taylor & Fiske, 1978). Rationality should be considered not as an attribute of ongoing control processes, but rather of the argumentative (cognitive and evaluative) foundations of action, which can be reconstructed even for habitual or routine action.

If becomes clear in this connection that changes in knowledge, experience, and information are important conditions of change in development-related action orientations. This holds not only for changes on the ontogenetic level, but on the cultural and historical level as well. It should be added parenthetically that predominant action orientations (beliefs, values, etc.) in turn influence the processing of information and the assimilation of knowledge (Rescher, 1969). For example, historical changes in educational attitudes are often related to altered cognitions concerning the developmental effects of certain patterns of child rearing; one remembers, e.g., the influence that psychoanalytic theory had on child rearing and education. With regard to adult development, too, there are syndromal changes of beliefs and values which can easily be interpreted in the sense of an information-induced value change. For example, the increasing preference for an active–participative life-style among the elderly seems clearly associated with the popularization of activity theories of aging according to which such a life-style can prevent functional deficits and contribute to the maintenance of role resources required for personal satisfaction in old age (see Birren & Schaie, 1977). The previously mentioned feedback of developmental psychological research on developmental processes is mediated by belief–value interactions of this kind.

We shall not go into the methodological problems of a valid reconstruction of historical decision processes here. The comparative analysis of the historical and cultural formation and modification of development-related beliefs and values is a promising research field that calls for the collaboration of all human and social sciences interested in human development. It may be added that such research may be not only of abstract scientific interest, but also of practical value. The individual actor has usually only a very limited comprehension of the argumentative underpinnings and functional values of the cultural demands and restrictions imposed on his development and behavior; in this regard, too, the postulate of the human agent's "bounded rationality" (Simon, 1957) seems justified. Such comprehension problems may become aggravated in periods of accelerated cultural change and of normative life transitions and may lead to experiences of alienation and helplessness as they are reported, e.g., for adolescent development (e.g., Coleman, 1980; Oerter, 1982) or in connection with obsolescence problems in old age (e.g., Schaie & Quayhagen, 1979). Efforts to reconstruct the historical decision processes and arguments from which social and institutional norm systems evolved thus may contribute to regain lost meaning contents and to make them accessible to reflection and criticism. Such efforts can further help to avoid certain unwanted side effects which frequently occur in connection with interventions in institutional contexts of development: The institutional conditions toward which such intervention efforts are targeted, being the result of historical problem solutions, may have latent functions and gratification values which *post festum* may be reactualized and then lead to adaptive crises and "dislocations" (Tenbruck, 1972) in the social need system—a problem that is well known from the field of innovation research (Boesch, 1971).

These last reflections lead to a closing consideration of some practical implications of an action-oriented developmental perspective.

## VI. Practical Implications of an Action-Oriented Developmental Perspective

If one conceives of actions as outcomes of argumentative discourses and reflective decisions, hence as behavior that is based upon, and accessible to argument, then some important practical implications may be derived for an applied developmental psychology (cf. Montada & Schmitt, 1982), as well as for problems of developmental goal planning across the life span.

### A. CONTRIBUTIONS TO DEVELOPMENTAL GOAL PLANNING

Obviously, it makes no sense to critically evaluate developmental processes in regard to criteria such as rationality, justice, and so forth, as long as one regards them from a strictly causal or deterministic posture (cf. Malcolm, 1977). Accordingly, there exists a certain danger for the advocates of such a position to be caught in self-contradictions when they engage in corrective, preventive, or optimizing interventions in development which presuppose or involve normative evaluations of the mentioned type (cf. Groeben, 1979). These self-contradictions disappear in an action-oriented developmental perspective: one can argue critically against actions, action demands, and action restrictions which rest upon cognitive or argumentative presuppositions. Hypotheses about probable action effects that were involved in the planning or justification of an action may be subjected to test, beliefs about available action alternatives or action competencies may be criticized, untoward side-effects and compatibility problems may be brought to attention. In short, the arguments involved in actions and decisions on the individual and social level may be evaluated in analogy to scientific hypotheses as to their validity and consistency, and even the semantic presuppositions inherent in the interpretation of actions may be critically analyzed. The above-mentioned phenomenon of information-induced value change reflects the fact that the invalidation of certain arguments also weakens the normative positions that were built upon them.

These considerations obviously presuppose an idealized concept of action that involves criteria such as accessibility to arguments, reflection on action outcomes, and so on. Factual processes of developmental goal planning often violate such criteria. The considerations above thus should not lead one to overestimate the "argumentative function" of language (cf. Popper, 1945) or the readiness of agents to organize their behavior on an argumentative basis. (It should be noted that the reception of arguments in itself may be considered as motivated or reasoned action: the credibility of a communication, its consistency with personal preconceptions, etc. are known to be relevant factors in this context.) Moreover, it should be clear that arguments affect individual actions only insofar as they fit into a context of beliefs and values which the agent takes for granted so far. Such more fundamental belief–value systems may be comprehensible only to the extent that one shares the agent's form of life ("empractical" understanding; see Kambartel, 1981).

These reservations notwithstanding, it seems evident that an action perspective on development offers the framework not only for a descriptive but also for a critical analysis of historical and current developmental orientations on individual and social levels. The developmental sciences seem by no means limited to a mere stock taking of prevailing developmental tasks and conditions. Rather, through investigating the realizability, the compatibility, and the effects and side effects of certain developmental demands they can substantially contribute to decisions about developmental goals over the life span—provided that such decisions conform to basic criteria of rational action. The deontological thesis, that no statement of value can be derived from a system of premises containing only statements of fact, remains undisputed here (see Hudson, 1969). The argumentative linkage of descriptive and normative premises, however, which is characteristic of action and decision processes, involves no such "naturalistic fallacy." From a practical point of view, there is not much reason at this juncture to bother about whether an "ultimate justification" for developmental goals is possible or not. The practical need for the critical evaluation and justification of certain developmental goals does not arise always and everywhere, but primarily in situations which call for the construction and reorganization of action orientations, that is, in connection with actual or potential developmental crises, conflicts, and so on. Only in the limited context of such problems does there seem to be a practical need for critical and justificatory efforts.

An action-oriented developmental perspective thus may be an effective antidote against the "value allergy" (Scriven, 1967) which seems to be widespread among developmental psychologists (and to be sure not only among them). At the same time, it leads to a broader conception of applied developmental psychology. This will be discussed in Section VII.

### B. DEVELOPMENTAL COUNSELING UNDER THE LIFE-SPAN ASPECT

Developmental problems and crises were characterized as situations in which special information and orientation needs arise. At any choice point in life-span development there is the complex decision problem of simultaneously taking into account the individual's developmental interests and potentials as well as social and cultural demands that result from the requirements of social coexistence. Such decisions often involve intricate problems of assessment, evaluation, and prediction that call for scientific and particularly for developmental psychological support.

A methodologically founded strategy of developmental counseling may be advocated as a mode of intervention to deal with this type of orientation problem across the life span. Developmental counseling represents a mode of applied developmental psychology that cannot fully replace, but may well supplement, technical interventions (see Herrmann, 1979). Since counseling is or should be an argumentative rather than a manipulative process, it seems that an action-oriented framework which conceives of development as related to action and action as related to arguments is especially suited to explicate this type of intervention (Brandtstädter, 1984b).

Demand for developmental counseling exists wherever the construction or revision of development-related orientations is at stake. Here again one thinks primarily of crises and conflicts related to life transitions; counseling opportunities across the life span may well be placed and timed according to the age–risk functions for normative developmental crises (Brim & Ryff, 1980; Danish, Smyer, & Nowak, 1980). The application range of developmental counseling is of course not limited to this problem type. Rather, a great variety of developmental difficulties such as educational problems, marital problems, problems of occupational development, and of obsolescence may be attributed to discrepancies or conflicts within or between personal aspirations or potentials and social demands or resources for development. Coping with such discrepancies or conflicts may require the critical revision of development-related action orientations, hence developmental counseling. It may now be asked in what respect developmental counseling can and should be distinguished from established approaches of counseling and consultation such as educational guidance, school counseling, marriage counseling, and occupational guidance. It seems that established approaches to counseling often limit their perspective to isolated problem areas as well as to only narrow segments of aging and development. Such a restriction is clearly inappropriate in regard to the task of optimizing development across the life span. In their antecedents, manifestations, and effects, developmental problems usually transcend isolated life spheres and age segments. School difficulties may develop out of familiar crisis situations, marital problems may result from problems of occupational development and coorientation within the partnership; occupational career decisions often simultaneously have to take extraoccupational developmental interests into consideration, and so forth (cf. Blocher, 1966; Van Hoose & Worth, 1982). Moreover, in choosing among developmental options (goals, tasks, opportunities) for certain periods of age and development, their compatibility with subsequent developmental tasks and options must also be taken into consideration. Developmental problems on individual and institutional levels often result from the mentioned narrowing of the counseling perspective. This justifies an attempt to integrate established area-specific approaches of counseling and consultation in a broader framework of life-span comprehensive developmental counseling.

The task of helping the individual in the evaluation and revision of developmental orientations surpasses the simple "giving away" of developmental psychological knowledge. Developmental counseling, if suited to the individual case, rather involves assistance in the interpretation and critical analysis of the subject's developmental themes and beliefs, the evaluation of objective and subjective developmental potentials and action competencies, the representation of alternative developmental options as well as of the effects and side effects of such alternatives, the localization of imbalances and conflicts between the subject's developmental orientations and the demands and requirements of his developmental ecology (including "codeveloping" individuals), and so forth. Such individualized assistance can contribute to preventing the above-mentioned "dislocation problems" that frequently result from personal life changes. For example, the dissolution of a partnership may enhance the individual's occupational development but at the same time threaten his needs for personal affiliation and security; the modification of a "stressful" life style may lessen the risk of coronary illness, but at the same time be discordant with the person's basic life themes and values and thus involve other developmental risks. Such negative side-effects come into view only in the comprehensive analysis of the individual's action orientations as should be attempted in developmental counseling. With regard to the need for a valid representation of personal developmental orientations, a nondirective context enhancing an unconstrained exchange of arguments seems to be a prerequisite for developmental counseling (cf. Kaiser & Seel, 1981). The explication of criteria for an authentic communication seems to be a methodological problem of prime importance (cf. the concept of the "ideal dialogue situation," Habermas, 1981).

The methodical regard for contextual conditions protects an action-oriented conception of developmental counseling from one-sided causal attributions in the analysis of developmental problems. As already mentioned, developmental difficulties and crises are indicative not only of personal competence deficits, but also of inadequacies in the person's social and institutional developmental ecologies with their specific demands and resources, their particular response patterns and potentials for conflict that result from prevailing rule and norm systems, and so on. Developmental counseling accordingly may of course be offered not only to single individuals, but also to policymakers and institutions (Brandtstädter, 1984b).

## VII. Summary

Development across the life span is controlled and modified by individual as well as social action orientations and constraints. An action-oriented conception of development across the life span involves some intricate problems as well as novel aspects for research and application in developmental psychology.

An initial group of questions concerns the possibility of general, context-independent theories of development. Obviously, general assumptions about the "normal" course of development already imply tacit assumptions about the restrictions and potentials for developmental modification given in the actual cultural and historical context. Developmental sequences involving an "actional" nexus cannot be nomologically universalized, but only locally generalized. Nevertheless, the widespread belief that the ideal of general theories of development has to be abandoned because of the context variability and "plasticity" of developmental patterns cannot be defended. The aspects of contextual variability and transcontextual invariance can be reconciled on the basis of an epistemological position that distinguishes between generated and generating functional levels of development.

A further complex of problems is related to issues of action explanation that are controversially discussed within philosophy of science today. If actions are conceived as "interpretative constructs" which are not causally determined but rather conceptually constituted by attributes such as expectancies, values, or control beliefs, then certain difficulties result for causal–nomological action explanations of the covering-law type. It seems, however, that a third position between the rival positions of causalism and logical intentionalism can be established that accounts for the "quasi-analytic" status of reduction statements.

An action perspective on life-span development offers a theoretical framework of great heuristic and integrative value. The research areas of social learning theory, of attribution, reactance, and helplessness, and of personal control and emotion may be integrated within an action framework. The extension of action–theoretical assumptions to the realm of human development across the life span generates numerous research themes. We have considered as examples processes of personal control over development and aging in their relationship to developmental values, expectancies, and efficacy beliefs; the dependency of the emotional–affective experience of development and aging on development-related action competencies and control beliefs; and the reconstruction of crises and critical life events as problems of the destabilization and reorganization of action orientations and action potentials. An action perspective further offers a common format for the analysis of ontogenetic and historical–cultural change, inasmuch as development on both levels depends on actions and decision processes.

The objectives of an applied developmental psychology are often restricted to the aspect of technical–manipulative interventions in development. An action-oriented conception of development that conceives of development as dependent on action and of action as behavior that is based on and accessible to argument leads also to a broadening of intervention perspectives. First, it becomes clear that the developmental sciences can also contribute to questions concerning the goal planning of human development across the life span and to a critical evaluation of prevailing developmental beliefs, values, and action patterns. From an action perspective, developmental crises and conflicts on individual as well as on social–cultural levels should be conceived as orientation problems that are characterized by special demands for information, argumentative exchange, and enhancement of personal control potentials. This highlights the practical importance of a life-span comprehensive developmental counseling as a mode of intervention that may be methodically elaborated within an action framework.

## Acknowledgment

The author is grateful to Michael Chapman for his valuable assistance in the translation of this article.

## References

Aebli, H. *Denken: das Ordnen des Tuns* (Vol. 1). Stuttgart: Klett-Cotta, 1980.
Ashby, R. W. Linguistic theory of the a priori. In P. Edwards (Ed.), *The encyclopedia of philosophy*. New York: Macmillan, 1967.
Ashby, W. R. *Design for a brain*. London: Chapman & Hall, 1960.
Baltes, P. B., & Baltes, M. M. Plasticity and variability in psychological aging: Methodological and theoretical issues. In G. Gurski (Ed.), *The effects of aging on the central nervous system*. Berlin: Schering, 1980.
Baltes, P. B., Reese, H. W., & Lipsitt, L. P. Life-developmental psychology. *Annual Review of Psychology*, 1980, **31**, 65–110.
Baltes, P. B., & Schaie, K. W. The myth of the twilight years. *Psychology Today*, March 1974, 35–40.
Bandura, A. Self-efficacy: Toward a unified theory of behavioral change. *Psychological Review*, 1977, **84**, 191–215.
Bandura, A. Self-referent thought: A developmental analysis of self-efficacy. In I. H. Flavell & L. Ross (Eds.), *Social cognitive development. Frontiers and possible futures*. London and New York: Cambridge University Press, 1981.
Beckermann, A. Intentionale vs. kausale Handlungserklärungen. In H. Lenk (Ed.), *Handlungstheorien interdisziplinär* (Vol. 2, Pt. 2). Munich: Fink, 1979.
Bell, R. Q., & Hertz, A. W. Toward more comparability and generalizability of developmental research. *Child Development*, 1976, **47**, 6–13.
Birren, J. E., & Schaie, K. W. (Eds.). *Handbook of the psychology of aging*. Princeton, New Jersey: Van Nostrand Reinhold, 1977.
Blocher, D. H. *Developmental counseling*. New York: Ronald Press, 1966.
Bloom, B. S. *Stability and change in human characteristics*. New York: Wiley, 1964.
Boesch, E. E. *Zwischen zwei Wirklichkeiten. Prolegomena zu einer ökologischen Psychologie*. Bern: Huber, 1971.
Boesch, E. E. *Kultur und Handlung*. Bern: Huber, 1980.
Brandtstädter, J. Relationships between life-span developmental theory, research, and intervention: A revision of some stereotypes. In R. R. Turner & H. W. Reese (Eds.), *Life-span developmental psychology: Intervention*. New York: Academic Press, 1980.
Brandtstädter, J. Apriorische Elemente in psychologischen Forschungsprogrammen. *Zeitschrift für Sozialpsychologie*, 1982, **13**, 267–277.
Brandtstädter, J. Individual development in social action contexts: Problems of explanation. In J.

Nesselroade & A. Von Eye (Eds.), *Individual development and social change: Explanatory analysis.* New York: Academic Press, 1984, in press. (a)

Brandtstädter, J. Entwicklungsberatung unter dem Aspekt der Lebensspanne: Zum Aufbau eines entwicklungspsychologischen Anwendungskonzeptes. In J. Brandtstädter & H. Gräser (Eds.), *Entwicklungsberatung unter dem Aspekt der Lebensspanne.* Göttingen: Hogrefe, 1984, in press. (b)

Brandtstädter, J. Emotion, Kognition, Handlung: Konzeptuelle Beziehungen. In L. Eckensberger & E. Lantermann (Eds.), *Emotion und Reflexivität.* Göttingen: Hogrefe, 1984, in press. (c)

Brim, O. G., Jr., & Kagan, J. (Eds.). *Constancy and change in human development.* Cambridge, Massachusetts: Harvard University Press, 1980.

Brim, O. G., Jr., & Ryff, C. D. On the properties of life events. In P. B. Baltes & O. G. Brim, Jr. (Eds.), *Life-span development and behavior* (Vol. 3). New York: Academic Press, 1980.

Bühler, C., & Massarik, F. (Eds.). *Lebenslauf und Lebensziele.* Stuttgart: Fischer, 1969.

Bunge, M. *Causality and modern science* (3rd ed.). New York: Dover, 1979.

Buss, A. R. Causes and reasons in attribution theory: A conceptual critique. *Journal of Personality and Social Psychology,* 1978, **36,** 1311–1321.

Clayton, V. P., & Birren, J. E. The development of wisdom across the life-span: A reexamination of an ancient topic. In P. B. Baltes & O. G. Brim, Jr. (Eds.), *Life-span development and behavior* (Vol. 3). New York: Academic Press, 1980.

Coleman, I. C. *The nature of adolescence.* London: Methuen, 1980.

Danish, S. J., Smyer, M. A., & Nowak, C. A. Developmental intervention: Enhancing life-event processes. In P. B. Baltes & O. G. Brim, Jr. (Eds.), *Life-span development and behavior* (Vol. 3). New York: Academic Press, 1980.

Feather, N. T. (Ed.). *Expectations and actions: Expectancy-value models in psychology.* Hillsdale, New Jersey: Erlbaum, 1982.

Festinger, C. *Conflict, decision and dissonance.* Stanford, California: Stanford University Press, 1964.

Filipp, S. H. (Ed.). *Kritische Lebensereignisse.* Munich: Urban & Schwarzenberg, 1981.

Flavell, J. H., & Ross, L. (Eds.). *Social cognitive development. Frontiers and possible futures.* London and New York: Cambridge University Press, 1981.

Garber, J., & Seligman, M. E. P. (Eds.). *Human helplessness.* New York: Academic Press, 1980.

Garn, S. M. Continuities and change in maturational timing. In O. G. Brim, Jr. & J. Kagan (Eds.), *Constancy and change in human development.* Cambridge, Massachusetts: Harvard University Press, 1980.

Gauld, A., & Shotter, I. *Human actions and its psychological investigation.* London: Routledge & Kegan Paul, 1977.

Gehlen, A. *Der Mensch. Seine Natur und seine Stellung in der Welt* (9th ed.). Frankfurt: Athenäum, 1971.

Gentner, D. Evidence for the psychological relation of semantic components: The verbs of possession. In D. A. Norman & D. E. Rumelhart (Eds.), *Explorations in cognition.* San Francisco: Freeman, 1975.

Gergen, K. J. The emerging crisis in life-span developmental theory. In P. B. Baltes & O. G. Brim, Jr. (Eds.), *Life-span development and behavior* (Vol. 3). New York: Academic Press, 1980.

Groeben, N. Widersprüchlichkeit und Selbstanwendung: Psychologische Menschenbildannahmen zwischen Logik und Moral. *Zeitschrift für Sozialpsychologie,* 1979, **10,** 267–273.

Habermas, J. *Theorie des kommunikativen Handelns* (Vol. 1). Frankfurt: Suhrkamp, 1981.

Hempel, L. G., & Oppenheim, P. Studies in the logic of explanation. *Philosophy of Science,* 1948, **15,** 135–175.

Herrmann, T. *Die Psychologie und ihre Forschungsprogramme.* Göttingen: Hogrefe, 1976.

Herrmann, T. Pädagogische Psychologie als psychologische Technologie. In J. Brandtstädter, G.

Reinert, & K. A. Schneewind (Eds.), *Pädagogische Psychologie: Probleme und Perspektiven.* Stuttgart: Klett-Cotta, 1979.

Horn, J. L., & Donaldson, G. On the myth of intellectual decline in adulthood. *American Psychologist,* 1976, **31,** 701–719.

Hudson, W. D. (Ed.). *The is–ought question.* New York: Macmillan, 1969.

Kagan, J. Perspectives on continuity. In O. G. Brim, Jr. & J. Kagan (Eds.), *Constancy and change in human development.* Cambridge, Massachusetts: Harvard University Press, 1980.

Kaiser, H. I., & Seel, H.-J. (Eds.). *Sozialwissenschaft als Dialog. Die methodischen Prinzipien der Beratungsforschung.* Weinheim: Beltz, 1981.

Kambartel, F. Friede und Konfliktbewältigung, handlungstheoretisch und ethisch betrachtet. In W. Kempf & G. Aschenbach (Eds.), *Konflikt und Konfliktbewältigung. Handlungstheoretische Aspekte einer praxisorientierten psychologischen Forschung.* Bern: Huber, 1981.

Kenny, A. *Will, freedom and power.* Oxford: Blackwell, 1975.

Klaus, G., & Buhr, M. (Eds.). *Philosophisches Wörterbuch* (Vol. 2). Leipzig: VEB Enzyklopädie, 1971.

Kohlberg, L. Moral stages and moralization. The cognitive developmental approach. In T. Lickona (Ed.), *Moral development and behavior. Theory, research and social issues.* New York: Holt, 1976.

Kohlberg, L., LaCrosse, J., & Ricks, D. The predictability of adult mental health from childhood behavior. In B. Wolman (Ed.), *Manual of child psychopathology.* New York: McGraw-Hill, 1972.

Krampen, G. *Differentialpsychologie der Kontrollüberzeugungen.* Göttingen: Hogrefe, 1982.

Lazarus, R. S. The stress and coping paradigm. In A. Bond & J. C. Rosen (Eds.), *Primary prevention of psychopathology* (Vol. 4). Hanover, New Hampshire: University Press of New England, 1980.

Lazarus, R. S., & Launier, R. Stress-related transactions between person and environment. In L. A. Pervin & M. Lewis (Eds.), *Interaction between internal and external determinants of behavior.* New York: Plenum, 1978.

Lehr, U. Sozialpsychologische Korrelate der Langlebigkeit. *Annual Review of Gerontology and Geriatrics,* **3,** 1984, in press.

Lenk, H. Über strukturelle Implikationen. *Zeitschrift für Soziologie,* 1975, **4,** 350–358.

Lenk, H. Handlung als Interpretationskonstrukt. Entwurf einer konstituenten- und beschreibungstheoretischen Handlungsphilosophie. In H. Lenk (Ed.), *Handlungstheorien interdisziplinär* (Vol. 2, pt. 1). Munich: Fink, 1978.

Lenk, H. *Wie philosophisch ist die Anthropologie?* Paper presented at the Conference "Erfahrung und Empirie," March 1982, Schloss Reisensburg, Günzburg, Federal Republic of Germany (unpublished).

Leontjew, A. N. *Tätigkeit, Bewusstsein, Persönlichkeit.* Stuttgart: Klett-Cotta, 1977.

Lerner, R. M. Individual and context in developmental psychology: Conceptual and theoretical issues. In J. Nesselroade & A. von Eye (Eds.), *Individual development and social change: Explanatory analysis.* New York: Academic Press, 1984, in press.

Lerner, R. M., & Busch-Rossnagel, N. A. (Eds.). *Individuals as producers of their development.* New York: Academic Press, 1981.

Macfarlane, J., Allen, L., & Honzik, N. *A developmental study of behavior problems of normal children between 21 months and fourteen years.* Berkeley, California: University of California Press, 1954.

Malcolm, N. Ist der Mechanismus vorstellbar? In A. Beckermann (Ed.), *Analytische Handlungstheorie* (Vol. 2). Frankfurt: Suhrkamp, 1977.

Meggle, G. Grundbegriffe der rationalen Handlungstheorie. In G. Meggle (Ed.), *Analytische Handlungstheorie* (Vol. 1). Frankfurt: Suhrkamp, 1977.

Miller, G. A., Galanter, E., & Pribram, K. H. *Plans and the structure of behavior.* New York: Holt, 1960.

Montada, L., & Schmitt, M. Issues in applied developmental psychology: A life-span perspective. In P. B. Baltes & O. G. Brim, Jr. (Eds.), *Life-span development and behavior* (Vol. 4). New York: Academic Press, 1982.

Neugarten, B. L., & Hagestad, G. O. Age and the life course. In R. H. Binstock & E. Shanas (Eds.), *Handbook of aging and the social sciences.* Princeton, New Jersey: Van Nostrand Reinhold, 1976.

Oerter, R. Jugendalter. In R. Oerter & L. Montada (Eds.), *Entwicklungspsychologie. Ein Lehrbuch.* Munich: Urban & Schwarzenberg, 1982.

Parsons, T., & Shils, E. A. *Toward a general theory of action.* Cambridge, Massachusetts: Harvard University Press, 1951.

Popper, K. *The open society and its enemies* (Vol. 2). London: Routledge & Kegan Paul, 1945.

Pörn, J. *Action theory and social science.* Boston: Reidel, 1977.

Rescher, N. What is value change: A framework for research. In K. Baier & N. Rescher (Eds.), *Values and the future.* New York: Free Press, 1969.

Riegel, K. F. Adult life crises: A dialectical interpretation of development. In N. Datan & L. H. Ginsberg (Eds.), *Life-span developmental psychology. Normative life crises.* New York: Academic Press, 1975.

Schaie, K. W. Translations in gerontology—from lab to life: Intellectual functioning. *American Psychologist,* 1974, **29,** 802–807.

Schaie, K. W., & Quayhagen, M. Aufgaben einer Pädagogischen Psychologie des mittleren und höheren Lebensalters. In J. Brandtstädter, G. Reinert, & K. A. Schneewind (Eds.), *Pädagogische Psychologie: Probleme und Perspektiven.* Stuttgart: Klett-Cotta, 1979.

Schank, R., & Abelson, R. P. *Scripts, plans, goals and understanding.* Hillsdale, New Jersey: Erlbaum, 1977.

Schulz, R. Aging and control. In J. Garber & M. E. P. Seligman (Eds.), *Human helplessness.* New York: Academic Press, 1980.

Schwemmer, O. *Theorie der rationalen Erklärung. Zu den methodischen Grundlagen der Kulturwissenschaften.* Munich: Beck, 1976.

Scriven, M. Science, fact and value. In S. Morgenbesser (Ed.), *Philosophy of science today.* New York: Basic Books, 1967.

Shaw, M. E., & Sulzer, J. R. An empirical test of Heider's levels in attribution of responsibility. *Journal of Abnormal and Social Psychology,* 1964, **69,** 39–46.

Simon, H. A. *Models of man, social and rational: Mathematical essays on rational human behavior in a social setting.* New York: Wiley, 1957.

Smedslund, J. Analyzing the primary code: From empiricism to apriorism. In D. R. Olson (Ed.), *The social foundations of language and thought. Essays in honor of J. S. Bruner.* New York: Norton, 1980.

Smith, M. J. *Persuasion and human action. A review and critique of social influence theories.* Belmont, California: Wadsworth, 1982.

Stegmüller, W. *Probleme und Resultate der Wissenschaftstheorie und Analytischen Philosophie* (Vol. 9). Berlin and New York: Springer-Verlag, 1969.

Stegmüller, W. *The structuralist view of theories.* New York: Springer Publ., 1979.

Stegmüller, W. *Neue Wege der Wissenschaftsphilosophie.* Berlin and New York: Springer-Verlag, 1980.

Taylor, S. E., & Fiske, S. T. Salience, attention and attribution: Top of the head phenomena. In L. Berkowitz (Ed.), *Advances in experimental social psychology* (Vol. 11). New York: Academic Press, 1978. Pp. 249–288.

Tenbruck, F. H. *Zur Kritik der planenden Vernunft*. Freiburg, Federal Republic of Germany: Alber, 1972.

Thalberg, J. *Perception, emotion and action. A component approach*. Oxford: Blackwell, 1977.

Thomae, H. Personality and adjustment to aging. In J. E. Birren & R. B. Sloane (Eds.), *Handbook of mental health and aging*. Englewood Cliffs, New Jersey: Prentice-Hall, 1980.

Toulmin, S. Concepts and the explanation of human behavior. In T. Mischel (Ed.), *Human action. Conceptual and empirical issues*. New York: Academic Press, 1969.

Toulmin, S. Rules and their relevance for understanding human behavior. In T. Mischel (Ed.), *Understanding other persons*. Oxford: Blackwell, 1974.

Van Hoose, W. H., & Worth, M. R. *Counseling adults: A developmental approach*. Monterey, California: Brooks/Cole, 1982.

Volpert, W. (Ed.). *Beiträge zur psychologischen Handlungstheorie*. Bern: Huber, 1981.

Von Wright, G. H. *Explanation and understanding*. Ithaca, New York: Cornell University Press, 1971.

Warren, N. Universality and plasticity, ontogeny and phylogeny: The resonance between culture and cognitive development. In J. Sants (Ed.), *Developmental psychology and society*. New York: Macmillan, 1980.

Watkins, J. W. N. Historical explanation in the social science. *British Journal for the Philosophy of Science*, 1957, **8**, 104–117.

Weiner, B. *Human motivation*. New York: Holt, 1980.

Weiner, B. An attributionally based theory of motivation and emotion: Focus, range and issues. In N. T. Feather (Ed.), *Expectations and actions: Expectancy-value models in psychology*. Hillsdale, New Jersey: Erlbaum, 1982.

Weiner, B., & Litman-Adizes, T. An attributional expectancy-value analysis of learned helplessness and depression. In J. Garber & M. E. P. Seligman (Eds.), *Human helplessness*. New York: Academic Press, 1980.

White, R. W. Motivation reconsidered: The concept of competence. *Psychological Review*, 1959, **66**, 297–333.

Winch, P. *The idea of a social science and its relation to philosophy*. London: Routledge & Kegan Paul, 1958.

# New Perspectives on the Development of Intelligence in Adulthood: Toward a Dual-Process Conception and a Model of Selective Optimization with Compensation[1]

*Paul B. Baltes, Freya Dittmann-Kohli, and Roger A. Dixon*

MAX PLANCK INSTITUTE

FOR HUMAN DEVELOPMENT AND EDUCATION

BERLIN, FEDERAL REPUBLIC OF GERMANY

[1]This article is based on a manuscript to appear in A. Sørenson, F. Weinert, & L. Sherrod (Eds.), *Life-course human development: Multidisciplinary perspectives,* in preparation. Any effort aimed at providing for an interdisciplinary conception risks the danger of oversimplification. Without relegating responsibilities for errors and deficits to others, the first author would like to express his appreciation for continued interdisciplinary dialogue and support to the members of the "Life-Course Perspectives on Human Development Committee" of the United States Social Sciences Research Council. In this instance, D. L. Featherman, A. Sørenson, E. Markman, M. W. Riley, and F. E. Weinert were especially helpful. The authors acknowledge also the constructive comments of Margret M. Baltes, Jochen Brandtstädter, Steven W. Cornelius, David F. Hultsch, Reinhold Kliegl, Richard M. Lerner, Ellen A. Skinner, and Doris Sowarka on an earlier version of this manuscript.

**33**

# Abstract

Major themes in current research on adult intelligence and its development are presented from a life-span perspective. First, a total of eight propositions aimed at guiding future research and theoretical endeavors is derived. The propositions are based on present trends in life-span research on intelligence, and are informed by other domains such as personality, biology, and sociology. Together, these propositions circumscribe a context for the formulation of new theoretical perspectives. On the most general level, the propositional framework acknowledges stability, growth, and decline as coexisting features of intellectual development. In addition, it emphasizes the need to consider the developmental pragmatics of intellectual functioning. Specifically, some propositions include statements about the continued potential (reserve) and possible directions of further intellectual growth, as well as about aging decline, especially in maximum level of certain facets of cognitive processing. Other propositions focus on the adaptive function of intelligence vis-à-vis the life tasks defined by the structure of psychological, biological, and sociological conditions associated with the context of adult development and aging. Finally, some of the propositions specify conditions for differential intellectual change, including aspects of specialization, compensation, and limits of progression.

Finally, two new models are briefly outlined to illustrate how the propositional scheme may be used to promote theoretical development. The first is a dual-process conception of intellectual development. Whereas the first process (cognition *qua* cognition) relates to the ontogenesis of the basic mechanics or operations of intellectual functioning, the second process (pragmatics of intelligence) emphasizes the contextual elaboration and application of intelligence in terms of knowledge systems and procedural skills. The second model characterizes intellectual aging as selective optimization with compensation. Selective optimization with compensation is seen as a prototypical mechanism of adult development, one that permits an integrative view of the interplay between growth and decline. Wisdom and scientific productivity are used to illustrate. Throughout, we describe the potential usefulness of a testing-the-limits strategy for the identification of specific aspects and conditions of growth and decline in intellectual aging.

# I. Introduction

## A. OBJECTIVE

In the first part of this article, eight propositions about the development of intelligence during adulthood and old age are described. The goal is to educe from the existing body of data (including its conflicting interpretations; e.g., Horn & Donaldson, 1976, 1977 vs Baltes & Schaie, 1976; Schaie & Baltes, 1977) a set of propositions aimed at the integration and coordination of distinct perspectives. The propositions are derived from existing data and from our current characterizations of the evidence pertaining to the development of intelligence throughout adulthood. In addition, the propositions are informed by research in other domains such as personality, biology, and sociology. Their juxtaposition illustrates the embeddedness of intelligence in a larger system of human development. In concert, the propositions form the heuristic core and boundaries for future theoretical developments.

In the second part of this article, two general theoretical conceptions are discussed as illustrations of how the propositional framework can be translated into theory. These conceptions are further elaborations of ideas presented in earlier and related work (e.g., Baltes & Baltes, 1980; Baltes & Willis, 1982; Dittmann-Kohli & Baltes, 1984; Kuhn, Pennington, & Leadbeater, 1983; Labouvie-Vief, 1981, 1982; Pascual-Leone, 1983). The first general conception is a dual-process model of life-span intelligence. The first process of this model refers to the development of cognition *qua* cognition. This process deals with the "content-free" architecture of cognitive information processing. The second process of the dual scheme is called the pragmatics of intelligence. It represents the contextual and functional elaboration of intelligence in terms of knowledge systems and procedural skills.

The second general theoretical orientation derived from the propositional framework is a prototypical process of adult intellectual development labeled "selective optimization with compensation." This model represents one concrete illustration of the dual-process approach to life-span development of intelligence and specifies how growth and decline interact in shaping a person's intellectual development. The continuing growth in some domains of expertise and in wisdom are examples of the former trend (Dittmann-Kohli & Baltes, 1984). A sample case for decline is speed of basic information processing (Horn & Donaldson, 1980; Kliegl, Kramer, & Baltes, 1984; Salthouse, 1982).

As a conclusion, research examples are given to illustrate application of the dual-process scheme and the selective optimization model. In addition, we argue for the potential usefulness of testing-the-limits as a research strategy. Under testing-the-limits conditions (i.e., requiring maximum effort), aspects of both growth and decline are exaggerated and thereby can be studied more directly. Current research focuses on the normal conditions of intellectual aging and thus may systematically overlook some unique features of development.

## B. THE CURRENT RESEARCH SCENE

The field of intelligence has been a longstanding testing ground for theoretical and methodological advances in life-span developmental psychology. This is not surprising because it is this area that has enjoyed perhaps the longest and most intensive interest and study in the history of developmental psychology (e.g., Baltes, 1983a; Carus, 1808; Galton, 1883; Hollingworth, 1927; Quetelet, 1835; Sanford, 1902; Tetens, 1777). This observation on the historical significance of intelligence-related life-span work is not intended to suggest that we know more about this substantive topic when compared with other domains of life-span study. What is suggested, however, is that this strand of work has pushed the field in a number of innovative and necessary ways.

For example, life-span work on intelligence has articulated with much clarity issues such as the problem of age-related measurement validity, the role of cohort-related historical variation in level and structure of intellectual functioning, the performance–competence distinction, and the question of intraindividual plasticity vs trait-oriented conceptions of stability (Baltes & Labouvie, 1973; Botwinick, 1977; Labouvie-Vief, 1977; Willis & Baltes, 1980). In each of these instances, it has become customary to list what life-span work has contributed to the corpus of data and concepts on intellectual development during adulthood and old age. Among the central contributions, for example, are concepts such as multidimensionality, multidirectionality, interindividual variability, and plasticity.

At the same time, however, life-span work has also illustrated several chronic deficits of its own dominant research strategy. With regard to the topic of appropriate developmental measurement, for example, life-span research on psychometric intelligence has been steadfastly using intelligence tests that were originally developed for children or younger adults in school-related performance contexts. Yet, the perseverance of a youth-centric and potentially unsatisfactory measurement of intellectual aging has demonstrated, most conspicuously by its very existence, a serious gap in age- and cohort-fair assessment. Similarly, research on modifiability (plasticity) of intelligence in old age, while emphasizing a substantial amount of reserve in many elderly persons, has also exemplified the lack of a theory of adult intelligence that would entail information about the possible directions of intellectual development and pragmatic use of intelligence.

A number of introductory observations may help to set the stage for the present article. First, we need to acknowledge that, although this article is written from a life-span perspective (Baltes, Reese, & Lipsitt, 1980), it does not offer life-span coverage. The substantive focus is on the second portion of life. For articles emphasizing intellectual development in earlier parts of the life span, see Bayley (1970), McCall (1979), and Wohlwill (1980).

Second, we need to acknowledge that our treatment of the data base is influenced more strongly by research on psychometric intelligence than by research on cognitive processes associated with topics such as learning, memory, information processing, and problem solving (thinking). In the recent decade, we have witnessed renewed enthusiasm for weaving together these separate lines of work (Friedman, Das, & O'Connor, 1981; Kluwe & Spada, 1980; Resnick, 1976; Sternberg, 1981; Sternberg & Detterman, 1979). This is an important integrative enterprise. At the same time, the extent of our knowledge about specific linkages between cognitive processes and psychometric intelligence is scarce. In fact, in some efforts to examine the degree of correlational convergence between information processing measures and psychometric intelligence in the aging adult (e.g., Cornelius, Willis, Nesselroade, & Baltes, 1983), the outcome shows that information processing tasks may index a fairly narrow range (predominantly the factor Perceptual Speed) of the variance covered in the multifactor space provided by psychometric intelligence. It appears from such results that psychometric intelligence covers more complex and diverse phenomena than is accounted for in memory and information-processing measures.

Thus, whereas in the long run we need to continue our search for an integrative view of the diverse approaches to cognition and intelligence, at present we have little option but to proceed in a somewhat separatist fashion. We will make some preliminary efforts, however, to show where linkages might exist between psychometric intelligence and cognitive psychology and to what degree the propositions, derived primarily from research on psychometric intelligence, have implications for research on memory, information processing, and cognitive problem solving as well.

## II. Propositions about Intelligence in Adulthood and Old Age

### A. RELATIONSHIP TO EARLIER WORK

In earlier writings (Baltes & Labouvie, 1973; Baltes & Willis, 1979b; Willis & Baltes, 1980), four concepts—multidimensionality, multidirectionality, interindividual variability, and intraindividual plasticity—were used to communicate our interpretation of the existing data on intelligence during adulthood and old age. Together, these concepts reflect the viewpoint that the development of adult intelligence is not a monolithic and highly regularized phenomenon with a fixed and unitary trajectory. To the contrary, one can demonstrate that (1) there is a myriad of mental abilities and distinct structural properties to be considered (multidimensionality); (2) there are distinct change patterns (multidirectionality); (3) there are large differences in the life course patterns of individuals (interindividual variability); and (4) there is clear evidence for modifiability (interindividual plasticity).

The interpretative orientation, of which the four themes (multidimensionality, multidirectionality, interindividual variability, and intraindividual plasticity) are an expression, is not intended to suggest that there is no regularity at all in the development of intelligence during adulthood and old age. The strong focus on the dynamic and yet diverging pattern expressed in this orientation, somewhat as the different emphasis on the half-fullness or the half-emptiness of a waterglass, was very much the reflection of a compensatory intent. The explicit goal was to achieve a posture on adult intelligence (Baltes & Schaie, 1976) that is not dominated by an orthodoxy of universal (general) and gradual decline (Botwinick, 1977; Horn, 1970, 1978).

At this time, this compensatory task has been accomplished and the next step is to move beyond the earlier dialogue. Indeed, let us emphasize that some regularity coexists with all the irregularity. There is, for example, good evidence for distinct trajectories for fluid vs crystallized intelligence (Horn, 1970, 1982) and for verbal vs nonverbal or psychomotor categories of intellectual functioning (Botwinick, 1977). Similarly, it is rather clear that, beginning around age 60, naturally occurring decline (i.e., decline observed in samples not selected for interventive treatments) becomes more likely for more people and for more classes of intellectual functioning (Schaie & Hertzog, 1983). This is particularly true if "testing-the-limits" tasks are used, i.e., tasks that require maximum mental effort and/or that are infrequently practiced in everyday life (Cornelius, 1984; Denney, 1982; Hasher & Zacks, 1979). Our view, however, continues to be that the early onset and regularity of intellectual decline with aging are less conspicuous and less inevitable than claimed by others (e.g., Horn, 1982) and need to be seen in the context of the four themes mentioned above. Thus, we believe that any comprehensive interpretation of phenomena associated with intelligence throughout adulthood needs to consider multidimensionality, multidirectionality, interindividual variability, and plasticity as salient features requiring attention and possibly integration.

The following set of propositions represents one approach to the task of summarization that is quite different from that reflected by the four themes contained in earlier writings. Nevertheless, the propositional framework is consistent with the themes outlined above; in addition, however, it incorporates a wider range of information and includes the positions stressed by proponents of a decline orientation (Botwinick, 1977; Denney, 1982; Horn, 1970, 1982; Salthouse, 1982). Thus, the propositions comprise our view of the overall data base, a portion of which contributes to the four themes described above, and a portion of which shows decline in intellectual functioning. Furthermore, propositions are derived not only from work in intellectual development, but also from ancillary areas of the psychology of adult development. Finally, propositions derived from outside psychology, namely sociology and biology, are also incorporated. Embedding research on adult intellectual functioning into a larger context of human aging makes it possible to articulate the reciprocal relationships between intelligence and other systems of psychological, biological, and societal functioning. It permits us also to show that intelligence is not a self-contained system; rather, intelligence develops interdependently with other modalities of the system and is used for both general and particular tasks of human adaptation.

## B. PROPOSITIONS DERIVED FROM RESEARCH ON ADULT DEVELOPMENT OF COGNITION AND INTELLIGENCE

The challenge before us now is to communicate a view that acknowledges the possibility of decline but, at the same time, asserts the existence of plasticity and the possibility for continued progress or growth. The position that growth *and* decline can be part of intellectual change with aging is historically well founded dating at least to Tetens (1777), and is currently preferred by writers such as Gisela Labouvie-Vief (1980, 1982). In other words, the key question may be how one can combine, for example, Horn's (1970, 1980) general view of systematic (though differential) decline with a theoretical orientation that emphasizes plasticity and the possibility of progressive change (e.g., Baltes & Willis, 1982; Dittmann-Kohli & Baltes, 1984; Labouvie-Vief, 1982; Riegel, 1973; Schaie, 1977)? The propositions are aimed at accomplishing this task of integration.

*Proposition 1. A First Central Feature of Adult and Gerontological Intelligence Is One of Constancy (Stability) in Intellectual Potential or Capacity for Functioning in the "Average" Range*

This first proposition states that there is no general (across abilities) and normative (applicable to most persons) change in the intellectual potential of adult individuals until they reach age 60–70. This applies particularly to the average or normal range of functioning. At present, there is no clear-cut definition of what constitutes the average or normal range of functioning. Thus, a negative definition must do. The normal range of functioning applies to tasks and cognitive resources for which maximum functioning has not been approximated for a given individual. We believe that this is true for the majority of tests used in intelligence research.

The key evidence to be marshalled in support of the first proposition is described in more detail in earlier publications beginning perhaps with Baltes and Labouvie (1973). Three major rationales and data bases provide such support: (1) cohort-related variation in intellectual functioning, (2) within-cohort longitudinal change studies, and (3) intervention research on intellectual plasticity. Implicit in our approach is a fourth rationale that invokes the distinction between potential and performance. A major question in aging research is whether and under which conditions a given performance can be taken as an index of potential or latent capacity. In general, we tend to believe that when elderly persons exhibit performance deficits relative to younger adults, it is often possible to interpret such deficits in terms of performance factors (e.g., practice, lack of skills, and task-relevant knowledge) rather than in terms of an aging-related decline in potential or capacity.

The first data base supporting a conclusion of stability or invariance in intellectual potential involves historical, *cohort-related variation* in level of functioning in tests of psychometric intelligence. Schaie's (1979) pioneering research is the best known illustration. It shows, for instance, between-cohort differences in level of functioning for same-age adults that are of the same magnitude as the age changes obtained when studying longitudinally a given cohort as it moves from adulthood into old age. Because such cohort differences for same-age adults are not likely to reflect biological or genetic differences between generations, the conclusion that they are largely related to differing environmental conditions (e.g., life histories) for the cohorts studied seems warranted. As a consequence, one can conclude that, if life conditions would have been different, all age groups (from about midlife to the early 70s) would have had the potential to function at comparable levels of intellectual performance. Similarly, it appears from Schaie's cohort-sequential data that age-related peaks of performance exhibit major historical, cohort-related shifts (up and down the age ladder) that differ also by class of ability. Cohort-related shifts are illustrated in Fig. 1. Again, such cohort-related shifts in peak indicate that the potential for higher or lower performance exists at most ages across the adult and early old-age range.

Schaie's (1979, 1983; Schaie & Hertzog, 1983; see also Rudinger & Lantermann, 1980) research dealing with onset, directionality, and rate of *within-cohort longitudinal change* during adulthood into advanced old age is exemplary for the second base as well. In short, normative or general decline (across persons and abilities) of intellectual performance does not seem to occur until the seventh or eighth decade of life in most individuals of presently aging cohorts in the United States. When longitudinal change is plotted for age groups into the 60s (separately for mental abilities but averaged across several cohorts) the evidence is one of invariance or relatively little change in performance for most longitudinal participants. For example, when decline is observed, it is relatively small in terms of standard deviation, perhaps approximating one-half of a standard deviation for the age range 50–70. Furthermore, as also shown in Fig. 2, a fair proportion of individuals shows invariance in average level of performance into the 70s with some even exhibiting increases. It is only when the late 70s and 80s (i.e., advanced old age) are considered that a picture of more general and regular decline emerges; again, however, a substantial degree of interability and individual variation in onset and course is observed.

The third data base evincing support for the proposition of stability or invariance of capacity or potential for functioning in the average range derives from *cognitive intervention* work (Baltes & Willis, 1982; Denney, 1979; Labouvie-Vief, 1976; Sterns & Sanders, 1980; Willis & Baltes, 1980). Such intervention work is aimed at exploring the range of intellectual performance exhibited by individuals when exposed to conditions designed to enhance or interfere with performance. There are two interrelated rationales for such research on plas-

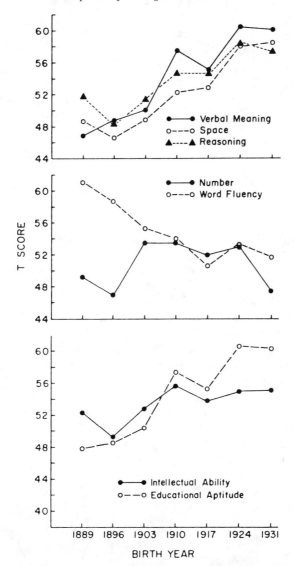

**Fig. 1.** Cohort gradients for the primary mental abilities. From Schaie, Labouvie, and Buech (1973; see also Schaie, 1979, 1983). Copyright by the American Psychological Association. Reproduced by permission.

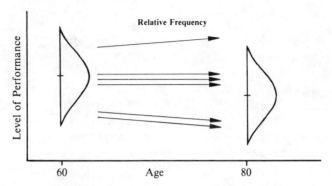

**Fig. 2.** Individual change patterns of intellectual performance in aging. After Schaie (1979, 1983).

ticity. The first rationale derives from the competence–performance distinction or from related efforts aimed at distinguishing between different indicators of intelligence such as capacity or potential vs actual performance (Botwinick, 1977; Overton & Newman, 1982; Willis & Baltes, 1980). The second rationale involves an assumption about ecological or practice deficits for intellectual functioning in the elderly (Baltes & Willis, 1982; Denney, 1982; Labouvie, Hoyer, Baltes, & Baltes, 1974). In this second line of reasoning, it is assumed that elderly persons, because of their practice deficits, benefit markedly from the experiential opportunities provided by additional practice.

In such intervention research (see Fig. 3), it is usually found that elderly persons continue to have the potential to improve their performance, relatively easily, in fact, up to the level shown by "untreated" average young adults. In our own research (Baltes & Willis, 1982), such training or experience effects go

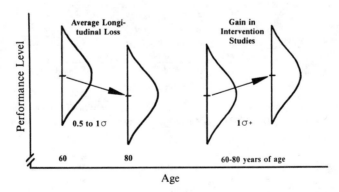

**Fig. 3.** Fluid intelligence: average aging loss (descriptive) and magnitude of amount of gain following training. After Baltes and Willis (1982).

beyond the tasks trained and show near transfer to other dimensions within the same cluster of abilities. They are maintained also for several months following training. Moreover, when the enhancement effect of a relatively short training program (five 1-hour sessions) on near-transfer measures in elderly persons (average age approximately 70) is assessed in terms of magnitude, the magnitude of enhancement is approximately one standard deviation of baseline variation. As it turns out, this amount of enhancement of intellectual performance is at least as much or more than what Schaie (1983) reports as the best estimate for 21-year longitudinal age decrement in the primary mental abilities from age 60 to 80. Performance enhancement in elderly subjects based on five 1-hour training sessions, then, is roughly equivalent to 20-year longitudinal age decline observed in the same age range for subjects not participating in any known training activities. Such evidence shows further how relatively minor the naturally observed aging decline in intellectual functioning appears to be when compared with information based on plasticity research.[2]

At present, there is no clear-cut delineation of the different aspects of intelligence such as actual performance vs ability vs capacity vs potential, etc. In analogy to research in biology and medicine (Fries, 1980; Fries & Crapo, 1981), we have added the term "reserve" to this collection (Baltes & Willis, 1982). In our own emerging conceptualization (see also Kliegl *et al.*, 1984) we distinguish between baseline performance, baseline reserve capacity, and maximum reserve capacity. Baseline performance indicates a person's initial level of performance on a given task, i.e., what a person can do in a specified setting without intervention or special treatment. Baseline reserve capacity denotes the upper range of an individual's performance potential, when at a given point in time all available resources are called upon to optimize an individual's performance. It is measured by tests of "maximum" performance. When adding a time dimension (past, present, future) and other conditions of enhancement, it is possible to speak of an individual's maximum reserve capacity. Strictly speaking, the maximum is not an ideal maximum, it is something akin to a "local" maximum.

The term reserve is of particular importance in this context. It permits separa-

---

[2]We need to emphasize three conclusions that our training research on older persons does not warrant but which are, however, occasionally attributed to us. First, we do not conclude that older adults benefit more from training than younger adults. This is an interesting hypothesis (Baltes & Willis, 1982, p. 382), but there are no good age- and cohort-comparative data available. Second, we do not conclude that our training research with elderly persons has improved level of performance in the total spectrum of intelligence to the level of untreated younger adults. Rather, the effect pattern is restricted to those domains of abilities included in the training program. We have reason to believe, however, that comparable improvement in other abilities (not yet trained) is possible in principle. Third, we need to stress that extant cognitive training is restricted to samples of relatively healthy older persons. For the samples studied, however, there is but scant evidence for subject by treatment interaction effects involving, for example, level of initial performance, sex, or educational background.

tion of knowledge about capacity into several categories. First, there is observable baseline performance indicating what a person can do. Second, there is baseline reserve capacity indicating what a person can do under better assessment conditions than those associated with baseline assessment. Third, there is maximum reserve capacity indicating what a person was able to do in the past or might be able to do in the future if conditions were or would be near optimal. Thus, the term reserve, like the concept of plasticity, explicitly recognizes, more so than other concepts (e.g., ability), that individuals have resources that are not yet activated. The distinction between baseline reserve capacity and maximum reserve capacity implies that aging individuals, just as younger individuals, have both as yet unactivated intellectual reserves in their repertoire that could be utilized if necessary or developed if conditions were suitable. Second, the term reserve is intended to convey a "dialectical" property. The range and level of one aspect of reserve, maximum reserve, is inherently unknowable; it can only be approximated. There is always the possibility that new conditions or agents that produce new levels and forms of intellectual performance on a given task, such as digit span (Kliegl *et al.*, 1984), may be found.

### Proposition 2. If Aging Decline in Capacity for Intellectual Functioning Exists, It Will Be Manifested Primarily in Functioning at "Maximum" and Difficult Levels of Performance

This proposition acknowledges the possibility of decline in intellectual potential. If it occurs, it applies primarily to *maximum* rather than average potential and, correspondingly, in terms of observable indicators, to maximum or near-maximum levels of performance. What is the evidence?

The evidence for this proposition comes from at least three areas of research: (1) multidimensional conceptions of intelligence and associated notions of differential change (including decline); (2) studies aimed at testing the limits of intellectual functioning; and (3) research linking health (or disease) and distance from death to level of intellectual functioning. In concert, results from these three areas can be interpreted to indicate that for aging individuals maximum reserve capacity is reduced by some quantitative amount.

However, it has not been shown yet (except in cases of severe brain disease) that such reduction in maximum capacity is relevant for everyday intellectual functioning in aging individuals nor that it would interfere with possible further "progressive" growth of intellectual functioning with aging in select ability domains. An example, taken from sports, may help to clarify this latter point. Whereas the maximum potential for elderly persons to run the 100 meter dash on the average is less than that of most younger persons (let us assume approximately 20 vs 15 seconds), it is not immediately evident that the slower maximum running speed for elderly adults is dysfunctional for the bulk of everyday locomotor behavior.

The first body of data providing some evidence for this proposition reveals a pattern of *differential change* for different classes of abilities of the multidimensional construct of intelligence during the adult life span (Botwinick, 1977; Horn, 1970, 1982; Schaie & Hertzog, 1983; Steuer & Jarvik, 1981). In descriptive age-comparative research, some classes of abilities do show a fairly general process of decline beginning somewhere around age 60. Two ability domains stand out as being most sensitive to this age-related decline. The first is fluid intelligence (Cattell, 1971; Horn, 1982) which, in contrast to crystallized intelligence, evinces aging decline. The other and related phenomenon is that of aging decline in speeded psychomotor tasks (Botwinick, 1977; Steuer & Jarvik, 1981). Together, these data suggest that performance for some abilities does decline beginning perhaps as early as age 50–60. This evidence is perhaps not persuasive to those researchers who argue that such differential change in performance does not necessarily index differential change in potential, but is a product of disparate living conditions among aging individuals (e.g., dissimilar quantity and quality of practice for distinct abilities in different age groups).

The second body of data supporting the proposition of some decline in maximum potential with aging involves data gathered with an approach that we categorize as *testing-the-limits* (Baltes & Willis, 1979a, 1982; Brown & French, 1979; Glaser, 1981; Guthke, 1980; Pawlik, 1976; Schmidt, 1971). Similar to tolerance or stress tests in biology (e.g., Andres & Tobin, 1977), the testing-the-limits strategy focuses on assessment of performance potential under varying conditions of support and difficulty. Most likely, for example, negative age differences in intellectual functioning are found when difficult tasks are used in age comparisons (see also Cornelius, 1984; Denney, 1982; Hasher & Zacks, 1979). In principle, there are two strategies to define level of difficulty. A first is statistical and specifies difficulty in relation to an individual's range of observed performance. A second, of more interest here, focuses on the internal structure of tasks or tests. In the latter case, tasks are of a high level of difficulty if they require the following for effective solution: (1) sustained effort, (2) multiple cognitive operations, (3) speeded operations, and (4) sequential changes in cognitive operations. Using such an orientation, our interpretive posture is that most fluid intelligence tasks are more difficult than crystallized tasks. Similarly, memory and information-processing tasks that often show negative age differences (Arenberg & Robertson-Tchabo, 1977; Botwinick, 1978; Craik, 1977) are those that could be characterized as more difficult, i.e., as requiring more mental effort (Hasher & Zacks, 1979; Pascual-Leone, 1983). The evidence, then, is that negative age differences are obtained if intellectual tasks are used that test the limits of cognitive information processing, and that such results can be marshalled in support of the proposition that maximum capacity and maximum reserve are reduced in advanced old age.[3]

---

[3]In a later section and in the context of a dual-process conception of intellectual development, we are restricting the conclusion of a decline in maximum capacity and reserve to the first of the two

The third body of data supporting Proposition 2 involves research on the interrelationship between *conditions of health* and *distance from death* and level of intellectual functioning (Jarvik & Blum, 1971; Riegel & Riegel, 1972; Siegler, 1975, 1980; Steuer & Jarvik, 1981). Because health and distance from death are correlated with age, both strands of research are similar to the study of "advanced" old age. Declining health and decreasing distance from death are a predominant feature of advanced old age. As a consequence, findings from the three foci of research should exhibit some correspondence.

To begin, it is clear that as one moves into the 70s and 80s there is increasing evidence for general decline in intellectual functioning (Schaie & Hertzog, 1983). Because of their age correlation, health status and disease can be expected to figure most prominently as explanatory variables. As to the role of health and disease in accounting for decline, research findings are perhaps less clear-cut than one might expect. First, there is evidence that a sizable proportion (perhaps 20%) of very old individuals (beyond 80) appears to suffer from chronic brain-related diseases or mental disorders variously described as senility, dementia, Alzheimers disease, cerebral arteriosclerosis, or some other appelation (Steuer & Jarvik, 1981). However, based on the longstanding effort to distinguish between primary, secondary, and tertiary aging (Busse, 1978), it is open to question whether one should consider such disorders as indicative of normal or primary aging rather than disease. If one attempts to exclude diseases from the process of normal aging, the evidence on senility, etc., is not relevant for the present situation.

What about other health-related factors? There is some evidence that other health-related factors, such as aging-related increases in hypertension or physical debility, have an impact on level of intellectual functioning, but the size of this relationship is not very persuasive either (LaRue & Jarvik, 1982; Steuer & Jarvik, 1981). There is only moderate support for the notion that reduced health, more prevalent in older than in younger adults, results in lower potential. However, because pertinent work has focused primarily on standard instruments with their focus on the normal range of functioning, one wonders whether the research findings are incomplete. Perhaps the application of new types of tasks and

---

processes (cognition *qua* cognition). It is possible for older adults to function at highest levels of performance in the second process (pragmatics of intelligence). As yet, it is unclear also whether older adults (if exposed to long-term practice or other performance-enhancing conditions) would reach levels of performance comparable to young adults who have experienced equivalent amounts of training. Denney (1982) does not think so. However, relevant studies with truly extensive training programs are lacking. In order to settle the question of adult age differences in maximum performance, a number of design criteria would need to be met including longitudinal information on past performance of elderly subjects as well as the use of treatments that would capture the frequency and pattern of experience associated with preexperimental age differences in life history.

systematic use of testing-the-limits procedures aimed at assessment of near-maximum functioning would result in a more clear-cut profile of outcomes.

The strongest evidence for a relationship between health and intellectual functioning in the normal aged comes from studies on distance from death or the terminal drop hypothesis (Jarvik & Blum, 1971; Riegel & Riegel, 1972; Siegler, 1975, 1980). If one plots the course of intellectual development backward from point of death rather than forward from time of birth, there appears to be more regularity in decline patterns of change (see Baltes & Labouvie, 1973, p. 174, for a graphic illustration). As distance from nonaccidental death can be interpreted as an overall measure of health or biological aging, the preferred interpretative posture is to view such a terminal drop as a reflection of decline in intelligence-related adaptive potential. This drop, however, is not gradual with aging but is specifically related to the individual onset and course of the dying process. The terminal drop finding is relevant also for understanding the occurrence of decline patterns in advanced old age. This is so because the relative frequency of being in a terminal process increases markedly as persons move beyond the range of average life expectancy.

### Proposition 3. There Is Evidence for the Possibility of Progressive or Growthlike Intellectual Change in Adulthood and Old Age

This proposition is the necessary counterpart to Proposition 2. Decline *and* growth can exist concomitantly (Baltes, 1983b; Hollingworth, 1927; Labouvie-Vief, 1980, 1982; Tetens, 1777). Progressive change is possible in those cognitive functions that are associated with a cumulative and experientially based build-up and transformation of skills and knowledge systems.

There are at least four bodies of research relevant for this proposition: multidirectional conceptions of intelligence (Horn, 1970, 1982), research on cognitive training (Baltes & Willis, 1982; Denney, 1979), efforts to extend cognitive structuralism into adulthood (Kramer, 1983; Labouvie-Vief, 1980, 1982), and work in expertise and knowledge systems (Brown, 1982; Chi, Glaser, & Rees, 1983; Dittmann-Kohli, 1984b; Dittmann-Kohli & Baltes, 1984; Kliegl *et al.*, 1984).

*Multidirectional conceptions* of the development of intelligence (Cattell, 1971; Horn, 1970, 1980) include abilities that continue to grow or, at least, remain stable during adulthood. Thus, in the model of Cattell and Horn, crystallized intelligence—abilities involved in reasoning associated with acculturated materials such as language—is shown to increase or remain stable into advanced adulthood. Could it be that crystallized intelligence might show further growth if one were to develop and use intellectual tasks more appropriate to the life ecology of aged individuals? As we shall see below, cognitive training research demonstrates that the potential for continued learning appears to be present in most elderly persons (Baltes & Willis, 1982; Denney, 1979). Thus, one of the prerequisites for continual evolution and transformation of crystallized intelligence is met.

One possible form of growth is found in research aimed at the articulation of concepts such as wisdom as possible forms of intellectual progression during adulthood (Baltes & Dittmann-Kohli, 1982; Clayton, 1982; Clayton & Birren, 1980; Dittmann-Kohli, 1984b; Dittmann-Kohli & Baltes, 1984; Meacham, 1980). Another form of further growth is related to aspects of *expertise* and *knowledge systems*. The likelihood of such progression is enhanced by the existence of ecological settings and tasks that would tend to elicit or accelerate the generation of new kinds of problem-solving and knowledge structures. Indeed, Baltes and Dittmann-Kohli (1982; see also Dittmann-Kohli, 1984b) have argued that there are new patterns of task demands that are conducive to the development of new knowledge structures and problem-solving skills in aging individuals. Such potentially beneficial conditions for adulthood growth might result, for example, from a novel and more complex combination of tasks involving the three settings and demands described in life-span conceptions of human development: viz. age-graded, history-graded, and nonnormative ones (Baltes *et al.*, 1980). With aging, experiences with such complex task characteristics may accumulate and, thereby, result in growth-type increments in intellectual abilities such as social intelligence and wisdom. Similarly, new kinds of problem-solving skills, or perhaps some varieties of metacognition may emerge or become predominant, in part because of the demand characteristics of adult and aging life. The use of select cognitive heuristics (see also Kahneman, Slovic, & Tversky, 1982; Newell & Simon, 1972; Tversky & Kahneman, 1981), especially "satisficing," may be such an example.

Another major strand of work suggestive of growthlike intellectual change during adulthood and old age is focused explicitly on possible *structural transformations in cognitive processes*. It is represented, on the one hand, by scholars who attempt both to extend cognitive structuralism into adulthood (Riegel, 1973) and to explore the possibility of further change in cognitive structures (e.g., Kramer, 1983; Kuhn *et al.*, 1983; Labouvie-Vief, 1980, 1982; Pascual-Leone, 1983). On the other hand, as mentioned already and less Piagetian in orientation, there is work influenced especially by action theory and functionalist cognitive psychology, which focuses on expertise and knowledge as a domain of further growth (Dittmann-Kohli & Baltes, 1984). The general argument is that adult cognitive development is not necessarily a representation of cognitive structure *qua* formal logic, a position that is inherent, for example, in Piaget's theory of cognitive stages. Rather, adult development may represent (1) trade-off principles between components (e.g., short- vs long-term memory) and stages of cognitive functioning, (2) the further organization and transformation of skills and knowledge systems, and (3) the further organization and transformation of cognitive structures into alternative forms of logic. Within a neo-Piagetian framework, Labouvie-Vief (1980, 1982), in her work aimed at showing how intellectual aging can be seen as a reorganization of structures associated with self-regulation, is perhaps the most persuasive on this point (see also Edelstein & Noam, 1982). Specifically, Labouvie-Vief (1982) proposes three adult stages of logic: intrasystemic (formal realism), intersystemic (contextual relativism), and autonomy.

On the empirical level, there is some preliminary corroborative evidence. With some memory tasks, e.g., those that focus on certain operationalizations of global meaning or main idea, rather than detail, recall, it *may* be possible to demonstrate positive age changes. For example, some recent research focusing on gist recall of presumably ecologically valid text materials has failed to find the same pattern of systematic age-related performance deficits so evident in list recall work (Hultsch & Dixon, 1984). Still, because other researchers do find such age-related deficits, this evidence must be considered inconclusive. In addition, some components of metacognition (e.g., some memory monitoring, prediction, and confidence ratings) show little or no decline with advancing age (Dixon & Hultsch, 1983; Perlmutter, 1978), although other important components clearly do. Other evidence comes from cognitive training research mentioned already (Baltes & Willis, 1982; Denney, 1979). Older individuals have been shown to have the reserve to raise their level of performance in intelligence tests to that of younger adults. Thus, in principle, older adults are able to engage in further evolution of their cognitive skills.

We need to acknowledge, however, that at present the conceptual contributions to Proposition 3 are more advanced than the empirical evidence, and that the available data base for such growthlike advances in intellectual aging (especially of the structural type) is not yet compelling. The least one can conclude, however, is that the possibility of growthlike intellectual change in adulthood and old age has not been falsified and that there is convergence between several bodies of data that make the proposition reasonable. This is particularly true if one acknowledges that such growthlike change is not normative, but that it *can* occur in some (or most) individuals *if* conditions are supportive, and further that, if it occurs, it is likely to apply to *select* cognitive skills and expert knowledge systems.

## C. PROPOSITIONS DERIVED FROM A GENERAL VIEW OF THE PSYCHOLOGY OF ADULT DEVELOPMENT AND AGING

The next set of propositions is aimed at placing intellectual aging into the larger context of psychological aging. It is likely that intellectual aging does not proceed independently of other domains of behavior; on the contrary, both its nature and course are embedded in the larger system of psychological functioning and development. What are the propositions about this larger context of psychological development that we consider especially relevant?

*Proposition 4. With Aging, the Life Goals or Developmental Tasks*
*of Most Individuals Are Less Oriented toward Cognitive Efficacy*
*(as Traditionally Defined) Than Is True for Childhood,*
*Adolescence, and Early Adulthood. Correspondingly, Domains*
*of Psychological Functioning Other Than Performance*
*on Intelligence Tests Gain in Relative Significance*

Most work on the goal or task structure of the individual life course suggests that the central tasks of adult and aging life are not focused on acquisition and maintenance of cognitive skills as defined by school-related criteria of intellectual functioning and knowledge structures. Rather, the substantive focus during adulthood is increasingly on domains such as family life, personality development, professional life, social intelligence, as well as issues of health and, by implication, death and dying.

Work by Havighurst (1948) on developmental tasks through the life span, by Bühler and Massarik (1968) on the structure of life goals, and by Erikson (1959) on adult personality development with its focus on identity, intimacy, generativity, and integrity are examples, as is Ryff's (1982) effort to consider progressive forms of personality functioning in the context of successful aging. Another illustration is the work by Neugarten (1977) and Gutmann (1977). The latter authors suggest an active-to-passive-mastery sequence for adult development and a change from an outer-world to an inner-world orientation. In the area of intelligence, work by Cornelius (1984) is consistent with this view. Cornelius finds that older adults judge fluid-type tasks to be more unfamiliar to them (1) than crystallized-type tasks and (2) than do younger adults.

It is reasonable to assume that the mastering of adult life tasks as described by Havighurst (1948), Neugarten (1977), Ryff (1982) and others involves intellectual competencies as well. However, it is also likely that their mastery extends beyond the use of basic cognitive skills as required in formal logic and beyond that knowledge dependent primarily on school-related content. This is certainly true for real-life accomplishments associated with careers and career settings (Featherman, 1983). For example, in contrast to the assessment of both child and adult intelligence, it is likely that criteria for success in the adult tasks described do not involve primarily a single criterion of logical truth (or accuracy). Rather, application of contextual knowledge systems and of multiple criteria of efficacy may be involved. The focus, in addition to logical principles, could be on such criteria as adaptive social efficacy and the evaluation of loss/gain functions in a complex framework of individual and social functioning (see also Schaie, 1978). Cognitive heuristics like that of Kahneman and Tversky (Kahneman et al., 1982) rather than the ability to process information in tight logical operations may figure more prominently in the daily cognitive activity of adults than it does in children. Thus, assessment of problem solving and reasoning in the somewhat artificial context of formal reasoning and unfamiliar laboratory tasks would not be a satisfactory indicator of an aged individual's intellectual potential (Baltes & Willis, 1979a).

As is true throughout the life span, in order to understand better intellectual functioning during adulthood and old age, we need to consider the pertinent developmental tasks of this age period and its location in the life-span sequence. Based on existing models of adult personality development and a life-span conception of developmental tasks, one can tentatively conclude that cognitive problem solving involving abstract content and principles of formal logic may be less relevant for everyday functioning during aging than is true for earlier age periods.

A first specific implication of this view is that, whenever intellectual performance deficits are observed in older individuals, they could reflect the fact that traditional measurement of cognitive functioning is biased toward substantive and evaluative criteria of the young adult and his/her world. In the life-span literature, a number of researchers have discussed this in more detail (Baltes & Willis, 1979b; Labouvie-Vief, 1980, 1982; Schaie, 1978). There is a counterpart literature in the field of cognitive psychology, in which it is argued that, in general, tests of general intelligence are loaded in the direction of scholastic aptitude (e.g., Glaser, 1981) or may be criterion centric in some other respect (Cole, Gay, Glick, & Sharp, 1971; Cole, Hood, & McDermott, 1978; Dörner, 1981, 1982; Fleishman, 1982).

A second implication of Proposition 4 is that we are in need of research aimed at examining what forms of problem solving are characteristic of adult intellectual life and its development. This quest has a long tradition in gerontology (Demming & Pressey, 1957). Similar questions are raised in cognitive psychology, for example, when constructing and using new tasks dealing with complex real-life situations such as being the mayor of a town (e.g., Dörner, 1981, 1982), or examining the procedural skills and knowledge structures involved in problem solving by experts such as chess master players or physicists (Chi, Glaser, & Rees, 1983). Thus far, however, in the study of adult intellectual development, the evidence is largely conceptual rather than empirical.

Schaie (1977) for example, has emphasized that during adult development intellectual performance may require, increasingly, modalities of executive and evaluative operations; moreover, the criteria for evaluation of effectiveness of intellectual functioning may involve, increasingly, dimensions of subjective life adaptation and perceived social consequences rather than dimensions of logical accuracy. In a related vein, but with a focus on adolescence, Dittmann-Kohli (1982, 1983a) has developed a conception of problem solving and problem interpretation in everyday life (intra-, inter-, and extra-personal life domains) that may serve as an analog for futher work on adult intelligence.

*Proposition 5. The General Process of Adult Development and Aging Has a Feature of Individual Specialization: Specialization Implies Increasing Individualization and Interindividual Differentiation of Life Trajectories*

For such a process of individual specialization and interindividual differentiation to occur throughout the life span one general condition must be met: viz. homogenizing forces associated with each life stage must be smaller than those generating individualization. Such forces—either toward interindividual homogeneity or heterogeneity of adult development and aging—can be located either in the psychological and biological make-up of individual development or in the social structure of the life course. What is the evidence?

Four areas of developmental scholarship serve to illustrate the available evidence for the case of specialization and interindividual differentiation: (1) age-comparative work on the extent of interindividual variability, (2) conceptual work on models of life-span development, (3) research on life career and professional specialization, and (4) evolutionary considerations on the nature of aging.

As for *interindividual variability,* there is a widely held posture that the variability between adults increases with aging, although the factual status of this conclusion has been recently questioned (Bornstein & Smircina, 1982). Increased interindividual variability would imply that a correlation between an increase in individuality and chronological age exists. McKenzie (1980), for instance, summarizes: "as we grow older, a communality of characteristics does not develop. Just the opposite is true. With increased age comes increased diversity, individuality, and uniqueness" (p. 9). This generalized observation of McKenzie may be an oversimplification in light of Bornstein and Smircina's (1982) assessment. However, except for the point of death itself, there is surely no general evidence for the opposite alternative, i.e., the existence of a common endpoint of psychological life-span development toward which individuals move.

Various *models of life-span development* have features corresponding to a view of increased specialization or uniqueness as well. Leland Van den Daele's writings (1969, 1974; see also, Meacham, 1982; Singer & Spilerman, 1979), for example, represent a genre of scholarship that is aimed at offering a taxonomy of different developmental change processes. This kind of work is based essentially on the premise of alternative pathways and the existence of "multiple" progressions, thereby including divergent or individualized forms of developmental branching. Another sort of developmental model building relevant for an individualization view is inherent in a trifactor scheme of influences on development formulated by life-span researchers (Baltes *et al.,* 1980). In addition to normative age-graded and history-graded influences, attention in this scheme is drawn to the role of idiosyncratic or nonnormative life events (Brim & Ryff,

1980; Filipp, 1981; Hultsch & Plemons, 1979). Nonnormative life events are defined as events and event structures that—while significant in their influence—have little generality in occurrence and patterning. It is assumed that such events play an increasingly prominent role in shaping the nature of adult development and, thereby, generate a higher degree of idiosyncratic change than is true for earlier phases of the life span.

The third area of research suggestive of a life-span process of individualization is associated with the concepts of *differential life careers or life trajectories*. A first line of evidence for the existence of differential life careers relates to the question of long-term stability of interindividual differences in psychological functioning. If such interindividual stability is high, people as they move through their lives tend to maintain their relative positions within a matrix of individual differentiation. For abilities and psychometric measures of personality (Costa & McCrae, 1980; Schaie, 1983), stability during adulthood is sizable and is thus supportive of a view of continued interindividual differentiation. More direct evidence comes from a recent summary of psychological development from childhood to adulthood as reflected in the Oakland and Berkeley longitudinal studies (Eichorn, Clausen, Haan, Honzik, & Mussen, 1981). Changes in personality and family life show a remarkable degree of typological or individual differentiation. Distinct life trends, not a unitary life process, characterize the midlife development of the longitudinal subjects.

Another relevant research area with a long tradition is that of the study of professional careers and achievements in worldly success (e.g., Featherman, 1980) and their anchoring in the structure of inter- and intragenerational processes of socioeconomic stratification. Social mobility between levels of stratification appears larger in earlier than in later phases of the adult life span. As life-span development proceeds during adulthood, individual commitments to certain professional careers, including their knowledge foci and skill constraints, may become more and more embedded and frozen. As a consequence of such a process of professional commitment and specialization, individual differentiation in psychological functioning is either maintained or further enhanced. As Featherman (1983) has shown, similar conclusions about the possibility of increased differentiation and continued specialization can be deduced from Matilda Riley's age/cohort stratification model (Riley, Johnson, & Foner, 1972; Riley, 1979), and also from the social–psychological work of Kohn and Schooler (1978, 1982) that links the stable differences in substantive complexity of occupational contexts to psychological functioning during adulthood.

A fourth rationale for considering a process of specialization as a central feature of adult development and aging has its conceptual base in *evolutionary perspectives*. Evolutionary perspectives include the question of the particular role that aging behavior and older individuals may play either in the process of differential reproduction or the maintenance of population functioning. Two notions stemming from evolutionary thinking are particularly relevant for the ontogenetic processes of specialization inherent in Proposition 5. A first general idea is Waddington's (1975) concept of the canalization of development. Canalization implies (1) multiple though differentially probable pathways of development, and (2) with age, increasing restrictions on mobility between such pathways. A second notion based on evolutionary thinking has been described by Brent (1978; Mergler & Goldstein, 1983). He argues that the unique role of older cohorts within a population is to provide as a collective, on the one hand, the specializations necessary for maintaining the gene pool within those environmental niches to which the species has already adapted. Younger age cohorts of the population, on the other hand, in addition to acquiring existing specializations, fulfill the additional functions of adapting to changes in the existing environment and expanding into new niches. Such a view suggests that, with aging, individuals may tend to exhibit a process of individual specialization and invest special efforts into maintaining or further increasing their specialized skills and knowledge.

## D. PROPOSITIONS FROM NEIGHBORING DISCIPLINES

The following propositions consider the context beyond psychology within which intellectual development occurs. The argument is that possible growth and decline of intellectual aging as seen by developmental psychologists should be consistent with notions about human aging as they have been formulated in other disciplines of the life sciences. This criterion of consistency is more one of plausibility than one of inductive–deductive reasoning.

*Proposition 6. From a Sociological Point of View, Aging in Many Countries Is Associated with a Social–Structural Process of Loss of Development-Enhancing Expectations and Social Resources: This Process Occurs Differentially across Domains of Functioning and Social Clusters*

This proposition is derived from a larger sociological framework dealing with the life course (Brim & Wheeler, 1966; Elder, 1975; Featherman, 1983; Kohli, 1978; Meyer, 1981; Riley, 1979, 1984; Riley *et al.*, 1972; Rosenmayr, 1978; Rosow, 1976). In general, sociologists tend to conceptualize the sequence and dynamics of life-span development as resulting from an age-graded allocation of resources, and socialization or movement into social positions such as roles and statuses. Roles and statuses (or similar indicators) in turn are strongly associated with institutional structures, and this association continues as these structures evolve through history.

Such a general approach explicitly recognizes that adulthood and old age involve continual adaptation within a social system that is organized in part by life-course criteria. Some observers (e.g., Rosow, 1976) also argue that with aging there is not only a dearth of new role expectations but also a movement toward a larger relative share of so-called tenuous and informal roles [see also Meyer's (1981) concept of increased privatization of the old]. Also relevant for this proposition is that such a sociological approach emphasizes further—based on its comparative stratification perspective—that there is interindividual differentiation in life-course patterns and in access to social resources (Bertram, 1981; Elder, 1975; Riley *et al.,* 1972).

Formulated within this larger sociological framework, Proposition 6 is more specific and focuses on adulthood and old age. It has two implications for the present topic. First, it implies that the general performance context for elderly persons is, on the average, less conducive to high cognitive efficacy than is true for younger adults. The profile of roles (or similar indexes) assigned to or possessed by aging individuals entails fewer roles of cognitive efficiency and worldly accomplishment than roles of the more private and personal sectors, such as retirement. It follows that, whatever intellectual changes, including decline, are observed with aging, the account of such changes needs to include information pertaining to the performance conditions associated with social structure, in addition to factors of individual competence or potential.

Second, the proposition states that sharing or possession of societal resources is unequal, e.g., it varies by social class and other social cluster variables such as gender and ethnicity (Bertram, 1981). Implied in this aspect of the proposition is that some aging individuals, notably those among the higher strata of the socioeconomic system, continue to participate in and take advantage of a relatively larger share of conditions that would potentially support intellectual performance. Such differential sharing of performance-elevating resources at the macrosocietal level is relevant for the present topic in the following respect. It provides one means for interpreting why (1) there is much interindividual variability and increasing specialization in intellectual development, and (2) why neither progressive (growthlike) nor regressive (declinelike) change in intellectual functioning during adulthood and old age is universal.

*Proposition 7. From a Biological Point of View, a Central*
*Feature of Normal Aging Is a Process of Increased Vulnerability*
*and Reduced Adaptability to Environmental Variation: Reduced*
*Adaptability Implies a Reduction Especially in Biological Reserve*
*for "Optimal" or "Maximum" Functioning*

It is beyond the scope of this article and the expertise of the authors to summarize and evaluate the diverse body of work in the biology of aging (e.g., Comfort, 1979; Finch & Hayflick, 1977; Fries & Crapo, 1981; Shock, 1977; Strehler, 1962/1977). As nonbiologists, we deduce from the literature known to us, however, that a predominant position in the field of biology of aging is to associate with normal aging a "decreased survival capacity on the part of the individual organism" (Strehler, 1962/1977, p. 11). Such decreased survival capacity implies a reduction in the boundary range of demand characteristics that is managable by the aging individual.

In this vein, Shock (1977) emphasizes that biological aging may be more than the summation of changes that take place at the cellular, tissue, or organ level. Rather, the essence may involve the level of systems integration and the notion that, with advancing age, there is "reduced effectiveness of adaptation" (p. 660). In fact, when it comes to Shock's review of the empirical literature, there is much similarity in approach to the testing-the-limits argument espoused by some psychologists and summarized in Proposition 2. Specifically, Shock examines evidence in support of the "reduced effectiveness of adaptation" position as obtained in research on biological responses to stress-type conditions (temperature variation, physical exercise, intensive work, etc.). Fries and Crapo (1981) continue this line of argument and conclude that biological aging decline is most notable in measures of optimal or maximum performance.

Recent work on the plasticity of the aging brain (Lerner, 1984; Lund, 1978; Lynch, 1983) is equally relevant to understanding the nature of biological change as a context for intellectual aging. Lynch (1983), for instance, argues that on the level of cellular and dendritic functioning, growth and deterioration (e.g., sprouting of dendrites) exist *conjointly* at all stages of life from birth to death. However, it is the relative proportion (and rate) of growth vs deterioration that may change as one moves into old age. With aging, there may be, overall, less new growth in the face of relatively more deterioration. Such a model is consistent with the notion (and Propositions 2 and 3) that growth and decline coexist, although during old age the potential for further growth is increasingly reduced.

As to implications of Proposition 7 for the present topic, we do not want to resurrect a simple-minded notion of mind–body parallelism. However, we believe there are at least two implications of Proposition 7 for work on intellectual development during adulthood and old age. A first implication for psychological conceptions of intellectual aging is the similarity in approach noted already between the testing-the-limits view in psychology and the stress (Shock, 1977) and optimal performance (Fries & Crapo, 1981) conception in biology and medicine. The likelihood of finding decline in biological functioning with aging increases if functions are studied at high levels of load or demand. In psychological research, the concepts of difficulty or mental effort reflect comparable views.

A second implication is that aging individuals, for biological reasons, experience with greater frequency situations of biological vulnerability (Skinner, 1983). One intuitive example of biological aging as a contextual feature of psychological aging is that most individuals do indeed experience reduced levels of biological energy or biological health. Such conditions may influence the type of intellectual behavior that is exhibited by individuals and the kinds of problem-solving strategies that are employed. Such experiences with one's biological status may affect what aging individuals do and think and may promote selective (what cognitive performances do I remain good at?) and compensatory (what do I need to do to maintain effectiveness?) actions or reactions. Such selective and compensatory actions bear an unmistakable resemblance to potentially progressive forms of cognitive change of the metacognitive kind (see Proposition 3). Experiences with one's biological aging, then, provide a context for intellectual performance. The nature of this experience with one's biological aging will become more relevant in Section III,D, in which we advance "selective optimization with compensation" as a prototype mechanism of intellectual aging.

Considering the role of biological aging it is not important whether or not there is a *direct* link between biology and cognition. There are also various indirect mechanisms that could be used to articulate the nature of a biology–cognition relationship. For example, applying Bandura's work on self-efficacy (1977, 1982; see also Lachman, 1983), one can argue that the impact of biological functioning on intelligence could be mediated through such belief systems. It is important to note that for this interpretation, it is arguably irrelevant whether cognitive potential itself is affected by reduced biological effectiveness or not.

There is another feature of the biological evidence on aging, not stated directly in Proposition 7, that is important to consider. As is true for psychological functioning, there are large interindividual differences in onset, course, and patterning of biological aging. As a consequence, the direct or indirect relationships between biological aging and intellectual aging should vary markedly. Furthermore, depending on the biological specifics (e.g., brain vs other organ dysfunction), whatever selective and compensatory action or reaction is taken on the psychological level should evince notable individuality. This is true, at least up to the possible phase of a generalized, terminal process associated with natural death (see Proposition 2).

*Proposition 8. The Biological Status of Aging Individuals Is Not a Fixed Phenomenon: It Is Plastic and Can Be Modified, Both during the Life Course of Individuals and over Evolutionary Time*

Because of a widely held belief among behavioral and social scientists that biological aging is more fixed and universal than psychological aging, it is not clear whether this proposition is trivial, or whether it needs to be stated explicitly. Our reading of the biological evidence suggests that the degree of openness of biological aging is not so different from that of psychosocial functioning.

Consider the following observations. As in psychological development, there is multidimensionality and sizable interindividual variability in biological aging. Information about differential age changes for distinct tissue and organ systems and about sizable individual differences abounds in studies of biological aging

(Finch & Hayflick, 1977). Furthermore, there is evidence for intraindividual plasticity. Fries and Crapo (1981), for example, review evidence on modifiability and plasticity for the period of adulthood and old age and argue that individual actions and environmental conditions (related to health) codefine the developmental course of biological functioning (see also Gollin, 1981; Lerner, 1984; Lund, 1978; Lynch, 1983; Parker, 1982). Organ reserves (e.g., lung capacity) can be increased by physical exercise. Many facets of biological reserve and performance during adulthood and old age, according to Fries and Crapo, continue to be subject to optimization.

The second class of information suggestive of modifiability of biological aging (e.g., in terms of aging and age-dependent vulnerability to disease) is derived from both animal-comparative (e.g., Rockstein, Cheskey, & Sussman, 1977; Sacher, 1977) and history-comparative research dealing with the human species (Fries & Crapo, 1981; Upton, 1977). A good illustration of the latter case— historical-comparative work—is the evidence for historical changes in disease patterns associated with aging during this and the preceding century. From such historical changes, Fries (1980) deduces a model of "compressed morbidity" that is especially relevant in the present context. A central proposition of this model is that presently in Western countries, aging-related illnesses (largely chronic in nature) are being postponed increasingly until the end of an individual's lifetime. As a consequence, future aging cohorts on the average may continue to experience a relatively longer lifetime of biological health and an increasingly compressed period of senescence at the end of life.

Based on plausibility and consistency arguments, there are several implications of Proposition 8 for the topic of adult and gerontological intelligence. First, for much of adulthood and old age, there is no definite knowledge about a fixed and constant limit imposed by biological conditions on the nature of intellectual aging. Evidence on modifiability (plasticity) of biological aging and the continual growth–decline scheme advanced by Lynch (1983) encourage the view, in analogy, that some aspects of the potential (reserve) for intellectual functioning can be enhanced at *all* points of the life span. Whereas it appears that in aging, for reasons of decline in a generalized maximum potential, such enhancement cannot be pervasive and applicable to all domains of cognitive functioning, enhancement can be achieved if focused and concerned with dimensions that are not affected in the biological aging of a given individual.

Furthermore, because of an increasingly longer ontogenetic span of healthy functioning, the biological context is such that it in itself does not pose a fixed barrier preventing the possibility of further intellectual growth or efficacy. Note in this context also Klix's (1980) evolutionary argument of much advancement in cognitive structure and functioning over the last several thousand years despite invariance in the basics of the nervous system. Specifically, Klix concludes that the structure of the human nervous system has been rather invariant for much of recent evolutionary history. Nevertheless, due to cultural evolution and generational transmission, major changes were possible in cognitive structure and functioning during this period. Such a focus on the plasticity and untapped reserve of brain functioning, in analogy, could be applied to life-span intellectual development.

## III. Implications of Propositions for Novel Conceptualizations of Intellectual Development and Aging

How do the propositions coalesce into a framework for theory development about adult intelligence? In principle, there are several ways in which this can be done. We will focus on two ways of special interest to us. First, some general implications for questions of rate, regularity, and directionality of adult intellectual development and the concept of intelligence will be discussed. Second, a tentative conception of a dual-process approach and one concrete prototheoretical model of intellectual aging, the model of selective optimization with compensation, will be sketched. The model of selective optimization will then be applied to two areas of research: scientific productivity and wisdom.

### A. GENERAL IMPLICATIONS

Earlier in this article it was stated that there are alternative approaches for the translation of evidence for multidimensionality, multidirectionality, interindividual variability, and plasticity into the next generation of scholarship in the field of adult intelligence and its development. This fact of multiple interpretations also applies to the present framework of propositions. Moreover, note that in order to maintain a developmental orientation in the face of overwhelming evidence of variability, it is necessary to delineate at least some forms of predictable, time-ordered regularity. Ubiquitous flux and complete age-independent variability are antithetical to any developmental orientation (Baltes, 1983a; Montada, 1979).

In our view, the propositional framework presented offers some guidance for articulating the outlines of a developmental conception of adult intelligence. The orientation derived does not resurrect a monolithic or fixed conception of intellectual development, e.g., of growth followed by decline. On the contrary, it emphasizes multiple pathways, plasticity, and joint occurrence of growth and decline. However, within such a framework of differential development and plasticity (Lerner, 1984), some additional specifications of directionality and of the conditions for variability in the course of adult intellectual development can be provided.

## 1. On Rate, Regularity, and Directionality

Questions pertaining to regularity, rate, and directionality of intellectual development are fundamental to the study of intellectual development. How regular (across persons and abilities) are changes? What is their rate? Their directionality? And what are the conditions that lead to variation in processes and outcomes? As monolithic conceptions of growth and decline have been rejected, such questions will continue to arise unless, of course, one is willing to treat intelligence during adulthood and old age as a nondevelopmental phenomenon.

Indeed, the propositions suggest some order within a system of change and variability. For example, as to rate and regularity, the propositions not only draw attention to large interindividual variability but also to conditions that provide for an organized or "aleatoric" account of development (Gergen, 1980).

Proposition 1 (invariance of an individual's average or normal-range intellectual potential), Proposition 2 (decline in abilities involving maximum performance, especially in speeded information processing and fluid intelligence), and Proposition 3 (possibility of growthlike changes) set the stage for the possibility of continued but selective intellectual efficacy. While showing decline in some abilities, older adults are able to increase their intellectual skills in circumscribed areas as well. Proposition 4 (change in life goal structure) provides suggestions for the substance of problem-solving and knowledge tasks to which intellectual capacity will be increasingly applied during adulthood. Proposition 5 (individual specialization) maintains that certain domains of intellectual functioning exist where individuals are likely to continue growth or maintain peaks of efficacy.

The propositions derived from outside psychology add to these specifications, either by providing support or by indicating directions for further expansion. Proposition 6 (social structure of the life course) derived from sociological research suggests that, on the average, performance conditions and environments found in old age are less conducive to high intellectual performance than those of younger age groups. However, as indicated in Proposition 5 (specialization), the social structure of the life course suggests facets of life ecology where continued support is available (e.g., professional specialization). In addition, Proposition 6—because of its comparative stratification perspective—enables one to specify which subgroups of the population may exhibit further growth and which are likely to evince earlier decline in observed performance (although not necessarily in reserve or potential).

The two propositions derived from biology provide further information on directionality and interindividual differentiation. Proposition 7 (increased vulnerability and aging-related reduction in maximum biological functioning) supports the general idea that intellectual growth in adulthood and old age, if it exists, is not likely to be found in tasks that require highly speeded performance and, complementing this, that individual adaptation and selection in the direction of less demanding (or better supported) ecologies and tasks become increasingly important. Proposition 7 also implies that, because aging individuals may be aware of their growing biological vulnerability, it is plausible that they make efforts to compensate for possible loss in performance and thereby optimize their functioning. Proposition 8 (modifiability and optimization of biological reserve) further reinforces the view of selective efficacy or optimization. Together, Propositions 7 and 8 make it evident also that reserves exist at the biological level as well and that they can be used to maintain or increase high levels of functioning, although probably at some expense to functioning in other areas. For example, if an older individual works at maintaining a high level of speed in jogging, he or she will have less time and energy for other activities and tasks. Selective compensation and optimization, therefore, will require trade-offs between alternative goals and domains of intellectual functioning.

Clearly, these suggestions regarding the nature of rate, regularity, and directionality derived from the propositional framework are at present primarily conceptual. The empirical evidence from them is primitive and indirect. However, taken as a whole, the suggestions are precise enough to permit the formulation of some specific and testable hypotheses. Prior to examining these formulations, however, some implications are offered for our view on the concept of intelligence (see also Dittmann-Kohli & Baltes, 1984).

## 2. Implications for Conceptions of Intelligence: Role of Context and Pragmatic Factors

A second general implication derived from the propositional framework relates to conceptions of intelligence, how they have developed historically, and how present conceptions may require modification in order to be more useful for developmental work relevant to adulthood and old age. Specifically, it is suggested that a theory of adult intellectual development needs to consider more explicitly than has yet been true the role of intelligence in the general context of aging and adaptation. According to our framework, that context is codefined by at least three interrelated systems: psychological aging, biological aging, and the social structure of the life course.

Within the history of cognitive psychology (e.g., Beilin, 1981), a focus on the function or pragmatics of intelligence covaries with the recurring attention directed to the relationship between structure and function, as well as between structure and content. Considering the life situation and goals of older adults implies an emphasis on function and content. Similar efforts in the study of intelligence outside the field of adult development and aging (e.g., Friedman *et al.*, 1981; Sternberg, 1980, 1982) also suggest that a consideration of the role of intelligence in human adaptation requires a reorientation in the general conception of intelligence. Note at the outset that such a view is not without potential pitfalls. For example, there is the perennial risk of elevating intelligence to such a superconstruct that it loses any specificity. Furthermore, it is not immediately evident that a theory of function (application of intelligence) should be inherently intertwined with a theory of structure. Alternatively, all or part of a theory of function could be developed separately, for example, as a general theory of intellectual behavior with cognitive structure and skills being one of several antecedent and necessary "performance" conditions.

One illustration for the quest for a more comprehensive theory of intelligence (including a strong concern with function and content) is reflected in the recent work of Sternberg (1980, 1982). In a historical and theoretical essay on the nature of intelligence, he draws attention to the incompleteness of extant models of intelligence. Sternberg emphasizes four "macrocomponents" as essential to a complete theory of intelligence. He defines intelligence as (1) the ability to learn and profit from experience and the products of this experience (e.g., crystallized intelligence and metacognitive strategies), (2) the ability to think or reason abstractly (e.g., fluid intelligence), (3) the ability to adapt oneself to the vagaries of a changing and uncertain real-world environment (e.g., including practical intelligence), and (4) the ability to motivate oneself to accomplish expeditiously the tasks one needs to accomplish (e.g., performance factors such as achievement motivation). Sternberg argues that traditional research on intelligence has concentrated on the first two macrocomponents and neglected the last two (those dealing with adaptation and performance) and that a new and coordinated look at all four macrocomponents is necessary to advance the field.

The propositions about adult intelligence outlined here are consistent with such a view. The concept of intelligence needs to be expanded in order to bring into focus the adaptive, functional, or pragmatic use of intellectual functioning. On the one hand, the propositions and the available evidence converge on the conclusion that the first macrocomponents of Sternberg's model (ability to learn and profit from experience as in crystallized intelligence, ability to think or reason abstractly as in fluid intelligence) have been studied widely and we know quite a bit about them, at least with regard to test and laboratory-type tasks. Aging individuals, for the most part, continue to maintain the requisite mental abilities, although when it comes to fluid intelligence elderly individuals may exhibit reduced levels of maximum performance. These two macrocomponents represent, however, only part of the construct intelligence as defined by Sternberg. The dimensions that represent the functions and contexts involved in life-long use of intellectual abilities have been neglected thus far. Thus, on the adaptive and motivational dimensions (Sternberg's third and fourth macrocomponents) of intellectual development, there is a paucity of research. The following section describes our emerging view of how to deal with the distinction between structure and function in the study of intellectual development, and to consider content as a salient dimension in its own right.

## B. TOWARD A DUAL-PROCESS CONCEPTION OF INTELLECTUAL DEVELOPMENT

The preceding observations on the conception of intelligence and on our interest in emphasizing the role of life tasks in delineating adult intelligence and its development (i.e., our concern with the developmental pragmatics of intelligence) suggest an approach that emphasizes the role of pragmatics and context in addition to the study of intelligence as a system of basic cognitive operations. Our emerging dual-process approach to intellectual development has the following characteristics. In the dual-process model two interrelated processes are postulated. Although these processes are intrinsically related, not only for the sake of communication we shall describe them separately. There are also arguments why one may want to proceed as if their study is best accomplished if they are initially separated rather than viewed as part and parcel of the same system.

The first process of the dual-process scheme refers to *cognition qua cognition,* i.e., the mechanics or basic architecture of information processing and problem solving. Cognition *qua* cognition (or the mechanics of intelligence) deals with the basic cognitive operations and cognitive structures associated with such tasks as perceiving relationships, classification, and logical reasoning. The acquisition and construction of formal logic and its requisite cognitive operations are also an essential part of this first process. Similar to Fischer's (1980) and Piaget's theory, the acquisition of these cognitive operational skills is assumed to result in more and more elaborate cognitive structures and higher levels of associated skills. We maintain that these cognitive operations defining the first process are content free, perhaps similar to a Weberian conception of an "ideal type." Max Weber used the notion of an ideal type as a heuristic device by which one approaches the study of a social phenomenon.

The second process of the dual-process scheme refers to the function and application of intelligence. We tentatively call this second process the *pragmatics of intelligence,* thereby emphasizing adaptation as a central feature of intellectual behavior. Our intent is to subsume under this second process (1) systems of knowledge that are fairly generalized, such as crystallized intelligence, (2) specialized dimensions of knowledge, and (3) knowledge about factors of performance, i.e., about skills relevant for the activation of intelligence in specific contexts requiring intelligent action. This second process, then, deals with the context-related application of the mechanics of intelligence.[4]

---

[4]Note that the dual-process distinction is similar to Cattell (1971) and Horn's (1970, 1982) model of fluid vs crystallized intelligence. Conceptually, our distinction is different in several respects, however. First, its underlying rationale is not factor analytic but associated with views of cognitive psychology and functionalism (see also Dittmann-Kohli & Baltes, 1984). Second, its formulation is

Why do we think that a dual-process scheme is useful in understanding adult intelligence and its development? There are several reasons. First, the distinction between the two processes might help in sorting out theoretical and empirical priorities and in avoiding pseudoissues. For example, the question of whether there are structural transformations in cognition beyond young adulthood (e.g., Kramer, 1983; Labouvie-Vief, 1982; Riegel, 1973) appears to be primarily an issue related to the first process, cognition *qua* cognition. The conceptual status of structure is less crucial (or at least different) where the second process is concerned. When it comes to aspects of "crystallized" forms of intelligence and the role of pragmatics (second process), questions of structure and structural transformation are less of a basic paradigm issue (Reese & Overton, 1970) than is true for similar questions arising in cognitive structuralism (or the first process in our model). A basic paradigmatic entailment of cognitive structuralism is that, unless there is evidence for qualitative–structural change, there is no further development of any major kind.

In a similar vein, our position would be that the major features of possible further development of intelligence in adulthood can be found in the second process (pragmatics) and not in the first. Cognitive development in the first sense (including the cognitive structuralism of Piaget) makes its primary contribution during the first third of life. Aside from aspects of décalage, we assert there is not much further developmental activity in that process after formal operations have been achieved (see also Flavell, 1970; Piaget, 1972). If any, the developmental changes in the first process, cognition *qua* cognition, involve adjusting to losses in related functions with aging. On the other hand, intellectual pragmatics appear to be the centerpiece of intelligence during adulthood and old age. The pragmatics or functions of adult intelligence are likely to undergo further changes during these periods due to developmental changes in goals and contexts. It is proposed that this new centerpiece, the second component of the dual-process scheme, is better approached if it is kept conceptually (and perhaps also empirically) clear rather than as a simple variation of cognition *qua* cognition. The general assumption should be that whatever basic cognitive operations (in the first sense) are requisites for pragmatic mastery, they are already in the repertoire of aging adults or, at least, they could be activated if necessary.

## C. TESTING-THE-LIMITS AND THE DUAL-PROCESS MODEL OF INTELLECTUAL DEVELOPMENT

It was mentioned earlier (e.g., Propositions 1–3) that most research in intellectual aging is conducted within the normal range of functioning. At the same

---

informed primarily by the propositions outlined. However, it is possible to consider the dual-process model as a modification of the fluid/crystallized theory, although we tend to believe that the relationship is more superficial than basic.

time, it was argued that intraindividual plasticity during adulthood and old age is sufficiently large that possible age changes are easily masked or modified as long as they are studied within this normal range. As an alternative, it was proposed to begin research focused on high levels of functioning approaching "local" maxima of capacity and reserve. At maximum levels, developmental (or aging) differences are expected to be robust, perhaps even approaching the criterion of irreversibility (Baltes & Goulet, 1971; Wohlwill, 1973).

The dual-process model suggests a more systematic approach than has been available. It implies that aging-related processes of growth and decline are best studied at near-maximum level. As shown in Fig. 4, it is predicted that near-maximum level of functioning will (1) exhibit robust age differences and (2) yield differential aging patterns for the two processes defined in the dual-process scheme. Conversely, if the same processes were studied within the normal range of functioning, age differences would be labile and modifiable. This is so because—within the normal or average range of functioning—it would be possible to arrange for performance enhancement (or decline) sufficient to eliminate whatever age differences were obtained. This is a lesson learned, for example, from cognitive training research with the elderly (Baltes & Willis, 1982; Denney, 1982).

In order to study maximum or near-maximum functioning, it will be necessary to search for analogs or research models that are intrinsically tied to long-term experience thereby simulating life-long development (Baltes & Goulet, 1971). It is reasonable to expect that maximum functioning is reached only after extensive amounts of experience. Examples of such analogs are prolonged practice or,

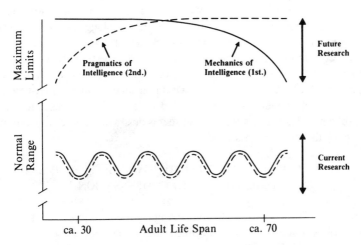

**Fig. 4.** Two-process model of intellectual aging: normal range versus maximum limits of performance. After Baltes (1983a); see also Denney (1982).

more recently, the study of expertise in select areas of factual and procedural knowledge (Chi *et al.,* 1983; Hoyer, 1984; Kliegl *et al.,* 1984).

What are some more concrete examples for studying the two processes at a level approximating maximum performance? A further example for the first process (cognition *qua* cognition) would be the extensive study of cognitive processing in difficult tasks such as multiple-choice tasks or tests of fluid intelligence under speeded conditions (see also Proposition 2). This difference should be robust and ideally without exception. As shown in Fig. 4, at maximum levels younger adults would be expected to outperform older subjects (strictly speaking, the best design would be to do this within-subject longitudinally). An example for the second process, the pragmatics of intelligence, would be the study of social intelligence or wisdom. At high levels of difficulty, in that instance, it would be expected that older adults would do as well (or better) than younger adults, at least in select facets of the second process.

The conceptualization of wisdom as a prototype of the second process of the dual-process model has been the topic of another paper (Dittmann-Kohli & Baltes, 1984). Following earlier suggestions on this topic (e.g., Baltes & Dittmann-Kohli, 1982; Clayton, 1975, 1982; Clayton & Birren, 1980; Hall, 1922; Meacham, 1982; Sowarka, 1982), Dittmann-Kohli and Baltes defined wisdom as a mental ability indexing "good judgment about important but uncertain matters of life." They proposed five criteria to define wisdom. Wisdom and tasks entailing wisdom involve (1) an expertise in selected domains of knowledge, (2) the pragmatics of life as the content domain of expertise, (3) contextual richness in problem definition, (4) uncertainty of problem definition, and (5) relativism in judgment. Classifying wisdom as an expertise in the pragmatics of life connotes that it is an ability involving a highly developed form of factual and procedural knowledge and, thus, it represents the outcome of a long-term developmental process. Furthermore, Dittmann-Kohli and Baltes (1984) speculated that *maximum* level of functioning in cognition *qua* cognition (the first process of the dual scheme) is not a necessary prerequisite for wisdom. As a consequence, our expectation is that healthy older adults would be superior in wisdom-type tasks, both at the outset as well as after extended practice. In any case, testing-the-limits research with such or similar tasks seems desirable in order to examine the usefulness of the dual-process model.

### D. A MODEL OF INTELLECTUAL AGING: SELECTIVE OPTIMIZATION WITH COMPENSATION

In this section, a model of intellectual aging is described that is consistent with both the propositional framework outlined and a dual-process scheme. At present, this model can be used as a heuristic for further research.

In earlier writing, one of us has proposed (Baltes & Baltes, 1980; Baltes &

Willis, 1982; see also Brent, 1978) the use of the term selective optimization as a characterization of a process of individual adaptation with aging. The propositions outlined give further credence to and specification of this notion. The process of selective optimization was posited to (1) index the continual evolution of individual life histories; (2) reflect the adaptation to further nonnormative life events and to the differing onset and conditions of social and biological aging; and (3) result in individual selective and compensatory efforts for the purpose of life mastery and "successful" aging. While the process of selective optimization is assumed to be general and prototypical of psychological aging, its specific manifestations would vary from individual to individual. In agreement with a life-span view, it is also assumed that the process of selective optimization has some of its origins in earlier life.

At the risk of redundancy, we summarize here how the propositions presented above permit further specification of this emerging model of selective optimization with compensation as applied to the topic of intellectual aging. Proposition 1 (invariance of intellectual capacity for average range of functioning) sets the stage for the possibility of intellectual efficacy as long as high levels of capacity of the fluid type (Proposition 2) are not required or compensation for such loss in capacity is achieved. Proposition 3 (possibility of growthlike changes) and Proposition 4 (change in life goal structure) provide suggestions for the substance of tasks to which intellectual capacity will be increasingly applied. Proposition 5 (individual specialization) specifies trajectories and domains of intellectual functioning where individuals are likely to continue to grow, obtain additional resources, and thereby maintain peaks of efficacy.

By providing support or by indicating directions for expansion, the propositions derived from outside psychology add to these specifications. Proposition 6 (the role of social structure of life course), derived from sociological work, suggests aging-related changes in the general environmental conditions of performance, such as the notion that particular career patterns channel intellectual resources in a continual manner along lines of expertise as well as decline. In addition, this proposition—because of its comparative stratification perspective—indicates how subgroups of the population may differ in change patterns, both in regard to directionality as well as in regard to domains of knowledge (e.g., academic vs everyday intelligence).

The two propositions derived from biology contain information also consistent with a selective optimization model. Proposition 7 (increased vulnerability and aging-related reduction in maximum biological functioning) strengthens the general idea that proactive or reactive selection (in the direction of less demanding ecologies and tasks) becomes increasingly important. Proposition 7 also implies that, because aging individuals may be aware of their growing biological vulnerability, it is plausible that they may make efforts at compensation and optimization. Proposition 8 (modifiability and possible optimization of biological reserve) further reinforces the view of selective optimization. It makes it evident that reserves exist and that they can be used to maintain or increase high levels of functioning, although probably at the expense of functioning in other areas. Selective compensation and optimization will require trade-offs (see also La- bouvie-Vief, 1982) between alternative goals and domains of intellectual functioning.

The study of age and scientific productivity is an example of how selective optimization with compensation operates. Research on this topic has undergone a trend rather similar to research on intellectual aging. Early cross-sectional studies (Lehman, 1953) revealed an aging-related decline in scientific productivity. Recent work (e.g., Cole, 1979), based on cohort analysis and the use of citation indices, suggests a different conclusion. For the age range up to retirement (approximately 60–65), and for scientists who remain active, there appears to be little if any decline in scientific productivity with age. Surprisingly, this finding of age invariance applies to all scientific fields examined by Cole (1979) includ- ing physics and mathematics. The latter fields traditionally have been assumed to be very sensitive to aging decline.

What is the interpretation of these findings offered by a selective optimization with compensation point of view? On a psychological level, the argument is that older scientists have the cognitive reserve to remain efficient and that such reserves can be used to continuously evolve the second process of the dual- process scheme, i.e., the one dealing with factual and procedural knowledge in expert-type settings. In addition, however, there is further compensatory support at the sociostructural level. As scientists are successful and remain active, they have increased access to societal resources and power in the community of science. With age, their work therefore can be accomplished and communicated more easily. Thus, the model of selective optimization with compensation has a psychological as well as sociological facet.

What additional recommendations for future work on adult intelligence and its development can be derived from a selective optimization view?

First, the model emphasizes further and from a different theoretical posture the importance of searching for new evaluation criteria and tasks by which to mea- sure intellectual functioning. If intellectual functioning during adulthood and old age is essentially a question of pragmatics (proactive and reactive application of available cognitive skills and knowledge to new substantive domains and task clusters) rather than the further transformation of cognitive structures (in the logical sense), then we need to have measures that index such forms of intel- ligence. Furthermore, as selective optimization includes efforts at compensation (e.g., for losses in the first process of the dual-process model), there is need for investigation of compensatory cognitive skills. How and under which conditions do compensatory skills evolve in the face of reduced effectiveness of maximum functioning in the mechanics of intelligence (see also, Skinner, 1983)?

Furthermore, the model of selective optimization provides further specification of directional processes related to intellectual development. There are at least five trends that need to be considered when identifying aspects of selection and compensation in intellectual aging: (1) the changing structure of life tasks, (2) the process of specialization, (3) the general trend toward reduced biological and environmental resources which lead to a reduction of reserve capacity, (4) an increasing occurrence of environmental and biological deficits or vulnerabilities that require compensatory mastery, and (5) the counterpart decrease in domains of functioning that are neglected in favor of others. Each of these age-related developmental trends is suggestive of particular forms of intellectual functioning relevant for the processes of achieving adaptation and selective optimization.

Finally, the model of intellectual aging as selective optimization also has some implications for metatheory (Reese & Overton, 1970). It implies that, with age, an increasingly larger share of adult intellectual functioning is best represented by a theory of performance than by a theory of cognitive structuralism à la Piaget. In other words, if fairly regular changes in intellectual functioning occur with aging, these changes are more likely to be of a reorganization and quantitative redistribution within existing cognitive skills and knowledge systems than a qualitative transformation of basic cognitive structures in the sense of Piagetian qualitative stages. In our view, and contrary to a view associated with cognitive structuralism (Riegel, 1973), the focus of intellectual change during adulthood and old age should be more on function and less on structure. Of course, there may be changes in the organization of knowledge systems and cognitive skills during adulthood, but these changes are not likely to be of the genotype inherent in "classical" cognitive structuralism and cognitive stages.

# References

Andres, R., & Tobin, J. D. Endocrine systems. In C. E. Finch & L. Hayflick (Eds.), *Handbook of the biology of aging*. Princeton, New Jersey: Van Nostrand Reinhold, 1977.

Arenberg, D., & Robertson-Tchabo, E. A. Learning and aging. In J. E. Birren & K. W. Schaie (Eds.), *Handbook of the psychology of aging*. Princeton, New Jersey: Van Nostrand Reinhold, 1977.

Baltes, P. B. Life-span developmental psychology: Observations on history and theory revisited. In R. M. Lerner (Ed.), *Developmental psychology: Historical and philosophical perspectives*. Hillsdale, New Jersey: Erlbaum, 1983. (a)

Baltes, P. B. Zur Psychologie der Intelligenz im Alter: Nur Abbau oder auch Entwicklung? In Max-Planck-Gesellschaft (Ed.), *Max-Planck-Gesellschaft Jahrbuch 1983*. Göttingen: Vandenhoeck & Ruprecht, 1983. (b)

Baltes, P. B., & Baltes, M. M. Plasticity and variability in psychological aging: Methodological and theoretical issues. In G. Gurski (Ed.), *Determining the effects of aging on the central nervous system*. Berlin: Schering, 1980.

Baltes, P. B., & Dittmann-Kohli, F. Einige einführende Überlegungen zur Intelligenz im Erwachsenenalter. *Neue Sammlung,* 1982, **22,** 261–278.

Baltes, P. B., & Goulet, L. R. Exploration of developmental variables by manipulation and simulation of age differences in behavior. *Human Development,* 1971, **14,** 149–170.

Baltes, P. B., & Labouvie, G. V. Adult development of intellectual performance: Description, explanation, and modification. In C. Eisdorfer & M. P. Lawton (Eds.), *The psychology of adult development and aging.* Washington, D.C.: American Psychological Association, 1973.

Baltes, P. B., Reese, H. W., & Lipsitt, L. P. Life-span developmental psychology. *Annual Review of Psychology,* 1980, **31,** 65–100.

Baltes, P. B., & Schaie, K. W. On the plasticity of intelligence in adulthood and old age: Where Horn and Donaldson fail. *American Psychologist,* 1976, **31,** 720–725.

Baltes, P. B., & Willis, S. L. The critical importance of appropriate methodology in the study of aging: The sample case of psychometric intelligence. In F. Hoffmeister & C. Müller (Eds.), *Brain function in old age.* Berlin and New York: Springer-Verlag, 1979. (a)

Baltes, P. B., & Willis, S. L. Life-span developmental psychology, cognitive functioning, and social policy. In M. W. Riley (Ed.), *Aging from birth to death: Interdisciplinary perspectives.* Boulder, Colorado: Westview Press, 1979. (b)

Baltes, P. B., & Willis, S. L. Plasticity and enhancement of intellectual functioning in old age: Penn State's Adult Development and Enrichment Project (ADEPT). In F. I. M. Craik & S. E. Trehub (Eds.), *Aging and cognitive processes.* New York: Plenum, 1982.

Bandura, A. Self-efficacy: Toward a unifying theory of behavioral change. *Psychological Review,* 1977, **84,** 191–215.

Bandura, A. Self-efficacy mechanism in human agency. *American Psychologist,* 1982, **37,** 122–147.

Bayley, N. Development of mental abilities. In P. Mussen (Ed.), *Carmichael's manual of child psychology* (Vol. 1). New York: Wiley, 1970.

Beilin, H. *Piaget and the new functionalism.* Unpublished manuscript, City University of New York, 1981.

Bertram, H. *Sozialstruktur und Sozialisation: Zur mikrosozidogischen Analyse von Chancenungleichheit.* Darmstadt: Luchterhand, 1981.

Bornstein, R., & Smircina, M. T. The status of the empirical support for the hypothesis of increased variability in aging populations. *The Gerontologist,* 1982, **22,** 258–260.

Botwinick, J. Aging and intelligence. In J. E. Birren & K. W. Schaie (Eds.), *Handbook of the psychology of aging.* Princeton, New Jersey: Van Nostrand Reinhold, 1977.

Botwinick, J. *Aging and Behavior.* New York: Springer Publ., 1978.

Brent, S. B. Individual specialization, collective adaptation and rate of environmental change. *Human Development,* 1978, **21,** 21–23.

Brim, O. G., Jr., & Ryff, C. D. On the properties of life events. In P. B. Baltes & O. G. Brim, Jr. (Eds.), *Life-span development and behavior* (Vol. 3). New York: Academic Press, 1980.

Brim, O. G., Jr., & Wheeler, S. *Socialization after childhood: Two essays.* New York: Wiley, 1966.

Brown, A. L. Learning and development: The problem of compatibility, access, and induction. *Human Development,* 1982, **25,** 89–115.

Brown, A., & French, L. The zone of potential development: Implications for intelligence testing in the year 2000. *Intelligence,* 1979, **3,** 255–277.

Bühler, C., & Massarik, F. (Eds.). *The course of human life.* New York: Springer Publ., 1968.

Busse, E. N. Duke longitudinal study I: Senescence and senility. In R. Katzman, R. D. Terry, & K. L. Beck (Eds.), *Alzheimer's disease: Senile dementia and related disorders.* New York: Raven, 1978.

Carus, F. A. *Psychologie. Zweiter Theil: Specialpsychologie.* Leipzig: Barth, 1808.

Cattell, R. B. *Abilities: Their structure, growth, and action.* Boston: Houghton, 1971.

Chi, M. T. H., Glaser, R., & Rees, E. Expertise in problem solving. In R. J. Sternberg (Ed.), *Advances in the psychology of human intelligence*. Hillsdale, New Jersey: Erlbaum, 1983.

Clayton, V. Erikson's theory of human development as it applies to the aged: Wisdom as contradictory cognition. *Human Development*, 1975, **18**, 119–128.

Clayton, V. Wisdom and intelligence: The nature and function of knowledge in the later years. *International Journal of Aging and Development*, 1982, **15**, 315–323.

Clayton, V. P., & Birren, J. E. The development of wisdom across the life span: A reexamination of an ancient topic. In P. B. Baltes & O. G. Brim, Jr. (Eds.), *Life-span development and behavior* (Vol. 3). New York: Academic Press, 1980.

Cole, M., Gay, J., Glick, J. A., & Sharp, D. W. *The cultural context of learning and thinking*. New York: Basic Books, 1971.

Cole, M., Hood, L., & McDermott, R. *Ecological niche picking: Ecological invalidity as an axiom of experimental cognitive psychology*. Unpublished manuscript, Laboratory of Comparative Human Cognition and Institute for Comparative Human Development, Rockefeller University, 1978.

Cole, S. Age and scientific performance. *American Journal of Sociology*, 1979, **84**, 958–977.

Comfort, A. *The bridge of senescence*. Amsterdam: Elsevier, 1979.

Cornelius, S. W. Classic pattern of intellectual aging: Test familiarity, difficulty, and performance. *Journal of Gerontology*, 1983, **7**, 253–269.

Cornelius, S. W., Willis, S. L., Nesselroade, J. R., & Baltes, P. B. Convergence between attention variables and factors of psychometric intelligence in older adults. *Intelligence*, 1983, **7**, 253–269.

Costa, P. T., Jr., & McCrae, R. R. Still stable after all these years: Personality as a key to some issues in adulthood and old age. In P. B. Baltes & O. G. Brim, Jr. (Eds.), *Life-span development and behavior* (Vol. 3). New York: Academic Press, 1980.

Craik, F. I. M. Age differences in human memory. In J. E. Birren & K. W. Schaie (Eds.), *Handbook of the psychology of aging*. Princeton, New Jersey: Van Nostrand Reinhold, 1977.

Demming, J. A., & Pressey, S. L. Tests "indigenous" to the adult and older years. *Journal of Counseling Psychology*, 1957, **4**, 144–148.

Denney, N. W. Problem solving in later adulthood: Intervention research. In P. B. Baltes & O. G. Brim, Jr. (Eds.). *Life-span development and behavior* (Vol. 2). New York: Academic Press, 1979.

Denney, N. W. Aging and cognitive changes. In B. B. Wolman (Ed.), *Handbook of developmental psychology*. Englewood Cliffs, New Jersey: Prentice-Hall, 1982.

Dittmann-Kohli, F. Theoretische Grundlagen der Analyse von Lebensbewältigung und Umwelt. In F. Dittmann-Kohli, N. Schreiber, & F. Möller (Eds.), *Lebenswelt und Lebensbewältigung*. Constance, Federal Republic of Germany: Constance University, 1982.

Dittmann-Kohli, F. Die Bewältigung von Entwicklungsaufgaben bei Lehrlingen: Analyse- und Interventionsgesichtspunkte. In E. Olbrich & E. Todt (Eds.), *Probleme des Jugendalters*. Berlin and New York: Springer-Verlag, 1984. (a)

Dittmann-Kohli, F. Weisheit als mögliches Ergebnis der Intelligenzentwicklung im Erwachsenenalter. *Sprache und Kognition*, 1984, in press. (b)

Dittmann-Kohli, F., & Baltes, P. B. Towards a neofunctionalist conception of adult intellectual development: Wisdom as a prototypical case of intellectual growth. In C. N. Alexander & E. Langer (Eds.), *Beyond formal operations: Alternative endpoints to human development*, 1984, in press.

Dixon, R. A., & Hultsch, D. F. Structure and development of metamemory in adulthood. *Journal of Gerontology*, 1983, **38**, 682–688.

Dörner, D. Über die Schwierigkeiten menschlichen Umgangs mit Komplexität. *Psychologische Rundschau*, 1981, **3**, 163–179.

Dörner, D. The ecological conditions of thinking. In D. R. Griffin (Ed.), *Animal mind–human mind (Dahlem Konferenzen)*. New York: Springer Publ., 1982.

Edelstein, W., & Noam, G. Regulatory structures of the self and "post-formal" stages in adulthood. *Human Development*, 1982, **6**, 407–422.

Eichorn, D. H., Clausen, J. A., Haan, N., Honzik, M. P., & Mussen, P. H. (Eds.). *Present and past in middle life*. New York: Academic Press, 1981.

Elder, G. H., Jr. Age-differentiation in life course perspective. *Annual Review of Sociology*, 1975, **1**, 165–190.

Erikson, E. H. *Identity and the life cycle*. New York: International University Press, 1959.

Featherman, D. L. Schooling and occupational careers: Constancy and change in worldly success. In O. G. Brim, Jr., & J. Kagan (Eds.), *Constancy and change in human development*. Cambridge, Massachusetts: Harvard University Press, 1980.

Featherman, D. L. The life-span perspective in social science research. In P. B. Baltes & O. G. Brim, Jr. (Eds.), *Life-span development and behavior* (Vol. 5). New York: Academic Press, 1983.

Filipp, S. H. (Ed.). *Kritische Lebensereignisse*. Munich: Urban & Schwarzenberg, 1981.

Finch, C. E., & Hayflick, L. (Eds.). *Handbook of the biology of aging*. Princeton, New Jersey: Van Nostrand Reinhold, 1977.

Fischer, K. W. A theory of cognitive development: The control and construction of hierarchies of skills. *Psychological Review*, 1980, **87**, 477–531.

Flavell, J. H. Cognitive changes in adulthood. In L. R. Goulet & P. B. Baltes (Eds.), *Life-span developmental psychology: Research and theory*. New York: Academic Press, 1970.

Fleishman, E. A. Systems for describing human tasks. *American Psychologist*, 1982, **37**, 821–834.

Friedman, M. P., Das, J. P., & O'Connor, N. (Eds.). *Intelligence and learning*. New York: Plenum, 1981.

Fries, J. F. Aging, natural death, and the compression of morbidity. *New England Journal of Medicine*, 1980, **303**, 130–135.

Fries, J. F., & Crapo, L. M. *Vitality and aging*. San Francisco: Freeman, 1981.

Galton, F. *Inquiries into human faculty and its development*. New York: Macmillan, 1883.

Gergen, K. J. The emerging crisis in life-span developmental theory. In P. B. Baltes & O. G. Brim, Jr. (Eds.), *Life-span development and behavior* (Vol. 3). New York: Academic Press, 1980.

Glaser, R. The future of testing: A research agenda for cognitive psychology and psychometrics. *American Psychologist*, 1981, **36**, 923–936.

Gollin, E. S. (Ed.). *Developmental plasticity: Behavioral and biological aspects of variations in development*. New York: Academic Press, 1981.

Guthke, J. Die Relevanz des Lerntestkonzepts für die klinisch-psychologische Diagnostik—demonstriert am Beispiel der Diagnostik der geistigen Behinderung und der frühkindlichen Hirnschädigung. *Probleme und Ergebnisse der Psychologie*, 1980, **72**, 5–21.

Gutmann, D. The cross-cultural perspective: Notes toward a comparative psychology of aging. In J. E. Birren & K. W. Schaie (Eds.), *Handbook of the psychology of aging*. Princeton, New Jersey: Van Nostrand Reinhold, 1977.

Hall, G. S. *Senescence: The last half of life*. New York: Appleton, 1922.

Hasher, L., & Zacks, R. T. Automatic and effortful processes in memory. *Journal of Experimental Psychology*, 1979, **108**, 356–388.

Havighurst, R. J. *Developmental tasks and education*. New York: McKay, 1948.

Hollingworth, H. L. *Mental growth and decline: A survey of developmental psychology*. New York: Appleton, 1927.

Horn, J. L. Organization of data on life-span development of human abilities. In L. R. Goulet & P. B. Baltes (Eds.), *Life-span developmental psychology: Research and theory*. New York: Academic Press, 1970.

Horn, J. L. Human ability systems. In P. B. Baltes (Ed.), *Life-span development and behavior* (Vol. 1). New York: Academic Press, 1978.

Horn, J. L. Concepts of intellect in relation to learning and adult development. *Intelligence*, 1980, **4**, 285–317.

Horn, J. L. The aging of human abilities. In B. B. Wolman (Ed.), *Handbook of developmental psychology*. Englewood Cliffs, New Jersey: Prentice-Hall, 1982.

Horn, J. L., & Donaldson, G. On the myth of intellectual decline in adulthood. *American Psychologist*, 1976, **31**, 701–719.

Horn, J. L., & Donaldson, G. Faith is not enough: A response to the Baltes–Schaie claim that intelligence does not wane. *American Psychologist*, 1977, **32**, 369–373.

Horn, J. L., & Donaldson, G. Cognitive development in adulthood. In O. G. Brim, Jr., & J. Kagan (Eds.), *Constancy and change in human development*. Cambridge, Massachusetts: Harvard University Press, 1980.

Hoyer, W. J. Aging and the development of expert cognition. In T. M. Schlechter & M. P. Toglia (Eds.), *New directions in cognitive science*. Norwood, New Jersey: Ablex, 1984, in press.

Hultsch, D. F., & Dixon, R. A. Memory for text materials in adulthood. In P. B. Baltes & O. G. Brim, Jr. (Eds.), *Life-span development and behavior* (Vol. 6). New York: Academic Press, 1984.

Hultsch, D. F., & Plemons, J. K. Life events and life-span development. In P. B. Baltes & O. G. Brim, Jr. (Eds.), *Life-span development and behavior* (Vol. 2). New York: Academic Press, 1979.

Jarvik, L. F., & Blum, J. E. Cognitive decline as predictor of mortality in twin pairs. A twenty-year-long study of aging. In E. Palmore & F. C. Jeffers (Eds.), *Prediction of life span*. Lexington, Massachusetts: Heath, 1971.

Kahneman, D., Slovic, P., & Tversky, A. (Eds.). *Judgement under certainty: Heuristics and biases*. London and New York: Cambridge University Press, 1982.

Kliegl, R., Kramer, D. A., & Baltes, P. B. *Cognitive reserve capacity, expertise, and aging: A research proposal*. Unpublished manuscript, Max Planck Institute for Human Development and Education, Berlin, Federal Republic of Germany, 1984.

Klix, F. *Erwachendes Denken: Eine Entwicklungsgeschichte der menschlichen Intelligenz*. Berlin: VEB Deutscher Verlag der Wissenschaften, 1980.

Kluwe, R. H., & Spada, H. (Eds.). *Developmental models of thinking*. New York: Academic Press, 1980.

Kohli, M. (Ed.). *Soziologie des Lebenslaufs*. Darmstadt: Luchterhand, 1978.

Kohn, M. L., & Schooler, C. The reciprocal effects of the substantive complexity of work and intellectual flexibility: A longitudinal assessment. *American Journal of Sociology*, 1978, **84**, 24–52.

Kohn, M. L., & Schooler, C. Job conditions and personality: A longitudinal assessment of their reciprocal effects. *American Journal of Sociology*, 1982, **87**, 1257–1286.

Kramer, D. A. Post-formal operations: A need for further conceptualization. *Human Development*, 1983, **26**, 91–105.

Kuhn, D., Pennington, N., & Leadbeater, B. Adult thinking in developmental perspective. In P. B. Baltes & O. G. Brim, Jr. (Eds.), *Life-span development and behavior* (Vol. 5). New York: Academic Press, 1983.

Labouvie, G. V., Hoyer, W. J., Baltes, P. B., & Baltes, M. M. Operant analysis of intellectual behavior in old age. *Human Development*, 1974, **17**, 259–272.

Labouvie-Vief, G. Toward optimizing cognitive competence. *Educational Gerontology*, 1976, **1**, 75–92.

Labouvie-Vief, G. Adult cognitive development: In search of alternative interpretations. *Merrill Palmer Quarterly*, 1977, **23**, 227–263.

Labouvie-Vief, G. Beyond formal operations: Uses and limits of pure logic in life-span development. *Human Development*, 1980, **23**, 141–161.

Labouvie-Vief, G. Proactive and reactive aspects of constructivism: Growth and aging in life-span perspective. In R. M. Lerner & N. A. Busch-Rossnagel (Eds.), *Individuals as producers of their development*. New York: Academic Press, 1981.

Labouvie-Vief, G. Dynamic development and mature autonomy: A theoretical prologue. *Human Development*, 1982, **25**, 161–191.

Lachman, M. Perceptions of intellectual aging: Antecedent or consequence of intellectual functioning. *Developmental Psychology*, 1983, **19**, 482–498.

LaRue, A., & Jarvik, L. F. Old age and biobehavioral changes. In B. B. Wolman (Ed.), *Handbook of developmental psychology*. Englewood Cliffs, New Jersey: Prentice-Hall, 1982.

Lehman, H. C. *Age and achievement*. Princeton, New Jersey: Princeton University Press, 1953.

Lerner, R. M. *On the nature of human plasticity*. London and New York: Cambridge University Press, 1984.

Lund, R. D. *Development and plasticity of the brain*. London and New York: Oxford University Press, 1978.

Lynch, G. S. *Aging and brain plasticity*. Invited address (Div. 20), 91st Annual Convention of the American Psychological Association, Anaheim, California, August 1983.

McCall, R. B. The development of intellectual functioning in infancy and the prediction of later IQ. In J. Osofsky (Ed.), *Handbook of infant development*. New York: Wiley, 1979.

McKenzie, S. C. *Aging and old age*. Glenview, Illinois: Scott, Foresman & Company, 1980.

Meacham, J. A. Research on remembering: Interrogation or conversation, monologue or dialogue? *Human Development*, 1980, **23**, 236–245.

Meacham, J. A. Wisdom and the context of knowledge: Knowing that one doesn't know. In D. Kuhn & J. A. Meacham (Eds.), *On the development of developmental psychology*. Basel: Karger, 1982.

Mergler, N. L., & Goldstein, M. D. Why are there old people? Senescence as a biological and cultural preparedness for the transmission of information. *Human Development*, 1983, **26**, 72–90.

Meyer, J. W. The institutionalization of the life course and its effects on the self. Unpublished manuscript, Department of Sociology, Stanford University, Stanford, California, 1981.

Montada, L. Entwicklungspsychologie auf der Suche nach einer Identität. In L. Montada (Ed.), *Brennpunkte der Entwicklungspsychologie*. Stuttgart: Kohlhammer, 1979.

Neugarten, B. L. Personality and aging. In J. E. Birren & K. W. Schaie (Eds.), *Handbook of the psychology of aging*. Princeton, New Jersey: Van Nostrand Reinhold, 1977.

Newell, A., & Simon, H. A. *Human problem solving*. Englewood Cliffs, New Jersey: Prentice-Hall, 1972.

Overton, W. F., & Newman, J. L. Cognitive development: A competence-activation/utilization approach. In T. Field, A. Houston, H. Quay, L. Troll, & G. Finley (Eds.), *Review of human development*. New York: Wiley, 1982.

Parker, D. M. Determinate and plastic principles in neuropsychological development. In J. W. T. Dickerson & H. McGurk (Eds.), *Brain and behavioral development*. Glasgow: Surrey University Press, 1982.

Pascual-Leone, J. Growing into human maturity: Toward a metasubjective theory of adulthood stages. In P. B. Baltes & O. G. Brim, Jr. (Eds.), *Life-span development and behavior* (Vol. 5). New York: Academic Press, 1983.

Pawlik, K. (Ed.). *Diagnose der Diagnostik: Beiträge zur Diskussion der psychologischen Diagnostik in der Verhaltensmodifikation*. Stuttgart: Klett-Cotta, 1976.

Perlmutter, M. What is memory aging the aging of? *Developmental Psychology*, 1978, **14**, 330–345.

Piaget, J. Intellectual evolution from adolescence to adulthood. *Human Development*, 1972, **15**, 1–12.

Quetelet, A. *Sur l'homme et le développement de ses facultés.* Paris: Bachelier, 1835.

Reese, H. W., & Overton, W. F. Models of development and theories of development. In L. R. Goulet & P. B. Baltes (Eds.), *Life-span developmental psychology: Research and theory.* New York: Academic Press, 1970.

Resnick, L. B. (Ed.). *The nature of intelligence.* Hillsdale, New Jersey: Erlbaum, 1976.

Riegel, K. F. Dialectical operations: The final period of cognitive development. *Human Development*, 1973, **16**, 346–370.

Riegel, K. F., & Riegel, R. M. Development, drop, and death. *Developmental Psychology*, 1972, **6**, 306–319.

Riley, M. W. (Ed.). *Aging from birth to death: Interdisciplinary perspectives.* Boulder, Colorado: Westview Press, 1979.

Riley, M. W. Age strata in social system. In R. H. Binstock & E. Shanas (Eds.), *Handbook on aging and the social sciences.* Princeton, New Jersey: Van Nostrand Reinhold, 1984, in press.

Riley, M. W., Johnson, M., & Foner, A. (Eds.). *Aging and society: A sociology of age stratification.* New York: Russell Sage Foundation, 1972.

Rockstein, M., Chesky, J., & Sussman, M. Comparative biology and evolution of aging. In C. E. Finch & L. Hayflick (Eds.), *Handbook of the biology of aging.* Princeton, New Jersey: Van Nostrand Reinhold, 1977.

Rosenmayr, L. (Ed.). *Die menschlichen Lebensalter.* Munich: Piper, 1978.

Rosow, I. Status and role change through the life span. In R. H. Binstock & E. Shanas (Eds.), *Handbook of aging and the social sciences.* Princeton, New Jersey: Van Nostrand Reinhold, 1976.

Rudinger, G., & Lantermann, E. D. Soziale Bedingungen der Intelligenz im Alter. *Zeitschrift für Gerontologie*, 1980, **13**, 433–441.

Ryff, C. D. Successful aging: A developmental approach. *The Gerontologist* 1982, **22**, 209–214.

Sacher, G. A. Life table modification and life prolongation. In C. E. Finch & L. Hayflick (Eds.), *Handbook of the biology of aging.* Princeton, New Jersey: Van Nostrand Reinhold, 1977.

Salthouse, T. A. *Adult cognition: An experimental psychology of human aging.* New York: Springer Publ., 1982.

Sanford, E. C. Mental growth and decay. *American Journal of Psychology*, 1902, **13**, 426–449.

Schaie. K. W. Toward a stage theory of adult cognitive development. *Journal of Aging and Human Development*, 1977, **8**, 129–138.

Schaie, K. W. External validity in the assessment of intellectual performance in adulthood. *Journal of Gerontology*, 1978, **33**, 695–701.

Schaie, K. W. The primary mental abilities in adulthood: An exploration in the development of psychometric intelligence. In P. B. Baltes & O. G. Brim, Jr. (Eds.), *Life-span development and behavior* (Vol. 2). New York: Academic Press, 1979.

Schaie, K. W. The Seattle Longitudinal Study: A twenty-one year exploration of psychometric intelligence in adulthood. In K. W. Schaie (Ed.), *Longitudinal studies of adult psychological development.* New York: Guilford, 1983.

Schaie, K. W., & Baltes, P. B. Some faith helps to see the forecast: A final comment on the Horn and Donaldson myth of the Baltes–Schaie position on adult intelligence. *American Psychologist*, 1977, **32**, 1118–1120.

Schaie, K. W., & Hertzog, C. Fourteen-year cohort-sequential analyses of adult intellectual development. *Developmental Psychology*, 1983, **19**, 531–543.

Schaie, K. W., Labouvie, G. V., & Buech, B. U. Generational and cohort-specific differences in adult cognitive functioning: A fourteen-year study of independent samples. *Developmental Psychology*, 1973, **9**, 151–166.

Schmidt, L. R. Testing the limits im Leistungsverhalten: Möglichkeiten und Grenzen. In E. Duhm (Ed.), *Praxis der klinischen Psychologie* (Vol. 2). Göttingen: Hogrefe, 1971.

Shock, N. W. System integration. In C. E. Finch & L. Hayflick (Eds.), *Handbook of the biology of aging.* Princeton, New Jersey: Van Nostrand Reinhold, 1977.

Siegler, I. C. The terminal drop hypothesis: Fact or artifact? *Experimental Aging Research,* 1975, **1,** 169–185.

Siegler, I. C. The psychology of adult development and aging. In E. W. Busse & D. G. Blazer (Eds.), *Handbook of geriatric psychiatry.* Princeton, New Jersey: Van Nostrand Reinhold, 1980.

Singer, B., & Spilerman, S. Mathematical representations of developmental theories. In J. R. Nesselroade & P. B. Baltes (Eds.), *Longitudinal research in the study of behavior and development.* New York: Academic Press, 1979.

Skinner, B. F. Intellectual self-management in old age. *American Psychologist,* 1983, **38,** 239–244.

Sowarka, D. *Überlegungen zu naiven Theorien über Weisheit.* Unpublished manuscript, Max Planck Institute for Human Development and Education, Berlin, 1982.

Sternberg, R. J. Sketch of a componential subtheory of human intelligence. *Behavioral and Brain Sciences,* 1980, **3,** 473–504.

Sternberg, R. J. Toward a unified componential theory of human intelligence: I. Fluid ability. In M. P. Friedman, J. P. Das, & N. O'Connor (Eds.), *Intelligence and learning.* New York: Plenum, 1981.

Sternberg, R. J. The nature of intelligence. *New York University Education Quarterly,* 1982, **12,** 10–17.

Sternberg, R. J., & Detterman, D. K. (Eds.). *Human intelligence: Perspectives on its theory and measurement.* Norwood, New Jersey: Ablex, 1979.

Sterns, H. L., & Sanders, R. E. Training and education of the elderly. In R. R. Turner & H. W. Reese (Eds.), *Life-span developmental psychology: Intervention.* New York: Academic Press, 1980.

Steuer, J., & Jarvik, L. F. Cognitive functioning in the elderly: Influence of physical health. In J. L. McGaugh & S. B. Kiesler (Eds.), *Aging: Biology and behavior.* New York: Academic Press, 1981.

Strehler, B. L. *Time, cells, and aging* (rev. ed.). New York: Academic Press, 1977. (Originally published, 1962).

Tetens, J. N. *Philosophische Versuche über die menschliche Natur und ihre Entwicklung.* Leipzig: Weidmanns Erben und Reich, 1777.

Tversky, A., & Kahneman, D. The framing of decisions and the psychology of choice. *Science,* 1981, **211,** 453–458.

Upton, A. C. Pathobiology. In C. E. Finch & L. Hayflick (Eds.), *Handbook of the psychology of aging.* Princeton, New Jersey: Van Nostrand Reinhold, 1977.

Van den Daele, L. D. Qualitative models in developmental analysis. *Developmental Psychology,* 1969, **4,** 303–310.

Van den Daele, L. D. Infrastructure and transition in developmental analysis. *Human Development,* 1974, **17,** 1–23.

Waddington, C. H. *The evolution of an evolutionist.* Edinburgh: Edinburgh University Press, 1975.

Willis, S. L., & Baltes, P. B. Intelligence in adulthood and aging: Contemporary issues. In L. W. Poon (Ed.), *Aging in the 1980's: Psychological issues.* Washington, D.C.: American Psychological Association, 1980.

Wohlwill, J. F. *The study of behavioral development.* New York: Academic Press, 1973.

Wohlwill, J. F. Cognitive development in childhood. In O. G. Brim, Jr. & J. Kagan (Eds.), *Constancy and change in human development.* Cambridge, Massachusetts: Harvard University Press, 1980.

# Memory for Text Materials in Adulthood

*David F. Hultsch*

UNIVERSITY OF VICTORIA
VICTORIA, BRITISH COLUMBIA, CANADA

*and*

*Roger A. Dixon*

MAX PLANCK INSTITUTE FOR
HUMAN DEVELOPMENT AND EDUCATION
BERLIN, FEDERAL REPUBLIC OF GERMANY

## Abstract

Research examining the development of memory abilities in adulthood has consistently revealed age-related differences in secondary memory performance, with younger adults routinely performing better than older adults. However, recent research focusing on substantive recall of meaningful, presumably ecologically valid text materials has failed to find such systematic age-related performance differences. Whereas a number of recent studies report age-related differences in quantity and quality of recall, several others report no such differences. Certainly, some of the discrepant results are attributable to contrasting empirical emphases, representational schemes, and scoring procedures. Many of the remaining differences, however, may be related to variables more substantively relevant to the study of cognitive development in adulthood. In this article the current state of understanding of text processing in adulthood is organized heuristically. Results of both major research programs

77

and isolated studies are cast in terms of the interactional scheme of Jenkins (1979). Thus, observed age-related performance differences on text recall tasks are viewed as dependent upon interactions among characteristics of the subjects (e.g., intellectual abilities), materials (e.g., texts), acquisition conditions (e.g., incidental learning), and criterial tasks (e.g., verbatim recall). Examination of these factors and the interactions among them serves to orient the observer not only to the present body of results but to future avenues of research.


# I. Introduction

Research examining the recall of text materials is a category of the larger field investigating discourse comprehension (Kintsch & van Dijk, 1978; Lachman, Lachman, & Butterfield, 1979; van Dijk & Kintsch, 1978). The consensus emerging in this literature is that text comprehension is a constructive process. That is, the reader does not semantically process each input sentence in its entirety and simply "store" it intact. Rather, the reader processes the material selectively, using information from the input sentences together with stored knowledge about the world to generate a semantic interpretation that "fits" the input "data" (Fass & Schumacher, 1981; Freedle, 1979; Grover, 1979; van Dijk & Kintsch, 1978). The classical evidence for this view comes from Bartlett's (1932) observation of distortions in the recall of unusual folk tales. For most texts, the constructions are not as sweeping as those observed by Bartlett. Nevertheless, it is clear that the reader's comprehension and memory for a text go far beyond the information contained in its surface structure (Cofer, 1976). Because of this fact, much of the recent work on text memory has emphasized substantive rather than verbatim recall of the target material (Kintsch, 1974, 1977; Loosen, 1981). Indeed, it is possible to argue that substantive recall is more representative of the individual's everyday cognitive experience than verbatim recall, particularly in the case of complex materials (Dooling & Christiaansen, 1977).

The implications of these observations are significant for our understanding of adult memory. During the last several decades, research examining the development of memory abilities in adulthood has clearly shown that age-related differences in secondary memory performance are widespread (Burke & Light, 1981; Craik, 1977; Fozard, 1980; Smith, 1980). With few exceptions, younger adults routinely outperform older adults when the focus of the task is on verbatim recall of supraspan lists of numbers, symbols, words, and so forth. However, when the focus of the task is on the substantive recall of meaningful text materials, the nature and extent of age-related performance differences are considerably less systematic, consistent, or clear. A number of recent studies have reported age-related deficits in text memory which conform to the general pattern observed in verbatim recall of word lists (Cohen, 1979; Dixon, Simon, Nowak, & Hultsch, 1982; Taub, 1975, 1976; Taub & Kline, 1978; Zelinski, Gilewski, & Thompson, 1980). Other studies have found that younger and older adults appear to be equally adept at comprehending and remembering texts (Hartley, Harker, & Walsh, 1980; Meyer & Rice, 1981). The primary goal of this article is to examine this emerging literature and to identify some of the variables which appear to influence adult age differences in memory for text materials.

## II. Early Investigations

Significant interest in text memory in adulthood and aging has emerged only within the last decade (Hartley *et al.*, 1980; Hultsch, 1977; Hultsch & Pentz, 1980a,b; Meyer & Rice, 1981). A search of the literature published prior to 1977 reveals only a handful of studies. This early research was characterized by simple age comparisons within a cross-sectional paradigm. Two distinct types of criterial tasks were used. In some instances the focus was on verbatim recall of the text (Botwinick & Storandt, 1974; Gilbert, 1941; Schneider, Gritz, & Jarvik, 1975), while in other instances attempts were made to measure the recall or recognition of the substance of the text (Gordon & Clark, 1974; Moenster, 1972; Monge & Gardner, 1976; Taub, 1975, 1976). In both instances, the results of these studies suggested that older adults performed more poorly than younger adults.

It may be argued, however, that the conclusions drawn by these early studies were premature. At least two major problems emerge. First, the studies examining verbatim text recall may be of limited interest. While some real life circumstances may require the verbatim reproduction of lengthy discourse passages, most do not. Thus, a concern for ecological validity directs our attention toward the comprehension and memory of the substance of texts rather than retrieval of their surface structure (Dooling & Christiaansen, 1977). Herein lies the second problem of the early research. In order to examine memory for the substance of texts, a theoretically consistent framework for representing their meaning is required. The early developmental research on adult text memory did not apply such a framework; rather, it relied on the intuitive (or, at least, pretheoretical) identification of idea units by the investigator. As a result, mechanisms for the specification of the nature of the texts used and for reliably scoring the recall protocols generated by the participants were limited. In the mid-1970s, the development of several theories for the representation of meaning provided a sound basis for more systematic research on adult age differences in text processing. We now turn to a brief description of these theories.

## III. The Representation of Meaning

A number of investigators have proposed models for representing the meaning of discourse (Anderson, 1976; Frederiksen, 1975; Kintsch, 1974; Meyer, 1975;

Norman & Rumelhart, 1975). Although all of these theories represent the surface form of discourse with a set of abstract units called propositions, the specific formulations of the various proposals differ significantly. However, because in the present context we are interested more in the use to which such models are put than in the models themselves, these differences may be legitimately ignored. Accordingly, the following discussion will focus on Kintsch's (1974) system of modeling text meaning, a system which is representative of these models and which we have used extensively in our own work (see Meyer, 1982, 1983, for comparisons between different prose analysis and scoring systems as applied to aging research).

Within Kintsch's system the meaning of a text is represented by a structured set of propositions known as a text base. A proposition consists of a predicate and one or more arguments. Predicates tend to be verb forms and specify a relation among the arguments. Arguments are word concepts or other propositions themselves. Propositions are written with the predicate first followed by the arguments, and the word concepts of the proposition are written in capital letters to distinguish them from words. For example, in the proposition (DRAFT, PROFESSOR, CHAPTER) the predicate is DRAFT, the first argument is PROFESSOR in the semantic role of Agent, and the second argument is CHAPTER in the semantic role of Goal. In English this proposition could be expressed as *The professor drafted the chapter,* or *The chapter was drafted by the professor,* and so on. For convenience, word concepts are expressed as words. However, it is important to note that they actually denote abstract concepts. A word concept, then, can be expressed by more than one word or phrase, and a proposition by more than one phrase or sentence.

Within Kintsch's system, propositions are also considered to be connected and hierarchically ordered. Two propositions are connected in the text base if they have an argument in common or if one proposition serves as an argument in another. Propositions are also ordered according to this repetition rule to form a hierarchical structure. The superordinate proposition(s) are determined according to the theme(s) of the text. From this point, when an argument is repeated in another proposition, the proposition containing the repetition is subordinated to the first. Applied repeatedly, this repetition rule defines a set of propositional levels such that the first level propositions represent the main ideas of the text, and successively lower level propositions represent the details of the text. This hierarchically ordered set of propositions constitutes the microstructure of the text.

An example of the repetition rule is shown in Table I. In this text fragment the main theme appears to be Proposition 4 (COLLIDE, TANKER, SHIP). From this starting point the hierarchical stucture of the text can be specified. Thus, Proposition 5 is subordinated to Proposition 4 because it repeats the argument SHIP. Similarly, Propositions 1 and 9 are subordinated to Proposition 4 because

**TABLE I**

**Fragment of Text and Text Base**

Text: A tanker loaded with 12 million gallons of crude oil collided with an empty ship off the French Coast and sank yesterday.

Text base

| Number | Level | Proposition |
|--------|-------|-------------|
| 1 | 2 | (LOAD, TANKER, OIL) |
| 2 | 3 | (QUALIFY: CRUDE, OIL) |
| 3 | 3 | (EXTENT OF: OIL, 12 MILLION GALLONS) |
| 4 | 1 | (COLLIDE, TANKER, SHIP) |
| 5 | 2 | (QUALIFY: EMPTY SHIP) |
| 6 | 2 | (LOCATION: OFF, P4, COAST) |
| 7 | 3 | (QUALIFY: FRENCH COAST) |
| 8 | 2 | (CONJUNCTION: AND, P4, P9) |
| 9 | 2 | (SINK, TANKER) |
| 10 | 3 | (TIME: PAST, P9, YESTERDAY) |

of the repetition of TANKER. Hence, these propositions are assigned to Level 2. Other propositions are assigned to Level 3 because they are subordinate to one or more Level 2 propositions, and so on.

Beyond the microstructure of the text, propositions are organized into some overall structure. This process is necessary in order to deal with the concepts of gist and summary. The organization of propositions into the overall structure takes place within the context of schemas—or sets of expectations the reader has about the structure and content of a text. The schemas specify certain text units, and the reader determines from the text and extralinguistic cues their particular labels. These labels constitute the text macrostructure.

A task analysis of the various psychological processes engaged when an individual reads or listens to a text is shown in Fig. 1. It is important to note that, for Kintsch (Kintsch, 1979b; Kintsch & van Dijk, 1978), text comprehension involves both top–down (schema use) and bottom–up (text cues) processes. Thus, from this perspective the reader does not comprehend and remember merely what is directly mentioned in a text. Rather, as Kintsch (1979a) notes, the text serves as a "stimulus for the construction of a complex edifice in the reader's mind" (p. 219).

## IV. A Classification of Variables and Interactions in Adult Text Processing

The perspective outlined in the previous section emphasizes that text processing is complex and contextually determined. It is apparent that the observed

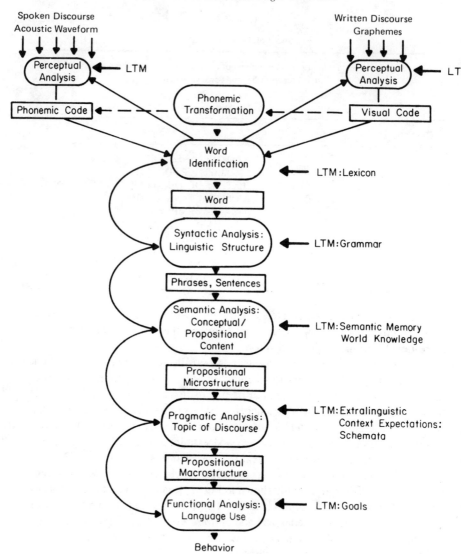

**Fig. 1.**   Processing stages in comprehension. From Kintsch (1977).

variance in this behavioral domain will not be described and explained by a fundamental "law" relating a small set of variables. Rather, consideration of multiple, potentially interactive variables is required. Jenkins (1979) has offered one classification of such variables as shown in Fig. 2. From this perspective, memory performance depends on the characteristics of the subjects we study (e.g., education, age), the kinds of material we ask them to remember (e.g., digits, texts), the nature of the acquisition conditions under which we ask them to remember it (e.g., incidental, intentional), and the kinds of criterial tasks we use to determine performance (e.g., recall, recognition). Historically, memory researchers have tended to use narrow paradigms emphasizing the variables of a single vertex of the tetrahedron. However, as Jenkins points out, it is the interactions, including the more complex interactions, that appear to most accurately characterize the emerging literature on text processing in adulthood. We will examine these factors and interactions in the following sections.

## A. ORIENTING TASKS

Craik and Lockhart (1972) have suggested that the durability of a memory trace is a function of the depth of processing carried out on the to-be-remembered material. Depth in this context refers to degree of semantic analysis. If encoding depends on depth of processing, then knowledge of a subsequent requirement to

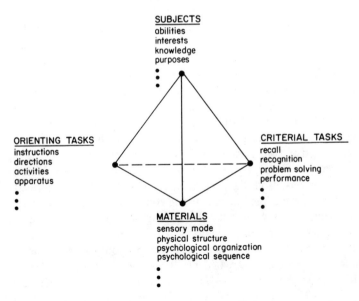

**Fig. 2.** The problem pyramid or theorist's tetrahedron. Each vertex represents a cluster of variables of a given type. Each edge represents a two-way interaction important to learning and memory. Each plane calls attention to a three-way interaction, and the whole figure represents the four-way interaction of all the variables. From Jenkins (1979).

reproduce the material should be relatively unimportant. Accordingly, the incidental memory paradigm has been used extensively to investigate this perspective. Within this paradigm, orienting tasks requiring shallow (nonsemantic) processing should result in relatively poor memory performance, while orienting tasks requiring deep (semantic) processing should result in comparatively good memory performance. Studies using this approach have supported the usefulness of the levels of processing framework (Craik & Tulving, 1975; Jenkins, 1974; see also Cermak & Craik, 1979).

Most of the research using this paradigm has used word lists as stimuli. Developmentally, it has been found that age-related differences in list recall are related to a deficiency on the part of older adults in deep or semantic processing (Eysenck, 1974; White, cited in Craik, 1977). In one study using the orienting task paradigm in order to examine adult age differences in text processing, Simon, Dixon, Nowak, and Hultsch (1982) asked younger, middle-aged, and older adults to process a 500-word narrative under one of four text reading conditions: (1) a syntactic condition in which subjects were asked to circle spelling and grammatical errors present in the story; (2) a stylistic condition in which subjects rated the story on a five-point scale for the dimension of interest, organization, readability, and the degree to which the story was true to life; (3) an advice condition in which the subjects wrote down their advice to the family depicted in the story; and (4) an intentional condition in which subjects were told to read and remember the substance of the story. Following presentation of the text, all participants were asked for written recall. It was emphasized that verbatim recall was not required. Kintsch's (1974) system was used to score the recall protocols. The major finding of this study was the interaction of age with orienting task as shown in Fig. 3. The recall of the younger adults was affected by the three orienting tasks in the manner predicted by the levels of processing framework. The syntactic (shallow) condition produced significantly lower recall than the two semantic (deep) conditions and the intentional learning condition. The middle-aged and older adults exhibited a different pattern. For these groups, no significant gains were registered from the syntactic condition to either of the semantic conditions. Both the middle-aged and older adults performed significantly better under the intentional learning condition than under the three orienting task conditions. Note that the three age groups did not differ significantly under the intentional learning condition.

Additional analyses demonstrated that younger adults recalled the main idea propositions of the text best when recall was preceded by the deep orienting tasks. In contrast, the middle-aged and older adults recalled the main idea propositions worst when recall was preceded by such tasks. The two older groups remembered the main idea propositions better in the intentional learning condition than in any other condition. That is, when alerted to the impending memory

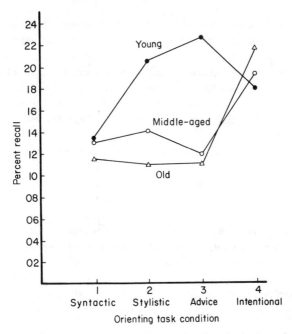

**Fig. 3.**    Mean percentage of propositions recalled as a function of orienting task and condition. From Simon, Dixon, Nowak, and Hultsch (1982).

test, the middle-aged and older adults were better able to grasp the main ideas of the text than when the memory test was unexpected.

A series of two experiments were conducted investigating the cross-cultural applicability of the depth of processing model to text recall research in adulthood (Dixon & von Eye, 1983, 1984). The personal narrative text used by Simon *et al.* (1982) was adapted slightly to a West German language and cultural setting, while the procedures of the American study were directly translated. A rather different pattern of results was obtained. In the first experiment, conducted with community-dwelling adults, young adults performed better than middle-aged adults who, in turn, performed better than old adults under all four conditions. Most importantly, for all three age groups, subjects in the two deep conditions performed only slightly (if at all) better than their counterparts in the shallow condition and at a lower level than those in the intentional condition. Similarly, in the second experiment, conducted with adults diagnosed as acute psychotics and residing in a mental health clinic in West Germany, little evidence was found for the effectiveness of the deep orienting tasks, although subjects in the advice condition tended to recall more of the text than those in the other two orienting task conditions.

Considering these three experiments together it appears that some evidence for the validity of the depth of processing model across ages, languages, and cultural settings has been obtained. Still, when improvement in recall rates does occur under deep processing conditions, this improvement is often not equivalent to performance under a simple intentional learning condition. Thus, a principle rationale for applying this model in aging research—viz. forcing older adults to process semantically might improve their recall of meaningful materials—is not fully supported.

One other study provides evidence that difficulty in processing semantic material may characterize older adults. Cohen and Faulkner (1981) used a task in which subjects listened to a text and then were asked to recognize changes in a represented (written) target sentence. The target sentences were selected from different points in the text so the delay between hearing the spoken version of the text and reading the written target sentence was approximately 10, 25, or 40 seconds. The target sentences were either identical to the spoken version or they were changed. Half the changes were semantic and half were nonsemantic. Based on list work suggesting older adults have difficulty processing material deeply, Cohen and Faulkner hypothesized that age differences should be greater in the recognition of semantic changes than in the recognition of nonsemantic changes.

The results showed that there were age differences in the recognition of both types of changes, but these varied as a function of delay. After 10 and 25 seconds, the younger adults were better than older adults at detecting nonsemantic changes, but after a delay of 40 seconds neither group was able to detect such changes. Younger adults, then, appeared to detect changes in the surface structure of the text more readily than older adults, but both groups quickly converged toward poor performance. In contrast, the age groups diverged in their ability to detect semantic changes. After delays of 10 and 25 seconds, both age groups were equally adept at detecting such changes. However, after a delay of 40 seconds, the older subjects detected only 33% of the semantic changes while the younger subjects detected 88% of them. Thus, memory for the meaning of the text was lost more rapidly by the older adults than by the younger adults. These findings suggest that the deeper levels of encoding achieved by the older adults are not sufficiently robust to be retained.

## B. CRITERIAL TASKS

### 1. Recall vs Recognition

Research using list materials has rather consistently shown that age differences are greater when subjects are asked for recall of the items than when they are asked to recognize them (Craik, 1977; Smith, 1980). However, studies contrasting these criterial tasks with text materials have produced conflicting results.

On the one hand, some studies have found age-related deficits in both recall and recognition performance (Gordon & Clark, 1974; Spilich, 1983). Spilich, for instance, examined this issue with a sample of younger and older adults. The latter were differentiated a priori on the basis of the Wechsler Memory Scale into high- and low-scoring groups. The subjects read two stories followed by a free recall test and then a recognition test. In the latter test they were given one sentence from the text along with three distractor sentences and were asked to judge which one was the exact sentence presented in the story. In some distractor sentences the semantic meaning was retained but the syntax was changed; in others the meaning was changed while the syntax was retained. Spilich's results showed that the younger subjects recalled and recognized more information than both older groups. On the recognition task, the older subjects had more difficulty than the younger subjects in detecting both syntactic and semantic changes in the text. In another study, Taub (1979) found age differences on a recognition memory task for low-verbal subjects, but not for high-verbal subjects.

On the other hand, a different pattern of results has been shown by other studies. For example, Spilich and Voss (1983) asked younger, "normal" older, and memory-impaired older adults to read short passages which differed in their contextual relatedness to target sentences. The subjects were then asked for free recall, cued recall, and finally for recognition of the target sentences. Large differences were found in favor of the young on the free recall task. Age differences were present with cued recall as well, but the normal-aged benefited more than the memory-impaired aged. Finally, no significant differences were found in recognition performance between the young and the normal-aged group whereas the performance of the memory-impaired aged group was significantly poorer than either of these two groups. In another study, Labouvie-Vief, Schell, and Weaverdyck (1981) assigned younger and older adults to one of three criterion task conditions: summary, recall, and recognition. The latter involved answering multiple choice questions about the content of the text. This study found no significant age-related differences in performance on either the recall or recognition conditions.

## 2. Delay Interval

Studies observing age-related deficits in text performance have generally observed these deficits both immediately after presentation of the materials and after delays of varying length (Gordon & Clark, 1974; Dixon *et al.*, 1982; Hultsch & Dixon, 1983; Hultsch, Hertzog, & Dixon, 1984). In some instances, there has been weak evidence of an interaction between age and delay interval such that age differences are greater at immediate recall than following a delay of 1 week (Dixon *et al.*, 1982; Hultsch & Dixon, 1983; Hultsch *et al.*, 1984). However, these interactions may reflect floor effects for the old at delayed recall.

### C. MATERIALS VARIABLES

*1. Input Modality*

Research examining the input modality issue with young adults has typically found that performance is similar after both reading and listening when reading time is equal to listening time. However, if the reading condition is self-paced (thus permitting review), as is the case in most nonlaboratory situations, then recall after reading is superior to recall after listening (King, 1968; Kintsch, Kozminsky, Streby, McKoon, & Keenan, 1975). In an early study, Taub (1975) examined adult age differences in immediate recall of short texts following reading and listening. Taub found self-paced reading was superior to listening for all age groups. However, he also observed a trend toward an Age by Modality interaction in which younger adults benefited more from the opportunity to read the material than the older adults.

A study conducted in our laboratory has also found evidence for this type of interaction. In this study, Dixon *et al.* (1982) asked younger, middle-aged, and older adults to read or listen to short newspaper articles. The subjects were asked to recall the substance of the texts immediately following presentation and after a delay of 1 week. The findings indicated a triple interaction of age, modality, and delay interval (see Fig. 4). At the immediate delay interval, the younger and middle-aged adults recalled a significantly greater percentage of propositions after reading than after listening. No significant differences between the two input conditions were observed at the immediate delay interval in the case of the

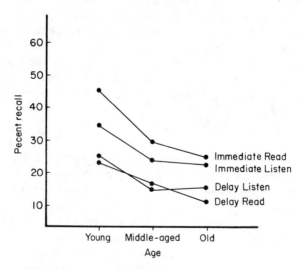

**Fig. 4.**   Mean percentage of propositions recalled as a function of input condition, delay interval, and age. From Dixon, Simon, Nowak, and Hultsch (1982).

older adults. In contrast, at the 1-week delay interval, the older adults recalled a significantly greater percentage of propositions after listening than after reading. No significant differences between the two input conditions were observed at the 1-week delay interval in the case of the younger and middle-aged adults.

Thus, the younger and middle-aged adults benefited more from the opportunity to read the material than the older adults. One explanation for this finding might simply be that the older adults were unable to understand the texts because of poor reading comprehension skills. However, the data indicate that the older individuals recalled as much after reading as they did after listening. Kintsch and Kozminsky (1977) have argued that listening is a highly overlearned process that provides a relatively pure reflection of the comprehension process. Hence, the absence of a reading–listening difference among the older adults weakens the reading comprehension explanation. A more plausible explanation for the pattern of results observed under the immediate recall condition is that the older adults did not take as much advantage of the opportunity to review the material during reading as the younger and middle-aged adults. Studies by Taub and Kline (1976, 1978), which have manipulated the subject's opportunity for review, support this explanation.

## 2. Text Structure

As noted in Section II, theorists have argued that the meaning of a text may be represented by a hierarchically structured set of propositions (Kintsch, 1974; Meyer, 1975; Norman & Rumelhart, 1975). Superordinate propositions, located at the top of the hierarchy, correspond to the main ideas of the text while subordinate propositions, located at the bottom of the hierarchy, correspond to the details of the text. Research has consistently shown that superordinate propositions are more likely to be remembered than subordinate propositions (Kintsch *et al.*, 1975; Mandler & Johnson, 1977; Meyer, 1977; Thorndyke, 1977).

The position that text information is hierarchically organized and that this organization is related to recall is particularly significant for developmental research since, based on previous work with list materials, it may be hypothesized that older adults will find it difficult to discover and utilize the organization of the text. In the case of list materials, there is considerable empirical support for the presence of age-related differences in organizational processes (Craik, 1977). Generally, the older adult's difficulty appears to be of the production deficiency or inefficiency variety. That is, older adults do not spontaneously use organizational strategies as extensively as younger adults, or, if they do, they use them less effectively (Denney, 1974; Hultsch, 1974; Sanders, Murphy, Schmitt, & Walsh, 1980). However, when various organizational strategies are built into the situation, the performance of older adults improves significantly, typically producing attenuation of observed age differences (Hultsch, 1969, 1971).

In contrast to the work with list materials, research examining the role of organizational factors in adult age differences in text recall has produced conflicting results. On the one hand, several studies have found that age-related differences are greater for the recall of the main ideas of the text than for the details of the text (Cohen, 1979; Dixon *et al.*, 1982). For example, Dixon *et al.* asked younger, middle-aged, and older adults to read or listen to short news articles. The subjects were then asked for written recall. The hierarchical structure of the texts was identified using procedures developed by Kintsch (1974) and described above. In general, the younger adults recalled the articles better than the middle-aged or older adults, and all individuals recalled the main ideas of the article better than the details. However, age-related differences in recall were slightly greater in the case of the superordinate (main idea) propositions than in the case of the subordinate (detail) propositions (see Fig. 5). Similarly, Cohen (1979) asked younger and older adults to listen to a short story modeled after Dawes' (1966) Circle Island passage. She found the older adults recalled significantly less information about the story than the younger adults. Further, the older adults produced fewer summary statements which represented the "gist" of the story than did the younger adults. Unfortunately, Cohen did not

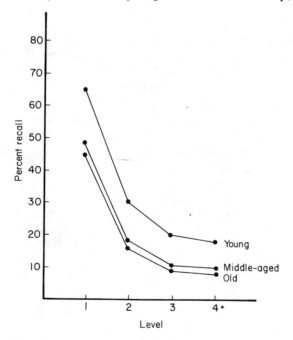

**Fig. 5.**   Mean percentage of propositions recalled as a function of propositional level and age. From Dixon, Simon, Nowak, and Hultsch (1982).

use any of the extant theories to specify the hierarchical structure of her text. However, to the extent that such summary statements reflect the discovery and utilization of the underlying structure of the text, Cohen's findings suggest the presence of age-related organizational deficits.

On the other hand, several studies have found that age-related differences are greater for the details of the text than for the main ideas of the text (Byrd, 1981; Labouvie-Vief *et al.,* 1981; Spilich, 1983; Zelinski *et al.,* 1980). For example, Zelinski *et al.* (1980) asked younger and older adults to read and recall a relatively lengthy passage. The recall protocols were scored using a modification of the system developed by Meyer (1975). They found no age differences in recall at the superordinate levels of the text, but older subjects recalled significantly fewer propositions than the younger adults at the subordinate levels of the text. Similarly, when Byrd (1981) asked younger and older adults to recall a structurally complete and temporally ordered story, he found that both age groups recalled the main ideas of the story equally well. However, the older adults recalled significantly fewer of the details than the younger adults. Finally, Labouvie-Vief *et al.* (1981) presented younger and older adults with a short story and, in one condition, asked them to summarize it. The age groups did not differ significantly in recall of the ''gist'' of the story, but the older subjects remembered fewer of the details of the story than the younger adults.

One other study suggests that younger adults are more sensitive to the hierarchical structure of texts, but that younger adults recall fewer details than older adults (Meyer & Rice, 1981). In this study, younger, middle-aged, and older adults read the text and then produced written recall. Using procedures developed by Meyer (1975), the subjects recall protocols were scored for idea units within a 17-level hierarchical structure. (Note that the passage developed by Meyer was also used by Zelinski *et al.;* however, in their analysis they scored idea units from only the first eight levels of the hierarchy.) Meyer and Rice found no overall age differences in text recall. However, younger subjects tended to be more sensitive to the organization of the text than the middle-aged and older adults. That is, the younger adults showed more differentiation in their recall of information from the various levels. In particular, their recall of information from the lower levels of the hierarchy tended to drop off more sharply than that of the middle-aged and older adults. Examination of age differences in number of correct answers to questions about the passage for three types of information confirmed this conclusion. All three age groups were able to answer questions about the main ideas of the text. In contrast, age differences were present for ideas consisting of major details supportive of the main ideas of the text and ideas consisting of minor details not essential to the main ideas of the text. In the case of the major details, the younger adults were able to answer more questions than the middle-aged and older adults. In contrast, in the case of the minor details, the middle-aged and older adults were able to answer more questions than the younger adults.

Thus, in some instances there appear to be greater age-related differences at the superordinate level of text information, while in other instances there appear to be greater age-related differences at the subordinate level of text information. There are several possible reasons for this discrepancy in the literature.

First, it is reasonable to expect that clarity of the text structure is related to recall performance. Research examining the text recall of college-aged subjects has consistently demonstrated that well-organized passages are recalled better than poorly organized ones (Frase, 1969; Kintsch *et al.*, 1975; Kintsch, Mandel, & Kozminsky, 1977; Thorndyke, 1977). For instance, Kintsch *et al.* (1975) report that the recall of superordinate propositions is somewhat reduced relative to the recall of subordinate propositions when the former occur in the middle of the text rather than at the beginning or the end. More recently, several studies have shown that text structure interacts with age (Byrd, 1981; Dixon, Hultsch, Simon, & von Eye, 1984; Meyer & Rice, 1981; Smith, Rebok, Smith, Hall, & Alvin, 1983). In general, age differences in performance and in the discovery and utilization of the organization of the text are attenuated when the text is well organized and exacerbated when it is poorly organized. For example, Byrd (1981) asked younger and older adults to listen to three stories differing in the organization of their structural elements: (1) a normal story (all structural elements present in normal temporal order), (2) a no-theme story (thematic elements removed and the remaining elements presented in normal temporal order), and (3) a random story (all structural elements present but no temporal order). Byrd found that in the normal story condition, the older adults recalled as many of the main ideas of the story as the younger adults. However, they recalled fewer of the details of the story. The same trend occurred in the no-theme condition, although overall recall was generally lower in this condition than in the normal story condition. However, in the case of the random story condition, the younger subjects recalled more of the main ideas of the story than the older adults. These data suggest that with well-structured texts, age differences may be found at the subordinate level, while with less well-structured texts they may be found at the superordinate level.

In a similar effort, Smith *et al.* (1983) asked younger and older adults to listen to four stories based on Mandler's story grammar. In this framework, a story is seen as consisting of at least one episode having several nodes: (1) setting— describes the time and place of the episode; (2) beginning—describes an event which starts the plot; (3) reaction—describes the response to the initial event; (4) goal—describes the formulation of the plan to deal with the event; (5) attempt— describes the attempt to attain the goal through some action; (6) outcome— describes the success or failure of the attempt; and (7) ending—describes the resolution of the episode. Smith *et al.* asked younger and older adults to listen to four simple double-episode stories with each story having a common setting for the two episodes. Three types of story structure were compared: (1) a standard structure in which the two episodes followed one another; (2) an interleaved structure in which the nodes of the two episodes were alternated, keeping the original order of nodes for both episodes; and (3) a scrambled structure in which the common setting was presented and followed by a random ordering of the nodes from both episodes. Recall was tested orally after a delay of 48 hours. Smith *et al.* found that both age groups performed well when the standard structure was used and poorly when the random structure was used. However, when the interleaved structure was used the young adults performed as well as in the standard condition, whereas the older adults performed as poorly as in the random condition. Again, these data suggest that age differences will be exacerbated when the text is poorly structured.

Both of these studies modified the structure of the text in relatively radical ways. One other study suggests that structural differences within "standard" texts may also interact with age. Dixon *et al.* (1984) examined the impact of the structure of the text by varying the number of arguments (concepts) introduced to the reader. That is, some texts may say a lot about relatively few concepts, while others may say a little about relatively many concepts. In either case, with short texts the concepts may be relevant to the same main idea. In such an instance, the main idea would be repeated in the subordinate propositions more frequently in a few-argument text than in a many-argument text. Previous work with young adults suggests that texts introducing relatively many arguments take significantly longer to process, but are remembered as well as texts introducing relatively few arguments (Kintsch *et al.*, 1975). In the study by Dixon *et al.*, younger, middle-aged, and older adults were asked to read and recall three texts containing relatively many arguments and three texts containing relatively few arguments. The results showed a triple interaction among age, number of arguments, and level of information in the text. The younger adults were able to grasp the main idea of either type of text, but recalled more of the details of the texts when they contained many arguments than when they contained few arguments. The middle-aged adults recalled more main ideas when the texts contained few arguments than when they contained many arguments. Apparently, the repetition of the main ideas in subordinate propositions in the few-argument texts facilitated their encoding and retrieval. Like the younger group, the middle-aged adults also recalled more details when the texts contained many arguments than when they contained few arguments. The pattern of results was somewhat less clear for the older adults. They tended to recall texts containing many arguments better than texts containing few arguments, although this effect was only marginally significant at two of the four levels. It appears that, overall, older adults had difficulty retaining the main ideas and details of the texts regardless of the number of arguments they contained. Again, this suggests decreasing sensitivity to the organizational structure of the text with increasing age.

In addition to text structure variables, it is reasonable to expect that individual differences in education and verbal ability will partially account for performance differences in text recall. Further, it is reasonable to expect that such individual difference variables may be related to the nature of age differences in performance (cf. Taub, 1979). In this context, it may be noted that the studies reporting age differences in recall of superordinate level propositions have generally tested subjects with relatively low levels of education and verbal ability (i.e., high school graduates), while the studies reporting age differences in recall of subordinate level propositions have generally tested subjects with relatively high levels of education and verbal ability (i.e., college graduates). Two studies suggest that the discrepancies in the literature concerning age differences in the discovery and utilization of the structure of texts may be related to such variables. Dixon *et al.* (1984) asked younger, middle-aged, and older adults to read and recall short texts. As described earlier, the texts varied according to the number of arguments they contained. In addition, within each age level, the subjects were differentiated on the basis of their verbal ability level as measured by the Advanced Vocabulary Test from the Kit of Factor Referenced Cognitive Tests (Ekstrom, French, Harman, & Dermen, 1976). Dixon *et al.* found that, as hypothesized, age-related differences in the discovery of the organizational structure of texts are mediated by the verbal ability of the individuals processing them. The interaction is shown in Fig. 6.

In the case of adults with relatively low levels of verbal ability, age-related differences in recall were greatest for the main ideas of the texts. Younger adults recalled a significantly greater percentage of main idea (Level 1) propositions than middle-aged adults who, in turn, recalled a significantly greater percentage of these propositions than older adults. The younger and middle-aged groups did not differ significantly in recall of the details of the texts (Levels 2, 3, and 4+). However, both younger groups recalled significantly more details than the older adults. In the present instance, then, the older adults showed a deficit in recall of both the main ideas and the details of the texts, although the size of the deficit was greater at the level of main ideas than at the level of details.

In contrast, in the case of adults with relatively high levels of verbal ability, age differences in recall were greatest for the details of the texts. There were no significant differences among the three groups in the recall of Level 1 propositions. However, young adults recalled a significantly greater percentage of detail (Levels 2, 3, 4+) propositions than the middle-aged adults who, in turn, recalled more of these propositions than the older adults.

A similar finding is reported by Spilich (1983) who compared younger adults and two groups of older adults differentiated on the basis of the Wechsler Memo-

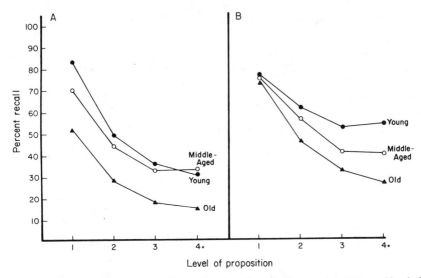

**Fig. 6.** Mean percentage of propositions recalled as a function of age, verbal ability, and level of proposition. (A) Low verbal; (B) high verbal. From Dixon, Hultsch, Simon, and von Eye (1984).

ry Scale. Spilich found that young adults and old adults scoring high on the Wechsler Memory Scale were equally adept at recalling the main ideas of the text. However, the young adults recalled significantly more of the details of the texts than the high-scoring older adults. In contrast, the older subjects scoring low on the Wechsler Memory Scale showed poorer recall compared to the other two groups at all levels. The low-scoring older adults showed no differential recall of information from different levels at all, suggesting an inability to discover the underlying structure of the texts.

Thus, the studies by Dixon *et al.* (1984) and Spilich (1983) suggest that among individuals with low levels of verbal or memory ability, older adults may have greater difficulty identifying and utilizing the organizational structure of text materials than younger adults. This may reflect an encoding inefficiency problem similar to that found with list materials (e.g., Craik, 1977; Hultsch, 1974). Alternatively, among individuals with relatively high levels of verbal or memory ability, the tendency of older adults to recall fewer details of the story may reflect the use of qualitatively different retrieval strategies and criteria for remembering (Labouvie-Vief *et al.*, 1981).

## D. SUBJECT VARIABLES

### 1. Prior Knowledge about the Topic

Memory is rooted in the articulation of a new information with past experiences and prior knowledge. Based largely on Bartlett's (1932) notion of schema,

Bransford, McCarrell, Franks, and Nitsch (1977) suggest that past experience "sets the stage" for the integration of new events. That is, preexisting schemas serve to guide the processing of novel texts. In many contexts, increasing integration of the event with preexperimental knowledge enhances remembering of the total event, but not the specific components of the event. Thus, recall for text materials may become increasingly reconstructed over time as the individual integrates the text event into preexisting knowledge (Bartlett, 1932; Dooling & Christiaansen, 1977; Kintsch et al., 1975). For example, Kintsch et al. (1975) asked subjects to read two types of texts varying in familiarity: unfamiliar topics from natural sciences or familiar topics from classical history. Immediate recall for both types of paragraphs was largely reproductive. However, when recall was delayed for a day, this pattern changed drastically for the familiar texts. Subjects were unable to differentiate between what they read and what they knew, and mentioned many things which they knew about the topic that were not part of the original material (i.e., elaborations). Such results illustrate the importance of examining reconstructive recall as well as reproductive recall.

There are many levels at which new input may be articulated with past experience. That is, acquisition processes may be conceptualized as a hierarchy of levels of processing involving wider and wider contexts (Craik & Lockhart, 1972; Kintsch, 1979a). In general, however, the more extensively the material has been integrated with prior knowledge at these multiple levels the better the information will be comprehended and remembered. That is, extant schemas and prior knowledge are important components in the comprehension process (Stevens, 1980). When appropriate schemas are not activated at the time of acquisition, recall of text information is impaired (Townsend, 1980). Further, it has been shown that the amount of known and new information in a passage, as well as their interaction, affect this activation process (Potts, Keller, & Rooley, 1981).

Given that different age and cohort groups have experienced relatively unique cultural and historical events, it is an intuitively sensible expectation that these groups will differ in terms of schemas or prior knowledge about historically relevant topics (Baltes, Cornelius, & Nesselroade, 1979). In a recent study, Hultsch and Dixon (1983) examined the importance of prior knowledge for age differences in substantive recall of text. In this study, younger, middle-aged, and older adults were asked to read and recall short biographical sketches of famous entertainment figures. An attempt was made to select the figures so that there was age-related variation in the amount of preexperimental knowledge possessed about them. The intent was to discover figures that were very well known to one age group and less known to the two other age groups, as well as figures that were generally well known to all age groups. A pilot study using a separate sample was conducted to determine the amount of knowledge about 28 entertainment figures evinced by the age groups of interest. This procedure yielded a set of four figures consisting of Steve Martin (young), Susan Hayward (middle-aged), Mary Pickford (old), and Bob Hope (general) who conformed relatively well to the desired pattern. Short biographical sketches on these figures were then developed and subjects were asked to read and recall these immediately after presentation and again after a delay of 1 week.

As shown in Fig. 7, the results suggest that age differences in recall performance may be present or absent depending on the level of preexperimental knowledge about the to-be-remembered topic possessed by the various age groups. Such a conclusion is supported rather clearly in the instance of the "young" and "old" stories. In the case of the "young" story (Steve Martin), younger subjects recalled significantly more material than both older age groups. In the case of the "old" story (Mary Pickford), the older subjects recalled more than both younger age groups, although the difference was significant only in the case of the middle-aged subjects. The pattern of results was less clear in the case of the "middle-aged" story (Susan Hayward), where none of the age groups differed significantly. It is interesting to note also that, comparing within-age groups across stories, the following results were obtained: (1) young adults achieved their best performance on the "young" and "general" stories; (2) middle-aged adults achieved their best performance on the "middle-age" story; and (3) old adults performed best on the "old" and "general" story.

## 2. Education and Verbal Ability

In general, research examining adult age differences in the verbatim recall of lists has found that, when comparing equated groups, younger adults recall more

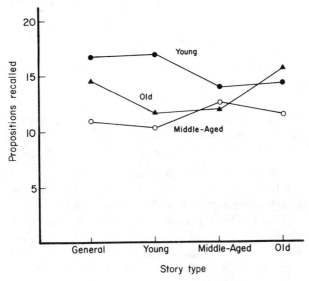

**Fig. 7.** Mean number of propositions recalled as a function of age and story type. From Hultsch and Dixon (1983).

items than older adults regardless of the educational or verbal ability levels involved (Gardner & Monge, 1977). For example, Perlmutter (1978) reports such an outcome even for individuals with doctoral-level training. However, it may be that a major portion of the variance in adult age differences in text processing is mediated by variables indexed by education, vocabulary score, and other measures of intellectual ability. Indeed, it may be noted that studies report-ing adult age differences in text recall have generally tested subjects with rela-tively low levels of education and verbal ability (i.e., high school graduates), while studies reporting no age differences have generally tested subjects with relatively high levels of education and verbal ability (i.e., college graduates).

The significance of education and verbal ability has also been demonstrated by studies which have specifically incorporated these variables into their designs. Taub (1979), for instance, divided younger and older adults into low-, middle-, and high-scoring groups on the basis of the vocabulary subtest of the Wechsler Adult Intelligence Scale. Taub found that in the case of the low- and middle-vocabulary subjects, the young adults performed significantly better than the old adults on measures of both comprehension and recognition memory. However, in the case of the high-vocabulary subjects, there were no significant age dif-ferences on any measure.

The most comprehensive examination of the education/verbal ability issue has been carried out by Meyer and Rice (1983). They present an analysis of four subsamples selected from a group of 314 younger and older adults, all of whom had read and recalled two expository texts. The subsamples were formed on the basis of their vocabulary scores on the Quick Test. The comparison groups were formed as follows.

1. Random Young vs High Verbal Old—young adults selected at random versus the 50 highest scoring old.

2. High Verbal Young vs High Verbal Old—the 50 highest scoring young versus the 50 highest scoring old.

3. Low Verbal Young vs Low Verbal Old—the 50 lowest scoring young versus the 50 lowest scoring old.

4. Low Verbal Old vs Matching Young—the 50 lowest scoring old versus 50 young with comparable scores.

The education, vocabulary, and performance data for the four comparisons are shown in Table II. These data suggest rather clearly that there are age-related deficits in memory performance for adults with average or below average abili-ties and little post-high-school education. The situation is not as clear for indi-viduals with above average verbal ability and college education. The age groups in comparisons 1 and 2 were equivalent in education. However, the vocabulary differences were greater for comparison 1, where no age differences in recall were found, than for comparison 2, where moderate age differences in recall

**TABLE II**

**Four Comparisons of Different Young and Old Age Groups**[a,b]

| Group | Subject variable | | Performance variable | |
|---|---|---|---|---|
| | Education | Vocabulary | Total recall | Logical relations |
| Random young vs | 15.4 | *52* | .35 | .40 |
| high verbal old | 16.1 | *80* | .37 | .45 |
| High verbal young vs | 16.5 | *67* | *.42* | *.48* |
| high verbal old | 16.1 | *80* | .37 | .45 |
| Low verbal young vs | 13.3 | *32* | *.31* | *.36* |
| Low verbal old | 12.5 | *46* | .25 | .31 |
| Low verbal old vs | *12.5* | 46 | .25 | .31 |
| matching young | *15.0* | 46 | .38 | .41 |

[a] From Meyer and Rice (1983).
[b] Within a given comparison, means in italics are significantly different.

were observed. Meyer and Rice (1983) suggest that in these groups, age differences in memory performance may be present or absent depending on how the investigator equates the age groups on education and verbal ability.

Although results like those of Taub (1979) and Meyer and Rice (1983) suggest that age differences in text recall interact with level of verbal ability, there are limitations to inferences drawn from such extreme groups designs. Age-related selection in the populations makes it difficult to equate age/cohort groups partitioned on variables such as educational attainment and verbal ability (Krauss, 1980). At a given level of education, a sample of older adults is probably more highly selected than a sample of younger adults because of cohort-related differences in educational attainment. Similarly, at a given level of verbal ability, a sample of older adults is probably less highly selected than a sample of younger adults because of age-related changes in vocabulary. There are other potential problems with the extreme groups approach as well. The extreme groups design ignores strength of prediction in the inner quartiles of the variables distributions. Further, group assignment on the basis of scores on a single fallible variable may cause measurement error to have an unacceptably high influence on the group assignment. Finally, other intellectual abilities and individual differences variables may mediate age differences in text processing. A comparison of groups differing on a single ability, however well measured, cannot address the determination of individual differences in text processing by well-defined domain abilities.

In an attempt to circumvent some of these problems, Hultsch *et al.* (1984) related text performance at three age levels to a set of intellectual ability factors (General Intelligence, Verbal Comprehension, Verbal Productive Thinking, and

Associative Memory) derived from scores on 12 tests. The analysis suggested that the potential contribution of ability factors to age-related differences in text recall is more complex than previous reports might indicate.

First, it is apparent that abilities other than Verbal Comprehension are predictive of text recall performance. In particular, the results suggested that General Intelligence (g), Verbal Productive Thinking, and Associative Memory also correlated with text recall performance. In fact, the ability with the largest overall relationship with text memory was g, not Verbal Comprehension. Second, the results showed that age differences in text recall covary highly with age differences in intellectual abilities. Regression analyses indicated that age differences in text recall performance were drastically reduced, but not eliminated, when partialled for intellectual ability. Third, the results did not support the notion that there is an Age × Verbal Comprehension interaction across the range of verbal abilities such that age differences are progressively reduced with higher ability levels. If anything, the results suggested larger age differences at the highest Verbal Comprehension levels. The type of interaction predicted by previous extreme groups designs was found only at immediate recall for Verbal Productive Thinking and Associative Memory; moreover, the small magnitude of the effects and their transience with respect to delay interval suggest, at minimum, that such interactions should be interpreted conservatively. These results need not be viewed as contradictory to previous findings if one considers the fact that the sample studied was from a community population which apparently contains small proportions of high-ability and highly educated elderly. It may well be that age differences are smaller only at the highest ability or educational levels. Nevertheless, the results of the study by Hultsch *et al.* speak to the generality of the results from previous extreme groups comparisons. For much of the ability range, there is little evidence of elimination of age differences at the higher ability levels.

The final complexity in ability–text memory relationships discovered in the study by Hultsch *et al.* (1984) was a shift in patterns of within-group correlations between text recall and intellectual ability across the three age groups. In the case of the young and middle-aged adults, the largest amount of variance was accounted for by g and Verbal Comprehension. However, in the case of the old adults, the largest amount of variance was accounted for by Verbal Productive Thinking, Verbal Comprehension, and Associative Memory. General Intelligence was of little value in predicting performance in the elderly. Thus, with increasing age, text recall performance is increasingly related to specific intellectual abilities.

The data of Hultsch *et al.* do not provide the basis for explaining this shifting pattern of correlations. However, one hypothesis is the concept of differential loss of abilities which relate to text performance. According to this notion, most young persons would have sufficient semantic processing skills and memory for words to perform adequately on text comprehension and recall tasks. Thus, individual differences in text memory performance would not be predicted by individual differences in Verbal Productive Thinking or Associative Memory. In older populations, on the other hand, it is possible that a subpopulation of older persons would have suffered a sufficient level of decline in their semantic processing skills to cause declines in text recall performance, while other older persons would have maintained their skills. Such a pattern would increase the predictive value of individual differences in associative memory and other semantic processing skills for text recall performance in the older groups, because the range of individual differences would include levels that would have an adverse impact on recall performance. This speculative interpretation is consistent with Spilich's (1983) findings of poorer text performance in normal-aged subjects compared to younger adults, but no qualitative age differences in text processing strategies. In contrast, he found evidence for such qualitative differences between the normal-aged and memory-impaired aged subjects.

In sum, poor text recall performance in later life might reflect two different phenomena which are hopelessly confounded in a cross-sectional design: (1) low-ability subjects whose poor text performance reflects the continuation of poor verbal skills over the life span, and (2) low-ability subjects whose poor text performance reflects a loss of skills from previous higher levels.

## 3. Metamemory

Metamemory—which refers to the knowledge one possesses about the functioning, development, and use of the human memory system in general, and one's own memory in particular—has been the subject of increasing attention among cognitive developmentalists (Brown, 1975, 1978; Flavell & Wellman, 1977). An underlying assumption of this research is that metamemory is closely related to, and perhaps predictive of, memory performance. While several inventive methods have been employed to assess and relate these two domains, most have used an experimental procedure in which metamemory is operationalized unidimensionally and memory performance is indicated by list recall materials. This is especially true for the child development literature, where such metamemory–memory performance studies reveal rather ambiguous age-related trends (Appel, Cooper, McCarrell, Sims-Knight, Yussen, & Flavell, 1972; Cavanaugh & Borkowski, 1979, 1980; Wellman, 1978).

The lack of clarity extends to the adult development literature as well. Although the bulk of this research is explicitly univariate, it does appear to suggest that deficiencies in some realms of metamemory may control a portion of memory performance variance. Such factors may include knowledge of task demands, memory capacity, memory monitoring, and memory motivation (Bruce, Coyne, & Botwinick, 1982; Carroll & Gray, 1981; Lachman, Lachman, & Thronesbery, 1979; Murphy, Sanders, Gabriesheski, & Schmitt, 1981). To date, the extent to which this memory performance variance is age related and extends to presumably ecologically valid textual materials has been investigated by only two sets of researchers.

Zelinski *et al.* (1980) investigated self-assessment of memory ability, one aspect of metamemory. A questionnaire was developed to assess the individual's awareness of memory abilities, as well as the perceived importance and changes in those abilities over time. In addition to list recall and recognition measures, Zelinski *et al.* related metamemory performance to text recall. Their findings generally indicated that metamemorial awareness was related to text recall in the old subjects but not in the young. Thus, it appeared that older adults more accurately evaluated their memory abilities vis-à-vis their performance than did younger adults.

A somewhat different approach was employed by Dixon and Hultsch (1983a,b). Using a cross-validation procedure, in which three separate samples of adults in three age groups were compared at every phase of the analyses, a psychometrically reliable and valid instrument was developed to represent a multidimensional construct of *metamemory in adulthood* (MIA) (Dixon & Hultsch, 1983b). Eight theoretically and empirically meaningful dimensions were defined: (1) use of memory strategies (Strategy), (2) knowledge of memory tasks (Task), (3) knowledge of own memory capacities (Capacity), (4) attitudes toward own memory: perception of change (Change), (5) activities supportive of memory (Activity), (6) memory and state anxiety (Anxiety), (7) memory and achievement motivation (Achievement), and (8) locus of control in memory abilities (Locus). The relationship between each of these dimensions and memory for text performances across two and three occasions was investigated.

Overall, it appeared that Task (knowledge about general memory processes), Change (knowledge about memory development), and Locus (the sense of control over memory functioning) were the best predictors of memory performance for all adults in the three samples (Dixon & Hultsch, 1983a). Certain age-related differences, however, were found. For younger adults, Strategy (knowledge about retrieval strategies and physical reminders), Change, and Task were the best predictors of memory for text performance. For older adults, Strategy, Task, Achievement (level of motivation to achieve in memory performance), Locus, and to some extent Anxiety (level of anxiety associated with memory demands) best predicted memory for text performance. Thus, whereas memory for text performance by young adults was best accounted for by a "knowledge" component of metamemory, the performance of older adults was considerably more related to "affective" dimensions.

## V. Summary and Conclusions

The study of memory for text materials in adulthood began as though it were possible to replicate the methods and results of several decades of research on age differences in memory for list materials. However, it soon became clear that the task of investigating the comprehension of and memory for meaningful discourse would be considerably more complex. An initial step was the use of the various theoretically powerful frameworks for representing the semantic properties of a given text that had been developed within cognitive psychology. However, application of these frameworks has not suggested any simple answers to questions about the nature of age-related differences in text processing. Instead, recent research based on these models has suggested that (1) age differences in text memory performance are not nearly as prevalent as those typically observed with list materials, and (2) the presence or absence of these age differences depends on multiple contextual factors that appear to mediate text processing.

In this article, we have tried to organize extant results with respect to Jenkins' (1979) framework. Viewed in this way, the seemingly disparate results from various programs of investigation, as well as several isolated studies, begin to be somewhat more coherent. Our review suggests that age interacts with multiple classes of variables to produce differences in text memory performance. In general, age differences appear to be attenuated when the text is well organized, when there is prior knowledge about the topic, and when the subjects possess superior levels of semantic abilities. However, the present effort is meant to be heuristic rather than complete. A more complete and complex taxonomy of contextual factors which interact with age to produce differences in text processing will have to be constructed through further research.

## Acknowledgments

The research reported in this article from D. F. Hultsch's laboratory was supported by research Grant 1 RO1 AG00910 and predoctoral fellowship T32 AG00048 from the National Institute on Aging. The authors would like to express their appreciation to J. Bornstein, S. Jennings, C. Kaus, C. Nowak, and E. Simon for their assistance in conducting this research. In addition, the authors would like to thank Fergus I. M. Craik and Bonnie J. F. Meyer for their comments on an earlier draft of this article.

## References

Anderson, J. R. *Language, memory, and thought.* Hillsdale, New Jersey: Erlbaum, 1976.

Appel, L. F., Cooper, R. G., McCarrell, N. S., Sims-Knight, J., Yussen, S. R., & Flavell, J. H. The development of the distinction between perceiving and memorizing. *Child Development,* 1972, **43**, 1365–1381.

Baltes, P. B., Cornelius, S. W., & Nesselroade, J. R. Cohort effects in developmental psychology. In J. R. Nesselroade & P. B. Baltes (Eds.), *Longitudinal research in the study of behavior and development.* New York: Academic Press, 1979.

Bartlett, F. C. *Remembering.* London and New York: Cambridge University Press, 1932.

Botwinick, J., & Storandt, M. *Memory, related functions, and age.* Springfield, Illinois: Thomas, 1974.

Bransford, J. D., McCarrell, N. S., Franks, J. J., & Nitsch, K. E. Toward unexplaining memory. In R. Shaw & J. D. Bransford (Eds.), *Perceiving, acting, and knowing: Toward an ecological psychology.* Hillsdale, New Jersey: Erlbaum, 1977.

Brown, A. L. The development of memory: Knowing, knowing about knowing, and knowing how to know. In H. W. Reese (Ed.), *Advances in child development and behavior* (Vol. 10). New York: Academic Press, 1975.

Brown, A. L. Knowing when, where, and how to remember: A problem of metacognition. In R. Glaser (Ed.), *Advances in instructional psychology.* Hillsdale, New Jersey: Erlbaum, 1978.

Bruce, P. R., Coyne, A. C., & Botwinick, J. Adult age differences in metamemory. *Journal of Gerontology,* 1982, **37**, 354–357.

Burke, D. M., & Light, L. L. Memory and aging: The role of retrieval processes. *Psychological Bulletin,* 1981, **90**, 513–546.

Byrd, M. *Age differences in memory for prose passages.* Unpublished doctoral dissertation, University of Toronto, 1981.

Carroll, K., & Gray, K. Memory development: An approach to the mentally impaired elderly in the long-term care setting. *International Journal of Aging and Human Development,* 1981, **13**, 15–35.

Cavanaugh, J. C., & Borkowski, J. G. The metamemory–memory "connection": Effects of strategy training and maintenance. *Journal of General Psychology,* 1979, **101**, 161–174.

Cavanaugh, J. C., & Borkowski, J. G. Searching for metamemory–memory connections: A developmental study. *Developmental Psychology,* 1980, **16**, 441–453.

Cermak, L. S., & Craik, F. I. M. (Eds.). *Levels of processing in human memory.* Hillsdale, New Jersey: Erlbaum, 1979.

Cofer, C. N. On the constructive theory of memory. In F. Weizman & I. C. Uzgiris (Eds.), *The structuring of experience.* New York: Plenum, 1976.

Cohen, G. Language comprehension in old age. *Cognitive Psychology,* 1979, **11**, 412–429.

Cohen, G., & Faulkner, D. Memory for discourse in old age. *Discourse Processes,* 1981, **4**, 253–265.

Craik, F. I. M. Age differences in human memory. In J. E. Birren & K. W. Schaie (Eds.), *Handbook of the psychology of aging.* Princeton, New Jersey: Van Nostrand Reinhold, 1977.

Craik, F. I. M., & Lockhart, R. S. Levels of processing: A framework for memory research. *Journal of Verbal Learning and Verbal Behavior,* 1972, **11**, 671–684.

Craik, F. I. M., & Tulving, E. Depth of processing and the retention of words in episodic memory. *Journal of Experimental Psychology: General,* 1975, **104**, 268–294.

Dawes, R. Memory and distortion of meaningful verbal material. *British Journal of Psychology,* 1966, **57**, 77–86.

Denney, N. W. Clustering in middle and old age. *Developmental Psychology,* 1974, **10**, 471–475.

Dixon, R. A., & Hultsch, D. F. Metamemory and memory for text relationships in adulthood: A cross-validation study. *Journal of Gerontology,* 1983, **38**, 689–694. (a)

Dixon, R. A., & Hultsch, D. F. Structure and development of metamemory in adulthood. *Journal of Gerontology,* 1983, **38**, 682–688. (b)

Dixon, R. A., Hultsch, D. F., Simon, E. W., & von Eye, A. Verbal ability and text structure effects on adult age differences in text recall. *Journal of Verbal Learning and Verbal Behavior,* 1984, in press.

Dixon, R. A., Simon, E. W., Nowak, C. A., & Hultsch, D. F. Text recall in adulthood as a function of level of information, input modality, and delay interval. *Journal of Gerontology,* 1982, **37**, 358–364.

Dixon, R. A., & von Eye, A. *Validation of the depth of processing model in aging research.* Paper presented at the 91st Annual Meeting of the American Psychological Association, Anaheim, California, August 1983.

Dixon, R. A., & von Eye, A. Depth of processing and text recall in adulthood. *Journal of Reading Behavior*, 1984, in press.

Dooling, J. D., & Christiaansen, R. E. Levels of encoding and retention of prose. In G. H. Bower (Ed.), *The psychology of learning and memory* (Vol. 11). New York: Academic Press, 1977.

Ekstrom, R. B., French, J. W., Harman, H. H., & Dermen, D. *Manual for kit of factor referenced cognitive tests*. Princeton, New Jersey: Educational Testing Service, 1976.

Eysenck, M. W. Age differences in incidental learning. *Developmental Psychology*, 1974, **10**, 936–941.

Fass, W., & Schumacher, G. M. Schema theory and prose retention: Boundary conditions for encoding and retrieval effects. *Discourse Processes*, 1981, **4**, 17–26.

Flavell, J. H., & Wellman, H. M. Metamemory. In R. V. Kail, Jr. & J. W. Hagen (Eds.), *Perspectives on the development of memory and cognition*. Hillsdale, New Jersey: Erlbaum, 1977.

Fozard, J. L. The time for remembering. In L. W. Poon (Ed.), *Aging in the 1980s: Psychological issues*. Washington, D.C.: American Psychological Association, 1980.

Frase, L. T. Paragraph organization of written materials: The influence of conceptual clustering upon level of organization. *Journal of Educational Psychology*, 1969, **60**, 394–401.

Frederiksen, C. H. Effects of context-induced processing operations on semantic information acquired from discourse. *Cognitive Psychology*, 1975, **7**, 139–166.

Freedle, R. O. (Ed.). *Advances in discourse processes: New directions in discourse processing*. Norwood, New Jersey: Ablex, 1979.

Gardner, E. F., & Monge, R. H. Adult age differences in cognitive abilities and educational background. *Experimental Aging Research*, 1977, **3**, 337–383.

Gilbert, J. G. Memory loss in senescence. *Journal of Abnormal and Social Psychology*, 1941, **36**, 73–86.

Gordon, S. K., & Clark, W. C. Application of signal detection theory to prose recall and recognition in elderly and young adults. *Journal of Gerontology*, 1974, **29**, 64–72.

Grover, S. The application of prior knowledge to the interpretation of text. *The Journal of General Psychology*, 1979, **101**, 271–278.

Hartley, J. T., Harker, J. O., & Walsh, D. A. Contemporary issues and new directions in adult development of learning and memory. In L. W. Poon (Ed.), *Aging in the 1980s: Psychological issues*. Washington, D.C.: American Psychological Association, 1980.

Hultsch, D. F. Adult age differences in the organization of free-recall. *Developmental Psychology*, 1969, **1**, 673–678.

Hultsch, D. F. Adult age differences in free classification and free recall. *Developmental Psychology*, 1971, **4**, 338–347.

Hultsch, D. F. Learning to learn in adulthood. *Journal of Gerontology*, 1974, **29**, 302–308.

Hultsch, D. F. Changing perspectives on basic research in adult learning and memory. *Educational Gerontology*, 1977, **2**, 367–382.

Hultsch, D. F., & Dixon, R. A. The role of pre-experimental knowledge in text processing in adulthood. *Experimental Aging Research*, 1983, **9**, 17–22.

Hultsch, D. F., Hertzog, C., & Dixon, R. A. Text processing in adulthood: The role of intellectual abilities. *Developmental Psychology*, 1984, in press.

Hultsch, D. F., & Pentz, C. A. Encoding, storage, and retrieval in adult memory: The role of model assumptions. In L. W. Poon, J. L. Fozard, L. S. Cermak, D. Arenberg, & L. W. Thompson (Eds.), *New directions in memory and aging: Proceedings of the George A. Talland Memorial Conference*. Hillsdale, New Jersey: Erlbaum, 1980. (a)

Hultsch, D. F., & Pentz, C. A. Research on adult learning and memory: Retrospect and prospect. *Contemporary Educational Psychology,* 1980, **5**, 298–320. (b)

Jenkins, J. J. Remember that old theory of memory: Well, forget it! *American Psychologist,* 1974, **29**, 785–795.

Jenkins, J. J. Four points to remember: A tetrahedral model of memory experiments. In L. S. Cermak & F. I. M. Craik (Eds.), *Levels of processing in human memory.* Hillsdale, New Jersey: Erlbaum, 1979.

King, D. J. Retention of connected meaningful material as a function of modes of presentation and recall. *Journal of Experimental Psychology,* 1968, **77**, 676–683.

Kintsch, W. *The representation of meaning in memory.* Hillsdale, New Jersey: Erlbaum, 1974.

Kintsch, W. On comprehending stories. In M. A. Just & P. A. Carpenter (Eds.), *Cognitive processes in comprehension.* Hillsdale, New Jersey: Erlbaum, 1977.

Kintsch, W. Levels of processing language material: Discussion of the papers by Lachman and Lachman and Perfetti. In L. S. Cermak & F. I. M. Craik (Eds.), *Levels of processing in human memory.* Hillsdale, New Jersey: Erlbaum, 1979. (a)

Kintsch, W. On modeling comprehension. *Educational Psychologist,* 1979, **14**, 3–14. (b)

Kintsch, W., & Kozminsky, E. Summarizing stories after reading and listening. *Journal of Educational Psychology,* 1977, **69**, 491–499.

Kintsch, W., Kozminsky, E., Streby, W. J., McKoon, G., & Keenan, J. M. Comprehension and recall of text as a function of content variables. *Journal of Verbal Learning and Verbal Behavior,* 1975, **14**, 196–214.

Kintsch, W., Mandel, T. S., & Kozminsky, E. Summarizing scrambled stories. *Memory and Cognition,* 1977, **5**, 542–552.

Kintsch, W., & van Dijk, T. A. Towards a model of text comprehension and production. *Psychological Review,* 1978, **85**, 363–394.

Krauss, I. K. Between- and within-group comparisons in aging research. In L. W. Poon (Ed.), *Aging in the 1980s: Psychological issues.* Washington, D.C.: American Psychological Association, 1980.

Labouvie-Vief, G., Schell, D. A., & Weaverdyck, S. E. *Recall deficit in the aged: A fable recalled.* Unpublished manuscript, 1981. (Available from author at Department of Psychology, Wayne State University, Detroit, Michigan).

Lachman, J. L., Lachman, R., & Thronesbery, C. Metamemory through the adult life span. *Developmental Psychology,* 1979, **15**, 543–551.

Lachman, R., Lachman, J. L., & Butterfield, E. C. *Cognitive psychology and information processing: An introduction.* Hillsdale, New Jersey: Erlbaum, 1979.

Loosen, F. Memory for the gist of sentences. *Journal of Psycholinguistic Research,* 1981, **10**, 17–25.

Mandler, J. M., & Johnson, N. S. Remembrance of things parsed: Story structure and recall. *Cognitive Psychology,* 1977, **9**, 111–151.

Meyer, B. J. F. *The organization of prose and its effects on memory.* Amsterdam: North-Holland Publ., 1975.

Meyer, B. J. F. The structure of prose: Effects on learning and memory and implications for educational practice. In R. C. Anderson, R. Spiro, & W. E. Montagne (Eds.), *Schooling and the acquisition of knowledge.* Hillsdale, New Jersey: Erlbaum, 1977.

Meyer, B. J. F. Text structure and its use in studying comprehension across the adult life span. In B. A. Hutson (Ed.), *Advances in reading/language* (Vol. 2). Greenwich, Connecticut: JAI Press, 1982.

Meyer, B. J. F. Prose analysis: Purposes, procedures, and problems. In B. K. Britton & J. Black (Eds.), *Analyzing and understanding expository text.* Hillsdale, New Jersey: Erlbaum, 1983.

Meyer, B. J. F., & Rice, G. E. Information recalled from prose by young, middle and old adult readers. *Experimental Aging Research,* 1981, **7,** 253–268.

Meyer, B. J. F., & Rice, G. E. Learning and memory from text across the adult life span. In J. Fine & R. O. Freedle (Eds.), *Developmental studies in discourse.* Norwood, New Jersey: Ablex, 1983.

Moenster, P. A. Learning and memory in relation to age. *Journal of Gerontology,* 1972, **27,** 361–363.

Monge, R. H., & Gardner, E. F. Education as an aid to adaptation in the adult years. In K. F. Riegel & J. A. Meacham (Eds.), *The developing individual in a changing world. (Vol. 2): Social and environmental issues.* The Hague: Mouton, 1976.

Murphy, M. D., Sanders, R. E., Gabriesheski, A. S., & Schmitt, F. A. Metamemory in the aged. *Journal of Gerontology,* 1981, **36,** 185–193.

Norman, D. A., & Rumelhart, D. E. *Explorations in cognition.* San Francisco: Freeman, 1975.

Perlmutter, M. What is memory aging the aging of? *Developmental Psychology,* 1978, **14,** 330–345.

Potts, G. R., Keller, R. A., & Rooley, C. J. Factors affecting the use of world knowledge to complete a linear ordering. *Journal of Experimental Psychology: Human Learning and Memory,* 1981, **7,** 254–268.

Sanders, R. E., Murphy, M. D., Schmitt, F. A., & Walsh, K. K. Age differences in free recall rehearsal strategies. *Journal of Gerontology,* 1980, **35,** 550–558.

Schneider, N. O., Gritz, E. R., & Jarvik, M. E. Age differences in learning: Immediate and one-week delayed recall. *Gerontologia,* 1975, **21,** 10–20.

Simon, E. W., Dixon, R. A., Nowak, C. A., & Hultsch, D. F. Orienting task effects on text recall in adulthood. *Journal of Gerontology,* 1982, **31,** 575–580.

Smith, A. D. Age differences in encoding, storage, and retrieval. In L. W. Poon, J. L. Fozard, L. S. Cermak, D. Arenberg, & L. W. Thompson (Eds.), *New directions in memory and aging: Proceedings of the George A. Talland Memorial Conference.* Hillsdale, New Jersey: Erlbaum, 1980.

Smith, S. W., Rebok, G. W., Smith, W. R., Hall, S. E., & Alvin, M. Adult age differences in the use of story structure in delayed free recall. *Experimental Aging Research,* 1983, **9,** 191–198.

Spilich, G. J. Life-span components of text processing: Structural and procedural changes. *Journal of Verbal Learning and Verbal Behavior,* 1983, **22,** 231–244.

Spilich, G. J., & Voss, J. F. Contextual effects upon text memory for young, aged-normal, and aged memory-impaired individuals. *Experimental Aging Research,* 1983, **9,** 45–49.

Stevens, K. C. The effect of background knowledge on the reading comprehension of ninth graders. *Journal of Reading Behavior,* 1980, **12,** 151–154.

Taub, H. A. Mode of presentation, age, and short-term memory. *Journal of Gerontology,* 1975, **30,** 56–59.

Taub, H. A. Method of presentation of meaningful prose to young and old adults. *Experimental Aging Research,* 1976, **2,** 469–474.

Taub, H. A. Comprehension and memory of prose materials by young and old adults. *Experimental Aging Research,* 1979, **5,** 3–13.

Taub, H. A., & Kline, G. E. Modality effects and memory in the aged. *Educational Gerontology,* 1976, **1,** 53–60.

Taub, H. A., & Kline, G. E. Recall of prose as a function of age and input modality. *Journal of Gerontology,* 1978, **33,** 725–730.

Thorndyke, P. W. Cognitive structures in the comprehension and memory of narrative discourse. *Cognitive Psychology,* 1977, **9,** 77–110.

Townsend, M. A. R. Schema activation in memory for prose. *Journal of Reading Behavior,* 1980, **12,** 49–53.

van Dijk, T. A., & Kintsch, W. Cognitive psychology and discourse: Recalling and summarizing stories. In W. U. Dressler (Ed.), *Current trends in text linguistics*. Berlin: de Gruyter, 1978.

Wellman, H. M. Knowledge of the interaction of memory variables: A developmental study of metamemory. *Developmental Psychology*, 1978, **14**, 24–29.

Zelinski, E. M., Gilewski, M. J., & Thompson, L. W. Do laboratory tests relate to self-assessment of memory ability in the young and old? In L. W. Poon, J. L. Fozard, L. S. Cermak, D. Arenberg, & L. W. Thompson (Eds.), *New directions in memory and aging: Proceedings of The George A. Talland Memorial Conference*. Hillsdale, New Jersey: Erlbaum, 1980.

# Parent–Child Behavior
# in the Great Depression:
# Life Course and Intergenerational Influences

*Glen H. Elder, Jr.*

UNIVERSITY OF NORTH CAROLINA
CHAPEL HILL, NORTH CAROLINA


*Jeffrey K. Liker*

UNIVERSITY OF MICHIGAN
ANN ARBOR, MICHIGAN


*and*


*Catherine E. Cross*

CORNELL UNIVERSITY
ITHACA, NEW YORK

## Abstract

This article applies a life-course perspective to some causes and consequences of parent–child behavior in the Great Depression of the 1930s. The study is based on the premise that parent–child behavior is shaped over time by the reciprocal interactions of mother, father, and child, and that family interactions are influenced by a changing social and economic order. Using the longitudinal archive of the Berkeley Guidance Study, the first part of the analysis assesses a theoretical model linking economic loss to relations in the family, with emphasis on the first half of the 1930s. Measures of parental behavior include arbitrariness (inconsistency) and extreme modes of discipline, either highly permissive or punitive. Three reliable measures of child behavior were developed: temper outbursts, a syndrome of difficult behavior (quarrelsome, irritable), and social introversion. All three types of problem behavior (ages 5–7) are correlated with teacher perceptions of unhappiness and social rejection in grade school among boys and girls. Ill-tempered, difficult children also tended to be judged highly assertive and hostile with peers in junior high school.

Heavy economic loss influenced only two types of problem behavior among boys and girls: temper tantrums and difficult behavior. In both cases the effect is indirect; it occurs primarily through the arbitrary discipline of father. In addition to this link, the problem behavior (ill-temper, irritability) of father and child *before* hard times also sharply increased the arbitrariness of father during the worst years of the Depression. The causal process varied significantly by the initial attitude of fathers toward the study child; the more negative the attitude, the more economic pressures increased the arbitrariness of father. The arbitrary behavior of fathers with hostile attitudes was *not* influenced by the child's acting out or problem behavior. By comparison, such behavior made a substantial difference in the arbitrary conduct of more affectionate fathers; the more troublesome the child, the higher the risk of father's arbitrariness. The arbitrary behavior of mothers was likewise influenced by the problem behavior of their children, though family income losses were not a source of variation.

The final section considers three implications of strained family relations and problem behavior for the lives of the study children: worklife, marital, and parental. A history of problem behavior in the 1930s enhanced men's prospects for an erratic worklife with spells of unemployment and career switches, for an unstable or broken marriage, and for generally undercontrolled behavior in the adult years. The relation between temper outbursts in childhood and erratic work was most pronounced for men who entered low-status trajectories. For women, a history of temper outbursts, irritability, and quarrelsomeness in childhood was not a disruptive marital influence. Neither the timing nor the stability of their marriage reflected such a history. However, these women were less successful in marrying high status or mobile men and they were characterized by undercontrolled behavior. In parenthood, only the Berkeley females show a connection between problem status in childhood and in the parental role many years later. Ill-tempered and difficult girls during the 1930s were likely to be seen by their own children as "ill-tempered" in 1970. Ill-tempered mothers and fathers were not attractive figures to most of their sons and daughters.

# I. Introduction

Hard times are generally coupled with increasing rates of problem behavior, from alcoholism, crime, and the health impairment of adults to the victimization of children in unstable households (Nelson & Skidmore, 1983). Contemporary understanding of the causal processes involved leaves much uncharted, especially regarding variations in adaptations to loss. Not all children are exposed to economic deprivation and similar exposure does not ensure uniform consequences. Hardship influences are contingent on what people bring to the situation, on how they define the situation and respond to it (Elder, 1974). The chemistry of this sequence offers clues concerning both short-term and more enduring outcomes over the life course.

This article is part of an ongoing effort to investigate parent–child behavior in the 1930s and its relation to the adult lives of a small sample of Depression children. The perspective is that of an emerging perspective on life-course dynamics (Elder, 1984; Featherman, 1981) which is challenging traditional ways of viewing early socialization. Until recently, studies of parent–child interactions focused exclusively on the mother–child dyad, removed from social context, with a tacit assumption that children are passive recipients of maternal influence. Recent theoretical advances (Bell & Harper, 1977; Belsky, 1984; Lerner & Spanier, 1978; Osofsky & Conners, 1979; Parke, 1979) bring fathers into the family system, depict families as embedded in a changing social and economic order, allow for the possibility that children can be important influences in the lives of their parents, and view the developmental trajectory of children and parents within the context of their life course.

Using data from a panel of Berkeley families in the 1930s, with some extensions to the 1970s, we view the problem behavior of parent and child in terms of what each brought to the Depression crisis as resource and liability (strong ties vs parent hostility) and consider the impact of severe income loss on parent behavior in different family contexts. Long-term implications of problem conduct during childhood are traced out in subsequent work and family behavior over the adult years. Do "problem" children become "problem" adults? In the 1930s era, problem child behavior refers to three behavior patterns: temper outbursts, the child syndrome of irritability, negativism, and quarrelsomeness, and social withdrawal. Problem parent behavior refers in particular to inconsistent, conflicted, and extreme forms of child discipline, punitive and neglectful, or indifferent. The core sample of 111 families and their children (born 1928–1929) are members of the Berkeley Guidance Study (Eichorn, Clausen, Haan, Honzik, & Mussen, 1981; Macfarlane, 1938), Institute of Human Development, Berkeley, California.

Research to date on Depression influences in the Berkeley sample follows two general lines. The first entails a study of the children and their course to adulthood, including a comparative assessment of the impact of the Depression on children of different ages (Elder, 1979): the Berkeley children with birthdates of 1928–1929 and the Oakland cohort with birthdates of 1920–1921. This comparison tested a life stage hypothesis on historical change and the life course: that the influence of such change varies according to the age status of individuals at the time. Reflecting their young age and gender, the Berkeley males emerged as the most disadvantaged subgroup in relation to the hard times of the 1930s. The second line of inquiry examines the influence of the Depression on the Berkeley parents from marriage to parenthood and old age (Elder, 1982; Elder & Liker, 1982; Elder, Liker, & Jaworski, 1984; Liker & Elder, 1983). Both short-term and long-term effects on mental health were more adverse for men than for women. In combination, these studies underscore two important principles: that families are changed through people, and that people are changed through families. In both cases, the change may involve an accentuated level of problem behavior. The adverse influence of income loss on families and individual members depended on what people brought to the Great Depression.

These two lines of inquiry come together in this study of Depression parents and children in an evolving system of relationships. We investigate relations between the actual *behavior* of parents and children in changing circumstances. The Oakland archive did not permit such focused inquiry because parent behavior was largely unstudied at the time; developing children were the foci of study. By comparison, the Berkeley study under Jean Macfarlane's direction specialized in the study of parent–child behavior. The Berkeley study offers one other unique feature to the research at hand; a sizable number of adolescent sons and daughters of the 1928–1929 cohort were interviewed in 1969–1970. Data on this third generation enabled empirical study of the enduring implications of problem behavior during the 1930s from the vantage point of postwar America.

We begin by outlining a theoretical model that links economic deprivation to relations in the family triad of father, mother, and child. Measurement issues structure the next section: the measurement properties of both child and parent indicators, their association, and a broader pattern of correlates, social and psychological. Child behaviors that correlate with the arbitrary and punitive behavior of parents may be both cause and consequence over time. Explosive children are apt to elicit such behavior from parents (Patterson, 1982). Using path analytic methods on two waves of data, we attempt to disentangle the influence of parents and children on each other. The family setting of this dynamic process and its implications are taken up next. At issue here is the conduciveness of initial family contexts (hostility toward child) for arbitrary parent behavior under mounting economic pressures. In Section V we examine problem conduct in childhood as a precursor of a problematic life course involving work, marriage, and parent behavior.

## II. Economic Decline and Family Relations in Children's Lives

Over a decade ago, Maccoby (1968, p. 267) observed that "work is needed on the socialization practices of parents functioning under different social, ecological, and economic conditions." The conclusion still applies today, though some advances have been made (Moen, Kain, & Elder, 1983; Nelson & Skidmore, 1983). What we know about parents in varying ecological contexts includes very limited parental behaviors, such as extreme physical abuse. Economic pressures are among the best documented correlates of physical child abuse (Garbarino, 1976; Gil, 1970; Kadushin & Martin, 1981; Light, 1973; Straus, Gelles, & Steinmetz, 1980; Young, 1964). Cross-sectional studies of this sort are suggestive of a causal sequence from economic pressures to parental behavior, but they are limited in the causal inferences possible.

Cross-sectional designs cannot distinguish social causation from social selection processes. For example, it is unclear whether fathers become punitive because of job loss, or whether some fathers, because of emotional or personality problems, are unstable as parents and also unsuccessful in relating to co-workers. Another example comes from clinical populations of problem children. Their mothers tend to rank high on anxiety, depression, and somatic complaints, qualities that have been viewed as etiological factors in children's antisocial behavior. Patterson's (1982, p. 284) observational research on parent–child interaction over time leads to a contrary view: that the problem behavior of children increases the risk of mood disorders among mothers.

The Great Depression provides a unique opportunity to study the consequences of economic decline on parent behavior and resolves an important issue in causal inference—the direction of effect. Available evidence on the Berkeley sample indicates that the deprived and nondeprived did not differ before the Depression on factors such as marital quality, personality characteristics of fathers and mothers, family size, and other factors that might lead to selectivity biases in contemporary samples. Hence, we view the Depression as a natural field experiment which created an exogenous change in the social and economic situations of families.

Our theoretical model linking economic loss to family dynamics in the 1930s includes personality characteristics, qualities of relationships, and reciprocal influences between parents and their children. Personality is defined here as a characteristic way of responding to environmental stimuli, a relatively enduring quality of individuals. Like personality, social relationships have their own developmental history. Though partly dependent on the unique dispositions of individuals engaged in interaction, relationships evolve over time as emergent interaction patterns that cannot be explained solely in terms of individual personality (Gottman, 1979; Hinde, 1979; Patterson, 1980). Moreover, social relationships in the home are structured by family roles and respond to environmental change.

The analytic model presented in Fig. 1 assumes that aggressive and withdrawn child behavior are linked to economic loss in the 1930s through the irritability of parents, their conflict over disciplinary matters, and their arbitrary–punitive discipline. On a general level this formulation bears some resemblance to Gerald Patterson's schematic outline of factors contributing to antisocial child behavior (1982, p. 219): a major crisis such as unemployment increases the likelihood of a disruption of family management practices (such as family rules, parental monitoring of child, and effective problem solving) which in turn increases the risk of antisocial child behavior. Multiproblem families are distinguished by a chaotic state of child supervision and discipline.

Among the most destructive features of an irritable, explosive parent is the recurrence of unpredictable, hostile outbursts which foster an incoherent, turbulent environment. As long as discipline is consistently applied and avoids the extremes of punitive behavior, children seem to be highly resilient under a wide range of parental styles (Moss & Susman, 1980). It is the inconsistent, arbitrary lashing out (Antonovsky, 1979; Rutter, 1980) that appears most problematic for healthful development. Moreover, consistency between parents may be just as crucial as the consistency of each parent across situations. Conflict between mother and father over disciplinary matters presumably increases the arbitrary, punitive discipline of each parent, and the latter feeds back to influence marital relations. The child's influence on parents should be especially prominent when economic pressures and discord are overwhelming. A quarrelsome, explosive child could readily exacerbate the irritability and arbitrariness of parents.

Assuming that deprivation increases the likelihood of punitive and incoherent discipline by increasing the irritability of each parent, theory and our Berkeley

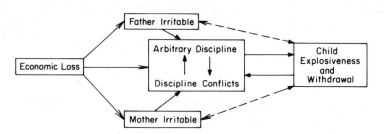

**Fig. 1.** Parent–child behavior under economic decline. The strength of economic influences may vary depending on the developmental history of parent–child interactions and adaptive resources of parents. The dotted paths are not directly tested here. That is, we are unable to empirically distinguish the effects of parent personality on child behavior directly from the effects operating through punitive discipline and discipline conflicts.

research to date underscore the pathway through father's behavior (Lamb, 1975, 1981). Hard times most directly influenced the behavior of the male breadwinner; men became more worrisome, explosive, and irritable (Liker & Elder, 1983), while very little change of this sort was observed among mothers. These women were deprived of family support and peace of mind when husbands lost jobs and income, but men lost a core element of their social significance. The latter commonly regarded unemployment and income loss as symptomatic of personal inadequacy. The sequence through men appears in many hardpressed families of the 1930s and of the post-1970 economic downturn. Acknowledging depressed feelings and the profound hurt of failing one's family, a contemporary unemployed professional observed that "everyone is angry around here. . . . I fly off the handle. My wife can't take it, the kids can't take it. The problems with my son are terrible" (Leventman, 1981, p. 210). Another professional recalled (p. 156) "the tremendous tension with wife and children" during the first "horrible year" of joblessness—"we were always angry at each other—the kids, too."

Apart from the specific stress of income loss, mother's irritability has been identified as a principal factor in children's acting out behavior. From his longitudinal studies, Patterson (1982, p. 277) views mother and her irritability as the key "variable for the understanding of children's social aggression. Mothers provide the reactions that are crucial to the maintenance of high levels of coercive performance." They do so by scolding rather than training the child; by negative verbalizations and threats rather than by confronting the child with efforts to actually change the undesirable behavior (cf. Elder, 1980, Chapt. A2). In many respects, the maternal disposition to react irritably was expressed in ways that reflect a generalized coping response which has short-term purposes and long-term disadvantages. Irritability among the mothers in Patterson's study undermined family management practices, the rule structure of the household, the supervision of child behavior, and problem solving. Unresolved crises were added to the list of past failures. The irritable mother (p. 280) "feels angry about her family and the uncontrollable situation in which she finds herself."

There is considerable evidence that children are active agents in the maltreatment process (Kadushin & Martin, 1981). Vivid characterizations of the "difficult child" that parents find troubling come from the New York Longitudinal Study by Thomas, Chess, and Birch (1969). Using factor analytic techniques, they identify a constellation of behaviors that include children who are negative in mood, intense, withdrawn, and nonadaptive. Such children were often described by their mothers as "difficult children." This undoubtedly had much to do with the intensity of the children's reactions. They tended to shriek more than whine and threw violent temper tantrums when frustrated, particularly in new situations to which they had not yet adapted. Case studies suggest that parenting responses and "difficult" child behavior are mutually reinforcing (p. 80):

"When the parents responded by insisting on compliance with all their demands, the child's intense negative responses were heightened. A chain reaction then began in which the parents' responses to the difficulties of daily handling intensified the behavioral characteristics of the child that had initially made his care difficult." The child behaviors most often correlated with varying forms of abusive parenting are precisely those that provoke punishment, behaviors that parents perceive as defiant and disruptive.

Quantitative research also supports the view that children play an active role in their own maltreatment (see review by Kadushin & Martin, 1981). First, is the consistent finding that one particular child is consistently singled out for punishment while siblings are treated relatively well (Bryant, 1963; Burland, Andrews, & Headston, 1973; Gil, 1970). In a study of 580 abused children and their families, Herrenkohl and Herrenkohl (1979, p. 265) found that children who were targeted for abuse, as compared with their nonabused siblings, were described by mother as presenting difficulties in "excessive eating or refusal to eat, eating bizarre material, frequent temper tantrums, sleeping problems, head banging, behavior problems and moodiness." Second, observational studies of dyadic interaction over time support the view of parent–child relationships as reciprocal dynamic transactions. According to Gottman (1979) and Patterson (1982), negative behaviors have a reinforcing influence that perpetuates *patterns* of mutually reinforcing negativity which can ultimately become a stable quality of the relationship.

A third approach to distinguishing parental influences and child influences is panel analysis and path modeling procedures. A path model applied to cross-sectional data from interviews with 127 male adolescents and their parents in Sweden (Olweus, 1984) finds suggestive evidence of reciprocal influences. Power assertion by parents and their permissiveness of aggression in adolescence are related to retrospective reports of "hot-headed" preschool behavior. Adolescent aggression is linked also with retrospective reports of parents' negativism toward the boy earlier in life.

This brief overview suggests the following hypotheses. First, income loss between 1929 and the low or worst year of the 1930s adversely influenced the behavior of children and father during the early 1930s. Children became more ill-tempered and difficult to manage while father became more explosive and arbitrary in the parent role. Second, the influence of economic deprivation on children's problem behavior occurred largely through father's behavior as parent. Third, the problem behaviors of fathers and children in the Depression reflected dispositions of this sort before the economy collapsed. Hard times served to enhance such tendencies. And fourth, economic hardship was most likely to increase the problem behavior of father under conditions of initial hostility toward the study children. This condition should weaken the moderating constraints on father's behavior, and identify the study child as a target for maltreatment.

All of these hypotheses apply to parent–child behavior in the Depression and preadult years of the Berkeley sample. The legacy of such early behavior patterns will be explored by relating them to problem behaviors in adulthood, from work to marriage, and parenthood. As a guiding hypothesis, we assume that the more problematic the *early* life course in explosive and difficult behavior, the more unstable the subsequent life course. Accordingly, men who were difficult and explosive as a child should rank higher on the risk of an erratic worklife and unstable marriage, when compared to other men. The same prediction applies to women in the realm of marriage. Last and most importantly, there is reason to expect a tendency for problem children to become problem parents. Irritable, ill-tempered responses to childhood frustrations may establish a pattern of behavior for the parental role.

An empirical test of the interaction and feedbacks effects sketched in Fig. 1 cannot be reduced to a single model, at least not with the Berkeley sample at hand. Accordingly, we shall proceed through a sequence of stages, with each one providing a partial test of the whole model. The first stage identifies valid indicators of parent and child behaviors, and their social correlates. This is followed by estimates of the mutual influence of parents and children, along with the influence of family setting. The final part views children's problem behavior in the 1930s as precursors of problem behavior through the adult years.

## III. Measurement Issues

The Berkeley Guidance study was launched in 1928 with every third birth in the city of Berkeley over a period of 18 months. The original sample includes an intensive group, which provided detailed information on family patterns in the 1930s, and a less intensively studied group, which was matched on social and economic characteristics in 1929. All analyses of parent–child behavior in the 1930s are based on the intensive sample (maximum $N = 111$). This sample and the less intensive group ($N = 103$) were combined in tracing out the legacy of childhood problem behavior through the life course to 1970. Most of the Berkeley families are white, Protestant, and native-born; only 6% are black. Slightly more than 60% were positioned in the middle class as of 1929. Two-fifths of the mothers were daughters of foreign-born parents (mostly in the United Kingdom, Germany, Scandinavia, and the Mediterranean region). Foreign parentage applies to about half of the fathers. Berkeley is distinctive as a university town, but few parents were university employees. A substantial majority of the fathers

commuted to work settings in other Bay Area communities, especially Rich-
mond, Oakland, and San Francisco.

The archive of childhood and adolescent data (1929–1945) includes annual
information on income, worklife of father and mother, and consumption patterns, annual teacher ratings concerning academic and social behavior, annual
interviews with mother and child within the intensive sample, and staff assessments based on observations and interviews. Of the 214 original subjects, 182
provided information at the age of 40. Most of these men and women participated in two adult follow-ups (1959–1960 and 1969–1970) which entailed
lengthy interviews and a battery of psychological, medical, and mental tests.
Educational, occupational, and family histories were constructed from the interview materials. A comparison of the childhood and adult samples produced no
reliable differences in distributions on IQ, 1929 social class, and ethnicity.

Three types of measurements require discussion at this point: measures of
economic deprivation or Depression hardship, child problem behavior, and parent behavior. Income records provided data for estimating economic deprivation.
An interview with mother each year (1928–1944) included reports on the problem behavior of her child. After entering school, the children were also interviewed about such behavior. To maximize the sample size, the Institute staff
averaged yearly measurements of parent behavior within a set of periods: before
the Depression (1930 and earlier), during the collapse (1933–1935), and after
(1936–1938, 1939–1941). Staff assessments of parent behavior were made each
year on the basis of interviews *and* home observations. All fathers and mothers
were interviewed in 1930. Subsequent interviews were carried out with the
mothers. Each period score represents the average value for the annual data at
hand. For example, fathers with scores on inconsistent or arbitrary discipline for
each of the 3 years between 1933 and 1935 were assigned the average of the three
scores for this period. Persons with missing data in one of the 3 years were
assigned the average of the available scores in this period. Only 1 year of data
was available for a period in a few cases and that score became the period score
(the 1930 interviews contained few missing data so aggregation was unnecessary). The original yearly scores are no longer available.

## A. DEPRESSION HARDSHIP

Family income for households in the sample averaged $2300 in 1929 and all
but a few of the fathers were fully employed. Some 3 years later, in the trough of
the Great Depression, family income had declined by some 30%, a figure which
is comparable to that of California families in general. Between 1929 and the low
point of the Depression, the number of Berkeley families at the bottom of the
economic ladder (below $1500) more than tripled. Using income records by year
for the intensive Berkeley sample, we find that families were most likely to reach

the bottom of their economic descent in 1933, followed at a distance by 1932 and 1934. Though economic changes between the three lowest years (1932–1934) were relatively minor, we relied upon the low-year figure to calculate percentage loss since it provides the best estimate of maximum change.[1] Depression losses varied greatly in the sample. Some families lost heavily while others suffered modest hardship or managed to avoid misfortune entirely. It is this variation that enables an assessment of deprivation effects.

## B. THE PROBLEM BEHAVIOR OF CHILDREN

Children in a disorganized family under economic stress may learn that "emotional expression and autonomy are dangerous and that survival entails withdrawal, passivity, and keeping things to self" (Elder, 1979, p. 122). An alternative or additional reaction may take the form of aggressive, defiant behavior that is known to be coupled with family discord and punitive parenting (Patterson, 1982; Rutter, 1980). Temper tantrums, an especially vivid and disruptive expression of self-will, include elements of social aggression, defiance, and control seeking. From infancy to adolescence, Macfarlane and associates (MacFarlane, Allen, & Honzik, 1954) found that the frequency of tantrums reached a peak at age 3 for boys and girls in the Berkeley Guidance Study, followed by a more abrupt decline in late childhood for girls than for boys. One-half of the boys and girls up to age 7 engaged in temper tantrums. Whether tantrums express angry feelings of hope or despair (Tavris, 1982), their value as a weapon of personal control can be learned as a way of dealing with frustrating and seemingly uncontrollable situations. Children who get their way (more atten-

[1]Data assembled by the United States Bureau of Labor Statistics indicate that the cost of living among Bay area communities declined by as much as 26% as of 1933. On the basis of this trend, economic losses up to one-fourth of pre-Depression income would not qualify as hardship. Substantial deprivation of one kind or another occurred as the income loss exceeded one-third of the 1929 figure. These deprivations include both general and severe budgetary restrictions (moving to a cheaper rental, etc.), rapidly mounting indebtedness, exhaustion of savings and credit, and the loss of assets, from insurance policies to furniture, the family car, and home.

These effects were also observed in a 1930s study of middle and working class families in Oakland (Elder, 1974). Families with an income loss of 35% or more between 1929 and 1933 were classified as economically deprived. All other families were classified as relatively nondeprived. We shall use this classification for both the intensive and less intensive samples in the Berkeley study when the analysis moves into the adult years and the postwar era. The procedure enables us to classify all members of the less intensive sample; only slightly more than half of these families had complete income records. With complete records on the intensive sample, we shall use the full range of percentage change values for a measure of Depression hardship, as calculated between 1929 and the low year. This index makes the best of available information on economic change. However, we have not found reliable differences between the effects of these different measures. Their results are virtually identical.

tion, love, etc.) by screaming, hitting, or smashing things are learning a behavior that may persist across their life span.

Using the Berkeley archive on problem behavior (see Macfarlane *et al.*, 1954), we focused on measures of aggression, defiance, and social withdrawal— a set of eight five-point ratings based on annual interviews with the mothers: severity and frequency of temper tantrums, irritability, negativistic, quarrelsome, excessive reserve, shy, and socially introverted. The most *severe tantrums* involved "biting, kicking, striking, throwing things" and such negative vocalizations as "screaming." In these cases, "anger completely dominated behavior." The measure of *tantrum frequency* ranged from once per month to several times a day.

Three ratings bear upon the discussion by Thomas *et al.* (1969; see also Thomas & Chess, 1977) of the "difficult child"—the intense, high-strung child that parents find difficult to manage. In the Berkeley inventory of behavior problems, the *quarrelsome* child tended to "have a chip on shoulder, to instigate quarrels with no apparent provocation"; the *negativistic* child had a "compulsive habitual urge to do the opposite of what is expected"; and the *irritable* child was "explosive and overreactive."

Three ratings described a pattern of social introversion. At the extreme, the child who ranked high on "*excessive reserve*" was "extremely reserved, practically never expressed feelings,—extremely inhibited emotionally." The *shy* child was "exceptionally shy, showed acute discomfort to the point of panic, withdrawal or antagonism in social situations or in meeting new acquaintances." The *socially introverted* child was "dominated by inner feelings, very unresponsive to feelings of others or to social pressure, and was also rigid, made adjustments and compromises with great difficulty." As described above, the children characterized by temper tantrums, difficult behavior, and social introversion shared an inability to interact successfully with others and to cope with demands or social pressures. Such behavior is deficient in effective ego control and resilience (Block & Block, 1980), as adaptation under stress.

Each of these five-point measures are averages of at least two yearly ratings across the periods of 1933–1935 and 1936–1938. The children were approximately ages 5–8 in the first period and 8–10 in the second. Examination of the frequency distributions across each behavior item indicates that only one end of each scale includes cases with a problem classification. Thus the temper tantrum distribution ranges from extreme outbursts to none and similarly "difficult" behavior ranges from extreme problems to the absence of problems. All cases on the introversion items range from extreme withdrawal to nonproblematic social involvement.

The three constructs of problem behavior (tantrums, difficult child, and social introversion) perform well at explaining the variance among the eight behavioral indices. Confirmatory factor analysis (Jöreskog & Sörbom, 1979) was used to test the fit of this model to the eight behavioral indicators. A technical description of this analysis is included in Section VII. The three construct model fit the data in 1933–1935 at a marginal level without any specification of correlated measurement error [$\chi^2(24) = 36.7$, $p = .05$]. According to the latent correlations, temper tantrums and difficult child behaviors are highly related (.87), and neither bears much of a relation to social introversion (.11 and .21, respectively). Consistent with the research of Pulkkinen (1982), outgoing and withdrawn children may respond to frustration with either explosive or even-tempered behavior.

Most indicators across the three constructs are at least moderately reliable. Because of these high reliabilities, and for a number of technical reasons,[2] we did not use confirmatory factor analyses for the structural models. Instead, we used ordinary least-squares regressions with indices constructed by averaging the item values. The only exception to this is the index of temper tantrums which is based on the product of severity times frequency for 1933–1935, with the same procedure followed for 1936–1938. Difficult child is measured by an average of scores on irritable, negativistic, and quarrelsome in each of the two periods. The scores on excessive reserve, shy, and socially introverted were averaged to form indices of introversion for the two periods. The three behavioral types are relatively stable between time 1 and time 2. Children who ranked high on temper tantrums at ages 5–7 were also likely to continue their stormy career into the next age group ($r = .57$), even though such behavior generally declines by age. The stability of "difficult" behavior is roughly similar. Even greater stability appears on social introversion ($r = .73$), a result that is consistent with Bronson's observation (1966) on the Berkeley sample.

The full meaning and implications of problem behavior among children are most likely to emerge through perspectives beyond the family, those of teachers and other adults, as well as those of classmates or peers. Were ill-tempered children generally viewed as troublemakers by teachers, as rebellious by other adults in the community, and as highly assertive and hostile by peers? Are there sex differences in these behavioral patterns? To answer these questions, we correlated the problem types for 1933–1935 among boys and girls with selected ratings from the child interview at ages 6 and 7, with averaged teacher ratings for grades 3 and 4, and with nine-point $Q$ ratings on interpersonal relations in junior high school (see Block, 1971). In combination, the three sets of ratings describe behavior at successive stages of the life course.

According to self-reports, we find that ill-tempered, difficult boys were far

---

[2]A main strength of LISREL is the ability to simultaneously estimate the measurement model and structural model. We did not carry through with the LISREL model in the structural analysis for a number of practical reasons. First, most of our independent variables include only one indicator. Attempts to identify multiple indicators of constructs such as parental discipline resulted in LISREL models that did not fit. For example, it became clear that arbitrary discipline and extreme discipline were not simply two facets of the same phenomenon. Second, with the absence of multiple indicators and the multitude of models we wished to run it was simply not cost effective to use LISREL.

more troubled than such girls at ages 6 and 7 (see Table I). They were more likely to rank high on anxiousness and irritability, and on feelings of insecurity in the home. These outcomes apply to both temper tantrums and the difficult child syndrome. The introverted child, whether boy or girl, is distinguished by relational problems in general, from insecurity at home to social maladjustment among peers and adults. Whether ill-tempered, difficult, or socially withdrawn, the problem child was generally perceived by teachers as less sociable and cheerful than classmates. Sex-typed expectations may account for the tendency of teachers to attribute misbehavior to ill-tempered, difficult girls to a greater extent than to boys in this problem category.

The overall pattern of correlations in the junior high period is consistent with expectations, although the sample is very small and many of the coefficients unreliable. Thus strained relations with parents are more common to all problem types, but especially to ill-tempered boys. A pattern of rebelliousness with adults is associated with all problem types, though particularly among the ill-tempered and difficult. Aggressive involvement in peer culture is especially characteristic of boys who were ill-tempered and explosive in early childhood. At the other extreme of isolation from peers we find the withdrawn child. These children and the "difficult" girl were least valued and appreciated by classmates. Interestingly, explosive children of either sex did not experience such disadvantage. Whether boy or girl, they were most likely to be perceived as assertive and hostile toward peers. Within the limits of these data, it is clear that boys and girls in each problem category were not simply problems for their parents.

To obtain a pre-Depression measure of problem behavior on the Berkeley children (used in the investigation of reciprocal influences), we must rely upon a general problem behavior index that was constructed with a recognition of the difficulty of child assessment at the age of 18 months or about 1930. The institute staff encountered some difficulty in achieving an accurate reading on many aspects of personality and behavior at 18 months, even with the detailed reports of mother. For many cases, no codes were available in the archive on specific items. The "problem child" index represents the percentage of all assessments on the child (35 items) that indicate some form of behavior problem. As might be expected, items that had the most variance and hence dominated the index were typically overt, disruptive behaviors such as temper tantrums. Indeed, severity of temper tantrums shows the highest correlation ($r = .40$) with the general problem index.

## C. PARENT BEHAVIOR IN 1930 AND 1933–1935

The very young age of the Berkeley children in 1930 pre-Depression ruled out the assessments of parental discipline made in 1933–1935, such as parent arbitrariness or inconsistency. Nevertheless, the archive does include pre-Depres-

Behavior Patterns and Social Relations as Correlates of Problem Types in Childhood (Ages 5–7): Assessments by Interview, Teachers, and Clinicians

| | Correlates with problem types (ages 5 through 7) by sex | | | | | |
|---|---|---|---|---|---|---|
| | Tempers | | Difficult | | Introverted | |
| Behavior and social relations | Boys r | Girls r | Boys r | Girls r | Boys r | Girls r |
| Interview with child, ages 6–7 (1=low, 5=high) | N = 49 | N = 51 | N = 49 | N = 51 | N = 49 | N = 51 |
| Open during interview | -.25 | -.20 | -.14 | -.27 | -.53*** | -.56*** |
| Anxious, irritable | .40** | .03 | .50*** | .07 | .23 | .25 |
| Poor social adjustment | .25 | .24 | .26 | .31* | .52*** | .39*** |
| Insecure in family | .38** | .01 | .38** | -.03 | .38** | .54*** |
| Teacher ratings, grades 3–4 (1=low, 5=high) | N = 49 | N = 48 | N = 49 | N = 48 | N = 49 | N = 48 |
| Sociable | -.31* | -.09 | -.06 | -.28 | -.20 | -.26 |
| Cheerful | -.19 | .13 | .03 | -.15 | -.34* | -.28 |
| Inactive | -.25 | -.34* | -.21 | -.18 | .23 | .13 |
| Misbehaves | -.01 | .45** | .18 | .40** | -.26 | -.21 |
| Q-sort ratings, Junior High (1=low, 9=high) | N = 34 | N = 37 | N = 34 | N = 37 | N = 34 | N = 37 |
| Respects parents | -.31 | -.28 | -.14 | -.11 | -.26 | .16 |
| Parents reasonable | -.35* | -.18 | -.17 | -.05 | -.18 | .15 |
| Rebellious with adults | .24 | .40* | .22 | .22 | .09 | -.09 |
| Adult oriented | -.35* | -.06 | -.26 | .09 | .03 | .20 |
| Covertly hostile with adults | .23 | .09 | .02 | .00 | .28 | .12 |
| Claims adolescent privileges | .32 | .05 | .22 | .05 | -.09 | -.03 |
| Knows peer culture | .13 | -.17 | .19 | -.16 | -.27 | -.33* |
| Talkative with peers | .11 | .31 | .30 | .11 | -.34 | -.35* |
| Attention getting | .28 | .30 | .45** | .27 | -.24 | -.03 |
| Assertive with peers | .32 | .54*** | .51** | .12 | .07 | -.35* |
| Hostile toward peers | .43* | .38* | .36* | .01 | .01 | -.32 |
| Is well liked | .06 | -.10 | .13 | -.18 | -.23 | -.12 |

* p < .05.
** p < .01.
*** p < .001.

sion measures on marital conflicts concerning discipline, parental attitudes toward the child, and parent irritability or explosiveness. Each rating in 1930 represents an average of the interviewer's judgment (based on interviews with mother and father) and that of a home observer. For 1933–1935, the ratings are based on the mother's interview and on home observations. In each case, the single rating was made by the interviewer. Though measures of father's behavior in 1933–1935 are not based on an interview with him, this restriction does not appear to handicap the study as the patterns of correlation discussed below suggest. Under stressful circumstances, mother's appraisal of father's parent behavior may well be the source which is most perceptive.

Five scales for 1930 were included in the analysis.[3] *Discipline conflicts* indicate the extent of differences between mother and father on matters of discipline; a high score indicates "marked differences with real conflict." *Hostility toward child* (father, mother) is indexed by a five-point scale with values that range from "exceptionally friendly, easy relationship" to "extreme hostility or distrust." *Irritability* (father, mother) refers at the extreme level to "very frequently irritable or explosive."

The discipline conflicts and irritability measures were also available for 1933–1935, but the parental hostility measures were not. Two other parent measures were available for 1933–1935: *arbitrary* behavior (father, mother)—a high score measures inconsistent discipline that reflects the mood of the parent—"the child never knows what to expect"; *extreme* discipline refers to parents who may be consistent, but tend to be either unusually punitive or laissez faire and indifferent. Both extremes are commonly experienced by children as parental rejection (Elder, 1980).

The five parental measures in 1933–1935 are highly interrelated, as shown in the correlation matrix of Table II. Fathers judged arbitrary tended to follow an extreme course as well ($r = .68$) and the correlation between these indicators for mothers is almost identical. Moreover, when fathers were extreme and arbitrary, mothers showed similar characteristics (correlations about .40). Finally, parents who were extreme or arbitrary toward their child tended to be in conflict with each other over discipline (correlations from .50 to .66). It is tempting to conclude from these substantial correlations that all parental measures reflect one underlying factor. However, we see a different picture in correlations between these behaviors and measures of parental irritability.

Fathers who were irritable tended to be arbitrary ($r = .40$) and extreme ($r = .53$) toward their children and this is true of mothers who were irritable as well (correlations of .33 and .55, respectively). However, we find no correlation between the irritability of one parent and the parental behavior of the spouse. In

---

[3]Two data sets include these ratings. The 1930 set is called Early Family Ratings; the 1933–1935 set is called "parental composite."

# TABLE II

## Correlations among Parent Characteristics and Socioeconomic Conditions from 1930 to 1935

| | | 1 | 2 | 3 | 4 | 5 | 6 | 7 | 8 | 9 | 10 | 11 | 12 | 13 | $\bar{X}$ | SD | N |
|---|---|---|---|---|---|---|---|---|---|---|---|---|---|---|---|---|---|
| 1933–1935 measures[a] | | | | | | | | | | | | | | | | | |
| Father arbitrary to child | (1) | | | | | | | | | | | | | | 1.6 | .84 | 104 |
| Father extreme to child | (2) | .68 | | | | | | | | | | | | | 2.0 | .77 | 105 |
| Mother arbitrary to child | (3) | .43 | .39 | | | | | | | | | | | | 1.8 | .84 | 106 |
| Mother extreme to child | (4) | .35 | .43 | .67 | | | | | | | | | | | 1.9 | .85 | 106 |
| Discipline conflicts | (5) | .50 | .66 | .57 | .51 | | | | | | | | | | 1.7 | .85 | 102 |
| Father irritable | (6) | .40 | .53 | .03[b] | −.04[b] | .33 | | | | | | | | | 1.7 | .98 | 104 |
| Mother irritable | (7) | −.02[b] | .00[b] | .33 | .55 | .08[b] | .03[b] | | | | | | | | 1.9 | 1.42 | 107 |
| 1930 measures[c] | | | | | | | | | | | | | | | | | |
| Father hostile to child | (8) | .21 | .39 | .09[b] | .22 | .19 | .42 | .08[b] | | | | | | | 2.4 | .84 | 110 |
| Mother hostile to child | (9) | .10[b] | .17 | .26 | .35 | .22 | .08[b] | .10[b] | .53 | | | | | | 2.2 | .74 | 111 |
| Discipline conflicts | (10) | .45 | .52 | .27 | .30 | .63 | .36 | .00[b] | .47 | .34 | | | | | 3.3 | .88 | 110 |
| Father irritable | (11) | .31 | .47 | −.07[b] | −.05[b] | .26 | .71 | −.12[b] | .39 | .10[b] | .46 | | | | 1.9 | .98 | 110 |
| Mother irritable | (12) | .12[b] | .14[b] | .31 | .40 | .29 | −.23 | .36 | .17 | .34 | .29 | −.19 | | | 2.3 | .85 | 111 |
| Socioeconomic conditions | | | | | | | | | | | | | | | | | |
| Class, 1929 (1=low, 5=high) | (13) | −.26 | −.16[b] | −.18 | −.08[b] | −.07[b] | .04[b] | .03[b] | .12[b] | .06[b] | −.01[b] | .03[b] | .02[b] | | 2.0 | 1.3 | 112 |
| Income loss (%), 1929 to low year | (14) | .32 | .17 | .11[b] | −.02[b] | .20 | .24 | −.14[b] | −.03[b] | −.08[b] | .12[b] | .09[b] | −.10[b] | −.23 | 31.8 | 28.0 | 111 |

Characteristic/condition

[a] Five-point clinical ratings based on home observation and interviews with mothers in 1933, 1934, and 1935. These yearly ratings were averaged, or if one year was missing, the average was based on the two available years of data.

[b] Not significant at .05 level, two-tailed test.

[c] Five-point clinical ratings based on home observations and interviews with mothers and fathers. Ratings of two judges were averaged into composite score.

addition, discipline conflicts are not strongly associated with the irritability of either parent, especially mothers. Finally, knowing the irritability of fathers tells us nothing about the irritability of wives. From these patterns we draw three implications.

1. The extent to which the 1933–1935 ratings are dependent on the reports of mothers raises some question about possible reporting biases with respect to the husband's irritability. Such bias could inflate correlations among the family measures. However this bias does not appear to be a problem if we are to judge from the lack of association between the irritability of husband and wife.

2. Parental irritability seems to represent one possible *source* of arbitrary parental behavior. It is not a consequence of such behavior. This conclusion is based on the association between each parent's irritability and parenting behavior, on the one hand, and on the lack of association from one parent's irritability to the other parent's discipline. For example, if fathers become irritable because of childrearing difficulties, why is this not expressed in a correlation with mother's arbitrariness?—particularly since mother's and father's parenting style tends to be similar.

3. Parents have more in common on disciplinary behavior than on irritability. The similarity may reflect the effort of each parent to achieve consistency or the common stimuli of a problem child which calls forth similar behavior.

Clearly, the discipline items effectively distinguish between the behavior of mother and father. Hence, we treat the five parental indicators as measures of distinct constructs rather than as multiple indicators of an underlying construct. More support for this conclusion comes from other correlations in Table II. First, the irritability and hostility of each parent in 1930 correlates with that parent's behavior in 1933–1935, but not with their spouse's behavior. Most noteworthy is the correlation of .71 between father's irritability in 1930 (when he was interviewed) and his irritability in 1933–1935.

Also of interest in Table II is the stronger connection between father's behavior in 1933–1935 and both income loss and class standing in 1929, when compared to mother's behavior and its correlates. In particular, arbitrary behavior of father is most strongly enhanced by hardship. Both lower class standing and economic deprivation are moderately related to the arbitrariness of father ($-.26$ and .32, respectively). By comparison, an *extreme* mode of discipline by father (punitive or neglectful) is more connected to father's irritability and hostile feelings (to personality) than to either class or economic deprivation (latter coefficients are $-.16$ and .17). It appears from these results that arbitrary behavior is more closely linked to situationally induced stress, while extreme discipline is a more stable reflection of personality. As such, we shall focus on *arbitrary discipline* of fathers as the discipline index in the analysis of economic loss and parent–child interaction.

## D. TOWARD A CAUSAL ANALYSIS

How do the three types of child behavior vary with aspects of maternal and paternal behavior, such as arbitrary discipline and irritability? The hypothesized connection from economic distress through father's behavior to child behavior corresponds with available knowledge of deprivational effects on the family, but contemporary studies of social aggression also identify mother as a critical parent in the causal process. The two positions are not mutually exclusive, as we have noted. Father may represent the principal link between hard times and children's problem behavior, while mother is still primary in the developmental course of such behavior.

The relation between each type of child behavior (1930 and 1933–1935) and measures of parent behavior for the two periods is described by correlation coefficients in Table III. At least through the age of 7, the Berkeley boys did not rank higher or lower than girls on aggressive, problem, or introverted behavior. Also, neither social class nor income loss accounts for these child behaviors to any reliable extent, though deprivation is modestly related to temper tantrums ($r = .17$). Beyond this, we see five general patterns of association that are especially noteworthy.

1. Defiant, aggressive child behavior is highly related to the arbitrary, extreme, and conflicted discipline of parents. Correlations with arbitrary behavior are slightly greater than corresponding correlations with extreme behavior.

2. These discipline measures are more strongly associated with children's problem behavior than are measures of parent irritability in the Depression era. While general irritability may have some influence on the child by creating a turbulent home environment or an aggressive role model, it is arbitrary or extreme behavior directed toward the child that appears to be a more substantial influence. As related behaviors, arbitrary, extreme discipline may be one expression of parental irritability.

3. The differential association with mother's and father's behavior. Irritability of mother in 1930 is more closely associated with defiant, aggressive behavior of children for 1933–1935 when compared to father's behavior in 1930, although this pattern does not apply to the 1933–1935 irritability measures. Mother's arbitrary and extreme parenting, in comparison to that of father, is in most cases a stronger correlate of problematic child behavior (see also Patterson, 1983), although this difference is far from statistically reliable. These data provide weak support for the assertion that mothers are more primary in the etiology of aggressive child behaviors, though arbitrary fathers are almost as potent an influence in this study.

4. The irrelevance of parental behavior (as measured here) for social introversion. The socially withdrawn boy and girl were not more likely than extroverts to

**TABLE III**

**Correlations between Parent and Child Behavior in 1930 and 1933–1935**

| | Child | | | |
| --- | --- | --- | --- | --- |
| | 1930 problem score[a] (18 months) | 1933–1935 child behavior[b] (5–7 years) | | |
| | | Temper tantrums | Difficult | Introverted |
| Parents | r | r | r | r |
| **1933–1935 measures** | | | | |
| Father arbitrary | .28 | .47 | .34 | −.14[c] |
| Father extreme | .21 | .41 | .32 | −.08[c] |
| Mother arbitrary | .38 | .48 | .60 | .02[c] |
| Mother extreme | .44 | .41 | .52 | .21 |
| Discipline conflicts | .29 | .45 | .45 | −.06[c] |
| Father irritable | .17 | .22 | .14[c] | −.09[c] |
| Mother irritable | −.13[c] | .13[c] | .22 | .01[c] |
| **1930 measures** | | | | |
| Father hostile | .07[c] | .33 | .22 | −.03[c] |
| Mother hostile | .17 | .29 | .23 | −.01[c] |
| Discipline conflicts | .27 | .43 | .26 | .20 |
| Father irritable | .05[c] | .20 | .02[c] | .21 |
| Mother irritable | .36 | .40 | .33 | .07[c] |
| **Other measures** | | | | |
| Income loss (%) | .01[c] | .17 | −.02[c] | −.15[c] |
| Class (1=low, 5=high) | −.13[c] | .07[c] | .06 | .13 |
| Sex (0=boy, 1=girl) | −.05[c] | .01[c] | .01[c] | .01[c] |

[a] This index is the percentage of 35 problems that characterized the child at approximately 18 months old (e.g., temper tantrums, restless in sleep, food finickiness, overactivity, attention demanding, etc.). Ratings of problems are based on clinical ratings from observations of child and interviews with the mother. Accurate readings were difficult on many items leading to little variance in ratings. The "temper tantrum" item had the most variance and correlates with the total index at .40.

[b] The three items measuring each underlying factor (see Fig. 2) were averaged into "difficult" and "introverted" indices. The temper tantrum index is a composite based on the severity and frequency items such that low scorers practically never got angry and the highest scorers exploded into a tantrum at least once a day (Macfarlane, 1938). The tantrum item based on the children's interviews was not used because of its low reliability.

[c] Not significant at .05 level.

be members of disorganized or punitive homes. Social withdrawal was observed among hardpressed fathers in the 1930s (Elder, 1974, Chapt. 3), but we find no evidence of a connection between such behavior among Depression sons and daughters and family hardship.

5. The stimulus role of the child. This view of the child does not imply less attention to parental influence or to the transactional nature of the parent–child relationship. Our first view of the study children comes after the formative early months and we have no basis for determining the pattern of early parent–infant interaction or especially the influence of the mother. In any case, the stimulus role of the child is clearly indicated by the pattern of results. Correlations between the problem behavior measure of 1930 and subsequent parent behavior suggest that ill-tempered children increased the likelihood of parental arbitrariness.

The correlations in Tables II and III are the basis for important decisions that structure the causal modeling in the following phase. Since social introversion is related to neither income loss nor parent behaviors, the focal point of our causal analysis is on explosive, defiant behaviors. The principle parent behavior is "arbitrary behavior" of fathers since this behavior is more closely linked to economic loss and explosive child behaviors than "extreme discipline." Mother's parenting behavior may be more potent than father's behavior in the lives of children, but father's behavior was most influenced by income loss. Hence, the analyses that follow focus on fathers as the primary link between the economic changes of the 1930s and the development of problem behavior in their children. To the extent that mothers do enter the process, it seems most likely that they play a preventive role by moderating the arbitrary behavior of fathers under stress through the support of a nurturant marriage.


## IV. Family Hardship in Parent and Child Behavior

The conceptual model in Fig. 1 outlines a causal sequence in which drastic income loss between 1929 and the early 1930s adversely influenced the behavior of young children by increasing the irritability and arbitrary behavior of fathers. Though mothers were also influential, family income loss was not a significant influence in their irritability or parenting. This model also assumes children directed the course of parental responses, an assumption that must be reflected in the estimation of causal parameters.

The ideal modeling strategy would estimate all the paths of Fig. 1 simultaneously and also build in interaction terms to reflect nonlinearities in the effects of income loss. We have argued that these effects depend on the resources and definitions brought to the situation. Such a complex model cannot be estimated with the data at hand. For reasons discussed below, the strategy we follow is to present evidence on parts of the whole model and then bring these pieces together. Where appropriate we call attention to the limitations of the inferences made from this piecemeal approach. We begin with the most precarious part, a reciprocal influences model, and then proceed to the analysis of income loss which considers mediating processes and contextual variations.

## A. RECIPROCAL INFLUENCES OF FATHERS AND CHILDREN

Different approaches are available for estimating the reciprocal influence of fathers and children in the 1930s. One approach views the influence process in terms of a simultaneous, two-way stream; at time 1, child influences parent and parent influences child. A second approach views the influence process over time in a lagged fashion; an effect at time 1 makes a difference at time 2, not at time 1. If we assume that the influence process evolves through proximal exchanges (near events influence each other), then an expanding temporal spread between measurement points lessens the plausibility of the lagged model (see Kessler, 1982, p. 9–10). A third model brings time and sequence to a reciprocal process: parent behavior elicits child behavior which in turn elicits parent behavior. Patterson's (1982, p. 5) research uses conditional probabilities to represent such interdependencies between parent and child actions. Fine-grained measurements over time are required for this type of analysis, a requirement that is not met by the relatively crude temporal categories and global measurements of the Berkeley archive.

Estimation of the simultaneous model requires demanding assumptions. To estimate effects in the two-way process between father's arbitrariness and child temper outbursts in 1933–1935, we must use earlier measures of father and child (1930), such as irritable father and problem child, as "instruments" for later behavior. This approach assumes that the cross-time effect of the father instrument on child behavior at time 2 is indirect; it occurs through father arbitrary at time 2. Likewise, the effect of the child instrument on father's arbitrariness is assumed to occur solely through the child's temper outbursts at time 2. Estimation of this nonrecursive model with two-stage least-squares is based on the assumption that the unmediated cross-time effects are very weak. In reality, there is good reason to expect both mediated and unmediated effects.

Nevertheless our efforts to fit a nonrecursive model in this way produced outcomes which supported the premise of a mutually reinforcing process involving the problem behavior of father and child in the Depression decade. The arbitrariness of fathers increased the likelihood of children's temper outbursts, and the latter increased father's arbitrariness. In a two-stage least-squares model, with irritability of father and problem child (1930) as instruments, the reciprocal influences between the endogenous variables, effects of the child's tantrums and

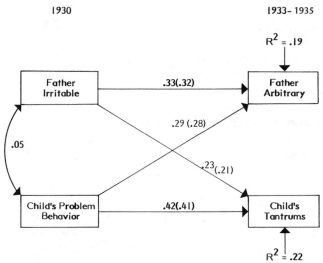

**Fig. 2.** A two-wave, cross-lagged model of father and child behavior. Minimal $N = 103$. Each path with a straight arrow is described by a standardized regression coefficient and a zero-order correlation coefficient within parentheses. The curved arrow relates exogenous variables and is described by a correlation coefficient. All regression coefficients are statistically significant at the .05 level.

father's arbitrariness in 1933–1935, were both statistically reliable, as indicated by $t$ values of 3.2 and 2.5, respectively. Given the many limitations of this model, we view these results as merely an indication of two-way influences, not as a statement of the timing of effects.

If we view the timing of influences as a lagged process taking several years for the behavior of parent to substantially alter the child's behavior and for children to change their parents, a lagged influence model is more appropriate as shown in Fig. 2. This model assumes a recursive process and was estimated in two separate ordinary least-squares regressions. The first equation links the arbitrariness of father in 1933–1935 to the problem behavior of father and child in 1930. Irritability was used for fathers since this was the best available measure of arbitrariness in 1930. The general problem index was used for children. Step 2 assessed the same independent variables in relation to child temper tantrums. The reciprocal effects of father and child are also suggested by this analysis.[4] Children's problem behavior before the onset of hard times increased the likelihood

---

[4]It is not surprising that the cross-lagged model ruling out contemporaneous paths and the contemporaneous model ruling out cross-lagged paths produced very similar results since it can be shown that the two models are equivalent in a sense. With the data on hand there is no way we can empirically distinguish cross-lagged from contemporaneous effects.

of arbitrary behavior by father during the first half of the 1930s, and men who entered the 1930s with irritable tendencies were likely to evoke temper outbursts from their children.

This is not a two-wave, two-variable model since we do not have repeated measures over time, yet it is encouraging that the 1930 parent and child measures substantially influence their respective measures in 1933–1935. Irritability of fathers forecasts arbitrariness for fathers ($\beta$ = .33) and the problem behavior index forecasts the temper tantrums of children ($\beta$ = .42). It is tempting but impractical to draw inferences about the relative strength of the father and child influences since standardized coefficients are presented. These coefficients are very sensitive to the sample variance of the particular indicators examined. In addition, either the 1930 father or child measures may include greater error variances which would dilute the cross-lagged effect.

Taken together, the evidence supports the assumption of reciprocal influences although little can be said about the relative efficacy of father and child in shaping the course of their relationship; nor can we say anything about the timing of influences. Comparable reciprocal models were estimated using the behavioral measures on mothers with almost identical results. We also considered the possibility that the strengths of the paths vary by sex of child, but found no evidence for this assumption in the early 1930s. Attempts to extend the lagged influences beyond 1933–1935 were hampered by the large number of missing data on father measures later in the 1930s.

Bearing in mind the likelihood of reciprocal influence, the analysis moves now to consider how income loss in the 1930s modified the family process. Does arbitrary behavior of father largely account for the effect of income loss on children's temper tantrums and difficult behavior? How does the effect of income loss on arbitrary parenting compare with the disruptive influences of a problem child? Is arbitrary parenting one aspect of a more generalized explosiveness or irritability of fathers or did economic stress alter the parent–child relationship without changing the personality of fathers? Does this process vary by the father's initial attitude toward the child, whether negative or positive?

## B. DRASTIC INCOME LOSS AND PARENT–CHILD BEHAVIOR

To model the process leading to child problem behavior, we set up two series of equations; one focused on temper tantrums and the other on difficult behavior. In both cases, we defined the problem status of child and father *before* the economic collapse (about 1930) as exogenous variables, or not to be explained. Degree of irritability in 1930 serves as an indicator of the father's disposition to lose control in moments of frustration. Child problem behavior in 1930 is measured by the single index described earlier. Income loss refers to the percentage change from 1929 to the low year.

In theory, arbitrary behavior by the father in the midst of the Great Depression (1933–1935) is linked to his general disposition of irritability, to the problem status of his child before hard times, and to the degree of economic pressure. In other words, a father's problem behavior in the Depression should reflect a family history of such behavior as well as the rising pressure of economic misfortune. The important question is whether father's arbitrariness actually mediates the influence of prior circumstances on children's tantrums and difficult behavior. The relevant models presented in Fig. 3 have been simplified for display by removing the weak paths, as defined by statistically unreliable path coefficients. Alongside each path with a causal arrow, we have placed a standardized regression coefficient and the original zero-order correlation coefficient within parentheses.

If we put aside considerations of reciprocal influence for the moment, the pathways outlined by Fig. 3 tell us much about father and child behavior in the depressed 1930s. First of all, the measure of father's arbitrary behavior provides valuable insight into the dynamics of family behavior under stress. *Drastic income loss increased the prospects of children's problem behavior, but only by increasing the arbitrariness of father's discipline. There are no direct effects.*

In addition to economic pressures, arbitrary discipline reflects the general personality of fathers who were inclined to be irritable prior to income loss. With only one marginal exception (the equation for difficult child behavior in 1936–1938) there is no *direct* effect of father's irritability on the child. All influences, family and individual, on the problem behavior of children in the last half of the Depression are mediated by such behavior during the early and most stressful phase of the Great Depression.

What do we lose by modeling the link from father arbitrariness to child outcomes without considering the influence of child on father? Evidence described above supports both paths, but because of our inability to specify the timing of influence we have no way of accurately adjusting the 1933–1935 influence of father on child. This leaves open the possibility of a direct influence of income loss on the children which does not appear because we in effect overadjusted for influences through fathers. But evidence discussed below on conditional effects suggests this is *not* a problem. The fathers who became arbitrary as a result of income loss were *not* affected by the stimulus of a problem child.

Another concern is the timing of the father irritability measure in relation to the measure of arbitrary parenting. The former is measured before income loss, yet the theoretical model of Fig. 1 suggests that irritability mediates the effects of income loss on arbitrary parenting. According to prior research (Liker & Elder, 1983), men who lost substantial amounts of income became more irritable and unstable (1933–1935). This research also shows that irritability was not the result of strained family relationships. The irritable behavior of men increased

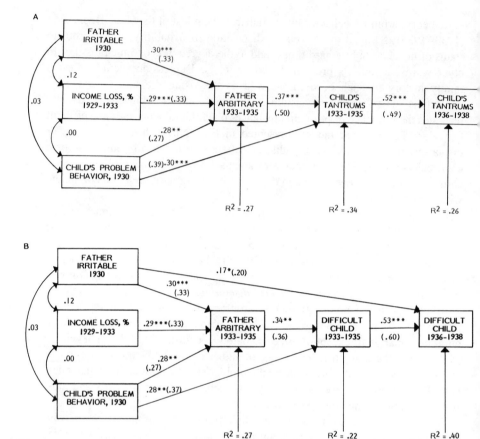

**Fig. 3.** Individual and family antecedents of children's temper tantrums and difficult behavior in the 1930s. (A) Temper tantrums ($N = 100$); (B) difficult child behavior ($N = 100$). As an exogenous variable, social class in 1929 did not alter the configuration of direct and indirect effects. Class has no reliable effect on father arbitrary or on the problem behavior of children. Each path with an arrow is described by a standardized regression coefficient and a zero-order correlation within parentheses. All paths with coefficients less than .16 have been deleted. *$p < .05$; **$p < .01$; ***$p < .001$.

marital discord; the latter made little difference in the degree of men's irritability. For the present study, this outcome suggests that irritability in 1933–1935 can be included in the equation for arbitrary discipline even though both measures refer to the same time period. Regression equations (see Section VIII) support the mediating role of irritability between income loss and arbitrary discipline. When irritability is added to the equation the direct effect of income loss on the arbitrary behavior of father is reduced ($\beta$ is reduced from .23 to .16), but it is not reduced to zero. "Losing control" partly reflects a general irritable syndrome of fathers under stress, but this does not entirely explain the process.

Two general conclusions and some questions emerge from the analysis to this point. First, the primary influence of Depression hardship on the problem behavior of children is indirect. The effect occurs mainly through the arbitrary discipline of father. Second, the problem behavior of Depression children, their temper outbursts and difficult behavior, also reflects the problematic behavioral history which parents and children brought to the 1930s: the irritability of father and disciplinary conflicts in particular, and the ill-tempered and generally troublesome conduct of the very young child (18 months or younger). Our questions concern what might be called the *generality* of the above process of antecedents, consequents, and linkages.

## C. THE CAUSAL PROCESS AS A GENERALIZATION

Can we assume that the process leading to the arbitrary behavior of father represents a general dynamic that applies to boys and girls, to middle and working class, and to all fathers regardless of initial regard for the study child? The first two factors are more easily addressed than the implications of fathers' attitude. Children's temper tantrums and difficult behavior did not vary by sex through the mid-point of the Depression decade (when the study children were 7 or 8 years old), and the general influence process outlined in Fig. 2 applies to both girls and boys in this time period.[5] Sex differences become more pronounced beyond this age level. The theoretical rationale for class differences is more complex, and we find no empirical basis for concluding that the causal sequence differs between middle and working class families in the 1930s.[6]

[5]The direct effects of income loss on father's arbitrary discipline were slightly more pronounced among the fathers of sons than among the fathers of daughters, but the difference is too small to be reliable. To test the generality for both sexes of a model with father arbitrary (1933–1935) as the dependent variable (as in Fig. 2), we used the two-group option of LISREL IV (Jöreskog & Sörbom, 1979). Unstandardized regression coefficients for the same path in the male and female groups were constrained to be equal. That is, we assumed that the general model would fit the data on boys as well as the data on girls. For each factor only a single indicator was used. Consequently, measurement error was not modeled. The results of this analysis clearly support the assumption of generality. The difference in $\chi^2$ between the constrained and unconstrained models was too small to reject the hypothesis that the effects were the same for boys and girls.

[6]The class standing of a child's family in 1929 bears directly on the problem behavior process by shaping ways of responding to stress and frustration. Physical force is more established in working class culture than in the middle class (Straus, Gelles, & Steinmetz, 1980). Class standing also subsumes a variety of cultural and resource differentials that influence vulnerability to loss. Economic hardships were more severe and prolonged for the working class, but middle class families lacked prior experience in coping with them. Higher class standing also involves educational advantages that enhance problem-solving ability and influence priorities or values. Better educated parents in the middle class are more apt to value self-control and are less likely to condone punitive behavior toward children than parents in the working class (Kohn, 1977). These variations do not lead to clear-cut predictions by class, except for the use of force in the lower strata, and class comparisons (middle vs working, 1929) produced no reliable differences on the determinants of father's arbitrary punishment.

Fathers' attitudes toward the study children (see Table II) have more direct or specific implications for father–child behavior under economic stress. When measured prior to the Depression as sentiment ranging from hostile to friendly, this affectional orientation tells us something about the directional nature of father's action under stress. Hostile feelings seem to identify the *study* child as a likely target of frustration and ill treatment. Such behavior is prompted less by what the child does than by the father's inner state. If we follow this logic, affectionate fathers were most strongly influenced by the disruptive, problem behavior of offspring since they were more responsive to the behavior of the child in question. For example, efforts by such fathers to control the angry outbursts of a child could take the form of trial and error, with persuasion and force applied at different times. Actions of this sort may vacillate over time and convey a sense of inconsistency or disorganization, though remaining always under the stimulus control of the child's misbehavior. Is this a process that may lead to negative escalation or reciprocal aggravation, as documented by Kadushin and Martin's (1981) analysis of child maltreatment records? In their account, a typical sequence begins with the child's temper outburst and the parent's request to desist which the child promptly ignores. Threatened by loss of control or authority, the parent responds with force which may intensify if the child fails to show a proper attitude and behavior.

This escalating dynamic was limited to some extent among men with positive feelings toward their child by the relation between this attitude and family solidarity with its normative regulation of behavior. Positive father attitudes are linked to marital quality: the more positive this attitude, the stronger the marriage. Family units with strong affective ties undoubtedly restrained the arbitrary and punitive treatment of children by Depression fathers. We find that the 1930 measure of father's hostility toward a child only 18 months old was symptomatic of weak family ties generally. As measured by disciplinary conflicts in 1930 (see Table II), such ties correlated .47 with hostile sentiment by father toward the study child. The correlation between mother's hostile feelings and discipline conflicts is substantial but lower ($r = .34$). The overall pattern implies a lack of father regulation in the household, or the absence of effective family constraints over men's impulses. One suspects that the situation is highly conducive to the outward expression of anger through physical and verbal force, especially when prompted by mounting economic pressures. Erratic or arbitrary punishment may be one such mode of expression. Conversely, children with warm, accepting fathers were under some protection from maltreatment by father, even if they were "difficult" or ill-tempered.

The analytic power that comes from both distinctions, marital and parent–child, is clearly demonstrated by the results of the subgroup comparisons (Table IV). Men with relatively "hostile" feelings toward the study child included those with high ratings on a five-point scale: (4) "chronic tension or hostility"

**TABLE IV**

Fathers' Arbitrary Discipline in 1933–1935 in Relation to Socioeconomic
and Individual Influences by Fathers' Initial Attitude toward Child:
Regression Coefficients

| Socioeconomic and individual influences | Influences on fathers' arbitrary discipline, 1933–1935, by their initial attitude toward child[a] | | | |
|---|---|---|---|---|
| | Hostile feelings | | Friendly feelings | |
| | *b* | β | *b* | β |
| Social and economic influences | | | | |
| Income loss, 1929 to low year (%) | .015* | .41 | .004 | .16 |
| Social class, 1929 (1=low, 5=high) | −.12 | −.19 | −.05 | −.08 |
| Discipline conflicts, 1930 | .62* | .53 | .04 | .04 |
| Individual influences | | | | |
| Problem child, 1930 | .00 | −.08 | .016* | .34 |
| Constant | 6.13* | | 4.53* | |
| $R^2$ | .66 | | .16 | |
| (Minimal *N*) | (43) | | (60) | |

[a] Statistical tests of the difference in unstandardized regression coefficients across hostile and friendly fathers found the following reliable differences: income loss, $t=2.2$; discipline conflicts, $t=3.4$; problem child, $t=2.6$.

* $p < .01$.

and (5) "extreme hostility or distrust." Four factors were included in regression equations for the hostile and friendly groups with father arbitrary (1933–1935) as the dependent variable: social class in 1929, income loss from 1929 to the low year, discipline conflict before hard times, and the problem status of the child in 1930.

Consistent with our hypothesis, income loss is strongly predictive of the arbitrary behavior of father in the Depression *only* among initially hostile fathers. By contrast, deprivation tells us very little about such behavior among initially friendly or accepting fathers. The large difference between these outcomes is statistically reliable (see footnote *a* to Table IV). Fathers' initial attitudes toward the study children differentiate contrasting family trajectories under economic pressure in the 1930s: one leads toward the maltreatment of children, the other involves a more benign course in which the child is responded to in terms of his or her behavior.

The impact of income loss on father's arbitrary behavior is restricted to the men with hostile feelings toward the study child, and, as noted earlier, these men were at odds with their wives over matters of discipline. From the analysis, we see that even among hostile fathers arbitrary behavior was highest when disciplinary conflicts were high. The less these hostile fathers agreed with their wives, the more they were apt to arbitrarily lash out at the child. Many features of this family situation reflect the breakdown of authority and civility. In the "affection" context, discipline conflicts are less pronounced and their variation has no bearing upon the arbitrary behavior of the Depression fathers. Only the problem behavior of a child evoked such action.

If we placed a hot-tempered child in the conflicted family environments of hostile fathers, one might expect accelerated family tensions and further disorganization. We would not expect these men to passively endure the outbursts of an unruly, combative child. Such behavior could serve as a precipitating event for maltreatment by the father, an event that justifies harsh, even cruel behavior. This scenario may apply to some hostile fathers, but the arbitrary conduct of these men did not require a child's provocation. Marital conflicts and increased economic hardship prompted their arbitrariness, not the child's behavior, however problematic. As such, this behavior of hostile fathers should appear arbitrary from the child's perspective. In line with the "contingency" argument, a problem child *did increase* the risk of arbitrary discipline by father when the latter felt positively toward that child. But since children of this type actually provoked a contingent response, they may not have experienced their father's behavior as arbitrary at all. Only among affectionate fathers were problem children more likely than other children to experience arbitrary discipline from father in the 1930s. The behavior of hostile fathers was more strongly governed by their own personal needs and preoccupations.

The contrasting dynamics of the two groups offer a way to address a problem of causal direction. One might argue that arbitrary behavior by father actually preceded the problem behavior of children, as measured before their second birthday. If this were the case, one should find problematic behavior associated with arbitrary discipline among *both* hostile and friendly fathers, though we know it applies only to the latter group. A more probable account suggests that the causal flow is reciprocal in the case of warm loving fathers, but unilateral among hostile fathers. The former are more sensitive to the stimulus of a difficult child because they are concerned with the child's own well being. Hostile, distant fathers are more driven by their own concerns. In both instances, children react to an arbitrary, inconsistent father with aggressive, defiant behavior. Up to this point in the research, *father's relation to the study child before the onset of hard times emerges as the most important contextual determinant of how children fared under economic hardship in Depression families.*

But we should note that the model presented in Table IV is only one of several plausible specifications. Instead of using father's attitude to define family contexts, one might rely upon marital relations to define weak contexts in which a father's hostility and income loss would increase his inconsistency. By comparison, a supportive marriage entails a shared outlook by father and mother in which the effects of income loss and hostility are likely to be moderated. We tested this specification by using groups defined by discipline conflicts as of 1930 and the results parallel those reported in Table IV. Father hostility and income loss emerged as significant determinants of father's arbitrariness only in conflicted marriages. Other research (Elder, 1979) on the Berkeley families and children shows that the most adverse effects of Depression hardship occur among families with initially discordant marriages. These studies used 1930 measures of each spouse's closeness and friendliness to the other.

Perhaps the most satisfactory specification would include all two-way interactions and a three-way interaction between father hostility, discipline conflicts, and income loss. Substantial loss of income should be most conducive to arbitrary discipline when fathers felt hostile toward the study child and also lacked the social regulation of a supportive spouse. Unfortunately, the correlations between these factors and the small sample size prevented use of such a model. Within the limits of our analysis, we conclude that either strong marital ties or warm affective ties to the child (or both factors) reduced the risk of arbitrary discipline by father under economic pressure.

A related limitation of the analysis concerns the absence of father irritability as a link between income loss and arbitrary discipline. This link is outlined by the study's conceptual model in Fig. 1 and its potential is documented by the correlation matrix of Table II. Irritable fathers in the worst years of the Depression were likely to have been irritable before their misfortune, but they became even more so following income loss and unemployment. That is, pre-Depression irritability and hardship interacted to heighten the explosiveness of men in the Depression (Liker & Elder, 1983). Despite these interconnections, father's irritability for 1933–1935 does not emerge as a mediating variable between family hardship and father arbitrariness in either group of men, hostile or friendly (see Section VIII). The explanation, it seems, has to do with the strength of the correlations between irritability and other father variables. A correlation coefficient of .42 between irritable in 1933–1935 and father hostile in 1930 means that the variance of irritable in each attitude group (hostile or friendly) is markedly reduced.

Though much remains unexplored among these Depression families and children, the results in hand provide important insights concerning the relation between hard times and bad times, between the build-up of economic pressures and the explosiveness of family relations. A good many Depression fathers became more explosive (irritable, arbitrary, punitive) under heavy income losses and thereby increased the psychological risk for their children. These fathers often brought some degree of child hostility and family difficulty with them as they experienced economic setbacks. They disagreed with their wives over discipline and were largely insensitive to the well being and behavior of their offspring. Another scenario involves family strengths and nurturance. Hard times were least likely to turn into bad times for untroubled children when they had the affection and emotional support of their fathers, along with a coherent family environment in which parents shared views on children, finances, and marriage.

If ill-tempered, difficult children emerged from bad times in the 1930s, were these behaviors mere adaptations to the times or did they forecast things to come, such as a problematic life course? At issue here is the assumed primacy of early experience in shaping the trajectory of development, a perspective long entrenched in psychoanalytic thought and developmental psychology. More recently, this position has been effectively challenged by empirical research and theory on personal changes through the life course. In the summary views of Brim and Kagan (1980, p. 1), "many individuals retain a great capacity for change, and the consequences of the events of early childhood are continually transformed by later experiences, making the course of human development more open than many have believed." Longitudinal research (Furstenberg, 1976; Vaillant, 1974) has begun to document the varied developmental paths in which childhood promise is not matched by well being or accomplishments in the adult years, and dismal life chances among youth are at least partially repaired by growth-inducing experiences later on in life.

A continuity theme on life-span development is complicated by the changing relation between disposition and behavior from childhood to adulthood. Thus lack of control over impulses may be expressed as temper outbursts in childhood and as hostility or hypercritical attitudes in adulthood. When a stable disposition underlies different behavioral manifestations, the process is generally described as heterotypic development. Available longitudinal evidence (Moss & Susman, 1980) on the sequelae of ill-tempered behavior in childhood is consistent with the heterotypic pattern. We turn now to this and related issues of continuity and change through work, marriage, and parenthood.

## V. Problem Children as Adults

As the Berkeley children entered adulthood in the late 1940s, they were called upon to perform roles they had learned in the past by "taking the perspective" of parents and other authority figures. Their work, marital, and parental relationships were subject in this manner to the self–other dynamics of family life in the 1930s. Arbitrary parental actions in a number of Depression families nurtured ill-tempered, explosive children. Did such behavior leave an imprint on adult relationships and accomplishments over the life course?

An explosive father and child pattern could be expressed in at least two ways. When faced with authority and its commands, the child component is likely to rebel or defy. In the role of adult authority, the individual would be inclined to act out the behavior of his father—punitive and erratic. The first situation applies most readily to the work settings of men in the lower strata who are least apt to exercise self-direction. Consider, for example, the case of a man named Otto, the son of a harsh, authoritarian (Cottrell, 1969, p. 563). He was "placed in an unskilled job but walked out of it after a reprimand by his supervisor. This same sequence repeated several times, and it became apparent that any exercise of authority evoked in Otto a very defiant reaction which usually lost him his job." Noting that he was likely to explode in such situations, Otto agreed to try not "to start fighting his old man" whenever people started "ordering him around."

Negative self–other patterns established in the Depression could increase the risk of marital instability through the social costs of harsh, inconsiderate behavior. This risk may also be enhanced through a process of social selection in which an ill-tempered, difficult person acquires a target for an established hostile response. Negativity is matched with negativity in the mating process and in the marriage of two people who are outspoken in their expression of displeasure and criticism. Another potential source of marital instability entails the projection of a harsh, arbitrary pattern of self–other interaction onto the marriage relationship (Cottrell, 1969). Expectations of ill treatment from the partner could lead to emotional distance and defensive forms of negativity. The end result is likely to resemble a self-fulfilling prophecy. Rough treatment is expected and elicits similar behavior.

The parent role is the third domain where behavior may be shaped by self–other patterns acquired in the Depression. The interactive analysis of Cottrell (1969, p. 564) suggests that any self–other relation that is learned in one setting is likely to be evoked by situations of comparable structure and content. The relevant situation is that of parent–child interaction. By taking the role of a punitive, arbitrary father, the child acquires a repertoire of behavior that forms a parental style for subsequent years. Thus, Otto's wife described him as "extremely harsh and strict" with his young son, and claimed that "he frequently struck the child hard enough to bruise him when the child did not respond to the father's directions" (Cottrell, 1969, p. 563).

## A. LACK OF SELF-REGULATION OVER TIME

To investigate these potential continuities, we used two measures of problem behavior in childhood, temper tantrums and the difficult child syndrome for 1936–1938. If we view these measures in terms of self-control and coping, the first question is whether this generalized pattern of behavior is a relatively stable disposition into the adult years. A set of ipsative ratings from the California $Q$ sort in the Berkeley mid-life follow-up (1970) provides an appropriate adult measure of ineffective coping and self control. Using a lengthy interview, two or more clinically trained judges sorted approximately 100 items on psychological functioning according to a nine-point scale with a fixed distribution (bell shaped). High scores on an item indicate that the behavior is characteristic of the person. We selected four intercorrelated items that collectively depict an under-controlled style of behavior: "self-indulgent," "pushes limits," "expresses hostility directly," and "undercontrolled." Using an index based on the average of these items, we find a very modest level of stability.

Men who ranked high on temper outbursts as children were slightly more likely to score high on an undercontrolled style of behavior at mid-life, age 40 ($r = .20, p < .10$). Slightly less predictive of this behavior is an early history of difficult behavior—quarrelsome, irritable, negativistic ($r = .16$). In the case of the Berkeley women, a history of problem behavior on both indicators weakly predicts an undercontrolled tendency in adulthood (mean $r = .22$), but it is not a relationship that generates confidence in the theme of behavioral continuity. Early problem behavior (temper outbursts, difficult behavior) does not predict a generalized pattern of uncontrolled behavior in adulthood, but it is far more consequential when we focus on role-specific behaviors in work, marriage, and parenting. To a notable extent, the Berkeley problem children did indeed follow a more troubled life course when compared to the lives of other children.

## B. WORKLIFE PATTERNS AND STATUS ACHIEVEMENT

An early history of problem behavior may not tell us much about the gener-alized problem of impulse control in adulthood, but does it forecast trouble in specific areas of life, such as work, marriage, and parenthood? Disorderly ca-reers are one example of trouble since they refer to a work course punctuated by discontinuities that might stem from fits of anger or explosiveness. Men with disorderly careers have moved between functionally unrelated lines of work (Wilensky, 1961). Their social ties are thin and relatively weak. To capture this discontinuity, we constructed a worklife index (scores from 0 to 7) that measures disorderly or erratic trajectories. The index refers to the span from 20 years to mid-life or about age 40, and draws upon information regarding spells of unem-ployment, number of employers, career switches between lines of work, and status fluctuations (an up and down pattern).[7] Nearly a third of the men had an erratic worklife, one which included incidents of suspensions and firings, object throwing, and angry backtalk.

---

[7]The index of erratic worklife represents the sum of values on the following attributes: (1) ever unemployed in adulthood (yes = 2, no = 0); (2) one or more shifts in line of work after 1955 (scored 1 vs no shifts = 0); (3) one or more fluctuations in worklife (up/down cycles)—scored 1 vs 0 = no fluctuations; (4) number of different employers prior to 1956 (3+ = 1, other = 0); and (5) number of years in a single line of work (less than 13 years = 2, 12–16 years = 1, and 17+ years = 0). Scores range from 0 to 7.

Ill-tempered Berkeley males were likely to follow an erratic worklife up to the middle years ($r = .33$), a risk which did not apply to those who were characterized as "difficult" children ($r = .07$). The erratic trajectory of men with a tantrum history in childhood is not surprising in view of the social repercussions of "blowing off steam" in the work setting. But there are some alternative explanations. Ill-tempered boys may end up with disorganized worklives because they lose out in formal education. This does not seem to be the case, however; neither type of problem behavior is a factor in men's educational attainment. Indeed, no plausible statistical controls altered the correlation between tantrums in childhood and an erratic worklife. The result remains the same ($\beta = .37$, $p < .01$) with statistical adjustments for class origin, childhood IQ, and educational level in a regression equation.

The long arm of child temper outbursts extends into men's worklife and makes a difference that cannot be matched by what we know at present about erratic work careers. Why do some men follow this course while others are more orderly? From the evidence at hand, we cannot answer this question with information regarding class origins, level of intelligence, or educational attainment. Not one of these factors proved useful in sorting out men who followed erratic and orderly trajectories. Their combined influence is far less than the total effect of child temper outbursts. An ill-tempered history may be a very modest help in charting an unstable worklife, yet it remains among the more useful points of departure for understanding a problematic life course.

Results of this sort gain meaning from the presumed disorganizing effect of erratic work. Various elements of an erratic worklife suggest less advancement or progression from first job to the middle years. Spells of unemployment, career switching, and status fluctuations do not bring to mind a successful career. Indeed, we find that the more erratic workers tended to end up in lower status employment by 1970: a correlation of $-.21$ between erratic work and occupational standing, as indexed by the seven-level Hollingshead measure. This is not a strong association, but it suggests an explanation for the association between tantrums in childhood and occupational status attainment by age 40. The effect of child tantrums is negative ($\beta = -.20$) even with IQ and parental social class in the analysis. Approximately one-third of this effect is explained by the costs of an erratic worklife.

The social implications of angry outbursts imply that this behavior should be most strongly linked to an erratic worklife among men who have much exposure to close and perhaps authoritarian supervision. In Robins' (1966) early research, we find that men with sociopathic tendencies were often successful in managing their adult life when employment entailed *minimal regulation* and out-of-doors activity. We do not have detailed work histories for classifying careers on autonomy or supervision, but a rough distinction along this line can be made by using the social position of the men in 1970. Self-direction is highly correlated with occupational status (Kohn, 1977). We divided the Berkeley men into the upper middle class (I and II on the Hollingshead index) and lower strata (III–V), the group with substantial close supervision. Much as predicted, child tantrums were predictive of an erratic worklife primarily among lower status men ($\beta$ = .62 vs .14), with adjustments for IQ and class origin. Spells of unemployment, career breaks, numerous employers, and status fluctuations were all most characteristic of lower status men with a record of temper outbursts in childhood.

Early problem behavior increased the probability of an unsettled or troubled career during the first half of men's worklife. In many respects, this time resembles a "worst" time in life and men's retrospective accounts at age 30 tend to document this conclusion. During the 1960 follow-up, the Berkeley men were asked to judge each year on a five-point scale relative to the "best and worst periods of life." The yearly scores were averaged to yield more stable assessments of three periods: 1942–1946, 1947–1955, 1956–1960. Child temper outbursts and difficult behavior were predictive of memories which portrayed the first two periods as bad times (mean $r$ = $-.22$, 1942–1946, and $-.33$, 1947–1955). Retrospective evaluations of the last years of the 1950s were unrelated to this behavioral history.

In theory one might expect to find a similar relation between problem behavior in childhood and women's occupational careers or worklife. Over one-half of the Berkeley women were employed by age 40, but the nature of their employment showed much greater variation and disorderly evolution when compared to the work histories of men. As such, the key elements of an erratic worklife (unemployment, for instance) were less applicable to the worklives of women. We find no evidence that temper outbursts or difficult behavior in childhood had implications for women's educational attainment or worklife. An early history of this kind does not distinguish between women who worked and those who did not, nor does it offer any insight into the duration and schedule of their employment.

## C. MARITAL PATTERNS

The most common experience of men and women in the sample is that of marriage. Do we find any evidence that early behavioral problems in the Depression years were predictive of marital instability? Were boys and girls who could not get along with parents (who were difficult and ill-tempered) likely to become men and women who had trouble sustaining a marital relationship? Three distinctions have special relevance to this question: the timing of marriage, the marital partner, and the permanence of the marriage. The timing of marriage has relevance to marital instability through the well-known risk of early marriage for divorce and separation. However, a history of behavior problems does not suggest a person who is likely to be attractive in the marriage market. A relatively late or delayed marriage seems more plausible. Examination of the data shows that neither type of behavior problem mattered for the timing of marriage among men and women. The correlation coefficients border on zero.

The marital partner has particular significance from the perspective of women's lives to the extent that their social position stems in part from husbands' accomplishments. If women with a history of temper tantrums and difficult behavior were at some disadvantage in the selection of a promising mate, the handicap would be expressed through the lower occupational achievements of their husbands. This outcome might also include a marital partner who resembles the arbitrariness and punitiveness of father, qualities that lessen chances for stable, productive work in occupational advancement. This is only one implication of an established self–other pattern of ill-tempered outbursts for marriage and the life course.

Whatever the causal mechanism, we find that women with a record of temper outbursts in childhood were likely to marry men of relatively low occupational status by 1970 (seven-point scale), when compared to more even-tempered women. The $\beta$ coefficient is $-.28$ ($r = -.36$) with adjustments for class in 1929 and women's educational level. Interestingly, the women who were judged "difficult" in childhood—as quarrelsome, irritable, negativistic—*did not* experience any disadvantage in status achievement through marriage ($\beta = -.04$). As in the case of the Berkeley men, it is a history of temper outbursts that has socioeconomic implications for women. This behavioral history tells us as much about their status achievement through marriage as their IQ and education, matched one at a time. The main effects are similar.

Marital impermanence represents a plausible explanation for this disadvantage through marriage. Women who came to marriage with a quick temper may have done so with a higher risk of marital discord and impermanence. Indeed, an early survey by Locke (1951) found poorer marital relations and greater instability when either partner claimed to "anger easily" and to fail to "get over anger quickly." If women with a history of behavior problems were especially difficult to live with, we find no evidence of this on divorce and separation. Neither child temper outbursts nor the cluster of difficult behavior increased the risk of marital impermanence among women.

When questioned in 1970 about their relation to spouse, women with an ill-tempered background were more likely to report that they were not "affectionate" and that they "expressed displeasure" openly. However, only the association with marital affection is reliable ($r = .32$, $p < .01$ vs .16 for expressed displeasure). The self-rating scale ranges from one to five. In the case of men, the link between early problem behavior and expressed displeasure is stronger for both indicators (mean $r = .37$, $p < .01$), but this connection does not appear for marital affection (coefficients border on zero). Despite these differences, the child problem behavior of men did anticipate an unstable marital career. Men with a background of temper outbursts in childhood were less apt to have an intact first marriage (tau $b = -.31, p < .01$) when they were interviewed in the 1970 follow-up. The correlation for "difficult" child is about half as strong.

In the adult domains of work and marriage, the long-term implications of problem behavior during the Depression decade largely center on temper outbursts. Men with this background were likely to have an erratic worklife, lower occupational attainment at mid-life, and an unstable marital history. Temper outbursts in the childhood of women offer few insights regarding their employment, marital age, or marital permanence. But they do predict life outcomes that suggest a relatively poor match in the marriage market of eligible, ambitious men. Women who were once ill-tempered children tended to end up with a status disadvantage through husband's occupational achievements up to the middle years. A summary of key correlations reflecting these patterns is shown in Table V.

### D. PROBLEM CHILDREN AS PARENTS

The third and last adult domain to be explored is parental experience. Were problem children in the Berkeley cohort likely to become problem parents in the postwar era? Were the more explosive children in the 1930s inclined to "lose control" of their feelings and actions as adults in parental situations? Retrospective reports of uncertain quality claim that poorly treated children are at risk of becoming adults who relate to their own children as their parents did to them (Finkelhor, Gelles, Hotaling, & Straus, 1983). But the evidence leaves much room for doubt. We addressed two issues that bear on this potential Depression legacy. The first concerns the relation between child behavior of a problematic nature and parent behavior in adulthood. The second issue centers on the enduring consequences of the Depression experience leading to more problem behavior, from economic pressures through father's arbitrary behavior in particular.

To address the first issue, we turned to the postwar children of the Berkeley cohort for reports of their parents' behavior, specifically the tendency to get angry and lose control in disciplinary situations. The children's interview of 1970 provided the very best measures of such parent behavior. In addition, use of the children's perceptions enables us to trace the Depression's influence into the lives of children who were born in the midst of affluence. During the 1969–1970 follow-up, the Institute staff at Berkeley attempted to interview all children of the subjects between the ages of 14 and 19. Approximately 60 males and an equal number of females completed interviews: 87 different families are represented by this total. The interview included two questions that pertain directly to the issue of self-control. One was stated in terms of parent anger, the other referred to loss of parental control. The four-point items ranged from even-temper to "usually bad-tempered," "evidence of screaming, physical abuse."

Sons and daughters generally agreed on the following portrait of parent behav-

# TABLE V

## Adult Correlates of Childhood Temper Tantrums and Difficult Behavior among Men and Women in the Berkeley Cohort

| | Correlations ($r$) between child problem behavior (1936–1938) and adult behavior | | | |
| | Males' problem behavior | | Females' problem behavior | |
| Indicators | Temper tantrums $r$ | Difficult $r$ | Temper tantrums $r$ | Difficult $r$ |
|---|---|---|---|---|
| Worklife and status | | | | |
| Men's occupational status,[a] 1968 (1=low, 7=high) | -.20** (81)[b] | -.22** (81) | — | — |
| Erratic worklife,[c] 1946–1968 | .33*** (60) | .07 (60) | — | — |
| Husband's occupational status,[a] 1968 (1=low, 7=high) | — | — | -.36*** (75) | -.23** (74) |
| Marriage | | | | |
| Intact first marriage, 1968 (1=yes, 0=no) | -.31*** (75) | -.17* (75) | -.04 (83) | -.13 (84) |
| Parenthood | | | | |
| Ill-tempered, as reported by child,[d] 1970 | -.08 (36) | -.07 (36) | .34*** (48) | .55*** (48) |
| Undercontrolled,[e] 1970 Q rating scale | .20* (61) | .16 (61) | .20** (72) | .24** (72) |

[a] Men's occupational status and husband's occupational status, 1968, are based on the Hollingshead seven-level index.

[b] Sample sizes are noted in parentheses.

[c] Erratic worklife, 1946–1968 is a summated index made up of five indicators of an unstable work pattern in adulthood (see text footnote 7).

[d] Ill-tempered, 1970, is the average of two interview items on children's perceptions of parents: ill-temper and lack of self-control.

[e] Undercontrolled, 1970, is the average of four Q-sort items: undercontrolled, self-indulgent, pushes limits, and expressed hostility.

\* $p < .10$.
\*\* $p < .05$.
\*\*\* $p < .01$.

ior. Over half of the fathers were described as ill-tempered when in a bad mood, compared to about 43% of the mothers. Loss of temper by either parent was far more common than loss of control through shouting, screaming, and using physical force. One-third of the fathers and one-fifth of the mothers were so described. The two intercorrelated items (mean $r = .51$) were averaged to produce an index for each parent.[8] We found no evidence that sex of child made a difference in parent perceptions. As a result, sons and daughters were pooled for the cross-time analysis.

Behavioral continuity appears only in the lives of the Berkeley women. Their temper outbursts and difficult behavior during childhood are predictive of ill-tempered behavior in the parent role, as judged by their own children. When included in a single equation, difficult behavior (1936–1938) has approximately twice the effect of temper outbursts ($\beta = .50$ vs .25). In combination they account for slightly more than one-third of the variance in perceptions of an ill-tempered mother. By comparison, the early problem behavior of men tells us very little about their parent behavior. Neither type of behavior is correlated with their children's perception of an ill-tempered father. The correlation coefficients do not exceed .07. The actual meaning of this sex difference is elusive and warrants further study.

The second issue on the enduring imprint of the Depression family concerns whether self–other relations learned in this setting were put to work in parenting many years later. Do the Berkeley men and women resemble their own parents in disciplinary situations? Did children of arbitrary fathers become out-of-control parents? A satisfactory answer to this question is not possible with the data and sample at hand, though some highly tentative observations are worth brief mention. We selected the index of economic deprivation and key mother and father variables of the 1930s (irritable, 1930 and 1933–1935; arbitrary, 1933–1935; extreme discipline, 1933–1935, and hostile attitude toward child, 1930), and correlated them with the children's perceptions of ill-tempered behavior for mother and father, 1970. The results show that early problem behavior remains by far the most important predictor of ill-tempered parenting among women. In the case of men, the only etiological clue appears in the parenting of mother rather than father.

Though much of the Depression's pathology involved men, their life experience and behavior have remarkably little bearings on the parental behavior of sons and daughters. Within the limitations of this sample, we find no evidence

---

[8]The ill-tempered index on mother and father represents an average of two four-category items from the child interview of 1969–1970: (1) ill-temper—1, exceptionally good tempered; 2, usually even tempered; 3, bad tempered when in a bad mood; 4, usually bad tempered; and (2) "self control"—1, no evidence of parental loss of control; 2, slightly uncontrolled, as in nagging too much; 3, parent swears, shouts, slams door; 4, parent shows widespread loss of control—evidence of screaming or crying in front of child, physical abuse. The two items are intercorrelated .51 (average $r$ across groups defined by sex of parent and child).

that Depression fathers who were arbitrary on disciplinary behavior were likely to have ill-tempered adult sons, as viewed by their children. The cross-time connection is equally weak between Depression fathers and mature daughters. As observed in this study, arbitrary fathers in the 1930s primarily made a difference in children's lives by accentuating their problem dispositions. The arbitrariness of Depression mothers was not a major force in daughter's lives, although these mothers represent the only notable influence on the parental behavior of sons. The irritable and arbitrary behaviors of mothers (1933–1935) are correlated .32 (mean $r$) with the ill-tempered behavior of adult sons, according to the perceptions of their children. As influenced by the Depression, the family environment warrants greater exploration as a source of parent styles in the postwar generation, a period known for its family-centered themes.

One might expect the legacy of undercontrolled behavior to persist across the generations. Using a 1970 index based on an average of four $Q$-sort ratings of uncontrolled behavior on the postwar children, we find that ill-tempered parents (mother and father, as described by children in 1970) were likely to have "undercontrolled" children ($r = .58$, both male and female). The correlation is equally strong for boys and girls, and for mother and fathers. The four items in the index are "rebellious," "pushes limits," "expresses hostility directly," and "undercontrolled." On the basis of simple correlations, we find that mothers with undercontrolled children were more likely than other women to have a record of problem behavior in childhood (e.g., $r = .32$ for difficult child), but the stronger cross-time link runs from the Depression problem behavior of females to their ill-tempered parenting.

In the 1930s an ill-tempered style of parent behavior is symptomatic of problems within and between mutually dependent lives, parent and child. Irritable, explosive fathers and angry, difficult children were sources of strain and polarization in the family. Such estrangement appears between the Berkeley "children of the Great Depression" who are ill-tempered in adulthood and their own children in 1970. These mothers and fathers were least likely to be described by their children as accepting, affectionate, and willing to listen.[9] The children reported spending relatively little time with them. They seldom shared ideas and

---

[9]The Berkeley "postwar" children were asked during interviews (1969–1970) about their perceptions of parental support and control, and about their orientation toward each parent on affection, values, and association. The support index for each parent represents an average score across four intercorrelated items that range from values of one to four: parent as supportive, as understanding, as having confidence in child, and as accepting of the child. For both mother and father, perceptions of ill-tempered behavior were negatively correlated with perceptions of parental support (mean $r = -.61$, for mother and father). Ill-tempered parents were also perceived by sons and daughters as not providing a democratic-type relationship in which views could be shared (mean $r = -.29$, for mother and father). In terms of orientation, the adolescents of ill-tempered parents were less likely to express feelings of satisfaction and acceptance, to claim that the parent is influential in their life, especially as a model and source of advice, guidance, and to report a free exchange of views with the parent. Intercorrelations range from $-.30$ to $-.62$.

feelings, or sought their advice. In this manner, Depression hardships initiated a cycle of alienation among the young who soon became parents of children in postwar America.

## VI. Hard Times, Bad Times, and the Generations

Cycles of deepening economic crisis have been expressed in rising public concern over the human toll. Hard times typically become bad times in the collective view with a legacy of misfortune that extends like a shadow across subsequent generations. As one state commission put it at the end of 1932: "unemployment and loss of income have ravaged numerous homes. It has broken the spirits of their members, undermined their health, robbed them of self-respect, destroyed their efficiency and employability."[10] By the end of the decade, community leaders and human service practitioners were troubled by the gloomy prospects of a child generation whose heritage included the "devastating" loss of parent morale and nurturance.

Broad generalizations of this sort do not match reality as we know it in the 1930s or in the 1980s. A large number of families did not suffer heavy income or job losses during the Great Depression, and even the severely deprived brought varied resources to the crisis and its adaptive requirements. These variations involve past experience with hardship, material and problem-solving assets, the strength of family bonds, personal confidence and self-esteem, and inner resilience. Such differences often made a difference in the ways families responded to hardship and in the experience of individuals. Depending on circumstances, the Depression experience impaired some lives and produced no ill effect in others.[11]

This conditional picture of the Depression experience in lives receives additional support and specification from the present study of parent–child behavior in the 1930s and its life course implications across three generations—parent,

---

[10]The report goes on to note that "many households have been dissolved; little children parcelled out to friends, relatives or charitable homes; husbands and wives, parents and children separated, temporarily or permanently. Homes in which life savings were invested and hopes bound up have been lost never to be recovered. Men, young and old, have taken to the road" (cited in Bernstein, 1970, p. 321). The intergenerational argument of lasting damage from the Depression parallels the notion that "growing up on welfare perpetuates dependence on welfare" in the next generation. Sophisticated panel studies have provided no convincing empirical foundation for this thesis on "dependency" transmission (see especially Coe, Duncan, & Hill, 1982).

[11]This conclusion is based on project research over the past 15 years, beginning with a class difference in life outcomes among the Oakland "children of the Great Depression" (birthdates, 1920–1921) and extending through the lives of the Berkeley children (birthdates, 1928–1929) and their parents (Elder, 1974, 1979, 1982; Elder, Liker, & Jaworski, 1984).

child, and grandchild. The parents were born around the turn of the century, the children just prior to the Great Depression in the city of Berkeley, and the grandchildren in the affluent age of postwar America. Data were collected annually on the parents and children from the late 1920s to the mid-1940s.

Using these data resources, we investigated the process by which Depression hardship made a difference in the problem behavior of children and in their adult life course of work, marriage, and parenthood. As measured, problem behavior refers to temper tantrums or outbursts, the difficult child syndrome (irritable, quarrelsome, negativistic), and social introversion in two time periods, 1933–1935 and 1936–1938. Building upon theory and cumulative knowledge regarding hard times, the resulting analysis supports four generalizations. First, father's behavior represents the principal link between Depression hardship and children's problem behavior. Second, the effect of hard times in the 1930s depended on whether father became more arbitrary and punitive toward the child. Third, such outcomes varied according to what parents and children brought to the deprivational experience, such as rejecting parent attitudes toward child and a conflicted marriage. Fourth, ill-tempered, difficult children are likely to experience a more troubled life course in work, marriage, and parenthood than other children from the Berkeley cohort, but life-span continuity and change depend on many factors.

This investigation of parent–child behavior in the Great Depression began with the premise that influence flows from parent to child and from child to parent. The results provide much evidence to support this premise, but more importantly, they specify conditions under which reciprocal and unidirectional patterns are most likely. The reciprocal model views fathers under economic pressure as more arbitrary and explosive figures who trigger behavior in kind from their children. The child's behavior in turn provokes further abuse from father, thereby perpetuating the punishment cycle. The Berkeley families suggest a more complex picture of parent–child interaction when we consider the different family dynamics at work in relations with friendly and hostile fathers.

Hostile fathers were most likely to become arbitrary under economic deprivation and marital strife, but the behavior of these men was not conditioned by child provocation. The men were primarily responding to their own concerns. A good many responded to economic loss by lashing out at an unliked child. The child thus became a target for maltreatment. Such ''out-of-control'' fathers most closely match Antonovsky's (1979) concept of an ''incoherent'' home environment. In contrast to hostile men, affectively close fathers were not ''out of control'' in the same sense. Their apparent arbitrariness was a response to the child as a problem stimulus. For these men, neither economic loss nor marital strife appreciably altered their behavior as parents. Among the factors examined, only the behavior of a ''problem child'' provoked arbitrary behavior by friendly, concerned fathers.

In the Depression era, mothers also played a major role in their children's development, but it was not strongly influenced by economic hardship. To understand the differing roles of father and mother in the 1930s, it is necessary to order them in relation to the course of economic crisis and family adaptation. Fathers loom very large in this analysis of the Depression crisis for families. Economic misfortune was typically the first-hand misfortune of men or fathers, and their response to this loss often intensified the social consequences of income loss. Examples include social withdrawal and explosiveness, depression, and anger. The behavior of fathers also provided clues as to how some deprived families were able to manage so well in severe hard times. A good many fathers coped effectively with the changes in their lives, and they were often men who displayed resourcefulness (e.g., calm under stress, marital stability) before the economic crisis.

Mothers in Depression families stand out as coping and recovery figures, a phase of the Depression experience which is not covered adequately in the present research. Following the trauma of economic crisis and the impairment or loss of husbands/fathers, the story of family survival is very much the story of women in the household economy, in the labor force, and in the lives of their children. Households became labor intensive under income losses, a change which expanded the women's responsibilites. The disruption and increasingly aimless character of men's lives in hard times were counterbalanced by the increasing family scope and authority of women.

The central issue concerning the Depression's influence is not life-span continuity or change, but rather knowledge of the conditions under which this influence is likely to be more or less enduring. Beginning with facts on the conditional effect of hard times in children's problem behavior, we looked for some long-term consequences of such behavior in three domains of adult life: work, marriage, and parenthood. Child temper outbursts were suggestive of adverse consequences in all three areas. Ill-tempered behavior is not compatible with stable work or marriage or with an even-tempered approach to child discipline. But some conditions lessened this minimal compatibility even more. A case in point is the "irritable" worker under close supervision. We find that men with a record of temper outbursts in childhood were likely to experience an erratic work history, one marked by job losses, status fluctuations, and career breaks, but this connection over time applies primarily to the men in lower status jobs, those with a high level of supervision. Here as elsewhere in the analysis, the results document both life-span continuity and change.

Girls as well as boys from the Depression era carried some imprint of their early behavior problems into major adult roles. Beyond worklife, the problem history of men and women is linked to undesirable outcomes in marriage. Men who were disposed toward temper flare-ups in childhood were less successful than other men in achieving a stable marriage, and women with a "problem past'' were less successful in marrying achievement-oriented men when compared to other women. Men's problem behavior in childhood produced few insights concerning their behavior as parents (reported by children, 1970), though women do show this continuity. Ill-tempered mothers in the descriptions of children generally ranked high on both temper tantrums and difficult behavior in their Depression childhood.

The costs of ill-tempered behavior are one unchanging theme across the generations, from broken relationships to misshapen lives. ''Problem behavior'' represents a multigenerational legacy of the hard times that turned bad in the 1930s, but competence and coping skills are also elements of this picture. Realistic accounts of the Depression's legacy require a concept of people as active agents in the coping process. Both parents and their young children often displayed remarkable stamina and resilience in hard times.

## VII. Appendix A: Confirmatory Model on Child Measures

To test whether the three constructs—tantrums, difficult child, and social introversion—characterize the available behavioral indicators a measurement model was tested with LISREL. Included are the eight behavioral indicators described above for 1933–1935 (see Fig. 4) in which each observed indicator is linked to one and only one construct. In addition, a self-report temper tantrum measure is included from interviews with the child which reflects an independent assessment apart from the interviews with mothers. The three-construct model fits the data in 1933–1935 at the .05 level without any specification of correlated measurement errors. According to the latent correlations, temper tantrums and difficult child behaviors are highly related (.87), and neither bears much relation to social introversion (.11 and .21, respectively). A model in which the tantums and difficult child behaviors were assumed to reflect a single latent construct did not fit the data and the fit was significantly poorer than the model of Fig. 4.

Most indicators across the three constructs are at least moderately reliable. The major exception is self-reported temper outbursts (*standardized factor loading* of .39). At ages 5 through 7, the children were apparently unable to give an accurate report of their own behavior. The same three-factor model also fit the data on child behavior at ages 8 through 10 (not shown here). Only two noteworthy differences emerged. First, self-reported tantrums became more reliable with age of respondent (*factor loading* of .61). Second, the correlations among all constructs were reduced, thus suggesting an age-related process of behavioral differentiation. Tantrums correlate with difficult behavior at only .68 and with introversion at .01. Difficult behavior is unrelated to social introversion, .13.

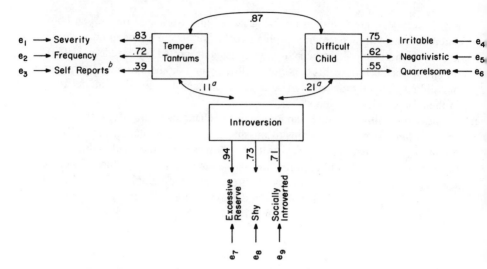

**Fig. 4.** Confirmatory factor analysis of child behavior items at ages 5 to 7 (1933–1935). All measures are the average of three yearly ratings for 1933, 1934, and 1935. If one of these years is missing, the average of the 2 years of available data is used. All coefficients are in standardized form and estimated with LISREL (Jöreskog & Sörbom, 1979). [a]Not significant at .05 level. [b]Clinical rating (five points) based on interview with child only. All other indicators are five-point ratings based on child's interview, direct observation, and interviews with teachers and mothers (Mac-farlane, 1938). $\chi^2(24) = 36.7$, $p = .05$, $N = 110$ (maximum $N$ in covariance matrix, hence $\chi^2/df$ is conservatively stated).

## VIII. Appendix B

Figure 1 depicts a causal process in which the irritability of father during the Depression mediated the effect of family income loss on his arbitrary discipline. The causal order for father irritable and arbitrary is based on empirical evidence which shows that the flow of influence runs from irritable to arbitrary (Liker & Elder, 1983). Theoretical and logical considerations support the same order. Table VI represents the results of an empirical test of this model using two regression equations. In the first model, the effects of socioeconomic influence (income loss and social class, 1929) and pre-Depression conditions (discipline conflicts, father hostility toward child, child's problem behavior) are estimated without father irritability in the equation. The second model includes father irritability.

A comparison of the two models provides modest support for the linking hypothesis. The influence of income loss and discipline conflicts on the arbitrary discipline of father occurs partly through father's irritability. Irritable men were often arbitrary fathers. The main effect of income loss on arbitrary discipline by

**TABLE VI**

**Effects of Economic Loss on Fathers' Arbitrary Discipline, 1933–1935, with Father Irritable as Linking Variable: Regression Coefficients**

| | Influences on fathers' arbitrary discipline, 1933–1935 | | | | | |
|---|---|---|---|---|---|---|
| | Without father irritable | | | With father irritable | | |
| Independent factors | $r$ | $b$ | $\beta$ | $r$ | $b$ | $\beta$ |
| Socioeconomic influence | | | | | | |
| Income loss, 1929 to low year (%) | .32 | .007*** | .23 | .32 | .005* | .16 |
| Social class, 1929[a] (1=low, 5=high) | -.26 | -.13** | -.20 | -.26 | -.13** | -.20 |
| Personality linkage | | | | | | |
| Father irritable, 1933–1935[b] | — | — | — | .40 | .28**** | .33 |
| Pre-Depression conditions, 1930 | | | | | | |
| Discipline conflicts | .45 | .316**** | .37 | .45 | .26*** | .27 |
| Father hostile toward child | .21 | .06 | .06 | .21 | -.04 | -.04 |
| Problem child index | .28 | .01** | .17 | .28 | .01*** | .23 |
| Constant | | 5.50*** | | | 4.20*** | |
| $R^2$ | | .35 | | | .41 | |
| $N$ | | (103) | | | (102) | |

[a] Two-factor Hollingshead index, occupational and educational status of father.
[b] Prior research finds father irritability substantially affected by income loss (Liker & Elder, 1983).
* $p < .10$.
** $p < .05$.
*** $p < .01$.
**** $p < .001$.

father declines by a fourth with father irritable in the model. In the case of discipline conflicts, the decline is only one-tenth.

## Acknowledgments

This study is based on a program of research on social change in the family and life course. Support from the National Institute of Mental Health (Grant MH-34172) and from the National Science Foundation (Grant SES82-08350) is gratefully acknowledged (Glen H. Elder, Jr., principal investigator). We are indebted to Jay Belsky for valuable editorial recommendations and to the Institute of Human Development, University of California, Berkeley for permission to use archival data from the Berkeley Guidance Study.

## References

Antonovsky, A. *Health, stress, and coping.* San Francisco: Jossey Bass, 1979.

Bell, R. Q., & Harper, L. V. *Child effects on adults.* New York: Wiley, 1977.

Belsky, J. The determinants of parenting: A process model. *Child Development,* 1984, **55,** 83–96.

Bernstein, I. *The lean years: A history of the American worker, 1933–1941.* Baltimore: Penguin Books, 1970.

Block, J. *Lives through times.* Berkeley, California: Bancroft, 1971.

Block, J. H., & Block, J. The role of ego-control and ego-resiliency in the organization of behavior. In W. A. Collins (Ed.), *Minnesota symposium on child psychology* (Vol. 13). Hillsdale, New Jersey: Erlbaum, 1980.

Brim, O. G., Jr., & Kagan, J. (Eds.). *Constancy and change in human development.* Cambridge, Massachusetts: Harvard University Press, 1980.

Bronson, W. C. Central orientation: A study of behavior organization from childhood to adolescence. *Child Development,* 1966, **37,** 125–155.

Bryant, H. D. Physical abuse of children: An agency study. *Child Welfare,* 1963, **42,** 125–130.

Burland, A., Andrews, R., & Headston, S. Child abuse: One tree in the forest. *Child Welfare,* 1973, **52,** 535–592.

Coe, R. D., Duncan, G. J., & Hill, M. S. *Dynamic aspects of poverty and welfare use in the United States.* Paper presented at Conference on Problems of Poverty. Clark University, Worcester, Massachusetts, August 1982.

Cottrell, L. S., Jr. Interpersonal interaction and the development of the self. In D. A. Goslin (Ed.), *Handbook of socialization theory and research.* Chicago: Rand McNally, 1969.

Eichorn, D. H., Clausen, J. A., Haan, N., Honzik, M. P., & Mussen, P. H. (Eds.). *Present and past in middle life.* New York: Academic Press, 1981.

Elder, G. H., Jr. *Children of the Great Depression.* Chicago: University of Chicago Press, 1974.

Elder, G. H., Jr. Historical change in life patterns and personality. In P. B. Baltes & O. G. Brim, Jr. (Eds.), *Life-span development and behavior* (Vol. 2). New York: Academic Press, 1979.

Elder, G. H., Jr. *Family structure and socialization.* New York: Arno Press, 1980.

Elder, G. H., Jr. Historical experience in later life. In T. K. Hareven (Ed.), *Aging and life course transitions.* New York: Guilford, 1982.

Elder, G. H., Jr. (Ed.). *Life course dynamics: From 1968 to the 1980s.* Ithaca, New York: Cornell University Press, 1984, in press.

Elder, G. H., Jr., & Liker, J. K. Hard times in women's lives: Historical influences across 40 years. *American Journal of Sociology,* 1982, **88,** 241–269.

Elder, G. H., Jr., Liker, J. K., & Jaworski, B. J. Hard times in lives: Historical influences from the 1930's to old age in postwar America. In *Life-span developmental psychology: Historical and cohort effects*. New York: Academic Press, 1984, in press.

Featherman, D. The life-span perspective in social science research. In *The Five-Year Outlook on Science and Technology, 1981 Source Materials* (Vol. 2, pp. 621–648). Washington, D.C.: National Science Foundation, Superintendent of Documents, 1982.

Finkelhor, D., Gelles, R. J., Hotaling, G. T., & Straus, M. A. (Eds.). *The dark side of families: Current family violence research*. Beverly Hills, California: Sage Publ., 1983.

Furstenberg, F. F., Jr. *Unplanned parenthood: The social consequences of teenage childbearing*. New York: Free Press, 1976.

Garbarino, J. Some ecological correlates of child abuse: The impact of socioeconomic stress on mothers. *Child Development*, 1976, **47**, 178–185.

Gil, D. G. *Violence against children: Physical abuse in the United States*. Cambridge, Massachusetts: Harvard University Press, 1970.

Gottman, J. M. *Marital interaction*. New York: Academic Press, 1979.

Herrenkohl, E. C., & Herrenkohl, R. C. A comparison of abused children and their non-abused siblings. *Journal of the American Academy of Child Psychiatry*, 1979, **18**, 260–270.

Hinde, R. A. *Towards understanding relationships*. New York: Academic Press, 1979.

Jöreskog, K. G., & Sörbom, D. *Advances in factor analysis and structural equation models*. Cambridge, Massachusetts: Abt Associates, 1979.

Kadushin, A. K., & Martin, J. A. *Child abuse: An interactional event*. New York: Columbia University Press, 1981.

Kessler, R. C. Life events, social support, and mental health. In W. R. Gove (Ed.), *Deviance and mental illness*. Beverly Hills, California: Sage Publ., 1982.

Kohn, M. L. *Class and conformity: A study in values* (2nd ed.). Chicago: University of Chicago Press, 1977.

Lamb, M. E. Fathers: Forgotten contributions to child development. *Human Development*, 1975, **18**, 245–266.

Lamb, M. E. (Ed.). *The role of the father in child development*. New York: Wiley, 1981.

Lerner, R. M., & Spanier, G. P. (Eds.). *Child influences on marital and family interactions*. New York: Academic Press, 1978.

Leventman, P. G. *Professionals out of work*. New York: Free Press, 1981.

Light, R. Abused and neglected children in America: A study of alternative policies. *Harvard Educational Review*, 1973, **43**, 556–598.

Liker, J. K., & Elder, G. H., Jr. Economic hardship and marital relations in the 1930's. *American Sociological Review*, 1983, **48**, 343–359.

Locke, H. J. *Predicting adjustment in marriage*. New York: Holt, 1951.

Maccoby, E. The development of moral values and behavior in childhood. In J. A. Clausen (Ed.), *Socialization and society*. Boston: Little, Brown, 1968.

Macfarlane, J. W. Studies in child guidance I: Methodology of data collection and organization. *Monographs of the Society for Research in Child Development*, 1938, 3 (Ser. No. 6).

Macfarlane, J. W., Allen, L., & Honzik, M. P. *A developmental study of the behavior problems of normal children between twenty-one months and fourteen years*. Berkeley: University of California Press, 1954.

Moen, P., Kain, E. L., & Elder, G. H., Jr. Economic conditions and family life: Contemporary and historical perspectives. In R. Nelson & F. Skidmore (Eds.), *American families and the economy: The high costs of living*. Washington, D.C.: National Academy Press, 1983.

Moss, H. A., & Susman, E. J. Longitudinal study of personality development. In O. G. Brim, Jr. & J. Kagan (Eds.), *Constancy and change in human development*. Cambridge, Massachusetts: Harvard University Press, 1980.

Nelson, R. R., & Skidmore, F. (Eds.). *American families and the economy: The high costs of living.* Washington, D.C.: National Academy Press, 1983.

Olweus, D. Development of stable aggressive reaction patterns in males. In R. Blanchard & D. C. Blanchard (Eds.), *Advances in the study of aggression* (Vol. 1). New York: Academic Press, 1984, in press.

Osofsky, J. D., & Conners, K. Mother–infant interaction: An integrative view of a complex system. In J. D. Osofsky (Ed.), *Handbook of infant development.* New York: Wiley, 1979.

Parke, R. D. Perspectives on father–infant interaction. In J. D. Osofsky (Ed.), *Handbook of infant development.* New York: Wiley, 1979.

Patterson, G. R. Mothers: The unacknowledged victims. *Monographs of the Society for Research in Child Development,* 1980, **45** (5, Ser. No. 186).

Patterson, G. R. *Coercive family process: A social learning approach.* Eugene, Oregon: Castalia Publ., 1982.

Patterson, G. R. Stress: A change agent for family process. In N. Garmezy & M. Rutter (Eds.), *Stress, coping, and development in children.* New York: McGraw-Hill, 1983.

Pulkkinen, L. Self-control and continuity from childhood to late adolescence. In P. B. Baltes & O. G. Brim, Jr. (Eds.), *Life-span development and behavior,* Vol. 4. New York: Academic Press, 1982.

Robins, L. *Deviant children grown up.* Baltimore, Maryland: Williams & Wilkins, 1966.

Rutter, M. *Changing youth in a changing society.* Cambridge, Massachusetts: Harvard University Press, 1980.

Straus, M. A., Gelles, R. J., & Steinmetz, S. K. *Behind closed doors.* New York: Anchor Books, 1980.

Tavris, C. *Anger: The misunderstood emotion.* New York: Simon & Schuster, 1982.

Thomas, A., & Chess, S. *Temperament and development.* New York: Brunner/Mazel, 1977.

Thomas, A., Chess, S., & Birch, H. G. *Temperament and behavior disorders in children.* New York: New York University Press, 1969.

Vaillant, G. E. Natural history of male psychological health: II. Some antecedents of healthy adult adjustment. *Archives of General Psychiatry,* 1974, **31**, 15–22.

Wilensky, H. L. Orderly careers and social participation: The impact of work history on the social integration of the middle mass. *American Sociological Review,* 1961, **26**, 521–539.

Young, L. *Wednesday's children: A study of child neglect and abuse.* New York: McGraw-Hill, 1964.

# Entry into Adulthood:
# Profiles of Young Men in the 1950s

*David L. Featherman*

UNIVERSITY OF WISCONSIN

MADISON, WISCONSIN


*Dennis P. Hogan*

UNIVERSITY OF CHICAGO

CHICAGO, ILLINOIS


*and*


*Aage B. Sørensen*

HARVARD UNIVERSITY

CAMBRIDGE, MASSACHUSETTS

**159**

## Abstract

The years of adolescence and early adulthood are a time of transition for American males involving changes in place of residence, school enrollment, labor force participation, military service, marriage, and procreation. Changes involving each state may occur more than once, and many of these changes are reversible. The timing of these changes is age graded, and different state-to-state transitions are linked so that certain changes ordinarily occur simultaneously or sequentially. However, these patterns differ among individuals and have changed over time.

Previous research on the patterns of early life activities and the timing and sequencing of changes in these activities has been hampered by (1) an inability to identify every change occurring in a state, (2) the exclusion of relevant states, (3) models of individual behavior that oversimplify the early life course, and (4) the use of synthetic cohort data instead of true longitudinal data for birth cohorts.

The research reported here represents a first step in overcoming these problems. The study uses retrospective life history data from the 1968 Hopkins Life Circumstances Study of American men born 1929–1939. For each month of age from ages 14 to 29 men are classified according to their school enrollment (enrolled/not enrolled), labor force participation (not working/working), military service (on active duty/not on active duty), marital status (unmarried/married), and parenthood (no children in the household/children in the household). These monthly data provide age-specific information on the person-months spent in each state and in combinations of states. The results are presented by birth cohort (1929–1934 vs 1935–1939), by race (white vs black), and by social class (father's occupation) origins (white collar vs blue collar or farm).

This research identifies the age-graded, statistically typical behaviors associated with adolescence and early adulthood. Combinations of activities that are rare are identified as atypical. Data on the usual age-graded patterns of behaviors provide a baseline against which future research can identify persons who are relatively early or late in their state-to-state transitions, or whose transitions are out of sequence. Appropriate strategies for the analysis of age-grading (nonstationarity and interindividual) differences (heterogeneity) in rates of transition events are discussed.

## I. Introduction

The early adult lives of American men are structured by their contacts with a variety of societal institutions. Schools, the Armed Forces, labor markets and career lines, and families provide examples. The patternings of school enrollment, labor force attachment, active military service, marriage, parenting, and residence are demographic markers in the life histories of men making the transition from adolescence to adulthood. These activities are age graded insofar as they conform to a relatively predictable schedule according to age. The extent of age grading in these transitions varies historically so that successive cohorts may not experience the same degree of age-related coherence and predictability in life events. Within a given cohort, all social groups (e.g., races, social classes) need not manifest the same pattern or pace of events across the life cycle.

The age grading of events over the life span has been a subject of increased attention by scholars in biology, psychology, social psychology, sociology, and anthropology. These multidisciplinary interests reflect the varied sources of age grading of life events. These sources include individual-level variables such as biological maturation and aspects of psychological functioning which define patterns of change in personality. Age grading also results from the use of age as an organizing principle by social institutions (e.g., schools, labor markets). While age grading is a pervasive societal phenomenon, considerable interindividual variability in age grading results from social change and variability in growth and development patterns associated with biological and psychological variables.

In this article we report statistical profiles of the age-graded timing of activities in each of several life domains among men becoming adults. Two cohorts born between 1929 and 1939 are compared to illuminate historical shifts. Differentials by race and social class are examined. Aside from the construction of a demographic history of these cohorts, the data provide a statistical portrait from which inferences about life-span development may be drawn (e.g., Clausen, 1972; Hagestad & Neugarten, 1984; Spanier & Glick, 1980).

## II. Background

Childhood, adolescence, and adulthood are commonly referred to as age-defined states. However, interindividual variation in the age boundaries of these states means that they usually are defined by a set of expectations regarding the roles and activities of individuals at each developmental level. In this article we are interested in interindividual variation in the age boundaries of these states. We define adolescence and adulthood by reference to the roles and activities of individuals in order to measure variations in the timing of adulthood.

Following social conventions, adolescence is taken to mean that a person is living with his family of origin, is unmarried, without children, enrolled in school, and not in the labor force. Adulthood is defined as living in one's own household, not enrolled in school, in the labor force, and (commonly) married with one or more children. The passage to adulthood consists of the state-to-state transitions which result in simultaneously being out of school, at work, living in one's own household, married, and the father of one or more children.

The social definition of adulthood as consisting of these developmental states is based on quite loose normative expectations rather than any rigidly applied criteria. This reflects several aspects of the states used to define adulthood. First, all of these states can be left as well as entered. Entering adulthood therefore usually is taken to mean first entry into the various states. Still, temporary sojourns are usually disregarded, as in the case of a teenage marriage of brief duration or a temporary stay away from home. Second, while the societal conception emphasizes the simultaneous occupancy of the various states, that is a normative expectation that for some is never realized (e.g., some adults remain single and/or childless). Third, the set of states that are used to define adulthood may vary over time and by culture. Different defining states may be applied to different population groups within the same society (for example, labor force entry has traditionally not been considered an essential aspect of women's transition to adulthood).

The process through which adolescents become adults may be characterized in several ways. First, to what extent are the component activities (and transitions between activities) age dependent or age graded? Second, to what extent are the various activities (and changes therein) synchronized (i.e., how closely are they spaced in time)? Third, to what extent is a particular order of transitions followed? Following such a description of the timing, synchronization, and sequencing of transitions, it is natural to identify characteristics associated with variations in these aspects of behavior.

The empirical part of this article describes the age-graded patterns of state distributions considered singly and in combination, rather than the transitions that produce these state distributions. As background for this empirical analysis we review the main mechanisms that may be assumed to cause variations in the timing, synchronization, and sequencing of transitions productive of age-graded patterns of life domains. As mentioned in Section I, life events in general may be seen as the result of an interplay among biological, psychological, and social structural variables. However, societal rather than individual-level variables appear most relevant for the life domains (activities) that are the subject of this article (Elder, 1984; Featherman, 1984a; Riley, 1984).

The age stratification model developed by Riley and associates (Riley, Johnson, & Foner, 1972; Riley 1976, 1984) draws attention to the age-graded character of roles and behaviors. Social expectations define the responsibilities and perquisites of incumbents in these age strata. The normative conception of adulthood as consisting of specified activities is a particular instance of this general pattern of age stratification. Thus, normative expectations arising from the American age stratification system may regulate the timing, synchronization, and sequencing of the various transitions to adult activities.

Empirical research documenting such normative expectations is quite limited (cf. Elder, 1974; Hagestad & Neugarten, 1984). Research with nonrandom samples of the population has indicated consensus about the appropriate chronological age ranges for life events, age ranges outside of which persons are either early or late (Neugarten, Moore, & Lowe, 1965). There appears to be considerable consensus about the timing of early life transitions. For example, a variety of groups in the population are able to specify appropriate age ranges for marriage, and most population groups adhere to the idea that couples should be economically self-sufficient at the time of marriage (Modell, 1980). However, these normative expectations differ among population groups and have changed over time (Fallo-Mitchell & Ryff, 1982; Modell, 1980). The behavior of American men displays a tendency to delay marriage until formal schooling is completed, but conformity to this typical pattern varies considerably for social groups and birth cohorts (Hogan, 1978, 1980; Winsborough, 1979).

Little is known about the sources of normative expectations regarding the youth-to-adult transitions. Such norms may reflect what is or has been typical behavior in middle-class and upper middle-class segments of society.[1] Also, norms appear to conform to the conventions of the market economy and intergenerational exchanges of economic resources which presuppose economic self-sufficiency for family formation. These bases of normative expectations change over time and differ among places, suggesting that norms about the temporal patterning of early life events are malleable.

The ability to achieve the simultaneous occupancy of states that define adulthood, to do so at the proper times, and to enter the states in the right order pose problems of coordination and adaptation for individuals and for social systems (Foner & Kertzer, 1978). Social structure and social institutions create constraints and opportunities for realizing adult status in the proper manner (Elder, 1984). Variation in these constraints and opportunities may in turn be seen as a major cause of variation in the timing, synchronization, and sequencing of the transitions to adulthood.

Norms regarding economic independence as a condition for marriage and parenthood point to the major role of economic independence in the timing of adulthood. Economic independence is partly a function of the general economic conditions in society. Delays in achieving economic independence postpone the overall achievement of adult status, and may affect the synchronization of transitions by spacing the various transitions more widely. Delays in achieving economic independence may also force the violation of norms about the timing of family formation (among those who postpone marriage in response to prolonged economic dependence) or norms about the sequencing of transitions (for those who marry at the normatively expected age despite the absence of economic emancipation).

Major social institutions modify the impact of economic conditions on youth-to-adult transitions. Schools, colleges, and universities are of major importance

[1]Indeed, the scientific writings on the subject frequently equate statistically typical or modal behaviors with normatively expected behaviors. While behaviors may, in fact, show statistical regularities as a result of conformity to normative expectations, this usage needlessly obscures essential distinctions (Hagestad & Neugarten, 1984). Normative expectations involve societal preferences, with positive and negative sanctions to enforce conformity by members of the society (Parsons, 1951). Statistical regularities in the temporal patterns of life events may arise as a result of the age-graded nature of individual contacts with institutions, individual preferences, or patterns of biological and psychological development.

in this regard. Schooling constrains a person's ability to engage in other activities and therefore usually imposes economic dependence. Leaving school is for this reason expected to be the first in the series of transitions into adult status. The timing of school leaving depends on economic resources (of the family of origin) and numerous other factors. These include the social and cultural variables that determine educational attainments (Featherman & Hauser, 1978). The organizing principles of schools also assume tremendous importance. For example, the greater diversity in school leaving age in traditional European educational systems should create differences in the transition to adulthood compared to the United States, where more comprehensive schooling is associated with greater uniformity in age at completion of formal education.

Labor market institutions impose opportunities and constraints on early life transitions. Labor markets structure career trajectories on the basis of firm and industry organization (Schrank & Waring, 1983; Spenner, Otto, & Cole, 1982; Spilerman, 1977). Career trajectories sometimes involve on-the-job training arrangements (as in apprenticeship systems), frequent job changes involving geographic moves (as in managerial positions in some large corporations), or the need to acquire capital (farmland or equipment) or clientele (legal and medical practices). Each of these aspects of career trajectories may delay the achievement of some adult statuses. Indeed, such an idea is the basis for the hypothesis that the prospects for improved occupational mobility are better for men who delay marriage and fatherhood (Blau & Duncan, 1967).

The military is an institution of particular importance for the timing of early life transitions for American males in the twentieth century. For many men service in the Armed Forces is involuntary (as a result of military conscription), and, because the wars and military manpower requirements are not fully predictable, the timing of military service often is subject to limited personal control. Since participation in military service, and its timing, are highly variable over time and across population subgroups, military service is a readily identified cause of variation in early life transitions.

Finally, governmental programs have impacts on the temporal structure of life events through their impact on educational institutions, the economy, and the Armed Forces. In addition, government social welfare policies may provide incentives or disincentives for marriage, parenthood, and independent residence in the absence of economic independence.

Thus, we expect that general economic conditions are important for the timing of entry into adulthood. This impact is modified and mediated by other social institutions such as schools, labor markets, the military, and government assistance programs. Further, we expect that the synchronization and sequencing of transitions are affected by these same forces, primarily through those variables that delay entering adulthood. The latter hinder the synchronization and proper sequencing of transitions because of the incompatability of the need for economic independence with the norms regarding the proper age grading of these events.

There is some empirical evidence for several of these hypotheses. Modell, Furstenberg, and Herschberg (1976) analyzed census manuscripts for late nineteenth century Philadelphia and public use sample data from the 1970 census to describe historical change in the transition to adulthood. Their research indicated that over the past century early life transitions have become more prevalent or uniformly experienced, and more age graded, with a narrowing of the typical age ranges for each transition. Transitions pertaining to entry into the economy (completion of school and beginning of work) have become more congruent with transitions relating to the formation of family of procreation (i.e., marriage, childbearing, and residence apart from family of orientation), narrowing the overall length of time needed to achieve adult status. The emerging connection of schooling to placement in the industrial work force, and the age grading of school matriculation, are crucial to the emergence of this new pattern of age grading of early life transitions (Featherman, 1980b).

Among men born during the twentieth century, there was considerable intercohort variability in temporal patterning of early life transitions (Hogan, 1981; Winsborough, 1978). This variability resulted from the intercohort upgradings of educational attainment, as well as the unique combination of historical circumstances (i.e., wartime or peacetime, prosperity or depression) experienced by each cohort. Cohorts undergoing the transition to adulthood during a period of peacetime and economic prosperity tend to prolong their human capital investment in education, delay beginning their first full-time jobs, and marry relatively early. During favorable economic circumstances, cohorts finish their schooling and enter the labor force relatively early, but delay marriage until relatively late. Men serving on active duty in the Armed Forces are more likely to experience disorderly transitions to adulthood, since military service often interrupts schooling and/or civilian occupational careers (Hogan, 1981).

The hypotheses of a historical nature concerning the impact of economic conditions, and the modifying and mediating influences of schooling and labor market conditions, all predict variation by social structural variables. Abundant evidence exists for strong differences by social class of origin in school leaving age, time of entry into the labor force, and age at marriage (Hogan, 1981). However, little evidence is available on the variation in the synchronization and sequencing of transitions by positions in social structure, or on how problems of adaptation and coordination of life events are resolved by different groups. On the latter point, Hogan (1981) shows that among men who graduated from college, those who were from lower social classes or smaller communities were more likely to experience interruptions in their schooling, had relatively late ages at school completion, and were more likely to work and/or marry prior to completing formal schooling.

## III. Shortcomings in Previous Research

The relationships of historical circumstances and subgroup membership to the timing, synchronization, and sequencing of early life transitions are not understood fully. Besides the problematic logical and empirical status of normative considerations, previous studies of behaviors have been hampered by limitations of the data analyzed and methods used. These shortcomings include the exclusion of relevant life domains, an inability to identify the timing of every transition occurring in a domain (e.g., the use of data on the first or more recent transition), and the use of age-specific data from a single period for synthetic cohort analyses (ignoring the pronounced intercohort changes in the temporal patterning of early life events).

Continuous-time life history data are required to overcome these problems. As event history records the exact *times* of *all* changes in some domain of interest during a specified period. Except for laboratory studies in which continuous observation of the subject is possible, event histories are necessarily retrospective. However, the length of the recall period may vary, with shorter periods ordinarily associated with more accurate recall (Featherman, 1980a; Hannan & Tuma, 1979). Event histories collected for a complete set of domains of interest generally are referred to as life histories. Life histories enable the researchers to identify (1) the status of individuals on each domain at a particular time (date or age), (2) the length of time spent in each domain from time of entry (or first observation) to time of exit (or last observation), (3) the date of occurrence of each state-to-state transition for a domain, and (4) the linkages of these three types of measures across domains.

## IV. Objectives

In this article we present a statistical portrait of adolescence and early adulthood using retrospective life history data for cohorts of American men born in 1929–1939. For each month of age from the fourteenth to the thirtieth birthday, men are classified according to their school enrollment (enrolled in a degree program/not enrolled), employment (not employed at a full-time job/employed), military service (on active duty/not on active duty), residence (living with family of orientation/living apart from family of orientation), marital status (unmarried/married), and parenthood (no children living in household/children living in household). These monthly "time-use" figures are summed to provide data on the amount of time spent in each state during each year of age. These data provide profiles of states (statistical "careers") within each of the life domains, describing how the cohort spent the years from ages 14 to 29. When such profiles are constructed for all domains, it is possible to characterize the members of the cohorts as to age-specific patterns of synchronization of domains.

This aggregate time-use analysis will permit us to characterize each year of age in terms of the mix of person-years in each domain, with the aim of identifying the age-graded patterns of behavior during adolescence and early adulthood. Age-graded patterns of combinations of activities across domains also will be identified. Activities and combinations of activities which are common at each age are statistically "normative" behaviors, and those that are rare are identified as atypical or statistically "nonnormative" behaviors. As discussed above, the timing and synchronization of activities are expected to vary between cohorts (to the extent their social histories differ) and among population subgroups. We therefore present the results of this analysis by birth cohort (1929/1933 vs 1934/1939), race (nonblack vs black), and father's occupation (white collar vs blue collar/farm) as an index of social class origin.

This method provides accurate descriptive data by which we can characterize the early lives of historically unique (see below) birth cohorts as they made the transition from adolescence to adulthood. Such descriptions are in the tradition of, but represent an improvement on, the research of Modell *et al.* (1976), Winsborough (1978), Sweet (1979), and Hogan (1978, 1981). However, this method does not show directly the rate of state-to-state transitions at various ages, but rather the distributions among states that result from these transitions. This means that our results may confound variations in rates of entering states with rates of leaving them.

As discussed below, the analysis of transition rates provides all of the information obtained with other analytic methods since the transition rates determine all other aspects of life histories (Tuma, Hannan, & Groeneveld, 1979). We believe that the preparation of statistical profiles of the early adult years represents an important first step in understanding the transition to adulthood. The information so obtained provides an empirical basis for decisions about the appropriate event history model specifications (e.g., what transitions occur with sufficient frequency and are persistent enough to merit attention, what linkages among transitions are worthy of further analysis, what classes of variables are probable independent variables associated with heterogeneity in transition rates, whether the age grading of states suggests nonstationarity in the transition rates).

## V. Hypotheses

Men from lower status social origins (farm or blue collar backgrounds) and blacks have lower educational attainments (Featherman & Hauser, 1978). We anticipate that these men will spend fewer person-years enrolled in school between ages 14 and 29. Men with lesser educational attainments enter the labor force earlier, and have somewhat earlier ages at marriage and shorter birth intervals (Coombs & Freedman, 1970; Hogan, 1981). Therefore, we expect the men from lower status family backgrounds and blacks to spend a greater proportion of their ages 14 to 29 employed at full-time jobs, and married, with one or more children living in their household.

Men from lower social status origins face greater difficulties in financing advanced schooling than those from higher social origins, since they cannot depend on as much economic support from their parental families. The available evidence suggests that blue collar men enrolled in school more frequently obtain financial support through employment or by marriage to a working wife (Hogan, 1981). We test this hypothesis about social class differences in the synchronization of education, work, and marriage.

As discussed below, men born 1929/1933 were more likely to serve in the military than men born 1934/1939. Therefore, we anticipate that more of the early adult lives of men from these earlier cohorts were spent in the military service, whereas they were enrolled in school or working full time at a civilian job for fewer years. Because high rates of military service prolong the period of school enrollment of birth cohorts (since some men return to school following military service), we expect that we may find somewhat higher rates of school enrollment at ages 23 and older among men born 1929/1933.

Aside from the descriptive goals of our analysis we seek an understanding of how and when age becomes a relatively more (or less) important basis of social organization. That is, we are searching for insights into the historical and societal antecedents of trend in the age grading of the life course. Age grading is viewed as a societal mechanism that schedules the access to and demands on social positions and the status rewards that accrue to incumbency in these positions (see Featherman, 1984b; Riley, 1976; Riley *et al.*, 1972).

To be sure, the data we analyze are not well suited to a broad historical analysis (because of the restricted historical range of the cohorts). At the same time they do permit us to explore several hypotheses about subgroup differentials that are derived from other historical research. For example, Modell *et al.* (1976) suggest that the trend toward a more compact age-graded transition into adulthood for American men after the middle nineteenth century was one consequence of specific institutional changes connected with industrialization and urbanization of the population and economy. We think it is equally likely that generally rising levels of family and personal income could have led to a similar outcome in life-course patterns [Modell *et al.* (1976) suggests as much]. Subpopulations at various locations in the socioeconomic hierarchy (e.g., white collar vs blue collar/farm occupational classes; whites vs blacks) displaying different patterns of age grading could be interpreted as evidence for the "rising affluence—greater discretion in timing" interpretation of trend. A more uniform pattern of age grading across these socioeconomic groups might be more in line with the broad industrialization/urbanization argument.

In any case, we expect that white males and the men from white collar backgrounds will evidence a more "modern" life-course timetable. That is, their life events within domains should be more predictable by age and manifest less variability across persons than in the instances of the less privileged subpopulations.

## VI. The Social Context of Development for Men Born 1929 to 1939

The cohort profiles of age grading we describe refer to a historically interesting and much-studied cohort of American men. The cohorts of 1929/1939 were born during the Great Depression, and were aged 2 to 12 at the beginning of World War II. These men completed their educations, entered the labor force, and began their families of procreation during the postwar period of prosperity. At the time the men born 1929/1933 were ages 16 to 20, the average unemployment rate was 4.2%, the average annual real growth in per capita GNP was 3.6%, and the average annual change in the Consumer Price Index was 3.8%. When men born 1934/1939 were age 16 to 20, the average unemployment rate was similar (4.3%), the annual real growth in per capita GNP somewhat slower (2.8%), and the average annual change in the Consumer Price Index was only 1.3% (United States Bureau of the Census, 1975).

The cohorts of men born 1929–1939 were relatively small compared to earlier birth cohorts. During the years the 1929/1933 cohort was age 16–20, the average number of persons age 15–29 was 55.2% as large as the number of persons age 30–64. For the cohort of 1934/1939, this figure was 50.3%. The comparable figure was an average of 63.3% among persons born 1907–1928 and 57.2% among persons born 1940–1952. Thus, the 1929/1939 cohorts had relatively few competitors among persons from earlier cohorts. This situation provided these men with a favorable demographic context for their transition to adulthood.

Due to the outbreak of the Korean War many of the men born 1929/1939 served on active duty in the Armed Forces. The experiences of men in these cohorts differ according to their age at the time of the Korean War. Whereas two-thirds (66.4%–67.7%) of the men born 1929–1932 served in the military, 60.4% of the 1933 cohort, 57.4% of the 1934 cohort, 53.7% of the 1935 cohort, and 44.8–48.5% of the cohorts of the 1936–1939 served in the military (Hogan, 1981, Table 3.3).

A number of researchers have argued that the placement of these cohorts in this uniquely favorable historical context, coupled with its small size, have marked it as an analytically important case for studying how structural features of the economy, population, and society affect the economic and family life courses of individuals (Easterlin, 1978; Elder, 1974). Rossi (1980) has observed that men from these cohorts have provided the life histories from which Gould (1978), Levinson (1978), and Vaillant (1977) have formulated various theories about adult development. None of these studies purports to rest on a representative cross-section of American men; neither do any of these analysts of adult development recognize the potentially important implications of the unique cohort characteristics and histories of the male subjects of inquiry. We comment below on the implications of this ahistorical oversight, but suffice it to say that our descriptive profiles are useful in putting the life courses of this analyzed group of men in perspective. The profiles gain additional value when used as an historical benchmark for the experiences of the subsequent baby-boom cohorts— the children of the 1929/1939 cohorts—who now are in or have recently completed this same life cycle transition into adulthood.


## VII. Data

The data are drawn from the Hopkins Life Circumstances Study (hereafter, HOPKINS) which recorded retrospective life histories for men aged 30–39 in 1968. The life histories included information on the educational, occupational, familial, and residential experiences of these men (born 1929–1939) from age 14 to the time of interview. All life events resulting in a change of state (for example, a new job or a change in marital status) of more than 1 month were registered by month and year of occurrence. Thus, the onset and termination dates of all states are known. HOPKINS also obtained information on the social, economic, and family backgrounds of all respondents.

The HOPKINS sample consisted of two components: (1) a national probability sample of all men, and (2) a supplementary national sample of black men. The survey fieldwork resulted in completed personal interviews with 851 whites and 738 blacks, for a total of 1589 survey respondents. Completion rates were 76.1% in the sample of all men and 78.2% in the supplementary sample of black men.

Because the life histories of individuals are complex, HOPKINS generated an enormous amount of information. This information is stored in a variable length record for each respondent that contains family background information and other constant characteristics of the respondent, an index to the life history which provides information on the number and timing of events in each area of activity, and, finally, information on each of the events.[2]

It appears that in almost all cases detailed and consistent descriptions of the life histories of the survey respondents were obtained. However, we discovered that coding errors had not been completely eliminated from the files. (These

---

[2]A special retrieval program, described in Karweit (1972), was developed by the HOPKINS investigators to permit the creation of analysis files from the life history data. The version of this program available at the Center for Demography and Ecology of the University of Wisconsin–Madison (named FETCH) was used to access the HOPKINS data for this research. (A variety of modifications to FETCH were necessary in order to facilitate the generation of the monthly domain activities analyzed here.)

errors become apparent in examining the sequencing of events.) For example, in the educational file several respondents have the same events recorded twice, or even their whole histories double reported, thereby increasing the number of events and preventing a clear definition of educational activity in some calendar months.

In reports of events in which the respondent failed to provide the month of the event, the missing data had been allocated to the midpoint of the calendar year by the HOPKINS investigators. This resulted in the heaping of transition points in the assignment of calendar months. The HOPKINS file was designed to permit the identification of allocated dates for many of the relevant domains. Of the 13,342 full-time employment events reported, 426 (3.1%) of the dates were allocated. Of 12,215 household composition events, 2914 (23.8%) were allocated. Of 4994 events involving children, 202 (4.0%) were allocated. Allocated dates on changes in education (7098 events) and marital status (2152 events) are not identifiable.

We edited the necessary data before carrying out our analysis, but the editing procedures were in some cases necessarily arbitrary since we did not have access to the original questionnaires. All coding errors were removed. Missing dates were reallocated according to the following procedures. In cases where the year of an event was missing, it was not possible to ascertain the experience of a man for that year and that domain. In such cases, the undefined experience of a man for that domain during the year in question was excluded from consideration in our analysis. In other cases, the year of an event is known, but the month of the transition had been allocated. In these cases, we first identified the patterning of event dates across months for each domain using only nonallocated data. A random procedure assigned months to missing dates, with the probability of a month being assigned directly proportional to its frequency of occurrence in the nonallocated data for that domain. This procedure has the advantage of eliminating heaping in the event dates of each domain considered singly. It has the potential disadvantage of randomly eliminating synchronization tendencies among domains with missing dates.

The oversample of blacks must be taken into account in the preparation of population estimates for the blacks and whites combined. Therefore, the probabilities of selection for blacks and whites under the sampling design of HOPKINS were used to calculate sampling weights for the cases. These weights were applied to the data in order to obtain unbiased population estimates of the experiences of the total population of blacks and whites combined. Where the results of our analysis are presented separately for the black and white populations, it was not necessary to weight the data.[3]

---

[3]In the course of employing the documented sampling weights for whites and blacks in HOPKINS, we discovered that errors had been committed in their construction through failure of the National Opinion Research Center (NORC) to enumerate the target populations appropriately. Back-

The HOPKINS study employed a cross-sectional strategy of data collection (i.e., a one-occasion interview) to retrospectively gather continuous longitudinal data. The problems of reliability and validity of retrospective data are well known (Bumpass & Westoff, 1970; Knodel & Piampiti, 1977; Potter, 1977). Featherman (1980a) has argued that such a strategy of research is both cost efficient and scientifically preferable to prospective panel designs for many inquiries. Indeed for some analytic purposes retrospective techniques are the only ones available. Featherman arrived at this conclusion by casting the trustworthiness of retrospective reports in relative terms: How valid are these data in relation to the reliability of contemporaneous reports? This statement of the issue in relative terms makes sense when the pertinence of the question is one of a choice between a long-term commitment to follow up one or more cohorts via successive interviews and a one-occasion retrospective design.

## VIII. Procedures

The HOPKINS data on activities within key life-course domains were analyzed to determine the monthly activities of all study respondents. These monthly activity data were summed to obtain the total months of each activity for individual respondents at each year of age. We then calculated the mean person-months of time these men spent in each domain by single years of age. These means provide a measure of the intensity of each activity by age. The total person-months spent in an activity from ages 14 to 29 measures the average volume of the activity during adolescence and early adulthood. Within each year of age, the standard deviation of the person-months spent in an activity was calculated to provide an indication of interindividual variability in the allocation of time to that state at that age. A small standard deviation indicates few differences among persons in regard to the time allocated to an activity; a large standard deviation indicates considerable variability (substantial differences) among individuals in their allocation of time to a particular activity.

As a crude measure of age grading, we calculate the coefficient of variation of months of time spent in each life domain over the 16 years. This measure (defined as the ratio of the standard deviation of the annual person-years in each domain to the mean figure for the 16 years between ages 14 and 29) measures the

---

ground data kindly provided by the current Director and the Librarian of NORC enabled us to track the source of the error to the loss of representativeness of the "master sample" based on a 1960 updating of a 1950 sampling frame that NORC used for this and other surveys during the late 1960s. Consequently, we recomputed a set of post hoc weights for sample elements, based on a race by age by region of residence table, deriving the weights in order to match population totals as estimated in the March 1968 Current Population Survey. Reweighting the data for time use by these post hoc computations made no appreciable difference in the outcome of the analysis we report here.

extent to which the distribution of time in each activity is unequally distributed over the duration. The coefficient has a minimum value of 0 (in the instance of equal person-months) spent in a domain at each year of age), with larger numbers indicating higher levels of variation and commensurately greater age grading.

In the analysis we examine a variety of life domains. The definitions for these domains were designed to delimit the activity of individuals at a given point in time. These definitions were intended to provide maximum information about integration into the roles and activities of the adult world. Each variable was conceptualized as being reversible from 1 month to the next, so that current activity (rather than a status based on a past action) was distinguished.

Any month in which a man is enrolled in a program of education (whether full time or part time) which is degree oriented is counted as a month in school. Any man working at a full-time job (35 or more hours per week) during a month is counted as working. Military service is defined as active duty in the Armed Forces. A person is counted as experiencing a month of marriage if he is currently married during a month (persons who are single, separated by marital discord, divorced, or widowed are treated as unmarried). A man who is head of a household with children present during a month is defined as parenting during that month, regardless of the biological relationship to the child. Being the biological father of a child living in a different household is not counted as parenting.

We attempted to define a sixth life domain—residence with family of origin—without success. Two sorts of HOPKINS data could be used in the definition of this variable. Information from the fixed record data file included the date the respondent "left home." These data have the disadvantage of defining an irreversible status. With such a variable, men who leave home and then return to live with their parents are either misclassified during their period away from home or their later return home is missed. The life history data collected in HOPKINS ascertained members of the household in which respondents lived. Respondents living with one or both of their parents could be defined as living in the parental household using these data. We were uncertain how to classify respondents living in households with other nonnuclear family members since either the respondents or these other relatives (e.g., uncle, aunt, grandparent) might be household head. While at the youngest ages it is likely that the nonparental relative is household head, at the older ages such a definition becomes progressively less certain. In addition, missing data problems in the household roster were especially severe at ages 14 and 15.

In hopes of overcoming these problems we defined a variable which used the fixed record data to ascertain family residence at ages 14 and 15 (for men reporting living apart from their parents), and the household roster data to determine family residence status for ages 16 to 29. The results of this attempt are shown in the "with parents" row of Table I. The results obtained using only the

# TABLE I

## Measures of Person-Months Spent in Each Life Domain by Age

| Life domain | Age | | | | | | | | | | | | | | | | |
|---|---|---|---|---|---|---|---|---|---|---|---|---|---|---|---|---|---|
| | 14 | 15 | 16 | 17 | 18 | 19 | 20 | 21 | 22 | 23 | 24 | 25 | 26 | 27 | 28 | 29 | Total |
| | Mean person-months | | | | | | | | | | | | | | | | |
| School | 10.3 | 10.0 | 9.0 | 7.0 | 4.0 | 2.9 | 2.5 | 2.2 | 1.8 | 1.5 | 1.3 | 1.1 | 1.0 | .9 | .6 | .5 | 56.5 |
| Work | 1.4 | 2.2 | 3.4 | 4.4 | 6.2 | 6.7 | 6.5 | 6.6 | 7.4 | 8.5 | 9.4 | 10.2 | 10.6 | 10.8 | 11.1 | 11.2 | 116.5 |
| Military service | .0 | .1 | .2 | .8 | 1.8 | 2.8 | 3.5 | 3.7 | 3.1 | 2.1 | 1.4 | .8 | .6 | .4 | .4 | .3 | 21.9 |
| With parents | 10.4 | 9.1 | 8.5 | 7.6 | 6.1 | 4.9 | 3.9 | 3.0 | 2.4 | 2.0 | 1.7 | 1.4 | 1.0 | .8 | .7 | .5 | 63.9 |
| With family of origin | 11.7 | 11.5 | 11.2 | 10.2 | 8.2 | 6.1 | 4.3 | 2.7 | 1.8 | 1.2 | .9 | .6 | .4 | .3 | .2 | .1 | 71.3 |
| Married | .0 | .0 | .0 | .1 | .6 | 1.5 | 2.6 | 4.0 | 5.3 | 6.5 | 7.6 | 8.4 | 9.1 | 9.6 | 10.0 | 10.2 | 75.4 |
| Parenting | .1 | .2 | .2 | .2 | .2 | .6 | 1.0 | 1.8 | 2.9 | 4.1 | 5.2 | 6.2 | 7.1 | 7.8 | 8.3 | 8.9 | 54.7 |
| | Standard deviation | | | | | | | | | | | | | | | | |
| School | 3.1 | 3.9 | 4.8 | 5.2 | 4.8 | 4.7 | 4.6 | 4.3 | 3.9 | 3.7 | 3.5 | 3.2 | 3.1 | 2.9 | 2.5 | 2.2 | — |
| Work | 3.0 | 3.8 | 4.5 | 4.8 | 5.0 | 5.2 | 5.2 | 5.3 | 5.2 | 4.9 | 4.4 | 3.8 | 3.5 | 3.3 | 2.9 | 2.8 | — |
| Military service | .3 | .8 | 1.5 | 2.6 | 3.4 | 4.8 | 5.1 | 5.1 | 4.8 | 4.2 | 3.5 | 2.7 | 2.4 | 2.1 | 2.1 | 2.0 | — |
| With parents | 4.1 | 5.0 | 5.3 | 5.6 | 5.7 | 5.6 | 5.2 | 4.8 | 4.4 | 4.1 | 3.9 | 3.7 | 3.2 | 2.9 | 2.6 | 2.4 | — |
| With family of origin | 1.7 | 2.2 | 2.9 | 4.0 | 5.1 | 5.7 | 5.5 | 4.8 | 4.1 | 3.6 | 3.1 | 2.5 | 2.0 | 1.8 | 1.3 | 1.0 | — |
| Married | .0 | .2 | .5 | 1.1 | 2.3 | 3.6 | 4.7 | 5.4 | 5.7 | 5.7 | 5.6 | 5.3 | 5.0 | 4.7 | 4.3 | 4.2 | — |
| Parenting | .9 | 1.4 | 1.4 | 1.3 | 1.5 | 2.3 | 3.1 | 4.1 | 4.9 | 5.5 | 5.7 | 5.8 | 5.7 | 5.6 | 5.3 | 5.1 | — |

## TABLE II

**Total Person-Months Spent in Each Life Domain from Ages 14 to 29 by Birth Cohort, Race, and Father's Occupation**

| Population group | Life domain | | | | | | |
|---|---|---|---|---|---|---|---|
| | School | Work | Military service | With parents | With family of origin | Married | Parenting |
| Total | 56.5 | 116.5 | 21.9 | 63.9 | 71.3 | 75.4 | 54.7 |
| Birth cohort | | | | | | | |
| 1929–1933 | 56.5 | 115.2 | 24.9 | 63.8 | 71.4 | 73.0 | 52.3 |
| 1934–1939 | 56.5 | 117.8 | 18.7 | 64.1 | 71.3 | 77.9 | 57.3 |
| Race | | | | | | | |
| Black | 45.0 | 121.3 | 19.2 | 60.4 | 76.2 | 72.2 | 56.4 |
| White | 58.0 | 115.9 | 22.2 | 63.1 | 71.3 | 74.1 | 53.9 |
| Father's occupation | | | | | | | |
| Blue collar, farm | 51.7 | 119.5 | 22.6 | 66.0 | 71.8 | 77.0 | 56.5 |
| White collar | 71.3 | 107.6 | 19.3 | 60.6 | 70.8 | 69.2 | 48.8 |

fixed record variable are shown in the "with family of origin" row of Table I. A comparison of the two variables indicates that the "with parents" variable underestimated residence in the family of origin at the early ages. This discrepancy is especially problematic among blacks who are less likely to have been living in a family of origin including a parent (Table II). The "with family of origin" variable appears to underestimate the frequency of living with family of origin from ages 21 to 29. We decided to exclude place of residence from our analysis since we were unable to develop a satisfactory operational definition of residence in the parental family with the HOPKINS data.

The analysis proceeds by first examining the measures of person-months spent in each of the other five life domains for all males born 1929–1939. We then discuss differentials in the allocation of time in each life domain by birth cohort (1929/1933 vs 1934/1939), race (black vs white), and father's occupation as a measure of social class (farm and blue collar vs white collar). Finally, we describe the ways in which these men combine activities across the domains.

## IX. Analysis Results

Measures of the allocation of time in each life domain from ages 14 to 29 for all males born 1929–1939 are presented in Table I. Of the total 192 person-months between ages 14 to 29, 56.5 months (29%) were spent enrolled in school, 21.9 months (11%) on active duty in the military, and 117 months (61%) working full time. On the average, 75 months were spent in marriage (39%), and 55 months (28%) involved parenting.

The allocation of time in each of the life domains is strongly age graded. Very rapid declines in school enrollment occurred between ages 14 and 19, with gradual but steady decreases thereafter. The greatest variability in school enrollment occurred from ages 16 to 21. Before age 16 most men were in school, and there was little variability in this status; after 21, relatively few men were enrolled in school. These birth cohorts were enrolled in high school during the later 1940s and early 1950s when high school completion rates were relatively low. Among more recent cohorts high school completion is the norm. Among such cohorts, rates of leaving school would be low from ages 14 to 17 but increase from ages 17 to 19 (as many men complete high school but forego college enrollment).

Labor force entry occurred at a rapid pace from age 14 when 1.4 person-months on average were spent in full-time employment to age 18, when about one-half year on average was spent in full-time employment. Full-time employment changed relatively little from ages 18 to 21, but increased steadily thereafter. It appears that a life-course branching point was reached by these men at about age 18. Upon finishing high school, the modal response was to enter the labor force directly. Other men chose to continue on to college or entered military service, postponing their labor force entry until ages 21 and after. By age 25 the number of person-months (10.2) occupied by full-time employment equalled that spent in school during the peak period of school enrollment at age 14. The transition of the cohorts from schoolboys to employed men thus was a gradual process occurring over a period of 11 years.

Military service occupied relatively little of the lives of these men prior to age 18 and after age 24. However, military service obligations occupied about one-third of the lives of these men at ages 20, 21, and 22. Indeed, these men devoted more time to military service than to school enrollment from ages 20 to 24. Thus, the early adult lives of these cohorts were characterized by military service as well as work and college enrollment.[4]

The marriage transition did not begin until age 18, but proceeded rapidly thereafter, with one-half of the lives of men at age 23 spent currently married. By age 29, fully 10.2 person-months per year were within marriage.[5] The timing of the parenting transition follows the marriage transition by about 2 years. By age 29, three-quarters of the lives of these men involved childrearing.

By our measures of age grading, the coefficients of variation (Table III), the allocation of time to work is the least age-graded domain (coefficient of variation equal to .44). The other domains display patterns of age grading for the domains close to 1.0, with marriage being somewhat lower (.86).

## A. COHORT DIFFERENTIALS

There are observable intercohort differentials in the total amount of time spent in each of the life domains, and in the age gradedness of those activities (see Table II, Figs. 1–5). The two cohorts devoted equivalent amounts of time to school enrollment (Table II). The 1929/1933 cohort spent about one-half year more time in the military, whereas the cohort of 1934/1939 spent 2.6 months more of their early adult lives working. The 1934/1939 cohort married earlier, as reflected in their greater number of months spent in the married state and oc-cupied by parenting (Hogan, 1981).

Military service requirements account in large part for these differentials. At

[4]A few men report military service at ages 14 to 17. Military service officially was not permitted at these ages. Either some men misreported the dates of their military service to the HOPKINS interviewers or they misrepresented their ages at the time of military service induction. In either case, the amount of military service reported at these young ages is relatively limited.

[5]This would correspond to the observation that about 85% of these men were currently married in a cross-sectional survey observing them at age 29. Census data indicate that the percentage of 29-year-old men who were currently married was 81.9% in 1960 and 82.3% in 1970 (United States Bureau of the Census, 1964, Table 176; 1973, Table 1). This provides independent evidence supporting the validity of the retrospective life history data collected in HOPKINS.

## TABLE III

**Coefficient of Variation of Person-Months Spent in Each Life Domain from
Ages 14 to 29 by Birth Cohort, Race, and Father's Occupation[a]**

| Population group | School | Work | Military service | Married | Parenting |
|---|---|---|---|---|---|
| | | | Life domain | | |
| Total | .99 | .44 | .94 | .86 | .97 |
| Birth cohort | | | | | |
| 1929–1933 | .94 | .43 | 1.05 | .89 | 1.02 |
| 1934–1939 | 1.03 | .45 | .89 | .84 | .93 |
| Race | | | | | |
| Black | 1.20 | .37 | .83 | .81 | .77 |
| White | .96 | .45 | .96 | .87 | .99 |
| Father's occupation | | | | | |
| Blue collar, farm | 1.07 | .42 | .92 | .85 | .95 |
| White collar | .82 | .51 | .91 | .91 | 1.05 |

[a] The coefficient of variation is the standard deviation of person-months of activity in each
domain divided by the mean person-months in that activity, calculated over the 16 years of life
experience.

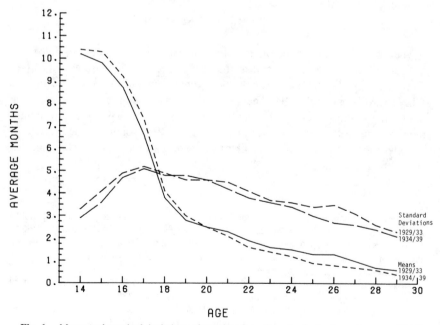

**Fig. 1.**   Means and standard deviations of months of regular school attendance by age and birth
cohort.

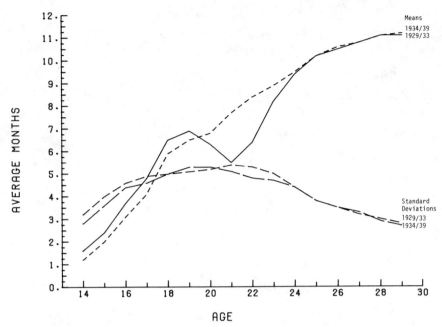

**Fig. 2.** Means and standard deviations of months of full-time civilian employment by age and birth cohort.

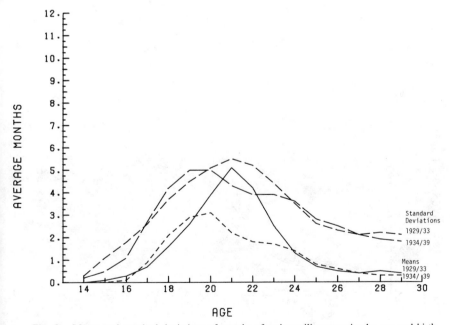

**Fig. 3.** Means and standard deviations of months of active military service by age and birth cohort.

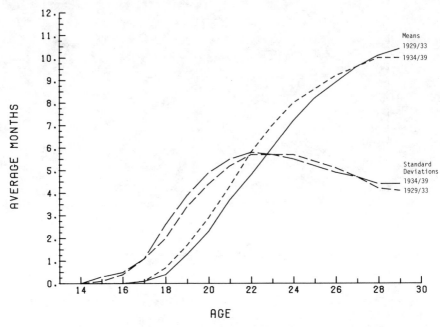

**Fig. 4.**  Means and standard deviations of months of marriage by age and birth cohort.

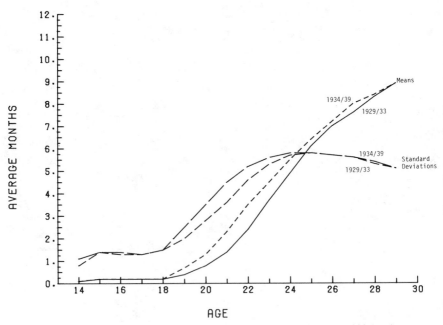

**Fig. 5.**  Means and standard deviations of months of parenting by age and birth cohort.

the beginning of the Korean War in 1950 about 1.5 million men were on active duty in the Armed Forces. The size of the Armed Forces expanded with American involvement in the war to 3.2 million in 1951, 3.6 million in 1952 and 1953, and 3.3 million in 1954. Thereafter the size of the Armed Forces declined to under 3 million men (United States Bureau of the Census, 1978, Table 602). Men born in 1929/1933 were age 17–21 in 1950 and 20–24 in 1953. The cohort of 1934/1939 was ages 11–16 at the beginning of the Korean War and 14–19 at its end. The brunt of the manpower requirements for the Korean War thus fell on the 1929/1933 cohort, from ages 20 to 23 (Fig. 3).

The school enrollment patterns of the two birth cohorts do not differ substantially, but there is consistent evidence of a slight tendency for higher school attendance among the 1929/1933 cohort at ages 21–29. This probably results from the higher rates of military service, and greater eligibility for GI Bill benefits for school enrollment of numbers of the 1929/1933 cohort. The employment levels of the 1934/1939 cohort increase monotonically with age (Fig. 2). In contrast, the level of employment in the 1929/1933 cohort declined from ages 19 to 21, corresponding to their ages at military service (Figs. 2 and 3). The employment levels of the 1929/1933 cohort did not recover fully until their unusually heavy military service obligations ended at age 24. Although the marriage and parenting transitions occurred slightly later in the cohort of 1929/1933, these differences do not appear to be related directly to its military service history (Figs. 4 and 5). These patterns are reflected in the cohort-specific measures of age grading of activities in domains (Table III). The age grading of military service was somewhat stronger in the 1929/1933 cohort. School enrollment was slightly less age graded for this cohort.

## B. RACIAL DIFFERENTIALS

The major racial differentials in early life activities involve schooling and employment (Table II). Black men spend 45 person-months in school compared to 58 among whites (a difference of 13 months). Black men worked at full-time jobs a total of 121 months from age 14 to 29, compared to 116 for whites (a difference of 5 months). Blacks had slightly lower levels of military service, married somewhat later, and began parenting earlier than whites.

These racial differences are distinctly patterned by age (Figs. 6–10). School enrollment is higher among whites than among blacks at every age. In other domains (employment, marriage, and parenting), the black men experience adult statuses more frequently than whites during the later teens, but the activities of white men begin to converge in the early 20s. By the mid-20s, a greater proportion of the lives of white men involves work, marriage, and parenthood.

At most ages, black men show less variability than whites in the allocation of time to schooling and military service, and more interindividual variability in employment, marriage, and parenthood. The coefficients of variation of person-

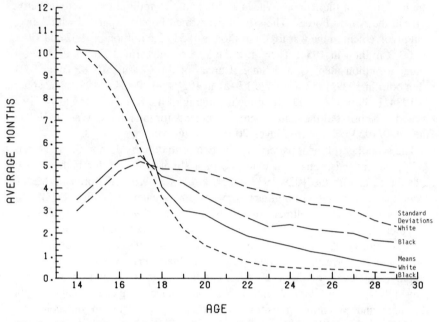

**Fig. 6.** Means and standard deviations of months of regular school attendance by age and race.

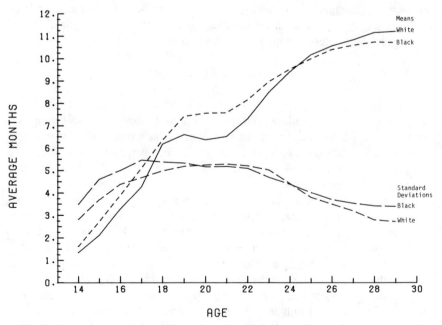

**Fig. 7.** Means and standard deviations of months of full-time civilian employment by age and race.

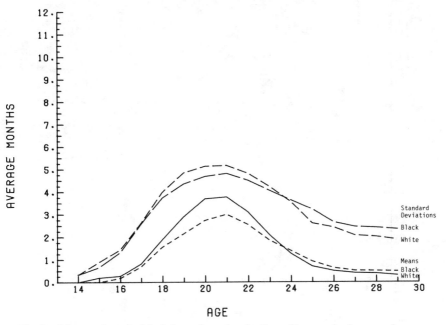

**Fig. 8.** Means and standard deviations of months of active military service by age and race.

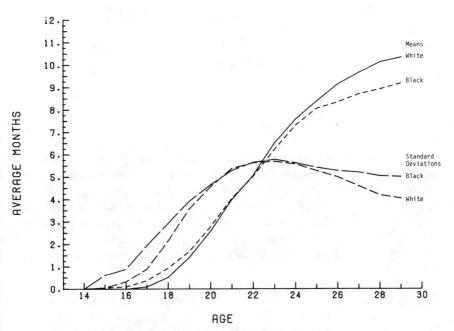

**Fig. 9.** Means and standard deviations of months of marriage by age and race.

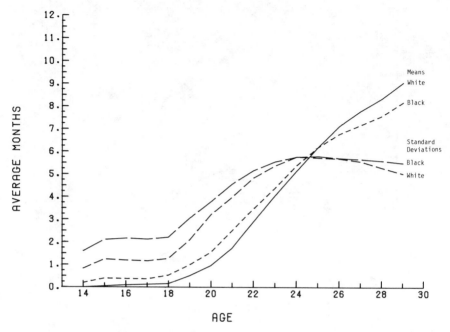

**Fig. 10.** Means and standard deviations of months of parenting by age and race.

months over the duration of 16 years indicate that school enrollment is more strongly age graded among blacks than whites (because relatively few of the black men enrolled in college and vocational school), but the age grading of other domains was slightly greater among whites (Table III).

## C. SOCIAL CLASS DIFFERENTIALS

There are major social class differentials in the life course activities in these men (Table II and Figs. 11–15). Men from blue collar or farm origins spend substantially less time from ages 14 to 29 in school (20 months) and considerably more time working (12 months), married (8 months), and parenting (8 months). Men of lower social status devoted slightly more time (3.3 months) to military service. These differences in school enrollment, marriage, and parenting are observed at nearly all ages, and the higher levels of employment among the lower social origins men persist until the mid-20s when they converge. In contrast to the racial differences the activities of the social classes do not cross over.

The activities of the lower social status men display greater interindividual variability at the younger ages (14–18 for school enrollment and employment and 14–22 for marriage and childbearing). Greater interindividual variability is observed among the higher social origins men at the older ages. These patterns

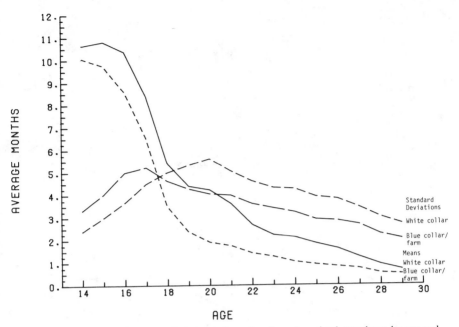

**Fig. 11.** Means and standard deviations of months of regular school attendance by age and father's occupation.

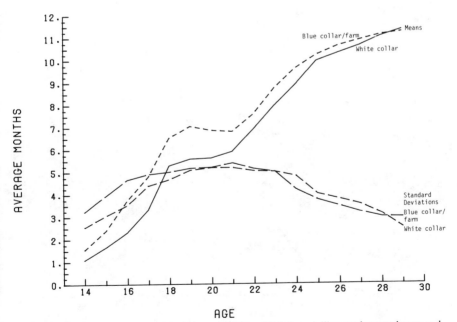

**Fig. 12.** Means and standard deviations of months of full-time civilian employment by age and father's occupation.

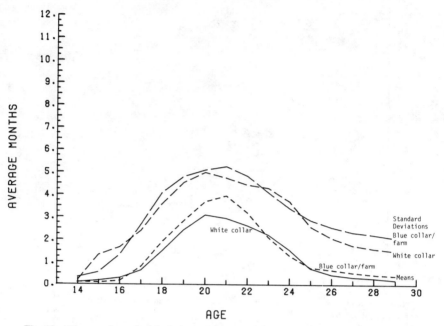

**Fig. 13.** Means and standard deviations of months of active military service by age and father's occupation.

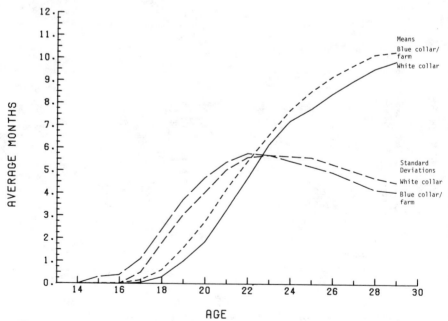

**Fig. 14.** Means and standard deviations of months of marriage by age and father's occupation.

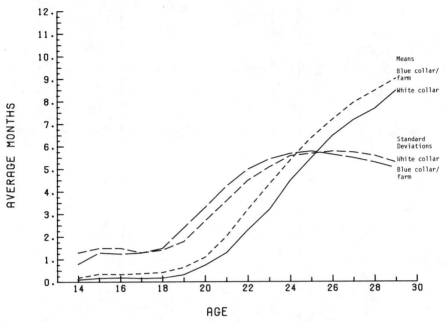

**Fig. 15.** Means and standard deviations of months of parenting by age and father's occupation.

result from the earlier transition to adulthood experienced by men of lower social class origins. This earlier assumption of adult statuses is closely related to the lower educational attainments (and earlier ages at school completion) of the lower status origin men. However, there are only minimal social origins differences in the age grading of the domain activities, with the exception of schooling (Table III).

## D. SYNCHRONIZATION OF DOMAINS

The total mean person-months spent in combination of activities in the five domains are displayed in Table IV.[6] Three combinations of life domains each consume an average of more than 40 months. These include (1) unmarried, childless, enrolled in school, not employed, and not in the military (the usual schoolboy); (2) unmarried, childless, not in school, not in the military, but employed full time (the usual unmarried working man); and (3) the man who is married with one or more children and working fulltime without school enrollment or active military service (the conventional working adult). About 15 months are spent working after marriage prior to the birth of a first child.

---

[6]By definition under the survey procedures, a man could not be employed full time at a civilian job while on active duty in the military. All other combinations are possible.

## TABLE IV

### Total Person-Months Spent in Each Combination of Life Domains from Ages 14 to 29

| Activity status | Family status | | | | |
|---|---|---|---|---|---|
| | Unmarried, childless | Married, childless | Unmarried, with child | Married, with child | Total |
| Enrolled, not employed, not in military | 41.2 | 1.1 | .5 | .8 | 43.6 |
| Enrolled, employed, not in military | 7.0 | .8 | .0 | 1.8 | 9.6 |
| Enrolled, not employed, in military | 2.5 | .5 | .0 | .1 | 3.1 |
| Not enrolled, not employed, not in military | 7.5 | .7 | .1 | 1.7 | 10.0 |
| Not enrolled, not employed, in military | 13.3 | 4.0 | .0 | 1.5 | 18.8 |
| Not enrolled, employed, not in military | 43.4 | 15.2 | .6 | 47.6 | 106.8 |
| Total | 114.9 | 22.3 | 1.2 | 53.6 | 192.0 |

Military service without school or work while unmarried consumes an average of 13 months, and an additional 4 months on average is spent in the military while married and childless. These men spent an average of 7 months enrolled in school and employed full time while unmarried. About 7.5 months were spent not enrolled, not employed, not in the military, and unmarried.

Together, these eight combinations of domains account for 179 of the 192 person-months between ages 14 and 29 (93% of the total). The remaining 16 combinations account for a total of 13 person-months (about 7% of the total). None of these rare combinations accounts for more than 1.3% of the total person-months of early adulthood. Thus, unusual combinations of life domains occur, but are relatively rare. The patterns of synchronization of early life-course activities of these men can be characterized in crude fashion with reference to eight combinations of domains.

These eight life-course patterns are strongly age related (Table V). At age 14, an average of 9.5 person-months involves the combination of domains that are socially defined as adolescent (enrolled in school, not employed, not in the military, unmarried, and childless). Young males quickly begin to depart this "schoolboy" state by leaving school and/or beginning work. By age 21, less than 10% of these young men's lives is spent in the schoolboy status. As young persons leave schoolboy status, they typically enter the labor force or the military without beginning a family of procreation. These statuses are intermediate stages between adolescence and adulthood. Such intermediate statuses are the most common combinations of domains from ages 19 to 21. Together, they account for 5 or more months of life activity at each age from 18 to 22. These men typically departed these intermediate statuses by marrying. Parenthood rarely preceded marriage among these men, although short first birth intervals during the 1950s and 1960s meant that parenthood typically occurred within 2 years of marriage (Hogan, 1983). We have argued that the usual social definition of adult status supposes a man is finished with school, working at a full-time job, and living in his own family (with a wife and, sometimes, children). This adult stage is rare before age 21, but becomes increasingly common thereafter. By age 25 more than 6 months of every person-year are spent in the adult activities. At age 14, 9.5 months were occupied by men in the schoolboy status; at age 29, 9.1 months of the person-years lived by these men involved socially recognized adult roles.

There are relatively small differentials by birth cohort, race, and social class origins in the total amount of time spent in these life-course combinations (Table VI). The index of dissimilarity comparing the percentage of the 192 months spent in each status was 5% for birth cohort, 7% for race, and 10% for social class origins. Thus, even in the case of social class, where differences are the largest, only 10% of the 192 person-months of time of one social class would have to be redistributed to make it identical to the other social class.

## TABLE V

### Mean Person-Months Spent in Selected Combinations of Life Domains by Age

| Life domains | Age | | | | | | | | | | | | | | | |
|---|---|---|---|---|---|---|---|---|---|---|---|---|---|---|---|---|
| | 14 | 15 | 16 | 17 | 18 | 19 | 20 | 21 | 22 | 23 | 24 | 25 | 26 | 27 | 28 | 29 |
| | | | | | | | Mean person-months | | | | | | | | | |
| **Unmarried, childless** | | | | | | | | | | | | | | | | |
| Enrolled, not employed, not in military | 9.5 | 8.8 | 7.5 | 5.6 | 2.9 | 1.8 | 1.3 | 1.0 | .7 | .5 | .4 | .3 | .2 | .1 | .0 | .0 |
| Enrolled, employed, not in military | .6 | 1.0 | 1.1 | 1.0 | .7 | .5 | .5 | .3 | .2 | .2 | .2 | .2 | .1 | .1 | .1 | .1 |
| Not enrolled, not employed, not in military | 1.0 | .7 | .6 | .9 | .9 | .6 | .5 | .5 | .4 | .4 | .2 | .2 | .2 | .2 | .1 | .1 |
| Not enrolled, not employed, in military | .0 | .1 | .2 | .7 | 1.5 | 2.1 | 2.4 | 2.3 | 1.7 | 1.1 | .6 | .3 | .1 | .1 | .1 | .0 |
| Not enrolled, employed, not in military | .7 | 1.2 | 2.1 | 3.2 | 4.9 | 4.9 | 4.1 | 3.4 | 3.2 | 3.0 | 2.8 | 2.5 | 2.1 | 1.8 | 1.6 | 1.4 |
| **Married, childless** | | | | | | | | | | | | | | | | |
| Not enrolled, not employed, in military | .0 | .0 | .0 | .0 | .1 | .2 | .5 | .7 | .7 | .6 | .5 | .3 | .2 | .1 | .1 | .1 |
| Not enrolled, employed, not in military | .0 | .0 | .1 | .1 | .3 | .6 | .9 | 1.2 | 1.4 | 1.5 | 1.6 | 1.7 | 1.6 | 1.6 | 1.5 | 1.2 |
| **Married, with child** | | | | | | | | | | | | | | | | |
| Not enrolled, employed, not in military | .0 | .0 | .0 | .0 | .1 | .4 | .9 | 1.6 | 2.4 | 3.5 | 4.4 | 5.4 | 6.2 | 6.8 | 7.5 | 8.0 |
| All other combinations | .2 | .2 | .4 | .5 | .6 | .9 | .9 | 1.0 | 1.3 | 1.2 | 1.3 | 1.1 | 1.3 | 1.2 | 1.0 | 1.1 |

## TABLE VI

**Total Person-Months Spent in Selected Combinations of Life Domains from Ages 14 to 29 by Birth Cohort, Race, and Father's Occupation**

| Life domains | Birth cohort | | Race | | Father's occupation | |
|---|---|---|---|---|---|---|
| | 1929–1933 | 1934–1939 | Black | White | Farm, blue collar | White collar |
| **Unmarried, childless** | | | | | | |
| Enrolled, not employed, not in military | 39.7 | 42.8 | 35.5 | 42.0 | 37.5 | 52.8 |
| Enrolled, employed, not in military | 7.5 | 6.6 | 4.6 | 7.4 | 6.6 | 8.7 |
| Not enrolled, not employed, not in military | 7.3 | 7.7 | 10.1 | 7.2 | 7.8 | 6.9 |
| Not enrolled, not employed, in military | 15.9 | 10.5 | 12.1 | 13.4 | 13.6 | 12.4 |
| Not enrolled, employed, not in military | 44.5 | 42.2 | 52.6 | 42.1 | 45.1 | 38.5 |
| **Married, childless** | | | | | | |
| Not enrolled, not employed, in military | 4.3 | 3.7 | 3.6 | 4.1 | 3.9 | 3.7 |
| Not enrolled, employed, not in military | 14.6 | 15.8 | 13.1 | 15.5 | 15.4 | 14.7 |
| **Married, with child** | | | | | | |
| Not enrolled, employed, not in military | 45.3 | 50.2 | 47.7 | 47.7 | 50.0 | 41.1 |
| All other combinations | 12.9 | 12.5 | 12.7 | 12.6 | 12.1 | 13.2 |

The cohort-specific patterns of military service account for the cohort differentials in time spent in the combination of domains. Most of the greater military service of the 1929/1933 birth cohort was served while unmarried and childless. This cohort spent fewer of its years as typical schoolboys, and experienced more of its school enrollment while employed. The cohort differences in school enrollment and employment described earlier occur among the unmarried, childless men.

Whites spend 6.5 more months as schoolboys than blacks. Blacks, in contrast, are single working men (the intermediate stage of the transition to adulthood) for 10.5 months more than whites. There are no racial differences in the average number of months spent devoted to fully adult statuses (married, parenting, and employed). However, white men spend an additional 2.9 months as husbands without children (either employed or in the military).

Social class origin differentials in the person-months spent in life domains resemble the racial differentials. Farm and blue collar background men spend many fewer months than those of white collar origins in the adolescent schoolboy stage (38 vs 53). The lower social status men spend 6.6 months more in the intermediate single working man stage. The lower social background men spend considerably more time (8.9 months) in the fully adult stage (working husband and father) during these transition years.

## X. Discussion

American males born between 1929 and 1939 entered early adulthood in a seemingly uniform age-graded sequence of transitions from schoolboy to full-employed parent. Whether their age-graded life course was influenced by their comparatively small cohort size, experience of the Korean military action, and a "growth" period in the business cycle remains as conjecture, inasmuch as the current analysis was limited to insufficient intercohort comparisons.

Given this apparent extensive age grading, it is perhaps not surprising that we failed to detect substantial and consistent interindividual and intergroup differentials and to confirm many of our hypothetical anticipations. Having divided the men's lives into two birth cohorts, we identified mainly the effects of differential participation in the Korean war. Race and socioeconomic differences (linked to paternal occupational group) became manifest as earlier versus later ages of leaving school to embark on a rather similar age-graded transition into adulthood.

Thus, our effort to gain some understanding of the historical and institutional bases of trends in the age grading of lives was only minimally successful. Consistent with our expectations, black men entered adulthood in a slightly less age-graded life course than whites, largely reflecting a less age-specific pattern of being married and living with one's children; at the same time, their experiences of schooling were less protracted into older ages than among whites. Somewhat parallel differentials separate the lower status occupational groups (blue collar and farm fathers) from their white collar counterparts. To be sure, the differentials are very small, but they tend to follow the broad historical, intercohort pattern reported by Modell *et al.* (1976), namely, a shortening of the duration of the transition into adulthood because of greater age regularity in establishing a family of procreation, even as exposure to extended secondary and postsecondary schooling became more pervasive in the population. Unfortunately, the two cohorts we created for this analysis apparently are too similarly placed in American historical experience to be of any use in construing causal inferences.

Why might the life-course patterns of blacks and other men from lower socioeconomic origins tend to recapitulate the historical trends in age grading? Our analysis is not very enlightening, but Featherman and Sørensen (1983, 1984), in similar analyses of time-use profiles of three Norwegian birth cohorts, offer some possible explanations.

Despite substantial economic and social change during the post-World War II years in Norway, neither these institutional transformations nor the preceding period of Nazi occupation and economic depression seem to have greatly altered the life courses of Norwegien men. To be sure, cohorts born in the early 1920s experienced different profiles of sociodemographic events in the transition into early adulthood than those born a decade or two later (viz 1941 and 1931 vs 1921). Prior to age 30, the three cohorts apparently spent different fractions of their lives in school, in active military service, in work, and as married parents. But except for the different volume of time spent in these different domains, the cohorts distributed their activities in a quite similar age-specific pattern that indicated little trend in the age grading of life events for individuals or in the age stratification of institutions in which adolescents and young adults participate. What little trend Featherman and Sørensen detected was consistent with prior research in North America: greater differentiation of the life course into more clearly articulated "periods" or age strata, with greater numbers of the successive cohorts leading a statistically typical or "normative" allocation of time by age.

Both individual variation in time use within each cohort and intercohort variation in age grading appeared to reflect two historical shifts in the institutional context of the adolescent and early adult life course: active military service and schooling beyond a compulsory minimum. Individual tendencies and aggregate trends toward greater participation or exposure to these age-graded institutions in the cohorts born in 1931 and 1941 versus 1921 appear to account for the small statistical association between age and the allocation of time (months per year) across the activity domains both within and among cohorts. Further, individual differences in time use were hypothesized to reflect social background contexts based on father's occupational type. Rather than a strict socioeconomic classification, this typology attempted to capture social groups with different levels of participation in the "modern" sectors of Norwegian society (e.g., factory-based industries, schools), following the logic of Inkeles and Smith (1974). Those men in each cohort whose fathers, by hypothesis, were less integrated with the modern political economy, the "traditional" category, manifested less age-graded life courses than those from "modern" and "privileged" origins. Across the cohorts, as the differences in schooling and military service among the social origin categories declined, so, too, did differentials in age grading by social origin.

These findings in Norway, based on somewhat more sophisticated statistical techniques of analyzing time allocation through age 30,[7] shed some light on the data for United States men born in the 1930s. Black men in these American cohorts, like the "traditional" Norwegians, were less likely as groups to be fully integrated into those institutional spheres which account for the segmentation of the early adult and adolescent life course into age strata. Ironically, their lesser ability or tendency to prolong school attendance produced a slightly greater degree of age grading among blacks than whites, although greater participation in the military, partly in a more extended career pattern, introduced decreased age grading than for whites. Decreased stability in marital life and residence with children for black men in these cohorts also diminished the extent of age grading of the life course. Inasmuch as differential participation in these rather substantially age-graded institutional spheres seems to lie at the heart of group differentials, it is likely that such differentials are heavily influenced by the socioeconomic opportunities and life chances of individuals and social origin groups. Based on other research, it is plausible to assume that, had blacks born in the 1930s been less heavily constrained by lower levels of income and restricted opportunity, they would have increased their school attendance beyond the compulsory years, been less inclined to use the military as a career option, and more likely to remain married and living with children (e.g., Featherman & Hauser, 1978; Hoffman & Holmes, 1976). The sum of these hypothetical effects would yield a more age-graded life course through age 30 and a more similar pattern with the profiles of whites.

This speculative interpretation is consistent with an explanation of intercohort or historical trends in age stratification. The prevalence of age-stratified institutional contexts of childhood, adolescence, and adulthood has increased in the

---

[7] In the Norway analysis (Featherman & Sørensen, 1983), the statistical association of activity domain and age was modeled by a series of hierarchical log linear models. This procedure provides a more determinant test of departures of time use from various hypothetical distributions, including the null of no net association with age.

twentieth century (e.g., Rosenmayr, 1979); coincident improvements in the socioeconomic levels of individuals and households increased the likelihood that greater fractions of successive birth cohorts would participate in these institutions and experience, as a consequence, a more age-graded course of life.

In light of this speculative interpretation, we return to the American data and the observations of quite modest differentials in age grading. There are two contending explanations for our apparent inability to detect substantial and consistent differences. The first is that they are subdued because of a unique set of period and cohort characteristics of this cohort up to age 30. Rossi (1980) has highlighted many of these and questioned whether a theory of adult development based on especially this one birth cohort has much generality. Given the analysis and discussion of this article, we can only echo that question. A second unresolved problem is methodological, namely, the optimal technique for identifying and estimating the association of behavior with time or age. In closing we offer some insights into the problematics.

## XI. Remaining Methodological Issues and Future Directions

The statistical profiles of time use presented in this article have a data base different from most other research on age grading: retrospective life history data. The longitudinal nature of the life history data provides obvious benefits for this type of research. Only some of these benefits have been capitalized upon in the present article, and it is a main objective of our present and planned research to utilize more fully the richness of retrospective life history data for research on age grading.

It is useful first to state in more formal terms what has been accomplished in the present article using life history data in comparison to the descriptions of age grading typically obtained from cross-sectional data. This will show more clearly both the advantages of the strategy used here and the limitations we hope to overcome in future research.

For the more formal recapitulation it is useful to see the life-course activities described here as forming a state space with discrete states (for example, the states of being married versus nonmarried). At any moment of observation an individual will occupy one of these states; and therefore we can form the proportion who, at any moment of time, occupy the various states. In the study of age grading we further classify individuals according to their ages. The proportion of persons who at age $t$ occupy state $i$ shall here be denoted $p_i(t)$.

Cross-sectional data provide information on age grading by allowing us to classify people according to their age and the state occupied at the time of the survey (typically the survey week). Assuming that a year of age is the time interval used in the age classification, the survey week is of course a much smaller time interval. Hence, cross-sectional data may be seen as sampling a smaller time interval within a year of age to provide an estimate of $p_i(t)$.

The life history data allow us to assign respondents to states at every moment of their lives (for the period covered by the retrospective questioning). Rather than sampling a time interval within an age interval as with cross-sectional data, we have in fact 12 observations for each year–age of the respondents. This will provide better estimates of $p_i(t)$ simply because we have more information on each $p_i(t)$. This may be an advantage with small samples or if there is substantial variation in the $p_i(t)$s that is unsystematic in relation to age (say seasonal variation). It is this feature of the retrospective life history data that is capitalized upon in our use of person-months in the tables shown here.

The main advantage of life history data over cross-sectional data is that the former offer comparisons of $p_i(t)$s across different values of $t$ which do not confound age and cohort variation. The longitudinal nature of the life history data allows us to separate age from cohort variation in $t$ since we can observe the same individual at different ages. This variation with age may of course still confound historical influences that are simultaneous with aging.

It should be noted that a panel study—where prospective observations of a cross-section of individuals are made at certain (say yearly) intervals—shares properties with both retrospective life history and with cross-sectional data in the study of age grading. As with life history data, repeated observations on the same individuals can be performed. As with cross-sectional data, a smaller time interval within a year is sampled to provide information on $p_i(t)$.

Since life history data provide information on $p_i(t)$s for each month of age, significant new information on age grading is available: information on the exact timing of change. This allows the investigation of the mechanisms that account for changes in the $p_i(t)$ and thus the observed age grading.

The relation between age grading in the $p_i(t)$s and the mechanisms that account for changes in the $p_i(t)$s is quite complicated because the observed variation in the $p_i(t)$ in general will not allow for the identification of the causes of such variation. This is best shown using a simple example. The example will also identify the main quantities focused upon in our current and planned research.

To make matters simple, assume that we are interested in age grading in only two activities or states so that a person at any age can be in either state 1 or state 2 (say married and nonmarried). A shift from one state to another is a transition. The frequency with which transitions occur in a certain time period can be seen as governed by the transition rates or transition intensities. These rates reflect the probability that a person in one of the states will move to the other state in the next small period of time. The rates may depend on how long a person already has been in a state; we speak then of duration dependence in the rates. Further, rates may (and usually will) depend on characteristics of individuals and their situation. (See Featherman, 1984b for a conceptual grounding for these distinctions and for empirical examples.)

In the most simple case, the rates are constant over time and homogeneous for a set of respondents. The proportion of these respondents in one of the two states at some time, $t$, will then estimate a probability of being in the state. This probability may be assumed to change as a function of the transition rates as

$$[dp_1(t)]/dt = -r_{12}p_1(t) + r_{21}p_2(t) \tag{1}$$

where $r_{12}$ is the rate of moving from state 1 to state 2 (say the rate of getting married) and $r_{21}$ is the rate of moving in the opposite direction (say the rate of getting divorced or widowed).

Assume now that we start observing the life course transitions at age $t_1$. Consider the probability that the person will be in state 1 by time $t_2$. This probability will be obtained by solving the differential Eq. (1). The solution will be

$$p_1(t_2) = p_1(t_1)e^{-(r_{12} + r_{21})\Delta t} + [r_{21}/(r_{21} + r_{12})] [1 - e^{-(r_{12} + r_{21})\Delta t}] \tag{2}$$

where $\Delta t = t_2 - t_1$, and $p_1(t_1)$ is the proportion of respondents in state 1 at time $t_1$.

It is clear from this expression that even under very simplifying assumptions $p_1(t_1)$ will be a function of these quantities: (1) the transition rates that govern the movements back and forth between the two states; (2) the length of the time interval $\Delta t$; and (3) the proportion in state 1 at time $t$.

The expression may be simplified by choosing $t_1$ so that $p_1(t_1)$ is 1 or 0, i.e., setting $t_1$ equal to the start of the process. In the example where the two states are marriage and nonmarriage this would mean setting $t_1$ equal to the age when people start marrying. Another type of simplification is obtained when $\Delta t$ is chosen so large that the term $\exp[-(r_{12} + r_{21})\Delta t]$ becomes zero. In that case $p_i(t_2)$ becomes

$$p_1(\infty) = r_{21}/(r_{12} + r_{21}) \tag{3}$$

This may be called the equilibrium state of the process since $p_i(t)$ will remain stable over time.

Two important implications for the study of age grading follow from this example. First, the simple example shows (by construction) that changes in $p_i(t)$ over time will take place even when the transition rates are constant over time. In other words, the proportion married will change with age (for a process like marriage, at least in the younger years) even though the transition rates do not change with age (i.e., even if the rates of getting married and the rates of marital dissolution are constant over time). In the general case transition rates will be functions of age and of other individual characteristics. However, it is not possible from the age variation in $p(t)$ to infer the age or time dependency in the transition rates.

It is often thought that age-graded activities reflect age-graded transitions. This is not necessarily so. A simple, perhaps trivial, example is provided by schooling. The schooling process could be modeled by Eq. (1) with state 1 being in school and state 2 being out of school. Assume $r_{21}$ is zero and everyone starts out in school; thus $p_1(t_1) = 1$ (choosing, for example, $t_1 = 16$) we will then have $p_1(t)$ decline and eventually reach zero as $t$ increases in a manner that is not completely unlike what is observed, even assuming $r_{12}$ is constant by age and also is independent of other characteristics. In other words, the age grading of schooling could have come about even if the rate of leaving school is not age (duration) dependent, that is, even if leaving school is not an age-graded transition.

A second major implication of the simple mode is that even when the process has reached an equilibrium state there is no one-to-one correspondence between $p_1(\infty)$ and the transition rates. The same value of $p_1(\infty)$ may be obtained (as long as there are at least two states and movement occurs in both directions) for very different levels of the rates. For example, this means that a certain proportion married may be observed in a given age group with very frequent changes in marital status and/or with very infrequent changes in marital status. On the other hand different values of $p_i(t)$ may be observed for two different groups because $r_{12}$ differs among the group or because $r_{21}$ differs. In words, two population groups may differ in the proportion married because the rates of entering marriage differ or because the rates of leaving marriage differ. Analysis of $p_i(\infty)$ cannot identify the sources of variation in the $p_i(\infty)$s.

A related ambiguity has to do with whether or not $p_i(\infty)$ in fact is reached in a particular process. Suppose one observes $p_i$ at two ages $p_i(t_a)$ and $p_i(t_b)$. The difference between the two proportions could then be due to the time difference $(t_b - t_a)$ if the process had not reached equilibrium. On the other hand, equilibrium may have been reached at both ages, but the $p_i$s differ because one or both of the transition rates have changed with age. Therefore, a difference in $p_i(t)$s can be attributed to an age change in transition rates only if one is willing to assume that the process is in equilibrium (as one must with cross-sectional data) or can observe that this is so (as one may be able to with longitudinal data).

It follows from these considerations that even with very simple processes it is not possible to link observations on age grading of life-course activities using (as in this article) measures of $p_i(t)$s to the mechanisms that govern age grading. Direct analysis of the transition rates is necessary. It is for this purpose that retrospective life history data have a major advantage over cross-sectional and panel data in the study of age grading. The continuous-time nature of the life history data allows for the direct observation of the lengths of the time intervals between transitions (or from the start of the process until the first transition). These time intervals or waiting times are governed by the transition rates (in general so that the lower the rate the longer the time interval between events) and thus permit the estimation of the transition rates. It is the nature of retrospective life history data as event history data that makes them uniquely suited for the analysis of life-course transitions. Cross-sectional data provide information on transition rates, and panel data usually provide very little or poor information on the rate at which events occur.

Numerous techniques now exist for the estimation of models that link variation in transition rates to characteristics of individuals and time (Kalbfleisch & Prentice, 1980; Tuma *et al.*, 1979). These techniques usually successfully overcome one major problem of using event history data—censoring. In most life history data there will be waiting times not completed by the close of the observation period. Incomplete waiting times are censored transitions or events.

Though the analysis of transition rates is a major step forward in the analysis of the mechanisms that produce age grading, several difficult problems must be solved before the full potentials of the estimation techniques and life history data can be realized. One problem is the proper determination of when a life-course process starts. For example, we do not know at what age most people enter a state of being at risk for becoming married. Therefore, one may use an arbitrary age (say age 16) as the start for the waiting time until the event. This will not be the true starting time for many respondents, and consequently some unmeasured variation in starting time will be introduced. This variation will show up as positive time or age dependence in the rates of marriage even though what varies are starting times and not necessarily the rate of entering marriage.

A similar problem of unmeasured variation has to do with variation in the transition rates that cannot be controlled statistically because of measurement error or omitted variables. This again will lead to time or age dependence that is not genuine. Here it often will be spurious negative time or age dependence in rates that will be observed. This arises because those respondents with high rates will experience the event first, leaving behind those with low rates, *ceteris paribus*.

A third major problem that occupies our current research has to do with the interdependence of life events. While it is theoretically plausible that many events (e.g., school leaving and marriage) are interdependent, it is difficult to model such processes with current methods. There are several different ways in which interdependence can be conceptualized, and they lead to quite different models and estimation methods. We need techniques for choosing among different models and for comparing alternative techniques [e.g., those relying on estimation of transition rates (Sørensen & Sørensen, 1983) and those relying on simultaneous probit models (Winship & Mare, 1983)].

*David L. Featherman* et al.

## Acknowledgments

Previous versions of this article were presented at the annual meeting of the Population Association of America (March 1981) and the Social Science History Association (November 1981). Support for this research was provided by grants to Featherman and Sørensen from the National Institute on Aging (AG02816-03) and to the Center for Demography from the National Institute of Child Health and Human Development (HD05876). Revisions of this article were completed while Dennis Hogan was a Fellow at the Center for Advanced Study in the Behavioral Sciences, supported in part by a grant from the John D. and Catherine T. MacArthur Foundation.

## References

Blau, P. M., & Duncan, D. O. *The American occupational structure.* New York: Wiley, 1967.
Bumpass, L. L., & Westoff, C. F. *The later years of childbearing.* Princeton, New Jersey: Princeton University Press, 1970.
Clausen, J. A. The life course of individuals. In M. W. Riley, M. Johnson, & A. Foner (Eds.), *Aging and society: A sociology of age stratification.* New York: Russell Sage Foundation, 1972.
Coombs, L. C., & Freedman, R. Pre-marital pregnancy, childspacing, and later economic achievement. *Population Studies,* 1970, **24,** 389–412.
Easterlin, R. A. What will 1984 be like? Socioeconomic implications of recent twists in age structure. *Demography,* 1978, **15,** 397–432.
Elder, G. H., Jr. *Children of the great depression.* Chicago: University of Chicago Press, 1974.
Elder, G. H., Jr. Perspectives of the life course. In G. H. Elder, Jr. (Ed.), *Life-course dynamics: From 1968 to the 1980s.* Ithaca, New York: Cornell University Press, 1984, forthcoming.
Fallo-Mitchell, L., & Ryff, C. Preferred timing of female life events: Cohort differences. *Research in Aging,* 1982, **4,** 249–267.
Featherman, D. L. Retrospective longitudinal research: Methodological considerations. *Journal of Economics and Business,* 1980, **32,** 152–169. (a)
Featherman, D. L. Schooling and occupational careers: Constancy and change in worldly success. In O. G. Brim, Jr. & J. Kagan (Eds.), *Constancy and change in human development.* Cambridge Massachusetts: Harvard University Press, 1980. (b)
Featherman, D. L. Individual development and aging as a population process. In J. R. Nesselroade & A. von Eye (Eds.), *Individual development and social change: Explanatory analysis.* New York: Academic Press, 1984, in press. (a)
Featherman, D. L. Biography, society and history: Individual development as a population process. In A. B. Sørensen, F. Weinert, & L. Sherrod (Eds.), *Human development: Interdisciplinary perspectives,* 1984, forthcoming. (b)
Featherman, D. L., & Hauser, R. M. *Opportunity and change.* New York: Academic Press, 1978.
Featherman, D. L., & Sørensen, A. Societal transformation in Norway and change in the life course transition into adulthood. *Acta Sociologica,* 1983, **26,** 105–126.
Featherman, D. L., & Sørensen, A. *Social origins and the transition into adulthood.* Center for Demography Working Paper. Madison: University of Wisconsin, 1984, forthcoming.
Foner, A., & Kertzer, D. I. Transitions over the life course: Lessons from age-set societies. *American Journal of Sociology,* 1978, **83,** 1081–1104.
Gould, R. *Transformations: Growth and change in adult life.* New York: Simon & Schuster, 1978.
Hagestad, G. O., & Neugarten, B. L. Age at the life course. In E. Shanas & R. Binstock (Eds.), *Handbook of aging and the social sciences* (2nd ed.). New York: Van Nostrand Reinhold, 1984, forthcoming.

Hannan, M. T., & Tuma, N. B. Methods for temporal analysis. *Annual Review of Sociology*, 1979, **5**, 303–328.

Hoffman, S., & Holmes, J. Husbands, wives, and divorce. In G. Duncan & J. Morgan (Eds.), *Five thousand American families—Patterns of economic progress* (Vol. 4). Ann Arbor Michigan: Institute for Social Research, 1976.

Hogan, D. P. The variable order of events in the life course. *American Sociological Review*, 1978, **43**, 573–586.

Hogan, D. P. The transition to adulthood as a career contingency. *American Sociological Review*, 1980, **45**, 261–275

Hogan, D. P. *Transitions and social change: The early lives of American men.* New York: Academic Press, 1981.

Hogan, D. P. *Demographic trends in human fertility and parenting across the life-span.* Paper presented at the Social Science Research Council Conference on biosocial life-span approaches to parental and offspring development, Elkridge, Maryland, 1983.

Inkeles, A., & Smith, D. *Becoming modern.* Cambridge, Massachusetts: Harvard University Press, 1974.

Kalbfleisch, J., & Prentice, R. *The statistical analysis of failure time data.* New York: Wiley, 1980.

Karweit, N. L. *Life history data.* Unpublished paper, Center for Social Organization Schools, The Johns Hopkins University, 1972.

Knodel, J., & Piampiti, S. Response reliability on a longitudinal survey in Thailand. *Studies in Family Planning*, 1977, **8**, 55–66.

Levinson, D. *The seasons of a man's life.* New York: Knopf, 1978.

Modell, J. Normative aspects of American marriage timing since World War II. *Journal of Family History*, 1980, **5**, 210–234.

Modell, J., Furstenberg, F. F., Jr., & Herschberg, T. Social change and transitions to adulthood in historical perspective. *Journal of Family History*, 1976, **1**, 7–31.

Neugarten, B. L., Moore, J. W., & Lowe, J. C. Age norms, age constraints, and adult socialization. *American Journal of Sociology*, 1965, **70**, 710–717.

Parsons, T. *The social system.* Glencoe, Illinois: The Free Press, 1951.

Potter, J. Problems in using birth history analysis to estimate trends in fertility. *Population Studies*, 1977, **31**, 335–364.

Riley, M. W. Age strata in social systems. In R. H. Binstock & E. Shanas (Eds.), *Handbook of aging and the social sciences.* Princeton, New Jersey: Van Nostrand Reinhold, 1976.

Riley, M. W. Age strata in social systems. In R. H. Binstock & E. Shanas (Eds.), *Handbook of aging and the social sciences* (2nd ed.). Princeton, New Jersey: Van Nostrand Reinhold, 1984, forthcoming.

Riley, M. W., Johnson, M., & Foner, A. *Aging and society (Vol. 3): A sociology of age stratification.* New York: Russell Sage Foundation, 1972.

Rosenmayr, L. Lebensalter, Lebenslauf und Biographie. In G. Klingenstein, F. Lutz, G. Stourzh, W. Bihl, & G. Heiss (Eds.), *Biographie und Geschichtswissenschaft.* Munich: Oldenbourg, 1979.

Rossi, A. S. Aging and parenthood in the middle years. In P. B. Baltes & O. G. Brim, Jr. (Eds.), *Life-span development and behavior* (Vol. 3). New York: Academic Press, 1980.

Schrank, H. T., & Waring, J. M. Aging and work organizations. In M. W. Riley, B. B. Hess, & K. Bond (Eds.), *Aging in society.* Hillsdale, New Jersey: Erlbaum, 1983.

Sørensen, A., & Sørensen, A. B. *Modeling interdependence of life course events with event history data.* Paper presented at the 78th Meeting of the American Sociological Association, Detroit, Michigan, 1983.

Spanier, G. B., & Glick, P. C. The life cycle of American families: An expanded analysis. *Journal of Family History*, 1980, Spring, 97–111.

Spenner, K. I., Otto, L. B., & Cole, Vaughn A. R. *Career lines and career.* Lexington, Massachusetts: Lexington Press, 1982.

Spilerman, S. Careers, labor market structure, and socioeconomic achievement. *American Journal of Sociology,* 1977, **83,** 551–593.

Sweet, J. A. *Changes in the allocation of time by young women among schooling, marriage, work, and childbearing: 1960–1976.* CDE Working Paper 79-15. Madison: Center for Demography & Ecology, University of Wisconsin, 1979.

Tuma, N. B., Hannan, M. T., & Groeneveld, L. P. Dynamic analysis of event histories. *American Journal of Sociology,* 1979, **84,** 820–854.

United States Bureau of the Census. *1960 U.S. Census of Population* (Vol. 1): *Characteristics of the population.* Washington, D.C.: U.S. Government Printing Office, 1964.

United States Bureau of the Census. *1970 U.S. Census of Population* (Vol. 1): *Characteristics of the population.* Washington, D.C.: U.S. Government Printing Office, 1973.

United States Bureau of the Census. *Historical statistics of the United States, colonial times to 1970* (Bicentennial edition, Pt. 1 & 2). Washington, D.C.: U.S. Government Printing Office, 1975.

United States Bureau of the Census. *Statistical abstract of the United States: 1978.* Washington, D.C.: U.S. Government Printing Office, 1978.

Vaillant, G. *Adaptation to life.* New York: Little, Brown, 1977.

Winsborough, H. H. Statistical histories of the life cycle of birth cohorts: The transition from schoolboy to adult male. In K. E. Taeuber, L. L. Bumpass, & J. A. Sweet (Eds.), *Social demography.* New York: Academic Press, 1978.

Winsborough, H. H. Changes in the transition to adulthood. In M. W. Riley (Ed.), *Aging from birth to death: Interdisciplinary perspectives.* Boulder, Colorado: Westview Press, 1979.

Winship, C., & Mare. R. Structural equations and path analysis for discrete data. *American Journal of Sociology,* 1983, **88,** 54–110.

# Mental Illness and the Life Course

*John A. Clausen*

UNIVERSITY OF CALIFORNIA

BERKELEY, CALIFORNIA

LIFE-SPAN DEVELOPMENT
AND BEHAVIOR, VOL. 6

## Abstract

Severe mental disorder is likely to be seriously disruptive of social roles and relationships. Whether or not preceded by the manifestation of vulnerabilities or deficits in performance, mental disorder frequently results in the patient's being "off-time" in the expectable schedule for the life course. Such effects may be less, however, for recent cohorts of patients who are hospitalized for shorter periods and perhaps feel less stigmatized than patients hospitalized 30 or more years ago.

A long-term study of first-admission married patients reveals that a majority remain married and functional in the community 15 to 20 years after their initial breakdown. Few of these patients make a career of mental illness, even among those recurrently or persistently symptomatic. Symptoms tend to become less severe and functional capacities to increase in successive decades after initial hospitalization. On the other hand, even when there has been no recurrence of mental disorder, former patients, especially schizophrenics, appear to have few close ties to others and to avoid situations that entail risking rejection from others. The meaning of mental illness for the life course depends in part on the patient's age at onset, on the social skills attained prior to onset, on the course of the disorder, and on the circumstances of social response and treatment as these are influenced by historical change.

## I. Introduction

Severe mental disorder constitutes a life crisis almost without parallel and inevitably entails a continuing stress for patient and family. Psychosis can be totally disabling for long periods. In any instance of hospitalization for mental illness, the life course is in a sense suspended for a time; subsequently, it is likely to be restructured, with relationships altered and aspirations scaled down. Mental disorder is widely held to be stigmatized. Whether or not an episode of hospitalization leads to the former patient being treated differently, most patients are likely to fear such a consequence. Regardless of the circumstances that led to an initial breakdown, the knowledge of one's vulnerability must perforce be a source of anxiety and a threat to self-confidence. We would thus expect both objective and subjective consequences for the patient's life course.

The rubric, mental illness, embraces a broad and diverse spectrum of behaviors and conditions. It is perhaps a bit presumptuous to entitle an article "Mental Illness and the Life Course." I shall risk that attribution in the hope that an examination of some of the ways in which severe mental illness affects the life course will serve to stimulate more thorough research and analysis. Until very recently there were no longitudinal studies of adequate samples of mental patients. Most follow-up studies were undertaken to ascertain treatment effectiveness or the course of symptoms and impairment over relatively short time periods. In the past two decades, however, several large-scale studies have followed patients for substantial segments of the life span in both the United States and Europe, and we begin to have preliminary formulations regarding the variety of short- and long-term effects of severe mental illness, especially schizophrenia.

If mental disorder were usually transitory, like an upper respiratory infection, there would be little reason to undertake the analysis here presented. On the other hand, if mental disorder were almost always totally debilitating and progressive, our analysis would be limited to describing how the life course is truncated, and the nature and rapidity of decline. Most severe mental disorder is not transitory, but neither is it indefinitely enduring nor destined to end in debilitation. Severe mental illness may have its onset at any time from mid-adolescence to old age. Onset may be gradual, it may be foreshadowed by problematic behaviors and personality difficulties, or it may be sudden. The disorder itself may consist of a single acute episode, a succession of such episodes, or persistent symptoms. It may be followed by complete recovery or may leave substantial residual psychological impairment. We shall therefore want to explore variations in effects on the life course associated with age of onset, character, and course of the disorder.

The first section of this article will briefly review what is known about the precursors, course, and outcome of severe mental disorder, drawing upon diverse sources. I shall deal primarily with psychosis resulting in hospitalization, though I shall touch upon the neuroses and personality or character disorders insofar as they may entail substantial impairment and hospitalization. In the second section, I shall present data from a 20-year study of the impact of the mental illness (hospitalization of a husband or wife) on the family, viewing the data from a life course perspective. The group of patients on whom I shall be reporting is relatively small (80), but they and their families were studied intensively during the period of hospitalization and a substantial amount of information on their subsequent functioning was obtained 15 to 20 years after admission to the hospital. I shall deal with topics such as features of onset (suddenness, symptoms, role impairment), variations in the response of others to the patient's problem, role performance and family relationships in the period immediately following hospitalization, and role performance, particularly marital histories and occupational careers, over the 15 to 20 years following initial hospitalization.

## II. Psychosis and Social Roles: A General Overview

Any one study of a group of mental patients, especially an intensive study, is likely to be so limited in scope and sample size as to make generalization to larger patient populations hazardous. Therefore it behooves us to learn what we can about those larger populations from statistical compilations of treatment data, from epidemiological studies, or from any other sources available. Our focus is on the life course, and it will be useful to know whether there are, in general, precursors of severe mental disorder that set the prospective patient on a different course well before symptoms become apparent. If so, what are they and how do they exert their influence? At what age or life stage is psychosis most likely to occur, and how does this relate to the achievement of social competence as a fully adult member of the community? Given a psychotic episode that results in hospitalization, what is the probability that there will be subsequent episodes? If there are no subsequent episodes requiring treatment, what are the expected long-term consequences for marriage, rearing children, occupational career, and participation with one's fellows in society? And how is that same set of expectations changed by subsequent episodes of psychosis or by continuing symptoms or impaired functioning?

## A. THE DISORDERS INCLUDED HERE

Before we can address these questions, it is necessary to specify the nature and frequency of the disorders with which we shall be concerned. They are the so-called functional disorders—schizophrenia, affective disorders, neuroses, and personality or character disorders—insofar as they result in hospitalization. Episodes of severe mental illness that last more than a few weeks will usually result in hospitalization, though many persons will be treated in outpatient settings for less severe episodes of the same type of mental illness. We lack accurate information on the proportion of the mentally ill who never enter treatment, but it is appreciable.

Schizophrenia is characterized by disturbances of thinking, mood, and behavior, usually involving delusions and/or hallucinations and often resulting in bizarre behaviors stemming from the misperception of reality (Neale & Oltmanns, 1980). Most often the onset of schizophrenia is gradual, with months or even years of increasing tension and difficulty in relating to others, but in some cases the symptoms and signs may develop in florid form in a few days or weeks. A distinction is frequently made between those who have a long history of seeming different—called "process" schizophrenics—and those whose development has appeared to be relatively normal but who manifest acute psychotic symptoms following an intensely stressful experience—called "reactive" schizophrenics (Garmezy, 1968).

The affective disorders include major psychotic depression and bipolar (manic-depressive) disorders. The affective psychoses are much less frequently diagnosed in the United States than is schizophrenia.[1] Nonpsychotic depression is,

---

[1]In the United States, schizophrenia has typically been defined more broadly than in Great Britain and Europe. A cross-national study of diagnostic comparability revealed that nearly half the patients diagnosed schizophrenic by hospital staffs in the United States would have received diagnoses of "affective illness" if the diagnosticians used criteria derived from the International Classification of Diseases and the British Glossary of Mental Disorders (Cooper, Kendell, Garland, Sharpe, Copeland, & Simon, 1972).

however, the single most frequent diagnosis in outpatient treatment settings, and for young adults the category "depressive disorder" is second only to schizophrenia in its frequency among mental hospital admissions.[2] The affective psychoses are disorders of mood; either extreme depression, or less often, elation (manic phase) dominates the mental life of the person to such an extent that he or she loses contact with reality. Nonpsychotic depression does not entail the extreme impairment of reality testing (delusions, hallucinations, confusion) found in psychotic episodes but may nevertheless be sufficiently severe to disrupt eating and sleeping patterns and destroy all motivation. In depressive disorders, self-destruction is always a danger.

Although the category neuroses is no longer used in the official nomenclature of the American Psychiatric Association, it has until recently been used in statistical reports of the National Institute of Mental Health. The neuroses include those disorders in which the person's sense of reality is intact but in which anxiety impairs functioning through phobias, immobilization, or other manifestations. The category personality or character disorders, on the other hand, subsumes a wide variety of deeply ingrained, inflexible, maladaptive patterns of relating to environmental circumstances, other persons, and self (Vaillant & Perry, 1980). While most personality disorders and neuroses are treated in outpatient settings, when either condition entails intense suffering and/or distinctly problematic behavior on the part of the patient, hospitalization may result.

The effects of mental illness on the life course have been markedly modified in recent decades through the transformation of mental health services. Until the 1960s, our state hospitals (many of them enormous, poorly staffed, and prisonlike) were the primary source of treatment for severe mental illness. Most patients were committed involuntarily and confined for months or years. Since then, many new facilities have come into being to offer short-term inpatient treatment. There has been a proliferation of small, private mental hospitals and of psychiatric wards within general hospitals. Most patients can be persuaded to enter such hospitals voluntarily. Patients diagnosed schizophrenic are now as likely to receive treatment in such facilities as they are in state and county mental hospitals. Indeed, on initial entry into treatment, they most often come into private hospitals and psychiatric services of general hospitals rather than into public mental hospitals.

The changed array of services, as well as changes in the way in which statistics on patient care episodes are now collected and presented, greatly complicate

---

[2]Statistics on the number and characteristics of mental patients seen in various types of facilities are published by the National Institute of Mental Health in several series of publications. In recent years, as a consequence of changes in diagnostic usage, psychotic and nonpsychotic forms of depression are lumped together in a single category, "depressive disorder," in most NIMH statistical publications. Therefore it is not possible to present statistics by finer diagnostic categories, but we can at least differentiate hospitalized patients from those treated in outpatient clinics.

efforts to get an overview of the incidence of initial episodes of severe mental disorder by diagnostic category, age, sex, and marital status.[3] Nevertheless, it is possible to get some sense of the frequency of hospital admissions—initial and readmissions—for various diagnostic categories by combining the separate reports for state and county mental hospitals, private mental hospitals, Veterans Administration hospitals, and psychiatric inpatient services of general hospitals.[4]

The total number of patients aged 18 and over admitted to these facilities in 1975 was roughly 1,170,000. Of these, roughly 325,000 were diagnosed as suffering from alcohol disorders, drug disorders, or organic brain syndromes. Eliminating this group as being quite different from the types of disorder that concern us in the present analysis, nearly 850,000 admissions per year remain. Schizophrenia accounted for approximately 38% of this total and depressive disorders another 35%. Finally, neuroses and personality disorders accounted for 15%. Thus, of the disorders resulting in admission to any form of mental hospital other than for alcohol and drug-related disorders and organic brain syndromes, fully 73% are accounted for by schizophrenia and the depressive disorders and 88% by these two categories plus neuroses and personality disorders.

## B. SEX AND AGE DIFFERENCES

Overall rates of treatment for mental disorder do not differ markedly by sex, but men are more often hospitalized and women are more often treated in outpatient settings. Beyond this, there are significant variations in rates of inpatient admission to different types of facilities and in the diagnoses received by men and women. Men are more likely to be admitted to a state or county mental hospital or to a Veterans Administration hospital, while women are more likely to be admitted to private mental hospitals or to the psychiatric services of general hospitals. Rates of inpatient admission of males for schizophrenia exceed rates for women by about a 4 to 3 ratio, while rates of inpatient admission of women for depressive disorders exceed those for men by nearly a 2 to 1 ratio. Women are somewhat more likely to be hospitalized with a diagnosis of neurosis, men with a diagnosis of personality disorder (National Institute of Mental Health, 1981).

Space will permit only a brief discussion of these variations and the explanations that have been advanced for them. There is strong evidence that women are

---

[3]As a consequence of securing data from some facilities in summary form rather than receiving individual specifications, it is not possible to get detailed cross-tabulations that allow one to examine marital status by age, sex, *and* diagnostic category simultaneously, nor is it possible to examine details of inpatient characteristics separately from those of data from outpatients in Federally funded mental health centers.

[4]The data reported below are from Tables 4a–d, National Institute of Mental Health, 1981, pp. 46–52.

more likely to be in touch with their feelings and to acknowledge emotional distress (Horwitz, 1982). They are therefore somewhat more likely to seek professional help (Kessler, Brown, & Broman, 1981). The higher rate of depression among women (found almost universally in epidemiological studies) may well be related to traditional sex roles and the effects of male dominance, but a biological basis cannot be ruled out. Hormonal variations have an unquestioned effect upon emotions but so do the burdens of unremitting care for small children when a mother is without assistance or emotional support (Brown & Harris, 1978).

The higher rates of hospitalization of males may largely reflect the possibility of maintaining a woman in the home, even if she is not functioning effectively, while a man is expected to be able to meet the demands of a job. Most families cannot long manage to maintain their economic status if the husband is unable to work, so action is likely to be taken if he loses his job or fails to go to work because of mental disorder. Under such circumstances a man is likely to be more problematic around the house, while a woman may still carry out a part of her normal responsibilities. Economic factors are also implicated in the choice of hospital; an employed husband can more readily send a mentally ill spouse to a general hospital or to a private mental hospital than can a wife, whether or not employed, unless the family has insurance that covers mental disorder.

The probability of developing a mental disorder of any kind or of being treated for a mental disorder changes dramatically over the decades of the life course.

**TABLE I**

**Admission Rates per 100,000
Population by Sex and Age, Inpatient
Mental Health Services,[a] United
States, 1975**

| Age | Male | Female |
|---|---|---|
| Under 18 | 129.9 | 121.6 |
| 18–24 | 988.9 | 569.6 |
| 25–34 | 1198.7 | 812.3 |
| 35–44 | 1081.5 | 822.3 |
| 45–54 | 1263.6 | 703.6 |
| 55–64 | 826.6 | 486.6 |
| 65 and over | 492.0 | 308.2 |

[a] Includes admissions to State and county mental hospitals, private mental hospitals, Veterans Administration inpatient units, and (discharges from) general hospital inpatient psychiatric units. Represents consolidation of data in Tables 1a–d from National Institute of Mental Health, 1981, pp. 17–22.

Table I consolidates data on rates of admission, including readmission, by age and sex to all inpatient psychiatric services except those incorporated in federally funded community mental health services (for which separate inpatient and out-patient statistics are not published).[5] It will be noted that inpatient admissions prior to age 18 are just over 1 per 1000 population, while in the 18–24 age group they approach 1 per 100 for males and somewhat over half that rate for females. Male rates of inpatient admissions exceed those of females most sharply in the early adult years and after age 45. The higher rates of hospitalization of males in the early years may reflect the greater tendency of young males to act out aggressively, while higher rates in the later years are accounted for largely by disorders associated with alcohol use.

Psychoses begin to bulk large among mental hospital admissions only after age 18. Rates of admission for functional psychoses peak in the 25–35 age group, with schizophrenia making up a very large segment of these admissions. The median age of initial diagnosis of schizophrenia revealed by a continuing register of all persons coming into treatment in a community (Monroe County, New York) was 25 years for men and roughly 30 for women (Babigian, 1980). Although schizophrenia was once called *dementia praecox* or adolescent demen-tia, and its first manifestations occur with high frequency in late adolescence, the disorder may occur well along in the adult years. Moreover, readmissions of persons diagnosed schizophrenic continue to constitute a substantial proportion of all mental hospital admissions right up to age 65. Beyond age 35, however, the depressive disorders account for roughly half of all persons admitted to inpatient services except for state and county and Veteran's Administration hos-pitals (where disorders associated with alcohol abuse are found in large num-bers).[6]

From a winnowing of these statistics, it is clear that the probability of develop-ing a severe mental disorder is greater in the early adult years than in the later adult years (except for the organic disorders of old age), that the contingencies relating to use of treatment services differ for the sexes, and that the type of disorder diagnosed varies by both age and sex.

## C. MARITAL STATUS

Married persons are substantially less likely to utilize mental health services than are nonmarried persons, and the highest utilization rates occur among per-sons whose marriages have been disrupted by separation or divorce (National

---

[5]These data were derived from Tables 1a–d, National Institute of Mental Health, 1981, pp. 17–20.

[6]As we shall see, many patients who develop psychoses or have severe personality disorders turn to the heavy use of alcohol. It is likely, therefore, that some proportion of those later hospitalized for disorders associated with alcohol use have previously been diagnosed as suffering from psychosis or personality disorders.

Institute of Mental Health, 1975). The same patterns are found in studies of the prevalence of untreated symptoms of mental disorder. Because men are generally expected to take the initiative in proposing marriage and to make a substantial economic contribution to the household, whether or not their wives work, we might expect a stronger relationship between marital status and mental disorder for men than for women. That is, men with emotional problems would be less likely to marry. This expectation is borne out by the bulk of epidemiological research on the topic. Single men tend to have higher rates of mental disorder than do single women, while the reverse is true of the married, though not for all disorders (National Institute of Mental Health, 1975).

When we examine marriage rates of hospitalized patients by diagnosis, regardless of age and sex, those patients diagnosed schizophrenic stand out sharply. Among admissions to public mental hospitals in 1975 (proportionally more men), only 21% of the schizophrenics were currently married, fully 51% had never married, 25% were separated and divorced, and the remaining 4% were widowed (National Institute of Mental Health, 1981). Schizophrenic patients admitted to private hospitals (proportionally more women) were more likely to have been married and, indeed, a majority were currently married at the time of admission. Admissions to private hospitals comprised less than 30% of all admissions of schizophrenics but more than half the admissions of married schizophrenics.

Patients with affective (depressive) disorders are much more likely to have been married at the time of hospital admission. Only a fifth of 1975 admissions had never been married and nearly half were currently married, while a fourth were separated or divorced (National Institute of Mental Health, 1981). Patients with depressive disorders tend to be a bit older than those diagnosed schizophrenic, but this accounts for only a small part of the difference between the two diagnostic categories. Relative to the general population, it would appear that depressives are only slightly less likely to marry but somewhat more likely to divorce.

Patients hospitalized with personality disorders tend to be younger than either of the major categories of psychotics and to be less often married as a consequence. Less than one-fifth were married at admission, and well over half had never been married. Age alone, however, does not explain the low marriage rate. A substantially larger percentage of persons admitted with personality disorders were divorced or separated than were currently married—27.4 vs 16.9%, respectively (National Institute of Mental Health, 1981). Divorces approximately balanced current marriages for patients receiving a diagnosis of neurosis.

Thus, persons hospitalized for mental disorder, especially men, are less likely to marry in early adulthood than are their nonhospitalized peers. If they do marry, they are much more likely to become separated or divorced from their partners. Further light on the relatively low rate of early marriage is afforded by studies that have sought to establish the precursors of mental disorder, especially schizophrenia.

## III. Antecedents and Course of Psychoses

To be human is to have the capacity for deep emotional upset or mental disorder. Life stresses may be so acute as to overwhelm even the healthiest of persons. Apart from such stress, however, most of us have vulnerabilities acquired in the course of socialization, whether from harsh mistreatment or from loving care that was overly protective or went otherwise awry at times. And apart from the developmental experiences by which our personalities are shaped, some of us bear genetic or constitutional vulnerabilities to mental as well as physical disorders.

Efforts to trace the consequences of early vulnerabilities for the later development and course of mental disorder are relatively recent. Longitudinal studies of "high risk" populations are in process, most of them following children who may have a genetic vulnerability to developing schizophrenia, or who have been subjected to extremely traumatic life circumstances, or whose behavior has been seriously problematic.[7] Until such studies have traced the long-term consequences of various sources of vulnerability, we have to rely on research based largely on retrospection for possible antecedents of disorders among persons who are followed up after treatment or on studies that examine early records relating to persons who become patients. Because schizophrenia is the most frequent and most ominous of severe mental illnesses, we have far more information about schizophrenia than about any other disorder.

### A. PRECURSORS OF MENTAL DISORDER

It has long been recognized that some persons who develop schizophrenia have from an early age seemed to differ from their peers in certain respects, while others who ultimately receive the diagnosis have been quite indistinguishable from their peers. Summarizing the data on precursors of schizophrenia, Goldstein (1980, p. 330) notes that there exists "a group of schizophrenics, the so-called poor premorbid group, who show severe withdrawal and social isolation during late adolescence and in some instances in late childhood as well." In an early study, Kohn and I (Clausen & Kohn, 1960) compared schizophrenics hospitalized over a period of two decades from a small Maryland city with a control group of their school classmates and discovered that roughly one-third of

---

[7]Garmezy (1974a,b) has provided an excellent discussion of the studies in progress at the time of his review. A major volume of reports from a consortium of high-risk investigators will soon appear.

the boys and girls who later were hospitalized with a diagnosis of schizophrenia had in early adolescence been characterized as socially isolated in their play patterns, with few ties outside the family. Only 4% of the controls had been similarly lacking in ties outside the family. The isolates who became schizophrenic had almost all been perceived by their families as shy and fearful or otherwise problematic during childhood. A study of young schizophrenics by Kreisman (1970) found that they were far less likely than normal controls to have had intimate ties with peers.

Several studies have followed-back persons who were identified as adult schizophrenics to seek early cues in school records (Bower, Shellhammer, & Daily, 1960; Watt, Stolorow, Lubensky, & McClelland, 1970). A number of statistically significant differences have been found, though again they reflect deviant performance for only a segment of the schizophrenic group. It is primarily the males who are easily discriminated from their normal peers. Schizophrenic males as a group were seen in their high school years as more irritable, aggressive, and negativistic, and more often behaved in deviant ways. Others who later developed schizophrenia were more apathetic, and less well liked by peers, attributes more closely related to the withdrawal–social isolation finding. Significant differences from normal peers have been found on a number of attributes relating to scholastic motivation, emotional stability, and agreeableness (Garmezy, 1974a). It has also been noted in the literature that insofar as preschizophrenics show acting out, aggressive behavior, it was primarily directed against members of their own family and not manifest in more common types of delinquency. Lack of heterosexual relationships and experiences is frequently noted as characteristic of males with early onset and those who tend to have poor prognosis.

Follow-back studies have shown somewhat different results for female schizophrenics. During their school years the girls who later became schizophrenic were seen as more immature, conforming, and introverted but more calm than their classmates. Only as they became withdrawn and isolated in middle adolescence did some of the girls who later developed schizophrenia diverge sharply from their normal peers.

There is little if any evidence that persons who develop affective psychoses were to a significant degree set off from their peers in childhood and adolescence. Euphoria and substantial mood swings are common in adolescence and it would require very careful monitoring to assess their incidence or other possible precursors of later affective disorder. There is some evidence that psychotic depression tends to be associated with early loss of a parent, but most children who lose a parent do not subsequently experience so drastic a consequence. There is little reason to suspect that most persons who will develop an affective psychosis differ substantially in their early life experiences or their personalities from their peers.

Personality disorders, on the other hand, are more likely to be linked to problematic socialization and to interpersonal difficulties during childhood and adolescence. Robins (1966) followed up into the adult years children who had been seen in a child guidance clinic an average of 30 years before. She found both a somewhat higher than expected proportion who developed schizophrenia and a much higher proportion who were labeled "sociopaths," many of them hospitalized and others sent to prison. Perhaps the most important experiential feature that characterized these children was the extent to which they were alienated and hostile, and therefore unable to fit into the normal developmental channels and carry out the tasks expected of them in school and family. This is not to say that the problem originated in the personality of the child; it was perhaps more often a reflection of extremely disturbed family relationships and flaws in the preparation these children had received to carry out expected tasks.

To sum up, a severely problematic childhood and adolescence is by no means the norm for men and women who develop a serious mental disorder during their adult years. Nevertheless, for a fraction of those who become schizophrenic and for some of those who are later diagnosed as suffering from personality disorders, adolescence is a seriously problematic time. Some preschizophrenics, especially males, have extreme difficulty in establishing heterosexual relationships. They are much less likely to engage in courtship or to marry at the age when most of their peers do. And to the extent that they drop out of school because of personal discomfort or difficulty in getting along with others, they are less well prepared for an average expectable life course.

## B. THE COURSE OF SCHIZOPHRENIA

Perhaps the most important thing to be said about the course of schizophrenia is that research has now quite conclusively demonstrated that schizophrenia has no typical course. There are many possible outcomes of an acute schizophrenic episode. One of the more common of these is complete recovery, with no recurrence. While some psychiatrists would speak of "remission" and regard the once-acute patient as always to some degree mentally ill, others would state that once the former patient has no detectable symptoms or signs of schizophrenia, he should be regarded as free of the disorder.

Kraepelin (1897/1918), who first characterized and described "dementia praecox," which Eugen Bleuler later termed "the group of schizophrenias," believed that the disorder led almost inevitably to mental deterioration. E. Bleuler (1911/1950) was somewhat more sanguine, but nevertheless tended toward the belief that schizophrenia most often led to a state of persistent thought disorder. Bleuler's son Manfred, however, who succeeded his father as head of the Burgholzli Hospital in Zurich, carried out long-term studies of schizophrenic patients which led him to a quite different conclusion (M. Bleuler, 1972/1978).

Of the patients whom Bleuler followed up, some had recovered completely after a single episode of illness, some had experienced repeated episodes but were capable of self-management most of the time, and some—less than a fifth of all patients originally admitted to the hospital with a diagnosis of schizophrenia— remained severely impaired. More recently, several other European investigators have come to very similar conclusions.

There is considerable evidence that long hospitalization is itself a cause of deterioration, rather than merely being a reflection of disease. Studies following up cohorts of patients on first admission with a diagnosis of schizophrenia have indicated that the longer a patient remained in the hospital beyond a year or two, the less the likelihood of that patient's ever being released to the community (Kramer, 1955). We now know, moreover, that short length of stay and ultimate recovery are not attributable to patients having been misdiagnosed as schizophrenic. Recent European follow-up studies (Ciompi, 1980; Huber, Gross, Schuttler, & Linz, 1980) indicate that schizophrenic patients diagnosed by rigorous criteria show no poorer prognosis than those who were clearly not affective but had less definitively schizophrenic symptoms.

The large scale, long-term follow-up studies of schizophrenia conducted in Europe in the past two decades and more recently reported in the United States, and the many follow-up studies in this country (e.g., Bland, Parker, & Orn, 1978; Vaillant, 1978) give a much more positive picture of outcome in schizophrenia than had been dreamed of 30 years ago. The following conclusions seem warranted: (1) between one-fourth and one-third of patients who receive a diagnosis of schizophrenia on first admission to a mental hospital appear to be completely free of symptoms or signs of mental disorder 20 years later; (2) at the other extreme, between a fifth and a third of patients show a substantial level of impairment due to symptoms of disorder, though few manifest the bizarre symptoms of the acute state, their impairment being more largely apathy and general lack of well-being; (3) well before the beginnings of pharmacotherapy and community care, a substantial proportion (from one-fourth up to perhaps almost one-half) of persons initially hospitalized with a diagnosis of schizophrenia experienced only a single episode of hospitalization; and (4) even among patients who show some residual mental impairment, more than half seem to be capable of independent functioning in the community as of 20 or more years following their initial hospitalization.

As might be anticipated, premorbid personality difficulties are associated with a relatively poor outcome in schizophrenia. So is a gradual as opposed to a sudden onset. In a survey of the world literature, Zubin, Sutton, and Salzinger (1961) located 177 studies that assessed type of onset as either sudden or gradual and in all 177, those patients with sudden onset had a superior outcome. More recently Turner and Gartrell (1978), in a sophisticated statistical analysis, found that the level of competence demonstrated prior to illness accounts for more variance in total time hospitalized (over a period of years) than do social class, marital status, and work performance, singly or in combination. Since demonstrated social competence is the best indicator of good premorbid personality status, we are left with the unresolved question of whether we are dealing primarily with an intrapersonal (perhaps constitutional) vulnerability or with the product of intrapersonal attributes and socialization experiences. In any event, earlier, gradual onset tends to be associated with poor premorbid personality, with lower educational and occupational attainment, and with a less favorable outcome in terms of symptoms and impairment.

The relationship between continued psychopathology and social functioning is far from perfect. Nevertheless, there is a strong relationship. Huber and colleagues (1980) found that 97% of their schizophrenic probands (drawn from a Bonn hospital) who showed complete remission of symptoms at follow-up were fully employed at their previous occupational level, or, in the case of female patients, were functioning as housewives at a normal level of performance. Of those who had a degree of psychiatric impairment but no severe symptoms at follow-up (two-fifths of the total group) 30% were fully employed at their previous level of performance and another 30% were fully employed but at a somewhat lower level than that at which they had previously functioned. For the entire group of former schizophrenics, 56% were fully employed as of an average of 22 years after onset. A majority of those schizophrenic patients whom Huber followed up not only escaped serious deterioration but appeared to be living reasonably normal lives outside the mental hospital.

A study of patients hospitalized from Lausanne, conducted by Ciompi (1980) between 1964 and 1969, followed surviving probands from all those hospitalized with a diagnosis of schizophrenia who had been born between 1873 and 1897. The median duration from initial hospitalization to follow-up was approximately 37 years. Half of these patients had been hospitalized only once in their lives, most often for less than 6 months. Because the average age of probands at follow-up was in excess of 75 years, and many had impairments of old age, Ciompi could not use the criteria of adequate functioning usually applied to younger persons. Nevertheless, 15% were employed full time and 37% part time among these older men and women who had at one time been hospitalized for schizophrenia. Fully 57% were judged to be better adapted than before hospitalization. On the other hand, only about one-third were judged to be "well adjusted" in terms of a combination of three criteria: ability to maintain themselves independently, good social relationships, and freedom from mental conflicts.

As previously noted, men and women diagnosed schizophrenic are less likely than their normal peers to marry. Unfortunately, few of the follow-up studies have obtained complete marital histories. Manfred Bleuler (1972/1978), who did obtain such histories, found that on initial admission only about a third of the men and less than half of the women who were hospitalized at Burghölzli with a diagnosis of schizophrenia had been married. Even at follow-up, 20 years later, only about half of the men had ever married, and a fourth of them had never had any kind of love relationship or, so far as Bleuler could ascertain, sexual relations. A third of the women were likewise "nonerotic," to use Bleuler's term. On the other hand, more than two-fifths of the women had been intimately involved with multiple partners, often in illicit relationships. It seems likely that the sexual behavior of many of these women was little different from that of their nonschizophrenic sisters, except for their inability to conceal it.

Finally, several follow-up studies have noted the impoverished social relationships of former patients, especially schizophrenics. Our own study of patients from a small Maryland city, compared with control subjects individually paired on the basis of age, sex, and father's occupation as of many years earlier, found that only 15% of the former schizophrenics met at least weekly with friends while 53% of controls did so (Clausen & Kohn, 1960).

## C. THE COURSE OF AFFECTIVE PSYCHOSES

When we turn to the affective psychoses—major depressive disorder and bipolar disorder (the latter being synonymous with the former manic-depressive disorder)—the picture is quite different. In the absence of antidepressive medications and lithium carbonate, recurrence of acute attacks is to be expected in the large majority of patients (ranging from three-fourths to nine-tenths), but symptoms and impairment are usually minimal in the periods between acute episodes.

While only a few follow-up studies of patients with affective disorders have inquired into the general functioning of the patients, Wolpert (1980, p. 1327) states "Without prophylactic treatment the usual course of recurrent episodic affective disorders is gradual loss of social, economic and psychological position in society." On the other hand, very high levels of occupational and artistic performance are noted for a number of manic-depressive patients after many years of recurring episodes. A major danger is that in the depressive phase the patient will commit suicide.

High levels of conflict have been noted in the families of manic-depressive patients and broken marriages are certainly more frequent than among the general population of comparable social status, but patients who develop affective psychoses do not appear to shy away from the opposite sex, as evidenced by the data on marriage rates earlier reported.

## IV. Description of the Research

### A. ISSUES AND THEMES

Given this overview, we are now in a position to identify what are likely to be the most salient influences of mental disorder on the life course. The life course is always anchored in a particular historical period and is therefore subject to pronounced cohort effects. Advances in psychiatric treatment and changed administrative practices over the past 30 years have led to marked cohort differences in the experience of patients in all diagnostic groupings. Diminished length of hospitalization is perhaps the most striking change. In place of a median duration of over 6 months for schizophrenic patients and just a bit less for patients with affective psychoses as of the early 1950s, a patient in the early 1980s is usually retained in hospital for substantially less than 1 month in most jurisdictions. Schizophrenics admitted to public mental hospitals stayed an average of less than 6 weeks in 1975; those admitted to private hospitals stayed about half as long and those admitted to general hospitals had an average stay of less than 2 weeks (National Institute of Mental Health, 1981). Moreover, despite the many shortcomings of our community mental health system, it appears that most patients hospitalized in metropolitan areas will receive some outpatient treatment as a follow-up to initial hospitalization.

Accompanying new treatments and administrative practices have come changes in the very concept of mental disorder, especially schizophrenia (Zubin & Spring, 1977). Both genetic and experiential elements appear to be involved in its etiology, and social response can shape its course. Most patients are now expected to be able to manage in the community after a brief period of hospitalization. There is some evidence that the dread and sense of stigma attached to mental disorder have been reduced, though not eliminated (Clausen, 1981b). Concern for the rights of the mentally ill and of handicapped persons generally has undoubtedly increased the probability that a former patient will be reemployed, if that person's work performance had previously been satisfactory.

In the data to be presented, I shall examine the consequences of these rather fundamental changes in outlook and in practice as they impinge upon the patient's life at the time of an acute episode: the degree of disruption of normal roles, the speed with which the patient is reincorporated in the family and other enduring relationships following such an episode, and the level of the patient's functioning in the community.

In a study of outpatients to a psychiatric clinic, Gould (1972, pp. 525–526) observed a decided relationship between types of problems presented and ages of the patients. Young adults (18–22) were most concerned with managing to achieve autonomy from their parents. From 22 to 28 "most of their energy [was] spent mastering what they [were] supposed to be," with commitments made and relatively high confidence that they were growing and building for the future. The early 30s, on the other hand, brought doubts about what they were supposed to be. They wished to be accepted as they were. Such "questioning of self, values and life itself" became more acute in the next decade, with an increasing sense of urgency.

Gould's patients were not psychotic. By and large they came to the clinic to deal more effectively with the problems that confronted them. But these problems clearly were posed by the major roles occupied and the patient's success in making expected transitions or consolidating role responsibilities. Psychotic patients often face additional problems, but they must certainly achieve autonomy from their parents, master an occupational role, or find an equivalent role that provides for personal growth as well as security, and they must in time form enduring relationships with others, most readily achieved through marriage. If they cannot master these role transitions, they cannot achieve full competence as adults.

Let us now consider how the life course might be affected by various aspects or correlates of severe mental disorder. Precursors such as premorbid personality and interpersonal difficulties as well as early onset may prevent attainment of the degree of interpersonal competence necessary for assuming adult roles on schedule. Attainment of autonomy and of the capacity for intimacy are tasks usually achieved in late adolescence and early adulthood. Knowledge of being "off-time" in making one's way, relative to peers and to general social expectations, may be a source of severe stress, especially when one lacks the skills needed to catch up (Neugarten & Hagestad, 1976). It would appear that at least one-third of the young men and women who will later develop schizophrenia and perhaps a like proportion of those with personality disorders and neuroses are likely to be "off-time" by virtue of such deficits or of the onset of the disorder prior to attainment of full adult competence.

Once a psychotic disorder is manifest in an acute episode, many role performances are likely to be markedly impaired and even the most intimate of relationships may be disrupted. There will frequently be a period of weeks, months, or even years of problematic behavior before the patient is hospitalized (Clausen & Yarrow, 1955). What happens to relationships and performances in this period may have substantial implications for reincorporation of the patient following hospitalization. For example, some patients may perform well on the job until immediately before hospitalization; others have blow-ups, quit their jobs, or perform in an unsatisfactory manner and lose their jobs prior to hospitalization.

In general, we might expect disturbed persons who were employed to be hospitalized more quickly than those not employed, for the former will be subject to more rigorous scheduling and assessment both of job performance and of general demeanor. Employed women whose husbands have adequate income might, however, be expected to withdraw from their jobs and perhaps enter outpatient rather than inpatient treatment. In the case of mothers, care of children is likely to be the crucial consideration in deciding how to deal with symptoms of severe mental disorder.

The period of hospitalization is itself a critical phase in the life course, for it almost inevitably brings to the patient a sense of failure and a loss of confidence. Unlike physical illness, where the patient is absolved of any blame for becoming ill, the hospitalized mental patient will frequently have a sense of having behaved badly. We may assume that an important element in the hospital experience is the degree of continuing contact with the circle of those who have been important to the patient. The longer the stay, the more likely is a break in such contact.

The immediate posthospital period is likely to be one suffused with anxiety on the part of both patient and significant others as to how relationships and role performances will work out. The patient's freedom from symptoms now and his ability to mobilize himself to cope with the problems of everyday life will become critical determinants of performance. The transition from the mental hospital to life in the community seems likely to be more stressful for patients who have been hospitalized for a long period than for those only briefly hospitalized, and may be especially difficult for those who are still experiencing disturbing thoughts and feelings related to their acute symptoms.

How much respite should one claim, after hospitalization, before resuming full responsibility in the family or at work? Should one try to return to one's old job or seek a new job? If the latter, should one acknowledge having experienced a psychotic episode? Quite apart from what one tells others, what does one tell oneself about the chances of another breakdown as against the chances of attaining the dreams that had guided one in the past?

We might assume that the former patient would achieve full confidence of ability to meet normal role obligations only after a period of demonstrated competence as a spouse, parent, employee, or valued member of the community. Recurrent symptoms or feeling overwhelmed by the challenge of taking up responsibilities would confirm an identity as mental patient.

Because successful role performance appears to be highly related to the level of episodic or persistent symptoms, it seems desirable to try to trace out the dominant life course features for at least three separate groups: (1) those who have been free of episodes of serious upset in recent years and seem capable of essentially normal role performance; (2) those who from time to time still experience episodes of upset severe enough to impair functioning, but who between episodes are able to cope reasonably well with adult roles; and (3) those who are persistently symptomatic or who manifest a considerable degree of residual impairment. As we shall see, the marital, occupational, and general social relational histories of these three groups tend to be quite different, though the groups are by no means homogeneous.

Mental patients are thus subject to major transitions that are quite unlike the expected transitions in a normal life course. If they negotiate the transition back to the community and are able to resume normal roles, they must then cope with expected transitions as well. If they do not return to full functioning, how do they fare? In either case, we may ask how these former patients cope with expectable life crises, and how they invest themselves in the process of living. The answers available from the data in hand are far less detailed than one might wish, but certain general patterns are manifest even in our somewhat sketchy evidence.

## B. SAMPLE AND RESEARCH DESIGN

The patients on whose lives I shall be reporting were selected for a study of the impact of mental illness on the family. The initial group (Phase 1) was a reasonably representative sample of married patients, not previously hospitalized, who experienced a functional psychosis or a severe neurosis or character disorder and were as a consequence admitted to public mental hospitals in the Washington, D. C. area between 1952 and 1959. Our intent was to study what happened to the family when either husband or wife was admitted to a mental hospital at a time when such admission was likely to be for a duration of many months. Patients' ages ranged from 21 to 49 in the original sample, with the median just under 35. Interviews in the initial sample were conducted between 1952 and 1959. Sixty-three Washington area patients, 36 men and 27 women, met our sampling specifications for inclusion in the original study (white, married, resident in the area at least a year, aged 20 to 49, not previously hospitalized with functional diagnoses). In our analyses we have combined data for this group with data from 17 women studied in California in the late 1950s by Sampson, Messinger, and Towne (1964), all first admissions to a California state hospital and diagnosed schizophrenic. The criteria of selection were essentially the same as those for the Washington study, but the California study was far more intensive.[8] Both the Washington, D. C. and the California samples were followed up in 1972 to ascertain the courses that the lives of patients and families had taken subsequent to the initial hospitalization.

A second cohort of patients was studied in the early 1970s (Phase 2), comprising some 39 patients (19 male and 20 female) in the same areas as those of the initial study. The Phase 2 study was designed to assess changes in the impact of mental illness on patient and family as a consequence of the revolution in mental health care that took place between the 1950s and the 1970s. Some patients were drawn from the public mental hospitals that provided the original sample, but most of the Phase 2 sample were drawn from psychiatric services of general

---

[8]The California study was originally undertaken to parallel, with a sample of female patients, the first phase of the Washington study, which concentrated on male patients. In the California study, both patient and spouse (and usually other informants as well) were interviewed intensively for up to 100 weeks after the wife's admission to the hospital. The verbatim interview transcripts prepared by the California research group were made available by Sheldon Messinger for abstracting and coding, using the set of codes developed for the Washington sample.

hospitals and private mental hospitals. The availability of insurance to cover brief hospitalization for mental disorder and the reorganization of institutional facilities for the care of mental disorder in the intervening 20 years sharply changed patterns of utilization of public mental hospitals. It was necessary to turn to private facilities in order to secure a sample of first-admission married patients who would be similar to those studied previously.[9]

For the patients and families studied, data were derived from a series of interviews beginning soon after initial hospitalization and usually lasting until after the patient's return home. Most often we have a series of four or more interviews during the period of hospitalization and just after, but for a few families we have only one or two. In addition, for most of the families studied in the 1950s, follow-up data were obtained by interview 15 to 20 years after the initial contact. The patient's spouse was the primary respondent in the first phase of the research and in the follow-up as well. In a few instances, where the marriage had been terminated, the patient was our follow-up respondent. And in the Phase 2 study, at least one posthospital interview was obtained with the patient in three-fourths of the families represented.

The initial interview focused on the onset of mental disorder, the symptoms presented, the roles impaired, and the spouses' response to the manifest difficulties of the patient. Thereafter we secured data on family relationships, occupational history prior to admission, and plans for the patient's return. In both phases, interviews were conducted with the spouse and often with the patient as well 6 months to 1 year after the patient's return home. Thus we were able to learn something about the process of adaptation immediately following hospitalization.

The long-term follow-up inquired into subsequent hospitalization or other treatment, the persistence of symptoms, the status of the marriage and of family relationships, the posthospital occupational history of the patient, current social activities, and an assessment of what the hospitalization had meant for patient and family. Thus, while the focus of the research was not on the patient's life history, we have data that bear upon many aspects of the life history.

---

[9]In both phases of the research, a substantial majority of the patients were diagnosed psychotic— 85% in Phase 1 and 70% in Phase 2. A review of diagnoses, using all data available as of time of initial hospitalization and the more rigorous Research Diagnostic Criteria for schizophrenia (Spitzer, Endicott, & Robins, 1978), reveals that at least one-third of the schizophrenic diagnoses must be considered suspect. In some instances, initially diagnosed schizophrenic, patients were subsequently reclassified as manic-depressives; in other instances they appear to have had brief psychotic reactions, and in a few instances they appear to have been suffering from character or personality disorders exacerbated in an episode of acute excitement or anxiety.

## V. The Prepatient Years

### A. THE EARLY YEARS

In Phase 1 of the research we did not secure data on the patients' early life experiences except as these were commented on by their spouses. Such comments were most often made in the context of the spouse's attempts to account for the patient's breakdown. Rejection by a parent or, more often in the case of male patients, being pampered by an overly protective mother were frequently mentioned. So was conflict within the family and difficulty in peer relationships. Deprivation and overt pathology were much more often reported for working class patients, especially women. But since there exists no control group with which comparisons can be made, our data do not permit anything more than the impression that the backgrounds of our married patients showed the same kind of patterned variations as are described in the literature on schizophrenia except for the somewhat greater heterosexual involvement of the males.

The heterosexual involvement of the men in itself suggests that they were "good premorbids" and would be expected to have relatively favorable outcomes. Nevertheless, half of these men were seen by their wives as having had problematic interpersonal relationships and were regarded as not fully "normal" prior to the onset of symptoms. Many men were characterized as immature or anxious, both among those diagnosed schizophrenic and those with personality disorders or neuroses. Of the female patients, only one-fifth were regarded by their husbands as having been "normal" before the episode that brought them into treatment. Nearly half were characterized as highly anxious, nervous persons. For both sexes, only among those diagnosed as having affective psychoses was the majority characterized by their spouses as essentially normal.

In the Phase 2 sample, in response to direct questioning, more than half the male patients and one-third of the female patients were reported to have a mentally ill parent or sibling but none of the spouses was reported to have had mentally ill parents or siblings. Otherwise there were no statistically significant or even appreciable differences in the reported occurrence of family crises or specific trauma in the early lives of the patients and their spouses. Patients did not view their childhoods as having been more unhappy than did spouses, despite the greater prevalence of psychopathology among parents and siblings.

### B. MARITAL HISTORIES PRIOR TO HOSPITALIZATION[10]

A few of the male patients were over 30 when they first married, but the median age of marriage was only slightly if at all above that for the general

---

[10]A more detailed description of the marriages and of the ways in which characteristics of the marital relationship influenced response to the patient's symptoms is contained in Clausen (1983). Data were secured from either spouse or patient or from both.

population. The great majority of the women married before 25. Perhaps the most striking finding was the frequency with which marriages occurred after only minimal acquaintance. Nearly a third of the wives of male patients and more than half the husbands of female patients in Phase 1 indicated that they had not really known the patient well at the time of marriage. Many marriages seem to have been made on impulse, after very short acquaintances. Depth of acquaintance was not related to diagnosis but, as would be expected, conflictful marriages predominated among those couples who had not been well acquainted. It is likely that recent conflict affected current reports of acquaintance at marriage. At the same time, the evidence of minimal acquaintance in many instances—sometimes no more than a few days of contact—is very strong.

The modal couple in our Phase 1 sample had been married 7 or 8 years and both members were in their early thirties. The great majority were in their first marriage, though several female patients had been previously married. Whereas 90% of the families of female patients contained children (an average of 2.5 each), only 75% of the families of male patients had children (an average of 1.5 each). Schizophrenic men and those with personality disorders were less likely to have children than men with affective disorders.

The marital relationship was much more often severely strained before the onset of mental disorder in families in which the wife became a patient. Substantial dissatisfactions and major conflicts had characterized a fifth of the marriages of male patients and half the marriages of female patients. Where symptomatic behavior long antedated hospital admission, it is likely that reports of the marital relationship prior to illness were more negatively tinged by the turmoil of recent events, but in many instances there was strong evidence of longstanding pervasive conflict.

Sampson *et al.* (1962, p. 88) noted a pattern that characterized roughly half the families of schizophrenic women in the California sample and a number of those in the Washington area sample as well:

> The marital partners and their children lived together as a relatively independent, self-contained nuclear family, but the marital relation was characterized by mutual withdrawal and separate worlds of involvement. At some point during the marriage, often quite early, one or both of the partners had experienced extreme dissatisfaction with the marriage. This was ordinarily accompanied by a period of violent, open discord; in other cases, the dissatisfaction was expressed only indirectly, through reduced communication with the marital partner. In either event, the partners withdrew from each other, and each gradually developed separate involvements.

This pattern occurred also, though less frequently, in the families of male patients. In general, wives were much more responsive to the emotional states of male prepatients than were husbands of female prepatients. Husbands of women who became patients often seemed almost totally unresponsive and lacking in empathy.

For a number of the couples it appears that the transition to marriage posed a demand for adjustment beyond the prepatient's capacities. Women, especially, often exhibited strong dependence on their mothers. Sampson and associates identified two forms of crisis that schizophrenic women experienced: crises of separation (from maternal dependence) and crises of identification, which frequently entailed the revival, in the marital family, of early identification with their mothers. Most often these crises of identification derived from the wife's own experience as a parent.

In a few of the families of male patients we find somewhat similar patterns, but more often the problem was the husband's inability to relate intimately to his wife. In the most extreme instance, the husband told his wife on the day after their marriage that he did not wish to be married. In several other instances, the husband continued to spend almost as much time in the parental home as in the marital home.

The Phase 2 sample was slightly older on the average and had been married a few years longer. The women patients in particular were of somewhat higher socioeconomic status and there was less extreme tension in these families than in those of many of the Phase 1 women patients. Nevertheless, there was again strong evidence that the husbands were relatively unresponsive to their wives' needs for companionship, affection, and communication.

From our data and from other research we can conclude that many of the marriages of mental patients are problematic not merely because of the prepatient's personality attributes and emotional problems but because of marital selection processes and the circumstances under which marriages are made. Women who subsequently develop schizophrenia often marry men who are emotionally unresponsive and not infrequently sociopathic (see also Mednick, 1978). Men who subsequently develop schizophrenia often marry women who were attracted by the men's sensitivity and apparent vulnerability (Planansky & Johnston, 1967). Kreitman (1964, 1968), in a series of studies of mental patients and their spouses, has concluded that persons who develop functional psychoses tend to select for marriage and be selected by other persons who are themselves mentally impaired. To the extent that such tendencies exist, they are likely to increase the difficulties of establishing a mutually supportive marital relationship. The transition to married life is then qualitatively different for many prepatients than for their peers who will never be hospitalized.

## C. OCCUPATIONAL EXPERIENCES

Most of the male patients had established themselves in an occupation prior to the onset of mental illness. Nearly half of the Phase 1 patients and well over half of the Phase 2 patients had been with the same employer for more than 5 years at the time of hospitalization. Two-thirds of the Phase 1 patients were white collar workers, though none were major professionals or executives. Of the male patients in Phase 2, half were white collar (several of them professionals) and the other half blue collar workers. A few men had not made a firm occupational commitment, and roughly a fifth of the Phase 1 men gave evidence of considerable instability, shifting from one job to another, sometimes quitting jobs for quixotic reasons well before the apparent onset of illness.

The great majority of the female patients in Phase 1 had been housewives. Roughly one in eight had been employed prior to the onset of symptoms, and of these, half had been with their employer for less than 1 year. Phase 2 female patients were more likely to have been employed, but of the two-fifths who worked half time or more in the year prior to admission, half had been with their present employer for less than 1 year. The primary reasons for working were most often a desire to have money for extras, coupled with a wish to establish a separate identity or degree of independence.

We do not have systematic information on the general level of competence with which those women who remained at home accomplished their housewifely chores. For the most part, however, it appeared that prior to the onset of illness, wives carried out their responsibilities adequately, so far as their husbands were concerned. Many of the husbands of female patients had themselves shown marked occupational instability and appeared emotionally problematic.

For our two samples of married patients, then, it appears that prior to the onset of mental disorder, most men had achieved a level of occupational competence and most women a level of competence either in a job or at home that permitted their meeting normal role responsibilities, though sometimes marginally. For both sexes, there were occasional interpersonal problems associated with working, but these appear to have been most acute in the year prior to hospital admission except for those prepatients who had not achieved a measure of occupational stability.

## VI. Becoming a Mental Patient

### A. SYMPTOMS AND ROLE IMPAIRMENT

The first signs of mental disorder were seldom seen as such. Most often the prepatient seemed out-of-sorts, easily upset, more than usually nervous, perhaps unable to sleep. Other persons responded to the distressed one in a variety of ways, depending on the quality of the relationship. Many husbands and wives were initially annoyed or angry, others puzzled, and, a few, sympathetic. Wives were in general more sympathetic and solicitous of their husbands than were husbands of wives who were upset (Clausen, 1983). Relatively few spouses of either sex interpreted the problem as a mental disorder until symptoms had become much more obviously deviant and role functions were seriously impaired.

It is of interest to note how symptoms and impairment related to the age of the patient at the time of onset. Except where the symptoms or signs included delusions, hallucinations, or extremely bizarre behaviors, most roles were not markedly impaired in the early stages of illness. Relationships between the spouses were often strained, and there might be anxiety about job performance or interpersonal difficulties on the job, but even markedly symptomatic patients were usually able to meet their basic role responsibilities for a time. Impairment was first evident in the role of spouse for nearly one-third of the Phase 1 patients, male and female alike. Accusations of infidelity, failure to involve the spouse in major decisions affecting the family, termination of sexual relationships, or violence against the spouse often occurred before other problems were apparent. Violations of role expectations in marriage were most acute in the case of younger men and those married less than 5 years and were unrelated to preexisting marital harmony. Men under 30 also more often were reported to have had problems on the job, and they were in general less well established and secure occupationally.

As symptoms intensified and stresses mounted, role impairment became more severe. In the period just before admission to the hospital the great majority of patients were performing very few roles adequately. As expected men were hospitalized more promptly than women in Phase 1; however, in Phase 2 there was little difference (Clausen, 1983). More of the female patients were employed in the Phase 2 sample, which may help to explain the prompter hospitalization of women in the later period. Age at onset was not significantly related to duration of symptoms prior to hospitalization for men, but women over 30 (and those married 10 or more years) were maintained at home longer than those under 30 at hospitalization among Phase 1 patients ($p<.05$). Most women managed to care for their children even when severely symptomatic, and as long as they could do so, their husbands were reluctant to propose hospitalization.

## B. THE PATIENTS' DESCRIPTION OF ONSET

In the Phase 2 study, we asked the patients (somewhat more than 1 month after their return home) to tell us about the nature of the problem they had experienced, its antecedents, how they had been feeling, and how they had attempted to cope. Women were far more likely than men to report episodes in which they had experienced delusions well before admission. In general, women acknowledged a longer, slower onset: four-fifths of the women reported some prelude or earlier period of difficulty, as against only one-third of the men. One-fifth of the women traced their problem back to childhood, some stating that they had "never been right."

Nearly one-fourth of the patients, male and female, made a suicide gesture or attempt, a slightly higher proportion than in the Phase 1 sample. In describing their feelings, fully half of the female patients said that they had felt over-whelmed by environmental stress or threatening events, as did one-fourth of the males. A fifth of both groups indicated that their feelings were predominantly reflective of delusions or hallucinations, while another fifth of the men charac-terized themselves as feeling personally inadequate.

When asked to describe themselves as they usually were, only two-fifths of the men and one-fourth of the women characterized themselves as essentially nor-mal. Of the remainder, men more often said they saw themselves as perfec-tionists, while women more often characterized themselves as being nervous and easily upset.

Men turned more readily to their wives for support; women turned more often to friends and relatives outside the nuclear family, often reporting they turned to their husbands only as a last resort. Help-seeking efforts have been described elsewhere (Clausen, Pfeffer, & Huffine, 1982), but we may note here that most saw a physician well before hospitalization was considered. Most of the women were taking tranquilizers during the period between early symptoms and hospi-talization. A fourth of the men were also taking tranquilizers, but fully half were using alcohol to excess, by their own later admission. Many recognized that they had a problem, but few could acknowledge the severity of that problem and most probably did not suspect it, even when they knew they needed help.

## C. THE PERIOD OF HOSPITALIZATION

Hospitalization was a crisis for all of the patients and families. The marital relationship had been severely disrupted in roughly half the families, and only about a third of the spouses were basically sympathetic to the patient just prior to hospitalization. Entry into the hospital afforded patient and spouse a moratorium from the turmoil of the preceding weeks and months. Where conflict had been most acute, a few spouses initially refused to visit the patient, and in other instances patients refused to meet with the spouses who came to visit. By and large, however, relationships were rebuilt once the patient's acute symptoms had abated and he or she seemed more like the person she/he had been prior to onset.

At the time our research was begun, drug therapy was not yet employed in American mental hospitals. Shock—electric or chemical—was the most usual treatment for psychotic patients in public mental hospitals. Spouses' reports of the patients' progress in the early weeks tended to bear out what they had been told by the hospital staff: one does not quickly recover from severe mental illness. A fourth of the female patients and a tenth of the male patients were reported to be worse when the spouse was interviewed a month or two after admission, but roughly half of both groups were seen as substantially improved.

In Phase 2, when the average duration of hospitalization was roughly 3 weeks, most patients had returned home as of the time we had been assessing hospital progress in Phase 1. No men and only two women were hospitalized more than 2 months. Most patients were reported to be showing improvement within the first week or so after admission, though a few seemed to be worse. It was, in fact, difficult to schedule interviews with spouses prior to the patient's release; 44% of the men and 14% of the women had been returned home before the initial interview could be carried out.

Thus, Phase 2 patients were only very temporarily separated from their families, and contacts were frequent in the period of hospitalization. Phase 1 patients, on the other hand, were less frequently visited, and in the early months of hospitalization were much more left out of decisions affecting their families and themselves. Wives of male patients more often involved their husbands in decisions affecting the family than did husbands of female patients (35 vs 20%, n.s.) but 39% of the male and 60% of the female patients were not involved in decisions and many were not even informed of important decisions during their early weeks and months in the hospital. Some were gradually brought back in by their spouses as they began to show substantial improvement, but others remained far from well informed as to what had been going on at home.

## VII. Return from the Hospital

### A. REESTABLISHMENT IN THE FAMILY[11]

Almost all of the Phase 1 patients returned to the marital home after their initial hospitalization, despite the high level of conflict and tension that had characterized many of their marriages. When husbands and wives were interviewed in the months after the patient's return home, their concerns suggested that a number of the marriages could not be expected to survive. Nevertheless, it was only after additional episodes of symptoms or evidence of blatant impairment that marriages tended to be terminated.

In the Phase 2 sample, separations after the first hospitalization were more frequent, and indeed in several instances had been in the offing at the time of the patient's acute symptoms. Nevertheless, a rating of the commitment of the spouse to the marriage at the time of the first posthospital interview (a median of roughly 7 weeks after discharge for male patients and 6 weeks for female patients) showed only one couple separated and three others (less than 10%) se-

[11]I am indebted to my colleague, Carol Huffine, for a portion of the data analysis drawn on in this section.

riously considering separation. Roughly 6 months later, the proportion separated or with one member seriously considering separation had risen to one-fourth.

Both patient and spouse tended to have a good deal of apprehension about the patient's return home. Husbands and wives frequently felt that the patient was not ready for release, while patients often exhibited anxiety about their ability to resume old roles. As might be expected, the longer the duration of symptoms and impairment prior to hospitalization and the more severe the degree of role impairment just prior to admission, the less likely was the spouse to regard the patient as ready to return home. Most of the Phase 1 patients were able to make trial visits on week-ends, affording husband and wife a chance to see how things would go. While trial visits were frequently reported to be extremely stressful for the spouse (and probably were for the patient as well) they eased the tensions occurring at the patient's discharge from the hospital. In some instances, trial visits gave rise to recriminations on both sides; spouses expressed outrage at the way they had been treated during the period of the patient's acute symptoms, and patients expressed their resentment at having been committed to the hospital. More often, however, there appears to have been tacit agreement to avoid discussion of the immediate prehospital period.

Patients returning home during the 1950s more often faced substantial changes in the social situation to which they returned than did those returning in the 1970s. Of the Phase 1 patients, a third were hospitalized for more than 6 months and another third for 3 to 6 months. Roughly half the wives of Phase 1 male patients had taken full-time jobs during their husbands' hospitalization. Some wives who had not previously driven the family car now depended upon it for their transportation. When the wife and mother was the patient, children had frequently been placed with grandparents or other relatives, often at a considerable distance from their homes. In general, the longer the patient's absence, the greater the changes that had occurred and the greater the need to renegotiate roles.

In roughly one-third of the Phase 1 sample, there was evidence of considerable stress relating to the resumption of life together at discharge. To our surprise, the length of the patient's hospital stay was not significantly related to the rating of stress after the patient's return, partly because shorter stays were associated with the spouse's feelings that the patient might not be ready to return and because longer stays were associated with a larger number of trial visits before the patient finally was released. Where there had been three or more trial visits, discharge stress was significantly less than when there had been fewer visits.

There was stress at the time of the patient's return home in Phase 2 as well. The number of cases is too small for reliable statistical analysis, but it would appear that often the much shorter stays in the hospital gave too little of a moratorium after the period of chaos that had gone before. Nevertheless, far less renegotiation of roles was required. More wives of patients left jobs than had taken new ones, and children of hospitalized mothers had been less often placed outside the home. In addition, fewer patients had been committed, and resentment of hospitalization was far less.

## B. RESUMPTION OF WORK[12]

Of the 36 men in the Phase 1 sample, 2 killed themselves while on trial visits. Of the remaining 34, half returned to their old jobs, the great majority doing so within 1 month of their release from the hospital. Men who had been older at onset, who had been longest with the same employer, and who had a short duration of symptoms were more likely to have their old jobs available and to return to them.

Those men who did not return to their old jobs, either because they had severe difficulties on the job or quit prior to their hospital admission, tended to take a considerably longer time to find employment. A dilemma facing these men was whether or not to acknowledge their hospitalization when they applied for jobs. This was especially acute for those who sought public employment, since failure to answer truthfully the question about hospitalization for mental disorder would be a criminal offense. Acknowledgment of the disorder would, however, almost certainly be a basis for not being hired. For a number of the men, reluctance to seek a job seemed to derive largely from uncertainty as to their own ability to perform adequately. As might be anticipated, such feelings of uncertainty were strongest among men who were still to some degree symptomatic.

Of the cohort of male patients admitted in the 1970s, the great majority returned to their old jobs. These men were older, were hospitalized much more briefly, and had been less impaired in their work roles from the onset of symptoms. Therefore it is impossible to separate cohort effects from changed patient characteristics, but almost certainly part of the greater continuity in the work role can be attributed to the men's having gotten into treatment more quickly and having been off the job for a much shorter period.

## C. THE PATIENT'S SELF-ASSESSMENT AFTER HOSPITALIZATION

Any major role failure is likely to be followed by efforts to explain to oneself what went wrong, unless there is complete denial of failure. As Goffman (1959) observed, "losing one's mind would seem to be one of the most threatening things that can happen to the self." It leads to efforts both at concealment and to find an explanation that one can live with. As noted earlier, many of the patients whom we interviewed acknowledged that in some ways they were not "normal"

[12]A fuller analysis is available in Huffine and Clausen (1979).

prior to the onset of acute mental disorder. Nevertheless, most attributed to themselves relatively innocuous deficiencies such as nervousness or perfectionism. Moreover, the great majority were able to attribute their problems to impossible levels of stress, prior physical illness, or the unreasonable behaviors of others. Few acknowledged having had a mental disorder. The extent of denial is evidenced by widespread unwillingness to admit to their bizarre behaviors. Only half the men and a fifth of the women who had presented bizarre symptoms (usually as a consequence of delusions or hallucinations) could be induced to give a frank account of their actions.

As of 6 to 7 months after release from the hospital, slightly more than half of the patients not only said that they felt they were back to normal but gave no evidence of serious anxieties about their functioning and displayed no signs of difficulty in the interview. Nevertheless, three-fourths of the men and more than half the women acknowledged that they had experienced substantial stress and uncertainty in the months since hospitalization, and nearly one-third of these patients had been briefly rehospitalized. For men, the most frequently mentioned sources of stress and concern were the job and the marital relationship. For women, the marital relationship and interpersonal relationships generally were most frequently mentioned.

Despite many feeling pressure on the job, most men reported that they did not expect their hospitalization to affect their careers in any way. A few, however, recognized that the effect on their careers would depend upon their own subsequent ability to function effectively. Apprehension was evident on the part of those who were experiencing continuing symptoms. Yet as they talked about themselves, their plans, their hopes, their fears, it appeared that except for those showing marked symptoms, more said that they had been strengthened or had become more understanding as a result of the illness than acknowledged a vulnerability not previously recognized. In the global classification of the patient's change in self-conception as a consequence of the illness, the modal category, applied to slightly less than half, was "no significant change." In the early months after hospitalization, then, most patients seemed to be working on redefining their experience as one in which they had learned something about themselves that they could put to good advantage in the future. A number felt that their marriages would be stronger as a consequence. Unfortunately, interviews with the spouses seldom bore out the patients' optimistic views in this regard.

There was evidence of some degree of feelings of stigmatization among roughly one-fourth of the patients and spouses in Phase 2, although such fears had been much more frequently expressed by spouses of Phase 1 patients. Less than 1 patient in 10 had experienced direct rejection, though a number were sensitive to the solicitousness of friends and job associates.

## VIII. Long-Term Outcomes

### A. SYMPTOMS AND TREATMENT

At the time of follow-up, 15 to 20 years after their initial hospital admission, we found only two patients currently hospitalized. Nevertheless, roughly one-fourth had either been repeatedly hospitalized or showed substantial impairment in their functioning.

Of those patients for whom we were able to secure data on functioning in the 5 years prior to follow-up or death (27 males and 32 females), 41% of the men had experienced no significant symptoms in the previous 5 years, 19% had experienced episodic symptoms but were able to function most of the time, and 41% had experienced persistent or frequently recurrent symptoms. For the women, the comparable proportions were 16% with no symptoms, 28% with episodic symptoms, and 56% with persistent or recurrent symptoms. All of the women with persistent symptoms had been rehospitalized at least once, as had most of those with episodic symptoms, but 3 of the 11 men who were persistently symptomatic had had no treatment following discharge. Moreover, 2 of these men continued to be employed at demanding jobs and their marriages remained intact despite persistent delusions in one instance and recurrent psychotic episodes in another.

More than half the women were in outpatient treatment at the time of follow-up, but of these, half received drug therapy only. The proportion of men in outpatient treatment was slightly smaller, yet numbered relatively more who were only mildly symptomatic. Outpatient treatment of men much less often entailed drug therapy alone. Nevertheless, even among those men who had been asymptomatic for the previous 5 years, nearly half took psychoactive medication at least occasionally. Those persistently symptomatic, both male and female, tended to be on a regime of regular drug prescription, though some did not always follow the prescription. The meaning of being dependent upon psychoactive drugs was clearly negative for most patients and spouses.

### B. MARITAL HISTORIES

Roughly one-third of the marriages had been terminated by separation or divorce at the time of follow-up, and in addition a fifth of the male patients and a tenth of the female patients had died. Despite the higher prevalence of conflict and tension in the marriages of female patients, the proportion remaining intact did not differ from marriages of male patients. In general, marriages rated good or fair prior to onset were more likely to persist than those rated poor, but even good marriages of male patients were very frequently terminated in those instances when symptoms and impairment persisted. Whether or not there were children, very few wives were willing to tolerate the uncertainties entailed in successive rehospitalization of their husbands unless the husbands were occupationally successful. Most of the men with affective disorders were successful, some highly so despite recurrent symptoms. Schizophrenic men with recurrent symptoms more often functioned marginally and their wives tended to separate and seek divorces after the second or third hospitalization. On the other hand, fully half the schizophrenic men had no recurrence of acute symptoms and no further treatment, and most of their marriages remained intact. One former patient who made a good recovery left his wife because he could not tolerate constant intrusive questioning as to whether he was going to be all right.

Among marriages that endured, relationships tended to be less conflicted than when these families were studied earlier. A major source of dissatisfaction on the part of wives of patients was the unwillingness of the men to help with household chores, even when their wives were employed. Husbands of female patients, on the other hand, frequently did a good deal of household work, even when their wives were not employed.

Despite some dissatisfactions, there was evidence of genuine warmth and mutual support in many of the families. A majority of both husbands and wives reported themselves as closer to the patient emotionally now than in the past. For roughly a fourth, however, the spouses are not at all close and have again returned to the kind of "separate worlds" accommodation to each other that was earlier described.

Where separation or divorce occurred, it was most often the spouse's decision. After separation male patients were more likely to return to their parents, and female patients, especially if they had children, to maintain a separate residence at least for a time. Minor children of female patients were as likely to be placed in the custody of their mothers as of their fathers.

Of those former patients whose initial marriages were terminated, remarriage was rare among schizophrenics but quite common among males with affective psychoses. Few of the wives of male patients remarried, but most of the divorced husbands of female patients did so.

The high rate of intact marriages came as a surprise, for it differs little from what might be expected of the general population. Again, however, it must be stressed that this sample of patients married as of the time of first hospital admission is select in that they had already demonstrated ability to coexist in a marital relationship, even if the relationship was often problematic.

## C. OCCUPATIONAL HISTORIES

As of 15 to 20 years after their initial hospitalization, two-thirds of the men who had survived were working at jobs of status equal to or higher than those they had occupied prior to admission. Of men whose hospitalization reflected a single episode of mental disorder, with no recurrence of symptoms, all had had orderly careers, many with an increase in occupational level. Of those who continued to experience mild symptoms or who had infrequent recurrences of serious symptoms, slightly more than half had advanced or at least maintained their occupational status. Only among men who had been persistently and seriously symptomatic in the years following index hospitalization did we find a majority working at lower levels, but even here it was only a slight majority. Several of the men who had been diagnosed schizophrenic have been unable to function more than marginally in occupational roles in the two decades since their first hospitalization. On the other hand, several men with recurrent episodes of affective psychosis and one man whose persistent symptoms were almost purely paranoid have managed to hold jobs requiring high levels of skill.

The persistence of symptoms is clearly an important determinant of occupational success, but prehospitalization occupational experience is an even more potent predictor. Even among those who have had subsequent episodes of illness, long-term employment, and short-term symptoms prior to hospitalization, coupled with resumption of the former job upon release, tend to ensure stable and upwardly mobile careers (Huffine & Clausen, 1979). This pattern was more frequent among men who had been hospitalized after age 34. Of this group, fully 80% had advanced or at least failed to regress in their careers, as contrasted with only 40% of the men whose illness resulted in hospitalization prior to age 35. Thus age at breakdown again appears to be important in terms of the acquisition of competences that remained with the individual despite mental disorder.

One of the most striking features of the subsequent careers of the men who were occupationally most successful, particularly those diagnosed schizophrenic, was their tendency to remain with the same employer. As compared with men of roughly the same age studied in the longitudinal projects of the University of California's Institute of Human Development, far more of the former patients (three-fourths) had been with the same employer for more than 10 years at the time of follow-up (Clausen, 1981a). In general, upwardly mobile men change jobs far more frequently than this, which suggests that the former patients may have been wary of entering new work situations. Accepted where they were, they may have preferred to play it safe by staying put.

## D. OTHER RELATIONSHIPS AND SOCIAL PARTICIPATION

Relatively few of the patients in this study had become totally detached from their families of orientation, if parents and siblings were still living, or from their children. In general, former patients were much closer to their spouses and to close relatives than to anyone else, and many seemed markedly to constrict their relationships outside the kin network. As might be expected, women were much more likely to maintain close ties with their siblings than were men, regardless of their psychological status. Female patients also had much closer ties with their children than did male patients, especially in those instances in which the marriage had been terminated.

Where the patient remained persistently symptomatic, close relatives very frequently provided major emotional and moral support and were often almost the only source of such support. Where former patients were asymptomatic or only episodically symptomatic, patterns of social support between patients and relatives were very much more balanced by mutual exchanges.

Even among those male patients who had successful careers, except for those diagnosed affective, most participated to only a very limited degree in any organization other than the church. Moreover, their social activities tended to be largely restricted to those that involved the spouse's social ties. Roughly half the former patients, male and female, reported having no close friends, and an additional fifth claimed a single close friend. Very few of the persistently symptomatic patients claimed more than a single friend, and spouses' reports suggested that many of these friendships were quite tenuous. Yet when we interviewed a number of the patients, they seemed warm and socially competent. The restriction of friendship and of casual social ties on the part of asymptomatic former patients did not seem to reflect an inability to form relationships, though a few of them expressed reservations about their abilities in this respect. In any event, most were full participants in family activities and, except for the most persistently symptomatic and impaired, did not appear markedly problematic in their relationships.

## IX. Further Observations and Conclusions

This inquiry into the life histories of married patients has illustrated an assertion made in the overview of prior research: there is no typical course for schizophrenia, or, for that matter, for most mental disorder. Twenty years after an initial psychotic episode, schizophrenics may or may not be impaired. Rather to our surprise, this turned out to be true of men and women with personality disorders or neuroses as well. If an episode of mental illness is severe enough to require hospitalization, it has a potential for long-term difficulties regardless of diagnosis.

The small size of the sample, its diagnostic heterogeneity, and the substantial differences in the experiences of men and women preclude an attempt to establish statistically the best predictors of different facets of outcome in this study. Late age of onset appears most generally to distinguish those with favorable outcomes; it serves both as a proxy for achieved social competence and as a reflection of good premorbid status. Yet there are instances in which persons who had late onset and good premorbid adjustment have become apathetic and persistently impaired while others with relatively poor premorbid status have become more effective. Perhaps we can look to the ongoing, long-standing studies of high-risk groups to permit more precise delineation of the various determinants of alternative courses of mental illness.

Despite recurring or persistent symptoms in a substantial proportion of these patients, especially the women, relatively few have been prevented from occupying useful roles in the community. Very few had become the kind of chronic patient that Estroff (1981) recently described in *Making It Crazy*. As has been repeatedly stressed, older, married patients had in general acquired greater interpersonal and occupational competence than had patients whose breakdown came earlier in life. Except for a very few of those who have been persistently symptomatic, the patients whom we have studied have not made a career of mental disorder. Even where the experience of mental disorder has led to the dissolution of marriages and to occupational marginality, these patients have not tended to associate primarily with other patients or to make the role of patient central in their lives.

Nevertheless, in writing on mental illness and the life course, it would be unthinkable not to consider the plight of chronic patients. Many of those who become chronic first break down in adolescence and young adulthood, before they have acquired competence and commitment to an occupation. Others have experienced long or recurrent hospitalizations and have lost whatever skills and motivations they may previously have had. It is among members of this group that a significant number embrace the career of mental patient. As Estroff notes, they come to see themselves as set apart, in part because of their dependence upon medication for the avoidance of acute symptoms:

> Clients who are told constantly in multiple ways that they need meds, probably for the rest of their lives, are also being told that they will never get well. They cannot persuade themselves that with perseverance and care, they will be cured. Rather they come to see themselves caught between a non-medicated world that is out-of-reach, and a medicated world that identifies them as crazy people with problems in their heads and in their lives. (p. 109)

Efforts of these chronic patients to hold a job often entail a series of short episodes of employment in dreary jobs which they quit or, less often, from which they are fired. Whether or not they were motivated to work prior to the onset of illness, their failures in the work situation become associated with a lack of motivation to work. Yet they recognize that being regularly employed and not needing drugs are the symbols of normality. They come, then, to a partial acceptance of the role "crazy" or at least to working the system to secure such benefits as are available. "Making it crazy," to use Estroff's phrase, entails a definition of self that is derogatory in the extreme. Despair and suicide are frequent in this group. Here the life history is blighted or sadly truncated.

We do not know the relative size of the group who come to see themselves as crazies or as incapable of functioning in normal society. Clearly it is a substantial group. Nevertheless, the large scale follow-up studies of cross-sections of patients hospitalized for the first time indicate that most persons hospitalized with severe psychosis do *not* become chronic.

There is, moreover, evidence that even patients who were at one time classified as chronic may have a far better life outcome than had been assumed. The initial findings of a long-term follow-up of 269 patients in a Vermont mental hospital rehabilitation program who had been defined as chronic in the early 1960s reveals that among those still living, only 5% were hospitalized on follow-up, a fourth were employed, another fourth retired, and only a third unemployed (Harding, Brooks, Ashikaga, & Strauss, 1982a,b). These patients had been continuously hospitalized for an average of 6 years. More than two-thirds were assessed as being improved at follow-up, compared with their condition 20 years earlier. It is of interest that nearly 90% still resided in the State of Vermont. Many are integrated into social networks, though, like the patients described in this article, only a relatively small proportion have intimate relationships with others.

To sum up briefly the major respects in which the life course is affected by severe mental disorder, all hospitalized patients experience a degree of discontinuity in their major roles and face a serious threat to self-confidence and self-esteem. It appears that even among those who experience only a single episode of acute symptoms many remain wary of venturing into new relationships. Although many mental patients marry late, if at all, and those earliest and most severely impaired do not achieve full occupational competence, severe mental disorder does not as a "social fact" preclude either enduring marriage or occupational success but it does tend to lead to restricted social ties.

We were unable to ascertain the extent to which these patients, in their middle years, came to feel more heavily stressed by the knowledge that they were not on schedule. Few of those who remained asymptomatic thought early on that their careers would be affected, and few subsequently thought that their careers had been detrimentally affected. Among men with persistent symptoms, however, most acknowledged that both their marriages and their careers had either been terminated or severely impaired by the effects of illness and hospitalization.

Soon after returning from their initial stay in a mental hospital, many patients claimed to have secured valuable insights that would make them subsequently more effective. Fifteen to 20 years later, relatively few appear to have held such views, though our primary source of data was their spouses, not the patients themselves. Most wished to let the dead past bury its dead, especially those who had had no recurrence.

In a recent, thoughtful analysis of the course of schizophrenia in the later years, Cohler and Ferrono (1982) suggest that the lowered morale associated with role and timing asynchrony may interact with the symptoms of disturbance so as each to intensify the effect of the other. The apathy of some of the patients who remain impaired may well result from such an interaction. In general, zest for life was not highly characteristic of patients or spouses in our study, though there were exceptions.

What one concludes about the effects of mental disorder, then, depends on one's focus as well as upon the course of symptoms and impairment in any particular case. In a short-term follow-up study conducted in the early years of the transition to community treatment, Angrist and associates (Angrist, Lefton, Dinitz, & Pasamanick, 1968) compared women patients returned to the community with their neighbors in demographic characteristics, instrumental role functioning, and psychopathology. The former patients differed little from their neighbors in role performance and in expectations for such performance when social and demographic characteristics were controlled. But the ex-patients were far more often single, separated, or divorced, had achieved less education, and were living in atypical residential arrangements. Moreover, even controlling for these attributes, the former patients showed far more symptoms and signs of psychological distress. To say that most mental patients are functioning in the community and that many seem to be as competent as persons who have not had a mental disorder is certainly not to say that the effects of mental illness on the life course are relatively minor.

Erving Goffman applied the concept "career" to the sequence of stages through which a person passes in becoming a hospitalized mental patient (Goffman, 1959). He traced out the prepatient and patient stages of this career, noting that the properly socialized patient is expected to come to think of himself as mentally ill in order to demonstrate insight. Few of the patients whom I have studied have come to think of themselves as mentally ill or as having been mentally ill, unless they have subsequently been markedly symptomatic and impaired. At present it seems fruitful to distinguish between those persons who experience a single episode of mental illness (or several episodes between which they are able to function effectively) and the much smaller group for whom the life course appears to be very largely a struggle with the manifestations and consequences of mental illness. It is for the latter that I would reserve the concept of a career of mental disorder. For most former patients, it appears that the turmoil and disjunction caused by episodes of mental illness create crises and a measure of continuing burden, but the expectable life course, taken as a whole, is not drastically blighted.

## Acknowledgments

This article reports data drawn from the author's research on the Impact of Mental Illness, which was supported by Grant MH 19649 from the National Institute of Mental Health and by supplemen-

240 John A. Clausen

tary assistance from the Grant Foundation. Shula Gubkin and Molly Haggard assisted with computer runs. I am grateful to Bertram J. Cohler and to Courtenay M. Harding for providing me with copies of recent, unpublished manuscripts bearing on the topic here discussed and for calling important issues to my attention. I am also indebted to James Greenley, Carol Huffine, Lee Robins, George Vaillant, and Davida Weinberg for many helpful comments. The article has greatly benefitted from their suggestions, though I have been unable to incorporate all of them.

# References

Angrist, S., Lefton, M., Dinitz, S., & Pasamanick, B. *Women after treatment: A study of mental patients and their normal neighbors.* New York: Appleton, 1968.

Babigian, H. M. Schizophrenia: Epidemiology. In H. J. Kaplan, A. M. Freedman, & B. G. Sadock (Eds.), *Comprehensive textbook of psychiatry,* (3rd ed.). Baltimore, Maryland: Williams & Wilkins, 1980. P. 1116.

Bland, R. C., Parker, J. H., & Orn, H. Prognosis in schizophrenia. *Archives of General Psychiatry,* 1978, **35,** 72–77.

Bleuler, E. *Dementia praecox or the group of schizophrenias.* New York: International Universities Press, 1950. (Originally published, 1911.)

Bleuler, M. *The schizophrenic disorders: Long term patient and family studies.* New Haven, Connecticut: Yale University Press, 1978. (Originally published, 1972.)

Bower, E., Shellhammer, R., & Daily, J. School characteristics of male adolescents who later became schizophrenics. *American Journal of Orthopsychiatry,* 1960, **30,** 712–728.

Brown, G. W., & Harris, T. *Social origins of depression.* New York: Free Press, 1978.

Ciompi, Luc. Catamnestic long-term study on the course of life and aging of schizophrenics. *Schizophrenia Bulletin,* 1980, **6,** 606–617.

Clausen, J. A. Men's occupational careers in the middle years. In D. Eichorn, J. A. Clausen, N. Haan, M. P. Honzik, & P. H. Mussen (Eds.), *Present and past in middle life.* New York: Academic Press, 1981. Pp. 321–351. (a)

Clausen, J. A. Stigma and mental disorder: Phenomena and terminology. *Psychiatry,* 1981, **44,** 287–296. (b)

Clausen, J. A. Sex roles, marital roles and response to mental disorder. In J. Greenley (Ed.), *Research in community and mental health* (Vol. 3). Greenwich, Connecticut: JAI Press, 1983.

Clausen, J. A., & Kohn, M. L. Social relations and schizophrenia: A research report and a perspective. In D. D. Jackson (Ed.), *The etiology of schizophrenia.* New York: Basic Books, 1960.

Clausen, J. A., Pfeffer, N., & Huffine, C. Help-seeking in severe mental illness. In D. Mechanic (Ed.), *Psychosocial epidemiology: Symptoms, illness behavior and help-seeking.* New York: Neale Watson Academic Publications, 1982.

Clausen, J. A., & Yarrow, M. R. (Eds.). The impact of mental illness on the family. *Journal of Social Issues,* 1955, **11,** No. 4.

Cohler, B. J., & Ferrono, C. L. *Schizophrenia and the adult life-course.* Paper presented at the Conference on Schizophrenia, Paranoia and Schizophreniform Disorders in Later Life, National Institute of Mental Health, Bethesda, Maryland, June 1982.

Cooper, J. E., Kendell, R. E., Garland, B. J., Sharpe, L., Copeland, J. R. M., & Simon, R. *Psychiatric diagnosis in New York and London: A comparative study of mental hospital admissions.* New York: Oxford University Press, 1972.

Estroff, S. E. *Making it crazy: An ethnography of psychiatric clients in an American community.* Berkeley: University of California Press, 1981.

Garmezy, N. Process and reactive schizophrenia: Some conceptions and issues. In M. M. Katz, J. O. Cole, & W. F. Barton (Eds.), *Classification in psychiatry and psychopathology.* Washington, D.C.: U.S. Government Printing Office, 1968.

Garmezy, N. Children at risk: The search for the antecedents of schizophrenia. Part I, Conceptual models and research methods. *Schizophrenia Bulletin,* 1974, No. 8, 14–90. (a)

Garmezy, N. Children at risk: The search for the antecedents of schizophrenia. Part II, On-going research programs, issues and intervention. *Schizophrenia Bulletin,* 1974, No. 9, 55–125. (b)

Goffman, E. The moral career of the mental patient. *Psychiatry,* 1959, **22,** 123–142.

Goldstein, M. J. The course of schizophrenic psychosis. In O. G. Brim, Jr. & J. Kagan (Eds.), *Constancy and change in human development.* Cambridge, Massachusetts: Harvard University Press, 1980.

Gould, R. L. The phases of adult life: A study in developmental psychology. *American Journal of Psychiatry,* 1972, **129,** 521–531.

Harding, C. M., Brooks, G. W., Ashikaga, T., & Strauss, J. S. *Social functioning in chronic patients 25–51 years after first admission.* Paper presented at the Conference on Schizophrenia, Paranoia and Schizophreniform Disorders in Later Life, National Institute of Mental Health, Bethesda, Maryland, June 1982. (a)

Harding, C. M., Brooks, G. W., Ashikaga, T., & Strauss, J. S. *What happens to chronic psychiatric patients as they grow old? The Vermont story.* Paper presented at the Conference on Schizophrenia, Paranoia and Schizophreniform Disorders in Later Life, National Institute of Mental Health, Bethesda, Maryland, June 1982. (b)

Horwitz, A. V. *The social control of mental illness.* New York: Academic Press, 1982.

Huber, G., Gross, G., Schuttler, R., & Linz, M. Longitudinal studies of schizophrenia patients. *Schizophrenia Bulletin,* 1980, **6,** 592–618.

Huffine, C., & Clausen, J. A. Madness and work: Short and long-term effects of mental illness on occupational careers. *Social Forces,* 1979, **57,** 1049–1062.

Kessler, R. C., Brown, R. L., & Broman, C. L. Sex differences in psychiatric help-seeking: Evidence from four large-scale surveys. *Journal of Health and Social Behavior,* 1981, **22,** 49–64.

Kraepelin, E. *Dementia praecox.* London: Livingstone, 1918. (Originally published, 1897).

Kramer, M. A historical study of the disposition of first admissions to a state mental hospital. *Public Health Monographs,* 1955, **32,** entire volume.

Kreisman, D. Social interaction and intimacy in preschizophrenic adolescence. In J. Zubin & A. M. Freedman (Eds.), *The psychopathology of adolescence.* New York: Grune & Stratton, 1970.

Kreitman, N. The patient's spouse. *British Journal of Psychiatry,* March 1964, **110,** 159–173.

Kreitman, N. Married couples admitted to mental hospital: Part I. Diagnostic similarity and relation of illness to marriage. *British Journal of Psychiatry,* June 1968, **114,** 699–709.

Mednick, S. A. Berkson's fallacy and high-risk research. In L. C. Wynne, R. L. Cromwell, & S. Matthysse (Eds.), *The nature of schizophrenia: New approaches to research and treatment.* New York: Wiley, 1978.

National Institute of Mental Health. *Marital status and mental disorders: An analytical review* [DHEW Publication No. (ADM)75-217]. Washington, D.C.: U.S. Government Printing Office, 1975.

National Institute of Mental Health. *Characteristics of admissions to selected mental health facilities, 1975: An annotated book of charts and tables* [DHHS Publication No. (ADM)81-1005] Washington, D.C.: U.S. Government Printing Office, 1981.

Neale, J. M., & Oltmanns, T. F. *Schizophrenia.* New York: Wiley, 1980.

Neugarten, B., & Hagestad, G. Aging and the life course. In R. Binstock & E. Shanas (Eds.), *Handbook of aging and the social sciences.* Princeton, New Jersey: Van Nostrand-Reinhold, 1976.

Planansky, J., & Johnston, R. Mate selection in schizophrenia. *Acta Psychiatrica Scandinavica,* 1967, **43,** 397–409.

Robins, L. N. *Deviant children grown up.* Huntington, New York: Robert E. Krieger Publishing Company, 1966.

Sampson, H., Messinger, S., & Towne, R. Family processes and becoming a mental patient. *American Journal of Sociology,* 1962, **68,** 88–89.

Sampson, H., Messinger, S., & Towne, R. *Schizophrenic women: Studies in marital crisis.* New York: Atherton, 1964.

Spitzer, R. L., Endicott, J., & Robins, E. Research diagnostic criteria: Rationale and reliability. *Archives of General Psychiatry,* 1978, **35,** 773–782.

Turner, R. J., & Gartrell, J. W. Social factors in psychiatric outcome: Toward the resolution of interpretive controversies. *American Sociological Review,* 1978, **43,** 368–382.

Vaillant, G. E. A 10-year follow-up of remitting schizophrenics. *Schizophrenia Bulletin,* 1978, **4,** 78–85.

Vaillant, G. E., & Perry, J. C. Personality disorders. In H. I. Kaplan, A. M. Freedman, & B. J. Sadock (Eds.), *Comprehensive textbook of psychiatry* (3rd ed.). Baltimore, Maryland: Williams & Wilkins, 1980.

Watt, N., Stolorow, R. D., Lubensky, A., & McClelland, D. C. School adjustment and behavior of children hospitalized for schizophrenia as adults. *American Journal of Orthopsychiatry,* 1970, **40,** 637–657.

Wolpert, E. A. Major affective disorders. In H. I. Kaplan, A. M. Freedman, & B. J. Sadock (Eds.), *Comprehensive textbook of psychiatry* (3rd ed.). Baltimore, Maryland: Williams & Wilkins, 1980.

Zubin, J., & Spring, B. Vulnerability—A new view of schizophrenia. *Journal of Abnormal Psychology,* 1977, **86,** 103–126.

Zubin, J., Sutton, S., & Salzinger, K. A biometric approach to prognosis in schizophrenia. In P. H. Hoch & J. Zubin (Eds.), *Epidemiology in the mental disorders.* New York: Grune & Stratton, 1961.

# Personality Development from the Inside: The Subjective Experience of Change in Adulthood and Aging

## Carol D. Ryff

FORDHAM UNIVERSITY

BRONX, NEW YORK

## Abstract

This article explores the question of whether adults are personally aware of change in themselves as they age. Previous theoretical perspectives have argued that personality transitions occur in adulthood and aging. Empirical studies have further supported this view. However, little research has examined adults' subjective experience of personal change. This work poses such inquiry within the phenomenological tradition. As such, the first section explores the meaning of phenomenology, its impact on psychology, and its relevance for the study of adult personality development. Emphasis is given to both the strengths and hazards of a phenomenological approach. The second section summarizes empirical studies conducted on self-perceived personality change in adulthood and aging. Evidence is provided for the subjective experience of change as well as stability. Developmental theory appears to play an important role in differentiating these two realms. A final section discusses future directions for research in this area, focusing on issues such as people's comparative needs for seeing change versus stability in themselves, cohort differences in subjective experience, and linking self-perceived change to the realm of everyday activities and meaning. Overall, the aim is to stimulate interest in the study of subjective experience, to illustrate the merit of exploring such topics from a life-span developmental perspective, and to broaden the range of questions appealing to those with related interests in phenomenology, personality, and development.

# I. Introduction

"Have I changed as I've grown older? In what ways? Do I expect to change in the future? How?" These are the questions that have guided the program of research to be presented in this article. They reflect a concern for subjective experience, particularly the inner awareness of change in self over time. Such change as "seen from the inside" is viewed as a significant component of human development and thereby essential to thorough understanding of life-span processes.

Two theoretical frameworks have been prominent in the evolution of the research that will follow. Phenomenology, a perspective perhaps more philosophical than psychological in nature, has been an implicit guide, though its influence has not been fully explicated. Thus, a beginning section will review the tradition of phenomenology, its influence on psychology in general, and its relevance for questions of self-perceived change in adulthood and aging. Hazards and benefits accompany the decision to work within a phenomenological framework, and these will also be discussed. The second theoretical influence stems from literature on adult personality development. Various perspectives have postulated changes in personality in the middle to old age transition. A summary of these views will be provided prior to the presentation of research conducted by myself and my colleagues. Our studies have attempted to determine whether people see themselves changing in ways that theory suggests occur in the second half of life. A final section will discuss future directions in the phenomenological study of personality development. Issues to be discussed include the extent of change versus stability in subjective perceptions, cohort differences in subjective experience, links between subjective experience and the life-world, the impact of perceived change, and the use of retrospective and prospective strategies in studying perceived change.

# II. Subjective Change Anchored in Phenomenology

## A. THE PHENOMENOLOGICAL TRADITION AND ITS IMPACT ON PSYCHOLOGY

Historical tracing of the meaning of phenomenology leads to the field of philosophy and the writings of Edmund Husserl (1859–1938). In phenomenology, Husserl saw a new way of understanding reality and a new content and method for philosophy. This newness grew out of Husserl's indictment against the positivistic orientations of his day. He rejected all forms of naturalism, objectivism, and the Cartesian dualism between the mind and the body in the sciences of human life, believing that such approaches distorted the phenomena being studied. From his point of view, the a priori source of all objective cognition was found in the person's self-intuition. His aim was to discover the "essence of things," which meant getting away from mathematical formulas or psychological constructs that were being substituted for human experience and going back to the experiences themselves. The method conceived of by Husserl was a laborious process wherein objects are brought to "self-givenness in intuition" (Husserl, 1911/1965). Thus, his motto "to the things" involved a turning away from concepts and theories toward the "directly presented in its subjective fullness" (Spiegelberg, 1972, preface). As such, phenomenology reflected a general attempt to develop a widened concept of experience than was allowed for by a sensation-bound positivism.

Specific to psychology, Husserl argued that too much emphasis had been placed on interpreting or classifying human experience rather than finding out what human experience actually is. The content of psychology, in his view, had not been taken from what was given in experience but from what psychologists *applied* to experience. He advocated a kind of pure description without interpretation or explanation. To understand reality as immediately given, one must free oneself of judgments or preconceptions; that is, "bracket" one's presuppositions so as to experience reality without bias. He was, therefore, not interested in theory-guided approaches to human experience, or, more generally, in any forms of causal determinism since such perspectives represented preconceptions that interfered with a pure understanding of reality. Other themes that have been associated with Husserl's work are the concept of intentionality (he was much influenced by the work of Brentano), the transcendental epoch referring to the act of pure philosophical reflection (the methods for which were never entirely clear), essential intuition (the perception of a perception or of a recollection or of a judgment), and the life-world (Lebenswelt) referring to the world of common sense language and everyday experience. In general, Husserl is associated with the general aim of understanding human subjectivity. As he stated, "the method of natural science must also embrace the mysteries of the spirit" (Husserl, 1911/1965, p. 184).

Despite the obscurity of Husserl's writings and methods and the fact that his work has not yielded a unified conception of phenomenology, it did influence a vast array of philosophical elaborations (see Spiegelberg, 1972) and psychological applications. Within experimental psychology, phenomenology has been more generally contrasted with behaviorism (Wann, 1964), which encompassed many of the same emphases (e.g., objectivism, positivism, determinism) against which Husserl was reacting in his day. MacLeod (1964) clarified the distinction between the phenomenologist and the experimentalist by noting that the former would accept as the subject matter of inquiry *all* the data of experience (subjective as well as objective), and that the former would begin observation of phenomena by suspending biases or putting implicit assumptions into brackets (i.e., concepts such as reinforcement or stimulus generalization would not be postulated). MacLeod recognized the impossibility of suspending all preconceptions, but stressed the need for identifying one's biases and attempting to shift systematically from one bias to the next. He also provided a much needed clarification between the phenomenological approach and the introspectionism of Titchener. For Titchener, introspection meant analyzing through disciplined observation the data of experience (sensations, images) into their irreducible elements (intensity, extensity, etc.). Thus, the introspectionist begins with the assumption that experience can be reduced to a finite number of conscious elements and attributes—a kind of bias the phenomenologist would attempt to bracket. More important, the phenomenologist would give much greater emphasis to the *meaning* of experience for the experiencing subject, a meaning that was separate from reducing experience to basic sensations and images. In MacLeod's view, there was no such thing as experience devoid of meaning: "Even a pinpoint of light in a dark room has meaning in that it is white and not red, small and not large, out there in space and not in here in me" (MacLeod, 1964, p. 68).

Much phenomenological research conducted in the traditional experimental areas of perception, learning, and memory has been published in the *Duquesne Studies in Phenomenological Psychology* (Giorgi, Fischer, & Von Eckartsberg, 1971; Giorgi, Fischer, & Murray, 1975; Giorgi, Knowles, & Smith, 1979). Colaizzi (1971), for example, analyzed the learner's perception of the learning material at various phases in the learning process. Participants were interrupted during the experiment to provide descriptions of their experiences. They spoke about the apparatus, instructions, experimenter, interruption, and unfamiliar letters, which clarified that the meaning of the learning situation included all of these, not just the nonsense syllables. The facts, contexts, and meanings were broader than the usual concern with performance. With regard to memory, Sardello (1978) critiqued traditional views concerned with storage, acquisition, and retrieval processes in which the past is treated as an impersonal fact, an abstract label, a thing rather than an experience that *lives* in the present. Sardello advocated the study of meaningful memory rather than memory for nonsense syllables, memory as experienced in the life-world rather than in the laboratory, and placed an emphasis on time as lived rather than an impersonal succession of moments. Straus (1966) also dealt with the phenomenology of the senses (spatiality, movement, remembering, awakeness) showing throughout the problems of attempting to reduce such experiences to the level of the nervous system. Overall then, these works emphasized the total range of experiences a person has in psychological experiments and the meaning the experiment would have for the individual. Further clarification of how phenomenology has influenced the study of traditional experimental topics is provided by Valle and King (1978).

In the personality realm, phenomenology has been closely related to humanistic and existential psychologies (Gatchel & Mears, 1982; Hall & Lindzey, 1978; Massey, 1981; Mischel, 1981; Pervin, 1980), all of which have rejected in varying degrees positivism, determinism, and materialism. The concern in these perspectives is with assessing the individual's subjective impressions or experiences and examining how they relate to external behavior and social circumstances.

> Modern phenomenology does not deny that there is a material or objective reality, but it focuses on consciousness and the individual's unique perception of a material or objective reality. It claims that reality is a private affair and that the appearance of things in the mind is more important than whatever actuality exists apart from human awareness. This viewpoint is therefore concerned with the study of subjective personal experiences of reality. Descriptions and analyses of reality are made according to the individual's unique frame of reference. (Gatchel & Mears, 1982, p. 417)

Taken as an emphasis on subjective experience and the unique frame of reference of the individual, phenomenology reflects an *approach* influencing the study of personality rather than a specific theory with formal postulates aimed at explaining disorders or adaptive functioning. Historically, the phenomenological influence in this realm has fluctuated from highs to lows. Snygg and Combs, pioneers in American phenomenology, asserted in 1949 that psychological causation or the explanations of behavior lie *entirely* within the phenomenal field of conscious experience. Contrasting the external, objective frame of reference with the internal, phenomenological frame of reference, they held that the causes for an individual's behavior reside completely within the realm of conscious experience. In response, Smith (1950) stressed that phenomenology should be seen as *one* rather than the only approach to scientific inquiry, since it could not deal with topics such as the subconscious or defense mechanisms, that it was only descriptive and not explanatory, and could not, therefore, give birth to constructs. Other aspects of this debate, generally focused on how much personality should be studied from the inside versus the outside, are summarized by Kuenzli (1959).

Phenomenology has been extensively articulated within the clinical realm, the therapeutic context where it is important to understand the subjective experiences of the individual. Carl Rogers (1951, 1959, 1961), for example, stressed understanding people in terms of how they view themselves and the world around them. He developed a theory of psychotherapy concerned with subjective personal experiences of reality.

> As he [the client] finds someone else listening acceptantly to his feelings, he little by little becomes able to listen to himself. He begins to receive the communications from within

himself—to realize that he is angry, to recognize when he is frightened, even to realize when he is feeling courageous. As he becomes more open to what is going on within him he becomes able to listen to feelings which he has always denied and repressed. He can listen to feelings which have seemed to him so terrible or disorganizing, or so abnormal, or so shameful, that he has never been able to recognize their existence in himself. (Rogers, 1961, p. 63)

Thus, the descriptions and analyses of reality are made according to the individual's unique frame of reference. The supportive context provided by the therapist enables the client to explore personal feelings and become more accepting of them. George Kelly's (1955) psychology of personal constructs represents another phenomenological perspective in personality. Kelly's model focuses on how behavior and thought are determined by the individual's interpretation and construction of reality. It is, therefore, a cognitive model that assumes behavior and personality are a function of belief systems and thinking processes within the individual. The emphasis on styles of thinking and perceiving is contrasted with psychodynamic theories that focus on concepts such as motivation, needs, drives. For Kelly, people operate much like scientists in generating constructs and hypotheses about their lives and what happens to them. The process of psychotherapy aims to elaborate, test, or modify these constructs. Both Rogers and Kelly stress understanding reality as the person sees or experiences it and build their program of therapy on altering the individual's view of self and of the surrounding world.

Within existential psychology, phenomenology has been seen as a *method* for studying the inner world of experience. It describes experience using the language of experience—a vocabulary of commonplace, everyday words as opposed to technical, scientific terms. Boss (1963) and Binswanger (1963) have stressed understanding human functioning rather than explaining it, thereby rejecting a concern for causality. They have also been suspicious of theory, mind–body dualism, and experimentation. The principles of existential counseling following from these views have been summarized by Anderson (1978). These include noninstrumentality (seeing the relationship in nontechnical, nondirective terms), self-centeredness (viewing the client's self as the primary focus of counseling), encounter (the counselor's willingness to confront the patient directly when appropriate), and incurable crisis (the aim is not to cure human crises since they are viewed as an inevitable part of the human condition). Again, phenomenology's role is to provide the means or methods for understanding the person's subjective experience of distress.

Throughout the previous perspectives, one can discern a continuum along which the works were integrated with the methods of science. Rogers and Kelly, · for example, both attempted to study the individual's subjective experiences with objective measures (structured interviews, content analyses, Q-sort methods, structured tests). At the other extreme one might consider Binswanger's (1958) case of Ellen West, which reveals a style of writing that is evocative, poetic, and oriented toward imagery rather than technical terminology. The ties in this work are stronger with literature than with scientific methodology. Thus, while phenomenology has led personality researchers to be concerned with how individuals experience themselves and their worlds, there has been considerable disparity regarding whether or not such aims can be pursued within the usual framework of the scientific method.

## B. PHENOMENOLOGY AND PSYCHOLOGICAL DEVELOPMENT

While phenomenology has influenced a broad array of topics in the field of psychology, minimal application of phenomenological principles to the study of psychological development has occurred. Except for Schachtel's (1959) work on the development of experiencing through changes in perception, focal attention, and memory from fetal to adult stages, the processes of development have held little interest for phenomenologists. Similarly, developmentalists have shown little attraction to phenomenology. What, then, would it mean to take a phenomenological approach to study of development, or, in this case, the study of personality development? First, it would mean that one does not just chart the directionality of change occurring over the life span (e.g., do people become more or less rigid with age?), or the nature of personality structure (e.g., does egocentrism in childhood mean something different than egocentrism in old age?), but that one would focus on the *personal experience* of change and the sense of transformation one feels on the inside. Second, emphasis would be placed on the *meaning* of such changes for the person—are they, for example, seen as changes for the better or the worse? Were they under the control of the individual, or the result of outside, unexpected forces? The concern is not just with monitoring the external facts of development, but with what the process of development means to the person. A further concern for the phenomenological developmentalist would be that of examining the process of development in the context of the *life-world* (Lebenswelt), the everyday world in which people are going about the normal course of living, the domain of practical meanings and experiences. Concern for the life-world could lead to the study of how individuals experience change in their relations to others in the family environment or at work. Do they attribute these changes to particular life events such as marriage or the death of a loved one? In short, how do people see themselves relating to their surrounding worlds (interpersonally, intellectually, physically); do they perceive change in these relations over time, and if so, what life experiences do they point to to account for such change? Overall, then, phenomenological principles would alert the developmentalist to studying the person's subjective experience of change (not just in the personality realm but also with regard to cognition, memory, physical functioning, etc.), would stress the importance of understanding the meaning such changes held for the individual, and would attempt to place such changes in the context of the person's surrounding world and past or future life experiences.

Life-span developmentalists have suggested that certain aspects of functioning may be more salient in some life stages than others. For example, biological processes may be more prominent influences during the early and later periods of the life span. On the other hand, phenomenological processes and the realm of subjective awareness may be particularly suited to the study of adulthood and aging. The history of aging research (Reinert, 1979) has shown a continued emphasis on the psychology of "inner life." Karl and Charlotte Bühler were among early researchers who studied reminiscences, biographies, and personal documents as a way of formulating the concerns and motivations of adulthood. Development in the second half of life was seen as more intrapsychic, concerned with self-knowledge and self-awareness. Unfortunately, many of these early aging researchers were not working in climates receptive to such inquiry.

> These paradigms [behavioristic–experimental paradigms] were not among the primary vehicles used by early leaders of the life-span movement (e.g., Bühler, Erikson, Havighurst, Neugarten, Thomae), who judged internal personological processes as most salient for adult development and aging. Such research questions and associated subjective–phenomenological methodologies were not in the zeitgeist of the epoch in psychology. (Baltes, Reese, & Lipsitt, 1980, p. 68)

The present work rests on the premise, or hope, that the zeitgeist has become more tolerant of differing theoretical orientations and methodologies, given that understanding of the psychology of adulthood and aging seems increasingly to require an attentiveness to the subjective, self-awareness realm. A telling indication of the need for such research comes from current adult developmentalists who have continued to call for studies of a phenomenological nature.

> In general, in studying the relations between personality, adaptation, and major life transition, psychologists will probably gain enormously by focusing more attention upon the issues that are of major concern to the individual—what the person selects as important in his past and his present, what he hopes to do in the future, what he predicts will occur, what strategies he elects, and what meanings he attaches to time, life, and death. In short, psychologists would do well to make greater use of the person himself as the reporting and predicting agent, and by gathering systematic and repeated self-reports along with other types of data, to combine the phenomenological and the "objective perspectives." (Neugarten, 1977, pp. 639–640)

For some, the above call has immediate appeal, while for others it is seen as inviting a host of scientific problems. As the decision to work within a phenomenological tradition carries such a mix of hazards and benefits, these will be further examined in the next section.

## C. THE POTENTIAL AND PERIL OF PHENOMENOLOGY

Phenomenology has been linked with the rejection of positivism, objectivism, experimentation, and determinism. Classic phenomenology, in its concern for understanding human experience, was atheoretical and solely descriptive, and saw each individual as having a unique frame of reference. Empirical researchers choosing to follow this tradition, therefore, embark on a perilous journey devoid of the usual scientific guideposts. Why, then, would one choose to work within this tradition, and what are its implications for theory and methodology?

My specific interest has been with the individual's view of his/her own personal change over time, though the question reflects a more general concern with understanding people's subjective experience of themselves and their worlds. As the issue of self and self-reflectiveness has a long-standing prominence in psychology and sociology, research of this nature could be pursued from many perspectives. For example, there is an extensive current theoretical and empirical literature on self-attribution or self-perception (see Cantor & Kihlstrom, 1981; Schneider, Hastorf, & Ellsworth, 1979; Wegner & Vallacher, 1980). Why the choice to study self-perceived personality change from a more dated, possibly murkier tradition? Despite the antiscience tone associated with phenomenology, there is a more constructive side to the tradition. This side has done more than vehemently reject positivism, it has, for example, repeatedly called for study of personal experience, personal choice and intentionality, the meaning of experience for the individual, and understanding experience in the context of the everyday world, the Lebenswelt. Giorgi (1970) provides a useful history of this tradition and its attempt to formulate psychology as a human science rather than pattern it after the natural sciences. Less known than the history of experimental psychology, the human science tradition can be traced to the works of Dilthey (1833–1911), a philosopher who drew inspiration from aesthetics, literature, and historical studies rather than mathematics and the natural sciences. Dilthey argued that the human sciences could not be observed directly nor could the science generate theories that could be tested by experiments, but rather they must be approached indirectly with awareness of the complexities of life. The human sciences must search for the understanding of meaning and the value of the unique individual, both of which must be studied in historical context. And they must attend to expressions of inner spiritual reality and higher functions of thought and action such as creativity, self-sacrifice, or religious devotion. Other works sharing this orientation included Brentano's concern with intentionality, Spranger's emphasis on understanding and the nexus of meaningful relationships rather than explanation or basic causality, and McDougall's concern for purposeful behavior. In contrast to the sequence from Wundt to James and Titchener, and its concern for controlled observation, experimentation, measurement, and explanation, this other tradition was concerned with description, meaning, intentional relations, and understanding behavior and consciousness in context; it emphasized the presence of the involved rather than the detached scientist. It is precisely these concerns that lead to the formulation of my research within the phenomenological tradition. Alternative approaches, such as those ensuing from cognitive, attributional, or social learning domains, follow more from the other tradition in psychology. As such, their concern is with the how rather than the what of self-perceptions, that is, with causality and explanation rather than naturalistic description. For example, the question of whether internal states are determined by situational or dispositional factors is given emphasis. Such questions lead to laboratory research in which situational or dispositional cues are manipulated to identify causal determinants. As my research orientation is more toward understanding than explanation, more concerned with the life-world than the laboratory, and more interested in naturally occurring rather than manipulated changes in self-perception, the phenomenological tradition provides the most suitable foundation for what has been done as well as a guide for what lies ahead.

What then are the implications of this choice? Does phenomenology prohibit theory-guided research? Are spontaneous, unstructured reports the only acceptable methodology? Is concern for measurement and quantification outlawed? Must one swear allegiance with those eager to attack the scientific method? I would respond negatively to each of the above questions. In my view, the concern with human experience, its meaning for the individual, and its connections to the world in which the person lives, do not automatically prescribe any particular approach or methodology. In fact, I would argue that quick dismissal of particular procedures belies a research orientation more concerned with ideological posturing than understanding the phenomenon of interest. In the interests of avoiding such a position, a more thoughtful examination of the implications for theory and methodology is warranted.

Husserl's approach called for pure, uninterpreted, presuppositionless description. Unfortunately, the call became a continuing stumbling block such that numerous phenomenologists later addressed the futility of the task. MacLeod noted that "there is no observation without bias, but there can be a deliberate attempt to identify bias and temporarily suspend it or at least shift observation systematically from one bias to another" (1964, p. 52). Giorgi made a similar point, stating that "presuppositionless descriptions are not possible because, at the very least, one cannot totally eliminate historicity and sociality" (1976, p. 312). As a result, many by-passed purely descriptive phenomenology in Husserl's tradition for more hermeneutic phenomenology as conceived by Heidegger, wherein the major function is interpretation or the unveiling of meaning (see Spiegelberg, 1972). The message here is that one *cannot* totally bracket one's preconceptions. To be totally atheoretical is, in short, impossible. What one can do, however, is be fully aware of one's theory, one's preconceptions, however implicit they may be. The worst phenomenological sin is not to have bias or preconception, but to be oblivious to it. For the present purposes, this imperative requires that I admit the reading of certain theoretical perspectives has influenced my thinking about adult personality development. The personal changes proposed by these models have guided the formulation of questions and the interpretation of results in the program of research that will follow. As such, I have tried to make those influences as explicit as possible by pointing to the specific words and passages from previous writings that have impacted each specific study. The aim has not been to eliminate theory, but to be precise in specifying what the theoretical influences were.

Still, there is the question of whether theories of adult personality development impose a kind of preformed meaning system that violates the real experiences of those being studied. Should adults be asked directly what their experiences and feelings about themselves have been over the years? A quick affirmative reply, while in the spirit of phenomenology, promotes a superficial view about theory, how it evolves, and the extent to which it should be a part of phenomenological research. To begin with, theories do not descend from some impartial, detached-from-life, abstraction forum in the sky. They are human constructions, created by particular individuals, and, as such, represent particular experiences of reality. The beginnings of theory construction are, in fact, in the best phenomenological tradition, given the emphasis on detailed accounting of experience and careful formulation of meaning. The question then becomes one of whether the theorist's experience or perceptions fit the experiences of other individuals. For example, does the psychosocial stage model of Erikson (1950) capture the personal experiences of others? Has he identified psychological changes that people can see happening in themselves? Such a question is ultimately empirical in nature. To answer a priori that every person has a unique frame of reference and that human experience is completely individualistic is to ignore the possibilities for similarities in people's experience of themselves, their human relations, and their connections to culture and society. Though the individual frame of reference is upheld as important, there is no guarantee that every frame of reference will be unique. Given that our experiences are influenced by the context in which we live, our surrounding culture, our period in the life span, and our place in history, there are likely to be significant parallels in subjective experience.

Thus, the phenomenologist need not begin by renouncing existing theory. One working within this framework would, however, be more likely to attend to the implicit theories of those being studied and try to incorporate them into the research. Theory construction would then entail a more involved interaction between the researcher and those studied, with both contributing to increased understanding of the phenomena investigated. In collaboration the psychologist and the research participant could differentiate what is unique from what is shared in meaningful human experience. To summarize, phenomenology does not require an atheoretical stance. In fact, it shows such attempts to be futile and thereby calls for explicit detailing of one's preconceptions. Nor does phenomenology prohibit the use of existing theory. Rather, it raises as an empirical question the extent to which existing theory fits the experience of more than the theorist or those studied in generating the theory. Finally, phenomenology mandates that the preconceptions of the researcher be integrated with the preconceptions of those studied so that both are contributing to the increased understanding of the phenomenon of interest.

What are the implications of a phenomenological orientation for methodology? Does it require that all concern with measurement, quantification, and research design be abandoned? Must the scientific method be seen as interfering with the study of pure human experience? Is there another procedure for unearthing people's experience to which one must adhere? Certainly phenomenology has revitalized interest in spontaneous reports, personal narrative, and protocol analysis (Colaizzi, 1978). Such methods enable persons to describe experiences they are having in their own words. But is this the only path to understanding personal experience, and is it a problem-free procedure? For example, there is the step of "formulating the meaning," the phase in which the protocol is condensed and interpreted by the researcher. Such activities are particularly open to bias, given that the guiding conceptions of the researcher become the lens through which the narrative is read and understood. Hence, unstructured interviews, despite allowing the person to provide an account of their experience in their own terms, are frequently the most suspect with regard to interpretive bias. The criteria for determining essential meanings are typically implicit, unstated, and perhaps not even evident to the researcher. In contrast to these procedures are structured questionnaires in which the person responds in fixed answer formats to particular statements. The spontaneity and naturalness of the person's own words are replaced with specific items, which make the guiding biases of the researcher explicit. There is less mystery regarding the researcher's influence in the process because one can review the actual data. The deficiency, of course, is that these strategies require individuals to respond to predetermined answer categories, thereby robbing them of their own spontaneous, potentially richer responses. Thus, structured measures provide better indicants of researcher bias but they do not allow for the fresh reporting of the participants. On the other hand, more open-ended procedures are limited by being unfair to the inarticulate, those who have difficulty finding the right words to express their experiences. Personal narratives presuppose individuals who are articulate, fluent, and expressive. To rely solely on those methods promotes a rather elitist methodology that works most effectively with the highly verbal. For those less verbal, responding to the words or descriptions of others might well capture their own experiences and feelings. Whether in terms of a structured personality inventory or the descriptions of a perceptive novelist, some experiences may be very well expressed by the words of others. Certain "hidden experiences" (Brim & Ryff, 1980) may, in fact, await the sensitivity of the writer to articulate what is being felt but cannot be expressed by others. Thus, phenomenological research would seem to benefit from many methods and procedures. Those of the unstructured variety allow for rich personal descriptions but are potentially unfair to the inarticulate, and open to interpretive biases of the investigator. Those of the structured variety lose the immediacy of personal expression, but equalize individual differences in personal fluency and minimize interpretive bias on the part of the researcher. Such a continuum of methodologies, each possessing certain hazards and benefits, should be fully utilized in the study of meaningful human experience.

In sum, though phenomenology has frequently been associated with atheoretical, idiographic, antiscience bandwagons, it has been drawn on here because of its emphasis on understanding human experience, the meaning of such experience for the individual, and the connection of experience to the life-world. There are implications for theory and methodology resulting from this choice, but they are not in the direction of discarding or renouncing either realm. Rather, the call is for a more thoughtful understanding of the process of theory construction, its ties to human experience, and an appreciation of the unique strengths and weaknesses of various procedures aimed at advancing knowledge of inner experience.

## III. Adult Personality Research

The previous section reviewed the phenomenological tradition with the aim of showing how it has, and, hopefully will, influence the present program of research. Most of the preceding topics were theoretical or metatheoretical in nature. The next section will ground these issues in more substantive research questions. Before presenting my own studies on self-perceived personality change, a brief review of the topic of personal change in adulthood and aging will be provided.

### A. SUMMARY OF BACKGROUND LITERATURE

Phenomenology has stressed the study of topics that have relevance and meaning for the person. In this sense, the field of adult personality research has an impressive showing, as can be seen through a quick scanning of recent popular literatures. The tremendous reception of Sheehy's (1976) popular work on predictable crises of adult life from the late teens to the mid-forties left little doubt regarding the relevance or timeliness of personal change in adulthood. Following in the wake of this bestseller and creating new enthusiastic responses were the work of Scarf (1980), which examined the psychological tasks encountered in a woman's life from the teens to the sixties, focusing on themes of loss, depression, and changing emotional bonds; the work of Rubin (1979), which dealt with the milestones of the midlife woman who had given over much of adult life to marriage and motherhood and was in search of new meaning now that the children were gone; and a further book by Sheehy (1981), that addressed how certain individuals successfully negotiate the passages of adulthood in expanding and self-renewing ways. Thus, people did seem to be experiencing changes in themselves as they aged; some felt compelled to write about them, and many more were interested in reading what others had written as a way of illuminating their own experience with change.

The literature on men reveals a further array of books dealing with change in adulthood. Exemplary research includes Levinson's (1978, 1981) extensive study of psychosocial development in adulthood. Employing biographical interviewing as a research method and a sample of men from four different occupational backgrounds, Levinson formulated a series of developmental periods. The focus within each of these was the life structure, or the boundary between personality structure and social structure. Various structure-building and structure-changing phases were postulated across the life course as the men dealt with internal changes in themselves and external changes in their environments. In another work, Vaillant (1977) conducted a longitudinal study of a sample of Harvard men following them over a period of 35 years. He explored the adaptive ego mechanisms employed by these men and formulated basic styles of adaptation. Gould (1978) also proposed a model of growth and change in adult life (based on studies of men and women) that involved a series of stages of adult consciousness in which the individual was striving to get beyond the constraints and ties of childhood consciousness. Each stage was characterized by major false assumptions that must be confronted and corrected so that a fuller, more independent adult consciousness could be achieved.

Taken as a whole, the above works reveal a broad range of interest in the topic of personal change in adulthood and aging. Beyond the personal experiences of change that have no doubt contributed to the writing and reading of such books, there is a small but significant theoretical base guiding many studies on personality development in the second half of life. These theories emerged in response to the once pervasive Freudian view that personality and one's sense of self were immutably fixed in early life. Jung (1933, 1958) was among the first to disagree with this perspective—he wrote of the process of self-illumination in old age and provided guiding ideas regarding potentially different patterns of change for men and women. He proposed that with age men become more aware of the feminine side of themselves, while women become more aware of their masculine nature. Karl and Charlotte Bühler (C. Bühler, 1935; C. Bühler & Massarik, 1968) provided a further model of change in their formulation of the basic life tendencies that work toward the fulfillment of life. Creative expansion and upholding internal order were the eminent tendencies in adulthood and aging. The most pervasive theoretical influence has undoubtedly come from the psychosocial stage model of Erik Erikson (1959). His theory is noted as an important influence in many of the aforementioned books. Erikson's adulthood and aging stages of ego intimacy versus isolation, generativity versus stagnation, and integrity versus despair have been referred to repeatedly in the recent surge of adult personality research.

The popular, empirical, and theoretical writings described above are not without their critics. Prominent among these are Costa and McCrae (1980) who argue on the basis of their longitudinal research that there is little evidence for maturational change in personality in adulthood and aging. Working within a trait model of personality that incorporates the dimensions of neuroticism, extraversion, and openness to experience, they contend that developmental psychologists have overstated the case for change and should be searching, instead, for the mechanisms that promote stability. Their research is founded on empirically based (factor-analytically derived) measures in contrast to the more open-ended interview or projective measures employed in many of the previous studies. Other studies using more structured measures (Schaie & Parham, 1976; Siegler, George, & Okun, 1979; Woodruff & Birren, 1972) have also supported the stability perspective.

Further criticism of certain theories and findings pertains to their relevance for the lives of women. Many theorists, investigators, and participants in the preceding research were men; hence, questions have been raised regarding their applicability to women. Barnett and Baruch (1978) were among the first to argue that the work of both Erikson and Levinson did not fit the experience of women. In their view women's lives involved varying role patterns that are not so centrally tied to chronological age. Numerous combinations of career, marriage, and children may exist, each with unique patterns of timing and commitment. Gilligan (1979, 1982) has strengthened this argument, contending that we have become accustomed to "seeing life through men's eyes" (1979, p. 432). Male life and male experience have implicitly been adopted as the norm. Women's development, in her view, is much more intricately tied to human relationships. While the male developmental model stresses autonomy, separation, and individuation, the female perspective places continuing importance on attachments, intimacy, and relationships across the life cycle. Gilligan further objects to the temporal patterning of psychological changes as formulated by male theorists—generativity, for example, is perhaps experienced by women earlier in the life cycle and sustained as a prominent concern thereafter.

Finally, Rossi (1980) has critiqued all of the above models for what she calls "cohort particularity." That is, nearly all of the findings from leading studies were based on people born between the early 1920s and 1930s. Thus, generalizations are being drawn from the lives of individuals who grew up during the Depression, spent early adulthood in war, parented large families, were pioneers in suburbia, and included wives who joined the labor force later in life due to financial pressure. In short the knowledge of adult personality development that is now available may be based on the experiences of a unique and distinctive cohort of both men and women. The extent to which cohort particularity limits the applicability of these studies to subsequent cohorts is, therefore, of critical concern.

In sum, considerable interest has been shown in the topic of adult personality processes in recent years. Many empirical studies as well as popular writings describe various psychological changes that adults experience at different life stages. Subsequent works have criticized these studies for overstating prevalence of change and failing to attend to dimensions of stability, for being irrelevant to the lives of women, and for neglecting the questions of cohort particularity. The controversies are further compounded by the discrepancies stemming from the type of research design employed (longitudinal, cross-sectional, sequential), the measures used (projective tests and unstructured interviews versus standardized, psychometrically based multivariate tests), and whether or not developmental theory guided the research as well as the instrument construction process (Whitbourne & Waterman, 1979). Thus, the adult personality realm is rich with personal experiences, conflicting empirical findings, and theoretical controversies that spur continued research and study.

## B. TOWARD A PHENOMENOLOGICAL FRAMEWORK

The above studies illustrate the magnitude of interest in the question of personality change in the second half of life. Change has typically been investigated by comparing individuals of different ages, or by following the same group of people across time. The question of whether people *perceive themselves changing* has not often been asked. That is, are men and women aware that certain aspects of their personalities are more prominent in some life phases than others? Do they have the subjective experience of transformation in self over time? Thus far, the work we have conducted has been largely descriptive, reflecting attempts to map the content of personal experiences of change. More interpretive questions (e.g., what is the meaning of such change for the person?) as well as broadened phenomenological themes (e.g., linking change with the life-world, examining the intentionality of change) have yet to be addressed.

Before presenting specific studies, I will summarize the general model guiding the program of research. Given the impossibility of studying these topics in a purely presuppositionless or idiographic way, the work has been explicitly theory guided. I have sought to make the guiding assumptions drawn from developmental theory as clear as possible so as to assess their relevance for the age groups studied. Theoretical guidance is drawn particularly from the writings of Erikson (1950, 1959) and his formulation of the stages of generativity versus stagnation and integrity versus despair, Bühler's (1935; Bühler & Massarik, 1968) work on basic life tendencies, especially the tendencies of creative expansion and upholding internal order, the Jungian (1933) process of self-illumination in old age, and

Neugarten's descriptions (1968, 1973, 1977) of the executive processes of middle age and the process of interiority in old age. The question has been whether individuals perceive themselves changing in the ways that are suggested by these theories. As explained previously, this theoretical guidance has occurred because reading these works has, in fact, influenced my thinking about these topics, and such preconceptions must be clarified. In addition, the theories are themselves products of individual experience, and, as such, responsive to the concerns of phenomenology. The question has been whether these conceptions fit the experiences of others. In terms of assessment procedures, structured self-report inventories have been employed. The trade-offs involved in such procedures are those of sacrificing the richness and subjective purity of spontaneous reports in order to make explicit the bias and preconceptions of the researcher. Such procedures also minimize problems associated with different levels of articulateness among participants, and they improve the potential for subsequent refutation or replication of the findings. While I view these priorities as a useful beginning, in the sense of clarifying bias both theoretically and methodologically, the long-term goals are to achieve a richer balance between more open-ended and structured procedures.

The question of whether individuals actually see personal change in themselves over time has been investigated by use of instructional variation. That is, participants have completed the personality inventories according to varying instructions aimed at assessing how they see themselves in the present (concurrent instruction), what they recall they were like in the past (retrospective instruction), and what they anticipate they might be like in the future (prospective instruction). The comparisons among these various instructional conditions are then used to provide a measure of subjective change. Finally, all of the studies have employed an analysis of variance paradigm. The factors in the model have included age, sex, and temporal focus (or target age). This general design is illustrated in Table I. The latter factor refers to the instructional variation and whether participants were asked to think of themselves in the present, or to focus on a previous or future age period. Most of the studies have included men and women and various combinations of three age groups (young adults, middle, and old-aged adults). The guiding research design will be further clarified as the findings from specific studies are reported. Four such studies will be summarized. As the works have been published in detail elsewhere, the following discussion will focus on key questions and findings.

## 1. Self-Perceived Change in Values

A first study (Ryff & Baltes, 1976) examined self-perceived change in the domain of values. The question was whether adults perceived that their values had, or possibly would, change as they aged. The Rokeach model of values (1973), which differentiates instrumental from terminal values, was the assess-

**TABLE I**

**General Research Design**[a]

| | Temporal focus (target age) | | |
|---|---|---|---|
| Age | Young adulthood | Middle age | Old age |
| Young adulthood (20–35) Male Female | Concurrent | Prospective | Prospective |
| Middle age (40–55) Male Female | Retrospective | Concurrent | Prospective |
| Old age (60+) Male Female | Retrospective | Retrospective | Concurrent |

[a] The above design was employed in Ryff and Heincke (1983). Total $N = 270$ (15 per cell). Variations of this design (differing combinations of age, sex, and temporal focus) have been used in all remaining studies.

ment procedure. Instrumental values refer to desirable modes of conduct such as being ambitious, capable, and courageous. Terminal values referred to desirable end-states of existence such as having a sense of accomplishment, freedom, or happiness. When considered in the context of developmental theories, particularly the description of the executive processes of middle age (Neugarten, 1968), which stressed qualities such as being active, controlling, achievement oriented, and the old-aged process of turning inward, becoming more reflective and contemplative (Bühler, 1935; Jung, 1933; Neugarten, 1973), we hypothesized that instrumental values would have greater salience in middle age, and that terminal values would be more prominent in old age. The subjective change hypothesis was that individuals would be aware of their changing value preferences over time. Two groups of women, one middle-aged ($n = 57$; mean age = 43.1) and one old-aged ($n = 62$; mean age = 70.4), rated their values under various concurrent, retrospective, and prospective instructional conditions. The findings showed that middle-aged women had a comparatively higher preference for instrumental values, and they anticipated that this preference would decline in old age. That is, they expected themselves to become less instrumentally oriented in old age. The older women, on the other hand, showed less of a preference for instrumental values in the present, and they recalled such values were more important when they were middle-aged. As the values instrument is ipsative in nature (i.e., the score on instrumental values determines the score on terminal values), the reverse change patterns were obtained for the terminal value preferences. Thus, the findings from this first study supported the view that there were age differences in value preferences, and, moreover, that women saw themselves changing in accord with these differences. Based on these outcomes, the next study attempted to broaden the subjective inquiry to the personality realm.

## 2. Subjective Change in Values and Personality

To identify what aspects of personality might be likely to show perceived change in the middle to old age transition, I again reviewed relevant developmental theories. The literature (Bühler, 1935; Erikson, 1959; Jung, 1933; Neugarten, 1968, 1973, 1977) presented an image of middle age that stressed traits such as being independent, bold, active, achievement oriented, energetic, controlled, and powerful. The vision of old age, however, revealed an emphasis on characteristics such as being reflective, philosophical, contemplative, accepting, accommodating, hedonistic, and non-work oriented. Based on these descriptions, personality inventories were sought that could operationalize the characteristics. The scales of achievement, dominance, social recognition, and play were selected from the Personality Research Form (Jackson, 1967). The former three were predicted to be most salient in self-descriptions focused on middle age, while the latter was predicted to be more salient in old age. Because these scales were predicted to show perceived changes, they were jointly referred to as Developmental Scales. To differentiate aspects of personality showing subjective change from those showing perceived stability, four Control Scales were also administered. These included measures of abasement, defendence, impulsivity, and order, characteristics that had not been included in the previous theoretical descriptions. Finally, the Rokeach values measure was again utilized with the hope of replicating the previous finding and examining its relevance for men. The study (Ryff, 1982a) was conducted with 160 individuals divided equally by age and sex.

The first outcome replicated the previous study (Ryff & Baltes, 1976), showing that women gave greater priority preference to instrumental values (and thereby lower preferences to terminal values) during middle age than old age, and they perceived themselves changing subjectively in the same fashion. The replication was particularly interesting given the sampling differences between the two studies, with the former including highly educated groups and the latter having more representative educational levels among the two age groups. A similar pattern was not obtained for men whose overall priority preferences were for terminal values during both age periods. It is possible that men do not experience a change in values orientations, or that a shift from instrumental to terminal values occurs at an earlier period in the life span for men.

The expected outcomes for the Developmental Scales were obtained, but only for middle-aged men. Their scores on achievement, dominance, and social recognition were higher than the ratings of old-aged men, and they anticipated that such dimensions would become less salient to them in old age. The play scale, also as predicted, showed the reverse pattern with scores being lower in middle age than old age. Old-aged men, on the other hand, rated themselves lower on the first three scales and higher on the fourth and recalled similar self-assessments from their middle years. The outcomes for women were in the predicted direction with higher scores on achievement, dominance, and social recognition (and lower on play) when focusing on middle age rather than old age, but the differences were not significant. Finally, the Control Scales of abasement, defendence, impulsivity, and order showed no age differences and no subjective change processes. As predicted, people did not see themselves changing on these dimensions of personality as they aged.

Following a similar research design, Ryff and Migdal (1984) investigated self-perceived personality change in the transition from young adulthood to middle age. Theoretical guidance was provided by Erikson's (1959) description of intimacy as the psychosocial task of young adulthood and generativity as the psychosocial task of middle age. According to Erikson, intimacy refers to interpersonal relationships where close friendships, affiliations, sexual unions, and self-disclosure with significant others are salient. Generativity in Erikson's model denotes a transition to a broader social orientation, an interest in teaching and guiding younger generations, and a concern with improving the nature of society. As in the previous study, an attempt was made to operationalize these constructs with structured personality inventories, specifically the Personality Research Form (Jackson, 1967) and the Jackson Personality Inventory (Jackson, 1976). Intimacy was measured by scales of affiliation, interpersonal affect, and succorance, and generativity by scales of breadth of interest, dominance, and innovation. Four Control Scales (i.e., abasement, anxiety, organization, and risk taking) were also used with the aim of showing perceived stability. The usual concurrent, retrospective, and prospective instructions were employed, and the sample consisted of 100 women divided equally between young adulthood (18–30) and middle age (40–55).

As predicted, women of both age groups saw intimacy as being more salient in their self-assessments during young adulthood than during middle age. In terms of self-perceived change, young adult women saw intimacy as more prominent in their present self-perceptions than they anticipated it would be when they reached middle age, while middle-aged women recalled that intimacy was more salient in their self-image during young adulthood than it was at present. For the generativity scales, middle-aged women rated themselves higher in the present than they recalled being in young adulthood, thereby supporting the predictions. The young adult women showed the reverse pattern in which their concurrent ratings were higher than their prospective ratings. Thus, the prediction of perceived change on generativity measures was partially supported. Finally, the Control Scales supported the predictions showing no systematic variation in self-perceptions from the period of young adulthood to middle age.

As a whole, the preceding studies provided mixed evidence for the subjective experience of personality change in adulthood and aging. Supportive findings were obtained on some measures for some age groups and occasionally for only one sex. The less than uniform outcomes may have been due to individual differences in the subjective perception of personality change. In other words, while adults may see personal change in themselves over time, the experience may not be so systematically organized by age or by personality dimension. It may, in fact, be more of an idiographic process. Another possible interpretation is that the developmental theories guiding the investigations may not have identified the key dimensions of change being experienced. Perhaps the participants must become the "theorists" through more open-ended, exploratory procedures in order to tap the personality dimensions along which people show pervasive subjective change. A third alternative explication for the mixed findings was that the above studies did not utilize assessment procedures sufficiently connected to the underlying theories. The problem may have been one of operationalization. The scales employed had been developed for other purposes and populations and were, at best, approximations of the developmental processes of interest. This third possibility served as a basis for the next study, which attempted a more direct empirical translation of the developmental dimensions that had guided the previous studies.

### 3. Toward Developmental Dimensions of Personality

Four dimensions of personality were selected from previous theoretical formulations as targets for scale construction. Two, generativity and integrity, came from Erikson's (1950) psychosocial stage theory of development. As noted before, generativity referred to having a concern for guiding the next generation and a sense of responsibility to those younger in age. Integrity was defined as adapting to the triumphs and disappointments of being and to viewing one's past life as inevitable, appropriate, and meaningful. The third dimension of complexity was derived from Neugarten's (1968) discussion of the "executive processes" of personality in adulthood. It referred to being actively engaged in a complex environment and to selectively manipulating and controlling activities in multiple spheres. Interiority, the final dimension, described the "turning inward" that had been addressed by several theorists (Bühler, 1935; Jung, 1933; Neugarten, 1973). It referred to one who was freely relinquishing signs of external status and becoming more reflective, contemplative, and individuated. The scale definitions, presented in terms of high versus low scorers, are provided in Table II. The scale construction and refinement procedures are detailed in Ryff and Heincke (1983).

With regard to predictions, generativity and complexity were viewed as key personality issues of middle age, while integrity and interiority were seen as prominent in old age. This meant that individuals would perceive the two former

TABLE II

**Definitions of Developmental Personality Scales**

Complexity
  High scorer is actively engaged in a complex environment, involved in elaborate
    planning and scheduling of work and personal activities; feels in command and has a
    sense of growth and achievement in multiple spheres; selectively manipulates and
    controls a diverse environment
  Low scorer feels bored and uninterested in daily routines; has empty time on hands;
    lacks a sense of growth or expansion; feels powerless in the face of a complex
    environment; possesses a sense of limited abilities; has no sense of purpose

Generativity
  High scorer expresses concern in establishing and guiding the next generation; possesses
    awareness of responsibilities to children or those younger in age; views self as a
    norm bearer and decision maker; shows awareness of leadership role and has a sense
    of maximal influence capacity
  Low scorer views self as having little impact on others; shows little interest in sharing
    knowledge or experience with others; reveals excessive self-concern and self-
    preoccupation; feels no obligation to guide younger generation

Integrity
  High scorer adapted to triumphs and disappointments of being; accepts personal life as
    something that had to be; views past life as inevitable, appropriate, and meaningful;
    is emotionally integrated; has resolved past conflicts and has a sense of having taken
    care of things
  Low scorer fears death; has feelings of disgust and despair regarding past life; is
    concerned with shortness of remaining time; fails to accept previous life as mean-
    ingful and appropriate; has a sense of insufficient time to start another life and try
    alternative roads to fulfillment; disappointed with choices made

Interiority
  High scorer is inward in orientation; invests less of self in outside life; freely
    relinquishes signs of external status and obligatory social roles; reflective; con-
    templative; more individuated and expressive; has a sense of freedom from norms
    governing everyday behavior
  Low scorer outward in orientation; emotionally invested in persons and events in
    external world; prefers interacting with others to being alone; avoids solitude;
    concerned with maintaining status in external world; unable to enjoy time with self;
    non-reflective

qualities as salient in their self-perceptions during middle age, while the two
latter qualities would be of increasing significance in old age. To examine these
predictions, concurrent and prospective responses were obtained from middle-
aged participants, and concurrent and retrospective responses from old-aged
individuals. The sample consisted of 270 individuals divided by sex and age
(i.e., young adulthood, middle age, old age). The former age group was included

for comparative purposes. The measures were completed according to the usual concurrent, retrospective, and prospective instructions.

The prediction of perceived change was supported for the scale of generativity, the dimension drawn from Erikson (1950). Self-perceptions of generativity were higher for the middle-aged ratings than any other period. Such a finding included several patterns of perceived change including the anticipated change of young adults, the recalled change of old-aged persons, and both the anticipated and recalled change of middle-aged persons. Regardless of actual age, all participants saw themselves as being the most generativity oriented in middle age. Integrity, also proposed by Erikson (1950), revealed the predicted high scores for self-perceptions focused on old age. Thus, old persons rated themselves higher on this dimension than they recalled being in the past, and young adults and middle-aged individuals anticipated scoring higher on integrity in old age than they saw themselves in the present.

The findings for the interiority scale were complicated, showing a variety of age and sex differences. There seemed to be little consensus regarding the inevitability or desirability of becoming more inward in the later years. For the complexity scale, measuring a sense of being in command and in control of a diverse environment, the outcomes supported the predicted age differences but not the patterns of self-perceived change. While the middle-aged group rated themselves higher on this dimension than the other two age groups, none of the participants indicated recalled or anticipated change on this dimension over time. This finding is perhaps related to the cohort issue (Baltes, Cornelius, & Nesselroade, 1978; Elder, 1981). Perhaps the juggling of multiple demands and responsibilities growing out of changing sex-role norms has left current middle-aged individuals, those caught between old and new role expectations, with a strong sense of complexity in themselves that appears to be stable over time.

The Control Scales that had been used in previous work (Ryff, 1982a) were again employed in this study. Three of the scales (abasement, impulsivity, order) replicated the previous finding of no perceived change across these age periods. The defendence scale showed subjective change in the direction of all age groups seeing themselves as becoming less defensive in old age. This was also the only scale on which clear sex differences were obtained with men scoring higher than women. The lack of sex differences for the majority of scales across all three age groups was an unexpected outcome given that previous research on self-perceived personality change had shown sex differences and that recent theoretical perspectives (Gilligan, 1979, 1982; Rossi, 1980) had questioned the utility of existing life-span theories for women.

## 4. Summary of Previous Studies

The objective of the previous research was to demonstrate empirically that people have a subjective experience of change in themselves as they age. To identify when change might occur and on what characteristics, theories of adult personality development were consulted. The personality changes described by these theories then served as the basis for instrument selection. The aim was to find scales that might approximate the theoretical descriptions. Overall, the findings suggested that adults do have a subjective sense of both change and stability in themselves over time. Two samples showed that women saw their values changing from an instrumental orientation in middle age to a terminal orientation in old age. Perceived change was demonstrated on some measures of personality though the findings were qualified by age and sex variations. When new measures were constructed that attempted a better connection with developmental theory, more clear patterns of subjective change were obtained. Particularly the dimensions of generativity and integrity, drawn from Erikson's theory, revealed the expected change processes. Other measures indicated more individual differences in these subjective processes. Finally, through the use of control scales it was possible to identify personality dimensions showing self-perceived stability. Developmental theory appeared to play an important role in differentiating the personality dimensions showing perceived change from those showing perceived stability.

These studies are the beginning of a research program aimed at understanding self-perceived personality change in adulthood and aging. Clearly, they need to be conducted with additional, more representative samples to strengthen the consistency and generalizability of the findings. As the studies were guided by existing theories and employed structured measures (both of which reflected a goal of making explicit the guiding biases), it would be useful to augment these works with more open-ended, exploratory procedures. Such research might illuminate new dimensions of perceived change as well as advance understanding of how these processes differ by subgroup (e.g., sex, socioeconomic status, ethnicity, etc.). To move in this more unstructured direction is to place a heavier burden on the articulateness of the respondents and to require careful interpretive efforts on the part of the researcher. However, as I have advocated throughout this article, the study of subjective personality processes will be advanced by partaking of the entire continuum of available methodologies.

Parenthetically, I should note one additional bias that has guided the research thus far. Self-perceived personality change could show various forms of directionality reflecting improved or worsened personal functioning. Given these possibilities we have chosen to document the ways in which people see themselves getting better, functioning at a higher level, developing. As such, the tone of the research is optimistic, aiming to articulate people's subjective experience of growth and improvement. Such endeavors show the positive changes of those we have studied, and they may also provide images or visions of becoming for those who will age in the future. They are visions intimately tied to the realities we will construct (Gergen, 1980, 1982), the aging alternatives we will generate.

We are, therefore, pursuing an alternative that emphasizes people's awareness of their own adaptive functioning, their personal experience of positive change in response to life's demands, and their successful negotiation of new life stages and new experiences (Ryff, 1982b, 1984). In so doing, we hope to understand not only what personal change has occurred, but to influence what personal change might occur.

## IV. Phenomenological Studies of Personality Development: Future Directions

The previous section summarized beginning descriptive research aimed at mapping the content of self-perceived personality research in adulthood and aging. There are many directions for broadening such a line of inquiry. The following section will highlight a number of these. Specifically, the focus will be on the balance of change versus stability in one's self-perceptions, cohort differences in subjective experience, the ties of subjective change to the life-world, the impact of subjective constructions about the self, and the use of retrospective and prospective research strategies. These topics were chosen because of their interest for the author and because most can be illustrated by way of related lines of research. As such, this section seeks to advance future research directions as well as identify contributors to the growing literature on subjective experience over the life course.

### A. CHANGE VERSUS STABILITY IN SUBJECTIVE PERCEPTIONS

The research conducted by myself and my colleagues has shown that people perceive both change and stability in themselves over time. Guided by developmental theory, the major thrust has been toward documenting transitions with change being viewed as development. However, does one tend to see primarily change versus stability in oneself over time? Though of an empirical nature, the question also has important theoretical implications regarding people's comparative needs for seeing change and growth in themselves over time versus seeing stability and consistency.

Cohler (1982) has contributed an impressive conceptual framework for the study of personal narratives, which he defines as "the most internally consistent interpretation of presently understood past, experienced present, and anticipated future" (p. 207) recounted at any point in the life course. Because of socially shared beliefs that lives must make sense and be connected over time, Cohler argues that people continually reconstruct their past lives so as to see stability and consistency in them. A good interpretation of a life history must have a consistency that is apparent both to the person and to others. Such consistency does

not mean that people do not change, but rather that through "continuing reconstructive activity" (p. 205) the past is reinterpreted so as to give the sense of
consistency and coherence. In this regard the interpretation of the personal past at
one point may show little association with what was constructed at another point.

Working within a transformational model that focuses on how earlier memories are revised as a function of subsequent experience, Cohler examined the
transformations occurring from early to middle childhood, from childhood to
adolescence and young adulthood, and from young adulthood to middle age. He
argued that the first two reformulations are shaped largely by maturational factors (particularly cognitive development), while the third transition is largely
socially determined. In these transitions, different use is made of the past,
present, and future—"maintenance of a continuing sense of congruence across
the course of life is a result both of shifts in the emphasis placed upon past,
present, and future time as well as in the manner in which memories of the past
are used" (p. 214). In adulthood, for example, the emphasis gradually shifts
from a concern with the future to a concern with the past. While emphasizing the
need for seeing consistency in one's life, Cohler makes clear that one's actual life
experiences may be quite change oriented and even disruptive.

> Studies of lives have suggested that the course of development may be much less predict-
> able and well-ordered than previously realized. Rather than viewing personality development
> either in terms of continuing stability over time or in terms of a number of well-ordered phases
> or stages, lives seem to be characterized by often abrupt transformations determined both by
> expected and eruptive live events and by intrinsic, but not necessarily continuous, developmen-
> tal factors, including biological aging. These events taking place across the life course are later
> remembered as elements of a narrative which provides a coherent account of this often disjunc-
> tive life course. (p. 227)

Cohler's writings strengthen the theoretical understanding of how people restructure their past lives and clarify the role such reconstructions play in general
psychological adaptation. He emphasizes that "the failure to maintain a coherent
personal narrative leads to feelings of fragmentation and disintegration" (p.
205). Cohler's work is also more truly life span in following transformations in
personal narratives from childhood to adulthood and, in so doing, provides
useful guidelines for expanding the present perspective to earlier age periods.
However, a notable element of contrast between Cohler's model and the research
presented herein is his focus on people's subjective experience of *consistency*,
while we have focused on their experience of *change*. In his view, change is seen
as rewarding only so long as it does not induce anxiety or interfere with the
maintenance of an ordered life account. I would argue, on the other hand, that
the subjective experience of growth or development would *require* that people
have a sense of change in themselves over time. Further, there may be important
differences between seeing consistency and coherence in one's past life, though
Cohler seems to use the terms interchangeably. Consistency implies a largely

stable narrative in which there is little room for change, while coherence seems more open to perceptions of change provided that they can be incorporated into the overall story in a meaningful fashion. In a related vein, Peskin and Livson (1981) have studied the role of the past in adult psychological health. Through the process of "discontinuous recoveries" (p. 154), they discuss how adults selectively reactivate certain traits or past resources that had been expressed in earlier life periods. Their discontinuous model, then, emphasizes change in personal characteristics with aging, although it is a change in the sense of reactivating previous traits rather than expressing new ones. Together, these studies indicate the growing interest in subjective profiles of change versus stability in life-span development and point to new issues regarding people's comparative needs for growth and development versus stability and consistency.

### B. COHORT DIFFERENCES IN SUBJECTIVE EXPERIENCE

Most of the preceding research has examined self-perceived changes in personality organized around age or life stage. The life-span perspective (Baltes, 1979; Elder, 1979), however, emphasizes possible changes in the surrounding sociohistorical context over time. The question for the present context would be whether introspective processes might vary across historical time. The research of Veroff, Douvan, and Kulka (1981) suggests that they do. These authors report findings from two national studies of the American population dealing with questions of how people assess their own mental health. Data were collected at two points in time, 1957 and 1976. Comparisons of responses from these two representative samples (involving over 4500 individuals aged 21 and over) provided an opportunity "to explore social change and social stability in American society from the perspective of people's own subjective experience" (p. 5). Noting the changes occurring in the country and the world (technological, economic, political) over these periods, they wanted to examine their impact on subjective well being. Their summary underscored the reduced social integration evident at the second assessment (status and roles were more often discredited as legitimate information about people in 1976), the increased search for intimacy, the increased dependence of men on the institution of marriage, and the general increase in taking a psychological orientation to experience. In terms of the perception of self, they provided the following summary:

> With regard to the two themes that emerged from the 1957 analysis, we can say that in 1976 men and women are more inwardlooking, or intraceptive, and that they have a more highly differentiated view of the inner world of self. In addition we find evidence that the 1976 population evaluate themselves more positively than the 1957 population did. (p. 115)

From a phenomenological point of view, such a finding is intriguing as it suggests cultural changes in the direction of individuals becoming more inward and differentiated with regard to self-perceptions. Thus, the study of subjective experience becomes increasingly relevant as the population as a whole tends toward being more inner oriented. With regard to the explanations for such changes they suggest the following:

> The sources of increased intraceptiveness, more psychologically framed and articulate self-concepts, and more positive self-regard must, we think be located in broad cultural currents which have affected the young and old, men and women, the educated and uneducated in similar ways. Certain subgroups may be particularly sensitized to the currents and show their effects in a heightened degree. But by and large, they diffuse through the society by means of the media, the schools, churches, and other organizations, and interpersonal exchange. (pp. 124–125)

Additional research could usefully clarify these trends. If individuals in our society are becoming more inner oriented, what are they thinking about? What specifically are the naturalistic categories of content (e.g., human relationships, the complexity of contemporary life, fears of the future, etc.) and are these changes toward increased reflectiveness adaptive? What are the possible disadvantages of our becoming a more reflective society? Such are the questions that move the study of subjective experience from the individual level to the broader sociocultural level with attentiveness to changes in each over time.

## C. LINKING SUBJECTIVE EXPERIENCE TO THE LIFE-WORLD

A phenomenological theme stressed repeatedly in this article is that of understanding people's experience in the context of the life-world. Defined as the world of everyday activities and concerns, the life-world encourages researchers to make their work more naturalistic, more tied to the spheres in which people actually conduct their lives. My preceding research has examined self-perceived change related to life-stage transitions. In more recent studies, we have tried to contextualize such change by linking it to the actual experiences. For example, self-perceived personality change has been examined in response to the event of widowhood (Dunn & Ryff, 1982) with the finding that both widows and widowers recalled being better adjusted (in terms of life satisfaction) during the final years of their marriage, than they saw themselves in the present. A further study (Zeren & Ryff, 1984) examined self-perceived change in response to the experience of fatherhood. In this study, men saw themselves becoming more nurturant, less impulsive, more generative, and having greater purpose in life after the fatherhood experience. This was true for men who actually were fathers as well as for men anticipating what they would be like in fatherhood. Another study (Ryff & Dunn, 1983) has looked at a composite of stressful life experiences and related them to personality development with the finding that men's self-ratings of personal growth seem to be better accounted for by their life experiences than women's. Finally, Fallo-Mitchell and Ryff (1982) have combined life event and historical change frameworks by examining cohort differences in the preferred timing of female life events.

Each of the preceding examples attempted to link personal development to the life-world via people's life events, with the events selected by the researcher. Another potential avenue is to investigate adult's spontaneous reports of what is or has been meaningful in their lives. McAdams (1982), for example, studied "human recollections of psychologically meaningful and complex events" (p. 293). He was interested in what event or experience is particularly salient for an individual and why. The study had people report experiences that were particularly meaningful for them, what might be considered "peak experiences" from Maslow's perspective. These recollections were then related to personality variables, specifically social motives of intimacy and power. The key finding was that these motives predicted the level of intimacy and power content in the recollections of personally meaningful experiences, thereby suggesting the role of personality in memory of the salient past. While the study was not developmental in nature, it provides an interesting example of subjective recollection of meaningful experiences, thereby bringing the research closer to the life-world of the individual and expanding understanding of "what the person selects as important in his past," to use Neugarten's phrase (1977, p. 640). Employing such procedures, developmentalists could begin to examine the age profiles of meaningful experiences and their relationship to changing personality profiles.

While the present examples have focused on pivotal or peak experiences, there is also the possibility of contextualizing through examination of more mundane though significant experiences (e.g., day-to-day boredom with one's job) as well as interpersonal relations, social and physical environments, and so on. Given the vastness of the life-world, researchers are wise to consult with those they study in identifying those aspects of day-to-day life most salient and worthy of social scientific investigation.

### D. THE IMPACT OF PERCEIVED CHANGE

Do our recollections or anticipations about ourselves matter? If so, in what ways? It is possible that our past memories and future dreams say much about who we are and what we will become. The recalling of past selves may, for example, be a component of self-evaluation related to the general question of "am I getting better or worse?" As such, present adjustment may be influenced by subjective comparison with recalled selves. One can also distinguish between adaptive and maladaptive reconstructions—from those that influence present feelings, motivations, and cognitions in ways that are beneficial to those that have detrimental effects. Gergen and Gergen (1984) in recent work on narratives of the self have provided useful questions and conceptual distinctions in this area. Self-narratives, which refer to the individual's account of the relationships among self-relevant events across time, are viewed as essential in giving one's life a sense of meaning and direction. Among the insightful queries that contribute to the building of one's narrative, they include the following:

"Am I improving?" "Is my life happier now?" "Are my abilities declining?" "Am I maintaining the high standards I once committed myself to?" or "Am I growing as a person?" To answer such questions the individual selects discrete incidents or images occurring across time and links them through evaluative comparison. (p. 6)

They provide useful distinctions between stability, progressive, and regressive narratives. Stability narratives link images and incidents in a way that the person remains unchanged with respect to evaluative position. In progressive narrative, experiences are linked to show increments in evaluations, while regressive narratives link events to show decrements in evaluative dimensions. The possibility of individual differences is noted here—"Some may gain proficiency in demonstrating the constancy or similarity among life events while others may be more proficient in techniques of seeing each day as an improvement over the past" (p. 13). They also distinguish between micro- and macronarratives, referring to whether events occur within brief durations or span broad periods of time. Finally, they emphasize the social origins of narratives, how narratives are molded by social interactions, and that one's narrative requires a supporting cast. With regard to the balance between seeing stability and change (preferably progressive) in one's narrative, they have stated persuasively the need for both. "Functioning viably in a relationship may depend on one's ability to show that one has always been the same, and will continue to be so, and yet contrapuntally to show how one is continuing to improve. One must be reliable but demonstrate progress; one must be changing but maintain a stable character" (p. 18).

The above perspective has focused on how people organize and interpret their past lives. There is also the question of impact with regard to one's future expectations. Looking ahead or anticipating what one will be like in the future, as obtained through the prospective reports, may be related to the process of anticipatory socialization. Whether drawing on aging stereotypes or ideal types, the projection of oneself into the future may indicate a preparation or readiness for change, and, as such, it may be a partial determinant of what one becomes. Bandura (1977, 1982), for example, has shown that people's beliefs in or expectations about their own effectiveness influence their behavior on several levels including their choice of activities, the effort expended, and their persistence. Extrapolating to a larger time frame, Sears (1981) has examined the role of expectancy in adaptation to aging, focusing on such topics as intellectual performance, family relations, and achievement motivation. Considered from these perspectives, retrospective and prospective reports provide insight as to how one maximally structures and uses the past as well as prepared for the future. Self-perceived change thus becomes not just a chronicling of subjective experience, but a source of information about present and future functioning.

## E. THE USE OF RETROSPECTIVE AND PROSPECTIVE RESEARCH STRATEGIES

The preceding research used retrospective and prospective designs to measure self-perceived change. In evaluating these strategies, many have focused on the issue of accuracy (e.g., Featherman, 1980; Fischoff, 1980; Ridley, Bachrach, & Dawson, 1979; Yarrow, Campbell, & Burton, 1970). The key concern is the extent to which retrospective reports provide accurate information about an actual previous condition. Answers to these questions vary from viewing recollections as inevitably fraught with distortion to seeing them as reasonable, sometimes very useful, data sources. While assessment of the accuracy of retrospective reports or their reliability (a somewhat different issue given that one can obtain repeatable reconstructions that are consistently inaccurate) is of concern, it is less so for phenomenologists. For them, the accuracy question would have little appeal, in part because of the difficulty in defining accurate (whose frame of reference is used to define the actual past condition), but also because of their assumption that the past is continually changed as it is remembered from new presents.

The past is not viewed as a former present that is completed and gone, existing as an abstract, impersonal fact, but rather as a past that endures and lives in the present. In the words of an existential philosopher:

> Our moments do not march past us like a procession of identical and faceless marionettes. Their unique qualities extend, distend, and leap over the continuum of time, if indeed it be a continuum at all. An event of ten years ago, charged with meaning, may be closer to me than last week's trivia. And, who knows, ten years from now some unpredictable cause may excavate those trivia and bring them closer than the bagatelles of that moment. Any experience may thus be located in a number of different temporal perspectives. (Barrett, 1972, p. 20)

Phenomenologists would argue that the future must also be studied as it is lived, not as the future of the clock. The future is that which comes to meet the now. "One is already in the day before one gets out of bed, and how one is in the day determines how one gets out of bed" (Sardello, 1978, p. 143). The past and future are intertwined into the now. The present constantly influences and alters the past, while the past and future give direction and form to the present. There is an intermingling of temporal frames and the experiences within each are continually open to reformulation and reconstruction.

The point of this discussion has been to clarify that retrospective and prospective research strategies can be evaluated by many different criteria. While one set of questions deals with how well these procedures match reality, those are not the only issues. Some argue that subjective reports are of critical importance even when they do not match reality. Thomae (1970), for example, has suggested that the perception of anticipation of change in self may be associated, even more than objective change, with immediate and significant behavioral outcomes.

Supportive findings have emerged in the perceived control and perceived health domains (Johnson & Sarason, 1979; Langer, 1979; Lefcourt, 1973; Maddox & Douglass, 1974; Rodin, 1980) where subjective perceptions of control and health have been found to be more influential in present functioning and behavior than actual control or health. However, such arguments fuel the antipathy between the subjective and objective realms, which is not the aim of the present work. The point, rather, is that the parallels between subjective constructions (retrospective or prospective) and objective conditions is but one issue to be raised in considering such strategies, and a question of lesser interest to phenomenologists.

The issue of how to most effectively measure perceived change remains open. While retrospective and prospective reports have provided evidence of subjective change, it has been derived through comparison with concurrent reports. Though change scores have not been employed, the assessment remains of an indirect nature. Future research would, therefore, benefit from the use of more direct procedures (structured or unstructured), which probed people's actual assessments of perceived change rather than examining what they recalled being like in the past, or what they anticipated being like in the future. Such inquiry could advance understanding of the methodologies best suited for the study of self-perceived personality change.

## V. Conclusion

In 1927 Karl Bühler wrote a psychological treatise entitled *Die Krise der Psychologie* (Bugental, 1966), which was viewed as a landmark in the history of psychology. In it, Bühler presented major associationist and psychoanalytic movements and argued for a systematic eclecticism. For him many schools of thought were necessary to study the three basic characteristics of human conduct: inner experience, meaningful behavior, and their relation to culture. Since Bühler's time, psychology has evolved in many directions and yet this list of the essentials of human conduct remains compelling. It was the emphasis on the first of these, inner experience, that has proved most inspiring for the present work. Prompted by the aim of understanding the personal experience of change, the objective has been to formulate a theoretical and empirical framework for the study of personality development as seen from the inside.

Research on adult personality development as inner experience was tied to the phenomenological tradition. Such anchoring was chosen because of phenomenology's emphasis on inner experience, the meaning of experience for the person, and the links between subjective experience and the life-world. Seeking to deemphasize the antiscience posturing of phenomenology, the objective was to advance a more thoughtful analysis of the theoretical and methodological implications of such an approach. Also, as adulthood and aging have repeatedly been seen as periods of heightened inner awareness, the relevance of adopting a phenomenological perspective during these periods was strengthened.

Four empirical studies conducted by myself and my colleagues were summarized. The findings suggested that adults do have a subjective sense of both change and stability in themselves as they age. The most consistent patterns of perceived change were obtained for the instrumental to terminal values transition in women and for the generativity to integrity personality transition for both sexes. Participants from their 20s to their 80s saw themselves changing on these dimensions as they aged and in the direction that had been predicted by theory. Such qualities of perceived changes were differentiated from personality characteristics on which people saw themselves remaining stable over time. Developmental theory appeared to play an important role in separating the subjective changes from the perceived stability.

Future research directions were discussed including the study of people's comparative needs for seeing change versus consistency in themselves, cohort differences in subjective experience, the linking of inner experience to people's everyday activities and meanings (i.e., the life-world), the impact of self-perceived change (i.e., its adaptive and maladaptive effects), and the use of retrospective and prospective strategies to measure perceived change. Such questions respond to the more immediate aim of advancing life-span developmental research on inner experience. Beyond those are more distant goals, those heralded by Bühler, in which the relationships between inner experience, meaningful behavior, and culture are explored.

## Acknowledgments

This article was prepared while the author was a Fellow at the Center for Advanced Study in the Behavioral Sciences. The author is grateful for financial support provided by the John D. and Catherine T. MacArthur Foundation and by Fordham University. Appreciation is expressed to Steven W. Cornelius, Glen H. Elder, Jr., Kenneth J. Gergen, David E. Leary, and Bernice L. Neugarten for comments on an earlier draft of this article.

## References

Anderson, T. G. Existential counseling. In R. S. Valle & M. King (Eds.), *Existential–phenomenological alternatives for psychology.* London and New York: Oxford University Press, 1978.

Baltes, P. B. Life-span developmental psychology: Some converging observations on history and theory. In P. B. Baltes & O. G. Brim, Jr. (Eds.), *Life-span development and behavior* (Vol. 2). New York: Academic Press, 1979.

Baltes, P. B., Cornelius, S. W., & Nesselroade, J. R. Cohort effects in behavioral development:

Theoretical and methodological perspectives. In W. A. Collins (Ed.), *Minnesota symposium on child psychology* (Vol. 11). Hillsdale, New Jersey: Erlbaum, 1978.

Baltes, P. B., Reese, H. W., & Lipsitt, L. P. Life-span developmental psychology. *Annual Review of Psychology,* 1980, **31,** 65–110.

Bandura, A. Self-efficacy: Toward a unifying theory of behavioral change. *Psychological Review,* 1977, **84,** 191–215.

Bandura, A. Self-efficacy mechanism in human agency. *American Psychologist,* 1982, **37,** 122–147.

Barnett, R. C., & Baruch, G. K. Women in the middle years: A critique of research and theory. *Psychology of Women Quarterly,* 1978, **3,** 187–197.

Barrett, W. *Time of need: Forms of imagination in the twentieth century.* New York: Harper & Row, 1972.

Binswanger, L. The case of Ellen West. In R. May, E. Angel, & H. F. Ellenberger (Eds.), *Existence.* New York: Basic Books, 1958.

Binswanger, L. *Being-in-the-world: Selected papers of Ludwig Binswanger.* New York: Basic Books, 1963.

Boss, M. *Psychoanalysis and daseinsanalysis.* New York: Basic Books, 1963.

Brim, O. G., Jr., & Ryff, C. D. On the properties of life events. In P. B. Baltes & O. G. Brim, Jr. (Eds.), *Life-span development and behavior* (Vol. 3). New York: Academic Press, 1980.

Bugental, J. F. Symposium on Karl Bühler's contributions to psychology. *Journal of General Psychology,* 1966, **75,** 181–220.

Bühler, C. The curve of life as studied in biographies. *Journal of Applied Psychology,* 1935, **19,** 405–409.

Bühler, C., & Massarik, F. (Eds.). *The course of human life.* New York: Springer Publ., 1968.

Cantor, N., & Kihlstrom, J. F. (Eds.). *Personality, cognition, and social interaction.* Hillsdale, New Jersey: Erlbaum, 1981.

Cohler, B. J. Personal narrative and life course. In P. B. Baltes & O. G. Brim, Jr. (Eds.), *Life-span development and behavior* (Vol. 4). New York: Academic Press, 1982.

Colaizzi, P. F. Analysis of the learner's perception of learning material at various phases of a learning process. In A. Giorgi, W. F. Fischer, & R. Von Eckartsberg (Eds.), *Duquesne studies in phenomenological psychology* (Vol. 1). Pittsburgh: Duquesne University Press, 1971.

Colaizzi, P. F. Learning and existence. In R. S. Valle & M. King (Eds.), *Existential-phenomenological alternatives for psychology.* London and New York: Oxford University Press, 1978.

Costa, P. T., Jr., & McCrae, R. R. Still stable after all these years: Personality as a key to some issues in aging. In P. B. Baltes & O. G. Brim, Jr. (Eds.), *Life-span development and behavior* (Vol. 3). New York: Academic Press, 1980.

Dunn, D. D., & Ryff, C. D. *Self-perceived adjustment in widowhood: Age differences, sex differences, and the role of mediating variables.* Paper presented at the Gerontological Society Meetings, Boston, 1982.

Elder, G. H., Jr. Historical change in life patterns and personality. In P. B. Baltes & O. G. Brim, Jr. (Eds.), *Life-span development and behavior* (Vol. 2). New York: Academic Press, 1979.

Elder, G. H., Jr. Social history and life experience. In D. H. Eichorn, J. A. Clausen, N. Haan, M. P. Honzik, & P. H. Mussen (Eds.), *Present and past in middle life.* New York: Academic Press, 1981.

Erikson, E. *Childhood and society.* New York: Norton, 1950.

Erikson, E. Identity and the life cycle. *Psychological Issues,* 1959, **1,** 18–164.

Fallo-Mitchell, L., & Ryff, C. D. Preferred timing of female life events: Cohort differences. *Research on Aging,* 1982, **4,** 249–267.

Featherman, D. L. Retrospective longitudinal research: Methodological considerations. *Economics and Business Bulletin,* 1980, **32,** 152–169.

Fischoff, B. For those condemned to study the past: Reflections on historical judgment. *New Directions for Methodology of Social and Behavioral Science,* 1980, **4,** 79–93.

Gatchel, R. J., & Mears, F. G. *Personality: Theory, assessment, and research.* New York: St. Martin's, 1982.

Gergen, K. J. The emerging crisis in life-span developmental theory. In P. B. Baltes & O. G. Brim, Jr. (Eds.), *Life-span development and behavior* (Vol. 3). New York: Academic Press, 1980.

Gergen, K. J. *Toward transformation in social knowledge.* Berlin and New York: Springer-Verlag, 1982.

Gergen, K. J., & Gergen, M. M. Narratives of the self. In T. Sarbin & K. Scheibe (Eds.), *Studies in social identity.* New York: Praeger, 1984, in press.

Gilligan, C. Woman's place in man's life cycle. *Harvard Educational Review,* 1979, **49,** 431–446.

Gilligan, C. Adult development and women's development: Arrangements for a marriage. In J. Z. Giele (Ed.), *Women in the middle years.* New York: Wiley, 1982.

Giorgi, A. *Psychology as a human science: A phenomenologically based approach.* New York: Harper & Row, 1970.

Giorgi, A. Phenomenology and the foundations of psychology. In J. K. Cole & W. J. Arnold (Eds.), *Nebraska Symposium on Motivation* (Vol. 40). Lincoln: University of Nebraska Press, 1976.

Giorgi, A., Fischer, C. T., & Murray, E. L. (Eds.). *Duquesne studies in phenomenological psychology* (Vol. 2). Pittsburgh: Duquesne University Press, 1975.

Giorgi, A., Fischer, W. F., & Von Eckartsberg, R. (Eds.). *Duquesne studies in phenomenological psychology* (Vol. 1). Pittsburgh: Duquesne University Press, 1971.

Giorgi, A., Knowles, R., & Smith, D. L. (Eds.), *Duquesne studies in phenomenological psychology* (Vol. 3). Pittsburgh: Duquesne University Press, 1979.

Gould, R. *Transformations.* New York: Simon & Schuster, 1978.

Hall, C. S., & Lindzey, G. *Theories of personality* (3rd ed.). New York: Wiley, 1978.

Husserl, E. *Phenomenology and the crisis of philosophy* (Q. Lauer, Ed. and trans.). New York: Harper Torchbooks, 1965. (Originally published, 1911.)

Jackson, D. N. *Personality research form manual.* Goshen, New York: Research Psychologists Press, 1967.

Jackson, D. N. *Jackson personality inventory manual.* Goshen, New York: Research Psychologists Press, 1976.

Johnson, J. H., & Sarason, I. G. Moderator variables in life stress research. In I. G. Sarason & C. D. Spielberger (Eds.), *Stress and anxiety* (Vol. 6). New York: Hemisphere Publ., 1979.

Jung, C. G. *Modern man in search of a soul.* New York: Harcourt, 1933.

Jung, C. G. *Psyche and symbol.* New York: Anchor Books, 1958.

Kelly, G. A. *The psychology of personal constructs.* New York: Norton, 1955.

Kuenzli, A. E. (Ed.). *The phenomenological problem.* New York: Harper, 1959.

Langer, E. The illusion of incompetence. In L. Perlmuter & R. Monty (Eds.), *Choice and perceived control.* Hillsdale, New Jersey: Erlbaum, 1979.

Lefcourt, H. M. The function of the illusions of control and freedom. *American Psychologist,* 1973, **28,** 417–425.

Levinson, D. J. *The seasons of a man's life.* New York: Knopf, 1978.

Levinson, D. J. Exploration in biography: Evolution of the individual life structure in adulthood. In A. I. Rabin, J. Aronoff, A. M. Barclay, & R. A. Zucker (Eds.), *Further explorations in personality.* New York: Wiley, 1981.

MacLeod, R. B. Phenomenology: A challenge to experimental psychology. In T. W. Wann (Ed.), *Behaviorism and phenomenology: Contrasting bases for modern psychology.* Chicago: University of Chicago Press, 1964.

Maddox, G., & Douglass, E. B. Self-assessments of health. In E. Palmore (Ed.), *Normal aging* (Vol. 2). Durham, North Carolina: Duke University Press, 1974.

Massey, R. F. *Personality theories: Comparisons and syntheses.* New York: Van Nostrand Reinhold, 1981.

McAdams, D. P. Experiences of intimacy and power: Relationships between social motives and autobiographical memory. *Journal of Personality and Social Psychology*, 1982, **42**, 292–302.

Mischel, W. *Introduction to personality* (3rd ed.). New York: Holt Rinehart & Winston, 1981.

Neugarten, B. L. The awareness of middle age. In B. L. Neugarten (Ed.), *Middle age and aging.* Chicago: University of Chicago Press, 1968.

Neugarten, B. L. Personality change in late life: A developmental perspective. In C. Eisdorfer & M. P. Lawton (Eds.), *The psychology of adult development and aging.* Washington, D.C.: American Psychological Association, 1973.

Neugarten, B. L. Personality and aging. In J. E. Birren & K. W. Schaie (Eds.), *Handbook of the psychology of aging.* New York: Van Nostrand Reinhold, 1977.

Pervin, L. A. *Personality: Theory, assessment, and research* (3rd ed.). New York: Wiley, 1980.

Peskin, H., & Livson, N. Uses of the past in adult psychological health. In D. H. Eichorn, J. A. Clausen, N. Haan, M. P. Honzik, & P. H. Mussen (Eds.), *Present and past in middle life.* New York: Academic Press, 1981.

Reinert, G. Prolegomena to a history of life-span developmental psychology. In P. B. Baltes & O. G. Brim, Jr. (Eds.), *Life-span development and behavior* (Vol. 2). New York: Academic Press, 1979.

Ridley, J. C., Bachrach, C. A., & Dawson, D. A. Recall and reliability of interview data from older women. *Journal of Gerontology*, 1979, **34**, 99–105.

Rodin, J. Managing the stress of aging: The role of control and coping. In S. Levine & H. Ursin (Eds.), *Coping and health.* New York: Plenum, 1980.

Rogers, C. R. *Client-centered therapy: Its current practice, implications and theory.* Boston: Houghton, 1951.

Rogers, C. R. A theory of therapy, personality and interpersonal relationships, as developed in the client-centered framework. In S. Koch (Ed.), *Psychology: A study of a science* (Vol. 3). New York: McGraw-Hill, 1959.

Rogers, C. R. *On becoming a person.* Boston: Houghton, 1961.

Rokeach, M. *The nature of human values.* New York: Free Press, 1973.

Rossi, A. S. Life-span theories and women's lives. *Signs: Journal of Women in Culture and Society*, 1980, **6**, 4–32.

Rubin, L. B. *Women of a certain age: The midlife search for self.* New York: Harper & Row, 1979.

Ryff, C. D. Self-perceived personality change in adulthood and aging. *Journal of Personality and Social Psychology*, 1982, **42**, 108–115. (a)

Ryff, C. D. Successful aging: A developmental approach. *The Gerontologist*, 1982, **22**, 209–214. (b)

Ryff, C. D. Adult personality development and the motivation for personal growth. In D. A. Kleiber & M. L. Maehr (Eds.), *Motivation in adulthood.* Greenwich, Connecticut: JAI Press, 1984, in press.

Ryff, C. D., & Baltes, P. B. Value transitions and adult development in women: The instrumentality–terminality sequence hypothesis. *Developmental Psychology*, 1976, **12**, 567–568.

Ryff, C. D., & Dunn, D. D. *Life stresses and personality: A life-span developmental inquiry.* Paper presented at the Gerontological Society Meetings, San Francisco, 1983.

Ryff, C. D., & Heincke, S. G. The subjective organization of personality in adulthood and aging. *Journal of Personality and Social Psychology*, 1983, **44**, 807–816.

Ryff, C. D., & Migdal, S. Intimacy and generativity: Self-perceived transitions. *Signs: Journal of Women in Culture and Society*, 1984, **9**, in press.

Sardello, R. J. A phenomenological approach to memory. In R. S. Valle & M. King (Eds.),

*Existential–phenomenological alternatives for psychology*. London and New York: Oxford University Press, 1978.

Scarf, M. *Unfinished business: Pressure points in the lives of women*. Garden City, New York: Doubleday, 1980.

Schachtel, E. *Metamorphosis*. New York: Basic Books, 1959.

Schaie, K. W., & Parham, I. A. Stability of adult personality: Fact or fable? *Journal of Personality and Social Psychology*, 1976, **34**, 146–158.

Schneider, D. J., Hastorf, A. H., & Ellsworth, P. C. *Person perception* (2nd ed.). Reading, Massachusetts: Addison-Wesley, 1979.

Sears, R. R. The role of expectancy in adaptation to aging. In S. B. Kiesler, J. N. Morgan, & V. K. Oppenheimer (Eds.), *Social change*. New York: Academic Press, 1981.

Sheehy, G. *Passages: Predictable crises of adult life*. New York: Dutton, 1976.

Sheehy, G. *Pathfinders*. New York: Morrow, 1981.

Siegler, I. C., George, L. K., & Okun, M. A. Cross-sequential analysis of adult personality. *Developmental Psychology*, 1979, **15**, 350–351.

Smith, M. B. The phenomenological approach in personality theory: Some critical remarks. *Journal of Abnormal and Social Psychology*, 1950, **45**, 516–522.

Snygg, D., & Combs, A. W. *Individual behavior: A new frame of reference for psychology*. New York: Harper, 1949.

Spiegelberg, H. *Phenomenology in psychology and psychiatry: An historical introduction*. Evanston, Illinois: Northwestern University Press, 1972.

Straus, E. W. *Phenomenological psychology*. New York: Basic Books, 1966.

Thomae, H. Theory of aging and cognitive theory of personality. *Human Development*, 1970, **13**, 1–16.

Vaillant, G. E. *Adaptation to life*. Boston: Little, Brown, 1977.

Valle, R. S., & King, M. (Eds.). *Existential–phenomenological alternatives for psychology*. London and New York: Oxford University Press, 1978.

Veroff, J., Douvan, E., & Kulka, R. A. *The inner American: A self-portrait from 1957 to 1976*. New York: Basic Books, 1981.

Wann, T. W. (Ed.). *Behaviorism and phenomenology: Contrasting bases for modern psychology*. Chicago: University of Chicago Press, 1964.

Wegner, D. M., & Vallacher, R. R. (Eds.). *The self in social psychology*. London and New York: Oxford University Press, 1980.

Whitbourne, S. K., & Waterman, A. S. Psychosocial development during the adult years: Age and cohort comparisons. *Developmental Psychology*, 1979, **15**, 373–378.

Woodruff, D. W., & Birren, J. E. Age changes and cohort differences in personality. *Developmental Psychology*, 1972, **6**, 252–259.

Yarrow, M. R., Campbell, J. D., & Burton, R. V. Recollections of childhood: A study of the retrospective method. *Monographs of the Society for Research in Child Development*, 1970, **35**, 1–83.

Zeren, A., & Ryff, C. D. *Psychological development in men during fatherhood*. Paper presented at the Eastern Psychological Association Meetings, Baltimore, 1984.

# Change in Self in Adulthood:
# The Example of Sense of Control

*Patricia Gurin*

THE UNIVERSITY OF MICHIGAN

ANN ARBOR, MICHIGAN

AND

RUSSELL SAGE FOUNDATION

NEW YORK, NEW YORK

*and*

*Orville G. Brim, Jr.*

FOUNDATION FOR CHILD DEVELOPMENT

NEW YORK, NEW YORK

## Abstract

Change in sense of control in adulthood is examined in data collected nearly every 2 years since 1952 by the Institute for Social Research of The University of Michigan. Two separate but related components of sense of control are considered. One component is judgment of the self as able to produce acts that should lead to desirable outcomes, here called personal efficacy. The second is judgment of the environment's likely response to individual action, here called system responsiveness. Personal efficacy has changed less, both historically and correlationally, than have judgments of responsiveness. This evidence about differential stability, admittedly limited to specific measures used in these repeated surveys, is used to raise questions about adult change in central aspects of self, as personal efficacy is held to be. Both psychological and sociological/situational explanations are offered.

Because personal efficacy is fundamental and central to self, events that challenge competence are also likely to arouse psychological needs that tend to foster stability. These include needs for consistency, self-respect, and control. They converge for people who expect to succeed, do well in life, and who think of themselves as highly efficacious, heightening their sensitivity to events that reinforce positive views of the self and their avoidance, reinterpretation, and externalization of threatening events and losses of valued roles. They diverge for people who expect to fail and who consider themselves incompetent. Their needs for self-respect and control may make them welcome success, while their needs for consistency may make them quite dubious about its credibility for self. Events must therefore be "psychologically compelling" if either success or failure is to change personal efficacy or other central aspects of self. However much desired, success must be incontrovertible if it is to influence the inefficacious. And, if not compelling, failure may go unnoticed or discounted by the efficacious. In contrast, because judgments of the environment's responsiveness are for most people less central to the self, these psychological needs should intrude much less to mute the potential impact of historical and life events.

The separate research traditions of naturalistic and laboratory studies of stressful life events are reviewed to suggest properties of events, and of the social situations in which they occur, which make them "psychologically compelling." These properties are analyzed for their pertinence to two aspects of individual change: attention and processing of social information as one step in change, and believing as well that the event has implications for the self. Some properties of events or situations contribute to their being compelling by daunting selectivity, increasing breadth of exposure, and helping people pay attention instead of ignoring the event. Some properties which initiate the change process in these ways may then militate against change in central aspects of self by decreasing the event's self-implications.

Understanding adult change in personal efficacy and other central aspects of self requires analysis of properties of historical and life events and their linkage to the change process. The important question for life-span theorists is not whether but when and how adults change in fundamental aspects of self.

## I. Introduction

The sense of control, inextricably linked developmentally to beliefs about causation, is fundamental to human life. Through interacting with the world the infant early on begins to grasp understanding of causality and at the same time develops good feelings about the self. Both occur together as the infant has effects on the world. In those moments when the infant tries to make interesting experiences continue, one of life's critical dramas takes place. During this drama the infant's earlier nearly exclusive dependence on external causation gives way to a sense of self as a causal agent. Eventually the infant no longer stops when bounced on an adult's knee or when tossed gently in the air. Instead, she appears to try to make the event continue. She bounces herself, reaching upward, causing the experience to last. Her pleasure usually causes the adult to remain engaged as well. Instead of depending on the adult's behavior, she is now able to cause pleasurable things to happen to herself and even cause others to respond. Causing things to happen is the medium through which the young infant begins to exercise control and to understand cause and consequence more fully.

This early drama is profound not only because of its implication for cognitive growth but also for development of self. These events are joyful. Causing things to happen feels good. This early omnipotence and pleasure in self will go through many vicissitudes en route to the adult's feelings about self and understanding of causal relations. Throughout, however, the sense of self as a causal agent will remain a fundamental theme through which personal theories of causality and conceptions and feelings about the self will develop.

This article focuses on adults' sense of control. How much control do adults feel they have over their lives? Has that changed in recent decades? Do older people report reduced feelings of control? How stable is the sense of control among individuals studied longitudinally in adulthood?

To answer these questions we trace historical and life-span trends in two interrelated but conceptually separable aspects of control that have been measured repeatedly in national surveys carried out by the Institute for Social Research (ISR) at The University of Michigan. One focuses primarily on judging the self as capable, as a person able to produce acts that should lead to desirable outcomes. We refer to it here as a judgment of one's personal efficacy. The other focuses on judging the environment's likely response to the act. We refer to it here as a judgment of the system's responsiveness.

We have two goals in the article: (1) to present some empirical evidence about differential stability of these two components of the sense of control, and (2) to use these admittedly instrument-bound results as an occasion to raise broader questions about ease and difficulty of adult change in beliefs about the self and about the environment. While the measures were not originally written to capture the distinction between self and environment, they nonetheless provide the most clearly pertinent data presently available for analysis of historical trends. Analyses of the national survey data collected over a 30-year period will show little historical change in Americans' answers to questions that ask primarily about their own personal efficacy. By contrast, responses to questions that ask about the responsiveness of political institutions and authorities have changed considerably more in recent decades. Why might this be?

In addressing this question, our second and major goal in this article, we begin by examining three psychological needs—needs for control, self-respect, and consistency—that partially explain why adults' views of their own efficacy may change less than their views of the system's responsiveness. Since judgments of personal efficacy are so central to the self, events that challenge competence are also likely to arouse needs that foster stability. Because judgments of environmental contingencies are less self-relevant for most people, psychological needs do not intrude as much to mute the potential impact of life and historical events. Then we turn to properties of events, and the situations in which they occur, which also apply to the issue of adult change. We will show that adults do change judgments and feelings about the self, including their personal efficacy, when events and situations are psychologically compelling. We review studies in both experimental and natural situations that delineate properties of events that do change individuals. We argue that aggregate change in adults' level of personal efficacy would be greater if more people experienced these compelling events. Paradoxically, however, the properties of events that press people to look at themselves and deal with the self-implications of the event are almost by definition too rare to alter a whole population's judgments of themselves as personally efficacious. Our goals will have been met in the article if the empirical evidence we present on efficacy and responsiveness stimulate questions about adult change and our discussion of psychological needs and properties of events suggests conditions when even very basic aspects of self may change in adulthood.

## II. Sense of Control: Judgments of Self and the Environment

Sense of control, or perceived control as it is sometimes called, has been defined in various ways, although nearly always the definitions include something about outcomes and something about causal reasoning. We define the sense of control as an actor's expectancy that he or she can control outcomes. While the expectancy itself is a probability assessment, developmentally and logically it is closely tied to causal questions. Control over outcomes logically involves judging and analyzing two interrelated connections: that between the self and an act, and that between the act and an outcome.[1] Causal explanations are impli-

[1]Skinner and Chapman (1984) define beliefs about control as the person's generalized expectancies that he/she is capable of producing intended outcomes. These control beliefs are further differentiated into two other sets of beliefs: condition Y results in outcome X, and, I have or can produce condition Y. They refer to the former as causality beliefs, the latter as agency beliefs. We can conceive that causality beliefs are involved in each, not exclusively in the belief about the connection between condition Y and outcome X; external causes should be stronger contenders in explaining that connection, while the connection between self and condition Y explicitly asserts personal causes.

cated in both these connections.

Let us consider the first connection, the relationship between self and the act. Here the actor judges his/her own capability, whether he/she is capable of performing an act that should lead to an outcome. We call it personal efficacy. While a person might feel inefficacious because of something external, for example, because the task is difficult or because materials needed to carry it out are unavailable, efficacy normally implies something about the actor's own qualities. People typically feel efficacious when they believe themselves to be competent. The very assessment of self–act connections invites internal, personal attributions, although external attributions are logically possible.

The sense of control also involves judgments of environmental contingencies. Will the act lead to an outcome? What is the likely response to the act? Sometimes the person judges a likely, fairly specific, response to his/her *own* act. Sometimes the person judges the environment's responsiveness to individual action in general. Responsiveness implies a causal theory about the way institutions operate. Is this an institution (work setting, classroom, political party) in which rewards/outcomes are supposed to and actually do result from individual acts? Or is it an environment in which outcomes are not contingent on individual action either because outcomes are delivered whimsically or according to rules or natural laws that make them dependent on something other than individual action? The self is normally a weak causal contender when act–outcome contingencies are judged, especially when it is the environment's responsiveness to individual action in general that is being judged.

In this article we are interested in tracing historical trends in Americans' views of their own personal efficacy and of the responsiveness of political institutions to individuals. These are two components of the sense of control which thus differ greatly in emphasis on self and the environment as causal forces. Had we focused on the individual's assessment of responsiveness to him or herself, the self-environment distinction would be less clear. As we will note later, the battery of items in the ISR studies does not include items asking about "responsiveness to me." For our purposes of raising questions about adult change, this marked separation between self in the efficacy items and environment in the political responsiveness items sharpens the issues.

Many of the important conceptual controversies about the value of the distinction between efficacy and responsiveness are not considered here. We do not discuss how they are combined to form an overall sense of control, whether this changes with development, whether it varies for different people or situations, for what kinds of action the distinction makes a difference.[2] Showing that

---

[2]We have discussed elsewhere the social structural conditions in which the distinction becomes especially pertinent to motivation (Gurin, Gurin, Lao, & Beattie, 1969), age trends in the two

efficacy and responsiveness have different historical trends and individual stabilities, as we do, adds to the growing literature on the validity of drawing this distinction, although we are concerned less with validity than with the implications of differential stability of efficacy and responsiveness for theories of change in adulthood.

The distinction we draw between self and environmental aspects of control has also been made by others in several different social science areas in which control plays a prominent theoretical role. Bandura's (1977, 1980) self-efficacy model of behavior change, for example, refers to both self and environment. Bandura delineates two expectancies that potentially influence a person's behavior in a specific situation. The environment is critical in one—the outcome expectancy which is the person's estimate of the extent to which a particular behavior will lead to a desired outcome in that particular environment. The self is critical in the other—the efficacy expectation which is the person's estimate whether he can successfully perform that behavior. Actual behavior theoretically depends on both expectancies, although Bandura's work primarily has dealt with the efficacy expectation. For Bandura both expectancies are specific to a particular situation whereas we are concerned with generalized expectancies. In the case of efficacy this means a view of oneself as generally competent rather than competent to produce a specific act. In the case of responsiveness this means a view of the environment's general responsiveness to individual action rather than response to a particular actor's specific act. In addition, we focus on the political system since the measures available for historical analysis pertain exclusively to the political arena.

Using different terminology, expectancy theorists in organizational psychology draw the same distinction (Vroom, 1964; Porter & Lawler, 1968). Instrumentality, the belief that performance will lead to rewards in a particular organizational setting, is analogous to Bandura's outcome expectancy. Expectancy, the belief that effort will lead to performance, resembles Bandura's efficacy expectation. Motivation theory in organizational behavior studies posits that the two together, sometimes additively, sometimes multiplicatively, influence behavior. Again, as in Bandura's work, the focus is on specific contexts.

A multidimensional conception of sense of control exists in political science and political sociology as well. Here the work emphasizes generalized beliefs, not beliefs about specific acts in particular contexts, and provides the measures we analyze below. There has been a much longer history of theoretical interest in sense of control in political science than in psychology.

---

components (Brim, 1974; Gurin & Gurin, 1975), and types of action for which the distinction makes a difference (Gurin, Gurin, & Morrison, 1978). See also our discussion here of the implications of the distinction for understanding the political action of challenging groups in the late 1960s and early 1970s.

Recognition of the importance of distinguishing judgments of self-competence and act–outcome contingencies did not occur when work on sense of control (called political efficacy in political studies) began with the introduction of the concept and measure of efficacy in the ISR presidential election study of 1952 (Campbell, Gurin, & Miller, 1954). Instead, political efficacy was cast just as an act–outcome contingency. Efficacy was the belief that individual political action can have an impact upon political outcomes.

The early political science literature primarily attempted to document a straightforward relationship between higher political efficacy and greater interest, involvement, and participation in political affairs. Participation measures in the early research in the 1950s were restricted to traditional, conventional political activity, such as voting and taking part in campaign activities. With these measures, participation generally was greater among people who were more politically efficacious. Participation effects of efficacy became more problematic, however, when nontraditional political activities, including direct action and protest activities, began to be measured during the turbulent decade of the 1960s. This suggested the need to look at conceptual and measurement problems in the sense of political efficacy.

Theoretical work on alienation during the 1960s also raised questions about the dimensionality of efficacy. Political scientists (Easton, 1965; Almond & Verba, 1965) and political sociologists (Gamson, 1968), interested in efficacy as the counterpart to alienation, drew the same distinction that became important in psychological work on control. They distinguished judgment of the self as competent from judgment of the political system's responsiveness. Gamson's (1968) treatment of alienation is representative of these conceptual developments. Gamson separates competence as an input dimension from trust as an output dimension of alienation. Competence refers to people's perceptions of their own abilities to influence authorities. Trust refers to the perception that political institutions and authorities do what they are supposed to do in a democratic system, that is, represent and respond to individuals. While trust sometimes denotes an expectation that others will pursue good outcomes independent of the opinions and actions of those to whom they are accountable, political trust as used in democratic theory specifically includes act–outcome contingencies. In the theory of democracy political authorities and institutions are supposed to be responsive to the will of the people. Barber (1983) refers to this responsiveness meaning of trust as the expectation that authorities will carry out their fiduciary responsibilities to place others' interests before their own. It is not the only meaning of political trust. Barber distinguishes it from a second meaning, the expectation that authorities will perform their roles with technical competence. It is the first meaning that relates particularly to our interest in sense of control.

Why did a number of years elapse before questions of the multidimensionality of political efficacy were raised? In fact, Lane (1959), a major contributor to the political science literature on political efficacy, noted the self-environment distinction in the 1950s. In a significant book Lane noted that political efficacy "has, of course, two components—the image of the self and the image of democratic government—and contains the tacit assumption that an image of self as effective is intimately related to the image of democratic government as responsive to the people" (Lane, 1959, p. 149).

While the dual judgments were recognized, the intimate relationship of the two was not questioned in the benign, quiet political environment of the 1950s. It took a period of activism and confrontation to demonstrate that a view of the self as politically competent and belief in the system's responsiveness are not necessarily intimately linked. The significance of distinguishing these judgments is clearly more impressive if they are not highly correlated, at least among some groups in society, and if they can be demonstrated to have discriminant validity. Studies of student protest of the Vietnamese War, participation in the civil rights movement in the South, and urban disturbances of the later 1960s and early 1970s provided the empirical justification for the significance of the distinction. Among challengers the two judgments were inversely related. Moreover, it was their disjuncture, rather than their connection, that was associated with action. In these groups, especially among minorities, the view of the self as competent and the system as unresponsive related to political action of both a traditional and nontraditional sort (Caplan, 1970; Gurin, Gurin, & Morrison, 1978; Paige, 1971). Research on the political environment and challenging activities of the 1960s and early 1970s thus made it clear that the effect of political efficacy on political behavior could not be understood without drawing the distinction between judgment of self and responsiveness of the political system.

## III. Stability and Change: Personal Efficacy and Judgments of Responsiveness

### A. MEASURES OF EFFICACY AND RESPONSIVENESS

The work at the Institute for Social Research, largely in the national election studies conducted nearly every 2 years since 1952, provides the nation's major data base for assessing trends in efficacy and perceptions of the responsiveness of political institutions and authorities. In most of these cross-section surveys, measures of both have been included, although more measurement attention has been devoted to the judgments of responsiveness than to judgments of the self as politically competent. However, these election surveys also include a measure of personal efficacy that is cast in global, rather than specifically political, terms.

Some limitations in the measures for our purposes should be noted at the outset. These become more apparent as we describe the measures in greater detail below. A first limitation has already been stated: the fact that the responsiveness judgments are restricted just to the political domain. Ideally we would like to know if perceptions of responsiveness of other institutions also have changed historically more than has personal efficacy.[3] Second, the surveys have included only a few efficacy items and the phrasing in some slips from judgment of self as competent to judgment of the overall sense of control itself. Ideally we would like more carefully worded questions that consistently maintain the distinction between self as competent and the environment as responsive. Dependence on extant measures that were not developed with a clear conceptualization of sense of control necessarily brings such limitations. However, these measures are the only ones on which long-term trends and individual stabilities are available, and also capture the distinction between self and environment reasonably well. Before turning to historical trends, we will describe them further to provide empirical evidence that the self is more critical in the efficacy items, the environment more critical in the responsiveness items.

Converse (1972) first noted that the measure of political efficacy introduced in these election studies in 1952 seemed to include two components, one emphasizing self, the other the political system. Noting that the two sets of items within the original efficacy index did not move in parallel over time, Converse suggested that the index should no longer be viewed as unidimensional. One component, the self as politically competent, is represented by the item: "Sometimes politics and government seem so complicated that a person like me can't really understand what's going on." Competence is demonstrated by disagreeing with this item. The other, a judgment of the political system's responsiveness to individuals, is represented by the item: "I don't think public officials care much what people like me think."

Recently, Mason, House, and Martin (1981) have gone further in providing conceptual clarity to the battery of items that have been included routinely in these election surveys. They scrutinize 27 items. Using exploratory factor analysis, Mason and colleagues accept an item as an indicator of a construct only if it meets two criteria: it represents only one latent construct and it means the same thing historically across time. They then apply canonical analysis to the items

---

[3]Lipset and Schneider (1983) report data from Opinion Research Corporation on attitudes toward business and industries and from Gallup on attitudes toward leaders of organized labor that show a sharp decline in public faith in these institutions since the mid-1960s, nearly the same time that Americans began in larger numbers doubting the responsiveness of political authorities and institutions. However, none of the questions about business, industry, and labor specifically refers to their responsiveness and accountability to people. Nor is it clear that trust in these institutions should involve the fiduciary element of expecting them to put the public's interests above their own. It is clear from the data compiled by Lipset and Schneider that there was an erosion from earlier positive attitudes about the position and power of large companies and specific firms and that this erosion, which started mid-1960s, has continued fairly unabetted to the present.

identified as historically stable clusters in the first exploratory stage. The essential validation criterion at the second stage is that the first canonical variate dominates all others in a series of models in which time trends, sociodemographic characteristics, and issue attitudes are taken into account. They require that historical trends, effects of sociodemographic variables, and relationships to issue attitudes be consistent across items within a cluster. The general position adopted is that a set of items should neither be considered indicators of a single underlying construct nor be combined into a multiitem index or scale of alienation unless the items not only covary with each other at a single point in time but also covary in the same way historically and manifest similar relations to external causes and consequences.

We are interested in 12 of the items which meet these criteria and form four unidimensional indices. These 12 plus a single item measuring political competence appear to represent the two basic themes suggested by Gamson (1968) and others. Results from a double constrained factor analytic model, in which constrained factors are themselves factored subjected to a priori restrictions, are consistent with the view that sense of control involves both input and output dimensions. The results show that the input dimension is represented by measures of self as competent, both in a general and in a specifically political sense. The output dimension is represented by measures of the responsiveness of political institutions and authorities.

These factor analytic studies of Mason and colleagues were intended to inform the use of the national election study data by the community of scholars interested in political behavior in the United States. It is used there to guide our examination of stability and change. We focus on two indicators of efficacy, the self as generally efficacious and as politically competent, and three indicators of responsiveness, the general responsiveness of political institutions/authorities, government responsiveness to what people think, and trustworthiness of government. The items on these three responsiveness indicators all ask people to judge how much authorities, the government itself, and political mechanisms such as elections and political parties respond to individuals. That they have been shown to represent separate unidimensional constructs in these factor analytic studies may stem partly from method or semantic issues. The items on each of the three indicators appear in different parts of the interview schedule and at least the government responsiveness and trust items may cluster together and separately from each other largely because of specific reference in the items to the words, "government" and "trust." For our purposes, however, we are less interested in this further differentiation within responsiveness than in the self-environment distinction which discriminates the two efficacy indicators from the three responsiveness indicators (Table I).

Additional evidence about the self–environment discrimination between the efficacy and responsiveness indicators is provided by their respective correla-

**TABLE I**

**Items Measuring Personal Efficacy and Perceptions of the Responsiveness of the Political System**

---

**Judgments of efficacy**

Generalized personal efficacy

  When you do make plans ahead, do you usually get to carry out things the way you expect, or do things usually come up to make you change your plans?

  Have you usually felt pretty sure your life would work out the way you want it to, or have there been times when you haven't been sure about it?

Political competence

  Sometimes politics and government seem so complicated that a person like me can't really understand what's going on.

**Judgments of responsiveness**

General responsiveness of political institutions/authorities

  People like me don't have any say about what the government does.

  I don't think public officials care much what people like me think.

  Generally speaking, those we elect to Congress in Washington lose touch with the people pretty quickly. (Asked beginning in 1968)

  Parties are only interested in people's votes but not in their opinions. (Asked beginning in 1968)

Government responsiveness to people's ideas

  Over the years, how much attention do you feel the government pays to what people think when it decides what to do—a good deal, some, not much?

  How much attention do you think most Congressmen pay to the people who elect them when they decide what to do in Congress—a good deal, some, not much?

  How much do you feel that having elections makes the government pay attention to what people think—a good deal, some, not much?

  How much do you feel that political parties help to make the government pay attention to what the people think—a good deal, some, not much?

Trustworthiness of government

  How much of the time do you think you can trust the government in Washington to do what is right—just about all the time, most of the time, only some of the time?

  Would you say that the government is pretty much run by a few big interests looking out for themselves or that it is run for the benefit of all people?

---

tions with the items of the Rotter Internal–External Control Scale that specifically refer to the self. These are the questions on that scale which are cast in the first person. [See Gurin, Gurin, Lao, & Beattie (1969) and Gurin *et al.* (1978) for validation studies of the personal theme in Internal–External (I–E) Control Scale.] The two personal efficacy items and one political competence item correlate quite highly with the personally phrased I–E items (range .64 to .76), while the 10 responsiveness items correlate very weakly (range .00 to .17). This pattern shows that self is more prominent in the efficacy than in the responsiveness items, although it can also be used as evidence that the efficacy items are limited for our purposes by reflecting the overall sense of control more than would be desirable.

The historical and age evidence we review comes from data collected in these national election studies (NES) and also from another research program at the Institute for Social Research, the Panel Study of Income Dynamics (PSID).

## B. CHANGE AND STABILITY

Change and stability connote different meanings that need clarification before we turn to empirical evidence about change in sense of control. In an important paper on change in party identification, Converse and Markus (1979) highlight one meaning of change that can be measured in successive independent cross-section samples. A trait or attitude has changed when the mean of the distribution shifts from one time to another. This is normally the sense in which we use the term "change or stability" when we are interested in historical effects. In addition, the variance of the distribution can move from one time to another. Variance can move independently of the mean, shrinking dramatically while the mean is stationary, remaining stationary while the mean shifts dramatically. The most striking change in party identification since 1965 was the shrinkage of variance by more than 10%. Mean shifts were very minor.

A second meaning of change, which cannot be assessed except from information provided by panel studies of the same individuals across time, concerns the ordering of individuals. Here stability and change is in the relative positions of individuals. Kagan (1980) calls this normative change/stability. Represented by the continuity correlation, it is the meaning of change most frequently invoked in psychological research. Unfortunately, it is often confused with change as a shift in a distribution's mean. Kagan (1980) notes, for example, that when textbooks say that children's cognitive ability is stable, they mean that the differences in test scores among a cohort of children remain stable, despite impressive shifts in abilities that accompany growth. The independence of these two meanings of change is stressed by Converse and Markus (1979).

> Although novitiates are constantly confused by the fact, continuity correlations formed on the same variable in two panel waves are as independent of temporal changes in the mean and variance of the distribution as the latter are independent of each other. That is to say, a continuity correlation can range from zero to perfection whether both mean and variance are constant, or one or both shift dramatically between the two time points. This is true by the very construction of the product–moment coefficient, which equates or normalizes the two means and variances, thereby partialling out whatever real change may have occurred with respect to those facets of the variable. (p. 37)

We can imagine historical events which are potentially powerful enough to shift the mean level of Americans' sense of control downward; for example, periods of economic recession and widespread unemployment. Still, even if sense of control does go down during some historical periods, it may be quite stable in a relative sense. If an historical event is to alter the ordering of individuals' sense of control from one time to another, the individuals' initial positions on a scale of control must be fairly independent of whether they are exposed to the event (the problem of selectivity) and/or how they react to it (responsivity). If highly efficacious people lose jobs less frequently than others during periods of high unemployment, their relative standing on sense of control will remain high after the event. If they respond to job loss more positively than less efficacious people, the ordering of individuals likewise will remain stable. Leapfrogging out of order may occur when an event capable of changing individuals operates independently of their earlier levels of control. And it will occur when the event is inversely related to initial positions on control. This can happen whether or not the mean of the distribution shifts downward/upward or remains the same before and after the event.

We are interested in both types of change/stability in sense of control. First, we examine evidence regarding historical shifts in both the self and the environmental components of control. Then we turn to the issue of correlational stability in both components.

*1. Mean Shifts*

The means of the distributions from the data collected in the national election studies from 1952 onward are shown in Table II. On all indicators the range is from one to five, five representing low personal efficacy and low system responsiveness. The table includes two indicators of personal efficacy and three indicators of judgments of responsiveness.

Several conclusions can be drawn from this table. In the years when both sets of judgments were measured, Americans tended to be more positive about the responsiveness of political institutions and authorities than about their own efficacy. This was particularly true in the early years when these measures were administered. Further, in 1952 when these measures were first introduced, both components of sense of control were unusually low. After 1952 both types of control increased through the latter part of the 1950s and up through 1964. Thereafter, the personal aspects of control decreased again, leveling out by 1968 at about the 1952 level and remaining stable through 1980. Thus, there was one period during the late 1950s and early 1960s when Americans felt fairly efficacious, although during most of the 30 years they considered themselves just moderately efficacious in a generalized sense and even less politically competent. Overall, the personal aspects of control have shifted very little since 1952.

The data on judgments of responsiveness are somewhat different. After the period of optimism in the late 1950s, ending about 1964, Americans increasingly came to view political authorities and institutions as more unresponsive. The increase in perceived unresponsiveness moreover continued beyond the period of

## TABLE II

### Historical Trends in Personal Efficacy and Judgments of Responsiveness

| | Year (number of respondents in survey) | | | | | | | | | | | | |
|---|---|---|---|---|---|---|---|---|---|---|---|---|---|
| | 1952 (1899) | 1956 (1762) | 1958 (1450) | 1960 (1181) | 1964 (1571) | 1966 (1291) | 1968 (1551) | 1970 (1580) | 1972 (2705) | 1974 (2149) | 1976 (2248) | 1978 (2304) | 1980 (1614) |
| **Judgments of efficacy** | | | | | | | | | | | | | |
| Generalized personal efficacy | | | | | | | | | | | | | |
| Two-item index; range 1–5, 5 = low control | — | 3.17 | 2.97 | 2.83 | 2.81 | — | 3.22 | 3.36 | 3.26 | 3.40 | 3.29 | — | — |
| Political competence | | | | | | | | | | | | | |
| Single item; range 1–5, 5 = low control | 3.86 | 3.55 | — | 3.32 | 3.68 | 3.89 | 3.85 | 3.95 | 3.93 | 3.93 | 3.91 | 3.93 | 3.86 |
| **Judgments of responsiveness** | | | | | | | | | | | | | |
| General responsiveness of political institutions/authorities | | | | | | | | | | | | | |
| Two items asked 1952 on; range 1–5, 5 = low responsiveness | 2.33 | 2.09 | — | 2.02 | 2.32 | 2.46 | 2.69 | 2.70 | 2.75 | 2.89 | 2.91 | 2.99 | 2.90 |
| Two items asked 1968 on; range 1–5; 5 = low responsiveness | — | — | — | — | — | — | 3.05 | 3.36 | 3.50 | 3.65 | 3.73 | 3.80 | 3.78 |
| Government responsiveness | | | | | | | | | | | | | |
| Three items; government, elections, congressmen; range 1–5; 5 = low responsiveness | — | — | — | — | 2.33 | — | 2.58 | 2.59 | 2.66 | 2.87 | 2.88 | 2.80 | 3.01 |
| Trustworthiness of government | | | | | | | | | | | | | |
| Two-item index, range 1–5; 5 = low trust | — | — | — | — | 2.69 | 2.88 | 3.17 | 3.49 | 3.57 | 4.07 | 4.09 | 4.15 | 4.27 |

Watergate up through 1980. There is no question that the judgments of responsiveness were not nearly as stable as were the judgments of self over this 30-year period.

The greater stability of personal than environmental components of control is supported by the canonical analysis of these data carried out by Mason *et al.* (1981) and by estimation of period, cohort, and age effects in the same data by Rodgers, Herzog, and Woodworth (1980). Both teams of investigators report very large period effects on all these measures of responsiveness. By contrast, the period effect in the political competence item, while significant, is much less pronounced (Rodgers *et al.*, 1980). Moreover, period effects in the generalized personal efficacy items are also less dramatic (Mason *et al.*, 1981).

Analyses of the PSID data, reported by Lachman (1984), also show stability in the generalized personal efficacy items. In fact, there were no significant period effects in these items over the 4-year period from 1968 to 1972. It should be remembered that the NES data also proved this period one of great stability in personal components of control. The small period effects in personal efficacy demonstrated in the NES data are explainable largely because personal efficacy increased in the 1950s. Except for that one period, however, all the analyses we have examined show marked stability in the personal aspects of control, and less stability in people's judgments of responsiveness.

Two other points should be made about historical shifts in sense of control. All these investigators report that the erosion of judgments of responsiveness was spread fairly evenly across different sectors of society. Both blacks and whites, men and women, old and young, better and less well educated began to view political authorities and institutions as less responsive after 1964. The persistence in this trend is found broadly in society. There is some evidence, noted by Mason *et al.* (1981), that the erosion was a bit greater among the less well educated. Otherwise, the shifts we have described were broadly and evenly based. Moreover, the stability we have noted in the more personal elements of control was equally true of the different sociodemographic categories.

Second, the changes in Americans' views of the responsiveness of political authorities and institutions should be seen in the context of other data which demonstrate clearly that their evaluations of the soundness of democracy itself remained intact. In 1976, when responsiveness was much in doubt, Americans nonetheless remained proud and positive about our form of government. When offered a choice between two statements: "I am proud of many things about our form of government," or "I can't find much in our form of government to be proud of," over three-quarters said they were proud. Also in 1976 only a quarter said we need "a big change" in our form of government to be able to solve the problems facing our country. And those who felt there should be some change largely talked about the ways the system is run, not changes in its underlying theory or structure. Erosion of sense of political control thus seems to have been produced by problems in the responsiveness of authorities and institutions, not by basic rejection of the viability of democracy itself or by Americans' competence to understand politics. This context and the fact that the mounting doubts about responsiveness were so broadly based in society have led many (A. Miller, 1979; Lipset & Schneider, 1983) to emphasize that genuine political institutional problems would have to be addressed to restore the public's perception of a responsive government.

Some comment should also be made about age differences. The literature on age effects in personal efficacy has to date been highly inconclusive, some showing a decrease in efficacy with age (Brim, 1974) and some showing efficacy highest in the middle years, lower among both the young and the old (Gatz & Siegler, 1981; Gurin & Gurin, 1975). Results from age analyses of the NES data are also inconclusive. Let us look first at judgments of responsiveness. Rodgers *et al.* (1980) report significant linear increases in perception of unresponsiveness, with those older than 50 less often believing that political system institutions are responsive. Mason *et al.* (1981), who examined several dimensions of responsiveness, report significant but not very consistent age effects. In some years the effect is linear, in others curvilinear, and in some years hardly present at all. Firm conclusions just cannot be drawn from these data about judgments of responsiveness as a life-span issue.

The same point can be made about the judgements of the more personal elements of control. The age effect on the measure of political competence is significant and curvilinear, the highest sense of competence expressed by persons in the middle years. Age differences in generalized personal efficacy, by contrast, are not very consistent across the repeated cross-section samples of the NES. And, while Lachman (1984) reports a significant age effect in the PSID data, it derives primarily from unusually high efficacy scores in just one age group. This group included 85 persons who were 60 to 63 in 1968 and aged 64 up to 67 by 1972 when efficacy was measured the last time. This group showed higher, not lower, efficacy compared to younger persons. However, the pattern of increasing efficacy with aging was not supported in the next youngest group as it aged over the same 4-year period. Thus, this age effect, restricted as it was to one very small group, does not seem reliable enough to provide a firm conclusion. It is also the first empirical evidence hinting that older people have greater feelings of control than those in the prime of life.

## 2. Correlational Stability/Change

Correlational stability, as we said, refers to stability of individual rankings on a characteristic over time. Certain measurement issues make the drawing of firm conclusions about correlational stability quite difficult. Many investigators report just raw continuity coefficients, which, of course, may greatly underestimate "true stability" because of measurement error. Morever, even when corrections for attenuation are made or when true stability is estimated with measurement models making explicit assumptions and estimations of error, the time interval between measures influences stability in two important ways. First, all dynamic processes are characterized by a "memory" so that the impact of an exogenous event is not limited to a single point in time. Instead, a trace of the event is reflected in the process for some span of time, the imprint of the event gradually fading out. Autoregressive models are explicitly dynamic. They possess a memory, the strength of which depends on the magnitude of the autoregressive parameter (G. Markus & Converse, 1984; Moss & Susman, 1980). Fading will clearly be greater the longer the time period. Second, time provides opportunity for change. There is just no time for events to affect the person if the underlying construct is measured moments apart. The longer the time interval between measurements, the greater is the likelihood that events may have affected the person. For this reason stability should be lower the longer the time frame. Unfortunately, stability coefficients, not just in the control literature but more broadly in social science writing, are often reported without sufficient attention to the time interval represented.

With these cautions in mind, some conclusions can be drawn about the stability of sense of control over at least short periods in adulthood. The personal components of control are moderately stable over a 4-year period and somewhat more stable over 2 years. Lachman (1984) provides estimates for an index of the personal efficacy items from the national sample studies in the PSID. She reports raw stability coefficients for 1968 to 1970, 1970 to 1972, and 1968 to 1972 of .49, .54, and .45, respectively. As expected, stability for the 4-year interval was somewhat lower than for either of the 2-year periods. The corresponding internal consistency reliability estimates were .55, .59, and .55. Lachman notes that stabilities close in value to the reliabilities indicated quite a high level of stability in personal efficacy. She also corrects the raw stability coefficients, with the added assumption of perfect measurement reliability, and the high values, .89, .92, and .83 confirm that little reliable change had occurred in personal efficacy over the period of investigation. Duncan and Liker (1983) similarly conclude that there is reasonably high stability in personal efficacy in the same national sample, in this instance based on estimation of true stability from a measurement model estimated by LISREL. The stability of personal efficacy was estimated to be .78 from 1970 to 1972. Of course, stabilities of this magnitude still mean there is considerable shifting among individuals. And even more change would be apparent if longitudinal data were available over longer time intervals in the adult years.

Analyses of the 1972–1976 panel data from the NES show less stability in the various measures which ask respondents to judge the responsiveness of political institutions and authorities. The 4-year raw stability coefficients for the three measures we have examined here range from .18 (government responsiveness), .21 (trustworthiness of government), to .24 (general responsiveness of political institutions/authorities. Stabilities corrected for attenuation are still considerably lower than the comparable 4-year stability estimates of the personal component of control. Historical events, actual shifts in responsiveness of authorities, and adult experiences with politics or other arenas of action seem to have influenced individuals' evaluations of the external world more than their evaluations of their own competence. This conforms to the conclusion offered by Moss and Susman (1980) in a major review of stability and change that social attitudes are less stable than personality.

## IV. Psychological Needs and Their Implications for Adult Change in Self

We have seen that Americans' views of their own efficacy shifted less historically and were also more stable in a correlational sense than were their judgments of the responsiveness of political authorities and institutions. Suppose this were reliable, true not only with these particular measures (with their limitations) but also with other indicators of the components of the sense of control. Suppose efficacy is the more stable and responsiveness judgments the less stable aspect of control. That responsiveness judgments do change is perhaps not very surprising. But why are the personal components of control more steadfast? Why do people's views of their own efficacy change less in response to historical and life-span events?

The rest of this article addresses this question. We turn first to some psychological reasons why adults might not change their views of their own efficacy as readily as their views of the environment's responsiveness. We look at three needs—for control, self-respect, and consistency of self—which, once formed, may produce forces for stability.[4] Then we turn to qualities of events themselves which also help explain the greater stability of efficacy. We are not suggesting that adults are incapable of personal change. There is now ample evidence that adults do change in their personality characteristics (Lerner, 1984; Brim &

---

[4]While we talk about these forces as needs, some theorists believe them to be features of the cognitive system itself. In a paper which conceptualizes the cognitive basis of personality, Cantor and Kihlstrom (1983) emphasize several cognitive heuristics that impair people's responsiveness to events which might otherwise result in adult change: a primacy effect such that a person's final judgment of an event is inordinately influenced by the earliest information received; an anchoring and adjustment heuristic whereby later adjustments do not depart far from the initial anchor point; a confirmatory bias in hypothesis testing toward data which confirm the person's hypothesis; and the tendency to read situations in terms of those domains about which the person is expert and has a rich and highly integrated body of knowledge. The debate about how much needs vs features of the cognitive system itself influence cognitive functioning and personal change is far from settled, as we will see again in the attribution literature (see footnote 5).

Kagan, 1980; Featherman, 1983), although the more central aspects of self are more difficult to change. Adult change would be greater if life events and role change were more discontinuous, demanding more change, and were compelling enough to counteract some of the psychological forces that press for stability. We will show that individuals in fact do change their judgments of their own efficacy in response to some life events and in some situations. Analysis of what makes some events psychologically compelling is essential for understanding when historical and life-span events will be powerful enough to produce change in the more personal elements of the sense of control.

## A. NEED FOR CONTROL

The importance of feeling competent, effective, and in control of one's life has been widely regarded as basic to self. Adler (1956) describes the need to exercise control as an intrinsic necessity of life itself. Ego psychologists (White, 1959, especially) look to effectance motivation, based on the need to master the environment, as a prompter of much behavior. deCharms (1968) and Deci (1975) credit the desire to be a causal agent as the prime base of intrinsic motivation.

Social psychologists, even in a period when motivation was downplayed in favor of cognitive theories, found themselves invoking a need for control in explaining many phenomena. Harold Kelley reflects this. He modified his own view of causal attributions to include a need for control. In 1967, Kelley wrote of the layperson as a pure scientist, simply seeking to understand his world. By 1972, Kelley's layperson had become an applied scientist who not only needs to understand but to apply his knowledge of causal relations in order to exercise control over his world.

The need for control is inferred from studies demonstrating that people often exaggerate their degree of control, even in situations of chance. They are easily misled that games of chance can be controlled (Henslin, 1967). The illusion of control in chance situations is fostered by familiarity and practice, allowing the subject to state an expectation (heads vs tails for example), long sequences of a particular outcome, choice and getting involved in the task (the subject, rather than the experimenter, throws the dice, for instance), and cultural expectations that the task requires skill (Rotter, 1966; Langer, 1975; Wortman, 1976). While many of these task and situational characteristics make the illusion of control plausible, the very ease by which confusion between contingency and noncontingency is created convinces many psychologists that people need to believe they can exercise control, even over outcomes they know rationally are determined by chance.

Research on psychological depression also suggests that people need a sense of control and that it is actually healthy to exaggerate one's causal power. In recent years a large number of studies, stimulated by Seligman's (1975) and

Beck's (1967) cognitive models of depression, have compared the causal attributions of depressed and nondepressed individuals. These studies expected to find an insidious attributional style among depressives. Depressives were expected to be unrealistic in assessing their roles in producing successes and failures in their lives—minimizing too much their responsibilities for success and exaggerating too much their responsibilities for failure. However, the research tends to show that it is nondepressed individuals who are unrealistic. They appear to live under an "illusory warm glow about themselves" (Lewinsohn, Mischel, Chaplain, & Barton, 1980). They exaggerate their causal significance in producing objectively noncontingent outcomes (Alloy & Abramson, 1979). They seem especially unrealistic when reinforcement is frequent, apparently misled by its frequency into believing that their own acts are bringing about objectively noncontingent reinforcement. They are also affected by the valence of outcomes. They take too much credit for noncontingent "good" outcomes, ones where they win money for example. They are even unrealistic when outcomes actually are contingent on their behavior, if the outcomes are "bad." Then they underestimate contingency, denying responsibility for producing "bad" outcomes, ones where they lose money. Moreover, compared to judgments made by observers watching them interact with other students, they have inflated self-evaluations (Lewinsohn *et al.,* 1980). Depressed students, by contrast, are more accurate in judging contingency and noncontingency. Their own self-evaluations also conform more closely to others' appraisals of them. They are perhaps too realistic and would be better off psychologically if they exaggerated their personal control. They are, in Alloy's and Abramson's words, sadder but wiser. Depression may be one of the costs of a more realistic view of the self, although, to be cautious, this body of research has not yet clarified the direction of causality between attribution and depression.

Need for control is also invoked as the motive behind assignment of blame. Walster (1966) suggests we often blame innocent victims for accidents that happen to them in order to preserve our own sense of control. To admit that something unfortunate is really an accident also means it could happen to us. This tendency to blame victims increases the more serious the outcome; presumably the need for control is even greater when consequences are severe. In similar vein, research on the "just world" (M. J. Lerner & Miller, 1978) suggests that people choose not to see an unjust world or one that is unpredictable. People believe that good things happen to good people, bad things to bad people. To think otherwise would be to imagine oneself unable to control what happens in one's own life.

If need for control is so basic to self and prompts so many other reactions and behaviors, some based on illusion, many at least unrealistic, it is understandable that social events, losses, and change in social roles over the life span which threaten personal control may be resisted. Change in personal aspects of the sense of control may occur in adulthood but probably in response to success experiences and to gains instead of losses. Threatening experiences and losses may not have much power to change people because there are many ways of protecting the self from threat. People avoid such experiences if they can. They hold on to illusions about their control. They try to manipulate relationships and the social environment to see themselves as effective. Life events which might lower feelings of control would have to be exceptionally compelling since there is such a strong need to preserve whatever level of control one has already achieved.

## B. NEED FOR SELF-RESPECT

Change also may be muted because other needs are basic to the sense of self. People need self-respect—to maintain the best possible opinion of themselves. By self-respect we mean the good or bad feeling that comes from appraising one's achievements and actions relative to personal standards and those set by other people who are important to us. Each person acquires a desire to live up to the standards or expectations held by others, internalizes those standards, and uses them to measure one's performance or achievement. The positive or negative affect which results from this appraisal, the good or bad feeling about performance, is what we mean by maintaining or losing self-respect. Many people use the term "self-esteem" for these evaluations. In our view, however, self-esteem has come to mean a general summary about the self—feeling good—which involves a mixture of self-respect and other components such as the satisfaction coming from a beach walk in the sun or soaking cold feet in a hot tub or having a full stomach after a day's hunger. Self-respect is one aspect of esteem, the feeling derived from positive appraisal of one's performance.

That human beings are motivated to maintain self-respect, indeed enhance it, has been advanced by many theorists from many different perspectives in psychology (Adler, 1956; Festinger, 1954; Heider, 1944; Snyder, Stephan, & Rosenfield, 1976). People seem to want information that assures them they are meeting standards, doing well. While people may also want to acquire accurate information about themselves (Thornton & Arrowood, 1966), most psychological writing gives the impression that people very readily distort, deny, and discredit negative information about their performance. Desire for accuracy seems overwhelmed by cognitive maneuvers which buffer information that threatens self-respect.

The desire to see oneself favorably is supported by several lines of research. One has explored people's reactions to evaluative feedback. In an extensive review of this work, Shrauger (1975) concludes that favorable information is accepted more readily than unfavorable. He does note, however, that the discrepancy between the feedback and the person's initial expectancy has generally not been equated in the experimental work on the impact of feedback. Studies which have controlled discrepancy seem to have produced much more equivocal results (Eagly, 1967; Harvey & Clapp, 1965; Snyder & Shenkel, 1976; Steiner, 1968). In these more controlled studies, it appears that the source of the feedback— whether it is given by an expert or not—influences its impact. Positive feedback is more readily accepted than negative feedback *except* when the negative feedback is given by an expert. Lacking an especially credible source, positive information is liked better, is more readily accepted, and produces greater change in self-evaluation. Shrauger also concludes that people generally are more attracted to positive than negative evaluators. And they like them better.

Research on causal attributions for success and failure also lends support to the idea that people have a need to maintain self-respect. Heider (1944) was the first social psychologist to suggest that people make attributions for success and failure in ways that protect and enhance evaluations of self. Labeled "self-serving" (Bradley, 1978), "egotistic" (Snyder, Stephan, & Rosenfield, 1978), and "beneffectance" (Greenwald, 1980), the attributional tendency to take credit for success and to deny responsibility for failure is now one of the best established, most replicated findings in social psychology. Many authors assume that this asymmetry in causal attributions reflects a motivational bias to maintain self-respect or a sense of control.[5] Taking credit for good outcomes enhances the self. Viewing bad outcomes as caused by forces outside the self protects self-respect [see reviews by Bradley (1978) and by D. T. Miller & Ross (1975)]. Snyder *et al.* (1978) stress that the threat to self-respect must be in an arena of life that is important to one's self-concept. Assuming an area critical to self is threatened, the need to maintain self-respect and these egotistic cognitive biases should work against change when people lose valued roles or experience failure in the course of their adult lives. To maintain respect people probably avoid such experiences, if at all possible. If avoidance is not possible, they may not attend to the meaning of the experience. They may not process or recall negative information about themselves very well. And even if negative information is not distorted or forgotten, they are apt to deny responsibility for it, seeing it as caused externally and thus not having much implication for the self. Of course, these very same needs and biases suggest that success ought to increase efficacy with great ease since people seem motivated to think well of themselves and to take credit for success, even undue credit.

[5]Some theorists remain skeptical about these motivational explanations for this asymmetry in attribution. That an attribution appears to serve an ego-protective function does not necessarily imply that asymmetry in attributing cause for success and failure is prompted by ego-protective needs (Bem, 1972; D. T. Miller & Ross, 1975; Miller, 1978; Nisbett & Ross, 1980; Ross & Fletcher, 1984). Note that until recently there has not even been direct evidence that the asymmetry in attributions for success and failure accomplishes its supposed aim, let alone is actually motivated by the need to maintain respect.

Individuals, by altering their aspirations, also manage to maintain self-respect in the face of failure, large gaps between their achievements and aspirations, and even overwhelming losses of critical roles and capacities. The thousands of experimental studies during the 1930s and 1940s, and the new research on achievement motivation, as well as many national surveys of income and mobility aspirations, all demonstrate that human beings are wondrously adaptive and flexible in adjusting to the realities of what in fact can be achieved, while still maintaining respect and a sense of control. Self-respect can remain stable by keeping goals at a just manageable level. Individuals and social groups adapt rather readily to fewer arrows, less corn, and poorer eyesight. Sometimes people lower their goals within arenas of life that have always been important to them. Sometimes they drop those arenas altogether and develop goals in new arenas. For the elderly "gentleman farmer" who can no longer roam the mountain trimming trees and brush, self-respect can be maintained by working a more manageable garden plot. When there is sufficient loss of sight so that even this is not possible, tree work, farm work, and gardening are at last given up. Energy is channeled into listening to the "talking books" of which there are many so that one can know the lives of the great poets, hear a good sampling of the world's drama, and specialize in novels of eighteenth century England; through this switch, self-respect can persist despite loss of a previously major activity and life role. Altering aspiration is an example of adult change, of course, but not a change in basic aspects of self, as we regard self-respect and the sense of control to be.

When motivated by need for respect, people also avoid social comparison that would tell them they are performing poorly or are somehow more worthless than others. In an important paper exploring the pain that sometimes comes from social comparison, Brickman and Bulman (1977) note that avoidance of comparison has received very little attention in the writing about comparison processes. Contrasting hedonic and adaptive forces, the former pressing for happiness and self-respect, the latter for useful information, Brickman and Bulman suggest that hedonic forces keep people from drawing comparisons that would be painful. In situations in which one party or the other will feel hurt or threatened by inferiority or insecurity or experience shame, individual proclivities and social norms both discourage comparison. If comparison cannot be avoided, hedonic forces press comparison with dissimilar, inferior others. The prevailing view in the social comparison literature that people tend to seek comparison with similar others or those slightly superior to the self was promoted, Brickman and Bulman contend, because Festinger (1954) originally made exclusively rational and adaptive assumptions about comparison processes. While desire to obtain accurate appraisal of one's abilities or opinions may prompt comparison, as Festinger suggested, desire for self-respect and hedonic forces also discourage it. Life-span theorists have perhaps too readily assumed that loss and failure will be interpreted negatively when in fact many individuals may avoid that implication by avoiding comparison altogether or by seeking comparison with those even worse off than they.

We know as social scientists that such changes in aspirations and shifts in comparison, to be effective, must be anchored in social reality. The shifts must be based in new reference groups, accepted by those groups, and validated by society. A vast social apparatus exists to confer such legitimation on falling aspirations for those who fail or lose previously valued skills and roles. Societies vary in how much they protect people who fail, some societies offering mechanisms that provide nearly complete "face-saving," and others emphasizing mechanisms that exaggerate failure and humiliation. An age-graded social system is one way (although there are many other mechanisms as well) in which society helps people manage sinking aspirations without losing self-respect or sense of control. Along with its economic and demographic functions, age grading also has another latent function: the establishment of reference groups for comparison of performance that will protect self-respect (Mayer, 1982; Mueller & Mayer, 1982). Sports perhaps provides the clearest illustrations. Many sports and athletic events have age categories so that one competes just as happily in marathons and tennis tournaments but matched against older age mates as one grows older. Countering William James's well-known example of the loss of esteem that comes from being the "second best pugilist in the world," there is also the maintenance of self-respect that comes for the fully happy, efficacious 90 year old in winning the old men's singles' championship at the local club.

## C. NEED FOR CONSISTENCY

The needs to feel in control and maintain respect bear similar implications for adult change in personal characteristics that are central to self. Both imply that success should produce change quite easily because people universally and desperately want to maintain respect and believe they control outcomes in their lives. By contrast, failure should prove less able to change central aspects of self because people employ many strategies that minimize its impact and allow them to preserve respect and sense of control.

Other psychological theories, however, question the universality of these needs and raise the possibility that other needs, to be consistent and think of oneself as the same person across time and space, press people not to change their views and feelings about themselves. They also make reactions to success and failure less universal than is implied by enhancement theories.

Consistency theory[6] challenges how much life events and experiences are able

[6]Although rejecting the nonchange implication of the need to maintain consistency, Cohler (1982) also suggests that people have a compelling need to experience their lives as coherent and consistent.

to alter well-formed views of the self because of motivation to maintain consistency. It predicts that people will selectively attend, encode, and remember information that is consistent with the view of the self, and ignore, distort, or forget inconsistent feedback. Disconfirming experiences, which potentially could change rather than simply reinforce prior views and feelings about the self, are thus robbed somewhat of their potential power.

Consistency and enhancement theories make the same predictions about ways people who have high esteem and expect to succeed will respond to success and failure. They will use the former to confirm their sense of self. They will ignore, distort, or forget the latter. However, these theories depart dramatically about the probable reactions of people who have low esteem and expect to fail. Instead of using success to enhance the self, consistency theory suggests that such people are apt to distort, discredit, forget, or attribute success to external causes. Instead of denying failure, they are apt to welcome it as an experience that confirms the self as ineffective and likely to fail.

Because consistency theory provokes important questions about the universality and exclusivity of the need to maintain/enhance respect, a review of the experimental work it has generated is in order. Assessing the evidence where predictions from enhancement and consistency theories depart is particularly pertinent to theories about adult change and development.

When Aronson and Carlsmith (1962) first tested consistency theory predictions about reactions to confirming and disconfirming information, they asked people to identify schizophrenic individuals from groups of photographs. Some subjects were led to think they were performing very well and others very poorly. On four trials, one-half of the subjects were told they had gotten 20% of the judgments correct; the other half were told 85% were correct. On the fifth trial, half of each group were then told they had 20% correct, the other half 85%. The outcome of the fifth trial was thus either consistent or inconsistent with the initial expectancies created on the first four trials. Under the guise that the experimenter had forgotten to record some information, subjects were asked to redo the fifth trial. Subjects who had been given consistent feedback changed fewer responses on the second take of the fifth trial. Those given inconsistent information changed more. The results supported consistency theory very well. Most important, those subjects initially led to think they were performing badly changed

---

While Cohler believes that people do change many aspects of their personalities, he emphasizes that people are strongly motivated not to see themselves as changing. By revising earlier memories and continually reconstructing and interpreting their personal narratives, people are able to maintain this sense of sameness, even as they are changing. The work from consistency theory explicitly argues, however, that experience primarily will be used to reinforce and verify rather than alter the self. It is not simply that people see and feel more stability than is actually the case but that their needs for consistency make them more attentive and responsive to experiences and feedback that confirm rather than disconfirm their already existing views and feelings about the self.

more answers after receiving positive than negative feedback. They seemed to be trying to "undo" success to keep their behavior and feedback consistent with their more negative views of themselves.

These results have generally not been replicated, however. The most thorough replication effort, carried out by Brock, Edelman, Edwards, and Shuck (1965), included six experiments. The first two, exact replications of the Aronson and Carlsmith procedures, produced similar results. In the four subsequent experiments frequency of feedback was varied. When feedback was clear and frequent, low expectancy subjects did *not* behave as consistency theory would predict. Instead, they seemed motivated to do well rather than trying to maintain consistency with initial expectancies. The findings that success feedback may be "undone" seems reliable enough under procedures identical to those of Aronson and Carlsmith but just not very robust. In fact, several later studies report differences opposite to consistency predictions for low expectancy subjects (Beijk, 1966; Cottrell, 1965; Frentzel, 1965; Kornreich, 1968; Lowin & Epstein, 1965).

Changing one's behavior need not be the only response to information that is inconsistent with one's self-image. People may also handle in emotional ways the discomfort that is presumably created by discrepancy, perhaps by expressing dissatisfaction with the message or annoyance at people who give it. They may adopt cognitive strategies, perhaps discrediting the information or in other ways disavowing it. A theory of personal change should be able to account for many different reactions to social experiences that disconfirm one's self-conception.

Isolating behavioral, emotional, and cognitive reactions is especially critical for testing self-enhancement and consistency theories' contradictory predictions for people with low esteem. Self-enhancement theory argues that people *want* to succeed and to think more favorably of themselves. Revising performance does not mean they necessarily dislike success or are not motivated to do well. They may want to succeed but question whether the success feedback is credible. This has important implications for adult change. Disbelief can be handled by making successes more compelling. However, if people who think badly of themselves really do not want to succeed and are motivated to keep a consistent image of themselves, experiences which give them more compelling, incontrovertible success information would still not produce change in the self.

In an important review of enhancement–consistency studies, Shrauger (1975) summarizes evidence not only about behavioral change but also about emotional and cognitive reactions to feedback. What does he conclude about *emotional* reactions? He finds no support for the strong consistency prediction that subjects with failure expectancies or low esteem are more dissatisfied with success than with failure feedback. In fact, their preferences for positive evaluations seem as strong as among high expectancy subjects. This is exactly what enhancement theory predicts. The only studies reporting more unpleasant emotions following positive than negative feedback are those in which tension is the emotion assessed. But tension and direct report of discomfort may reflect fear that the positive feedback is inaccurate, not lack of pleasure or satisfaction with it. Brickman (1972) indeed shows that subjects who receive feedback more favorable than expected are less confident of its accuracy. This may explain the fragility of expectancy changes that follow very large discrepancies in feedback. Low expectancy subjects may like and accept information that tells them they are considerably better than they believe themselves to be. But the effect may not last because its credibility may seem dubious (Baron, 1970; Gurin & Gurin, 1970). In a similar vein, Mettee (1971) proposes that low expectancy subjects are generally very gratified by success feedback unless it raises hopes that they fear will be destroyed by later experience, something much more apt to happen if the success message is outlandishly discrepant.

Research on *cognitive* reactions to discrepant feedback shows stronger support for consistency theory. Shrauger (1975) reviews a wide range of studies of this topic and concludes that information that is inconsistent with one's initial expectations or view of the self is processed less efficiently and accurately than consistent information. Discrepant information is less accurately recalled. It is not perceived as being as credible or as resulting from an enduring aspect of the self. Moreover, these cognitive disavowals characterize how people with failure expectancies handle positive feedback, not simply how people with success expectancies handle negative feedback.

Recent research on self-schemas (H. Markus, 1977, 1980) also suggests that experiences which disconfirm one's view of the self may not induce much change once schemas bave been formed.[7] A recent study by Swann and Read (1984) addresses how self-schemas are verified instead of changed. They offer an information/cognitive rather than motivation argument for self-verification.[8]

[7]Defining a self-schema as a knowledge structure about the self, H. Markus (1977) shows that self-schemas serve as filters of experience, making people particularly responsive to information that matches their view of themselves. While the writing about self-schemas explicitly asserts that people continually revise their schemas as a function of experience, the very notion that schemas function as filters for relevant, confirming social information questions how much revision occurs, at least after schemas are well formed. Perhaps responsivity to disconfirming social information is much greater during the period of schema formation. Self-schemas develop and are revised through repeated categorizations and reactions of others, through successes and failures, and through direct social experiences (H. Markus, 1980). While social interaction is the medium through which self-schemas develop, disconfirming communications in social interaction may not result in major revision after the schema has become articulated, rich, well organized, and operates to filter experience for confirmation.

[8]While consistency and self-schema research both emphasize receptivity to compatible information, there are different emphases in the two bodies of work as well. While it is assumed that self-schemas help people deal efficiently with vast and complex social information, a functional and motivational base is not always assumed as it is in consistency theory. Self-schema work moreover has focused primarily on information's relevance to the schema, while consistency research has focused on discrepancy per se. Self-schema research has emphasized the match with content of the self and has paid less attention to whether it is positive or negative. Consistency research has

It is not that people find discrepant information particularly uncomfortable. Rather, they argue, confirming information is just much more "informative." It tells us more about ourselves. We therefore seek, elicit, and recall it better than discrepant information. As in consistency theory, the nonobvious predictions about self-verification concern people who think poorly of themselves. Such people may want positive feedback about themselves. They may want people to like them. But Swann and Read argue that they will pay more attention to appraisals they suspect will confirm their negative views of themselves. They will elicit reactions that confirm their conceptions as the social interaction unfolds. After they leave the interaction, they will preferentially remember confirmatory feedback. Three experiments were carried out to examine self-verification at three steps of social interaction. Two focus on cognitive verification processes—seeking information and remembering others' appraisals of oneself. One focuses on behavioral strategies—eliciting reactions from others. The two experiments on cognitive processes support the verification predictions. The one probing behavioral strategies provides only partial support.[9]

Some general conclusions can be drawn from the experiments contrasting enhancement and consistency. The need to think favorably of oneself appears quite well supported in the studies that have focused on emotional reactions and on behavioral strategies people use in social interaction. Success seems to be gratifying to people in general. They like positive feedback and evaluators who give it to them. They act to elicit enhancing reactions from partners they expect to like them. On the other hand, consistency appears well supported in the

---

deemphasized content and dealt nearly exclusively with evaluative information.

[9] In these experiments college students were asked to rate themselves on 10 evaluative traits. Those who scored below the median were designated "self-dislikables," those above the median "self-likables." Half of each group was led to believe that a partner whom they were later to meet held one of two views about them. The partner presumably either liked them or found them somewhat disagreeable. The important measures in the information-seeking experiment were provided by timing how long subjects took to read a series of statements the partner purportedly had made about them. Subjects who held favorable views of themselves spent more time reading statements from partners who presumably liked them than from partners who did not. Most important to the enhancement–consistency controversy, subjects who held unfavorable views of themselves spent more time reading statements they thought came from partners who disliked them than from those who liked them. In the memory experiment subjects were asked to write down as many as possible of the partner's statements, which they had heard on a recording instead of read. Self-likables recalled more statements when they anticipated that the partner liked rather than disliked them. Self-dislikables recalled more when they anticipated that the partner disliked rather than liked them. Eliciting behavior, defined as complimenting and praising the partner, was rated in the behavioral study from videotapes of actual interaction. A careful look at the behaviors of subjects who disliked themselves supports self-enhancement more than consistency theory. When they expected partners to like them, they complimented and praised partners more, not less as they should if they were attempting to confirm negative views about themselves. They seemed motivated by the pleasurable anticipation of positive appraisal and acted to elicit enhancing reactions from their partners.

research on cognitive reactions. Confirming experiences are processed more efficiently than disconfirming ones. The critical test of this involves people who expect to fail, those with low self-regard, and those who expect others to dislike them. These people also process confirming information (that they have failed, that others do not like them) more efficiently. As a vehicle for personal change, success would therefore have to be unusually compelling for these people who tend to give it little attention, discredit it as invalid, forget it easily, or view it as externally caused, bearing little implication for the self.

## V. Properties of Events and Change in Adulthood

Life-span theorists emphasize the potential for personal change throughout the life cycle, as well as the power of historical events to alter the personalities of a broad spectrum of people in society. They credit major social upheavals in society and role discontinuities that occur even in periods of social stability as important sources of change. Adults gain new roles—new jobs, promotions, new residences and community involvements, marriage, parenthood. They lose old roles—the empty nest, lay-offs, demotions, retirement, divorce, widowhood. Americans have also lived through tumultuous social, economic, and political events in the past 30 years that one would think might have left us feeling less personally efficacious than in simpler, more predictable, and traditional eras. Why then is age only minimally and inconsistently related to judgments of self as competent? Why has there been little historical shift in the personal components of control since the early 1950s? Why is the ordering of individuals so stable? We have examined some psychological reasons that help explain stability, and have argued that they inhibit change in judgments of the system's responsiveness much less. We turn now to other reasons, more sociological, that also explain why change may not occur. Let us be clear that changes of many sorts do occur in adulthood. We have already stressed that adults alter their aspirations as they win and lose, succeed and fail, indeed often to preserve respect. We are not talking about change in the abstract but a particular kind of change—change in a central aspect of self as we believe personal efficacy to be.

The first point to note concerns *discontinuity/discrepancy*. That social roles available in different age strata may be discontinuous, making highly discrepant demands of individuals as they age, was first suggested many years ago by Benedict (1938). Benedict emphasized the discontinuity between the expectations of the child role and the adult role, the former emphasizing passivity and asexuality and the latter dominance and strong sexuality. Because of these discontinuities, adults need socialization after childhood and their personalities should change as they gain and lose social roles. Of late some role and life-span theorists have taken exception to the view that these role gains and losses really are discontinuous. Many of the role shifts that adults regularly experience are not very discrepant with their past skills and with other people's prior expectations of them (Mortimer & Simmons, 1978). Riley (1976) emphasizes that new roles may either provide direct substitutes for former roles, compatible with the values and attitudes of the previous roles, or alternatively they may present entirely different norms that require restructuring of orientations. Much depends then on the degree of normative congruence or discrepancy between roles available in adjacent age strata. Many theorists traditionally have described life-cycle changes in Western industrialized societies as generally requiring this kind of restructuring. Retirement particularly has been viewed as requiring a major restructuring. Western socialization emphasizes autonomy and productivity and yet at retirement we must suddenly adjust to more dependent and less productive roles. Still, even retirement may not be as discontinuous as once thought. Mortimer and Simmons (1978) point out that many of the role changes once considered stressful because of discontinuity—new parenthood, empty nest, and retirement—have been shown to be relatively positive experiences, at least for certain categories of people. There is just as much evidence of continuity as discontinuity. Even role changes in the work area, which many consider the most dramatic type of shift for adults in industrialized nations, may not actually demand much change in central aspects of self because some work role shifts involve movement between occupations with highly similar functions and demands, particularly after the mid-30s (Mortimer & Simmons, 1978).

A second point to consider is *selectivity/exposure*. Adults have considerable freedom to select their environments. They may physically avoid role shifts and other events that threaten the self. If they are unable to avoid exposure, they may psychologically avoid its implications by not paying attention, distorting its meaning, or in other ways blunting its impact. Brim (1966) and Mortimer and Simmons (1978) stress that the power to select one's environment is a major difference between adult and child socialization. Adults have more resources and alternatives. They are allowed greater choice. The failure to take account of the considerable selectivity and self-determination in adult socialization has led perhaps to an exaggerated conception of how much adults change.

We will argue below that some events are hard to avoid even for the most privileged, whose power to select their environments far exceeds that of the poor and least advantaged in society. Some events are more powerful than others. Events vary in properties which, when present, increase attention and make it more likely that people will seek rather than avoid information and accept rather than blunt the implications of the experience. Systematic concern with the properties of events is needed if we are to understand how events over the life course sometimes produce stability, other times produce change.

A third point to keep in mind is how events may have *implication for the self*. Even if truly discrepant events do occur, and we do not ignore, deny, or blunt them, we may not change if we feel they have little implication for the self. If I attribute the loss of my job to the closing of the plant, the job loss is not apt to daunt my sense of efficacy. If I attribute my recent promotion, or award for a recent book, to an insufficient pool of genuine talent, success is not apt to raise my sense of efficacy. The outcome of an event must be attributed to the self and the experience must have implications for the self if the event is to produce much change in such a central aspect of the self as personal efficacy. We believe that some properties of events are more likely than others to engage the self and thus foster change.

Our concern in the remainder of the article is to suggest what makes some events, or situations in which they occur, psychologically compelling enough to counteract the psychological needs that keep people from changing their sense of efficacy. What properties of historical and life-cycle events can blast apart the psychological forces for stability in central aspects of self?

Properties of life events are held to be in the events themselves, qualities that can be appraised objectively, such as whether or not their occurrence is highly correlated with age, whether they are enduring or temporary, and whether they occur to many or just a few people (Brim & Ryff, 1980). This approach to life events differs from some other treatments in two ways. Sometimes a property is assigned to an event in terms of the effect that event has on behavior. In this approach an event is stressful, for example, if prior research has shown it to cause high blood pressure. Other times life events are characterized by people's subjective evaluations. An event is stressful or undesirable if the person reports it to be. We are attempting here to delineate properties of events that can be objectively noted and that vary in measurable ways for different people. Birth of a child is in our view neither inherently stressful nor delightful, neither inherently likely nor unlikely to cause personal change in the parents. But if the child is born off-time, much later than is typical and normative, childbirth may be a far more powerful experience, at least in terms of producing change in central aspects of self. We will argue this is because off-time events do not allow as much anticipatory socialization or social support from age-mates, both of which help people adapt, even change in some ways but usually not in central views and feelings about the self. Off-time events also foster social comparisons that emphasize uniqueness and looking at the self.

We review two types of material that have developed largely in isolation: survey research on life events in natural situations and experimental work on events in the laboratory. The work in each is increasingly sensitive to qualities, not simply the number, of events. Researchers in both are more and more aware that events of different kinds may produce different effects. The experimental work on the effects of stressful events not only emphasizes properties of the event itself but especially the properties of the situation in which it occurs. The event, usually receiving an electric shock in these studies, varies in many properties such as intensity and frequency. The situation in which the shock occurs also varies in properties such as the presence or absence of warning signals, availability of distractors, whether or not the continuance of the shock is under the person's control. Studies of events in natural situations typically have not distinguished properties of the event from those of its context. The experimental material we review largely pertains to properties of situations, with a bit on properties of events; the survey research material covers both without a clear distinction. While weaving back and forth from these separate research traditions is treacherous at times, we believe that the gap between naturalistic and experimental work on stressful events should be narrowed. Life-span research will be improved by serious attention to these presently separate endeavors. We will see, for example, that laboratory work on attributions as a mediator of the impact of stressful events suffers from being insufficiently attentive to real-life issues, while naturalistic studies of life events lack a rigorous research approach for studying the self-implications of life events.

We attempt to relate properties to two aspects of the change process: attention and processing of social information as the first step in change, and believing that the event has implications for the self. Some properties may facilitate change by increasing likelihood of exposure, likelihood of attention if exposed, and likelihood of the information and demands of the situation being encoded. Other properties may influence change by making the individual instead of the environment highly salient so that the event, even when given attention, also implicates the self. Paradoxically, some properties that encourage people to face an event head-on, pay attention to it and seek information about it, may then mitigate against personal change because they allow the person to anticipate, prepare, and adapt without changing or because they foster external rather than self-attributions.

### A. PROPERTIES OF EVENTS: IMPACT ON ATTENTION AND INFORMATION SEEKING

A series of studies by S. M. Miller (1980) examined properties of the situation which help explain when people will seek information about a noxious event. In these studies the noxious event was electric shock. Typically the information people could attend to or ignore told when the shock would occur. Miller is interested in "blunting"—cognitive strategies that blunt the impact of a physically present danger signal. Her work has centered primarily on distraction, thinking about something other than the danger signal. Miller views distraction as just one of several blunting strategies; others include intellectualizing the event, denying its negative qualities, and reinterpreting it as a positive, beneficial experience. The aspect of Miller's work that applies most to our concerns has focused on choice—seeking or avoiding information. Do people choose to know about a danger signal for an aversive event, or do they prefer to think about something else? People can distract themselves spontaneously, of course, but Miller has focused on those properties of the situation that distract people who are facing an aversive event.

*Availability of external distractors* is an extremely important property of the situation. Without distractors, most subjects in Miller's experiment preferred to know when an aversive event was going to happen. This is seen using standard choice procedures in which subjects were offered a choice between listening to a tone signaling a shock or waiting passively with no signal. When the procedure offered a choice between listening for a tone or listening to music with no warning signal, the preference reversed and the majority chose distraction and not receiving information (S. M. Miller, 1984). In real life most situations do offer distractors. These studies imply that most people would then prefer not to be warned about aversive events. The elimination of distractors may partially account for the greater socialization power of institutions which bring recruits to an isolated setting without television, trips home, or visitors and then program most of their time. Organizers of professional meetings fully understand the influence of external distractors on attention to the substantive content and agenda of the meeting. Life events vary greatly in whether they happen with many or few external distractors.

The *instrumental value of the information for control of the event* likewise influences preference for information over distraction. People prefer information more when events are controllable, when they can do something about them—stop them, make them last, change their consequences (Averill, O'Brien, & DeWitt, 1977). For example, in the experiment in which S. M. Miller (1980) assessed preference for listening to music vs a warning tone, half of each group were told they could avoid shock altogether by pressing a button on those trials when they detected the warning tone. The other half were not given this opportunity to exercise control. They presumably believed the shock was uncontrollable. S. M. Miller reports that 71% of the subjects who could control the shock, as opposed to only 32% of the other group, monitored the tone on the majority of six trials. Paying attention to events and seeking information about their meaning are reasonable strategies when attention increases control. When events are truly uncontrollable, people are less likely to pay attention. Moreover, blunting or other psychological maneuvers to avoid their impact are also more adaptive. Life events vary in their controllability and thus in their power to influence people through the attention they draw.

Avoidance of information and preference for distraction are influenced by other properties of events as well. S. M. Miller (1980) concludes that distraction occurs less when the event itself or signals about the event are intense—when, for example, a tone which warns of a shock occurs at a *high level,* with *great frequency,* for a *long period of time,* and/or with *high probability.* These properties have also been noted by many researchers working on the impact of stress upon physical and psychological health.[10] Increasingly this literature suggests that frequent and/or chronic stresses may impair health more than a single though major stress (Brown & Harris, 1978; Pearlin, Lieberman, Menaghan, & Mullan, 1981). Highly probable, frequent, and durable events, even if small hassles (Lazarus & DeLongis, 1984), can cause illness or impair health partly because people are not able to escape them or blunt their impact by thinking about something else.

Events that happen with high probability and/or great frequency over longer time periods should be more powerful to change adults because they make distraction and ignoring the event more difficult. Meditation, relaxation exercises, focusing on something else, thinking "good thoughts," and all the other modern tricks used to mute stressors should work less when events with these properties occur. Whether good or bad, change is more likely to occur because the event will not be ignored.

Brim and Ryff (1980) propose a typology of life events which includes much the same properties that the experimental literature has delineated. Cross-classifying events by three properties (social distribution, age relatedness, and probability for the individual) produces eight events. Type I events, the familiar role changes discussed in the sociological tradition, are highly probable for the individual, highly age graded, and widespread or common in the society. The expectedness of these Type I events (marriage, starting to work, retirement, entering school, first birth, Bar Mitzvah, first walking, heart attack, birth of sibling) makes them potentially powerful life events by increasing the likelihood that people will pay attention to them.

The very same properties—commonality, age relatedness, and high probability of occurrence for the individual—may not result in change, however, despite their impact on attention. Brim and Ryff note, for example, that common events usually are accompanied by social support to help buffer change and to provide new reference figures. House (1981) concludes that the work environment and properties of the job are less influential in changing personality of workers who have positive, supportive relationships with their supervisors and co-workers. The stress literature nearly always discusses social support in positive terms because social support is viewed in the literature as buffering and protecting people's health from stress. The term buffer tells the story. People are insulated against change by social support. Wilcox (1981) describes that dense social support networks work against change in adulthood. Dense networks are

---

[10]Since this literature focuses on health and illness, event properties have not been discussed in general change terms. There is also a nearly universal negative tone in the literature on stress, that it is usually bad for us, will break us down, and make us ill. That stress can be positive by pressing for change or that people may thrive on stress is admitted but given little attention in the life events, health area (Kobasa, Hiker, & Maddi, 1979, is a clear exception).

often comprised of kin who frequently are not supportive of change but instead want relatives to remain the same. These networks rarely involve diversity that would allow adults to experience new ways of thinking and imagine new choices. Dense networks are often emotionally intense and based on long-standing emotional needs which mitigate against trying new patterns of life. They are more apt to operate around commonly occurring events because many others are experiencing the same event. Age-related events also allow people to prepare and learn through anticipatory socialization how to cope with these events. The psychological forces against change in central aspects of self are thus not likely to be countered by events which allow people to prepare ahead.

We also believe that widespread, highly probable, age-graded events militate against change because they encourage the individual to externalize the cause of the event, to keep the self unimplicated. By contrast, other properties which enhance attention to the event can also make the self salient. Events occurring with few external distractors and chronically and durably over time not only increase attention but also help us look at ourselves.

## B. PROPERTIES OF EVENTS: HEIGHTENING SALIENCE OF THE SELF

Social distribution and age relatedness both provide social comparisons that influence whether adults treat events as telling something about themselves. When events are widespread in a society, they encourage recognition of similarity. When events are rare, they heighten perception of uniqueness and difference from others. The same issue is involved in age-graded events. Events that are highly age related happen to many people in the age group. They help adults see themselves as similar to their age-mates. Events that are unrelated to age, or more impressively those that occur at atypical ages, help adults see themselves as unique and different from others. Atypical, off-time events should change the self more powerfully because they tell people something about themselves—that it is *their* actions, personalities, something about them that caused the event to happen. Widespread, age-graded events happen to so many people at such expected times that they tell more about the environment than the self. They help people externalize the causes of events.

The attribution literature in social psychology, while not reflecting a life-span orientation, is suggestive of possible reasons why widespread, age-graded events might foster stability by keeping the self unimplicated. One possibility is that widespread, age-graded events provide consensus information which tells how others act in the same situation. Consensus information, attribution research suggests, is a major determinant leading people to decide that the cause of an event lies in the circumstances, not in the person. If the impact of consensus information on drawing situational rather than self-attributions proved valid beyond the contrived tasks and limited settings in which it has been studied in attribution research, this would help explain why people might not change central aspects of themselves in response to events occurring broadly in society and predictably at given ages. Rare, off-time events, by contrast, provide very little consensus information. D. T. Miller and Ross (1975) note that the absence of a culpable external agent is a major determinant of attributing cause to the self. Experiencing an event nearly alone or at an atypical time may thus greatly narrow the range of explanations, decisively lower the likelihood of situational explanations, and raise the probability that the person will focus on the self. Increasing the salience of the self should increase the likelihood of change in central aspects of self.

Is there evidence that events that are rare or occur off-time do produce more change than those that happen more commonly or on-time? We consider first whether there is evidence of strong age grading in America, since being off-time is important only if many events are highly correlated with ge. When Neugarten (1968) offered the concept of on-time and off-time, she argued that a socially prescribed timetable for the ordering of major life events exists, that men and women are aware of the social clocks that operate in their lives and indeed describe themselves as being early, late, or on-time with regard to finishing school, marriage, first job, parenthood, top job, grandparenthood, and so on. Still, there is much debate about how strongly such life events are correlated with age. We take up the age correlation of life events and then examine research that has specifically looked at timing and change in personal efficacy.

## 1. Timing of Events

While the phenomenon of age grading is of broad significance in sociological and anthropological theory, much of the empirical evidence about its prevalence has been provided by research on stress, specifically by researchers attempting to measure life events as stressors. There is no need here to delineate previous limitations in this research tradition since that has been done elsewhere (Brim & Ryff, 1980; Dohrenwend & Dohrenwend, 1974). However, three points apply to its appropriateness for assessing evidence about age grading in America. First, much of the discussion has confused whether or not distress is age related with whether or not events happen with greater or less frequency in different age cohorts. This is largely because the theoretical interest in this literature is on stress, not age grading per se. But it is amply clear by now that occurrence of an event is not synonomous with distress since individuals have at their disposal many mechanisms to mute, distort, reinterpret, and alter the meaning of the event so it is not distressful. Shifting expectations and reference groups are two protective devices that reduce the age–distress relationship. Unfortunately, this literature has not always kept clear whether it is the age–distress or age–events relationship that is being discussed. Second, much of the work on life events in the stress literature has depended on cross-sectional studies of a single point in the individual's life. Evidence that comes from the same individuals across time would be much stronger. Third, practically none of this work has benefited from sociological thinking about age norms. Age grades imply more than an age correlation. Age grades involve norms about appropriate times to carry out particular acts or to have certain experiences. Age grading in this sense could not exist without high event–age correlations, but the obverse is not true. For an event to be "off-time," it implies that it happens at an age that is both atypical and somehow "wrong."

The PSID longitudinal study of adults, referred to in our examination of trends in efficacy, has addressed the first two of these three criticisms of stress–life events research. It assesses the occurrence of events unconfounded with distress, and it covers an 11-year period in the lives of the same individuals aging over this period.[11] We find it useful in addressing our two questions: Is there much age grading in the events experienced by adults, and do off-time events produce more change than those occurring on-time?

A picture of considerable age grading, in the frequency sense, emerges from assessments of life events of the same individuals from 1968 to 1978 (Duncan & Morgan, 1980). During this period, 22 different events were scored for each respondent. The events chosen for scoring follow the work of Sarason, Johnson, and Siegel (1978). In keeping with the economic concerns of this study there was much more information available on labor market events than on other life events in adulthood. Thirteen of the 22 tapped work and income experiences, another six tapped changes in family composition, and three the experience of moving residentially.

Virtually all respondents had experienced at least one of these events over the decade. On the average 10 events had occurred to the respondents in this panel. Moreover, most of these events were related to age, and in much the same way for married male heads of households, their wives, and female heads of households. (One exception is that death of a spouse was more sharply related to age for both groups of women than for men.) Only 4 of the 22 events were completely independent of age. All age cohorts had nearly equally experienced a decrease in family size, work loss due to illness, increase in family income, and decrease in family income. The remaining 18 events were age related, most of them quite highly.

The age patterns also show that most of the challenges and losses took place during the ages 18 to 30 (Duncan & Morgan, 1980). Nearly all of the family

---

[11]The Committee on Life Course Perspectives on Human Development of the Social Science Research Council (United States of America) held two workshops in June 1980 and November 1981 to encourage more intensive analyses of the PSID data, with special reference to questions arising from the life-span orientation to human development. A volume reporting this work has been prepared (Elder, 1984).

events (marriage, divorce/separation, remarriage, birth, growing family size) occurred much more frequently in that age group. In addition, entering the labor force, voluntarily or involuntarily changing jobs, as well as moving residentially both voluntarily and involuntarily, occurred considerably more frequently among people 30 or younger. Shifts in work hours, interestingly, in both directions— working more and working less—also characterized this group more dramatically, although this fluidity continued into the 30s as well, settling down after 40. Only disability, retirement, and death of a spouse increased with age. Very little occurred distinctively more in the middle years, a fact leading to the question of whether recent attention to "mid-life" change is focusing more on exceptions than common occurrences (Duncan & Morgan, 1980).

Exceptions are the issue, however, in off-time events. Thus the middle years potentially are times in which life events may influence personality in powerful ways because many events occur less frequently than among the younger and some less frequently than among the older. Middle-aged persons who enter the labor force, become parents, change jobs, or who become disabled, lose a spouse, or retire from the labor market are exceptions in their age cohort. It is exactly these kinds of events that Ryff and Dunn (1983) find influence personality of men in the middle years. One personality dimension, called complexity, involves items asking largely about self-perceived efficacy. Events which occurred off-time by being atypically early reduced middle-aged men's complexity. Events which occurred off-time by being atypically late increased their complexity, perhaps because they had more resources for handling such events.

Duncan and colleagues have examined the impact of the 22 events scored in the PSID data, specifically on the measure of personal efficacy listed in Table I. The data provide evidence that off-time events do change adults.[12] One analysis focused on the impact of events measured over the 11-year period (Duncan & Morgan, 1980) and a second examined shorter time periods of 2 and 4 years (Duncan & Liker, 1983).[13] We focus here on the results for men who were 40 to 49 when the study began in 1968 and aged 50 to 59 during the longitudinal follow-up.

Certain events happening to men in their 40s, rare in their own cohort, would mean sharing the events with younger persons for whom they occurred much

---

[12]Hogan's (1978, 1980) studies of temporal ordering of events marking men's transitions to adulthood also demonstrate that the timing of events influences adult development. Disorderly transitions—completing schooling after starting a career, marrying before completing schooling or beginning the first job—are associated with lower earnings returns to education, substantial deficits in total earnings, and higher rates of marital disruption in the later years. Hogan argues that deviating from the normative sequence in early adulthood produces these later effects.

[13]Both of these analyses involve a three-item measure of personal efficacy. Two of the three are listed in Table I. A third item on the index asked whether or not the respondent usually finishes things once he has started them.

more commonly. Other events, just as rare in the middle years, would result in sharing the events with older adults. Some of these off-time events did indeed influence personal efficacy. The very same events did not significantly alter efficacy when they occurred on-time. Two of these, off-time in the direction of doing something more typical of persons younger than 30, reduced the personal efficacy of the middle-aged men to whom they happened. Efficacy decreased among middle-aged men who changed jobs voluntarily or moved involuntarily atypically late. In the other direction, becoming disabled atypically early likewise lowered efficacy. These middle-aged men were atypical of their age-mates in one of two ways. They were less settled, more like the young, or they were more vulnerable, more like the old. McLanahan and Sørensen (1984), analyzing the same data using slightly different approaches, confirm the same pattern of off-time effects for middle-aged men.

The effect of timing is also seen in the impact of retirement on efficacy. While many role theorists suggest that loss of a valued social role should lower one's personal efficacy, analyses of the PSID data show that retiring after 60 does *not* reduce it. On-time retirement is not powerful enough to influence efficacy. Further, the results suggest that very early retirement, occurring for men who were 40 to 50 when the study began, lowered efficacy somewhat.

In our view, the evidence is not yet in for drawing firm conclusions about the relative power of on- and off-time events. Morgan and Augustyniak (1982) were not able to find greater impact of off-time events in an analysis which gave each individual an event-residual score capturing whether the event was on- or off-time for his 5-year age cohort.[14] Large residual scores represent events occurring for the individual which were rare for the cohort. Very few of the event-residuals appeared to have any effect on efficacy. These analyses were carried out, however, controlling for actual chronological age but not examining interactions among age, event-residuals, and efficacy. Our own view of the life events data reported by Duncan and colleagues is that off-time effects are more likely to be demonstrated for adults in the middle years. In fact, most of the evidence for off-time effects that can be marshalled from Duncan's earlier analyses of men in 10-year cohorts pertains to the middle years. The later effort to search for off-time effects may well have failed because it was *not* carried out separately for the young, middle, and older aged groups.

Let us return briefly to reasons why the timing of events may influence whether or not the events change central aspects of self in adulthood. Events that happen at ages deemed appropriate by societal norms allow people to anticipate,

[14]Cohort probabilities for each of the 22 events were calculated, indicating how common the event was for the cohort. Using the cohort probabilities a set of residual variables for individuals was calculated. A residual variable is one minus the probability of an event occurring for the individuals who experienced the event, and zero minus the probability of the event for those who did not. The magnitude of the residual variable gives a measure of the timeliness of the event.

prepare, and learn how to cope with the new situation. Moreover, since they occur to many others in the age cohort, age-mates can support each other in learning to adapt to the demands of the age-graded events. The shift in reference figures is societally validated. This may ease distress (a concern of the stress–life events researchers) but result primarily in stability, not change in self. In addition, events that happen to many people either in the population at large or in one's age group tell little that is unique about the individual. They are readily interpreted as externally caused and having little implication for the self. Indeed, the labels and definitions they are given by people sharing the experience and by the media emphasize the generality, not uniqueness of the experience. Off-time events, or those that in other ways make the individual feel unique compared to others in his or her family, social categories, or groups, press examination of the self. Often the individual even has to construct a label for such experiences.

The social psychology of an off-time experience involves two sets of comparisons that enhance awareness of self: comparison with one's age-mates who are not experiencing the event, and comparison with those, younger or older, for whom the event is far more common. Both comparisons heighten awareness that one is different. Going back to college at 40 enhances looking at the self because one stands out not only in one's age group but in the college scene. Parenting a 10 year old at age 55 fosters self-awareness partly because friends one's own age, whose children have long since left home, have no interest in discussing children, and partly because the Parent Teachers Association and the pediatrician's office are full of adults in their late thirties and early forties. None of the empirical work on timing has explicitly tried to measure comparisons with one's own age group, let alone the double comparisons, which make off-time events more powerful. Nor have other processes, anticipatory socialization for example, been measured directly.

## 2. Duration of Events

Pearlin and colleagues argue that it is the enduring presence of noxious circumstances that strips away the insulation that otherwise protects the self against threats.

> Hardships that are an enduring testimony to one's lack of success or to the inadequacy of one's efforts to avoid problems would seem to pose the most sustained affront to one's conceptions of self-worth and of being in control over personal destiny. By contrast, problems that by their very nature are rare and short-lived or those that are readily responsive to efforts to solve them do not leave people convinced of their own deficiencies; in fact, successful encounters with these kinds of problems might enhance the self. It is the abiding problems to which people can see no end, those that seem to become fixtures of their existence, that are intrinsically uncongenial with positive self-concept. (Pearlin *et al.*, 1981, p. 346)

While the language of causal attribution is only hinted here, the argument implies that it is self-attributions that give power to enduring events.

Empirical support for the import of enduring events was strong in the panel study carried out by Pearlin and colleagues. The stress process leading to depression was examined among 1106 men and women in Chicago. Efficacy was viewed as a mediator of stress, a personal resource that would lower its impact. For our purposes the factors which influenced efficacy itself are of interest. The critical factor that lowered the efficacy of these adults was durable economic problems (referred to as strain): having difficulty acquiring the necessities of life (food, clothing, housing, and medical care) and some optional accoutrements as well. Suffering a job disruption (referred to as a stressor) also lowered efficacy and produced economic strains as well. But the enduring strains of not being able to provide for oneself and one's family particularly daunted efficacy and their impact was strong even after the effect of job disruption itself was controlled.

Whether or not an enduring success experience increases one's sense of efficacy has been given much less attention in life events research. However, the durability of the experience would seem to be an important quality for making success compelling enough to convince people, even those who expect to fail, of its credibility. We have seen that people with low efficacy and high expectations of failure, because of consistency needs and self-verifying strategies, tend to pay more attention to failure information and to attribute success to some external cause which bears little implication for the self. However, such people seem to accept success information as credible and personally relevant when it has enduring qualities—when it is given frequently and unambiguously (Shrauger, 1975).

## 3. Other Event Properties That Heighten Salience of the Self

Bandura's work (1977) on self-efficacy impressively shows that some events—some successes—are far more potent than others in raising efficacy. Success changes efficacy more when feedback is tied to performance that is incontrovertibly the result of one's skills and talents. Making the self salient and helping the person understand that a given success is *not* distinctive, that he or she has succeeded on other tasks as well, have proved very important efficacy interventions. For these reasons, Bandura emphasizes the superiority of performance feedback over vicarious experience or verbal persuasion. He also points to other conditions that can make success more compelling. When success occurs on tasks that culturally denote skills and on tasks that are difficult enough that the individual believes ability is involved, when success occurs in varied circumstances, and when the pattern of performance implies improvement rather than leveling off, success is a more effective vehicle for change. All of these conditions would seem to influence change because they heighten self-awareness and attribution to the self. They may be specially important in countering the consistency force against change among people who expect to fail or feel inefficacious to begin with. However, Bandura stresses their importance for people in general and has not involved himself in the controversy generated by consistency–enhancement theories about the special issues facing people with low expectancies.

The self-relevance of the event is also noted by Duncan and Morgan (1980) in explaining why *earned* income affects the efficacy of male heads of households more than nonlabor income. While in a practical sense $100 is $100 no matter who receives it, income that these men could take personal credit for earning especially influenced their sense of efficacy. Recent analyses of the PSID that focused on the economically disadvantaged (household heads with average earnings in the bottom half of the average earnings distribution of male workers for a 3-year period) also show the importance of the event's self-relevance in altering efficacy. Increase in work hours raised the efficacy of both black men and black women heading poor households. Getting off of welfare likewise enhanced it among black women. By contrast, increase in total family income had no effect on either group's sense of efficacy. The events that seemed to matter were those the household heads could easily construe they personally caused. Efficacy was not influenced just by good things happening but by events this culture hails as resulting from the individual's own motivation.

Research on socialization for work roles also points to self-implicating properties of the work experience which produce change by heightening self-awareness. Kohn and Schooler (1978) emphasize the importance of work that requires self-directed thought. These investigators were concerned with qualities of work that might influence intellectual flexibility. On the basis of a 10-year panel study of the work experience, Kohn and Schooler conclude that work features which make adults look at themselves, exercise responsibility, and think about their work have the most powerful effects on intellectual flexibility. Properties that heighten salience of the self can alter the self, even dimensions which generally are quite stable, as Kohn and Schooler have shown intellectual flexibility to be.

In a similar vein, Mortimer and Lorence (1979a,b) stress the importance of work autonomy, a concept closely related to occupational self-direction. They examine the impact of work autonomy specifically on sense of competence. Their work thus applies directly to the personal aspect of control, the judgment of self as a competent person. The studies examine the early careers of a sample of men who graduated in 1966 from a prestigious mid-Western university. Eighty-eight percent of the graduates were located 10 years later. Work autonomy was measured using the men's own judgments of three qualities of their jobs during the 10-year period following their graduation: how much decision-making latitude the jobs had allowed, how much innovative thinking they had required, and how much personal challenge they had provided. The work autonomy measure averaged these qualities of the "early career" jobs. Personal competence was measured, again using the men's own judgments of whether they were: competent–not too competent, confident–anxious, active–quiet, and strong–weak. This measure of self-competence was taken as the men were seniors and again 10 years later. Men whose jobs had provided the most autonomy in the intervening years had increased their sense of competence the most. The causal analysis further indicates that it was work autonomy in particular, far more than income itself, that enhanced these young men's sense of competence beyond the level they had had as college seniors 10 years before. Moreover, the change that was brought about by work autonomy occurred despite considerable overall stability in the sense of competence. While the ordering of these men's sense of competence did remain fairly stable over the 10 years, some experiences were capable of producing individual change. And these were notably ones that heightened the salience of the self.

Still other research points to the significance of public events in heightening salience of the self. When success or failure occurs in a situation that others see and other people reaffirm one's causal role in the outcome, successes and failures are much more influential in altering self-esteem. Snyder *et al.* (1978) specifically argue that this is because the outcome cannot so easily be discounted or attributed to the situation. Self-serving attributions about failure are less plausible when others witness the failure and especially when others verbally hold the person responsible for it. Additionally, the expectation of having to face another future test of one's performance increases willingness to take credit for failure. Being scrutinized and expecting a subsequent test both heighten self-attributions, even for failure which many people would handle defensively or egotistically.

Studies of how to increase objective self-awareness also show that self-attributions are made more frequently in public than in private situations, notably so when the person is made an active observer of himself through techniques increasing self-consciousness. In experimental settings these techniques include telling the subject that the session is being videotaped, focusing a camera directly on the subject, actually playing back a videotape to the subject, requiring the subject to look in a mirror, playing back an audiotape of the subject's voice (Duval & Hensley, 1976; D. T. Miller & Ross, 1975; Storms, 1973).

### C. PSYCHOLOGICALLY COMPELLING EVENTS

We have examined two different research traditions, experimental work on stress from laboratory studies and survey research on life events in natural settings, and have offered some ideas about properties of events and the situations in which events occur that can overpower psychological forces for stability. We offer them as hypotheses, tying event properties to the change process, and not as established connections. We believe that forging links between these two traditions and uniting event properties and the change process form an important agenda for life-span research.

To review briefly: the psychological forces which at some times and for some people press for stability rather than change include needs for control, self-respect, and consistency. They converge for people who expect to succeed and those who think of themselves as highly efficacious, heightening their sensitivity to events that reinforce their positive feelings about the self and their avoidance and/or externalization of threatening events. These forces may diverge somewhat for people who expect to fail and who consider themselves incompetent. Their needs for self-respect and control make them welcome success. However, their needs for consistency may make them quite dubious about its credibility or its relevance for self. Events must therefore be psychologically compelling if either success or failure is to change personal efficacy or other central aspects of self. However much desired, success must be incontrovertible if it is to influence the inefficacious. And, if not compelling, failure will go unnoticed or discounted by the highly efficacious.

Some properties of events contribute to their being compelling by daunting selectivity, increasing breadth of exposure, and helping people pay attention to the event instead of ignoring it. Events are more apt to be noticed if they occur with few distractors, happen to many people in the society in general or in the age cohort, and endure over time, or, if not entirely durable, occur with high probability and high frequency. In addition, controllable events that make information instrumental draw attention and increase people's willingness to seek information.

Unfortunately, some of these properties which may initiate the change process by increasing the likelihood that people will be exposed to the event and attend to rather than avoid it may then militate against change by decreasing the event's self-implications. Events that are widespread in society, highly age graded, and extremely probable in the life of the individual produce these countervailing influences on change. While they heighten exposure, attention, and active processing of the experience, they also give consensus information that may well focus attention on the environment, not on the self.

Other properties, we have argued, not only encourage exposure but heighten the salience of the self. Enduring events that can be influenced, if not totally controlled, by individual action are of this sort. Moreover, some properties that impinge especially on attention or especially on self-salience at least do not appear to damage the other aspect of the change process. Events that occur with few distractors help people pay attention and learn about the event. Whether that increases self-awareness is perhaps debatable but there is at least no evidence that it interferes. Events that tie outcome inarguably to performance, occur in many different circumstances, require self-directed thought and self-initiated behavior, and provide public verification of the role of the self act to heighten self-awareness without decreasing the event's power to draw attention and avert willingness to seek information.

The paradox is that rare, atypical, off-time events which make people look at themselves and deal with the self-implications of the experience are by definition too rare to alter a whole population's judgments of themselves as competent.

Our analysis of properties of events illuminates why historical events, gains and losses of social roles, and other social experiences in adult life can so much more easily affect the aspect of control that involves evaluations of the system's responsiveness. We have seen that these evaluations have been much less stable, both historically and correlationally. Judgments of responsiveness have changed more, partly because they are much less central to self. Events thus arouse the motivational forces against change much less because the self is not threatened. People can pay attention to the functioning of institutions and recognize changes in the way political parties or authorities respond to individuals because the self is not much implicated in these situations. Of course, when views of the system's responsiveness are central to self, as they may be for political activists, minorities, executives on the rise, and public officials, for example, life events will need to be extremely powerful to change them as well. For many people this is not the case. We also argue that judgments of responsiveness change more easily because the very properties of events that should increase exposure and attention at the same time focus attention on the environment. Widespread, age-graded, highly probable events—Brim and Ryff's (1980) Type I events—yield exactly the kind of information that should change views of the environment. They give consensus information that tells more about the environment than the self. In addition, such events happen to enough people to produce aggregate shifts in people's judgments, and they uniquely provide information that encourages concern with the environment. Finally, correlational instability is more plausible because the events that should change judgments of responsiveness are likely to be fairly independent of people's initial beliefs about the environment's responsiveness. If we are correct that judgments of responsiveness are rarely central to the self, they should not function as powerful selectivity forces. Change in the ordering of individuals on a psychological dimension will not occur when exposure to an event is highly correlated with initial position. For all these reasons it is not surprising that major historical events and life-span role shifts influence people's views of responsiveness more easily than their views of themselves as efficacious.

## VI. Historical Events and Change in Personal Efficacy

To this point we have treated historical events and role shifts in much the same fashion, arguing that they quite easily influence judgments of responsiveness but only rarely change people's judgments of their own personal efficacy. However, in some ways historical events may be more powerful than the age-graded discontinuities normally considered by life-span theorists. The unexpectedness of major technological, economic, and political upheavals minimizes opportunities for anticipatory socialization. Societies do not socialize people for the massive layoffs that materialized in the Great Depression or in American industries most severely hit by energy costs. No one socializes adults for life after a revolution. And while social support and new reference groups will eventually emerge, initially there are few support systems to assist in the adaptation to major upheavals. The breadth and unexpectedness of their impact can make historical events potentially quite powerful. The issue is whether they not only demand major restructuring and affect people broadly but also endure long enough to heighten salience of the self and in other ways press for awareness of self. When they do, they should alter the level of personal efficacy in society. Events in recent history appear to have done that, at least for some sectors of society.

Inkeles and Smith (1974) discuss modernization as an enduring event, powerful enough to change adults even in a fundamental characteristic of self, as personal efficacy is considered to be. They argue that the creation of the factory in developing nations presents a powerful environment that should be able to impinge with sufficiently concentrated force upon individuals to bring about changes in core features of personality. Their analysis of the factory emphasizes many of the event properties that we have suggested influence two aspects of the change process: exposure/attention and seeing the experience as pertinent to the self.

The factory is a highly discrepant environment, one that demands major new learning from skills previously valued and demanded in village socialization. Moreover, the discrepancy is communicated with an invariant character which requires villagers to adapt to it rather than it adapting to them. Also, in the sectors of developing countries experiencing the process of modernization, the factory's impact is felt broadly, not only on those directly employed but on children through formal schooling and on others through the service industries which develop along with production industries. These effects endure in two senses. The worker's contact with the factory system is not fleeting or irregular and the modernization process itself irreversibly disrupts old ways. The chronicity of the demands and sheer importance of work heighten the salience of self as does awareness of some atypicality. While modernization impinges broadly, obtaining jobs with the pay and steadiness of factory employment in developing nations is rare enough to enhance awareness of uniqueness for those directly involved in the factory. Most of all, Inkeles and Smith point to the activities and organization of the factory which make it a powerful environment. While they may have other effects, the features stressed—*public, clearly delineated, unambiguous performance standards* and expectations of *space* and *place for the individual*—ought to make the self very salient.

The essential logic of machinery and mechanical processes must be rigorously observed, else the machine, or its attendant, or both, must break. It requires only a few instances in which hair, or a flowing gown, or fingers get caught in the machine, to impress the point indelibly on all who come in contact with it. This same sharpness of outline tends to be manifested in the organization of the factory. Departments, shops, even individual machines are distinctly set off and clearly demarcated. Division of labor is generally precisely and rigorously maintained. Hierarchies of authority and technical skill give a definite structure to interpersonal relations. Standards of performance tend to be objective and precise. And the system of rewards and punishments is highly relevant to all the participants, unambiguous, powerful, and by and large objectively calculated. (Inkeles & Smith, 1974, pp. 157–158)

Inkeles and Smith were studying the effects of modernization on personality and constructed an attitude scale to measure "modernity" of attitudes. They found that modernity of attitudes does increase during industrialization and that personal efficacy was a critical theme in the modernity scale. In all six nations studied, 3 of the 12 items important to the modernity scale were explicitly measures of personal efficacy and a fourth clearly reflected the same tendency.

The impact of World War II's mobilization of women into civilian and military work roles is also discussed in terms congenial to our analysis of powerful event properties (Anderson, 1981; G. H. Elder, Jr., personal communication, June 7, 1983; Rupp, 1978). The change in women's lives during this period was dramatic both in terms of presenting demands highly discrepant from those traditionally expected of wives and mothers and in affecting women across society. In both senses the mobilization was large enough to have altered the level of women's personal efficacy. The war effort lasted long enough for these women to learn about themselves and not to view the experience as a fleeting aberration. And while many of them returned home to traditional roles after the war, the employment experience itself was durable enough to cause aggregate change at the time. There was also enough atypicality to further increase the salience of the experience for learning about the self. While broad in its impact, not all women went off to the factory in the wartime mobilization. In much the same ways that Inkeles discusses the factory as setting for change during modernization, the factory also brought public, clearly delineated, universal performance standards to many women during World War II. Outside of schooling, girls' and women's lives in traditional roles provide much less public scrutiny of performance.

Elder (1982) describes the experience of women during the Great Depression in taking employment outside the home and managing family finances as having a similar positive effect on the efficacy of many women. While measures of personal efficacy were not collected in the early waves of the well-known Berkeley study in which Elder has investigated the impact of the Great Depression, it does show that qualities normally associated with efficacy were influenced when women became independent and coped with deprivation by taking on work outside the home (Elder & Liker, 1982).

While none of these studies has actually provided empirical evidence of aggregate efficacy shifts nor been able to tie efficacy specifically to the properties theoretically responsible for change, the studies do suggest that some events may alter the level of efficacy in a society. The events must be compelling in the ways we have noted.

None of the events that may have affected the level of personal efficacy—modernization, World War II, the Great Depression—would necessarily have disturbed the ordering that individuals had before the events. Correlational stability may still be very marked even when events are powerful enough to alter level of efficacy in a population because individuals initially more efficacious probably respond better to these events. While everyone may be hit by major historical events, there is no reason to assume that their responses and ways of coping with the events are independent of their earlier sense of efficacy. Indeed, current writing about life events as stressors typically treats personal efficacy as a resource for coping with stress. Elder and Liker (1982) make this argument in explaining why the Great Depression affected working and middle-class women differently. They assume that middle-class women were more efficacious to begin with, and that their initial efficacy gave them a resource for coping with economic loss during the Depression. The effects of the Depression were not simply less negative for middle- than for working-class women; they were actually positive for those from the middle class. The impact of the Depression on the efficacy of the two groups would thus accentuate rather than alter their initial differences. The same point is documented by Gleser, Green, and Winget (1981) in describing recovery from a community disaster. They followed up people initially studied by Erikson (1976) when a dam collapsed in a small community. Participation in the recovery efforts bolstered individuals' sense of efficacy, and people who felt more efficacious before the disaster were more likely to respond by participating in its recovery.

To disrupt the ordering of individuals on a scale of efficacy, events must either be uncorrelated or inversely correlated with the individuals' initial positions on the scale. What kind of events might those be? We believe them to be rare because the event must bring such unexpected consequences that initial efficacy is simply irrelevant to coping, or provide a set of entirely new social processes in which previous privileges, rights, and expectations are removed from the efficacious and provided to the inefficacious. Gottfried (1983) gives the example of the Black Death which not only killed between one-quarter to one-half of Europe's population in 4 years but severed the threads—political, economic, and religious—that had held medieval society together. The social rules were irreversibly altered in ways that indeed should have decreased the efficacy of the lords and increased the efficacy of the peasants. The old aristocracy was impoverished, its land made valueless by the fact that few people were left to farm it. And those peasants who survived were then able to demand high prices for their labor and work freely where they pleased. Political revolutions, in a like vein, restructure the rules of privilege, reversing opportunity and disadvantage in such a way that the ordering of efficacy should be greatly changed. But most events, we feel, are more apt to accentuate than alter initial individual and group differences in personal efficacy, even when they are powerful enough to lower or raise the aggregate level of efficacy in society.

# References

Adler, A. *The individual psychology of Alfred Adler.* New York: Harper & Row, 1956.

Alloy, L. B., & Abramson, L. Y. Judgment of contingency in depressed and nondepressed students: Sadder but wiser? *Journal of Experimental Psychology: General,* 1979, **108,** 441–485.

Almond, G., & Verba, S. *The civic culture.* Boston: Little, Brown, 1965.

Anderson, K. *Wartime women: Sex roles, family relations, and the status of women during World War II.* Westport, Connecticut: Greenwood, 1981.

Aronson, E., & Carlsmith, J. M. Performance expectancy as a determinant of actual performance. *Journal of Abnormal and Social Psychology,* 1962, **65,** 178–182.

Averill, J. R., O'Brien, L., & DeWitt, G. W. The influence of response effectiveness on the preference for warning and on psychophysiological stress reactions. *Journal of Personality,* 1977, **45,** 395–418.

Bandura, A. Self-efficacy: Toward a unifying theory of behavioral change. *Psychological Review,* 1977, **84,** 191–215.

Bandura, A. The self and mechanisms of agency. In J. Suls (Ed.), *Social psychological perspectives on the self.* Hillsdale, New Jersey: Erlbaum, 1980.

Barber, B. *The logic and limits of trust.* New Brunswick, New Jersey: Rutgers University Press, 1983.

Baron, R. The SRS model as a predictor of Negro responsiveness to reinforcement. *Journal of Social Issues,* 1970, **26,** 61–81.

Beck, A. T. *Depression.* New York: Harper (Hoeber), 1967.

Beijk, J. Expectancy, performance, and self-concept. *Acta Psychologica,* 1966, **25,** 381–388.

Bem, D. J. Self-perception theory. In L. Berkowitz (Ed.), *Advances in experimental social psychology* (Vol. 6). New York: Academic Press, 1972.

Benedict, R. Continuities and discontinuities in cultural conditioning. *Psychiatry,* 1938, **1,** 161–167.

Bradley, G. W. Self-serving biases in the attribution process: A reexamination of the fact or fiction question. *Journal of Personality and Social Psychology,* 1978, **36,** 56–71.

Brickman, P. Rational and non-rational elements in reactions to disconfirmation of performance expectancies. *Journal of Experimental Social Psychology,* 1972, **8,** 112–123.

Brickman, P., & Bulman, J. R. Pleasure and pain in social comparison. In J. M. Suls & R. L. Miller (Eds.), *Social comparison processes: Theoretical and empirical perspectives.* Washington, D.C.: Hemisphere Publ., 1977.

Brim, O. G., Jr. Socialization through the life cycle. In O. G. Brim, Jr. & S. Wheeler (Eds.), *Socialization after childhood: Two essays.* New York: Wiley, 1966.

Brim, O. G., Jr. *The sense of personal control over one's life.* Paper presented at the 82nd Annual Convention of the American Psychological Association, New Orleans, September 1974.

Brim, O. G., Jr., & Kagan, J. *Constancy and change in human development.* Cambridge, Massachusetts: Harvard University Press, 1980.

Brim, O. G., Jr., & Ryff, C. D. On the properties of life events. In P. B. Baltes & O. G. Brim, Jr. (Eds.), *Life-span development and behavior* (Vol. 3). New York: Academic Press, 1980.

Brock, T. C., Edelman, S. D., Edwards, D. C., & Shuck, J. R. Seven studies of performance expectancy as a determinant of actual performance. *Journal of Experimental Social Psychology,* 1965, **1**, 295–300.

Brown, G. W., & Harris, T. *Social origins of depression.* New York: Free Press, 1978.

Campbell, A. A., Gurin, G., & Miller, W. E. *The voter decides.* New York: Harper, 1954.

Cantor, N., & Kihlstrom, J. Social intelligence: *The cognitive basis of personality.* Technical Report No. 60. Cognitive Science Center, University of Michigan, 1983.

Caplan, N. The new ghetto man: A review of recent empirical studies. *Journal of Social Issues,* 1970, **26**, 59–73.

Cohler, B. J. Personal narrative and life course. In P. B. Baltes & O. G. Brim, Jr. (Eds.), *Life-span development and behavior* (Vol. 4). New York: Academic Press, 1982.

Converse, P. E. Change in the American electorate. In A. A. Campbell & P. E. Converse (Eds.), *The human meaning of social change.* New York: Russell Sage Foundation, 1972.

Converse, P. E., & Markus, G. B. Plus ça change . . . : The new CPS election study panel. *The American Science Review,* 1979, **73**, 32–49.

Cottrell, N. B. Performance expectancy as a determinant of actual performance: A replication with a new design. *Journal of Personality and Social Psychology,* 1965, **2**, 685–691.

deCharms, R. *Personal causation.* New York: Academic Press, 1968.

Deci, E. L. *Intrinsic motivation.* New York: Plenum, 1975.

Dohrenwend, B. S., & Dohrenwend, B. P. Overview and prospects for research on stressful life events. In B. S. Dohrenwend & B. P. Dohrenwend (Eds.), *Stressful life events: Their nature and effects.* New York: Wiley, 1974.

Duncan, G. J., & Liker, J. K. Disentangling the efficacy–earnings relationship. In G. J. Duncan & J. N. Morgan (Eds.), *Five thousand American families: Patterns of economic progress* (Vol. 10). Ann Arbor: Institute for Social Research, University of Michigan, 1983.

Duncan, G. J., & Morgan, J. N. The incidence and some consequences of major life events. In G. J. Duncan & J. N. Morgan (Eds.), *Five thousand American families: Patterns of economic progress* (Vol. 8). Ann Arbor: Institute for Social Research, University of Michigan, 1980.

Duval, S., & Hensley, V. Extensions of objective self-awareness theory: The focus of attention–causal attribution hypothesis. In J. H. Harvey, W. J. Ickes, & R. F. Kidd (Eds.), *New directions in attribution research* (Vol. 1). Hillsdale, New Jersey: Erlbaum, 1976.

Eagly, A. H. Involvement as a determinant of response to favorable and unfavorable information. *Journal of Personality and Social Psychology Monograph,* 1967, **7** (3, pt 2.).

Easton, D. *A systems analysis of political life.* New York: Wiley, 1965.

Elder, G. H., Jr. Historical experiences in the later years. In T. K. Hareven & K. J. Adams (Eds.), *Aging and life course transitions.* New York: Guilford, 1982.

Elder, G. H., Jr. (Ed.) *Life course dynamics: 1968 to the 1980's.* Ithaca, New York: Cornell University Press, 1984, in press.

Elder, G. H., Jr., & Liker, J. K. Hard times in women's lives: Historical influences across forty years. *American Journal of Sociology,* 1982, **88**, 241–269.

Erikson, K. *Everything in its path.* New York: Simon & Schuster, 1976.

Featherman, D. L. Life-span perspectives in social science research. In P. B. Baltes & O. G. Brim, Jr. (Eds.), *Life-span development and behavior* (Vol. 5). New York: Academic Press, 1983.

Festinger, L. A theory of social comparison processes. *Human Relations,* 1954, **7**, 117–140.

Frentzel, J. Cognitive consistency and positive self-concept. *Polish Sociological Bulletin,* 1965, **1**, 71–86.

Gamson, W. *Power and discontent.* Homewood, Dorsey, 1968.

Gatz, M., & Siegler, I. C. *Locus of control: A retrospective.* Paper presented at the American Psychological Association Meetings, Los Angeles, August 1981.

Gleser, G. C., Green, B., & Winget, T. C. *Prolonged psychological effects of a disaster: A study of Buffalo Creek.* New York: Academic Press, 1981.

Gottfried, R. S. *The black death.* New York: Free Press, 1983.

Greenwald, A. G. The totalitarian ego: Fabrication and revision of personal history. *American Psychologist,* 1980, **35,** 603–618.

Gurin, G., & Gurin, P. Expectancy theory in the study of poverty. *Journal of Social Issues,* 1970, **26,** 83–104.

Gurin, G., & Gurin, P. *Personal and political powerlessness among older Americans: A national probability sample.* Paper presented at Gerontological Society Meetings, Louisville, Kentucky, April 1975.

Gurin, P., Gurin, G., Lao, R. C., & Beattie, M. Internal–external control in the motivational dynamics of Negro youth. *Journal of Social Issues,* 1969, **25,** 29–53.

Gurin, P., Gurin, G., & Morrison, B. M. Personal and ideological aspects of internal and external· control. *Social Psychology Quarterly,* 1978, **41,** 275–296.

Harvey, O. J., & Clapp, W. F. Hope, expectancy, and reactions to the unexpected. *Journal of Personality and Social Psychology,* 1965, **2,** 45–52.

Heider, F. Social perception and phenomenal causality. *Psychological Review,* 1944, **51,** 358–374.

Henslin, J. M. Craps and magic. *American Journal of Sociology,* 1967, **73,** 316–330.

Hogan, D. P. The variable order of events in the life course. *American Sociological Review,* 1978, **43,** 573–586.

Hogan, D. P. The transition to adulthood as a career contingency. *American Sociological Review,* 1980, **45,** 261–276.

House, J. S. Social structure and personality. In M. Rosenberg & R. H. Turner (Eds.), *Social psychology: Sociological perspectives.* New York: Basic Books, 1981.

Inkeles, A., & Smith, D. H. *Becoming modern: Individual change in six developing countries.* Cambridge, Massachusetts: Harvard University Press, 1974.

Kagan, J. Perspectives on continuity. In O. G. Brim, Jr. & J. Kagan (Eds.), *Constancy and change in human development.* Cambridge, Massachusetts: Harvard University Press, 1980.

Kelley, H. H. Attribution theory in social psychology. In D. L. Vine (Ed.), *Nebraska Symposium on Motivation.* Lincoln: University of Nebraska Press, 1967.

Kelley, H. H. *Causal schemata and the attribution process.* Morristown, New Jersey: General Learning Press, 1972.

Kobasa, S. C., Hiker, R. J., & Maddi, S. R. Who stays healthy under stress? *Journal of Occupational Medicine,* 1979, **21,** 595–598.

Kohn, M. L., & Schooler, C. The reciprocal effects of the substantive complexity of work and intellectual flexibility: A longitudinal assessment. *American Journal of Sociology,* 1978, **84,** 24–52.

Kornreich, L. B. Performance expectancy as a determinant of actual performance: Failure to replicate. *Psychological Reports,* 1968, **22,** 535–543.

Lachman, M. E. Personal efficacy in middle and old age: Differential and normative patterns of change. In G. H. Elder, Jr. (Ed.), *Life course dynamics: 1968 to the 1980's.* Ithaca, New York: Cornell University Press, 1984, in press.

Lane, R. E. *Political life.* New York: Free Press, 1959.

Langer, E. J. The illusion of control. *Journal of Personality and Social Psychology,* 1975, **32,** 311–328.

Lazarus, R. S., & DeLongis, A. Psychological stress and coping in aging. *American Psychologist,* 1984, in press.

Lerner, M. J., & Miller, D. J. Just world research and the attribution process: Looking back and ahead. *Psychological Bulletin,* 1978, **85,** 1030–1151.

Lerner, R. M. *On human plasticity.* London and New York: Cambridge University Press, 1984, in press.

Lewinsohn, P. M., Mischel, W., Chaplain, W., & Barton, R. Social competence and depression: The role of illusory self-perceptions. *Journal of Abnormal Psychology,* 1980, **4,** 561–571.

Lipset, S. M., & Schneider, W. The decline of confidence in American institutions. *Political Science Quarterly,* 1983, **98,** 379–402.

Lowin, A., & Epstein, G. F. Does expectancy determine performance? *Journal of Experimental Social Psychology,* 1965, **1,** 248–255.

Markus, G. B., & Converse, P. E. Dynamic modelling of cohort change: The case of political partisanship. *American Journal of Political Science,* 1984, in press.

Markus, H. Self-schemata and processing information about the self. *Journal of Personality and Social Psychology,* 1977, **35,** 63–78.

Markus, H. The self in thought and memory. In D. M. Wegner & R. R. Vallacher (Eds.), *The self in social psychology.* London and New York: Oxford University Press, 1980.

Mason, W. M., House, J. S., & Martin, S. S. *Dimensions of political alienation in America: Theoretical and empirical.* Ann Arbor: Population Studies Center, University of Michigan, 1981.

McLanahan, S. S., & Sørensen, A. B. Life events and psychological well-being over the life course. In G. H. Elder, Jr. (Ed.), *Life course dynamics: 1968 to the 1980's.* Ithaca, New York: Cornell University Press, 1984, in press.

Mettee, D. R. Rejection of unexpected success as a function of the negative consequences of accepting success. *Journal of Personality and Social Psychology,* 1971, **17,** 332–341.

Meyer, J. *The institutionalization of the life course.* Paper presented at a conference sponsored by the Social Science Research Council's Committee on Life Course Perspectives on Human Development, Berlin, September 1982.

Miller, A. H. *The institutional focus of political distrust.* Paper presented at the Annual Meeting of the American Political Science Association, Washington, D.C., August 1979.

Miller, D. T. What constitutes a self-serving attributional bias? A reply to Bradley. *Journal of Personality and Social Psychology,* 1978, **36,** 1211–1223.

Miller, D. T., & Ross, M. Self-serving biases in the attribution of causality: Fact or fiction? *Psychological Bulletin,* 1975, **82,** 213–225.

Miller, S. M. When is a little information a dangerous thing? Coping with stressful events by monitoring versus blunting. In S. Levine (Ed.), *Coping and health: Proceedings of a NATO conference.* New York: Plenum, 1980.

Miller, S. M. Coping with impending stress: Psychophysiological and cognitive correlates of choice. *Psychophysiology,* 1984, in press.

Morgan, J. N., & Augustyniak, S. *Do events that happen to people affect their sense of personal efficacy?* Unpublished paper, Institute for Social Research, University of Michigan, Ann Arbor, 1982.

Mortimer, J. T., & Lorence, J. Occupational experience and the self-concept: A longitudinal study. *Social Psychology Quarterly,* 1979, **42,** 307–323. (a)

Mortimer, J. T., & Lorence, J. Work experience and occupational value socialization: A longitudinal study. *American Journal of Sociology,* 1979, **84,** 1361–1385. (b)

Mortimer, J. T., & Simmons, R. G. Adult socialization. *Annual Review of Sociology,* 1978, **4,** 421–454.

Moss, H. A., & Susman, E. J. Longitudinal study of personality development. In O. G. Brim, Jr. & J. Kagan (Eds.), *Constancy and change in human development.* Cambridge, Massachusetts: Harvard University Press, 1980.

Mueller, W., & Mayer, K. U. *The development of the state and the structure of the life course.* Paper presented at a conference sponsored by the Social Science Research Council's Committee on Life Course Perspectives on Human Development, Berlin, September 1982.

Neugarten, B. L. Adult personality: Toward a psychology of the life cycle. In B. L. Neugarten (Ed.), *Middle age and aging.* Chicago: University of Chicago Press, 1968.

Nisbett, R. E., & Ross, L. *Human inference: Strategies and shortcomings.* Englewood Cliffs, New Jersey: Prentice-Hall, 1980.

Paige, J. M. Political orientation and riot participation. *American Sociological Review,* 1971, **36,** 810–820.

Pearlin, L. I., Lieberman, M. A., Menaghan, E. G., & Mullan, J. T. The stress process. *Journal of Health and Social Behavior,* 1981, **22,** 337–356.

Porter, L. W., & Lawler, E. E. *Managerial attitudes and performance.* Homewood, Illinois: Dorsey, 1968.

Riley, M. W. Age strata in social systems. In R. H. Binstock & E. Shanas (Eds.), *Handbook of aging and the social sciences.* New York: Van Nostrand Reinhold, 1976.

Rodgers, W., Herzog, R., & Woodworth, J. *Extensions of procedures for the analysis of age, period, and cohort effects* (Working Paper Series, Institute for Social Research, University of Michigan). Ann Arbor: ISR, 1980.

Ross, M., & Fletcher, G. Social and cultural factors in cognition. In G. Lindzey & E. Aronson (Eds.), *Handbook of Social Psychology* (3rd ed.). Reading, Massachusetts: Addison-Wesley, 1984, in press.

Rotter, J. B. Generalized expectancies for internal versus external control of reinforcement. *Psychological Monographs,* 1966, **80** (1, Whole No. 609).

Rupp, L. J. *Mobilizing women for war: German and American propaganda, 1939–1945.* Princeton, New Jersey: Princeton University Press, 1978.

Ryff, C. D., & Dunn, D. D. *Life stresses and personality: A life-span developmental inquiry.* Unpublished paper, Fordham University, Bronx, New York, 1983.

Sarason, I. G., Johnson, J. H., & Siegel, J. M. Assessing the impact of life changes: Development of the life experience survey. *Journal of Consulting and Clinical Psychology,* 1978, **46,** 932–946.

Seligman, M. E. P. *Helplessness: On depression, development, and death.* San Francisco: Freeman, 1975.

Shrauger, J. S. Responses to evaluation as a function of initial self perceptions. *Psychological Bulletin,* 1975, **82,** 581–596.

Skinner, E. A., & Chapman, M. Control beliefs in an action perspective. *Human Development,* 1984, in press.

Snyder, C. R., & Shenkel, R. J. Effects of "favorability," modality, and relevance on acceptance of general personality interpretations prior to and after receiving diagnostic feedback. *Journal of Consulting and Clinical Psychology,* 1976, **44,** 34–41.

Snyder, M. L., Stephan, W. G., & Rosenfield, D. Egotism and attribution. *Journal of Personality and Social Psychology,* 1976, **33,** 435–441.

Snyder, M. L., Stephan, W. G., & Rosenfield, D. Attributional egotism. In J. H. Harvey, W. J. Ickes, & R. F. Kidd (Eds.), *New directions in attribution research* (Vol. 2). Hillsdale, New Jersey: Erlbaum, 1978.

Steiner, E. D. Reactions to adverse and favorable evaluations of one's self. *Journal of Personality,* 1968, **36,** 553–563.

Storms, M. D. Videotape and the attribution process: Reversing actors' and observers' points of view. *Journal of Personality and Social Psychology,* 1973, **27,** 167–175.

Swann, W. B., Jr., & Read, S. J. Self-verification processes: How we sustain our self-conceptions. *Journal of Experimental Social Psychology,* 1984, in press.

Thornton, D. A., & Arrowood, A. J. Self evaluation, self enhancement, the locus of social comparison. *Journal of Experimental Social Psychology* (suppl., 1966, pp. 40–48.

Vroom, H. J. *Work and motivation.* New York: Wiley, 1964.

Walster, E. Assignment of responsibility for an accident. *Journal of Personality and Social Psychology,* 1966, **3,** 73–79.

White, R. W. Motivation reconsidered: The concept of competence. *Psychological Review,* 1959, **66,** 297–333.

Wilcox, D. L. Social support in adjusting to marital disruption: A network analysis. In B. H. Gottleib (Ed.), *Social networks and social support.* Beverly Hills, California: Sage Publ., 1981.

Wortman, C. B. Some determinants of perceived control. In J. H. Harvey, W. J. Ickes, & R. F. Kidd (Eds.), *New directions in attribution research* (Vol. 1). Hillsdale, New Jersey: Erlbaum, 1976.

# Sibling Studies and the Developmental Impact of Critical Incidents

*Judy Dunn*

UNIVERSITY OF CAMBRIDGE

CAMBRIDGE, ENGLAND

## Abstract

Recent studies of siblings provide provocative findings in relation to the theoretical orientation of life-span psychologists. Two particular aspects of this orientation—the impact of critical life events and the question of the significance of early experience—are considered in the context of the sibling relationship. The changes accompanying the birth of a sibling demonstrate that the significance of critical incidents in developmental processes cannot be understood without reference to individual differences in personality and family relationships. Differences in the quality of the early sibling relationship persist into middle childhood and retrospective material shows that in late adulthood individuals attribute their closeness to their siblings to this early relationship. The sibling relationship is of much significance to the majority of individuals in old age. Critical incidents are of considerable importance in the dynamics of the sibling relationship throughout life, but the developmental significance of such incidents, again, can be understood only if the sibling relationship is studied within the context of other family relationships and of individual differences in personality.

## I. Introduction

The relationship which an individual has with his or her sibling is the longest lasting relationship of his or her life—longer than the relationship with parent, with child, or with lover or spouse. But how significant are sibling relationships in development, either in childhood or later in life? How does the sibling relationship change as an individual grows up and passes from childhood to adolescence and adulthood? Does the quality of the relationship between siblings at any stage of the life span influence an individual's personality, behavior, or intellectual development?

We are very far from being able to answer with any confidence these general questions on the significance of the sibling relationship in development. It has been argued by psychologists from a wide variety of backgrounds, including clinicians and behavioral geneticists, that the experience of being a sibling does have profound effects on an individual (see for example Adler, 1928, 1959; Bossard & Boll, 1959; Brim, 1958; Cicirelli, 1973, 1975, 1977, 1979; Koch, 1960; Lamb & Sutton-Smith, 1982; Levy, 1934, 1937; Rowe & Plomin, 1981; Scarr & Grajek, 1982; Sutton-Smith & Rosenberg, 1970; Wagner, Schubert, & Schubert, 1979; Zajonc & Markus, 1975). It has been suggested that the early interaction between siblings and the parents' socializing influence within the family set up a pattern of interaction between the siblings that persists throughout adulthood; it has also been proposed that at various points in the life span siblings act as role models, as challengers, and as reinforcers, and that the salience of the sibling for an individual lends power to this influence in adulthood.

The findings of the birth order and "sibling status" research are however often confusing or contradictory, and the methodology is unsatisfactory: the processes involved in the developing relationship between siblings are by no means clear. Reference to processes such as identification or deidentification are made with little direct evidence by which we can judge how plausible these are. Detailed developmental research on the nature of the sibling relationship is in fact very limited in scope and largely confined to the early years of childhood. Most of the psychological research discussed here comes solely from studies of siblings in the United States and in Great Britain. It is obvious from the anthropological material on siblings in other cultures that it may be misleading to draw broad generalizations from such a narrow source.

But in spite of its limitations, the recent work on very young siblings (Abramovitch, Corter, & Lando, 1979; Abramovitch, Pepler, & Corter, 1982; Dunn & Kendrick, 1982a,b; Nadelman & Begun, 1982) and on adult siblings (Cicirelli, 1982; Ross & Milgram, 1982) does offer some illumination for psychologists thinking about developmental processes within a life-span orientation—illumination which depends, I suggest, on our thinking about sibling relationships within a family context. To make any progress in answering the general questions on the development and significance of the relationship between siblings we must study the relationship not just in terms of age gap and sex of siblings—the variables which have been the focus of most previous research—but in terms of the quality of the relationship between the siblings, of the relationship which each child has with the parents and grandparents, and of the mutual influence of these family relationships. We should consider the siblings within a framework of family relationships—and one which extends beyond childhood. The sibling relationship develops within a family context, a family context which may itself be changing; change and development in the family relationships take place moreover within a society which also may be changing. When we consider sibling relationships within such a framework, a host of further questions are raised: What is the impact of the birth of a second child on marital relations, which in turn affect the parents' behavior to each child? How important is the life stage of the parents—their age and financial status—in its influences on their behavior to one another and to their children, and the relationship of the children to one another? What is the impact of social class and ethnic group? What is the role of support systems outside the home on parents and on siblings?

One of the important contributions of the life-span psychologists is that their concern with developmental issues beyond childhood and their examination of "nonnormative" historical events and cohort effects highlight the importance of these questions, and the limited scope of much developmental work in childhood. The life-span psychologists stress, for instance, that human development is a life-long process, and that no one period in the life span can claim primacy for the origin of developmental change. They argue that developmental research must be concerned with many different kinds of change with very different origins, and that account must be taken of "history-graded" influence by considering cohort effects and the role of "nonnormative events" in shaping the course of development (Baltes, Reese, & Lipsitt, 1980).

Now we are not in a position to speculate on a grand scale about the impact of historical events on siblings, nor even to discuss usefully the significance of changes such as the transition from childhood to adolescence for the sibling relationship. We simply do not have, as yet, sufficiently precise, systematic, or longitudinal information to do more than guess at such influences. But if we think about the recent research on siblings within a framework of family relationships, and in terms of the changes with which families have to cope, the studies of siblings do provide some provocative and interesting findings in relation to the theoretical orientation of life-span psychologists. A close look at the research on the birth of a sibling and the developing relationship between the young siblings does provide detailed and systematic data on how a major event in children's lives affects their relationships and their development. It presents the psychologist with the opportunity not simply to document the importance of a dramatic change in an individual's life but to explore the processes by which this event may be affecting his or her development. It hints at what psychological processes may be operating at different stages of the life cycle in this, the longest lasting of family relationships.

The research on siblings in later life supports the arguments put forward by life-span psychologists for the significance of critical events in adulthood; however it also presents a challenge to their approach both in its evidence for the stability of the sibling relationship over the life course and in the questions it raises about the significance of early experience in the development of sibling relationships.

In this article then I shall consider these two particular aspects of the life-span orientation, namely, the importance of critical life events and the question of the significance of early experience, in the context of the sibling relationship. I shall focus first upon the beginning of the sibling relationship—the arrival of a sibling and the changes in family relationships which follow this event. A close examination of this example of one kind of potentially stressful change, and its effects on an individual within a family, raises many more general issues about the links between environmental change and development, and about how we should study such processes. Second I shall consider what evidence we have for changes in the nature of the sibling relationship during the life span, and the bearing this evidence may have on the arguments put forward against the "primacy" of early childhood experiences, and for the significance of nonnormative events.

## II. The Arrival of a Sibling

The birth of a sibling can hardly be classed as a nonnormative life event since 80% of children grow up with siblings. But, while it is not an unusual event, clinicians have long regarded the birth of a sibling as a stressful event which can have long-lasting effects on the personality and emotional development of an individual (Aarons, 1954; Black & Sturge, 1979; Moore, 1969; Petty, 1953). (It should be noted that many of the events classified by life-span researchers as nonnormative, such as divorce, marital separation, or job loss, can hardly nowadays be considered uncommon.)

This view of the long-lasting nature of the effects of a sibling birth was based largely on clinical case histories and retrospective material. However, in the last few years systematic prospective studies of the response of children to the changes accompanying the birth of a sibling have been conducted. This research has shown that the effects on children are striking and of considerable developmental importance. The findings have, moreover, a number of more general implications for our understanding of the processes involved in the relation between development in early childhood and the experience of stress and change.

The studies show, first, that there are marked changes in children's behavior immediately following the birth of a sibling. Increases in demanding, difficult behavior, in tearfulness, clinging, and withdrawal are common, as are increases in problems with sleeping, feeding, and toilet training. However, developmental *advances* following the birth of a sibling are also reported to be common (Dunn

& Kendrick, 1982a; Nadelman & Begun, 1982; Trause, Boslett, Voos, Rudd, Klaus, & Kennell, 1978). Evidence for such advances needs replication; however, it seems reasonably well established that children often show increased independence and maturity, insisting on feeding or dressing themselves, showing new powers of independent play and mastery. While it has been argued previously by clinicians that mildly stressful situations can produce relatively mature behavior and developmental change as well as "retrogressive" change, there has been until now little convincing documentation of such developmental advances. The findings from the sibling studies provide strong support for the general argument. Another example from the research into early childhood is the demonstration by Emde and colleagues that weaning from the breast can be associated with rapid developmental change (Emde, Gaensbauer, & Harmon, 1976).

The sibling studies not only document the incidence of changed behavior following the sibling birth, they also raise questions about the processes underlying both the developmental advances and the problem behavior that so frequently accompany the sibling birth. One detailed study of the response of children to the sibling birth allows us to look closely at the nature of the changes in the firstborn children's behavior, and in their lives and relationships (Dunn & Kendrick, 1982a). The findings show that there were marked changes in the interaction between mother and firstborn child following the arrival of the sibling. It was not simply that the children became more difficult or withdrawn, but that their relationships with their parents changed in some distinctive ways. The mothers became less attentive and playful, and more punitive and restraining. They were less likely to initiate interaction with their firstborn; there was, in fact, a shift in the balance of responsibility for beginning the interaction, with the children becoming primarily responsible. These changes in mother–child interaction may well be of real significance in the increase in problem behavior shown by the children.

The "direction of effects" here is of course unclear. It could be that the increase in negative and demanding behavior by the children was the major cause of the changes in maternal behavior, or vice versa. The problems in making casual inferences are obvious. However, the analyses suggest that the changes in both maternal and child behavior may be important. For instance, a comparison of mother–child interaction at times when the mother was busy with the new baby and when she was not showed that, on the one hand, incidents of "deliberate naughtiness" by the children increased threefold when the mother was busy with the baby and that at such times confrontation escalated, but on the other hand, the decrease in maternal attentiveness and play with the firstborn occurred at times when the new baby was *not* present or awake.

There is a general point of some importance here. Studies of the response of children to stressful situations suggest that in any attempt to understand the processes linking the event and its outcome it is important to take account of the changes in parent–child interaction which accompany the event (Rutter, 1981; Dunn, 1984). It is interesting too that there is a striking parallel here with the results of studies of the response of infant rhesus monkeys to experiences of separation from their mothers. Hinde and colleagues found that every independent variable which affected infant rhesus depression also affected mother–infant interaction (Hinde & McGinnis, 1977).

After the sibling birth there were changes not only in the playful and punitive interactions between mother and firstborn, but in the nature of conversations between them. With the arrival of the sibling, discussions of the feelings, needs, and intentions of someone other than the child significantly increased. For the first time in the child's life, the wants, actions, and intentions of someone other than the child himself were extensively discussed, and in such discussions the firstborn children frequently began to use new terms and dimensions of self-categorization. The dramatic change in the discussion of self and other is surely an important transformation in the child's egocentric world, and may indeed contribute to the developmental changes in the child's behavior.

This suggestion that the changes in discussion of self and other may not only reflect but also contribute to the changes in the children's behavior raises a further question about the cognitive processes mediating the developmental changes which accompany the sibling birth. The implication is that even with such young children, reflection on the nature of self is of real significance in the children's developmental advances. How far then is the child's interpretation of the meaning of a major change implicated in the disturbed behavior? How does the parents' interpretation of the event, and of the child's response to it, influence the child's reaction? Analysis of family conversation with slightly older siblings shows vividly not only how common it is for a mother to give a running commentary interpreting the behavior of each child to the other, but also how closely each child monitors and responds to the conversation between the other two family members. It is clear that we should take seriously the point that very early in a child's life he attends to and reflects upon other people's perception and interpretation of his own and others' behavior; we should examine just how significant these "attributions" may be in development. The attribution and family discussion of "cause" which accompany changes within the family may be of considerable importance even with children as young as 2 years.

In addition to these changes in the patterns of interaction between mother and firstborn child, for many children major "lifestyle" changes accompanied the arrival of the sibling. In the 2 to 3 weeks following the birth, the firstborn children were frequently looked after by people other than their usual caregivers; they were taken out more, and the families were visited by other people more. Many of the mothers attributed both the problem behavior and the developmental advances in their firstborn to the change in caregiving that the child experienced at the sibling birth. It is certainly possible that a change in the child's accustomed routine and in what is expected of him by others might lead to his discovering that he can indeed master certain problems and that such mastery is enjoyable.

It is argued elsewhere (Dunn & Kendrick, 1982a) that there are a number of different ways of explaining these effects. One possibility is that, with a different caregiver and routine, different requirements are placed on the child; another possibility is that different beliefs and expectations about the child lead the caregiver to interpret the child's behavior very differently from the mother, and to attribute different intentions to him. The explanation for the changes in the child's behavior lies, in both these interpretations, with the moulding by the *adult* of the child's behavior. Detailed study of the caregiver and child in the days following the sibling birth is needed to assess these different possibilities. The changes in the *mother's* behavior toward her firstborn following the birth are also of course significant here. In the study, many of the mothers themselves commented on the changes in their own behavior—the changes in what they expected and demanded from the child as the following statement from one mother illustrates: "I'm expecting him to play more on his own than he used to—I'm not giving him so much attention. What he finds as occupations tend to be the 'come and stop me' ones. I try not to let it escalate, but quite often it does" (Dunn & Kendrick, 1982a, p. 55).

A third interpretation is that the changed behavior of the child is a response by the *child* to his or her altered world. The argument here is that by changing a child's world you not only draw his attention to new possibilities in that world, but also to new possibilities in himself as an actor in that world. With either of the first two types of change in the caregiver, the consequence is likely to be a change in the child's feelings, beliefs, and ways of acting in the world. Certainly the birth of a sibling is likely to involve a change of a symbolic kind in the child's conception of himself within his family. The analysis of conversations before and after the birth has already shown that such changes do take place. It is also possible that the emotional experiences that the child goes through at the time of the birth may themselves contribute to a heightened sense of self-awareness and thus to the developmental changes in behavior. Izard (1977) has argued very plausibly for the crucial part played by the emotions of shyness and anger in the process of differentiation of self and other: "Anger increases the infant's opportunities to sense self-as-causal-agent and hence to experience self as separate, distinct, and capable" (p. 398). We have no evidence on which to judge whether such processes may be involved in the developmental and behavioral changes following the sibling birth. What is clear, however, from the sibling research is, first, that young children are very susceptible to changes in their world, and, second, that such changes are accompanied by major changes in the children's interaction with their parents and their reflective discussion of themselves and others. Such findings highlight the importance emphasized by the life-span psychologists of research at different levels of analysis. To understand the changes in the children's behavior which follow the birth we must take into account the changes in the child's experience at many different levels, from the comparatively gross changes in life style and social experience, to changes in the sensitive responsiveness of the mothers, and in the family discussion of other people, as well as the symbolic dethronement which has been the focus of much psychoanalytic writing. To make any progress in clarifying the relative importance of these different kinds of changes in influencing an individual's development, we will have to try to understand the relationship between the changes at the different levels. At present we are very far from such understanding.

The third issue highlighted by the sibling research is the significance of individual differences in children's responses to major changes in their environment. The individual differences in children's responses to the constellation of events surrounding the birth were marked, and the nature of the reaction was closely linked to individual differences in children's temperament assessed before the birth of the sibling (Dunn & Kendrick, 1982a). For instance, children who were very "negative in mood" before the birth were more likely to increase in withdrawal and in sleeping problems after the birth. Those who were rated as "withdrawing" before the birth were less likely than the rest of the sample to be affectionate toward and interested in the baby. Second, individual differences in the quality of the mother–child relationship were also important. In families in which tension and conflict between mother and firstborn were high before the birth, the escalation of conflict between mother and firstborn after the birth was particularly marked. Third, the children's relationships with their fathers were important. In those families in which the firstborn had an intense relationship with the father, the increase in confrontation and the drop in maternal attentiveness were less marked.

Clearly other family relationships may well be important too. It is likely that the quality of the marital relationship and the child's relationship with its grandparents were of considerable importance in the sample of Dunn and Kendrick; in further studies these should certainly be examined. In the Cambridge study most of the firstborn had close relationships with their grandparents, whom they frequently saw, and it was usually the grandparents who took care of the children when the mother was in the hospital. This may well have "buffered" the children against some of the trauma of separation from the mother, and could explain why few differences were found between the reaction of children whose mothers delivered the second child at home, and those who went to the hospital. The role of support systems in such family changes is obviously an important area of enquiry. I would argue that to understand fully how such support systems affect the child's behavior and development we need to document not just the range and availability of support, but the details of how the family interaction patterns are affected by the presence or absence of such support. We need to know, for instance, whether the influence of father involvement on the changes in mother–firstborn interaction is a direct or an indirect one. A direct effect would be, for instance, that after the sibling birth the father's close relationship with the first child intensifies, and as a consequence the child shows a less pronounced increase in demanding and difficult behavior to the mother. An indirect effect would be that the fathers who were intensely involved with their firstborn also provide more support for their wives, and that this support contributes to a relatively smooth passage for mother and firstborn after the sibling birth.

The results of the Cambridge study reinforce the argument that the consequences of stressful life events are closely related to individual differences in personality and family relationships, and that the significance of such events for the child's development will only be fully understood when these differences in patterns of family interaction are taken into account. The sibling study shows moreover that these individual differences in the firstborn's response to the birth are not simply of short-term importance. It is true that many of the problem behaviors which increased at the birth did disappear over the next few months (Dunn & Kendrick, 1982a). However it is also the case that the individual differences in the affectionate interest which the children showed toward their newborn siblings were remarkably stable over the next few years. Individual differences in the children's behavior toward their siblings were marked over the year following the birth, and these differences were linked to the initial response of the children to the newborn baby. Not only were those children who had shown interest and affection toward the baby in the second and third week after the birth more friendly toward their siblings 14 months later, but also their siblings were more friendly to them than the younger siblings in the rest of the sample. And when the firstborns were interviewed 3 years later, as 6 year olds, those who had shown much positive interest and affection toward their newborn siblings talked with much more affection about their siblings than those who had not initially been affectionate (Stilwell & Dunn, 1984).

The detailed study of the beginnings of the sibling relationship does then highlight a number of more general developmental issues about the nature of children's responses to stressful events or changes in their lives. These can be summarized in the following points.

1. Such events are likely to have marked effects on children's behavior.
2. The events may also be associated with changes in the parent–child relationship.
3. It is these changes in the parent–child relationship which may mediate the effects on the children; any attempt to understand the consequences of stressful life events and the processes involved must study the mutual influence of family relationships.
4. Individual differences in the nature of children's responses to the events are marked, and are linked to personality differences, and to the quality of the

parent–child relationship before the event. Again to understand the origin of the individual differences the children must be studied in a *family* context.

## III. Sibling Relationships in Later Life: Critical Incidents and the Importance of Early Experience

Individual differences in reaction to the arrival of a sibling showed, as we have seen, a consistent relation to the striking differences in the quality of the relationship which developed between the siblings over the year following the birth. What kind of continuity do these differences show as the children grow up, and how does the nature of the sibling relationship change with adolescence and adulthood?

We have pitifully few data with which to address these questions. Studies are frequently based on retrospective or clinical data and longitudinal research is rare. Such evidence that we do have is usefully reviewed in a recent volume edited by Lamb and Sutton-Smith [1982; see especially the excellent chapter on sibling relationships in adulthood by Cicirelli (1982) and that on middle childhood by Bryant (1982)]. Since these chapters summarize the literature I shall not attempt a general review here but will focus instead upon the findings that relate to the particular orientation of the life-span psychologists and to the issues raised in the discussion of the research on the early sibling relationship. In particular, the significance of critical or stressful events and the question of whether the experiences of early childhood hold special significance for the course of the sibling relationship later in life will be examined.

In the early childhood years the distinctive features of the interaction between siblings—a very high frequency of imitation of older by younger, a close monitoring of the other child's behavior, marked and uninhibited expression of both positive and negative feelings, close matching of interests and cooperation in play, and a remarkably sophisticated understanding of the other's interests and feelings—all suggest that siblings may well be of considerable importance as an influence in domains of social understanding, as well as in mastery of the object world. It is clear that modeling, tuition, and emotional support as well as direct aggression, rivalry, and self-comparison are all important processes in the early years.

We know little about developmental changes in the sibling relationship during the middle childhood years, and about how the quality of the sibling relationship affects the way in which children cope with the various developmental tasks they face. We are ignorant about very basic questions such as how much time children aged 6–12 spend with their siblings, or what kinds of activities they engage in together. The findings of the only study to date which has followed siblings from infancy to childhood suggest that there is considerable stability in individual differences in the friendliness and aggression that children show toward their siblings over this period (Stilwell & Dunn, 1984). This finding is particularly striking given that the 6½-year-old firstborns had all entered the wider world of school and peers, and had made the transition to a whole new set of relationships and experiences, yet their relationship with their siblings had remained in affective terms very stable. The sample studied was, however, small, and the findings need replication. Whether the quality of the sibling relationship affects the way in which a child manages the transition to school is just one of the questions to which we do not as yet have an answer. Small scale studies suggest that there is no simple relationship between the quality of children's relations with siblings and with peers, but this is clearly an area where more research is needed.

Social comparison processes as well as ambivalence, rivalry, and conflict apparently continue in middle childhood, but support and caretaking seem also to be common (Bryant, 1982). It should be noted, however, that the research strategies employed in most studies do not make it possible to examine with much precision the processes involved. Take for instance the question of the extent to which social comparison processes are important. In studies such as that of Koch (1960), children were explicitly asked to compare themselves with their siblings. The answers are striking and vivid but, while it seems very plausible that such processes are of real significance developmentally, this approach cannot address the question of how far children spontaneously make such comparisons, or how far parents contribute to such comparisons. In contrast, the studies by Patterson and colleagues, employing fine grain observation of family interaction, demonstrate unequivocally the crucial role played by siblings in shaping aggressive behavior (Patterson, 1975; Patterson & Cobb, 1971). Patterson's work shows not only that rivalry and conflict persist into middle childhood, but that most conflict within the family involves both parents and siblings. It is research of this kind which will clarify both the nature and extent of sibling influence in middle childhood, and the processes involved. One other study which has systematically examined both maternal and sibling behavior—this time using a structured setting—again shows that the quality of the sibling relationship continues to be closely linked with the quality of the mother's relationship with each child (Bryant & Crockenberg, 1980).

For adolescence our information is even more incomplete. Without systematic prospective studies we do not know how the transition to adolescence affects the nature of the relationship, and/or whether individual differences in the quality of the sibling relationship persist in a relatively stable manner. Interview studies show that fifth and sixth graders (W. Furman, personal communication, 1982) and adolescents do frequently refer to the importance of their relations with their siblings (A. Peterson, personal communication, 1983), and we know from anecdotal, clinical, and literary sources that in many families the relationship between adolescent siblings can be of very great significance. The relationship between the Brontës provides a particularly vivid example (Gaskell, 1975). It is an example which illustrates dramatically the importance of considering the sibling relationship within the framework of the family and the broader social circumstances in which the young people were growing up. To understand the intense relationship between the Brontë siblings it is clear that the isolated circumstances in which the family lived, the repeated crises of illness and death within the family, the distinctive relationships of the children with their father, as well as the extraordinary talents and particular personalities of the sisters and their brother should all be considered.

Perhaps the clearest systematic account of the significance of middle childhood and adolescence in the sibling relationship comes from a study of adult siblings in which the quality of the individual's earlier relationships was explored in in-depth group discussions. Ross and Milgram (1982) worked with 75 adult participants ranging in age from 22 to 93 years. The discussions were held in groups of 4–6, and the individuals explored their sense of closeness to their siblings, their feelings of rivalry, and the changes in their feelings over time. Individuals were all white and middle-class. It was clear from the discussions that adolescence was, as Ross and Milgram comment:

> A time in which siblings grew together, forging their identities by similarity and contrast. Inspiring and teaching each other, modelling . . . exploring issues through intense discussion, even providing dates for each other, were all relatively frequent. Through these interactions close personal relationships between siblings developed. (p. 230)

In contrast, Ross and Milgram found that closeness rarely *originated* in adulthood. However, studies of sibling relationships in adulthood do consistently report that closeness is maintained through adulthood, and that especially in late adulthood many siblings are frequently very close (see Cicirelli, 1979; Cumming & Schneider, 1961; Larerty, 1962). For instance, Cicirelli found in a study of middle-aged adults that 68% felt close or extremely close to their siblings, and only 5% not close at all. Several studies suggest that this closeness between adult siblings increases with age (though none of these studies is longitudinal). In a study of individuals over 60 years, Cicirelli (1979) found 83% felt close or extremely close to their siblings. There are some differences in the frequency with which extreme closeness is reported in adulthood. Adams (1968), for instance, reports a lower instance than Cicirelli in young adults and more marked differences in the frequency with which rivalrous feelings are reported. Only 2% of the individuals in Cicirelli's study reported frequent feelings of rivalry, and Cicirelli argues plausibly that greater maturity of outlook and limited frequency of contact probably contribute to this decrease in rivalry with age. However Ross and Milgram (1982) report from their in-depth discussions a much higher frequency of rivalry between adult siblings than that found in studies using more conventional interview techniques. In Ross and Milgram's study 45% of individuals considered rivalry active between themselves and their siblings. Ross and

Milgram's findings suggest that where rivalrous feelings persisted in adulthood this frequently reflected a pattern of family interaction which continued into adulthood from childhood. Rivalry apparently is "reactivated" in adulthood when the individual's relationship with the parent is directly involved, for instance, when issues of inheritance or the care of the parents arise.

These differences between the studies may reflect differences in methods, or differences in the willingness of different cohorts to express their feelings about their siblings. But the striking findings remain clear. Although there is a decline in contact with siblings in late adulthood, there is no decrease in the closeness of feelings expressed. Indeed, there is almost certainly an increase.

What accounts for this closeness between siblings in adulthood? Where does it originate and why does it persist? It must be emphasized that we have no longitudinal data to help us answer such questions. However, two themes consistently stand out in the research on adult siblings, whether it is research based on interview, in-depth group discussion, or clinical material, and both themes relate in an important way to the orientation of the life-span psychologists. The first theme concerns the importance of the early experience of the siblings together. In Ross and Milgram's study (1982) the participants consistently maintained that the origin of the affectionate support and closeness between them and their siblings lay in their shared experiences in early childhood and adolescence—their experience as part of a close family. Common shared family experiences—eating together, going to church together—were frequently cited, and closeness was apparently enhanced if young siblings had shared bedrooms, had gone to school together, and had spent time together in groups. Shared experiences in adolescence increased such closeness, but, as we have noted, it was very rare for closeness to begin in adulthood.

This consistent reference to the significance of early shared experience, even by adults in their 70s and 80s, is very striking. Whatever reservations we may have about the methods of the studies, or the restricted nature of the samples, or the limitations of their particular historical setting, the implications of the findings—that what happens in the family context in the early years is of real significance to individuals at the end of the life span—must be taken seriously.

A second theme that stands out from the research on adult siblings concerns the significance of critical incidents in the lives of the siblings as events which bring about important changes in the sibling relationship. Throughout the life span, from early childhood to old age, such incidents apparently play an important part in the dynamics of the sibling relationship, increasing either closeness or conflict between the individuals. For the great majority of individuals in Ross and Milgram's study (1982) both "normative" incidents (events which occur at the expected time in the life cycle such as death of a parent in adulthood, marriage of a sibling in young adulthood) and "idiosyncratic" or unexpected events brought about changes in the relationship. Geographical moves away from or near to the sibling were largely seen as unemotional events, but resulted in decreased closeness or increased closeness, respectively. Other types of incidents frequently produced much more marked emotional changes in the relationship, but the nature of the change differed very much in different families. Marriage of the sibling, for instance, produced negative changes in the sibling relationship for 69% of the individuals but enhanced closeness in 31%. Sickness of the parents had negative consequences for 56%, but positive consequences for 44% of siblings. When death of a parent occurred at an expected time, the siblings were usually brought closer together; shared grief increased their feelings of closeness. Death of a parent when the individuals were children or adolescents produced much more complex reactions, but again the sharing of pain and confusion had positive consequences for the sibling relationship in most families. The consequences of sibling death had unequivocally positive consequences for the relationship between the remaining siblings, but the divorce of parents had a much more mixed response, with increased conflict between some siblings and increased closeness between others. Any incidents between the siblings which involved disagreements over life styles, morals, or value judgments were frequently accompanied by extreme emotional reactions; those in which parental favoritism was implicated generated especially violent and long-term feelings of resentment against the sibling.

These findings on the importance of critical events are echoed in other studies. Bank and Kahn's (1982) study of the intense loyalty which some siblings develop provides many vivid illustrations of the significance of such events, and of the supportive response of individuals to their siblings at such times. The following quotation comes from two middle-aged brothers from a group of four who were extremely close.

> Youngest brother, "There's four brothers, going through life. Instead of falling apart, as many would do at a crisis—like the death of our mother or the crumbling of our father as a 'figurehead' of the family—we didn't. We complement each other. If one is down, the others are up. At no time would all four of us be down, because whoever might be down at a particular time it will be recognised by the others, and they would help to get him up."
>
> Second oldest brother, "Whether that be financially or spiritually."
>
> Youngest brother, "Right! Regardless of what it is. For example, I know as I sit right here, if I ever got in any trouble, the first ones I go to is my brothers. I don't call my father. I don't call my in-laws. I don't call my wife. I call my brothers." (p. 255)

Bank and Kahn attribute special significance to loss or inaccessibility of a parent in the development of intense loyalty between siblings (Bank & Kahn, 1982). Townsend's (1957) work showed that in old age death of the mother frequently led to a change in sibling relationships, with older sisters assuming the mother's role in caring for the brothers in the family. Death of a brother's wife also led to increased closeness, and often led to a sister assuming the duties of the dead wife. Such incidents do then presumably contribute to the growth of the closeness between siblings in late adulthood and old age. The origins of such closeness may well lie in the early relationship between the siblings as children, but the dramas and stresses of adult life clearly help to maintain and enhance the siblings' affection for one another.

It is notable in Ross and Milgram's (1982) study that very similar incidents resulted in such strikingly different consequences for different sibling pairs. Ross and Milgram attribute the different responses to differences in the quality of the sibling relationship before the critical incident. If a sibling relationship was characterized by conflict and resentment, a critical incident frequently exacerbated the conflict. Where siblings were close and affectionate, a similar incident apparently increased the closeness. The findings illustrate an important general point. I have argued that young children's responses to stressful events in early childhood are closely linked to individual differences not only in children's personality and family relationships before the event, but in each family member's response to the others' altered behavior after the event. Family relationships before and after the arrival of a sibling were critically linked to the nature of the children's response to the event. Ross and Milgram's account of the association between individual differences in the relationship between adult siblings before a critical incident and the later consequences of the incident thus parallels the results from the study of Dunn and Kendrick (1982a) of the very beginnings of the sibling relationship.

To understand the significance of critical incidents for the dynamics of the sibling relationship it is then clear that we need careful study of the quality of the relationship between the siblings and between parents and siblings before the incident. Bank and Kahn (1982) argue that the personalities of the individual siblings as well as the quality of the parental monitoring of the sibling relationship in childhood and adolescence are of major importance in accounting for differences in the way in which the siblings' relationship develops in adulthood. It is the significance of the quality of the particular sibling relationship, rather than the sex of the individuals or the age gap between them, that stands out in the accounts of the consequences of critical incidents for adult siblings.

This is an important point. The recent observational research on very young siblings suggests strongly that to understand the nature and extent of sibling influence in childhood, the individual differences in the affective quality of the relationship, rather than simply the variables of sex and ordinal status, must be considered. This has been shown to be important for fifth–sixth grade siblings (Furman, personal communication, 1982), and seems likely to be equally true for the research on adult siblings. However, most writing on sibling influence in adulthood had focused on sibling constellation variables rather than on differences in the affective quality of the relationship—this in spite of the argument cogently put by Schooler (1972) that the birth order literature suffers from major methodological shortcomings and that most birth order effects may be spurious.

While much of the research investigating sibling constellation effects remains difficult to interpret in a coherent way, two sets of interesting findings reported by Cicirelli concerning sex constellation variables in adult siblings deserve comment. In one study of 200 elderly subjects, Cicirelli (1982) found that both sex of sibling and the quality of the sibling relationship were linked to the maintenance of an internal locus of control. First an external locus of control was more common with individuals who had several brothers, while an internal locus of control was more common with individuals who had fewer brothers. Second, individuals with a close sibling relationship were more likely to have an internal locus of control. Those who had frequent contact, felt close to, and shared values with their sibling felt in greater control of events and more able to act to improve their conditions. Of course we cannot be sure of the direction of effects in this case; however, in another study Cicirelli (1982) reported links between the emotional security of elderly men and women, and the sex of their siblings. Men with more sisters expressed greater emotional security and happiness. Women with more sisters were more concerned with helping others, maintaining social relationships, and were better able to deal with criticism from others. This work and that of Troll (1975) suggest that sisters are particularly important in the provision of emotional support in adulthood.

What we now need is research which will enable us to disentangle the salience of past factors—early parental reactions, early differences in status, early conflict—from current factors—current economic or marital status—in siblings of differing sex and age gap. An approach such as that of Brown and Harris' (1978) study of past and current variables affecting depression might begin to clarify the issues; however, to answer questions about process in family interaction and the mutual influence of family relationships, there can be no substitute for a combination of sensitive in-depth interviewing and direct observation of a longitudinal sample.

## IV. Conclusion

The detailed studies of very young siblings and the cross-sectional studies of adults do suggest the following general points, which relate to the approach of life-span psychologists.

1. Differences in the quality of the early sibling relationship do apparently persist into middle childhood, and retrospective material shows that individuals do attribute their closeness to their siblings in adulthood to this early relationship within a family context. It is important to pursue this finding longitudinally. The sibling relationship is of major importance to the great majority of individuals in old age, and its salience needs to be better understood.

2. Critical incidents in the lives of individuals are of considerable significance

in the dynamics of the sibling relationship. How such incidents affect the sibling relationship appears to be related to the quality of the sibling relationship before the event. The processes involved in the response of siblings to such incidents is certainly worth further study. It is clear from the study of the response of children to the arrival of a sibling that, in childhood at least, many different processes may be involved and these will require study at very different levels of analysis. The research on very young siblings illustrates the general point that the significance of "critical incidents" cannot be understood without reference to individual differences in personality and family relationships.

3. The sibling relationship must be studied within a family context, and explored with reference to an individual's relationships with other family members. In both early childhood and adulthood the quality of the relationship between siblings is linked to the parents' relationship with the siblings, and vice versa.

4. The developmental research on siblings which is discussed in this article comes solely from studies in the United States and Great Britain. Anthropological research in other cultures demonstrates how misleading it may be if broad generalizations are drawn from such a narrow source. Weisner (1982) argues that the norm throughout most of the cultures of the world is that "brothers and sisters are decisive participants in each other's fate concerning sexual access, marriage or property" (p. 323). He suggests that the distinctive features of middle-class American siblings are a product of a particular set of family pressures, and urges us to broaden the perspective within which we study siblings. It is a message which we should certainly take seriously.

# References

Aarons, A. Z. Effect of the birth of a sister on a boy in his fourth year. *Archivos de Pediatria*, 1954, **71**, 54–76.

Abramovitch, R., Corter, C., & Lando, B. Sibling interaction in the home. *Child Development*, 1979, **50**, 997–1003.

Abramovitch, R., Pepler, D., & Corter, C. Patterns of sibling interaction among preschool-age children. In M. E. Lamb & B. Sutton-Smith (Eds.), *Sibling relationships: Their nature and significance across the lifespan.* Hillsdale, New Jersey: Erlbaum, 1982.

Adams, B. N. *Kinship in an urban setting.* Chicago: Markham, 1968.

Adler, A. Characteristics of the first, second and third child. *Children*, 1928, **3**(5), 14.

Adler, A. *Understanding human nature.* New York: Premier Books, 1959.

Baltes, P. B., Reese, H. W., & Lipsitt, L. P. Life-span developmental psychology. *Annual Review of Psychology*, 1980, **31**, 65–110.

Bank, S. P., & Kahn, M. D. *The sibling bond.* New York: Basic Books, 1982.

Black, D., & Sturge, C. The young child and his siblings. In J. G. Howells (Ed.), *Perspectives in infant psychiatry.* New York: Brunner/Mazel, 1979.

Bossard, N. H., & Boll, E. S. *The large family system.* Philadelphia: University of Pennsylvania Press, 1959.

Brim, O. G., Jr. Family structure and sex role learning by children. *Sociometry,* 1958, **21,** 1–16.

Brown, G., & Harris, T. *Social origins of depression.* London: Tavistock, 1978.

Bryant, B. K. Sibling relationships in middle childhood. In M. E. Lamb & B. Sutton-Smith (Eds.), *Sibling relationships: Their nature and significance across the lifespan.* Hillsdale, New Jersey: Erlbaum, 1982.

Bryant, B. K., & Crockenberg, S. Correlates and dimensions of prosocial behaviour: A study of female siblings with their mothers. *Child Development,* 1980, **51,** 529–544.

Cicirelli, V. G. Effects of sibling structure and interaction on children's categorization style. *Developmental Psychology,* 1973, **9**(1), 132–139.

Cicirelli, V. G. Effects of mother and older sibling on the problem solving behaviour of the younger child. *Developmental Psychology,* 1975, **11,** 749–756.

Cicirelli, V. G. Children's school grades and sibling structure. *Psychological Reports,* 1977, **41**(3), 1055–1058.

Cicirelli, V. G. *Social services for the elderly in relation to the kin network.* Report to the NRTA-AARP Andrus Foundation, May 31, 1979.

Cicirelli, V. G. Sibling influence throughout the life span. In M. E. Lamb & B. Sutton-Smith (Eds.), *Sibling relationships: Their nature and significance across the life-span.* Hillsdale, New Jersey: Erlbaum, 1982.

Cumming, E., & Schneider, D. Sibling solidarity: A property of American kinship. *American Anthropologist,* 1961, **63,** 498–507.

Dunn, J. Commentary: Stress, development, and family interaction. In M. Rutter, C. Izard, & P. Read (Eds.), *Depression in childhood: Developmental perspectives.* New York: Guilford, 1984, in press.

Dunn, J., & Kendrick, C. *Siblings: Love, envy and understanding.* Cambridge, Massachusetts: Harvard University Press, 1982. (a)

Dunn, J., & Kendrick, C. Temperamental differences, family relationships, and young children's response to change within the family. In *Temperamental differences in infants and young children* (Ciba Foundation Symposium 89). London: Pitman, 1982. (b)

Emde, R. N., Gaensbauer, T., & Harmon, R. J. Emotional expression in infancy: A biobehavioural study. *Psychological Issues,* **10**(1), Monograph 37. New York: International Universities Press, 1976.

Gaskell, E. *The life of Charlotte Brontë.* Harmondsworth, England: Penguin Books, 1975.

Hinde, R. A., & McGinnis, L. Some factors influencing the effects of temporary mother–infant separation: Some experiments with rhesus monkeys. *Psychological Medicine,* 1977, **7,** 197–212.

Izard, C. E. On the ontogenesis of emotions and emotion–cognition relationships in infancy. In M. Lewis & L. A. Rosenblum (Eds.), *The development of affect.* New York: Plenum, 1977.

Koch, H. The relation of certain formal attributes of siblings to attitudes held toward each other and toward their parents. *Monograph of the Society for Research in Child Development,* 1960, **25** (No.4).

Lamb, M. E., & Sutton-Smith, B. (Eds.). *Sibling relationships: Their nature and significance across the lifespan.* Hillsdale, New Jersey: Erlbaum, 1982.

Larerty, R. Reactivation of sibling rivalry in older people. *Social Work,* 1962, **7,** 23–30.

Levy, D. M. Rivalry between children of the same family. *Child Study,* 1934, **11,** 233–261.

Levy, D. M. Studies in sibling rivalry. *American Orthopsychiatric Association Research Monographs,* 1937, No. 2.

Moore, T. Stress in normal childhood. *Human Relations,* 1969, **22**(3), 235–250.

Nadelman, L., & Begun, A. The effect of the newborn on the older sibling: Mothers' questionnaires.

In M. E. Lamb & B. Sutton-Smith (Eds.), *Sibling relationships: Their nature and significance across the lifespan.* Hillsdale, New Jersey: Erlbaum, 1982.

Patterson, G. R. The aggressive child: Victim and architect of a coercive system. In L. A. Hamerlynck, E. J. Marsh, & L. C. Hardy (Eds.), *Behavior modification and families.* New York: Brunner/Mazel, 1975.

Patterson, G. R., & Cobb, J. A. A dyadic analysis of "aggressive" behaviors. In J. P. Hill (Ed.), *Minnesota symposium on child psychology* (Vol. 5). Minneapolis: University of Minnesota Press, 1971.

Petty, T. A. The tragedy of Humpty Dumpty. *Psychoanalytic Study of the Child,* 1953, **8,** 404–422.

Ross, H. G., & Milgram, J. I. Important variables in adult sibling relationships: A qualitative study. In M. E. Lamb & B. Sutton-Smith (Eds.), *Sibling relationships: Their nature and significance across the lifespan.* Hillsdale, New Jersey: Erlbaum, 1982.

Rowe, D. C., & Plomin, R. The importance of nonshared ($E_1$) environmental influences in behavioural development. *Developmental Psychology,* 1981, **17,** 517–531.

Rutter, M. Stress, coping and development: Some issues and some questions. *Journal of Child Psychology and Psychiatry,* 1981, **22,** 323–356.

Scarr, S. W., & Grajek, S. Similarities and differences among siblings. In M. E. Lamb & B. Sutton-Smith (Eds.), *Sibling relationships: Their nature and significance across the lifespan.* Hillsdale, New Jersey: Erlbaum, 1982.

Schooler, C. Birth order effects: Not here, not now! *Psychological Bulletin,* 1972, **78,** 161–175.

Stilwell, R., & Dunn, J. *Continuities in sibling relationships: Patterns of aggression and friendliness.* Submitted, 1984.

Sutton-Smith, B., & Rosenberg, B. G. *The sibling.* New York: Holt Rinehart & Winston, 1970.

Townsend, P. *The family life of old people: An inquiry in East London.* New York: Free Press, 1957.

Trause, M. A., Boslett, M., Voos, D., Rudd, C., Klaus, M., & Kennell, J. A birth in the hospital: The effect on the sibling. *Birth and the Family Journal,* 1978, **5,** 207–210.

Troll, L. E. *Early and middle adulthood.* Monterey, California: Brooks/Cole, 1975.

Wagner, M. E., Schubert, H. J. P., & Schubert, D. S. P. Sibship-constellation effect on psychological development, creativity, and health. *Advances in Child Development and Behaviour,* 1979, **14,** 57–148.

Weisner, T. S. Sibling interdependence and child caretaking: A cross-cultural view. In M. E. Lamb & B. Sutton-Smith (Eds.), *Sibling relationships: Their nature and significance across the lifespan.* Hillsdale, New Jersey: Erlbaum, 1982.

Zajonc, R. B., & Markus, G. B. Birth order and intellectual development. *Psychological Review,* 1975, **82**(1), 74–88.

# Peer Interaction and Communication:
# A Life-Span Perspective

*Joan E. Norris*

UNIVERSITY OF GUELPH

GUELPH, ONTARIO, CANADA


*and*


*Kenneth H. Rubin*

UNIVERSITY OF WATERLOO

WATERLOO, ONTARIO, CANADA

## Abstract

The role of social interaction in human development has long been considered significant. However, researchers have tended to focus on the nature, function, and consequences of social contact in

LIFE-SPAN DEVELOPMENT
AND BEHAVIOR, VOL. 6

**355**

childhood rather than in later life. In this article we explore the strengths and limitations, from a life-span perspective, of research and theory concerning one type of social interaction, peer interaction. The opening section provides a state-of-the-art picture of the functional significance of peer interaction across the life span. The promotive aspect of peers is examined as well as the consequences of peer deprivation. In the second section, the life-span development of two components of social competence, the breadth of the social repertoire and sensitivity to the social context, are examined. In the third part of this article, one essential aspect of social functioning, communication, is discussed. Research on both quantitative and qualitative changes throughout the life cycle is examined. Finally, the article ends with a discussion of three potentially useful methodologies for the life-span study of social competence: hypothetical–reflective, observational, and simulated situation approaches. The strengths and weaknesses of each approach are examined. The article concludes with a call for more qualitatively oriented research, particularly with adults, toward our understanding of life cycle changes in social functioning.

## I. Introduction

In recent years the nature, function, and consequences of social interaction in childhood and adolescence have received a great deal of attention from social scientists. Of particular concern has been the role of peer relations in promoting normal social development during childhood. For example, *psychologists* have postulated that the quantity and quality of peer interactions in early and middle childhood have causal bearing on the development of social, social–cognitive, and cognitive skills (for a recent review, see Hartup, 1983). *Biologists, ethologists,* and *sociobiologists,* who are interested in individual adaptation and the evolutionary sources of social and cognitive abilities, also have stressed the importance of peer interaction. They have noted that contact with peers, especially when it necessitates the need to resolve effectively problems inherent in social exchanges, elicits the development of general intelligence (Hogan, Johnson, & Emler, 1978; Humphrey, 1976; Kummer, 1971). *Sociologists,* as well, have indicated that peer interaction in childhood influences the acquisition of cultural roles, rules, and values (Berger & Luckmann, 1966; Goffman, 1958; Mead, 1932).

Despite this breadth of interest in peer interaction during childhood, fewer researchers have been concerned with the development of peer relationships throughout the life span. We know very little, for example, about the peer experiences of young, middle-aged, and older adults, although researchers have provided information about how often and with whom adults interact socially (for recent reviews, see Kahn & Antonucci, 1980; Tigges, Cowgill, & Habenstein, 1980). Take, for example, the social interaction literature concerned with the aged individual. The frequency of visits from family members and friends has been well documented. The *function* of these interactions and the importance of them to the older adult remain less clear.

As well, we know little about the stability or change in the patterns and meaning of interaction from childhood to maturity, or about the age-graded phenomena and life events which could influence these patterns. In the following sections, we will explore, from a life-span perspective, some limitations of our knowledge about peer interaction, and how we might extend existing theory and research to overcome these limitations.

We have three specific purposes in writing this article. First, we will paint a state-of-the-art picture of research on peer interaction across the life span. We will be concerned with both the nature and function of peer relationships at various ages and developmental stages. We will examine the promotive aspects of peer relations as well as the effects of peer deprivation, and how both of these factors relate to development in a life-span context. Furthermore, we will explore some of the processes responsible for patterns of continuity or change in the nature and function of peer interaction throughout the life course.

Our second purpose is to discuss the development of social competence and its relationship to successful peer interaction. We will explore the concept of social competence as it was proposed to account for individual differences in the social development of children. We will continue the discussion by examining the life-span implications of this child developmental research. We will suggest, further, that the socially competent individual, regardless of age, requires two strengths: (1) the ability to produce a wide range of social behaviors, and (2) the sensitivity and flexibility to tailor these behaviors to specific situations.

Third, we will describe extant research concerning one area of social skill vital to successful peer relations at any point in the life cycle: communicative competence. Again, we will consider both the nature and function of the communication process as well as the factors potentially responsible for life-span variations.

In all three sections, we will attempt to highlight with quantitative and qualitative issues important for a life-span approach to the study of peer interaction. We consider qualitative analyses to be of particular importance. As a case in point, most existing studies examine only interaction frequency counts (e.g., how often does a given individual interact with others?). This simple reliance on quantitative methods may obscure the discovery of developmental and individual differences in the function and significance of peer relationships.

## II. Functional Significance of Peer Interaction

### A. PEER RELATIONS IN CHILDHOOD

We begin our article with an overview of the functions of peer relations in childhood. This discussion will serve to illustrate important developmental advances in children's social functioning. Furthermore, we will place these early developments in a broader life-span perspective by discussing their implications for peer interaction in adulthood.

In the child development literature, a youngster's peers are considered to be his or her age-mates, regardless of demographic characteristics such as sex, or of the nature of any interactions. Generally, it has been suggested that such peers or age-mates serve multiple causal roles in development (Asher, 1978; Hartup, 1983). First, peers provide children with challenges concerning their extant conceptions of their personal and impersonal worlds. These challenges have been postulated to aid in the acquisition of perspective taking, mature moral judgment, and communicative and other related social–cognitive skills (Piaget, 1926, 1932, 1970; Shantz, 1983). The process by which social challenges play a developmental role may be described briefly as follows.

Through social interaction children are inevitably faced with viewpoints of the social and nonsocial world that are different from their own. Exposure to these different perspectives is thought to engender an uncomfortable state of cognitive conflict (Piaget, 1970). Since conflict throws the organism into cognitive disequilibrium, a resolution is sought. One route to a cognitive resolution of the conflict is via the process of accommodation. By accommodating to the different perspectives of his/her peers, the child accepts, as feasible, alternate ways of conceptualizing the social environment. In short, children are thought to overcome their early egocentric perspectives by being forced *by peers* to accept social compromise. Experimental research has supported the Piagetian premise that peer conflict promotes cognitive and social–cognitive development. Concepts such as moral judgment, perspective taking, and conservation have all been trained by allowing children to experience alternative peer viewpoints (for relevant reviews, see Brainerd, 1977; Rest, 1983; Shantz, 1983).

Peers serve also as direct or indirect sources of learning for one another. Drawing from social learning theory, it has been found that models influence the acquisition of new and multiple forms of prosocial and agonistic behaviors in childhood (e.g., Bandura, 1969). Peers have also been found to play a *direct* tutorial role in the teaching of social and cognitive skills (Allen, 1976). Moreover, once children have an established repertoire of social skills, peers regulate acceptable, normative group behaviors (Combs & Slaby, 1978). Finally, peers appear to provide each other with emotional security and support, even in the early preschool years (Freud & Dann, 1951; Ipsa, 1977).

## B. PEER RELATIONS IN ADOLESCENCE AND ADULTHOOD

During adolescence, we see the continuing influence of age-mates as children begin to establish their autonomy from parents and siblings (Newman, 1982). These peers regulate and direct the behavior of the teenager, as well as provide a nonfamily group for whom he or she can feel a sense of emotional bondedness.

In early adulthood, age is still a significant factor in determining who are one's peers and one's friends (e.g., Newcomb, 1962). However, as young adults become less conforming and more independent in their thinking (Boyd, 1975), and as they experience a wider variety of life events, their peer group becomes increasingly differentiated and complex (Newman, 1982). Individuals who share similar interests, attitudes, occupations, or histories may now be considered the young adult's peers.

It seems clear that throughout most of the adult life course, peers continue to be selected on the basis of similarity. Various types of life events appear to determine this similarity. For example, an age-graded event such as the birth of a child provides a new referent group, parents. Similarly, history-graded events such as war may create groups that adults consider as peers, even though they vary in age, sex, or socioeconomic status. As well, nonnormative events such as divorce may provide a woman with peers of even greater variety. Only in late adulthood when ties to former roles are weakened may we see a return to considering age as the salient characteristic in defining one's peer group (Lowenthal & Robinson, 1976). However, even at this point, chronological age is rarely the only way one conceptualizes the peer group; for example, individuals in age-segregated housing quickly divide themselves into subgroups on the basis of common interests (Hochschild, 1973). The bottom line is that an individual's relationships with members of any defined peer group seem highly tied to perceptions of similarity between members of that group. This premise holds true not only in adulthood but also throughout the years of childhood (Rubin & Ross, 1982).

Researchers have not addressed directly the question of whether peers fulfill the same functions in adulthood as do age-mates in childhood. However, the accumulated evidence on social interaction in adulthood suggests that peers are important agents in maintaining perspective taking and social cognitive skills, acting as social models, and providing emotional support. Indeed, one theorist (Sinnott, 1978) has suggested that social cognitive growth may advance beyond formal operations as adults experience more variety in their social interactions, and are required to solve an increasing number of interpersonal problems. Presumably, upon reaching this fifth stage, the metatheoretical stage, adults are better able to understand more of the complexities and contradictions present in social relationships. Thus, Sinnott (1978) suggests that an older adult should be able to understand that a peer may be embedded in several mutually contradictory logical systems of behaviors. For example, she/he may be acting on a model of social determinism and rugged individualism simultaneously, although the two are contradictory in theory. Consequently, the awareness that such contradictions are possible should promote more skilled interactions.

There is also evidence that peers continue to function as models and to provide emotional support throughout adulthood (Kahn & Antonucci, 1980). A group of similar others seems to buffer stress and provide support during life crisis such as pregnancy (Nuckolls, Cassel, & Kaplan, 1972), or difficult work situations (French, 1974). As Gottlieb (1983) has pointed out, peers fulfill several functions in providing this support. First, initial levels of anxiety may be reduced as individuals are exposed to those who successfully have weathered a life crisis. Then, feedback from supportive companions may shortcircuit possible feelings of self-recrimination, and bolster self-esteem and self-efficacy. Finally, peers provide rational problem-solving strategies and tangible aid as the individual struggles to adjust to a novel life event.

Although much of the literature on social support deals with young and middle-aged adults, there is evidence that peers are also vital for the well being of older adults (Rosow, 1967; Shanas, Townsend, Wedderburn, Friis, Milhoj, & Stehouwer, 1968). Rosow (1967), for example, found that peers provided models of appropriate behavior for the elderly at a time in the life course when few norms are made explicit. While some older adults may be ambivalent about accepting role models who confirm their own aging (Tamir, 1979), most view peer relations as important and satisfying (Blieszner, 1980; Conner & Powers, 1975; Norris, 1982; Sherman, 1971). Indeed, there is evidence that strong affective ties to peers in later life are associated with fewer psychiatric disturbances (Lowenthal & Haven, 1968) and generally higher self-esteem and life satisfaction (Beck & Leviton, 1976; Kahana, 1982; Norris, 1979a).

For the most part, we still know very little about the positive roles that peers play among the aged. This seems due to the fact that much of the research concerning the elderly has followed a biodecremental model (Birren & Renner, 1977), and is therefore negatively tinged; that is, many developmental researchers have centered on the possible regression of abilities (Bielby & Papalia, 1975), or the lessening of the quality of life (George, 1980) in the aged. Thus, it is not surprising that the *promotive* aspects of peer relations and social interaction have been neglected in much of the literature, including research with a life-span perspective.

## III. Consequences of Peer Deprivation

### A. DEPRIVATION IN CHILDHOOD

Developmentally, there has been a lengthy history of theory and research concerning peer deprivation and rejection. Suomi and Harlow (1975), for example, indicated that rhesus monkeys raised by their mothers without exposure to their age-mates produced long-standing avoidant and aggressive behaviors when later placed in peer group play situations. Bronson (1966) has noted that young children rated initially as "reserved–somber–shy" were often found to evidence vulnerability, instability, and lack of dominance in their peer relationships. More recently, Rubin (1983) has found that children observed to be socially withdrawn in *kindergarten* are more likely to display immature play patterns and impulsive classroom behaviors, and to evidence poorer cognitive and perspective-taking skills when in *grade 1* than their more sociable kindergarten age-mates.

As for peer rejection, longitudinal research (Cowen, Pederson, Babigian, Izzo, & Trost, 1973; Roff, Sells, & Golden, 1972) has demonstrated clearly that rejection in the early and middle years of childhood appears to predict juvenile delinquency, psychopathology, school failure and dropout, and sexual disorders in adolescence (cf. Asher, 1978; Hartup, 1983, for relevant reviews).

## B. DEPRIVATION IN ADULTHOOD

The *life-span* consequences of negative peer relational experiences in childhood and adolescence are not, at present, clear. Some psychologists have suggested that negative experiences with age-mates in childhood may be associated with pathology in later life (e.g., Gaitz & Varner, 1980; Post, 1962). However, a causal relation has yet to be established. Nevertheless, it appears that the loss of access to peers in adulthood following a lengthy period of normal social relations does affect development. College students, for example, have been found to experience adjustment problems during the first few months spent in a dormitory separated from life-long friends (Norris, 1979a). At first, the pain of separation is particularly acute resulting in social withdrawal, depression, and occasionally severe psychological disturbances. When superficial relationships begin to emerge in the dormitory, however, and a new peer group evolves, improvements in overall social activity levels and morale may be marked.

During the middle years of adulthood, there is also evidence to suggest that disruption of the peer network may have negative consequences. For example, a study by A. M. Matthews (1979) of housewives who were forced to relocate repeatedly when their husbands were transferred found that these women experienced increasingly severe adjustment problems. At first, they managed to substitute adequately for close friends. However, as the number of relocations accumulated, the women had more difficulty in finding a new peer group. For some, the outcome was social isolation. In a similar vein, Levinson (1978) found that his sample of middle-aged men appeared devoid of social support because they had relinquished the intimate male peers of their adult years. They now relied heavily on their wives for support. However, these women, busy with children and with well-established social networks of their own, seemed unable to substitute adequately for the support of a male peer.

Research on marital separation and divorce in midlife also suggests that the loss of an intimate peer, a spouse, may also be highly disruptive to functioning even when the dissolution of the marriage was desired (Weiss, 1979). The outcome of this loss may be to make a spouse feel unwanted and vulnerable enough to avoid interaction with others in his or her peer network (Spanier & Casto, 1979). Thus a downward spiral in social functioning may take place. A similar process could also occur in the social support system of the unemployed worker who is often removed abruptly from an important peer group (Liem & Rayman, 1982).

In later life, researchers have agreed that many peer interactions may be curtailed due to age-related losses such as bereavement (e.g., Norris, 1980) or retirement (e.g., Friedmann & Orbach, 1974). They have not been in complete agreement, however, about the effect of diminished contact on the well being of the older adult, nor have they speculated about possible qualitative changes in remaining peer relationships. Disengagement theorists (Cumming & Henry, 1961; Neugarten, Havighurst, & Tobin, 1968) proposed that normal aging involves a withdrawal from many types of social contact. This process was considered to be a result of both intrinsic developmental change and societal pressure, and was proposed to be linked to high life satisfaction in old age. More recently, however, researchers have countered this view, finding that social deprivation represents a significant challenge to the coping skills of the older adult (Bengtson & Treas, 1980).

Generally, diminished social contact in old age has been shown to result in lowered life satisfaction (Cutler, 1979) and deterioration of physical and mental health (Larson, 1978). The loss of *peer* contact seems particularly devastating (Beckman, 1981; Edwards & Klemmack, 1973). B. B. Brown (1980), for example, found that older adults without a confidant, compared to those who had an intimate friend, had fewer interests, lower self-esteem, and fewer feelings of well-being, and were more bothered by the frustrations of old age but less likely to seek help from others. Furthermore, there is also evidence that older adults show a much greater disruption in their social lives and psychological functioning than do younger individuals after losing a spouse through separation or divorce (Chiriboga, 1982). Perhaps one of the reasons that the loss of peers has such a significant impact on the lives of older adults is that changes in psychological functioning may be occurring concurrently with social losses. These changes may then inhibit the elderly person's ability to make new friends. For example, egocentrism, resulting from inadequate social feedback (Looft, 1972), and lack of creativity in forming new alliances, resulting from an overemphasis on old habits (Kalish & Knudtson, 1976), could inhibit peer interactions at a time when social support is vital.

In summary, considering the extant data from child and late-adult research concerning peer relationships leads us to conclude that peers serve crucial life-long developmental functions. It should be clear from our brief review that depriving an individual of significant contact with age-mates at any point in the life cycle may have serious consequences. In the next section, we examine how attributes of social competence may promote healthy and satisfying peer relations throughout the life cycle.

## IV. Social Competence: Issues of Concern

Given extant theory and research, we have suggested that a relative lack of peer interaction may be debilitating at any age. However, we do not think that it is simply the frequency of peer interaction that promotes healthy social functioning; the quality of interaction, regardless of frequency, must assuredly have a significant impact. It would seem likely that socially competent individuals of any age should be better adjusted than their less competent age-mates. Over the years, social competence has, of course, been difficult to define (Krasnor & Rubin, 1981; Putallaz & Gottman, 1981). Nevertheless, we conceptualize the phenomenon as involving several related components.

First, the socially competent individual is one who has a behavioral repertoire that evidences some breadth. She/he should be able to employ multiple behaviors to achieve given social goals successfully. For example, the goal of object acquisition is more likely to be met if the goal-seeking individual has several alternate means to reach it (e.g., grab, threaten, ask, share, command, bribe). The socially competent individual should also be able to select from *within* categories of alternative behaviors (e.g., agonistic, prosocial) to achieve his/her social goals. For example, she/he may have many qualitatively different forms of aggression (e.g., physical force on person, grab object, threaten) in his/her repertoire.

Second, the socially competent individual is one who is cognizant of and sensitive to situational or contextual factors. This cognitive sensitivity allows the individual to choose among the various forms of social behaviors within his/her repertoire in order to deal effectively with the situation at hand. For example, Krasnor and Rubin (1983) have found that the social problem-solving behaviors of young children are highly predictable given information concerning the target of the social act (i.e., who has the desired object, who is the target of a request for action), the goal of the social act (e.g., gaining attention, object acquisition, gaining information, obtaining help), and the identity of the social problem solver. Moreover, Krasnor (1981) has indicated that the ability to solve social problems is widely variable in children. In a nutshell, some children are more socially competent than others.

The question that remains, however, is whether socially competent individuals are better able than their less competent peers to monitor contextual cues when choosing their social strategies. In a recent study, Rubin and Krasnor (1983) have found that the ability to choose *appropriate* social problem-solving strategies increases with age from preschool to early elementary school. Moreover, within any given age, large individual differences exist. For example, grade 1 children are more likely than kindergarteners to suggest that a 4 year old who desires an object from a 7 year old should employ prosocial means to do so (e.g., share, ask, say "please"). Alternately, when the target of the object acquisition is younger, grade one children are more likely to suggest agonistic (threaten, bribe, grab object) strategies to solve the social problem. Interestingly, from preschool to grade 1 the range of different object acquisition alternatives (i.e., the social problem-solving repertoire) does not vary; instead the *qualitative* use of these alternatives varies with age given situational cues. As for individual differences, those children in kindergarten and grade 1 who were found to be more sensitive to contextual factors were also (1) more popular among their peers, (2) more likely to play cooperatively with their peers, and (3) were judged by their teachers as being more socially competent than their less "sensitive" age-mates (Rubin & Daniels-Beirness, 1983).

Thus, in our conceptualization of social competence, we believe that the competent individual is one who will consider such situational factors as the age, sex, and psychological status (e.g., the thoughts, feelings, cognitive competencies) of the social target when choosing a social strategy to meet an intended goal.

Finally, we view the socially competent individual to be one who is successful in meeting his/her goals through culturally acceptable means. For example, she/he will not use agonistic tactics when negotiation is clearly the norm concerning a given social problem.

The examples we have employed in our discussion above have been taken from the child development literature. We believe, however, that the three criteria outlined above concerning the definitive properties of social competence are relevant to a life-span perspective. Certainly adults also benefit from having a large repertoire of social behaviors, as well as from having the ability to select those appropriate to differing situations. As Hultsch and Plemons (1979) have noted, these dimensions of competence seem particularly important as mediators in adjusting to critical life events. The individual will be more successful in meeting the demands of a novel situation if he or she possesses a variety of strategies that can be implemented within the constraints of that situation.

Such flexibility appears especially important for the older adult whose social network may be diminishing. Spence (1975) indicated that the ability to reinterpret changing social situations allows elderly individuals to adapt most quickly to novel settings. In support of this premise Sequin (1973) found that the successful inmovers to a retirement community were those who adjusted previous role-related behaviors to suit their new social situations. In this way, these "newcomers" avoided what Kuypers and Bengtson (1973) described as the social breakdown syndrome, an overreliance on societal definitions of aging incompetence without reference to personal strengths and coping strategies.

The literature discussed above suggests that the dimensions of social competence are similar in childhood and adulthood. What we require now is a body of life-span research that deals with developmental descriptions of these skills. For example, it is necessary to know when given social behaviors appear in the repertoire; it is also necessary to discover how such behaviors change with age. Currently, there is some evidence that social competence persists across the life span (e.g., Mussen, Honzik, & Eichorn, 1982). As Kahana, Kahana, and McLenigan (1980) have pointed out, however, researchers' foci on declines in functioning with age have not allowed us to examine areas of competence for the elderly. We need to explore further patterns of social involvement, engagement, and the seeking of social stimulation in later life.

It is important, moreover, to examine age-related changes in the social sensitivity to situational factors. Does sensitivity to contextual cues change with age? Does development follow a linear, progressive path? We know now that socially withdrawn children have more limited social repertoires and are less sensitive to situational factors than their more sociable age-mates (Rubin, 1982a,b). It is also possible that those aged persons who lack peer interaction experiences or who disengage themselves from the social community decline both in their social repertoires and sensitivity to the social milieu. However, more empirical work by life-span developmental psychologists must be carried out to substantiate this relation as well as to link it with other life-span phenomena.

## A. THE SOCIAL REPERTOIRE: AN EXAMPLE

Few psychologists have attempted to track the life-span developmental course of social behavior in general, and of specific social behaviors in particular. Any attempt to do so would require addressing one of two questions. First, *when* is it that the behaviors, in whatever form, enter the repertoire? Second, *how* does the production of such behavior *change* over time? Answers to both questions are important in that they provide us with information concerning developmental, age-related norms. Deviation from these norms in terms of developmental lag or regression may allow social scientists to identify individuals "at risk" for social alienation, isolation, and rejection.

In the following sections, we attempt to provide the reader with an example of how a given social phenomenon can be traced within a life-span framework. Our presentation will, of course, be brief given the constraints of article length. Our focus will be on *communication* within peer interactions—a social behavior that is significant because it relates to many other developmental variables such as physical–motor, language, cognitive, and social–cognitive growth.

### 1. Quantitative Dimensions of Socialized Speech

*a. Childhood.* Recently, researchers have indicated that the young infant is socially oriented and desirous of the company of others (for recent reviews, see Hay, Pederson, & Nash, 1982; Vandell & Wilson, 1982). This finding contradicts the early Piagetian treatise that infants, and indeed even young children, are egocentric and care little about their peers or the adults in their environments (Piaget, 1926). Early attempts by infants to communicate with others are obviously not verbal in nature. In the first few months, the infant attempts to communicate nonverbally through the media of smiles and cries (e.g., Ainsworth, Bell, & Stayton, 1974). Although much research indicates that infants are socially oriented (Hay *et al.*, 1982; Vandell & Wilson, 1982), it is nevertheless the case that the impetus for much of their communicative behavior is egocentered or self-serving. The infant may be uncomfortable because she/he is soiled, or she/he may wish to play a game with a familiar adult. Consequently, cries and smiles are produced and the responsive adult must infer the baby's needs or wishes. Interestingly, there is evidence to suggest that babies produce these early communicative behaviors with some, albeit limited, knowledge of the consequences of their actions.

Through parent–infant interactions, the nonverbal communicative network broadens. Parents point to objects and label them for their babies. This communicative strategy and others like it become salient for the infant and she/he begins to use it as a communicative device. Thus, smiles and cries are the first developmental communicative phenomena appearing within the first trimester of life (Trevarthen, 1979); pointing and other rudimentary forms of gestural communication (e.g., shaking the head ''no'') enter the repertoire shortly before the first birthday (Bates, 1979; Rheingold, Hay, & West, 1976).

During the second year of life the child produces her/his first holophrastic utterances that have referential meaning (Dore, 1974). Holophrases are expressed in prosodically different ways. One-word utterances are used to ask, to label, and to command. For example, requests for action and information from others are emitted through the complementary use of gestures and language (Escalona, 1973). Thus the holophrase *Ball* accompanied by a point to the referent and a gaze toward the auditor may be taken to mean that the young speaker wants the listener to play ball, or perhaps to verify that the object is a ball. Comprehension of the holophrase is aided by contextual cues and by inflection and intonation. Moreover, responsive parents tend to provide their young children with model utterances that expand the holophrase (R. Brown, 1973). Thus, in response to *Ball!*, the parent may utter, ''Yes that's a ball. Let's play ball.'' By 2 years the toddler begins to use short sentences reminiscent of the short expansions provided earlier by the parent (e.g., ''Let's play ball!'' instead of ''Ball!'').

In the third through fifth years, there is further rapid development of vocabulary and syntax. Nevertheless, researchers have indicated that *referential* communication during these years is marked by the supposed inability of the young child to take the listener's perspective or to monitor his/her own messages following communicative failure (Levin & Rubin, 1983). Thus, egocentrism

(Piaget, 1926) and/or metacommunicative deficiencies (Flavell, 1981) serve as useful variables to explain the relatively poor performance of young children in referential communication studies. However, other factors may play a role in the reported results. Competent referential communication performance on paradigmatic tasks such as those used by Glucksberg and Krauss (for a review of this work, see Glucksberg, Krauss, & Higgins, 1975) may result from the speaker's appreciation of task demands, or the ability to make fine-line comparisons between referent and nonreferent stimuli (Asher & Wigfield, 1981). When the referential communicative task is simplified (e.g., Maratsos, 1973) or when the young child is allowed to supplement his/her verbal vocabulary with gestures (Evans & Rubin, 1979), children of 3 to 5 years exhibit surprisingly competent referential communication skills. In short, the relatively poor referential communication performance of young children on the typical paradigmatic, laboratory tasks cannot be explained simply by reference to the inability to perspective take or to think competently about one's own messages. Task demands and other factors may mask the social communicative skills of young children.

Because of the problems with laboratory studies, socio- and psycholinguists have recently begun to study the communicative competence of children as it emerges in natural settings. In general, it has been reported that approximately 60–70% of all *preschool*-aged children's spontaneous utterances produced in social situations are socially oriented (e.g., Mueller, 1972; Rubin, Hultsch, & Peters, 1971). These percentages are higher than those reported for toddlers (Mueller, Bleier, Krakow, Hegedus, & Cournoyer, 1977). Interestingly, little is known of the percentage of speech that is socially directed beyond the preschool years! Thus, although many have assumed the young child to be communicatively egocentric, the findings that (1) two-thirds of all utterances are socially directed, and (2) there is a lack of developmental data beyond 5 or 6 years of age provide ample questions regarding this assumption. Does the proportion of socially directed speech to all speech in social situations change with age beyond the preschool years? If so, to what can this change be attributed?

Interestingly, in *The Language and Thought of the Child,* Piaget (1926) suggested that the decline of egocentric speech and thought would result from opportunities for peer interaction, conflict, and negotiation. However, few researchers have studied individual differences, regardless of age, concerning the relations between peer interaction and socialized and/or egocentric speech. In one recent investigation, Rubin (1982b) reported that socially withdrawn preschoolers do, indeed, produce more egocentric speech and less socialized speech during dyadic interaction than their more sociable counterparts. The causal connection between peer interaction and social speech, however, cannot be ascertained from the extant data. Consequently, longitudinal or cross-sequential research might be worthwhile. Such research might answer whether opportunities for peer interaction do lead to declines in egocentric speech *in childhood.*

*b. Adulthood.* The literature on communication indicates the importance of this skill to the social relationships of the developing child. Researchers interested in *adult* development have also stressed the importance of clear communication to successful interaction, especially in intimate relationships such as marriage. As Gottman (1979) has noted, distressed couples often have communication problems suggestive of difficulties in perspective taking. They tend to "cross complain," that is, to stress their individual viewpoints with little or no effort to understand the spouse's perspective. Jacobson (1982) has reported similar findings in his work with married couples. In his experience, communication strategies such as echoing or reflective listening may be misused by spouses to suit egocentric purposes, rather than to enhance understanding. As an example, Jacobson describes a situation in which reflection is used to contradict the speaker's own explanation of her behavior and make it more consistent with the spouse's perspective:

> *Wife:* I don't want to have sex tonight; I'm tired.
> *Husband:* What I hear you saying is that you don't feel close to me tonight probably because I was flirting with Jane at the party last night. (p. 236)

Examples such as this emphasize the necessity of skilled communication in adulthood, but provide less information about how this skill develops. Developmental issues emerge once again in the research, however, when older adults are considered. For example, in one of the few life-span cross-sectional studies of referential communication, Rubin (1974) found that performance improved in a linear fashion in grade 2, grade 6, and University (mean age = 21.07 years) subjects. However, noninstitutionalized elderly adults (mean age = 76.33 years) performed more poorly than the university students and only as well as the grade 6 students. These curvilinear findings, however, may be explained by task demands rather than by developmental factors. Older adults' abilities may be minimized by noncognitive factors such as test anxiety or lack of motivation (Hultsch & Deutsch, 1981). Moreover, inadequate controls for verbal fluency, intelligence, or for physical factors such as sight or hearing preclude any firm statements being made vis-à-vis the life-span development of referential communication skill.

Rubin's (1974) study suggests that paradigmatic investigations of referential communication in adults are as problematic as similar studies of children. Thus, it seems more fruitful to explore the possible causes for individual differences in skill at any point in the adult life course, than to look for developmental patterns based on chronological age alone. For example, it would be interesting to discover whether or not communicative competence varies in accord with available interaction with peers in the elderly. It may be, as Looft (1972) has suggested, that the loss of access to familiar peers (through their death, hospitalization, or relocation) leads to increases in production of egocentric speech during social interaction. In short, if the response of a given aged individual to the loss of peers is dissociation from social groups, will that person grow out of touch with societal norms, values, and expectations? If so, will such a loss lead to a re-generation of "egocentric thought" and will this eventuality result in declines in the ability to communicate socially? All of these questions would appear worthy of answer in future life-span research.

## 2. Qualitative Dimensions of Socialized Speech

*a. Childhood.* In the above discussion we have been concerned with quan-titative dimensions of egocentric/socialized speech. However, when speech is directed at others in natural settings, it involves *qualitatively* different speech acts (Searle, 1969) in which the speaker may express particular intentions (e.g., apologies, promises) that are designed to produce particular effects in the lis-tener. Recent developmental work carried out in the sociolinguistic tradition has focused on one specific form of speech act—the request for action. People request action when they want others to do things for them. Of course, there are many different ways to request action verbally from a social target. For example, in the following three requests, the speaker's intention is the same:

1. Give me that pen.
2. Can you give me that pen?
3. I need something to write with.

The requests, from 1 to 3 become less direct, more vague, and more reliant on the listener to infer the speaker's meaning. The first request has been labeled a *direct* request for action, the latter two are *indirect* requests for action (Garvey, 1975; Levin & Rubin, 1983). Actually, the second request (2) has the meaning of a directive and yet is posed as an interrogative. The third request (3) shares the same meaning as (1) and (2) and is posed as a "hint."

The alternative request forms may not be equally salient to children of differ-ent ages. When do children come to understand the relation between the syntactic meaning of an utterance and its intended meaning? When do children produce requests of different forms?

Shatz (1978) has indicated that the question directives [e.g., "(2)"] issued by mothers can be understood by approximately 2 years of age. In terms of request production, most early requests in the toddler years (2 and 3 years) are uttered in the imperative (Ervin-Tripp, 1977). With increasing age, from $3\frac{1}{2}$ to 6 or 7 years, the proportion of indirect to all requests increases (Garvey, 1975; Levin & Rubin, 1983). Thus, it would appear that with cognitive growth children come to understand that a given utterance (e.g., "Can you give me my dolly?") can be used and interpreted in two ways—as an imperative and as a question. This separation of literal from nonliteral meaning in the sociolinguistic domain ap-pears to enter the communicative repertoire at much the same time as other markers of naturalistic "decentration" (e.g., the onset of symbolic play during which a given object is used to designate something else).

In a developmental study of request production and its consequences, the only study which covered more than the preschool years, Levin and Rubin (1983) found that preschoolers were as likely as first and third graders to use direct and indirect requests. However, the older children were more likely to gain listener compliance. Moreover, when a given request failed, older children were more likely to use a different request form (e.g., switch from a command to a question-directive) in efforts to gain compliance. The greater degree of success and flexibility following noncompliance is reflective of the growth of social competence with age.

In a follow-up to the Levin and Rubin (1983) study, Rubin and Borwick (1983) examined the requestive skills of preschool and kindergarten children who varied with regard to sociability. Socially withdrawn children had communicative repertoires that were equal in breadth to their more sociable age-mates; that is, they were equally able to produce all the same request forms (direct and indirect requests). However, the requests of children with greater amounts of peer experience were more likely to be complied with. In addition, the requests of the more sociable children were more assertive (e.g., commands to obtain objects) and reflected a sense of self-assurance. The requests of the "isolate" children were less costly to their listeners (e.g., indirect requests for attention, "Look at this.") and were expressive of social anxiety and low assertiveness. Rubin and Borwick (1983) suggest that the communicative styles of the socially withdrawn children are the product of their lack of peer relational experiences and of their low positions in their classroom dominance hierarchies. Furthermore, these authors hint that early provisions for peer-related experience should constitute a "Headstart" program for young children deficient in peer relations and social skills.

*b. Adulthood.* There has been little, if any, research concerning requestive skills beyond the mid-childhood years. Yet it may well be that peer rejection and isolation at all points in the life span result, in part, from communicative deficiencies. Although their causes may differ, some problems in fact may be the same in individuals of widely varying ages. For example, the lack of *flexibility* following failure to gain compliance to requests may predict peer relational problems regardless of age. In children, requestive *rigidity,* or the continuous issuance of the same statement despite earlier noncompliance, has been related positively to independent measures of egocentricity in children (Levin & Rubin, 1983). In turn, egocentricity, or the inability to perspective take, has long been associated with peer relational problems (for a review, see Rubin & Everett, 1982). In late adulthood, continuous ineffective use of the same communicative strategy may also be problematic. As Kalish and Knudtson (1976) have pointed out, institutionalized older adults may have to be quite creative, even socially inappropriate, to elicit the attention of others. This strategy is not based on egocentrism, however, but on an understanding of the constraints of the social situation.

The use of requests that draw attention to the self rather than toward cooperative endeavors has been shown to predict rejection in childhood (Putallaz & Gottman, 1981). A similar strategy on the part of the institutionalized elderly, however, has been related to more extensive interaction with staff members and to better adjustment in the institution (Tobin & Lieberman, 1976). Thus, specific types of requests may have varying consequences given different life circumstances and developmental factors. Nevertheless, it seems logical to posit that the inability to issue requests that will lead to successful cooperative behavior may well predict peer rejection and isolation regardless of age.

In summary, communicative competence appears to increase with age until the early elementary school years. In some cases, as in referential communication, skill appears to improve beyond preadolescence. In others, as in the study of speech acts, the breadth of the communicative repertoire appears to remain the same beyond the preschool years. Yet the success of children's requests continues to increase beyond the early years. Obviously, then, there is more to social (or, in this case, communicative) competence than the breadth of a behavioral repertoire. What other factors are important in determining social skill? We have suggested that flexibility, or the ability to alter one's social strategies following failure, is one such factor. In the next section we examine another relevant area—the sensitivity of the social actor to her/his social environment.

## B. THE SOCIAL CONTEXT

### 1. Children's Sensitivity to the Social Context

The literature on referential communication has typically not allowed inferences to be drawn about young children's sensitivity to social, contextual cues. However, by reading between the lines of the extant literature, some evidence concerning early social sensitivity emerges. In the early referential communication work, Flavell (1968) and Glucksberg and Krauss (1967) made cursory notes concerning the presence of pointing and tracing movements when young children were required to describe a referent stimulus to listeners separated visually from them. Such gesturing was considered to constitute further proof of the egocentric nature of young children's communicative endeavors.

Another interpretation of such gestural behavior is that it represented the only means by which young children, with a limited verbal repertoire, could describe the novel, abstract figures employed in the typical referential communication study. Gesturing in these cases could be interpreted as resulting from the frustration of not being able to find the "right words" to describe the stimuli.

In more recent studies, the use of gestural communication in childhood may be taken as evidence of social sensitivity rather than egocentrism. Evans and Rubin (1979) found that kindergarten-age children were as capable as grade 2 and 4 children in explaining simple board games when allowed to use hand gestures to supplement their verbalizations. Maratsos (1973) found that the use of gestures in preschoolers varied in relation to the visual capacities of their listeners. Gestures were used to describe referent stimuli when their listeners could see the stimuli. However, when the listeners were blindfolded, young speakers rarely employed visual means of communication.

In more recent studies, researchers employing less structured methods have found a good deal of evidence for the sensitivity of preschool and kindergarten age children to social, contextual cues. *Age* of a listener is one characteristic that has been shown to produce variations in the verbal behavior of young children. Children apparently base the complexity of their language on the age of their listeners. For example, Shatz and Gelman (1973) asked 4½-year-old children to explain the workings of a toy to a 2 year old, an age-mate, or an adult. The average number of utterances and the mean utterance length decreased whereas the use of gestures increased with listener age. Furthermore, subordinate and coordinate clauses were produced more often in conversation with adults while visual attention getters such as *watch, look,* and *see* were used more often with 2 year olds. Similar studies have confirmed that young children vary their communicative behavior in response to relatively small differences in the ages of their listeners (e.g., Holmberg, 1980; Langlois, Gottfried, Barnes, & Hendricks, 1978).

The verbal means that children employ to "get others to do what they want them to" likewise varies with the age of the listener/target. Aggressive communicative demands are more likely to be addressed to younger than older children (Muste & Sharpe, 1947; Rubin & Krasnor, 1983) or adults (Holmberg, 1980). Similarly, investigators have discovered that the dominance status and the sex of the listener/target elicit varying forms of communicative behavior from young children. For example, Lubin and Whiting (1977) reported that children tend to escalate persuasive strategies with lower status targets and to deescalate or repeat strategies with higher status (older) listeners when first attempts are met with noncompliance. Imperatives are more likely to be directed by preschoolers to female than male listeners (Krasnor & Rubin, 1983) and to mothers than fathers (Lawson, 1976, cited in Ervin-Tripp, 1977). In short, recent data make it quite clear that children as young as 4 and 5 years can, and do, use different communicative strategies in accord with social, contextual factors. Some researchers have inferred, from these findings, that earlier conclusions concerning the egocentric status of young children were ill taken (e.g., Garvey, 1975). Others have suggested that the recent data indicate merely that young children categorize their listeners and that these categorizations invoke rules or social–cognitive scripts for appropriate speech styles (Higgins, 1981). As such, perspective taking is not considered a requisite skill vis-à-vis communicative competence.

Research by Levin and Rubin (1983) described earlier, however, suggests that such an anti-Piagetian stance may be as inadequate an explanation of the development of communication as is a view which does not consider contextual factors. In fact, it is likely that perspective-taking ability *and* sensitivity to the social context determine communicative competence. In their study of requestive strategies, Levin and Rubin (1983) found preschoolers to be as likely as elementary schoolers to initiate conversation through requests, and as likely to use alternative forms of requests such as indirect suggestion. Young children, however, lacked flexibility in developing rerequest strategies after failure, a probable consequence of less sophisticated perspective-taking skills. Thus, children of all ages in this study were socially oriented and sensitive to contextual cues; however, younger children seemed less able to predict behavioral outcomes from their requests due to a less well-developed understanding of their listener's point of view.

## 2. The Adult Communicator in the Social Context

Research concerning communicative competence with peers seems to end abruptly in the middle years of childhood. There have been few attempts to examine the phenomenon in the later years of childhood and in adolescence. This research vacuum probably exists because of the assumption that childhood egocentrism (and thus communicative incompetence) wains, and indeed is nonexistent during these later years.

Much of the research on communication beyond the childhood years has been conducted by social psychologists. These researchers have been concerned with the sensitivity of young and middle-aged social actors to listener characteristics and to the demands of the broader context. A major thrust of this work has been on identifying individual differences in sensitivity to three channels of communication: verbal (e.g., Bales, 1951), paraverbal (e.g., Wiener & Mehrabian, 1968), and nonverbal (e.g., Argyle & Kendon, 1967).

It is assumed that individuals having reached adolescence and early adulthood are capable of competent communication, including an enhanced ability to tailor language to the demands of the social context. Researchers have determined, for example, that some adults, high self-monitors, are particularly sensitive to the characteristics of their listeners (Berscheid, Graziano, Monson, & Dermer, 1976; Snyder & Gangestad, 1982). Consequently, they appear to have qualitatively better social interactions with their peers (Snyder, 1979). Certainly, adults who are less adept at determining social contextual factors and adapting their communication accordingly appear less socially competent (e.g., Schegloff, 1972) or even severely disturbed (e.g., Gladwin, 1967). Jones, Hobbs, and

Hockenbury (1982), for example, found that college students who were insensitive to their listeners' needs during dyadic interaction were also extremely lonely and generally unskilled in peer interactions.

As do children, competent adult communicators adjust their speech to different contextual variables. They must be aware of sociological characteristics of listeners such as age or social position as well as of specific variations in the setting or topic of conversation (Ervin-Tripp, 1968; Goffman, 1958). The infant–caregiver relationship, for example, illustrates communicative adaptation to listener age (Tamir, 1979). As the child's language becomes progressively more sophisticated, a mother correspondingly modifies both the complexity and content of her own speech (Escalona, 1973). At all points in development, the competent caregiver remains both accepting of and responsive to her child's nonstandard speech (Bloom, Rocissano, & Hood, 1976; Moerk, 1974). Further, a study by Rubin and Brown (1975) suggests that adults also modify their language to suit the perceived limited competencies of older adults. When asked to explain a set of game rules to figure drawings representing children, middle-aged adults, and elderly individuals, college students provided simplified explanations for both the young and the old. In actual communication, adult caregivers also modify their speech to accommodate the perceived childlike status of the institutionalized older person (Caporael, Lukaszewski, & Culbertson, 1983).

In addition to age, competent adult communicators consider listener differences in social status or position. Most adults are extremely sensitive to discrepancies in prestige or power, even when the cues are subtle (Goffman, 1958). Women, for example, have been found to adapt the volume and assertive content of their speech to the presence or absence of men in a discussion group (Kimble, Yoshikawa, & Zehr, 1981). Similar sensitivity to status factors has been shown in communicators, such as salesmen, who wish to influence their listeners. Depending upon the message, they may adjust their language to appear similar to (e.g., Brock, 1965) or more expert than (e.g., Bochner & Insko, 1966) their audience.

Adults have also been found to adapt language to the level of intimacy in their relationship with a listener. Both the amount and the content of information expressed may vary. In a close relationship, a competent adult may perceive that his respondent shares similar experiences and beliefs; thus he may provide less information in his speech than he would to a stranger (Clark & Haviland, 1974). Similarly, the adult communicator, especially a high self-monitor, is sensitive to norms regarding the type of information expressed in differing situations (Shaffer, Smith, & Tomarelli, 1982). Between strangers, a strict norm of reciprocity in self-disclosure exists (Gouldner, 1960); between close friends, this norm is considerably relaxed (Derlega, Wilson, & Chaikin, 1976).

Available research provides few insights into the roots of these individual differences in adult social sensitivity. As some current longitudinal work suggests (e.g., Mussen *et al.*, 1982), it may be that childhood patterns of competence persist into later life. For example, personality characteristics in general appear to remain constant across the life span (Costa & McCrae, 1980). Thus, it is quite possible that self-monitoring style, a relatively stable characteristic in adulthood, may be the product of childhood sensitivity to the social environment.

Even if communicative skill has some foundation in the childhood years, it is probable that it will be modified by the adult's life circumstances. The range and depth of social experiences should lead not only to a larger behavioral repertoire, but also to a greater awareness of which strategies are appropriate in a given situation. Environmental psychologists, for example, have suggested that the optimal situation for personal growth is one which offers challenges without completely surpassing the adult's abilities (e.g., Parr, 1980). It is likely, therefore, that providing an individual with varied, challenging situations which fit his or her social abilities should enhance social flexibility and sensitivity. The adult who does not have the opportunity for varied interaction may indeed appear socially insensitive with a new group of peers.

## 3. Changes in Sensitivity in Later Life

Researchers interested in early adulthood have typically been less concerned than gerontologists with developments in communicative competence and sensitivity. This concern appears to be the result of a focus on the deterioration of psychological abilities in old age. Thus, a great deal of attention has been paid to age-related changes in other aspects of functioning which could cause decrements in communication skill. For example, researchers have noted that severe physical illnesses such as Alzheimer's disease or multiinfarct dementia may produce an inability to recognize given situations as social phenomena, or an inability to recognize once familiar social interactors (Burnside, 1980). Sensory changes, such as hearing loss (Botwinick, 1978), or declines in the ability to understand both spoken and written discourse (Cohen, 1979) due to general cognitive deterioration, may result in blocked access to information required for successful communication, and may even be linked to a more generalized decline in day-to-day living skills (North & Ulatowska, 1981).

In later life, individual differences in personality may affect sensitivity to contextual variations. Researchers have found, for example, that well-learned strategies may result in an inflexible approach to novel situations (Botwinick, 1978). Thus, it is conceivable that an older adult who has just lost access to a spouse or to friends (via death or separation) might not be able to manifest the flexibility in social skills necessary to develop adaptive peer relationships in new settings. Instead, old, potentially inappropriate communicative "scripts" (Abelson, 1976) may be enacted automatically. If such inflexibility is compounded by feelings of personal powerlessness engendered by negative stereotypes about aging (Rodin & Langer, 1980), the initiation of communication with peers may be even less likely.

Age-related changes in an older adult's perception of the meaning of friendship (Loeb, 1973; Tierney, Zwicker, & Bush, 1982) may also influence communication by affecting the type of contextual cues which are monitored. There is evidence, for example, that the elderly, because of diminishing personal resources, look for the highest payoff (i.e., best quality) for the lowest cost (i.e., least energy expenditure) in a relationship (Duff & Hong, 1980). Thus, they may be considerably more selective than a younger adult in their choice of peer interactions and unwilling to adapt to the needs of a listener perceived to be different.

Changes in the immediate physical and social context have also been shown to affect significantly the communicative skill of older adults, espcially in their sensitivity to listener characteristics. Isolation caused by nonnormative life events such as role loss, illness, or institutionalization may block access to peers and to social feedback and begin a downward spiral in communicative competence. The consequences may be increased egocentrism (Looft, 1972), inconsistency in verbal behaviors (Norris, 1977), and "pseudocommunication" (Tamir, 1979), that is, communication based on misperception. The older adult may then appear quite primitive in his/her inability to adapt communication to listener needs and contextual demands.

Negative stereotypes of old age and aging may also cause declines in social sensitivity and communicative skill with peers. Kuypers and Bengtson (1973) have suggested that older adults may exacerbate declines in functioning by taking on characteristics of incompetence ascribed to them by society. S. Matthews' (1979) study of the social life of older women supports this view. Furthermore, results indicated that the elderly may compound the problem by seeking to avoid interaction in case they are perceived as old and incompetent. It is possible, then, that voluntary disengagement to avoid stigmatization may result in the same declines in competence as involuntary isolation.

Research discussed above suggests that any changes in communicative competence in later life will be regressive. It is possible, however, that because of their focus on age-related losses, researchers may have missed qualitative improvements in the communication skills of older adults. Recent work on person perception in later life provides some support for this view. Sinnott (1978), in a theoretical article, proposed that older adults acquire more advanced social inferential and perspective-taking abilities, allowing them to communicate on several apparently contradictory levels within any relationship.

This dialectical approach to interaction in the aged has not been confirmed by empirical research, but work by Norris and co-workers (Norris, 1979b; Norris & Pratt, 1980) suggests that older adults do possess sophisticated strategies for understanding their social world. In one study (Norris, 1979b), elderly adults perceived significant others in more complex and differentiated terms than did young adults. In another (Norris & Pratt, 1980), well-educated older adults outperformed young and middle-aged individuals in determining the motives of story characters from limited information. In actual social encounters, McGee and Barker (1982) have suggested that older adults are quite adept at interpreting subtle communication tactics. For example, the elderly readily recognize when younger adults express ritualistic deference (versus true respect), even if they do not choose to act upon this knowledge. Presumably, such social–cognitive abilities could produce more skillful communication with peers as adults grow older.

## V. Methodological Approaches to Social Competence

In Section IV, we have examined communicative competence, an aspect of social competence important to development throughout the life span. In our discussion, we have noted that both the individual's behavioral repertoire and his or her sensitivity to the social context will determine success in communicating with peers. It should also be apparent from this review, however, that research on social competence across the life span is fragmented in its approach and, at times, inconsistent in its findings. Thus, any attempt to articulate a theory of the development of competence, or to identify deficient social skills in individuals of various ages, is extremely difficult. In this section, we will examine three different methodological approaches to the study of social competence and peer relations throughout the life cycle. The strengths and limitations of each approach will be evaluated, as well as their potential contributions to life-span theory, research, and clinical application.

### A. HYPOTHETICAL–REFLECTIVE APPROACHES

Much of the research on the assessment of social competence in childhood has drawn on a hypothetical–reflective methodological approach (Krasnor & Rubin, 1981). Children are presented with hypothetical social situations and are asked to describe (1) how the story characters are thinking or feeling or (2) what the characters should do to solve major or minor social dilemmas. The perspective-taking, moral judgment, and social problem-solving research of Selman (1980), Kohlberg (1976), and Spivack and Shure (1974) is typical of the hypothetical–reflective approach. The method is heavily dependent on cognitive as well as verbal skills.

Hypothetical–reflective approaches also have formed the basis of research on social competence in adults. Using methods similar to those employed with children, researchers have investigated perspective taking (Bielby & Papalia, 1975; Looft & Charles, 1971; Rubin, Attewell, Tierney, & Tumolo, 1973), moral judgment (Pratt, Golding, & Hunter, 1982), and social problem solving, particularly as a component of skill-building therapies (Argyle & Kendon, 1967; Berger & Rose, 1977; Rotheram & Corby, 1980; Schinke & Rose, 1976). Typically, the abilities of adults on these tasks deteriorate in later life. In addition to intrinsic developmental change (e.g., Cumming & Henry, 1961), task demands (Tesch, Whitbourne, & Nehrke, 1978) and social isolation (Cooper, 1978) have been suggested as contributing factors in the purported social– cognitive decrements.

As a means of assessing social competence and extending our understanding of its development, the hypothetical–reflective approach is somewhat limited. In their analysis of the social problem-solving skills of children, for example, Krasnor and Rubin (1981) identified a series of restrictions on the usefulness of this method. Most of these related to the external validity of the hypothetical–reflective approach within any age group. For example, the domain of hypothetical situations is typically small, and may be of no personal relevance to the participant. Noncognitive factors such as lack of motivation may therefore affect performance. In addition, criteria for judging a successful verbal response are set in advance of the testing and have no flexibility for innovative strategies, some of which may be nonverbal or paralinguistic. The internal validity of studies using this method may also be in question. For example, the psychometric properties of many widely used hypothetical–reflective instruments are known to be weak (e.g., Rubin, 1978), and the relationship of results from them to independent measures of social competence (e.g., peer and teacher ratings) has not been consistently supported by research.

Despite these difficulties, hypothetical–reflective methods have increased our knowledge of how children and adults think about their social worlds and have provided clues about the nature of social–cognitive development across the life span. In addition, they have aided researchers in identifying individuals who may be at risk for problems of social competence, as well as suggesting means of altering dysfunctional thought patterns in those lacking social skill. Thus, for the life-span researcher a hypothetical–reflective approach may be a useful way of understanding the individual's thinking about social problems. It is important, however, to be sensitive to possible *qualitative* differences in ability that may exist among age groups even when the same instruments are used. Kalish and Knudtson (1976), for example, have suggested that elderly adults who strive to induce guilt in the relatives responsible for their institutionalization may be using a sophisticated strategy designed to foster attachment in a situation devoid of other options. If such a strategy were suggested in response to a hypothetical dilemma, it would appear primitive. Obviously, a flexible interpretation of common responses within any age group will add significantly to our understanding of social competence.

## B. THE OBSERVATIONAL APPROACH

A second approach to the study of social competence involves the use of observational methods. In contrast to hypothetical–reflective methods, where inferences are made about a child's "real-life" social competence, observational approaches allow an analysis of behaviors in naturalistic settings. Cognitive strategies may be inferred from these behaviors. For example, Krasnor and Rubin (1983) used this approach to study how preschool-aged children attained personal goals in social settings. Descriptions of the children's social behaviors were assessed for problem-solving attempts aimed at the same goal; these attempts were then analyzed for the amount of persistence a child exhibited in reattempting a failed goal and the amount of flexibility a child showed in altering strategies after failure. Thus, the authors were able to assess the nature and frequency of problem-solving strategies as well as their effectiveness, and could make inferences about cognitive strategies based on these observations.

Other researchers have employed observational techniques to discover why children are accepted or rejected by their peers. In their summary of the findings from this work, Putallaz and Gottman (1981) noted that popular children tend to initiate and receive more positive interactions with their peers than do less popular children. In addition, unpopular children appear insensitive to group norms. For example, instead of engaging in the ongoing activity of their peers, they draw attention to themselves through demands and questions. This behavior, combined with a tendency to be disagreeable and destructive, appears to lead to peer rejection (Dodge, 1983).

Observational methods have rarely been used to assess the social competence of young or middle-aged adults. Recently, however, there has been more interest in descriptive or qualitative approaches to the study of social interaction among older adults. Generally, this research has focused on the institutionalized elderly, a population more readily accessible and easily observed than their community-dwelling peers. The purpose has been to examine the nature of interaction among institutional residents. Baltes and colleagues (Baltes, Barton, Orzech, & Lago, 1980; Barton, Baltes, & Orzech, 1980), for example, have used behavior-mapping techniques to examine patterns of dependency among nursing home staff and patients. Other researchers (e.g., Davis & Smith, 1980; Waters, 1980) have investigated problematic social behaviors in geriatric patients with a view to developing intervention procedures.

Krasnor and Rubin (1981) have noted that an observational approach to the study of social competence is useful for a number of reasons. First, because behavior is observed in a naturalistic setting, it is likely to be more representative of the actual domain of behaviors which an individual possesses. Second, with this method, the researcher can determine not only the normal sequencing of behavior in a social setting, but also which sequences are most likely to be effective in a given situation. Finally, "real life" competencies obtained through observational methods may be compared with social–cognitive skills, such as perspective taking, assessed by more structured approaches. This may provide information about the relationship of social behaviors to cognitive development throughout the life span.

The observational approach, however, could have some drawbacks. It may be difficult to find a setting which can be easily and ethically accessed (Watson, 1979–1980). This is particularly true when, as in life-span studies, adults are a focus of investigation. Many gerontologists have attempted to circumvent this problem by observing readily available, institutionalized samples. This strategy, however, sacrifices one of the major benefits of observational techniques, ecological validity. In an artificial setting, the behavior of older adults may be very different than those of their community-dwelling peers. Goffman (1961), for example, has pointed out that a contained social environment develops its own norms; thus the competent social behaviors of its residents may appear very different from those of the general population.

As Webb and colleagues (Webb, Campbell, Schwartz, & Sechrest, 1966) point out, choosing a setting for naturalistic study need not be so problematic. Rather, it requires a flexible and creative approach on the part of the researcher. These authors have reviewed a wide variety of studies, many conducted in public areas such as waiting rooms or restaurants, in which nonobtrusive or nonreactive recording techniques have been used. Sommer's (1962) work on physical distancing between conversationalists is a good example. This investigator simply used a "waltz technique" in his own conversation to measure a listener's movement backward and forward in response to his movements. Although such techniques have rarely been employed directly to study social competence, they provide suggestions for innovative settings and techniques which could be adapted to this area of study. Following Sommer's work, for example, one might investigate life-span variations in conversational distance. Presumably, major deviations from the conversational distance from within one cohort in a given culture could indicate problematic social adjustment.

## C. THE SIMULATED SITUATION

A "simulated situation" approach to the study of social competence has been suggested as a solution to the problems of ecological validity inherent in hypothetical–reflective procedures, and to the lack of control characteristic of observational methods (Krasnor & Rubin, 1981). This procedure represents a blending of the other two methods: spontaneous verbal and nonverbal social behaviors are observed in a setting designed to elicit interaction. For example, in a series of studies by Sherif (e.g., Sherif, 1966), children at a camp were randomly divided into two groups. For 1 week the children engaged in activities designed to facilitate intergroup cooperation. After this period, between-group competition in the form of games was introduced, and the children's strategies for coping with this problematic social situation were observed. This method allowed the researchers to control the type and quality of social problem introduced to the children, while permitting them to choose spontaneously both verbal and nonverbal means of resolution.

The simulated situation approach has also been a popular method with social psychologists studying young adults. Using this procedure, researchers have investigated various problematic social situations such as those eliciting conformity (Asch, 1956), compliance (Freedman & Fraser, 1966), or prosocial behavior (Latane & Rodin, 1969). For example, Latane and Rodin (1969) used a simulated waiting room situation to investigate the conditions under which college students would be likely to go to the aid of an apparently injured experimenter. These researchers discovered that the social context made a significant difference vis-à-vis the amount of prosocial behavior evidenced. Students waiting alone were most likely to help the experimenter; the presence of a friend inhibited this response, but a friend was less inhibiting than a stranger, especially an unresponsive one.

In the literature on old age, there are few examples of the use of simulated social situations. It is true, however, that many studies of the elderly have been carried out in what is essentially a quasinaturalistic setting—the institution. Researchers have been interested in how being placed in a situation which has been structured by others affects the adult's spontaneous social behavior. Generally, it appears that admission to such a setting is correlated with the deterioration of autonomy and social skill, *except* when the older individual possesses characteristics which might be considered socially undesirable outside the institution— i.e., hostility and stubbornness (Tobin & Lieberman, 1976).

Finer grained analyses of institutional life have also employed what are essentially simulated situation methods. In one study by Langer and Rodin (1976), a situation was created for half the adults in a nursing home wherein control over their own lives was enhanced with extra choices and reminders of other opportunities available. The other residents continued to have decisions made for them. Based on this study and others like it (Schulz, 1976), it is clear that the competent social functioning and general well being of the institutionalized elderly are promoted by their increased control over significant events.

The simulated situation approach appears to have a great deal of potential for studying the social competence of healthy, community-dwelling aged as well. Planned research by the present authors, for example, includes a quasinaturalistic study of social problem-solving skills. In a waiting room setting older adults will be confronted with a common interpersonal problem, for example, a peer who expresses anxiety about an important personal concern. Of interest will be the variety and flexibility of approaches used by the older adult in responding to the confederate's problem.

As Krasnor and Rubin (1981) point out, the simulated situation technique allows observations of relatively naturalistic social behaviors in settings less constrained than those of hypothetical–reflective studies, but with more standardization than those usually found in observational studies. Because of this advantage we feel it is a useful method for studying peer interaction and communication across the life span. Each age group can be investigated in familiar social surroundings, and the variety of skills discussed in this article can be examined. How large and flexible is the behavioral repertoire of any one cohort? Are there differences in sensitivity to contextual factors between age-mates, and to what are these due? Through answers to these questions, life-span researchers and practitioners will have a more adequate understanding of the development and maintenance of social competence.

## VI. Summary

Social interaction has long been considered an important factor in human development. The nature, function, and consequences of social contact have been more clearly articulated for children, however, than for adults. In this article, we have explored the strengths and limitations, from a life-span perspective, of research and theory on one form of social interaction, peer interaction. We have stressed the importance of considering both the *quantitative* and *qualitative* aspects of peer contact.

Our first goal was to paint a state-of-the-art picture of the functional significance of peer interaction across the life span. In so doing, we explored the promotive aspects of peer contact as well as the results of peer deprivation. While research with adults is incomplete, it does appear that peers serve an important function in promoting competent social cognitive functioning and emotional well being throughout the life span.

Our second goal was to discuss the development of social competence in childhood and the implications of this development for adults. We identified several components of competent social functioning. The most important of these for individuals of any age are a large behavioral repertoire and sensitivity to the social context.

Our third purpose was to explore one area of competence vital to successful peer relations throughout the life span—communicative interaction. We noted that in childhood quantitative changes in communication, such as the expansion of vocabulary, as well as qualitative developments, such as increasing flexibility in requestive strategies, determine competent interaction. Adults, it appears, become even more adept at communication through an increasing sensitivity to contextual factors such as listener age, sex, or social status. In old age, however, the picture is less clear. Researchers have shown elderly adults to be less flexible in their choice of friends and in their interactions with them. Whether this is due to age-related loss of cognitive capacity, or whether it represents a qualitative change (not necessarily primitive) is an unresolved question.

We ended our article with a discussion of three methodologies useful in the life-span study of social competence. The first, the hypothetical–reflective approach, uses hypothetical situations to explore individual social cognitive abilities. The second, the observational approach, employs naturalistic settings to determine spontaneous social behaviors and problem-solving strategies. The third, the simulated situation, can be used to examine spontaneous social behaviors in a setting designed by the researcher. We consider this approach particularly useful for the study of social interaction because it allows the investigator some elements of experimental control, while providing the subject with a "real life" situation in which to interact.

In conclusion, we feel that social competence is a vital component of successful peer relations across the life span. Of particular importance is an individual's capacity to employ his/her cognitive and emotional resources in a flexible way while remaining sensitive to contextual factors. It is clear, however, that more research needs to be carried out before quantitative and qualitative developmental changes in these skills, across the life span, can be clearly articulated. The use of one or several of the methods discussed should enhance the process.

# References

Abelson, R. P. Script processing attitudes, formation, and decision making. In J. S. Carroll & J. W. Payne (Eds.), *Cognition and social behavior.* Hillsdale, New Jersey: Erlbaum, 1976.

Ainsworth, M. D. S., Bell, S. M., & Stayton, D. J. Infant–mother attachment and social development: "Socialization" as a product of reciprocal responsiveness to signals. In M. P. M. Richards (Ed.), *The integration of a child into a social world.* London and New York: Cambridge University Press, 1974.

Allen, V. L. *Children as teachers: Theory and research on tutoring.* New York: Academic Press, 1976.

Argyle, M., & Kendon, A. The experimental analysis of social performances. In L. Berkowitz (Ed.), *Advances in experimental social psychology* (Vol. 3). New York: Academic Press, 1967.

Asch, S. E. Studies of independence and conformity: In a minority of one against a unanimous majority. *Psychological Monographs,* 1956, **70**, 9.

Asher, S. R. Children's peer relations. In M. E. Lamb (Ed.), *Social and personality development.* New York: Holt Rinehart & Winston, 1978.

Asher, S. R., & Wigfield, A. Training referential communication skills. In W. P. Dickson (Ed.), *Children's oral communication skills.* New York: Academic Press, 1981.

Bales, R. F. *Interaction process analysis.* Reading, Massachusetts: Addison-Wesley, 1951.

Baltes, M. M., Barton, E. M., Orzech, M. J., & Lago, D. *Behavior mapping in a nursing home:*

*Observation of elderly residents and staff behavior.* Unpublished manuscript, Pennsylvania State University, 1980.

Bandura, A. *Principles of behavior modification.* New York: Holt Rinehart & Winston, 1969.

Barton, G. M., Baltes, M. M., & Orzech, M. J. Etiology of dependence in older nursing home residents during morning care: The role of staff behavior. *Journal of Personality and Social Psychology,* 1980, **38,** 423–431.

Bates, E. *Cognition and communication in infancy.* New York: Academic Press, 1979.

Beck, A. A., & Leviton, B. *Social support mediating factors in widowhood and life satisfaction among the elderly.* Paper presented at the annual meeting of the Gerontological Society, New York, 1976.

Beckman, L. J. Effects of social interaction and children's relative inputs on older women's psychological well-being. *Journal of Personality and Social Psychology,* 1981, **41,** 1075–1086.

Bengtson, V. L., & Treas, J. The changing family context of mental health and aging. In J. E. Birren & R. B. Sloane (Eds.), *Handbook of mental health and aging.* Englewood Cliffs, New Jersey: Prentice-Hall, 1980.

Berger, P. L., & Luckmann, T. *The social construction of reality.* Garden City, New York: Doubleday, 1966.

Berger, R. M., & Rose, S. D. Interpersonal skill training with institutionalized elderly patients. *Journal of Gerontology,* 1977, **32,** 346–353.

Berscheid, E., Graziano, W., Monson, T., & Dermer, M. Outcome dependency: Attention, attribution and attraction. *Journal of Personality and Social Psychology,* 1976, **34,** 978–989.

Bielby, D. D. V., & Papalia, D. E. Moral development and perceptual role-taking egocentrism: Their development and interrelationship across the life span. *International Journal of Aging and Human Development,* 1975, **6,** 293–308.

Birren, J. E., & Renner, V. J. Research on the psychology of aging: Principles and experimentation. In J. E. Birren & K. W. Schaie (Eds.), *Handbook of the psychology of aging.* New York: Van Nostrand Reinhold, 1977.

Blieszner, R. *Assessing qualities of social relationships.* Paper presented at the annual meeting of the Gerontological Society, San Diego, 1980.

Bloom, L., Rocissano, L., & Hood, L. Adult–child discourse: Developmental interaction between information processing and linguistic knowledge. *Cognitive Psychology,* 1976, **8,** 521–552.

Bochner, S., & Insko, C. A. Communication discrepancy, source credibility, and opinion change. *Journal of Personality and Social Psychology,* 1966, **4,** 614–621.

Botwinick, J. *Aging and behavior* (2nd ed.). New York: Springer Publ., 1978.

Boyd, R. E. Conformity reduction in adolescence. *Adolescence,* 1975, **10,** 297–300.

Brainerd, C. J. *Piaget's theory of intelligence.* Englewood Cliffs, New Jersey: Prentice-Hall, 1977.

Brock, T. C. Communicator–recipient similarity and decision–change. *Journal of Personality and Social Psychology,* 1965, **3,** 650–654.

Bronson, W. C. Central orientation: A study of behavior organization from childhood to adolescence. *Child Development,* 1966, **37,** 125–155.

Brown, B. B. *Social and psychological correlates of help-seeking behavior among urban adults.* Paper presented at the annual meeting of the Gerontological Society, San Diego, 1980.

Brown, R. *A first language.* Cambridge, Massachusetts: Harvard University Press, 1973.

Burnside, I. M. Symptomatic behaviors in the elderly. In J. E. Birren & R. B. Sloane (Eds.), *Handbook of mental health and aging.* Englewood Cliffs, New Jersey: Prentice-Hall, 1980.

Caporael, L. R., Lukaszewski, M. P., & Culbertson, G. H. Secondary baby talk: Judgments by institutionalized elderly and their caregivers. *Journal of Personality and Social Psychology,* 1983, **44,** 746–764.

Chiriboga, D. A. Adaptation to marital separation in later and earlier life. *Journal of Gerontology,* 1982, **37,** 109–114.

Clark, H., & Haviland, S. Psychological processes as linguistic explanation. In D. Cohen (Ed.), *Explaining linguistic phenomenon*. New York: Wiley, 1974.

Cohen, G. Language comprehension in old age. *Cognitive Psychology*, 1979, **11**(4), 412–429.

Combs, M. L., & Slaby, R. A. Social skills training with children. In B. Lahey & A. Kazdin (Eds.), *Advances in clinical child psychology* (Vol. 1). New York: Plenum, 1978.

Conner, K. A., & Powers, E. A. Structural effects and life satisfaction among the aged. *International Journal of Aging and Human Development*, 1975, **6**, 321–327.

Cooper, P. E. *Spatial and communicative egocentrism among middle-aged and elderly women*. Unpublished doctoral dissertation, Pennsylvania State University, 1978.

Costa, P. T., Jr., & McCrae, R. R. Still stable after all these years: Personality as a key to some issues in aging. In P. B. Baltes & O. G. Brim, Jr. (Eds.), *Life-span development and behavior* (Vol. 3). New York: Academic Press, 1980.

Cowen, E. L., Pederson, A., Babigian, H., Izzo, L. D., & Trost, M. A. Long-term follow-up of early detected vulnerable children. *Journal of Consulting and Clinical Psychology*, 1973, **41**, 438–446.

Cumming, E., & Henry, W. E. *Growing old*. New York: Basic Books, 1961.

Cutler, N. E. Age variations in the dimensionality of life satisfaction. *Journal of Gerontology*, 1979, **34**, 116–121.

Davis, A. D. M., & Smith, P. A. The social behaviours of geriatric patients at mealtimes: An observational and an intervention study. *Age and Aging*, 1980, **9**, 93–99.

Derlega, V. J., Wilson, M., & Chaikin, A. L. Friendship and disclosure reciprocity. *Journal of Personality and Social Psychology*, 1976, **34**, 578–582.

Dodge, K. A. Behavioural antecedents of peer social status. *Child Development*, 1983, **54**, 1386–1399.

Dore, J. A pragmatic description of early language development. *Journal of Psycholinguistic Research*, 1974, **3**, 343–350.

Duff, R. W., & Hong, L. K. *Quality and quantity of social interactions and the life satisfaction of older Americans*. Paper presented at the annual meeting of the Gerontological Society, San Diego, 1980.

Edwards, J. N., & Klemmack, D. L. Correlates of life satisfaction: A reexamination. *Journal of Gerontology*, 1973, **28**, 497–502.

Ervin-Tripp, S. An analysis of the interaction of language, topic and listener. In T. A. Fishman (Ed.), *Readings in the sociology of language*. The Hague: Mouton, 1968.

Ervin-Tripp, S. "Wait for me Roller Skate!" In S. Ervin-Tripp & C. Mitchell-Kernan (Eds.), *Child discourse*. New York: Academic Press, 1977.

Escalona, S. K. Basic modes of social interaction: Their emergence and patterning during the first two years of life. *Merrill-Palmer Quarterly*, 1973, **19**(3), 205–232.

Evans, M. A., & Rubin, K. H. Hand gestures as a communication mode in school-aged children. *Journal of Genetic Psychology*, 1979, **135**, 189–196.

Flavell, J. H. *The development of role-taking and communication skills in children*. New York: Wiley, 1968.

Flavell, J. H. Cognitive monitoring. In W. P. Dickson (Ed.), *Children's oral communication skills*. New York: Academic Press, 1981.

Freedman, J. L., & Fraser, S. C. Compliance without pressure: The foot-in-the-door technique. *Journal of Personality and Social Psychology*, 1966, **4**, 195–202.

French, R. R. P., Jr. Person-role fit. In A. McLean (Ed.), *Occupational stress*. Springfield, Illinois: Thomas, 1974.

Freud, A., & Dann, S. An experiment in group upbringing. *The Psychoanalytic Study of the Child*, 1951, **6**, 127–168.

Friedmann, E. A., & Orbach, H. L. Adjustments to retirement. In S. Arieti (Ed.), *American handbook of psychiatry*. New York: Basic Books, 1974.

Gaitz, C. M., & Varner, R. V. Preventive aspects of mental illness in late life. In J. E. Birren & R. B. Sloane (Eds.), *Handbook of mental health and aging*. Englewood Cliffs, New Jersey: Prentice-Hall, 1980.

Garvey, C. Requests and responses in children's speech. *Journal of Child Language*, 1975, **2**, 41–63.

George, L. K. *Role transitions in later life*. Belmont, California: Wadsworth, 1980.

Gladwin, T. Social competence and clinical practice. *Psychiatry*, 1967, **30**, 30–43.

Glucksberg, S., & Krauss, R. What do people say after they have learned how to talk? Studies of the development of referential communication. *Merrill-Palmer Quarterly*, 1967, **13**, 309–316.

Glucksberg, S., Krauss, R., & Higgins, E. T. The development of referential communication skills. In F. D. Horowitz (Ed.), *Review of child development research* (Vol. 4). Chicago: University of Chicago Press, 1975.

Goffman, E. *The presentation of self in everyday life*. Garden City, New York: Doubleday, 1958.

Goffman, E. *Asylums*. Garden City, New York: Doubleday, 1961.

Gottlieb, B. H. Social support as a focus for integrative research in psychology. *American Psychologist*, 1983, **38**, 278–287.

Gottman, J. M. *Marital interaction: Experimental investigations*. New York: Academic Press, 1979.

Gouldner, A. The norm of reciprocity: A preliminary statement. *American Sociological Review*, 1960, **25**, 161–178.

Hartup, W. W. The peer system. In E. M. Hetherington (Ed.), *Handbook of child psychology* (Vol. 3): *Social development*. New York: Wiley, 1983.

Hay, D. F., Pederson, J., & Nash, A. Dyadic interaction in the first year of life. In K. H. Rubin & H. S. Ross (Eds.), *Peer relationships and social skills in childhood*. Berlin and New York: Springer-Verlag, 1982.

Higgins, E. T. Role-taking and social judgment: Alternative developmental perspectives and processes. In J. H. Flavell & L. Ross (Eds.), *New directions in the study of social cognitive development*. London and New York: Cambridge University Press, 1981.

Hochschild, A. R. *The unexpected community*. Englewood Cliffs, New Jersey: Prentice-Hall, 1973.

Hogan, R., Johnson, J. A., & Emler, N. P. A socioanalytic theory of moral development. In W. Damon (Ed.), *New directions in child development* (No. 2): *Moral development*. San Francisco: Jossey Bass, 1978.

Holmberg, M. The development of social interchange patterns from 12 to 42 months. *Child Development*, 1980, **51**, 448–456.

Hultsch, D. F., & Deutsch, F. *Adult development and aging: A life-span perspective*. New York: McGraw-Hill, 1981.

Hultsch, D. R., & Plemons, J. K. Life events and life-span development. In P. B. Baltes & O. G. Brim, Jr. (Eds.), *Life-span development and behavior* (Vol. 2). New York: Academic Press, 1979.

Humphrey, N. The social function of intellect. In P. Bateson & R. Hinde (Eds.), *Growing points in ethology*. London and New York: Cambridge University Press, 1976.

Ipsa, J. *Familiar and unfamiliar peers as havens of security for Soviet nursery children*. Paper presented at the biennial meeting of the Society for Research in Child Development, New Orleans, 1977.

Jacobson, N. S. Communications skills training for married couples. In J. P. Curran & P. M. Monti (Eds.), *Social skills training: A practical handbook for assessment and treatment*. New York: Guilford, 1982.

Jones, W., Hobbs, S., & Hockenbury, D. Loneliness and social skill deficits. *Journal of Personality and Social Psychology*, 1982, **42**, 682–689.

Kahana, B. Social behavior and aging. In B. B. Wolman (Ed.), *Handbook of developmental psychology*. Englewood Cliffs, New Jersey: Prentice-Hall, 1982.

Kahana, B., Kahana, E., & McLenigan, P. *The adventurous aged. Voluntary relocation in the later years.* Paper presented at the Gerontological Society of America meeting, San Diego, November 1980.

Kahn, R. L., & Antonucci, T. C. Convoys over the life course: Attachment, roles and social support. In P. B. Baltes & O. G. Brim, Jr. (Eds.), *Life-span development and behavior* (Vol. 3). New York: Academic Press, 1980.

Kalish, R. A., & Knudtson, F. W. Attachment vs disengagement: A lifespan conceptualization. *Human Development*, 1976, **19**, 171–181.

Kimble, C. E., Yoshikawa, J. C., & Zehr, H. P. Vocal and verbal assertiveness in same-sex and mixed-sex groups. *Journal of Personality and Social Psychology*, 1981, **40**(6), 1047–1054.

Kohlberg, L. Moral stages and moralization: The cognitive–developmental approach. In T. Lickona (Ed.), *Moral development and behavior*. New York: Holt Rinehart & Winston, 1976.

Krasnor, L. R. *An observational study of social problem solving in preschoolers.* Unpublished doctoral dissertation, University of Waterloo, Waterloo, Ontario, Canada, 1981.

Krasnor, L. R., & Rubin, K. H. The assessment of social problem-solving skills in young children. In T. Merluzzi, C. Glass, & M. Genest (Eds.), *Cognitive assessment*. New York: Guilford, 1981.

Krasnor, L. R., & Rubin, K. H. Preschool social problem solving: Attempts and outcomes in naturalistic interaction. *Child Development*, 1983, **54**, 1544–1558.

Kummer, H. *Primate societies: Group techniques of ecological adaptation*. Chicago: Aldine, 1971.

Kuypers, J. A., & Bengtson, V. L. Social breakdown and competence. *Human Development*, 1973, **16**, 181–201.

Langer, E., & Rodin, J. The effects of choice and enhanced personal responsibility for the aged: A field experiment in an institutional setting. *Journal of Personality and Social Psychology*, 1976, **34**, 191–198.

Langlois, J., Gottfried, N., Barnes, B., & Hendricks, D. The effect of peer age on the social behavior of preschool children. *Journal of Genetic Psychology*, 1978, **132**, 11–19.

Larson, R. Thirty years of research on the subjective well-being of older Americans. *Journal of Gerontology*, 1978, **33**, 109–125.

Latane, B., & Rodin, J. A lady in distress: Inhibiting effects of friends and strangers on bystander intervention. *Journal of Experimental Social Psychology*, 1969, **5**, 189–202.

Levin, E. A., & Rubin, K. H. Getting others to do what you want them to do: The development of children's requestive strategies. In K. Nelson (Ed.), *Children's language* (Vol. 4). Hillsdale, New Jersey: Erlbaum, 1983.

Levinson, D. J. *The seasons of a man's life*. New York: Knopf, 1978.

Liem, R., & Rayman, P. Health and social costs of unemployment: Research and policy issues. *American Psychologist*, 1982, **37**, 1116–1123.

Loeb, R. Disengagement, activity, or maturity? *Sociology and Social Research*, 1973, **57**, 367–382.

Looft, W. R. Egocentrism and social interaction across the life span. *Psychological Bulletin*, 1972, **78**, 73–92.

Looft, W. R., & Charles, D. C. Egocentrism and social interaction in young and old adults. *Aging and Human Development*, 1971, **2**, 21–28.

Lowenthal, M. F., & Haven, C. Interaction and adaptation: Intimacy as a critical variable. *American Sociological Review*, 1968, **33**, 20–30.

Lowenthal, M. F., & Robinson, B. Social networks and isolation. In R. H. Binstock & E. Shanas (Eds.), *Handbook of aging and the social sciences*. New York: Van Nostrand Reinhold, 1976.

Lubin, D., & Whiting, B. *Learning techniques of persuasion: An analysis of sequences of interac-*

*tion.* Paper presented at the biennial meeting of the Society for Research in Child Development, New Orleans, March 1977.

Maratsos, M. Non-egocentric communication abilities in preschool children. *Child Development,* 1973, **44,** 697–700.

Matthews, A. M. *Age as a factor of experience of moving.* Paper presented at the annual meeting of the Canadian Association on Gerontology, Halifax, Nova Scotia, 1979.

Matthews, S. *The social world of old women.* Beverly Hills, California: Sage, 1979.

McGee, J., & Barker, M. Deference and dominance in old age: An exploration in social theory. *International Journal of Aging and Human Development,* 1982, **15,** 247–262.

Mead, G. H. *Mind, self, and society.* Chicago: University of Chicago Press, 1932.

Moerk, E. Changes in verbal child–mother interactions with increasing language skills of the child. *Journal of Psycholinguistic Research,* 1974, 3(2), 101–116.

Mueller, E. The maintenance of verbal exchanges between young children. *Child Development,* 1972, **43,** 930–938.

Mueller, E., Bleier, M., Krakow, J., Hegedus, K., & Cournoyer, P. The development of peer verbal interaction among 2-year-old boys. *Child Development,* 1977, **48,** 284–287.

Mussen, P., Honzik, M. P., & Eichorn, D. H. Early adult antecedents of life satisfaction at age 70. *Journal of Gerontology,* 1982, **37,** 316–322.

Muste, M. J., & Sharpe, D. G. Some influential factors in the determination of aggressive behavior in preschool children. *Child Development,* 1947, **18,** 11–25.

Neugarten, B., Havighurst, R. J., & Tobin, S. S. Personality and patterns of aging. In B. L. Neugarten (Ed.), *Middle age and aging.* Chicago: University of Chicago Press, 1968.

Newcomb, T. M. Student peer group influence. In N. Sanford (Ed.), *The American college.* New York: Wiley, 1962.

Newman, P. R. The peer group. In B. B. Wolman (Ed.), *Handbook of developmental psychology.* Englewood Cliffs, New Jersey: Prentice-Hall, 1982.

Norris, J. E. *Disengagement and eccentricity in young and old adults: Phenomena of old age?* Unpublished master's thesis, University of Waterloo, Waterloo, Ontario, Canada, 1977.

Norris, J. E. *Disengagement in young and old adults: Controversial, but measurable.* Unpublished doctoral dissertation, University of Waterloo, Waterloo, Ontario, Canada, 1979. (a)

Norris, J. E. *Social cognition in adulthood. Perceiving the complexity of others.* Paper presented at the annual meeting of the Gerontological Society, Washington, D.C., November 1979. (b)

Norris, J. E. The social adjustment of single and widowed older women. *Essence,* 1980, **4,** 135–144.

Norris, J. E. *Psychological assets of later life. The example of the older professional.* Paper presented at the annual meeting of the Canadian Association on Gerontology, Winnipeg, Manitoba, 1982.

Norris, J. E., & Pratt, M. *Adult usage of Kelley's causal schemes.* Paper presented at the annual meeting of the Canadian Association on Gerontology, Saskatoon, Saskatchewan, October 1980.

North, A. J., & Ulatowska, H. K. Competence in independently living older adults. Assessment and correlation. *Journal of Gerontology,* 1981, **36,** 576–582.

Nuckolls, K. B., Cassel, J., & Kaplan, B. H. Psychosocial assets, life crisis, and the prognosis of pregnancy. *American Journal of Epidemiology,* 1972, **95,** 431–441.

Parr, J. The interaction of persons and living environments. In L. W. Poon (Ed.), *Aging in the 1980's: Psychological issues.* Washington, D.C.: American Psychological Association, 1980.

Piaget, J. *The language and thought of the child.* London: Routledge & Kegan Paul, 1926.

Piaget, J. *The moral judgment of the child.* New York: Free Press, 1932.

Piaget, J. Piaget's theory. In P. H. Mussen (Ed.), *Carmichael's manual of child psychology* (Vol. 1). New York: Wiley, 1970.

Post, F. *The significance of affective symptoms in old age: A follow-up study of one hundred patients.* London and New York: Oxford University Press, 1962.

Pratt, M. J., Golding, G., & Hunter, W. J. *Adult moral judgment orientation: A construct validation study.* Paper presented at the annual meeting of the Canadian Psychological Association, Montreal, 1982.

Putallaz, M., & Gottman, J. Social skills and group acceptance. In S. R. Asher & J. M. Gottman (Eds.), *The development of children's friendships.* London and New York: Cambridge University Press, 1981.

Rest, J. Morality. In J. Flavell & E. Markman (Eds.), *Handbook of child psychology* (Vol. 2): *Cognitive development.* New York: Wiley, 1983.

Rheingold, H. L., Hay, D. F., & West, M. Sharing the second year of life. *Child Development,* 1976, **47**, 1145–1155.

Rodin, J., & Langer, E. Aging labels: The decline of control and the fall of self-esteem. *Journal of Social Issues,* 1980, **36**, 12–29.

Roff, M., Sells, S. B., & Golden, M. M. *Social adjustment and personality development in children.* Minneapolis: University of Minnesota Press, 1972.

Rosow, I. *Social integration of the aged.* New York: Free Press, 1967.

Rotheram, M. J., & Corby, N. Social power and the elderly. In D. P. Rathjen & J. P. Forest (Eds.), *Social competence: Interventions for children and adults.* Oxford: Pergamon, 1980.

Rubin, K. H. The relationship between spatial and communicative egocentrism in children and young and old adults. *Journal of Genetic Psychology,* 1974, **125**, 295–301.

Rubin, K. H. Role taking in childhood: Some methodological considerations. *Child Development,* 1978, **49**, 534–536.

Rubin, K. H. Non-social play in preschoolers: Necessarily evil? *Child Development,* 1982, **53**, 651–658. (a)

Rubin, K. H. Social skill and social–cognitive correlates of observed isolation behavior in preschoolers. In K. H. Rubin & H. S. Ross (Eds.), *Peer relationships and social skills in childhood.* Berlin and New York: Springer-Verlag, 1982. (b)

Rubin, K. H. *Longitudinal correlates of social isolate status in early childhood.* Paper presented at the biennial meetings of the Society for Research in Child Development, Detroit, May 1983.

Rubin, K. H., Attewell, P. W., Tierney, M. C., & Tumolo, P. Development of spatial egocentrism and conservation across the life span. *Developmental Psychology,* 1973, **9**, 432.

Rubin, K. H., & Borwick, D. The communicative skills of children differing with regard to social status. In H. S. Sypher & J. L. Applegate (Eds.), *Social cognition and communication.* Beverly Hills, California: Sage Publ., 1983.

Rubin, K. H., & Brown, I. D. R. A life-span look at person perception and its relationship to communicative interaction. *Journal of Gerontology,* 1975, **30**, 461–468.

Rubin, K. H., & Daniels-Beirness, T. Concurrent and predictive correlates of sociometric status in kindergarten and grade one children. *Merrill-Palmer Quarterly,* 1983, **29**, 337–351.

Rubin, K. H., & Everett, B. A. Social perspective-taking in young children. In S. Moore & C. Cooper (Eds.), *The young child.* Washington, D.C.: National Association for the Education of Young Children, 1982.

Rubin, K. H., Hultsch, D. F., & Peters, D. L. Non-social speech in four-year-old children as a function of birth order and interpersonal situation. *Merrill-Palmer Quarterly,* 1971, **17**, 41–49.

Rubin, K. H., & Krasnor, L. R. The development of social problem solving in early childhood. *Journal of Applied Developmental Psychology,* 1983, **4**, 463–475.

Rubin, K. H., & Ross, H. S. Some reflections on the state of the art: The study of peer relationships and social skills. In K. H. Rubin & H. S. Ross (Eds.), *Peer relationships and social skills in childhood.* Berlin and New York: Springer-Verlag, 1982.

Schegloff, E. A. Notes on conversational practice: Formulating place. In P. P. Giglioli (Ed.), *Language and social context*. London: Cox & Wyman, 1972.

Schinke, S. P., & Rose, S. D. Interpersonal skill training in groups. *Journal of Counseling Psychology*, 1976, **23**, 442–448.

Schulz, R. The effects of control and predictability on the physical and psychological well-being of the institutionalized aged. *Journal of Personality and Social Psychology*, 1976, **33**, 563–573.

Searle, J. *Speech arts: An essay in the philosophy of language*. London and New York: Cambridge University Press, 1969.

Selman, R. *The growth of interpersonal understanding: Developmental and clinical analyses*. New York: Academic Press, 1980.

Sequin, M. M. Opportunity for peer socialization in a retirement community. *Gerontologist*, 1973, **13**, 208–214.

Shaffer, D. R., Smith, J. E., & Tomarelli, M. Self-monitoring as a determinant of self-disclosure reciprocity during the acquaintance process. *Journal of Personality and Social Psychology*, 1982, **43**, 163–175.

Shanas, E., Townsend, P., Wedderburn, D., Friis, H. J., Milhoj, P., & Stehouwer, J. *Old people in three industrial societies*. New York: Atherton, 1968.

Shantz, C. U. Social cognition. In J. Flavell & E. Markman (Eds.), *Handbook of child psychology* (Vol. 2): *Cognitive development*. New York: Wiley, 1983.

Shatz, M. Children's comprehension of their mothers' question-directives. *Journal of Child Language*, 1978, **5**, 39–46.

Shatz, M., & Gelman, R. The development of communication skills: Modification in the speech of young children as a function of listener. *Monographs of the Society for Research in Child Development*, 1973, **38**(5, Ser. No. 152).

Sherif, M. *In common predicament: Social psychology of intergroup conflict and cooperation*. Boston: Houghton, 1966.

Sherman, S. The choice of retirement housing among the well elderly. *Aging and Human Development*, 1971, **2**, 118–138.

Sinnott, J. D. *Adult intellectual development as social cognitive growth*. Paper presented at the annual meeting of the Gerontological Society, Dallas, 1978.

Snyder, M. Self-monitoring processes. In L. Berkowitz (Ed.), *Advances in experimental social psychology* (Vol. 12). New York: Academic Press, 1979.

Snyder, M., & Gangestad, S. Choosing social situations: Two investigations of self-monitoring processes. *Journal of Personality and Social Psychology*, 1982, **43**, 123–135.

Sommer, R. The distance for comfortable conversations: Further study. *Sociometry*, 1962, **25**, 111–116.

Spanier, G. B., & Casto, R. F. Adjustment to separation and divorce: An analysis of 50 case studies. *Journal of Divorce*, 1979, **2**, 341–353.

Spence, D. The meaning of engagement. *International Journal of Aging and Human Development*, 1975, **6**, 193–198.

Spivack, G., & Shure, M. B. *Social adjustment of young children*. San Francisco: Jossey-Bass, 1974.

Suomi, S. J., & Harlow, H. F. The role and reason of peer relationships in rhesus monkeys. In M. Lewis & L. A. Rosenblum (Eds.), *Friendship and peer relations*. New York: Wiley, 1975.

Tamir, L. M. *Communication and the aging process*. Oxford: Pergamon, 1979.

Tesch, S., Whitbourne, S. K., & Nehrke, M. F. Cognitive egocentrism in institutionalized adult males. *Journal of Gerontology*, 1978, **33**, 546–552.

Tierney, M. C., Zwicker, C., & Bush, B. *Conceptions of friendship in well-adjusted older people*. Paper presented at the annual meeting of the Canadian Association on Gerontology, Winnipeg, Manitoba, 1982.

Tigges, L. M., Cowgill, D. O., & Habenstein, R. W. *Confidant relations of the aged.* Paper presented at the annual meeting of the Gerontological Society, San Diego, 1980.

Tobin, S. S., & Lieberman, M. *Last home for the aged.* New York: Wiley, 1976.

Trevarthen, C. Communication and cooperation in early infancy. A description of primary intersubjectivity. In M. Bullowa (Ed.), *Before speech: The beginning of interpersonal communication.* London and New York: Cambridge University Press, 1979.

Vandell, D. L., & Wilson, K. S. Social interaction in the first year: Infants' social skills with peer versus mother. In K. H. Rubin & H. S. Ross (Eds.), *Peer relationships and social skills in childhood.* Berlin and New York: Springer-Verlag, 1982.

Waters, J. E. The social ecology of long-term base facilities for the aged: A case example, *Journal of Gerontological Nursing,* 1980. **6,** 155–160.

Watson, W. H. Resistance to naturalistic observation in a geriatric setting. *International Journal of Aging and Human Development,* 1979–1980, **10,** 35–45.

Webb, E. J., Campbell, D. T., Schwartz, R. D., & Sechrest, L. *Unobtrusive measures: Nonreactive research with social sciences.* Chicago: Rand McNally, 1966.

Weiss, R. S. *Going it alone.* New York: Basic Books, 1979.

Wiener, M., & Mehrabian, A. *A language within language: Immediacy, a channel in verbal communication.* New York: Appleton, 1968.

# Author Index

# Subject Index